The
Professional
Secretary's
Handbook

The Professional

Secretary's Handbook

Houghton Mifflin Company   Boston

The two quotations from pages 200 and 3–5, respectively, of Thomas J. Peters and Robert H. Waterman Jr.'s book *In Search of Excellence: Lessons from America's Best-Run Companies* (New York: Harper & Row, 1982) that are found on pages 361 and 362 of this book have been reproduced by permission.

The quotation on page 447 is taken from page 225 of Robert Townsend's book *Further Up the Organization* (New York: Alfred A. Knopf, Inc., 1984) and is reprinted by permission.

The information in the section "United States Customs Information" on pages 475–476 appears courtesy of Pan Am CLIPPER magazine, from which it was adapted.

The author of Chapter Fifteen wishes to acknowledge reference to material having to do with the accounting process and bank reconciliation found on pages 217–219 and 670–673 of *Introduction to Financial Accounting* by Kirkland A. Wilcox and Joseph G. San Miguel (New York: Harper & Row, 1980).

All correspondence and inquiries should be directed to
Reference Division, Houghton Mifflin Company
One Beacon Street, Boston, MA 02108

Library of Congress Cataloging in Publication Data
Main entry under title:
The Professional secretary's handbook.
    Includes index.
    1. Office practice—Automation. 2. Secretaries.
HF5547.5.P7 1984   651.3'74   84-3756
ISBN 0-395-35604-0

Manufactured in the United States of America

Table of Contents

The Secretarial Advisory Board

Nancy B. Arrigo
Secretary to
   Robert B. Huff, President
Bell & Howell
Chicago, Illinois

Arlene L. Belli
Secretary to the Chairman
American Cyanamid
Wayne, New Jersey

Beth A. Carson
Assistant to the Corporate
   Vice President &
   Director
Reference Division
Houghton Mifflin
Boston, Massachusetts

Jeanne Dickover
Secretary to the President
Houghton Mifflin
Boston, Massachusetts

Anne T. Guerrette
Administrator, Office of
   the Chairman and Chief
   Executive Officer
Houghton Mifflin
Boston, Massachusetts

Paula C. Hardacre
Staff Assistant
Office of the President
Wang Laboratories, Inc.
Lowell, Massachusetts

Annie B. Kelly
Editorial Operations
   Secretary/Reference
Houghton Mifflin
Boston, Massachusetts

Kathleen M. Kelly
Secretary to the Chairman
Polaroid Corporation
Cambridge, Massachusetts

Barbara Matyskiel
Secretary to the President
Prime Computer Inc.
Natick, Massachusetts

Patsy Reynolds
Administrative Assistant
Chairman's Office
The Firestone Tire &
   Rubber Company
Akron, Ohio

Ann Satchwill
Assistant to the Divisional
   Vice President &
   Publisher/Reference
Houghton Mifflin
Boston, Massachusetts

Lynn Takahashi
Area Administrator
Office of the President
Apple Computer Inc.
Cupertino, California

Special Consultants

Richard B. Crawford
Science Writer
Lawrence Livermore
   National Laboratory
Livermore, California

Mary Ann Esser
Editor
Lawrence Livermore
   National Laboratory
Livermore, California

Mary Ann Fitzhugh
Product Marketing
   Manager
Digital Equipment
   Corporation
Merrimack, New
   Hampshire

Ruth Gallinot, PhD, CPS
Principal, Gallinot &
   Associates
Educational Consultant/
   formerly CEU
   Program Director,
   Professional
   Secretaries
   International®
Chicago, Illinois

Janet Galvin
Administrator,
   Personnel
National Broadcasting
   Company, Inc.
New York, New York

Kenneth M. Gordon
Editor
Lawrence Livermore
   National Laboratory
Livermore, California

Jan A. Meierbachtol
Product Planning Manager
Office Systems
   Division/3M
St. Paul, Minnesota

Peter W. Murphy
Editor/Writer
Lawrence Livermore
   National Laboratory
Livermore, California

The Authors

Harold Bogdonoff
Engineering Fellow
Xerox Corporation
Rochester, New York

Jeff Blyskal
Staff Writer
Forbes Magazine
New York, New York

Marie Blyskal
Co-author, *Agri Selling*
New York, New York

Edward F. Coyman, Jr.
Product Manager
Office Systems Product
  Group
Wang Laboratories, Inc.
Lowell, Massachusetts

Kaethe Ellis
Editor, Reference Division
Houghton Mifflin
  Company
Boston, Massachusetts

Linda Noble Gutierrez
Confidential Secretary
Human Resources
  Department
The Times Mirror
  Company
Los Angeles, California

James C. Hamilton, Esq.
Partner
Homans, Hamilton,
  Dahmen & Marshall
Boston, Massachusetts

Susan W. Hass, MBA, CPA
Assistant Professor
Graduate School of
  Business Administration
Simmons College
Boston, Massachusetts

Jacqueline L. Larkin
Telemarketing Manager
Warren, Gorham &
  Lamont Inc.
Boston, Massachusetts

Melissa Ludlum
Executive Secretary to
  M. S. Rukeyser, Jr.
Executive Vice President,
  Corporate
  Communications
National Broadcasting
  Company, Inc.
New York, New York

Heather Menzies
Author, *Computers on the
  Job* (Toronto: James
  Lorimer & Co.) and
  Women and the Chip
  (Toronto: Institute for
  Research on Public
  Policy)
Ottawa, Ontario, Canada

Donna L. Muise
Executive Assistant,
  Editorial & Production
Reference Division
Houghton Mifflin
  Company
Boston, Massachusetts

Gail Pennington, Esq.
Partner
Homans, Hamilton,
  Dahmen & Marshall
Boston, Massachusetts

David R. Pritchard
Associate Editor,
  Reference Division
Houghton Mifflin
  Company
Boston, Massachusetts

Ann Elise Rubin
Editorial Assistant to
  William Safire
The New York Times
  Washington Bureau
Washington, DC

William Saffady, PhD
Associate Professor
Department of Library &
  Information Science
Vanderbilt University
Nashville, Tennessee

Anne H. Soukhanov
Senior Editor, Reference
Reference Division
Houghton Mifflin
  Company
Boston, Massachusetts

M. Sue Strachan
Executive Assistant to the
  Chairman of the Board
Pan American World
  Airways, Inc.
New York, New York

Richard K. Turner
Product Manager
Office Systems Marketing
Wang Laboratories, Inc.
Lowell, Massachusetts

Palmer T. Van Dyke
Writer/Editor
Lawrence Livermore
  National Laboratory
Livermore, California

Lamont Wood
Professional Writer;
  formerly Public
  Relations Writer,
  Datapoint Corporation
San Antonio, Texas

Preface

The Professional Secretary's Handbook—a comprehensive, hands-on guide to automated and conventional office procedures, systems, and equipment—is an exceptional product. It is the only such book written and reviewed by secretaries and other business people who share with you their experience and expertise. Its in-depth coverage of automated and conventional practices and systems is unparalleled. And its content and direction reflect input from our Advisory Board composed of secretaries to the chief executive officers, presidents, and other top managers of selected Fortune 500 companies. The sixteen chapters in this book have been written by a team of twenty-one authors, six of whom are, or have been, secretaries; for instance, Sue Strachan of Pan Am on travel arrangements . . . Melissa Ludlum of NBC on telephone use . . . Ann Rubin of *The New York Times* on the mail . . . and Linda Gutierrez of The Times Mirror Company on meetings and time management. *The Professional Secretary's Handbook* devotes over 150 pages to automation: Heather Menzies, author of *Computers on the Job* and *Women and the Chip*, on the reconfigured role of the secretary in the automated office . . . Ted Coyman and Rich Turner of Wang Laboratories on word processors and electronic typewriters . . . Lamont Wood, high technology writer, on electronic mail and telecommunications . . . Harold Bogdonoff of Xerox Corporation on new copying techniques and technologies . . . and Bill Saffady of Vanderbilt University on automated and conventional records management.

The Professional Secretary's Handbook does not neglect conventional office practices. Eighty-one pages are given over to business English in a chapter by *Forbes* Magazine staff writer Jeff Blyskal and his wife Marie Blyskal, also a professional writer. Thirty-six pages are devoted to scientific document formats in a chapter unique to this book and of special interest to secretaries in scientific settings. Another eighty-one pages discuss in detail the formats of letters, memos, press releases, and reports, accompanied by special sections on graphic aids and audiovisuals. Still other chapters cover dictation and transcription, accounting, and business law. Those of you who work for traveling executives will find the 43-page Global Travel and Holidays Chart indispensable in planning international trips. The Chart gives you at a glance the geographic locations, capitals, currencies, climate conditions, languages, nationalities, religions, international dialing codes, and holidays by dates in all countries. But perhaps the chapter of greatest personal importance to employed secretaries, returnees to the job market, and business education students is the one having to do with career development. Written by Jackie Larkin—once a secretary herself, later a personnel placement manager, and now a telemarketing manager—this chapter provides thirty pages of the practical, forward-looking guidance that you need in order to enhance your career in a fast-changing corporate world.

The Professional Secretary's Handbook has also benefited immeasurably from the counsel of our Secretarial Advisory Board. Members of this Board responded to a survey questionnaire intended to assist us in focusing the content sharply and candidly on the realities of the American office from the secretarial vantage point. The Board's input appears throughout the book; see, for example, the Board's comments on time management problems (pages 453–454). The Board members also read and reviewed the chapters with a view toward accuracy, comprehensiveness, and up-to-date content.

The Professional Secretary's Handbook with its numerous photographs, facsimiles, line drawings, and tables, together with its readable text, contains all the resources that you require to move forward confidently as multifaceted managers in the dynamic corporate environment of this, the electronic age.

Anne H. Soukhanov
Senior Editor, Reference

1

The Reconfigured Role of the Secretary in the Automated Office

Heather Menzies • *Author*, Computers on the Job *(Toronto, Canada: James Lorimer & Company) and* Women and the Chip *(Toronto, Canada: Institute for Research on Public Policy)*

THE FUTURE FOR SECRETARIES IS BRIGHT, BUT NOT GUARANTEED

Information is at the center of secretaries' work, and always has been, for secretaries spend 90% of their workdays managing and supervising the flow of information through in-baskets, telephone calls, letters, memos, and filing systems; collecting and packaging information; ferreting out information, and so on. In the past, this fact has been hidden under the surface of standard secretarial tasks such as typing and filing. Now, however, it's been brought out in a most dramatic way, through the creation of computerized information systems in the automated office.

The technology is transforming the whole basis of office work. In doing so, it is changing the secretarial role more dramatically than it has been altered since women began entering this formerly male field nearly a century ago. For secretaries male and female, this change has to be both frightening and exciting. It's frightening because standard secretarial work is being substantially automated. It's exciting because the automated systems, once they're in place, will open the way to much more rewarding work, specifically information work in which secretaries already have substantial, though informal, experience. If secretaries are adequately prepared to recognize opportunities when they open up and if they are educated and trained properly to seize and capitalize on those opportunities, they should enjoy a wide range of challenging careers as information managers and professional information workers in the office of the future.

. Computers are only one half of the automated office. The other half is telecommunications, which takes in everything from telephones to satellites and private branch exchanges (PBXs). Communications devices move information around and shift it from one medium to another. Computers, in turn, massage information: they add and subtract it, list it, process and combine it, format and store it. When integrated, these technologies represent the single most powerful force for change since the invention of the steam engine which launched the Industrial Revolution about 150 years ago. These technologies are revolutionizing work not only in offices but also in factories, warehouses, mines, supermarkets, banks—in short, everywhere.

Inside the Automated Office

This new office is a computerized information system, with its information set down in electronic bits rather than on paper. The office is therefore freed from filing cabinets and the restrictive concrete walls of buildings. You can now enter your "office" wherever you have a computer terminal and a phone line for plugging it in. The terminal could be at your home, in a hotel room halfway across the country, or in someone else's office. Instead of inserting a key into a lock, you now "key" your personal access number onto the computer terminal and proceed to "call up" whatever information you need to do your work.

At the push of a key your electronic mailbox, or in-basket, appears on the computer screen, listing its contents: mail, telephone messages, memos and reminders for meetings, or whatever. You deal with what you can, then route material to various other people in the management group in which and for which you work. (These people also have desktop terminals, called workstations.) Next, you call up the electronic calendar to confirm the time for any meeting you're expected to attend or you prepare material needed for that day. Then you call up the files on some research project you're involved in and settle down to work—still possibly in the comfort of your own home, which has been turned into an auxiliary office called an *electronic cottage* by the technology's ability to relay office work and automated support systems to it. Instead of commuting to a fixed piece of real estate to go to work, you will increasingly have the option of "telecommuting" to work, via telecommunications technology.

Forces Behind Office Automation

This new electronic office with its changing roles for office workers is being shaped by a number of forces, of which technology is but one. Not surprisingly, those who are designing and installing automated information systems are not driven by the desire to save secretaries the boring legwork of filing or the frustrating time wasted in routing memos from one person's out-basket to another person's in-basket. They're being driven by cold pressure to improve productivity—that is, the volume of work performed per person per day. During the 1970s when computers were introduced to automate work in factories, the productivity of that sector rose by approximately 40%. The productivity of office workers, meanwhile, increased by a mere 4%. By the 1980s the lesson was clear: use computers to eliminate paperwork, legwork, and unnecessary finger work in running an office. That's the way to increase office productivity and, through that, the competitiveness of business and industry.

Other influences are in play as well. For instance, a new management style has begun to emerge, replacing the bureaucratic, hierarchical approach of top-down administration. The new style is looser and more decentralized, emphasizing involvement, teamwork, personal initiative, and entrepreneurship. The style is in keeping with the times of ongoing change and of current values, among them those of the women's movement. This second influence has already had an effect on secretarial work, helping to free it from the past when the work was restricted to simple support services such as typing and reception, when it was largely seen as "women's work" and restricted primarily to women, when it was often equated with the traditional role of women as mothers and housewives, and when it lacked real opportunities for advancement into more responsible work in management and administration and consequently was tarnished with the label "female job ghetto."

As the new information technologies move into offices across the country, secretaries could come into their own at last as professional information workers: as managers of information systems, as packagers of information, and as information go-betweens or brokers. For this to happen though, secretaries must know what the technology is all about. They must be aware of the inherent hazards so as to avoid them. Most important of all, they must know what they can do both to make their work more productive and to make the new high technology work for them, rather than allowing themselves to be used by that technology.

LOOKING AT THE PIECES OF A COMPUTER SYSTEM

There are many ways of describing the new automated office systems: in terms of the gadgets involved, through the functions they perform, as extensions of traditional equipment and types of corporation involved, and so on. To avoid confusion it is best to ignore such techno-talk as ROM 16K bit memory etcetera and to concentrate instead on simple concepts and applications. Just as one uses the telephone every day without having to understand how it works, so too will thousands of office workers soon use computer-based office equipment every day without having to know that the computer has a 16K RAM electronic brain inside. But it does help to know that every computer system, no matter how complicated it looks, still consists of only four basic parts:

1. An input unit puts information into the computer.

2. A processing unit, or "brain," does something with that information according to instructions given to it through software—such as combining numbers or shifting paragraphs in a letter.

3. A storage unit files the information in the computer's memory or outside it on disks or computer tapes.

4. An output unit produces the information in a usable and legible form.

Functions and Functional Devices

This is a way of looking at the automated office system according to the basic operating components of a computer system, and relating them to general office functions.

Input.   This function corresponds to taking notes or dictation, typing, listening, and other traditional office activities whereby information is recorded or taken in. In office information systems, the most common input device is the computer keyboard. Most keyboards are alphanumeric—that is, they have keys for the alphabet and for numbers. Some are attached to television-like screens, self-contained computer terminals. Others are freestanding and can be plugged into a terminal, a printing unit, or another unit used for output.

Another input device is the mouse, a device moved across or beside the computer-terminal screen for electronically "pointing" to symbols displayed there. These symbols will be the menu of the computer's services—filing, information retrieval, and so on. The mouse's moves are mimicked by an electronic light point called a cursor, located inside the terminal screen. Once it has been positioned over the symbol for the desired service, the mouse button on the keyboard is pressed to execute the command to perform the desired service. Light pens can perform similar pointing functions. Other light pens communicate information directly through the terminal screen and can be used for drafting, drawing, and other design work.

Optical-character recognition (OCR) devices take in a variety of printed information by optically scanning or reading it off the surface of printed material. While OCRs are most common in supermarkets and department stores where they read product bar codes, their office use is rapidly growing as well. Here, they're used to input draft text of documents into a word processing system.

Finally, there is voice input which, though still at a primitive stage of development, is already being used in some offices. An office automation project in France has been using voice input to activate certain office support functions, such as calling up one's electronic in-basket. Another variation on voice input is the voice-messaging capability incorporated in some automated office systems. Users can store voice messages as one would on an answering-service machine, but with the added advantage that the message can be routed to several people and the replies automatically routed back to the originator's voice mailbox.

Once the information has passed through an input device to become digitized—that is, made electronic in form, it then can be processed, moved, stored, and regurgitated as printed text or as graphs or drawings—all automatically.

Output devices or peripherals.   Output corresponds to all the end products of office work: final texts of speeches, reports, letters, and so on. The most common output devices in automated offices are the printer and the computer screen, called either a cathode-ray tube (CRT) or a video display terminal (VDT). Other peripherals include intelligent copiers that produce photocopies automatically and facsimile machines that handle information originating in print form. Offices generating a lot of printed information—publishing houses and advertising agencies are good examples—would probably also have photocomposition units to transform texts automatically from a word processing memory unit into hard printed copy. New computer-operated laser printers are capable of printing out 20,000 lines a minute—much faster than mortal fingers can fly.

Micrographic devices that transfer information from computer memory onto microfilm for storage tend to be found more often in libraries and offices with large volumes of fixed information, such as personnel files and general ledgers. Finally, plotter devices associated with design work generate information in the form of line graphs and drawings, and can produce these either on regular paper or in a number of media such as acetate for overhead slides. Voice input is also available, but the synthesized voice is dull to the ear and is still very restricted in its range of "vocabulary."

Processing unit.   This unit is the center of any computerized office system and the seat of its power to automate. It corresponds to the brains involved in actually running an office, setting up a letter correctly, managing a filing system, and so on. In transforming a typewriter into an automatic word processor, the computer's processing unit allows the typist to shift paragraphs around automatically, to store material in files locally and in remote office locations, to hyphenate and justify the text automatically, and to have it checked for spelling errors before being printed out automatically. The processing unit does these things following instructions contained within computer programs or software. Computer systems often are categorized by either the power of their processing unit or the distribution of that power throughout a particular operating system. For instance, a stand-alone word processor has its own internal processing unit, while shared-logic or distributed systems have a number of terminals plugged into one mini- or mainframe computer, in ascending order of memory size and operating speed.

Memory or storage unit.   In traditional offices, this function and equipment category corresponds to the filing cabinets, the in-house library, ring binders of instructions and personnel procedures, and the stacks of unfiled paper on desk tops, tables, and windowsills. In the automated office, this chaotic array is replaced by electronic storage at different levels of accessibility and related cost. If the information is stored within the computer terminal, or word processor, it is said to be stored on-line and is therefore the most accessible and expensive. But if the information isn't to be reused immediately, it can be stored at lower cost on floppy disks, usually having random-access memory (RAM). This means, as it sounds, that you can instantly retrieve specific information stored on the disks. Computer tapes, perhaps the cheapest form of information storage, are magnetic tapes similar to those in a tape recorder; you have to read through the stored material to find the information sought.

Communications.   Traditionally, communications has been the action binding offices together, making the information flow from decision to outcome and back again. In automated offices, communication devices link word processors to intelligent copiers, to other computer terminals around the company and, through them, to databases or electronic files, as well as the corporation's software. The media used in communication can take many forms, from the familiar telephone to the two-way coaxial cable or the more modern technology of fiber optics, which can carry forty times as much information as telephone wires can. Outside specific office buildings and geographic locations, information can be moved via satellite from city to city and around the world at minimal cost and in virtually no time at all.

In addition to the transmission component, communications also involves switching mechanisms, which route messages through the maze of transmission lines and operating systems to a variety of destinations—desktop executive and secretarial workstations, word processors, automatic printing presses, and so on. Many companies have their own in-house switching system called a private-branch exchange or PBX—an automated, much more sophisticated version of the old-fashioned telephone switchboard. The latest models of these switchboards can handle data as well as voice transmissions. Essentially they serve as traffic cops, directing information traffic electronically.

The communications component is a major reason for the excitement generated around office automation, for it weaves a whole series of computer devices and functions into an integrated array of office services—everything from decision support to administrative support—and all on an automated basis.

PUTTING THE PIECES TOGETHER

In the 1970s, there was a tendency to see office automation and its effects in isolated and limited terms. The sales talk went like this: electronic mail eliminates the paper flows and the related delays associated with interoffice memos and traditional postal service. Voice mail eliminates telephone ping-pong and the need for secretaries to keep interrupting more important work to once again try placing an executive-consultation telephone call. Word processing eliminates retyping, which can account for up to 70% of a secretary's traditional typing time. In the early 1980s, however, a more integrated perspective emerged, both in the managers' approach to the computerized office and among the companies selling its equipment. Office equipment companies, which first introduced the intelligent typewriter with floppy disk storage, see the text-editing and production unit as the keystone to an integrated technology with communications, computing, printing, and graphics as peripheral support systems. Computer companies, on the other hand, tend to view word and text processing as mere extensions of data processing, which was the original application of computers. In turn, these computer companies are now adding on additional features such as electronic files. Finally, telephone and other telecommunications companies present themselves as the centerpiece of all this activity, orchestrating the entire array of office information through their switching units and along their vast communications networks, both on an in-house basis and around the globe. From there, they're expanding to offer access to various automated office services such as payroll processing and even management information systems and services.

Not to be outdone or forgotten, office equipment companies that specialized in, for instance, photocopying, have launched their own versions of the office of the future, linking high-speed automated printing and photocopying machines into a network also including word processing, data processing, and electronic filing. Companies that used to make just filing cabinets are now venturing into automatic filing and information retrieval systems. And so it goes. The office of the future is a giant jigsaw puzzle being assembled day by day, in different ways by different players.

Different Looks, Different Settings

The final shape of the office of the future will probably be as varied as the gadgets and systems marketed. And so it should be; the configuration of the office of the future should vary from industry group to industry group, from small company to large company, and from one management philosophy to another.

Company size. Company size and information volume are probably the two most important determinants of the future look and shape of the automated office. In large companies with large amounts of paperwork, office automation will most likely involve a major reorganization of work, generally along the lines of specific tasks and functions. Large word processing and data processing centers might be established, with the equipment arranged in a shared-logic system to which all major information-processing work would be routed. Although this centralization was fairly common in the 1970s, a more diversified pattern has begun to emerge since then. While there will probably be a large central word processing pool, there might also be some smaller satellite centers for more specialized or urgent work requirements in certain departments, plus some stand-alone word processors for a management group or senior executive. Medium-sized companies would tend to have one or two fairly small word processing centers, perhaps in a shared-logic configuration supported by a minicomputer. A stand-alone word processor or two plus a few microcomputers or personal computers with word processing software would probably be found there as well. In small companies with a relatively small central office staff, drastic task reorganization is the least likely, while the most informal approach to office automation is the most likely option. Computer equipment can be installed in such companies on a fairly ad hoc basis, being gradually integrated with other equipment and upgraded as specific needs are identified over time. A small company might start by buying a stand-alone word processor and a couple of personal or microcomputers. It might then acquire the components for integrating different offices through a local area network or private branch exchange. As office

Office Automation Configuration in Small, Medium, and Large Organizations

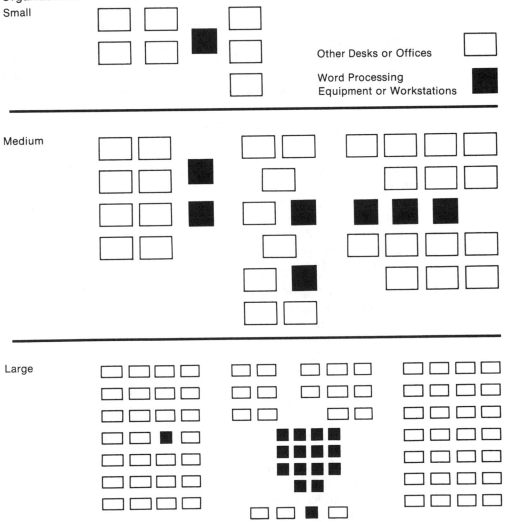

Small

Other Desks or Offices

Word Processing
Equipment or Workstations

Medium

Large

managers and secretaries become used to the system, they might augment it with different application-software packages sold off-the-shelf just like other office products. The most common application-software programs are those for word processing and financial calculations. Functioning as an automated spreadsheet, the financial package can free secretaries from tedious bookkeeping, thus enabling them to do much more interesting research or financial analysis.

Nature of the work being done. The shape of the automated office will be greatly influenced by the type of information work involved. A law office, a company involved in technical research, or a public relations firm would undoubtedly require a very sophisticated system, while a company processing vast volumes of similar information—an insurance company or a bank, for example— would need something simpler but more powerful. In some offices, the emphasis might be on routing information; that is, getting it to where it's needed as fast as possible—to government policymakers and senior corporate executives, for example. In this setting, the communications component, i.e., the local area networks and the PBX, would be vital. In other offices, the emphasis might be on effective record-keeping, as in a medical research facility or a library. Here, the system would be geared toward good database management and related systems software. These systems structure each record's content in such a way that it is linked by logic to every other record in the system and thus can be retrieved instantly through a "key word search." This research, in turn, would be facilitated through software designed for information retrieval including content searches.

Still other offices might require computer graphics capability. If computer graphics software is incorporated into a word processing unit—used, for instance, in a public relations department—it will enable the user to display graphic information quickly, dramatically, and in a way that instantly communicates the desired message. Computer graphics capabilities combined with photocomposition are now enabling many companies that formerly contracted report-formatting/printing out to local graphic artists and printing firms to do more of this work in-house. For secretaries, this means the opportunity to do more artistically challenging work. The amount of time spent on manual layouts is eliminated, and in the end, the company saves money.

The organization of work, or télématique/privatique. The French term télématique is strongly associated with a differentiation made among computer systems in a major report written in 1978 for the President of France. Commonly called the *Nora-Minc Report* after its authors, it anticipated a vast electronic highway or utility (a *télématique*) as the central feature of the computerized world to come. This utility would be worldwide in scope and would provide access to a host of information-based computer services. The approach both favored and reflected a management model of centralized planning and control. A year after the *Nora-Minc Report* was published, two other Frenchmen authored a dissenting view that came to be called the *privatique* approach. *Privatique* featured a decentralized, locally autonomous arrangement of computer users, an arrangement that articulated the new emerging model of decentralized, even participative, management.

Applied strictly to office automation and word processing, a *télématique* approach would feature a shared-logic setup with several so-called dumb terminals linked to one central processing unit. On the other hand, the *privatique* approach could take two forms, depending on the size and nature of the setting: a few stand-alone word processors distributed throughout the organization; or a distributed-logic system, with some shared-logic features for high-volume word processing jobs plus some distributed processing capabilities, thereby making each terminal smart and allowing for some local autonomy by the users. These differences in approach are critical, for the secretary's future depends less on the size of the company, the type of work it does, or even the technology introduced than it does on the organization of the work and the management philosophy underlying it. In progressive companies where an open decentralized style is encouraged, secretaries should find their careers expanding in a variety of challenging and rewarding ways. However, in companies maintaining tight centralized control, with scientific management segmenting work into discrete tasks, secretaries could find themselves pushed into less rewarding jobs and working under assembly line conditions.

WHAT SECRETARIAL WORK IS AUTOMATED

Anyone taking a strictly functional view of secretarial work would conclude that the future for secretaries is rather grim. Such a view focuses on the specific tasks that secretaries have tended to perform: answering the telephone, taking dictation, typing, handling and routing mail, filing, and routine office administration. While these routine tasks take up a great portion of most secretaries' time, there are other more challenging duties such as composing drafts of correspondence, reports, and speeches; researching and preparing briefing notes; general financial and personnel administration; editing copy prepared and typed by others; and advising others on a host of subjects from office equipment purchase to office procedures. These more challenging tasks cannot be automated by computer technology; however, since they account for only a minority of most secretaries' time they are often excluded from secretarial job descriptions. On the other hand, the tasks occupying most of a secretary's time are quite negatively affected by computers: almost all of these tasks are markedly reduced if not completely eliminated by electronic technology. Word processors, for instance, allow you to move words and paragraphs around, edit and correct spelling and grammar errors automatically, and produce a clean document without having to retype it. Some of the first research into the effects of office automation concluded that word processors contributed to labor savings of between 33 and 50%, although generally only in word processing centers.

It is more difficult to plot the indirect changes that occur with the advent of the integrated office automation systems, but their cumulative effect is enormous, as I discovered in my research for *Women and the Chip*. Here I studied a large corporate head office and an insurance company, and found a variety of changes which together reduced traditional secretarial workloads. In the corporate head office, for instance, a year after computer terminals had been installed on the desks of the professionals and executives, these individuals were using them to do up to 75% of the work that secretaries had once done for them. They were doing their own filing; their mail was automatically placed into their electronic in-baskets and coded according to priority. Software within the system was placing telephone calls and routing information according to addresses stored within the system's on-line memory. Although most of these executives couldn't type, they nevertheless managed fine with two fingers. In fact, some of them had even developed their own shorthand, typing things like "I want 2 CU 4" instead of a full, written-out message. Over the course of adopting automated information systems through the 1970s, this company also underwent a major reorganization. In one development, what had been a rather minor department dealing with data processing was renamed the Information Systems Department, having taken over the traditional paper-based work of the old Administrative Services Department and having enlarged its focus from just number crunching to the inclusion of every aspect of information work going on in the company. Although the new Information Systems Department and its workload grew dramatically, the number of clerical and administrative support workers (a category including not only secretaries but also mail and filing clerks) actually dropped by 130 during this transition period. Jobs had disappeared by being simplified or by being completely automated. Workloads had been reallocated along more functional lines to make more efficient use of the new, more expensive computer equipment. Most of the routine correspondence and report preparation activities had been centralized into a word processing unit, a trend prevalent in large companies and one that became apparent throughout the United States and Canada during the 1970s. Only two secretaries were left in the new Information Systems Department.

The productivity of secretarial work—that is, the amount of work performed per secretary per day, or at its simplest, output over input—is increased enormously through office automation. Retyping is eliminated. Boilerplate, or stock paragraphs (e.g., clauses in legal documents) held on-line because of repeated use, cuts down on the overall amount of typing to be done. Other software programs allow for information to be pulled from a variety of electronic files and databases and inserted into a text automatically. Still other software photocopies or prints texts automatically. And the final result is that more and more work can be taken on with no increase in staff. This productivity increase won't immediately eliminate job openings for secretaries. In fact, the secretarial profession is forecast to continue growing throughout the 1980s. However, increased productivity due to electronics will eventually reduce job growth from the rate that reflected a rise in U.S. secretarial employment from four million to five million between 1970 and 1980.

Post-secretarial Work

While secretarial productivity is increasing, there are some indications that the complexity and challenge of the work might actually be decreasing. Two issues are pertinent to this development: deskilling of general secretarial work and, on the upper end of the occupation, an erosion of post-secretarial work in middle-management and administration. Here, the cause lies in a rapid increase in availability of varied software capable of performing semiautomatically a host of activities at this level, while at the same time eliminating the need for many of the organizational skills traditionally used by secretaries for achieving upward mobility. For example, software can make reporting redundant, for once information has been input into the system, no matter where, it becomes instantly accessible to anyone anywhere else in the system. Information is gathered, collated, and processed automatically, then formatted and displayed or printed out automatically complete with bar graphs and color where called for. Other software (called general ledgers or spreadsheets) updates and even helps to prepare and modify budgets. There's software to handle payroll and employee records; and software for managing production schedules, for setting up new files, and for establishing and maintaining accounting procedures, everywhere from factories to banks. One bank in Canada has begun to replace traditional office and branch managers with technical specialists having programming and other computer skills.

Deskilling

The term *deskilling* refers to a reduction in the complexity, variety, and actual skills involved in doing a job. It has come to be associated with office automation throughout North America, especially in large companies where technological change is often implemented in a *télématique* style. Here secretarial work is often reorganized into two categories: administrative support and word processing. Deskilling is inherent in that simple division, for each of the new job types immediately becomes less varied than when both were combined into the one job of secretary. In large corporate reorganizations the administrative support workers are generally located in satellite work areas from which they perform tasks for an entire management team or professional group. Their duties range from telephone answering and reception to research and some administration. The word processor operators are generally clustered together as well, either in small satellite word processing pools (sometimes referred to as "puddles") or in large centralized pools. Here they spend their entire days typing material for "clients" throughout the company who send work to the center and generally remain anonymous. In a situation like this, secretarial social skills are obviously no longer needed. As Anne Machung said in a speech to the International Conference on Office Work and New Technology in Boston, Massachusetts, a meeting organized by the U.S. Working Women Education Fund in 1982, "new 'machine skills,' then are replacing 'outmoded' social and organizational skills."

These machine skills aren't even very exciting in many cases. Although the software available with word processing systems is rich with potential to enlarge the work variety—i.e., it has the capability to generate color graphics, different typestyles, and so on—there is a tendency for the systems to be underutilized, and for the operators to be restricted to routine typing that soon becomes repetitive and boring. Software does the hyphenation and justification. Software checks spelling and wipes away typing errors. Any challenge once associated with development of good typing and language skills has now been eliminated and those skills made redundant.

In a study of word processor operators in San Francisco conducted by and then reported on by Anne Machung at the same Boston conference, one of the operators was quoted as saying, "After a while you realize that even the most ridiculously lousy typist and beginner could still come up with a perfect letter, but at first it's like magic; it looks good."

In the same study it was pointed out that a word processing supervisor had to replace operators after two or three years because of "burn-out," from "using their minds too little and their eyes too much," as she herself put it.

Health Issues

In the past several years, video display terminal (VDT) operators have been the single largest group reporting health complaints to the U.S. National Institute of Safety and Health (NIOSH). (An estimated 10 million people now work with VDTs.) Some of the health problems include cataracts, birth defects and miscarriages, blurred vision, headaches, backaches, and neck and shoulder pain. Concern about cataracts, birth defects, and miscarriages relates to suspected, but scientifically unsubstantiated levels of radiation emitted by VDTs. Concern about VDTs and cataracts surfaced when, in 1977, two *New York Times* copy editors who worked on VDTs developed radiation-induced cataracts. However, independent scientific examination of the *Times* VDTs revealed that the machines themselves were incapable of emitting enough radiation to produce the cataracts. And in 1983, experts assembled by the U.S. National Research Council to examine the effects of VDTs on vision concluded that the use of such equipment does not increase the risk of cataracts. Nevertheless, NIOSH is conducting a five-year study to determine whether any visual impairment is resulting from its own workers' use of VDTs.

The question of birth defects and VDTs is more controversial. On the one hand, statistical clusters of birth defects and miscarriages have been associated with women who operated VDTs while pregnant. (A *statistical cluster* refers to instances in which the rate of occurrence of a given phenomenon is far above the average.) Such clusters have occurred throughout Canada and the United States. In Washington, DC there were seven miscarriages out of twenty pregnancies among clerical employees in a computer-equipped office between 1979 and 1980. In Atlanta, Georgia, three birth defects were reported and seven spontaneous abortions occurred among nineteen pregnancies during 1979–1980 at the U.S. Army Defense Logistics Agency. Other instances have been reported in Dallas, Texas; and in Toronto, Ottawa, and Gander, Newfoundland, in Canada. While the facts themselves are not in question, scientists nevertheless have been unable to link conclusively the birth defects and miscarriages to VDT radiation. Conversely, no other cause for these birth defects has been found that would dispel the fears of many women working on VDTs during their childbearing years. As an interim step, however, some union contracts in the U.S. and Canada have won for VDT operators the right to be transferred off this equipment when pregnant. NIOSH has embarked on a three-year study that will examine 6,000 women workers, half of whom are VDT operators, and the other half are not. NIOSH intends to record any miscarriages among the subjects and any cases of infant mortality and birth defects among the subjects' children. Other factors, such as on-the-job stress and the general health histories of the subjects, will also be evaluated. The Canadian Occupational Health and Safety Research Institute in Montreal is conducting a similar study in which about 50,000 pregnancies are being monitored.

Eye strain and back and neck pain are other health issues often linked to ergonomics—that is, one's physical work environment. The lighting might not be right; hence, an adjustable reading lamp is often recommended. The chair might not be adjusted to the right height or it might not provide sufficient back support. The unit generating the image on the screen might be inadequate or faulty, thus causing a slight flicker. Though often too faint to be perceptible, this flicker will fatigue the eyes, bring on headaches and weaken one's eyesight.

The psychological and social side effects of working in word processing pools represent a third category of health issues. Scientists in Europe and in North America are studying possible links between stress symptoms such as headaches, sleep problems, and drug dependency with assembly-line conditions such as the ones found in large centralized word processing pools. One of the most interesting studies was conducted by NIOSH in the 1970s. It monitored certain stress indicators among two groups of clerical workers and two groups of professional workers, with one group in each of the occupational categories using VDTs and the other using conventional office equipment. The professional VDT operators scored the lowest in stress and strain, the clerical VDT operators scored the highest, and the clerical workers not using VDTs placed somewhere in between. The study concluded that the source of stress lies in the organization of work and job content. Subsequently in 1983 NIOSH launched a three-year study to explore the relative importance of different stress sources: variety versus routine in the job, control and discretion over how the job is done, degree of self-esteem, and the nature of one's working relationships with others.

Organization of Work

In 1982 a New York consulting firm was engaged by the Professional Secretaries International (PSI) to survey PSI members' views on office automation. On the surface, the findings were very encouraging. Although office automation was still only a minor development in most of the firms where the responding secretaries worked, they looked forward to its opening up new career opportunities for them while at the same time relieving them of dull tasks such as filing and photocopying. Specifically, they anticipated moving on to more challenging work in office management and administration. However, that was not the view of the executives for whom these secretaries worked, who were also included in the survey. Responding executives anticipated that secretaries would move on to "specialized positions in data processing or office automation."

This difference in expectations on the part of secretaries and executives is critical to the future of the secretary. Taking the more functional view expressed by the executives in the PSI survey, secretarial work could be severely restricted and reduced in scope. Furthermore, the physical separation of word processing pools and data processing centers could lead to the eventual emergence of companies specializing in word processing and data processing services, to which large corporations would contract out all of this sort of work. Employees of these word and data processing service bureaus could be located in satellite offices scattered throughout an urban or suburban area. They could even be located in their own homes or apartments, turned into electronic cottages by computer and communications technology. In an electronic cottage work situation, material would be transmitted to one's home computer terminal via a telephone line.

This latter development in the organization of work is still largely speculative; however, some U.S. companies are excited about its potential for reducing overhead and giving part-time work to housebound people (usually mothers) unable to find or afford daycare facilities allowing them to take on regular office work. If these trends continue, there is a real possibility that instead of blossoming the secretarial profession itself could change very little, and that in numbers it could shrink to become the preserve of only a small minority, a secretarial elite.

But there is another way of looking at secretarial work, a way that sheds a much more positive light on the future of people currently employed as or training to become secretaries. This is a strategic view focusing on the process of running an office, not on specific tasks and functions performed within that process. Secretaries themselves tend to have this broader strategic conception of their role, and it is a laudable one. However, in an age of increasingly specialized and science-influenced management, a personal expression of that role—stressing one's personal skills and working relationships—might no longer be appropriate or even sufficient. Secretaries could do well to rethink their strategic roles within the organizations for which they work, with a view toward achieving specialized skills and abilities in the context of high technology. This means, for instance, that secretaries with a keen sensitivity for inspiring people to work together and smoothing ruffled egos should now start learning about such technologies as teleconferencing and electronic files so that they can advise the experts how to fine-tune these technological devices to fit and reflect the personal style and individual needs of the people within their organizations.

NEW CAREER PATHS

Back in the good old days when businesses were small and run by rule of thumb, the secretary was a generalist—an office manager, an administrator, an executive assistant, and a correspondence assistant. Promotion into management wasn't guaranteed, but it happened often enough to establish secretarial work as a pre-management training ground. Today, when businesses are large, infinitely more complex, and almost of necessity run by technical experts on productivity and scientific management, the secretary is at a critical crossroad. One route could lead to drudgery as a machine operator in data or word processing. The other could lead to a meaningful career in office management, information management, or some other professional information segment of the workforce. The gateway to this latter route involves at least two things. It requires both specialization and personal initiative on the part of the women and men who either have or wish to have careers in the secretarial field. Potential areas of specialization include computer graphics, systems analysis, and database management. Viewed strictly as computer applications, they are foreign territory to most secretaries now. However, they are really only a technological extension of traditional secretarial work. There is a lesson in this: your best hope for the future will likely be tied to an evolution of some aspect of what you're doing now. So take some time to think about secretarial work—not in terms of narrow functions and tasks, but rather in terms of broad, strategic themes. Most of it is information work of three kinds, each being a steppingstone to new computer-assisted information work:

1. information management and administration
2. information formatting and packaging
3. information brokerage and research

The first career path, leading into administration and management, would be appropriate for those with strong organizational skills and a natural interest in that area. The second could lead to work in some of the neophyte companies specializing in computer-based information goods and services; it would appeal to someone with artistic talent and a flair for creating good layouts. The third specialization would be attractive to secretaries who relish research assignments, for as the number of commercially available databases increases, so too will the scope for information brokerage, thus opening up a whole new career area previously nonexistent.

Information Management and Management/Administration

While secretarial work involves many activities, information management is perhaps the most important for it is around the success of this activity that the health and success of the organization depend. Good secretaries know how to organize information according to subjects and priorities, and route people and their information (verbal or written in form) through an organization—and with efficiency, tact and grace. With office automation, however, there is less paper and fewer people in transit to manage. Instead you have more electronic bits of information to route through more hard- and software components. As a result, one of the first possible steps in developing a career path in this new area is by specializing in database management. Computer languages and systems specifically designed for this application already exist. Besides having a general knowledge of how organizations work and how information flows through them—knowledge which most secretaries acquire almost intuitively on the job—it would also be helpful to study library referencing and indexing systems. The difference between running an ordinary filing system and running a library is largely one of degree; however, the larger systems associated with libraries require more formal systematized procedures for categorizing and cross-referencing information. Database management systems are similarly formal and systematic in approach. A career path here might begin with your helping a technical expert set up an electronic filing system or corporate database. A next step might involve your working with the database—sorting and updating its files. Although many of the database management systems available off-the-shelf—that is, through computer stores and consultants—are flexible enough to make it unnecessary for you to change the computer program, you would still probably find it useful to master a programming language. This mastery will give you the option of modifying existing database software, to fine-tune it to your office's needs, so to speak. It would also give you the option of moving into the more technical areas of program analysis, systems design, and systems analysis. In offices dealing with specialized information (e.g., law and medical offices), database management takes on an added dimension because the stored information therein can be vital to later research carried on in-house or by outsiders. A law office specializing in malpractice suits might make some database information available to doctors wishing to avoid malpractice suits or to patients wishing to launch such suits. The database manager and administrative assistant would have to anticipate such ancillary uses when organizing the database and coding its information for future retrieval. The same law office also might use its database as the prime source for a short course in malpractice law to be packaged in videotex form for insurance company in-house training purposes.

If you want to get into more generalized management, it would be useful for you to take courses in business and office administration and perhaps in accounting as well as in computers. A secretary with a good knowledge of how the office works could be employed as an assistant to a computer programmer, advising how to design the automated office system that would best harmonize with that organization's particular style, workflow, and procedures. After having taken some computer courses—e.g., introduction to computer systems, the principles of programming, and programming in BASIC or FORTRAN—the programming assistant could then advance to a job as office-systems administrator, a position that could later lead into middle management.

Middle management is becoming much more technical. Although its human-resource aspect is by no means disappearing, the new technical aspect of it demands that managers be able to control the technological resources of the automated office, putting them to use both cost effectively and flexibly (i.e., according to the changing needs of the professional and executive personnel). Moving into this work doesn't require that you become a computer scientist or electrical engineer. But you must keep abreast of developments in office automation, be comfortable working with computer systems and technical experts, and have a good knowledge of business administration and the systems theory associated with computer technology. Although occupational titles will remain in a state of flux for some time to come, the new middle manager will likely be similar to a systems administrator.

Information Formatting and Packaging

This career path picks up where ordinary typing leaves off. It involves the use of creative talent in conjunction with computer graphics and the color and typographic features associated with computer printers. It can lead to paraprofessional and professional information work within the company you work for, most likely in the public relations or personnel departments, or in a new company expanding the horizons of what seems to be a new sector in the economy—the information sector. In this sector, employment will involve creating and marketing new information goods and services.

The path to this career might lie in word processing, although not necessarily. The important thing for you to do is to acquire a working knowledge of word processing and text-editing systems and their software, and to find imaginative opportunities in which to apply that knowledge and those related skills. There is software for creating columns and charts; software for drawing pictures and graphs; software for underlining, coloring, and shading areas. There ought to be a fair amount of scope for applying all this software in public relations, where the goal is to communicate information and a particular corporate image at the same time. Personnel should offer possibilities too, since personnel manuals and instructional materials are increasingly prepared in electronic form for display on employees' computer terminals at home or in the office. Since the technology allows packaging of this material in a much more accessible and pleasing way, it's likely to raise the expectation that some real effort be put into the work of packaging and display. To augment one's basic typing and information display skills, one could take courses in graphic arts and computer graphics. It might also be good to study public relations and advertising if you're interested in the media, or education or organizational behavior if you're interested in preparing training materials or in other aspects of personnel work.

Outside traditional organizational structures and occupations, you should watch for developments in some of the new information industries such as videotex. In one videotex application, several retail shopping firms in the United States have launched a new form of shopping called "teleshopping." In fact, teleshopping is a variation of the old-fashioned mail-order system, but the catalogue has been transformed into pages of computer graphics relayed to the consumers' home television sets or computer terminals via their telephones. The system, as well as its computer graphics, is called videotex. Several occupations are associated with the packaging and delivery of this advertising information for videotex. First, the page creator composes the actual pages of the catalogues (updated daily in some cases). This work involves word processing, text editing, and formatting together with computer graphics and pictorials. Often, companies specializing in this work will provide their own training for page creators, although they expect recruits to have typing skills and at least some experience in graphic design or illustration. Many people going into this field have backgrounds in newspapers and advertising agencies. But there's no reason why secretaries with some report-writing experience can't move into the field as well.

Editing is another videotex occupation. Editing requires good organizational abilities, an ability to relate material to an intended audience, and a sense for communicating. In a bank wanting to prepare packages of financial information and how-to advice for customers using telebanking (that is, bank customers doing their banking via home computers), the editor would help design the overall package and rough out the information to be contained on each page of videotex display. The page creators would take over from there.

Incidentally, some companies are experimenting with videotex for use in in-house training programs. Secretaries employed by such companies could move into this challenging information field without ever leaving the companies. As an example, secretaries in law offices might become involved in creating information packages for in-house or outside training and for research aids. In medical offices similar opportunities might exist for developing various information packages out of medical files to be used as educational and self-help aids. A third and rather more technical occupation in videotex work involves structuring the entire system first to mount the pages for display and then to deliver them through communications networks. Some knowledge of computer programming, plus some training in library science would be almost essential.

Information Brokerage and Research
While the first career path focuses on information organization and management and the second, on information packaging and display, the third career path concentrates on information usage. As such, it can lead all the way to the executive ranks. From simply getting information according to given specifications, the work leads to taking on more and more research initiative and, from there, to analysis and decision-making. The work should attract those secretaries who are interested in finding answers, solving problems, and getting results—all essential attributes for success as an executive. At its most junior level, the work would be little different from that most tedious of secretarial tasks, finding information located in files or lurking at the bottom of somebody else's in-basket. But instead of file searches, the work involves dialing up a database to relay the specifications on information needed by a professional such as a chemical or electrical engineer designing a new product and needing the latest data on the properties of a particular chemical or material. At a higher level, an information broker would be responsible for formulating the key word search—that is, the specifications on the basis of which information is pulled from the database and then relayed to the

client company. It takes some learning and experience to become proficient at formulating key word search commands. Watch for articles in specialized trade journals dealing with commercial database services; there are well over 200 commercial databases, or electronic reference libraries, available across North America. At a higher level, a middle manager in charge of information brokerage would be responsible for keeping abreast of developments in the field of commercial databases, knowing their access protocols (call numbers really), and also being able to advise senior management on the most useful databases to subscribe to on a regular basis, and to budget for the company's research needs.

Although research and information brokerage can become a full and rewarding career in itself, the option of moving beyond research into analysis work also exists, either in production planning, financial analysis, or marketing. Of course, one's own interests and aptitudes as well as the available opportunities will affect one's choice of career path.

There's a good deal that secretaries can do for themselves in helping to create new career opportunities. For instance, it's worth reminding employers that it is often more costly to hire outside technical experts than it is to retrain existing staff who already know, at an intuitive level, how the organization runs and how to get things done. The technical-expert recruit must flounder through a long and very expensive adjustment period before understanding the organization well enough to work effectively within it.

OTHER ISSUES TO THINK ABOUT

The PSI survey findings seem to contradict themselves. On the one hand, responding secretaries were very positive about their future in automated offices, expecting to work with the automated information systems in new and rewarding ways. On the other hand, half of the secretaries said that they were dissatisfied with existing opportunities for advancement. Among the secretaries in the under-thirty age bracket, only a third were sure they really wanted to be secretaries in the first place. And, in a third finding, 40% of the secretaries felt that they were overqualified for their jobs.

Reading between those lines, one could wonder whether the job title *secretary* is becoming more of a liability to women's office careers and less of the treasured asset it has been in the past. Perhaps the time has come to modify this title to reflect more appropriately the work being done and the aspirations and qualifications of those doing the work.

Job Title

The original meaning of the word *secretary* had nothing to do with people; it was a piece of furniture used for writing. Today, as executives routinely refer to their desktop computer terminals as "my electronic secretary," there is a real temptation to let evolution take its course, and to let *secretary* come to mean the electronic equipment or furniture used to provide automated information and office management services. But what of the millions of people who've invested time and energy into becoming good secretaries? Surely there is a way of affirming the importance of their traditional identity, but in an enlarged definition of their occupation. It would be appropriate to the times as information management and information work are expanding. It would also be more appropri-

Table 1. Career Paths from Secretary to Information Worker

Level	Occupational Title	Work Function
Pre-secretarial	Information technician/machine operator	electrical technician fixing, testing equipment, etc. computer operator word processor operator data entry clerk
Secretarial	Information processor a) Administrative-systems assistant	database maintenance software support programmer/assistant programmer
	b) Paraprofessional	computer graphics text composition information brokerage
Post-secretarial	Information processor a) Office systems administrator	database management computer-assisted administration programming
	b) Professional	manager, reference and research manager, information display
Middle Management	Systems administrator	systems maintenance and management systems analysis and design
	Executive team	computer-aided research, analysis, planning, and decision-making

ate to the increasing specialization of white-collar work. Finally, it would more adequately accommodate the career developmental and mobility expectations among the people currently entering or considering the secretarial field.

The single job title *secretary* can refer to an information manager, an information packager, and an information broker. Within the secretarial position there are also many levels of responsibility ranging from following instructions to bearing at least some responsibility for administration and office management. It is important to recognize these differing levels of responsibility, as well as the diverse secretarial functions that can be channeled into more specialized careers, and to formalize them into an occupational standard. At the least, thinking about alternate job titles will help us to clarify what is now only a vague outline of potential career paths.

Table 1 illustrates how a new series of occupations could be created. In it, I have taken each aspect of work implicit in the secretarial role and made it explicit. Hence, secretarial services becomes administrative services and, at the most senior level of responsibility, systems management services. The titles are arbitrary; I have invented them purely for demonstrating what I mean. They're intended simply as something for you to think about and be guided by as you prepare for the future.

Education

When the Canadian philosopher Marshall McLuhan coined the phrase "learning a living" back in the 1960s, hardly anyone knew what he was talking about. Today, people are still only beginning to realize how clearly he understood that ongoing technological change was going to make continuous adult education a necessary constant of our working lives. Office workers everywhere—whether they call themselves secretaries, information managers, systems administrators, or whatever—must keep abreast of new technological developments in their area of specialization: database management, electronic and voice messaging, or financial spreadsheets. They must take courses pertinent to computer applications in their specialization. And they must add computer literacy to a solid basic education.

Basic education.   A good basic education is the foundation on which you can learn more, relatively easily. But the three traditional Rs deserve a bit of revision for this day and age. Instead of reading alone, all forms of information intake should be stressed: good listening skills, the ability to read graphs, and so on. Instead of writing alone, techniques of preparing computer graphics, slides, transparencies, and oral presentations should be taught. And instead of just arithmetic, there is a need for teaching good reasoning skills. These range from the discipline of thinking in a systematic way and being able to break down complex problems or projects into a logical series of discrete steps to, on a more technical level, the methodologies associated with higher mathematics and computer programming.

Computer literacy.   It seems that the definitions of computer literacy are as plentiful as the experts offering them. This author takes the term to mean a general ability to work in a computerized work environment and to exploit the computer systems in it. Many colleges and schools offer weekend workshops in computer literacy or computer awareness. They might start by reviewing the four basics of computers and their different applications in offices, factories, warehouses, banks, hospitals, and so on. They might explain some of the fundamental principles involved in programming, in data inputting and database management systems. They might also deal with some of the more common computer languages. The point to remember is that, just as you use the telephone every day without having to know much about its technology, so will you soon be using the computer without having to know a thing about bits and bytes and RAMs and ROMs.

Further education.   With the technology changing so fast, schools and colleges are still scrambling to understand what kind of education is required to master it, and they have barely begun to design the necessary additions to their curricula. It is a time, therefore, when individuals must take the initiative, and almost custom-design their own educational agenda. Secretaries interested in an information management career are advised to take some courses in business administration from a secretarial or business administration school, as well as courses in computer systems theory and, perhaps some courses in programming. Those interested in information packaging should take a course in graphic arts from an art school, plus one in computer graphics. For those interested in information brokerage, a course in research and reference systems at a school of library science would be useful, along with a course in database management systems.

Other forms of education. It is vital that you keep abreast of technological developments and continue to learn and grow in your work. But that doesn't have to mean spending the rest of your life going to night school. In an age of lifelong learning, when learning and earning are becoming more intertwined, a host of educational options are available for continuing your education on formal and informal levels. On a formal level, many colleges and schools now offer "distance education"—that is, courses made available to people in their homes or places of work, with the traditional classroom teacher having been replaced or augmented with an audio- or videotape or a computer disk. You can also learn through a variety of informal channels, such as subscriptions to journals specializing in computer applications in your own area of work—be it information brokerage in a law firm or a government office, information management in a library or a hospital, or layout and information packaging in a publishing house or an advertising agency. In addition, you can join associations in your occupational or professional group. There are traditional associations like Professional Secretaries International and younger, more technical associations in fields such as information processing, database management, and systems administration. These associations usually publish authoritative newsletters and magazines full of information useful in advancing your career. They often sponsor educational programs or at least can counsel members on the best local educational opportunities available. And they hold annual and/or monthly meetings focusing on continuing education and self-improvement. Besides learning through listening to lectures and so on, you can learn by volunteering to organize meetings, by preparing and giving a talk, by looking after membership dues, and so on. Having recorded these credentials on your curriculum vitae (CV), you can impress potential future employers with your talent, maturity, and intellectual flexibility.

THE ELECTRONIC COTTAGE

The term *electronic cottage* was coined by Alvin Toffler to mean a new option in working; i.e., home-based work. A modern version of the home-based craftsmanship and cottage industry that flourished before the Industrial Revolution, the concept involves working via a telephone hookup between a home-based computer and another one in an office building downtown. Also known as "telecommuting," the concept holds out many advantages, not the least of which is greater flexibility in one's working lifestyle. Enthusiasts rave about the savings in gasoline, time, and nervous energy, for one can go to work at home instead of via rush-hour traffic, with dry-cleaning bills and the expense of restaurant lunches having been eliminated. By working at home, you "go to work" when you feel like it; you make your work fit the schedule of children's school hours, college classes, or fitness activities. You're also in the comfort of your own home away from annoying interruptions and the strain of office politics.

The electronics of the automated office are also a boon for small businesses. You can literally establish a whole business in a spare bedroom, for you can seek out customers or clients and deliver finished work all by way of a simple computer installation. As a former secretary, your electronic cottage industry might be in information processing (data and word processing and text-editing services), in computer graphics for public relations, or perhaps in research services. In recent years there has been a proliferation of such little companies, some of which are based in private homes; others, in shopping malls.

There are, however, some negative aspects to the electronic cottage that must be acknowledged and guarded against. The one most feared by women secretaries is the danger of the electronic cottage's becoming a new job ghetto for women. They fear a scenario in which a woman takes home-based word processing work as a means of earning some money while tending small children, but then is stuck doing only that kind of work with no chance of promotion. Not only would she be physically cut off from the larger organizational whole, thereby being kept unaware of possible career advancement opportunities, but also she might be paid on a piecework basis (i.e., paid by the quantity of work produced and not by the hour). This situation would reinforce the narrow focus of her work identity.

POSTSCRIPT

It has seldom been more appropriate to remember that the present is where the past encounters the future. Change always accompanies that intersection, inevitably bringing some fears but at the same time offering an equal number of new opportunities to be taken advantage of. The change that computers are bringing is so profound that it has been described as a second Industrial Revolution. Nowhere else will that revolution be felt more acutely than in the office setting and in particular by the secretarial profession. While the electronic revolution will eliminate many of the tasks involved in your job, it also should widen the scope of your job considerably, for secretaries are at the information center of every office. Just as this center is made richer and more vital through office automation, so too should secretaries come into their own as office professionals, as they learn new ways of gathering, packaging, routing, and managing information.

Making the transition from traditional secretary to modern, computer-literate information worker requires fitness in the fullest sense of the word. This means your becoming informed about the nature of the new technology that is transforming North American offices and other places of work; your acquiring the necessary skills to work effectively with that technology; and your being open to change, to exploration of new career options, to acceptance of new responsibilities and a willingness to embrace new challenges. This might require leaving behind the traditional job title of *secretary* in favor of *information processor* or *systems administrator*. It might require a greater commitment to education and some adjustments in personal lifestyle. All of these changes, though, are up to you. You, the reader, are standing on the springboard to the future; it's only by jumping clear sometimes that you can truly enter the future.

2

Successful Career Development and Personnel Interaction

Jacqueline L. Larkin • *Telemarketing Manager, Warren, Gorham & Lamont; formerly Manager of Administration/Training, Transitional Employment Enterprises*

THE SECRETARY'S CHANGING, UPSCALE ROLE IN THE CORPORATION

The role of the secretary in today's office environment has changed dramatically with the introduction of high technology and with changing attitudes toward the office worker's function. In addition to having office proficiency, secretaries now must be able to work independently and make more decisions within the scope of their individual responsibilities. Instead of merely "taking care of" their supervisors, today's secretaries are taking on aspects of their supervisors' jobs. Secretaries make an important contribution to business, academia, human services, and government. The fact that nearly three million secretaries are currently employed in the United States demonstrates the widespread need for qualified people to fill the many job slots available. The secretarial profession is unique in that its scope is as diversified as the number of businesses and agencies that require office workers.

A recent study describes the typical secretary as a married woman in her forties with a teen-aged child at home. Five out of six of those profiled had more than a high-school education. Just as the profile of the office worker has radically changed in the last ten years, so have the responsibilities of the typical secretary. A job description of general secretarial duties would probably include the following:

1. answer customer correspondence

2. gather research data for reports

3. prepare statistical reports involving sales figures or budgetary information

4. attend meetings in place of supervisor and report activities that took place

5. set up conferences and meetings

6. purchase office equipment and participate in the evaluation and selection of some automated office systems

7. write a company newsletter
8. keep department expenditure records in accordance with a budget
9. transcribe documents from dictated media
10. make travel arrangements and plan itineraries
11. read and sort incoming mail and answer it when necessary
12. maintain and organize filing systems
13. take minutes at company meetings
14. make appointments
15. acquaint new employees with company systems and equipment
16. supervise one or more employees

Thus the duties required of today's secretary are far different from those of the stenographer who, in the past, was neither expected nor advised to use independent judgment and initiative in making substantive decisions. Nowhere is this difference more apparent than in the definition of *secretary* written by Professional Secretaries International:

> an executive assistant who possesses a mastery of office skills, who demonstrates the ability to assume responsibility without direct supervision, who exercises initiative and judgment, and who makes decisions within the scope of assigned authority.

As we have seen in Chapter One, office automation has permanently affected the role of the secretary. And with the continued development of new telecommunications equipment, secretaries now must be prepared to learn new and more technologically oriented procedures. The secretary who has "technophobia," or a fear of computers, will not survive long in today's office. The widespread introduction of this new office technology has created many new career paths for the secretary. For example, many companies have established word processing centers that handle standardized contracts, reports, and proposals. As a result, the position of word processing supervisor and trainer has become common in large organizations. Depending on the sophistication of the equipment itself, word processing can be highly technical and can require some data processing knowledge. Sophisticated equipment like the laser printer and graphics terminal may be part of the word processing center. If the word processing equipment is connected to the company's mainframe computer, access to confidential information and password-protected documents may be the responsibility of the word processing supervisor. This is a job requiring far more ability than that needed to supervise a space-age typing pool.

How can you keep up with office automation? Many courses are available for those interested in word processing and data processing. Or, when your company installs word processing equipment, appropriate training will usually be provided by the vendor. Make sure you are trained on the new equipment and that you keep up with the ever-changing, ever-improving software. Computer technology will be an integral part of every office in the near future. Don't sell yourself short by avoiding it. (See Chapter One for a detailed discussion of avenues of career advancement opened up to you by way of high technology.)

PROFESSIONAL SECRETARIAL COMPETENCY

Education has become an important factor for today's secretary. Many secretarial jobs require a college background as well as technical skills. For that reason, continuing education is a must for the secretary aspiring to advance to a higher professional level. More and more companies have made tuition assistance available for employees at the secretarial level to encourage career advancement. The abilities discussed in the next paragraphs are basic requirements for most secretarial jobs.

Business Writing

You have to be able to write effectively, clearly, and correctly. Since most business communications are read by a number of people inside and outside the organization, the content of any outgoing document must be grammatically correct, concise, and easy to understand. Many guides designed to help you enhance your writing ability are available. Along with a basic writing guide, you should also have a dictionary, a style manual, and a thesaurus at hand. In many ways, business writing is like newspaper reporting. If you follow the "who," "what," "when," "where," and "why" formula used by reporters, you will be able to cover every essential angle of your communication. If you have trouble with writing, many courses are open to you—some of which are geared specifically to the needs of the administrative assistant or secretary. A course in business writing is a sound investment for your career. (See also Chapter Eleven, "A Guide to Business English," herein.)

Knowledge of Business Math and Accounting

Knowing basic arithmetic is a necessity in a business environment. Many executives depend on the capability of administrative personnel to compile reports involving percentages of increase and decrease in sales, to perform departmental bookkeeping, or to write budget variance reports. In many cases, a knowledge of simple accounting techniques can mean the difference in job status between a secretary and an administrative or executive assistant. Chapter Fifteen, "Accounting and Data Processing," has been written to assist you with basic, on-the-job accounting procedures.

Organization and Planning

Time management and organizational skills are solid ingredients for success in any secretarial position. The ability to set priorities and juggle several different tasks at once is necessary to command an efficient workflow. People have different ways of organizing their tasks and you should choose the one most comfortable for you. A common way to organize one's time is to make a list of things to do and set the order of priority for each item on the list. Some workers plan their time in blocks with different activities scheduled for certain times of the day.

Since your time is valuable, it is necessary that other people in the office understand it and realize that you must complete your own scheduled activities on target. If you are in the middle of a detailed, high-priority project and someone else wants to speak with you, schedule a time later on when you can meet with that person. While interruptions are part of your job, you nevertheless need to determine the importance of each interruption. Otherwise, you will never get anything done. If your workload is too heavy and help is at hand, take advantage of it. And don't be afraid to delegate tasks that can make your own job easier. If you try to do everything yourself in a short time, you may not produce the kind of quality work you can be proud of.

Typing and Shorthand

Typing speed is still a prerequisite for many secretarial jobs. Top-level administrative positions often require a typing speed of 60 words per minute or above. Shorthand also is used as a benchmark to measure the skill level of applicants for secretarial positions. Therefore, both of these should be kept at an acceptable performance level. They are of potential value in almost any profession. Shorthand is particularly useful when taking notes or gathering information for research.

INTERPERSONAL RELATIONS

Communication

The American Heritage Dictionary, Second College Edition, defines communication as "... exchange of thoughts, messages, or information as by speech, signals, or writing." Communication skills are needed in any profession, but they are especially crucial to the secretary since a major function of the job is handling communications, whether they be verbal or written. We have already mentioned written communications and the need to be clearly understood when executing a well-written document. But two other communication skills must be addressed.

Oral skills. You may have good ideas to contribute to your business environment, but if you can't articulate them effectively, they will be lost. Speaking well requires a command of the English language, good diction, and the self-confidence to speak up. If you are shy and have little experience speaking in front of a group, take a continuing-education course in public speaking. Such a course can help you overcome your fear of addressing a group. Most of the other students in the class will be there for the same reason you are and will understand your own difficulties. If you are to take on a career role as a supervisor or trainer, chances are you will have to speak in front of one or more persons on a regular basis. And the more you speak publicly, the easier it gets.

Body language. The signals we use to communicate are often called *body language*. Your posture and gestures convey a number of attitudes and emotions including pride, anger, hostility, fear, self-esteem (or lack of it), and defensiveness. If you are nervous or jittery, you can appear uncertain or insecure about your abilities. Try to be as aware of your appearance as possible without becoming self-conscious, of course. If you want to send a self-assured, confident signal, look directly into the eyes of the person who is talking with you. A smile or nod will assure the person with whom you are speaking that you agree with or understand what they are trying to convey. Analyze some of the gestures and nuances of your nonverbal communication style and try to determine what kind of mes-

Table 1. Body Language and the Messages It Conveys

Negative action/mannerism/gesture/posture	Negative message/impression thus conveyed
hands tightly folded across chest	insecurity; defensiveness
clasped/unclasped hands; fiddling with rings, necktie, lapels	nervousness; stress
biting of fingernails	deviousness and deceit; nervousness and general insecurity
sitting with crossed legs, skirt hitched up; fiddling with hair (used of a woman)	flirtatiousness
lack of eye contact with the person to whom you speak	disinterest in the other party, the conversation, or instructions being conveyed to you; deviousness
slouching, either while standing or while sitting	boredom; laziness; disinterest in job or conversation
holding hand over mouth while talking, especially during a meeting	fear
typing, filing, etc., while wearing a transistorized radio headset	tuned completely out of the job and its responsibilities
Positive action/mannerism/gesture/posture	**Positive message/impression thus conveyed**
hands held loosely at sides, in jacket pockets, or behind back	ease; confidence; relaxation; openness with others
steady eye contact with the person to whom you speak	interest in the other party, the conversation, or instructions being conveyed to you; straightforwardness, candor, and honesty
erect yet relaxed posture while standing, walking, or sitting	energy; control; self-confidence

sage you are conveying. It is easy to develop bad habits in conversation and in the gestures we use to support our speech. If you become more aware of what you are doing, it will be easy to correct any bad habits.

Effective Listening

It has been said that we hear 20% of what is being said and we only listen to 10% of what we hear. In order to take direction and do many of the tasks a secretary must perform, listening ability must be markedly improved above the norm. The first step is learning how to listen actively. Try to clear your head of all other thoughts and concentrate only on what is actually being said. Take notes and avoid interrupting the speaker until his or her thought has been completed. Try not to analyze what you are listening to until you have heard the complete message. If you don't take the time to listen carefully, you may end up having to do projects over several times. Sometimes the speaker does not convey a thought as clearly as you may need to follow directions. But if you have taken notes, you may be able to ask the right questions to clarify the instructions. Remember that it is very irritating to a busy executive when a secretary continually returns with numerous questions, the answers to which were already given in previous instructions.

Your Image

In the 1960s it became acceptable to wear dungarees and long hair to public school. Offices then reflected the trend of more casual dress, and as a result women began to wear slacks, jeans, and pantsuits to work. Although casual dress for professionals became commonplace, it never became the preferred mode.

Table 2.   Dressing for Success: Questions and Answers

Question	Answer
Do many companies have dress codes?	No, but they do have unwritten rules or standards of attire. We suggest that you observe the dress of the executives—both men and women—and of their secretaries to discern the overall style of the company. Some companies do state in their employee handbooks that personnel are requested to come to work in dress "appropriate to the business environment."
Please characterize a typical business environment in which corporate style is considered important.	A typical conservative, or traditional, business environment might be that of a publishing house, a large TV network, a city newspaper, a law or accounting firm, or a government office where the general public, outside clients, and perhaps authors or public figures are often received. In such an environment, the importance of a positive public image is keenly felt.
Who is most influential with respect to dress and general style in a company?	The chief executive and operating officers set the overall style and tone of the business environment. This style is often reflected in the dress and manner of the employees at all levels. But in some companies, studied informality in itself is an indicator of the desired image.
What attire is generally acceptable in a relatively conservative business environment?	Jeans, stiletto heels, yards of gold chains, and satin shirts are out, for starters. We recommend for women and men a conservative tailored suit (or two) together with easily mixed and matched separates, conservative sweaters, shirts, and ties. Jewelry, shoes, and hairstyles ought to convey an image of businesslike self-confidence. In short, the employee—not the clothes—should stand out.

Many competent secretaries have been passed over for promotions because their appearance did not fit the corporate image. Employers still ask employment agencies and recruiters for so-called "front office types" when they look for executive secretaries and administrative assistants. If you are trying to make a positive impression on an employer, you should project a professional image by the way you are dressed.

HUMAN RELATIONS

Getting along with other people is an essential part of your job. You don't have to like someone personally to foster a good working relationship. If you present an even-tempered, positive image to all of your coworkers, they will more than likely respond to you in the same fashion. Your ability to get along with many different personalities will play a major role in your ultimate career development. It's a challenge to deal with a difficult person successfully—one that you will encounter many times over. To survive in a business environment, you must be objective and aware of the ways in which you interact with other people. Everyone has prejudices or predetermined ideas about others affecting their communication ability. Avoid stereotyping people or putting them into set categories. To deal with people effectively you yourself must be perceptive and understanding. Stereotyping builds an immediate barrier against open communication—a barrier that will hold you back from effective, sensitive interactions with others. Learn to evaluate your reactions to other people as well as their reactions to you. If you have an innate understanding of why people project certain images, it will be easier for you to interact positively with people from all walks of life.

Personal contact with visitors, service people, and customers should always be pleasant and businesslike. People associate a business with the person from that organization with whom they have had direct contact. Keep in mind that you are The Company to anyone from the outside, and the corporate image projected by you should be above reproach at all times.

You and Your Supervisor

Getting along with your supervisor is of major consequence to you. To a great extent, your supervisor will have a marked effect on your future. Many qualified secretaries have lost chances to advance because of personality conflicts with supervisors, situations that have resulted in poor recommendations. Learning to control your temper and emotions in business is therefore essential to your professional development. If you take criticism from your supervisor personally and harbor resentment about it, you will probably not be able to handle your job well. Learn to control your temper and evaluate a situation before you take any oral or written action. Sometimes the criticism is warranted and is meant to help you improve rather than to hurt your feelings. Of course, there will be times when you are called upon to deal with an extremely difficult person. Even though you may make every effort to get along with that person, it just won't work. In a case like that, you should consult Personnel for a transfer or look for another job.

Trust is another factor in a successful relationship with your supervisor. Many executives are under a great deal of pressure and will use you as a sounding board for confidential matters, particularly if you display good judgment. Never divulge any confidential information to your coworkers. Juicy secrets have a way of getting around a company fast. If word of this should get back to your supervisor, it could ruin your working relationship and eventually result in the loss of your job. Thus, absolute loyalty to your supervisor is essential. It can mean the difference between working with instead of for someone. Keep in mind also that the image you project is associated with that of your supervisor. If you are able to look upon your working relationship as a team effort, you will be considered capable of assuming as much responsibility as your supervisor is willing to delegate.

Good Human Relations

Certain qualities make a good secretary stand out from the crowd and progress quickly. You should try to develop the qualities discussed below in order to become exceptional at your job.

Responsibility and teamwork with the supervisor.   Your ability to accept responsibility and be accountable for your tasks will be judged on a daily basis. If you are conscientious and well organized, you should be able to perform those tasks well. Your willingness to assume additional responsibility will also be looked upon as an asset when your superior evaluates your performance. Acceptance of increasing responsibility by the secretary results in closer teamwork with the executive.

One way of increasing your worth in the eyes of your supervisor is to assist him or her actively in managing the flow of on-line projects in the office. To effect true executive/secretarial teamwork you should meet with the executive at least once a day, preferably early in the day, to set priorities for the day's activities—including appointments, anticipated telephone calls, dictation, correspondence keyboarding, and incoming/outgoing mail. Try to bypass crises by knowing your executive's daily plans in advance; in this way you can at least attempt to expedite the influx and outflow of people and paper. Ensure that the executive's appointment book and the entries in your copy of it match. Take the initiative to call expected visitors if you know that the executive is running behind schedule. Try to remember what took place the day before (consult your calendar, diary, or appointment book) so that you can, if possible, anticipate tomorrow's events to some extent. If your supervisor travels a lot, know where he or she can be reached at all times, and find out what is required of you in your supervisor's absence.

Understand the goals of your executive within the corporation and familiarize yourself with the goods, services, and products of the corporation. Only by exercise of initiative, use of common sense, and acceptance of responsibility can you work as a real team player with the executive.

Flexibility.   Business environments change rapidly due to growth, change in management, the fluctuating economy, and many other factors. In order to maintain a position in a business that is going through such changes, you must be able to adapt easily to new situations and be flexible enough to accept change. Changes can be upsetting if you are not forward-thinking.

A good disposition.   Moodiness is not acceptable in an office. It is necessary to be even-tempered and good-natured to maintain a pleasant working atmosphere. A moody or irritable employee can adversely affect the morale of the entire office. A good sense of humor can help you through stressful situations. Many times you will be asked to do a rush job that will keep you overtime or you will be requested to perform a task in an unreasonably short time. If you allow the situation to upset you emotionally or make you lose your temper, you could be displaying an immaturity that will haunt you when you want to make a career move later. People remember unpleasant situations. Think before you act and above all don't ever cry in the office.

Courtesy.   Since most offices are fairly formal, courtesy should be an integral part of your work habits. If you share an open space with others, care should be taken not to disturb your coworkers. If you smoke and your coworkers don't, find a place where you can have a cigarette break or ask to be moved to a spot where you will not irritate anyone else when you smoke. More and more offices are now providing specific smoking areas instead of allowing smoking in the entire office area.

Stability.   A well-integrated personality stands out in a crowd. If you are able to keep calm when an upsetting situation develops, you will become known as a very stable employee. Problem-solving is also part of the secretary's job: a clear and logical approach to a problem would be to identify it, break it down into components, and then determine a workable solution. Much valuable time and energy can be wasted by overreacting to a situation instead of trying to devise a sensible way to change the situation for the better. The more responsibility you assume, the more problems you will encounter. If you learn to deal with problematic situations as they occur in a step-by-step fashion, your self-confidence to assume more and more responsibility will be enhanced.

Assertiveness.   You can stand up for your own rights without being hostile. And you should be able to deal with those who may be rude or who try to take advantage of you without becoming emotionally upset, intimidated, or overly aggressive in response. Assertiveness training teaches us to express our opinions and feelings freely and candidly without playing the silly power game called The Big Putdown. Aggressive people (who are often very insecure) seem to be masters at this game. The loser, of course, is the nonassertive mouse (equally insecure) who flees the area of combat, licking his or her wounds, taking every putdown to heart, and often complaining to everyone else about the situation. A few mannerisms, particularly in conversations with superiors and coworkers, serve as assertive (but not hostile) signals to them. The message to be conveyed consistently is this: Don't play silly games with me because I won't bite. For example, when you and your superior have a crisis situation, say *we,* as in "*We* have a big problem today. What should *we* do about it?" as opposed to "*I* just can't deal with this. Whatever am *I* going to do?" (i.e., I can't handle it, Boss, *please* help me). And when talking with your coworkers use *you* as much as possible in all situations. Reserve the trump card *I* for instances in which you sense an impending conflict. If you use *I-I-I* and *me-me-me* constantly you will be (and sound) aggressive, thus generating hostility from those around you.

Firm repetition of your position in a conflict is another signal of healthy assertiveness. This technique is especially useful when you are attempting to get a reluctant employee to perform a task that you've been authorized to delegate. The key to effective use of this technique is sticking to the issue at hand, keeping calm, and not allowing yourself to be sidetracked into ancillary discussions by the other party. A number of excellent books and courses in assertiveness training are available and are well worth the time spent on them. In the highly competitive business environment of today, a sensitivity to the well-documented profiles of the assertive personality, the nonassertive personality, and the aggressive/hostile personality is essential to job survival and enjoyment.

Office Politics

The term *office politics* almost always has a negative connotation. It's true that getting involved in office politics in terms of gossip and deceitful behavior is negative. But in order to get your job done you will find it necessary to understand the overall political structure of your office and your place within that structure. Whether the office is large or small, there is a political structure based on power and decision-making. And people striving for advancement in business constantly develop and apply new strategies to enhance their positions within the corporate political structure. The secretary lacking keen political savvy can easily be caught in the middle of some very difficult, tricky situations. You must be observant and aware of other people's positions within the organization. Determine who gets certain jobs done and who makes the really important decisions. Treat those people accordingly. Read the company's organizational chart and determine the structure of your own office first and then that of the corporation in general. This kind of knowledge will help you when dealing with other departments and disseminating information outside your own office. Nothing is more embarrassing than making political faux pas because of your ignorance regarding someone else's position.

THE ADVANCEMENT LADDER

Deciding what career path to take is often determined by what you do best. When thinking about pursuing another position within your company or in another company, it is important to take certain steps before you make a move. First you must determine if you are qualified for the position you aspire to. If you are not so qualified, are you willing to upgrade your capabilities by taking courses and participating in seminars that will assist you in advancing to a higher level?

Basic Job Descriptions

Entry-level positions.   Clerk-typists and receptionists are considered entry level in most companies because they require only basic communication skills and keyboarding. No substantive responsibilities are included in such positions. Entry-level jobs rarely require shorthand and are considered the first step toward a secretarial career in business.

The secretary.   As we have indicated, certain basic competencies are required for any position labeled *secretarial*. Although shorthand may not be required, Dictaphone skills will usually substitute for it in an average position. Typing speed and accuracy are a must, as well as a good command of English. The specific level of the position may be defined by the number of tasks the secretary must perform without supervision. Depending on the type of business, a secretary may be asked to type and/or compose letters for the executive, order office supplies, make travel arrangements, plan on- and off-site meetings, write a company newsletter, screen callers and visitors, sort the executive's mail according to priority, and perhaps plan some of the company's recreational activities.

The two secretarial positions usually described as specialized are those of the legal secretary and the medical secretary. Although the required training for these positions is very specific, many other positions rely just as much on experience in the field as they do on specialization. For example, if you look in the business section of your newspaper, you will see that most of the secretarial jobs advertised have specific titles like "marketing secretary," "sales secretary," "publishing secretary," "personnel secretary," and "advertising secretary." Some of these jobs require extensive experience in a particular field and the employers equate such experience with X number of years in a secretarial school or college. A personnel secretary should have prior experience with personnel record-keeping systems and should be able to work under rules of strict confidentiality. A marketing secretary should be familiar with different aspects of advertising, production, copywriting, and publicity. Good research skills are extremely desirable. The ability to speak with many people on the telephone is an essential attribute. A sales secretary should be familiar with active lead follow-up and sales record-keeping as well as with customer files and correspondence. The ability to use a computer and to perform basic business mathematical operations is important. The sales secretary also must interact with various members of the company's sales force in a positive, organized manner. Planning sales meetings and covering for the executive(s) when absent are also important tasks. A publishing secretary should have an excellent command of the English language as well as some proofreading and copyediting experience, for the paperwork load in such a position is often quite heavy. An advertising secretary should be able to work under intense pressure and meet close deadlines. Excellence in communication is essential, for such a secretary is often called upon to assist in the preparation of ad copy or press releases. In addition, the ability to project a highly professional image through person-to-person contact and by way of manners and attire is requisite. These are just a few examples of the way you can specialize in a specific field. As you can see, each field of specialization focuses on and demands from you particular abilities that you can hone down and fine-tune as you gain more and more experience in the workplace.

Executive secretary.   This position is a big step up from a general secretarial position and usually involves a high degree of confidentiality and formality. Working for a high-level executive often involves scheduling meetings, taking minutes at board meetings, and then transcribing/typing them, doing public relations work, composing letters and instructions on your own initiative, and performing many other tasks such as screening calls/visitors and reading/evaluating mail with little or no supervision. Interpersonal skills come into play heavily in an executive secretarial position since it is a highly visible and very political position. You must be mature, honest, sophisticated, and diplomatic at all times.

Administrative assistant.   Every company seems to have a different definition for administrative assistant. In many cases it refers to an administrative support job performed with little or no supervision, and one that is a step higher than executive secretary. For example, an administrative assistant may handle dissemination of contract information or work with the chief financial officer of a company in preparing corporate reports. This position usually involves supervision of others and may require a college degree. A secretary is often promoted to administrative assistant when the manager decides to delegate additional responsibilities requiring more intensive effort than a strictly executive secretarial position does. Since so many companies differ in their definitions of administrative support positions, you should clearly understand the job description and the opportunities for advancement in the particular company offering such employment.

Medical secretary.   This highly specialized position requires training in medical terminology, medical office ethics and practice, and medical dictation/transcription procedures. The medical secretary is often required to manage an entire office, taking responsibility for its billing, records management, medical and office supply organization, and appointments. The position also requires good knowledge of accounting procedures and financial record-keeping. The medical secretary—usually called a *medical assistant/administrative* or a *medical assistant/clinical*—must be able to understand and process many kinds of complex health insurance forms. This position also requires excellent human relations skills, as well as the ability to deal with sick people, often in emergency situations. Colleges and some business schools offer certificate programs lasting from six months to two years. Medical secretarial positions can be obtained in hospitals, medical schools, private doctors' offices (single-physician or group practices), and clinics.

Legal secretary.   The job opportunities for one seeking this position are abundant. There are positions for legal secretaries in private law offices, courts, and corporate law departments. The training is also highly specialized and requires knowledge of legal and court procedures and familiarity with a myriad of forms and legal documents. There are all types of law practices. Many jobs are available in single-attorney offices where the legal secretary may serve really as an office manager, performing duties such as appointment scheduling, court appearance scheduling, preparing documents, billing, bookkeeping, and record-keeping. If the lawyer is a generalist, the legal secretary has to be proficient in a broad spectrum of procedures and documentation such as handling subpoenas, mortgages, deeds, closings, pleadings, briefs, wills, proxies, and abstracts. Working for a generalist is good experience for the neophyte legal secretary who would like to sharpen basic skills and gain wide experience. Positions are also available with lawyers specializing in real estate, criminal law, insurance, taxation, divorce, estate planning, government contract law, and bankruptcy. Large corporations often have their own in-house law departments specializing in labor law, insurance law, and taxation law. Opportunities to work in corporate law departments are available to those interested and qualified. The court systems—federal, state, and local—have to fill legal secretarial positions from time to time. A secretary therein might work for a district attorney, for a judge, or perhaps for a clerk of a court. Community colleges and secretarial schools offer career courses for legal secretaries. And if a secretary wants to achieve a higher level of specialization in the legal field, he or she may decide to become a paralegal aide—a position demanding further education.

Before deciding on any area of concentration, you may want to work in a temporary capacity in a law office, a medical office, or a business office to see if the atmosphere and job responsibilities suit your needs. Working for a temporary agency affords you the opportunity to try out different types of professions and companies. In this way you can get a clear view of the real world. It also may help you avoid making a serious, often expensive, career mistake.

Opportunities abroad.   The United States Department of State offers positions in over 300 countries around the world to secretaries who meet criteria for foreign service. When applying for the Foreign Service, you must be willing to work anywhere in the world. Candidates for Foreign Service also must meet the following criteria:

1. The candidate must be in excellent health and must be able to pass a physical examination.
2. The candidate must have a high school diploma or G.E.D. certificate.
3. The candidate must be a U.S. citizen. If married, the candidate's spouse also must be a U.S. citizen.
4. The candidate must be able to pass the U.S. Civil Service Examination requiring a shorthand speed of 80 words per minute and typing speed of 40 words per minute.

If the candidate successfully meets the requirements, the Department of State conducts a security check including an interview with the Central Intelligence Agency. If the candidate passes the investigation, he or she is then assigned to the Foreign Service Institute for orientation and further training before receiving a posting. For further information on opportunities in the U.S. Foreign Service, write to the Recruitment Branch, Employment Division, U.S. Department of State, Washington, DC 20520.

The government is not the only overseas employer, though. Large multinational corporations often recruit personnel in the United States for foreign assignments. Foreign job opportunities are advertised in major newspapers such as *The New York Times*, *The Christian Science Monitor*, and *The Washington Post*. If you enjoy travel and variety, you should consider applying for such a position.

PROFESSIONAL EXAMINATIONS AND CERTIFICATION PROGRAMS

Your professional development should involve the constant learning of new skills and the sharpening of those already acquired. This is the only way to survive and advance in the high technology business place of today. One way to enhance your professional status is by achieving certification through some of the examinations administered for professional secretaries. Certification is a valid goal for the truly career-oriented secretary. The following sections detail some of the steps you may have to take in order to acquire the credentials reflecting generally accepted standards of excellence in the secretarial profession.

The Certified Professional Secretarial (CPS®) Rating

Professional Secretaries International® (PSI) sponsors the Certified Professional Secretary (CPS) rating—probably the most well known and respected credential a truly professional secretary can attain. To obtain this certification, you must pass a two-day, six-part examination administered by the Institute for Certifying Secretaries. The exam is given on the first Friday and Saturday in May at about 338 examination centers in the United States, the Virgin Islands, Puerto Rico, and

Malaysia. Versions of the exam are also administered in Jamaica and Canada. The exam was first given in 1951 by the National Secretaries Association. (The name of that organization has since been changed to Professional Secretaries International.) Since 1951, the program has been accepted by many colleges and universities to the extent that it equals academic credit hours toward various degree programs.

The CPS rating does not guarantee an automatic salary increase or change in job status, but recent surveys show that a CPS may make an average of 15% more in salary than a secretary without the CPS status. This is an important factor to keep in mind. Furthermore, many companies in both the public and private sectors are encouraging their secretaries to take the CPS exam; this incentive takes the form of tuition aid plans for preparatory class studies and review courses as well as fee-paid examinations.

Qualifying for the CPS.   A secretary must have twelve months of continuous employment with one employer within the last five years prior to applying for the CPS exam. If you are currently employed, length of employment will be measured through December 31 prior to the examination. One of the following requirements also must apply to you:

1. If you have no college degree, you must have 4 years of verifiable secretarial experience.

2. If you have an associate degree, you must have 3 years of verifiable secretarial experience.

3. If you have a bachelor's degree, you must have 2 years of verifiable secretarial experience.

You may take the CPS exam prior to meeting the requirements as stated above, but you will not be granted the certification until the requirements for secretarial experience have been met.

Business educators and business education students also can take the CPS exam. A business educator in the secretarial field must submit the equivalent of a minimum of 12 months' cumulative secretarial experience within the past 25 years. The candidate must submit a letter of employment verification for the educational institution where he or she is employed. Business education students must meet the requirements listed above, and must also submit a certificate stating that they will receive a specific degree on a specific date.

The CPS examination.   There are six parts to the CPS examination:

I. Behavioral Science in Business
   Human relations, including an understanding of one's peers, oneself, and other work-related business relationships. Other focus areas include fundamental needs and motivations, the nature of conflict, leadership styles, essentials of supervision and communication, and an understanding of the informal organization.

II. Business Law
   Knowledge of business law as it relates to the working environment and the operation of government controls on business. History of the development of business controls.

III. Economics and Management
An understanding of the business relationships between Canada, Jamaica, and the United States (35%). Principles of management, finance, production, and marketing (65%).

IV. Accounting
A knowledge of accounting procedures and business mathematics, including computing interest and discounts, analysis of financial statements, and interpretation of financial data.

V. Office Administration and Communication
Proficiency in office administration and communications including, under administration (50%) executive travel, office management, records management, and reprographics; and under communication (50%) written business communication, editing, abstracting, and preparing communications in final format.

VI. Office Technology
An understanding of secretarial responsibilities created by data processing, communications media, advances in office management, technological applications, records management technology, and office systems.

Preparing for the CPS examination.   The Institute for Certifying Secretaries offers preparatory material for the CPS exam. These materials include sample questions, an outline of the examination's general topics, a study bibliography, and a time schedule for CPS review. Information on applying for the exam and ordering preparatory study materials may be obtained by writing to Professional Secretaries International, 301 East Armour Boulevard, Kansas City, MO 64111–1299. (CPS® and Professional Secretaries International® are registered trademarks.)

Professional Legal Secretary (PLS) Rating

Like the CPS exam, the PLS exam offers the legal secretary the opportunity to acquire career-enhancing professional credentials. The National Association of Legal Secretaries offers this seven-part exam nationally on the last Friday and Saturday of March and October. The candidate must have five years of legal secretarial experience to qualify for the exam. Two years' experience will be waived if the applicant has a degree. The major parts of the exam are as follows:

I. Written Communication Skills and Knowledge

II. Human Relations and Ethics

III. Legal Secretarial Procedures

IV. Legal Secretarial Accounting

V. Legal Terminology, Techniques, and Procedures

VI. Exercise of Judgment

VII. Dictation

Write to the National Associates of Legal Secretaries, 3005 East Skelly Drive, Tulsa, OK 74105.

Certified Medical Assistant (CMA) Rating

The American Association of Medical Assistants (AAMA) sponsors the Certified Medical Assistant examination twice a year on the first Friday in June and the last Friday in January. This three-and-one-half hour exam is national, and certification is recognized nationwide. The CMA examination covers general knowledge of medical procedures, clerical procedures, and administration:

I. Anatomy and Physiology

II. Medical Terminology

III. Medical Law and Ethics

IV. Psychology

V. Written and Oral Communications

VI. Bookkeeping and Insurance

VII. Administrative and Clinical Procedures

In addition to the general certification—the CMA—you may earn specialized certification in administrative—CMA-A—and clinical—CMA-C—areas. Those candidates earning certification both in the administrative and in the clinical categories may use the initials CMA-AC with their names. For more information on application procedures and qualifications, write the American Association of Medical Assistants, 20 N Wacker Drive, Suite 1575, Chicago, IL 60606.

Certified Administrative Manager (C.A.M.) Rating

For secretaries who have reached the administrative management level of the profession, an examination for the Certified Administrative Manager rating is provided by the Administrative Management Society (AMS). To obtain the C.A.M. certificate, you first must apply for candidacy and then complete the C.A.M. program standards within a seven-year period. To qualify for the C.A.M. certificate, you must:

1. Take C.A.M. exams in personnel management, financial management, administrative services, information systems management, management concepts, and an in-depth case study;

2. Have three years of administrative management experience;

3. Exhibit superior standards in personal and professional behavior;

4. Have participated in voluntary service organizations;

5. Have demonstrated innovative ability in developing administrative procedures and standards through written and oral communications.

When the program has been satisfactorily completed, candidates become members of the Academy of Certified Administrative Managers. For more information write to The Administrative Management Society, Maryland Road, Willow Grove, PA 19090.

Administrative Studies Program for Secretaries

Roosevelt University in Chicago now offers a program called Administrative Studies for secretaries. The program is fully accredited and results in a baccalaureate degree. Secretaries who have passed the CPS exam are given credit toward the degree. The program is designed for adults over twenty-five and offers electives in the following specialty courses: accounting, communicative arts, foreign language and culture, public administration, women's studies, computer science, management, marketing, personnel management, and health care administration. More information may be obtained by writing to the Dean of Admissions, Roosevelt University, 430 S Michigan Avenue, Chicago, IL 60605.

Seminars

In addition to certification, you may want to take advantage of helpful seminars that may focus on skills that you need to improve or refresh. Seminars usually condense a full course or a lengthy study program into a short time span. Most seminars run from one to three days, and if well structured, they can give you a mini-course that is as valuable as a semester's worth of study. Many organizations sponsor useful secretarial seminars. The American Management Association is well known in this area. Some of the topics covered in its seminars include career development for executive secretaries and administrative assistants, assertiveness training for first-line women supervisors, time management, organizational style, fundamentals of finance and accounting for secretaries, and fundamentals of data processing. For information on courses for secretaries write the American Management Association, Human Resources Division, 135 W 50th Street, New York, NY 10020.

The Institute for Certifying Secretaries also offers a variety of seminars. Some of them are "The Secretary in the Management Process," "Oral Communication and Effective Listening," "The Public Relations Image of the Secretary," "The Secretary in the Computer Age," "Interpersonal Communication," and "Career Growth for the Professional Secretary." Information on these courses can be obtained by writing to Professional Secretaries International, 301 East Armour Boulevard, Kansas City, MO 64111–1299.

Dun & Bradstreet has secretarial career development courses dealing with topics such as "How to Control Secretarial Stress," "Managerial Techniques for Better Job Control," "Working with People on the Job," "Writing Techniques for Secretaries," and "Computer Basics and the Electronic Office." For more information write to Dun & Bradstreet, Business Education Services, P.O. Box 803, Church Street Station, New York, NY 10008.

You may not realize it, but your company's own personnel department is an excellent source of information for continuing-education seminars and academic courses for career development. Most modern companies are concerned with upscaling their employees' skills and therefore require Personnel to maintain up-to-date information relevant to professional development opportunities.

THE ORGANIZED JOB SEARCH

Before setting out on an active job search, you should first determine your own marketability and your position in the job market itself.

Researching the Job Market

The U.S. Department of Labor publishes annually the *Occupational Outlook Handbook*. The *Handbook* describes major industries, including information such as growth potential and general business trends. Over 300 occupations are covered in it, along with information on salaries and working conditions. This is a good place to start when trying to determine your value in the marketplace.

Another publication that will provide you with valuable job classification information is *The Dictionary of Occupational Titles* (4th ed., 1977), and may be obtained by writing the Superintendent of Public Documents, U.S. Government Printing Office, Washington, DC 20402. Over 20,000 job titles are listed in this book, together with descriptions of each one. These publications and many others dealing with the job market are available in your public library. The U.S. Department of Labor publishes newsletters and labor statistics reports that you can also use in your research efforts. Before you apply for any job, however, you should assess your overall proficiency so that you can match your skill level with the various jobs you may apply for. A realistic, objective assessment of your own qualifications (including strong and weak points) will help you to avoid disappointments and failed expectations during the job search.

Your First Job

If you have recently graduated from secretarial school or have achieved a certificate in business training, you should have an accurate idea of your performance level in the most basic areas of typing, shorthand, filing, transcription, word processing, and office machine technology. But since you may have little or no job experience, it is often difficult to decide what kind of job suits your abilities and personality the first time. You might ask yourself some of the following questions at the outset:

1. Am I a people-oriented person? If so, would I enjoy a job where I will be dealing with the public on a regular basis, like a job in a sales or customer service department?

2. Would I rather work in a large, mid-size, or small company?

3. Is there a profession or business that I find particularly fascinating? If so, what is it?

4. What are my salary requirements? (NOTE: If you are a recent graduate of a secretarial school, your placement office may provide you with information on salary levels that you should pursue. Many employment agencies can provide current salary surveys and job classifications useful to you in assessing your own marketability.)

5. Where do I want to work? In the city or in the suburbs?

If you have no idea of the kind of job you are looking for or where to start, a temporary employment agency may be the answer. With basic secretarial training, you can find work easily in a temporary agency. This is an excellent way to try out different types of jobs without making a commitment until you are ready to decide where you want to work permanently. With temporary employment, you can work in almost any type of company and have the advantage of being able to observe the diverse jobs open in different businesses.

Companies require temporary help when there is an overload of work to be done, or if someone has left the company unexpectedly or is on vacation. If you are filling in for someone who has left the company and you make a favorable impression, more often than not you will be offered the job. Temporary agencies usually charge a fee to an employer who hires a temporary worker on a permanent basis. Since the fee is usually less than the ones charged by most permanent placement agencies, more and more companies are hiring temporaries with permanent jobs in mind if the people fill the jobs well. Use of temporary employment services gives the employer a chance to observe a candidate in action and to see if that person fits in well with the company.

Returning to the Workforce

For those secretaries returning to the workforce after a considerable amount of time has passed, the first step is to brush up on proficiency. A good investment is a keyboarding course and/or a course in basic word processing. Although you may have a better idea of the kind of job you want from previous work experience, you too may want to try temporary work. In addition to familiarizing you with the business world once again, temporary work will provide you with some recent work history to be included on your résumé. Temporary employment is a means of building up the self-confidence that may be lacking after a long absence from the workforce.

The Job Change

If you are presently working at a job and feel it is time for a change, you should consider several things before looking elsewhere:

1. What conditions do I expect to improve or change by looking for another job?
2. Have I been at my present job long enough to have exhausted all possibilities of increased responsibilities or promotion?
3. Have I considered seeking employment in another part of my company?
4. Does my company encourage career-pathing? If so, have I talked with my supervisor or with Personnel to determine what my next step for advancement would be?

If you have done all of these things and truly feel that you need a change, then you need to set some goals for yourself to achieve the kind of change that will be beneficial to your career. When you already have a job, you have the security affording you time to search out another position that meets all of your needs and standards.

Before preparing your résumé, take an inventory of your present abilities and all of the responsibilities you have had in your present job and any previous jobs. After completing the inventory, decide which tasks you like the most and which ones you like the least. By doing this you will have a basis for comparing what you want to do with what is available to you when looking for your new job. It will also help you to avoid getting into a pattern similar to the one causing you to want to leave your present job. When you have completed an accurate ability and task analysis, you will then be ready to prepare your work history.

The Résumé

Your personal vitae or résumé should be thought of as a marketing tool for selling yourself to a prospective employer. Since you will have limited page space on which to present everything relevant about your work history, you should go back to the "who," "what," "where," "when," "why" formula and be concise and clear in your presentation and format. A lot of people out there are looking for jobs—all of them with résumés in one form or another. An employer may have to look through as many as 100 résumés of applicants for the same job before selecting the people to be interviewed. Therefore, your résumé must be eye-catching and brief so that a person scanning a page can immediately pick out your best assets and work experience.

The first step is to take the abilities and tasks you have listed and put them into categories similar to the ones in the following list:

Planning	Supervising
Organizing	Training
Coordinating	Purchasing
Editing	Record-keeping
Writing	Budgeting
Developing	Negotiating

If you have a career objective you may want to state it on your résumé. There are two schools of thought on this subject, however. If you state your job objective, i.e., executive secretary, you may be limiting or categorizing yourself into a specific job market. There may be a job out there that can combine all of your skills with a title that does not even resemble that of executive secretary. On the other hand, you may have determined in your research that you definitely want the particular type of job atmosphere associated with the title *executive secretary*.

The format.   You may put identical information into several different formats and thereby present totally different images with each. The choice of format will depend on the way you want to focus attention on your proficiencies.

Guidelines for résumé presentation.   The appearance of your résumé is almost as important as its content, for your résumé is a reflection of your professionalism. As such, it should project a businesslike image. Here are a few general guidelines for résumé preparation that will help you:

1. Paper should be $8\frac{1}{2}'' \times 11''$ and white or off-white. If you are going to use colored paper, it should be conservative in tone or shade.

2. Use a high-quality copying process such as offset printing or laser printing.

3. Don't include personal information other than your name, address, and telephone number. Employers do not need to know your marital status, height, weight, sex, etc. Most of that can be determined at your interview.

4. Use the active voice throughout and be careful not to change tenses in the body of the résumé.

5. Try to keep the format pleasing to the eye. Avoid overuse of underlining and capitalization.

6. Spell out names of organizations and agencies. Titles also should be spelled out.

7. Proofread your résumé carefully. In fact, have someone else proofread it for you a final time before you have it printed. There is nothing more embarrassing than finding a mistake on your résumé after having given it to a prospective employer!

The chronological résumé. The chronological format is one of the most commonly used. It starts with your latest job experience and works backward. It is easy to follow and focuses on your career development. Since tasks for each position are detailed separately in the chronological format, try not to repeat elements of job descriptions. Only the inclusive years should be used to designate employment dates; there is no need to specify the months. If you want to highlight skills instead of chronological work history, you should not use this format.

The functional résumé. If you want to highlight your skills as opposed to the individual tasks for each position that you have held, you may want to use the functional format for your résumé. This format details your skills under the specific function areas that you choose to highlight. A disadvantage to use of this format is the possibility that your interviewer might want to relate your duties to each previously held job. However, this format may give you an opportunity to cover each position in more detail at your interview. If you have had more than three or four jobs or if your experience looks scattered, this is an excellent format to use. Because the functional résumé focuses on your marketable skills rather than on your job history, it also can be used advantageously if you are worried that a prospective employer will be concerned with too many moves.

Where to Find Your Niche

Having done some research and having determined your job target, it's now time to begin the actual search. Several avenues can be taken in looking for a job.

The newspaper. This is probably the first place that people look when they are trying to get information on available jobs. The classified section breaks down job opportunities by section, usually by the general headings of professional help, medical help, business help, and sales. Most secretarial jobs are advertised in the business section of the classifieds, but specialized positions like medical secretarial jobs would probably appear under the medical section of the classifieds. Look through all the jobs. One suiting all of your qualifications might be listed in any section of the classifieds.

Be sure to keep a file on all of the ads that you have answered so that you do not answer the same ad twice, and also so that you remember what positions you have applied for. This may sound odd, but if you have ever been involved in an active job search during which you might have answered twenty-five or more ads, you know that mix-ups can happen. You also can confuse the contact names in

Chronological Résumé Format

LINDA LEE WEB
19 Monroe Drive
Cambridge, Massachusetts 02140
(617) 354-8261

Experience

1983 - Present   DATRONICS, INC.
Burlington, Massachusetts

Executive Secretary to Vice President/Personnel
Scheduled Executive Committee Meetings and
recorded minutes for distribution to Committee
members. Acted as liaison between employees
filing grievance procedures and Executive
Committee. Maintained company activity calendar
of social functions. Composed reply letters to
applicants for executive positions. Typed and
scheduled newspaper ads for corporate job openings.
Disseminated confidential personnel information to
regional branch offices.

1981 - 1983   DUNN AND TAYLOR ADVERTISING, INC.
Medford, Massachusetts

Account Secretary
Organized and maintained client files for three
account executives. Scheduled layout and design
meetings with freelance designers. Corresponded
with clients relative to scheduled advertising
activity. Arranged travel and planned itineraries
for account executives. Recorded meetings with
clients for files. Scheduled launch meetings
with staff writers and prepared account agendas.

Education

1979 - 1981   Secretarial Training Program
Katharine Gibbs School
Boston, Massachusetts

1979   B.A. - Liberal Arts
University of Massachusetts
Amherst, Massachusetts

References furnished upon request.

Functional Résumé Format

GENEVIEVE F. WARD
119 Oakley Boulevard
Chicago, Illinois 60606
(312) 753-1324

Experience

ADMINISTRATION

Standardized contract filing systems for sales department.
Prepared schedules and agendas for national sales meetings.
Developed active lead follow-up system for sales staff.
Maintained department personnel records. Developed standard-
ized sales call report format. Formatted sales inquiries
on word processor. Planned exhibits and trade shows.

COMMUNICATION

Corresponded with customers regarding product information
and shipment schedules. Handled customer complaints.
Communicated operational procedures to field sales managers
in five regional offices.

PUBLIC RELATIONS

Coordinated and wrote sales department newsletter detailing
sales achievements and new product information. Acted as
company representative at trade shows and exhibits. Acted
as department liaison with all levels of personnel.

TECHNICAL SKILLS

Operational knowledge of Wang OIS 140 Word Processor, IBM
Displaywriter, Data General SSI Word Processor, and IBM
Memory Typewriter. Working knowledge of most common office
machines.

Work History

1981 - Present

Administrative Assistant to National Sales Manager
Parker-Hill Chemical Company
Chicago, Illinois

1979 - 1981

Sales Support Secretary
Bona Pharmaceuticals Company
Chicago, Illinois

Education

1981

Certified Professional Secretary
Institute for Certifying Secretaries
Kansas City, Missouri

1979

Bachelor of Arts - English
University of Chicago
Chicago, Illinois

References furnished upon request.

the ads if you are not careful. Do not call the company unless a telephone call is requested. If the ad requests a résumé, send one with a cover letter.

Try to stay away from blind ads using newspaper box numbers instead of company names. Companies placing blind ads usually want to avoid sending out reply letters to the applicants. If the ad sounds like just what you've been looking for, apply; but don't get your hopes up for a quick answer. If you answer an ad placed by an employment agency, be sure to call first to see whether or not the job is still available. Agencies often run tantalizing ads to draw clients into the agency, or they run ads for jobs that have already been filled.

Trade journals and specialty publications. If you are looking for a job in a specialized industry, you may want to check out the classifieds in professional trade journals. For example, if you are looking for a job in advertising, you may want to look through *Advertising Age* or *New England Advertising Week.* Your local library will have trade journals and specialty publications available for you to browse through.

Employment agencies. If you are going to use an employment agency to find a job, be sure to find one specializing in secretarial jobs. You will be able to tell from the newspaper ads and from the listings in the Yellow Pages which agencies are best suited to your needs and qualifications. Agencies screen and test job candidates before sending them on interviews. Hence, an agency interview should be treated exactly like an interview with a prospective employer.

Companies requiring confidentiality and desiring prescreened candidates usually use employment agencies. If the hiring company has experienced success with employee placements from a particular agency, the employment counselor at that agency may be your ticket to a good job. Try to stay away from high-pressure agencies. You'll know which ones to avoid next time when you sit in a counselor's office whose walls are adorned with high-performance plaques for best placement records. Agencies like these are more interested in the fee paid by the hiring company than in putting you into a job that fits your abilities.

Most agencies give skill tests to applicants for secretarial jobs. Typing and shorthand will be tested as well as transcription skills. If you are unfamiliar with the equipment on which you will be tested, ask to practice for a while before taking the test. It will give you a chance to get used to the touch of the typewriter or the operation of the transcription machine. If you do poorly on the test, ask to take it again. Most employment counselors are understanding in testing situations since people are usually nervous. Some applicants, especially the highly experienced ones, have expressed resentment at being tested, mainly because the agencies often equate *secretarial* with what is really *stenographic.* One should realize, however, that many other professional jobs require some degree of testing. A good example is that of a foreign language translator who is tested as to oral and written translation ability before being hired. And in some states, physicians are periodically tested for relicensing, as are teachers for recertification. In some instances, stenographic skills testing is waived after the interviewer has contacted the previous employers and has received exceptional recommendations for the candidate.

When the agency sends you on an interview, they will do all of the communicating and negotiating with your prospective employer before and after the interview. Do not call the company where you have been interviewed until you hear from your employment counselor. If a job has been advertised as "fee paid," the hiring company will pay for the placement services. If the job has not been so advertised, you should ask what the fees are before signing any employment contracts.

School placement services.   If you are a recent business school graduate, you should register with the school's placement office. Companies will often list job openings with school registers. Katharine Gibbs School, for example, has an active placement agency depended on by many companies.

The application cover letter.   When you answer an ad through the mail, you should always send a descriptive cover letter with your résumé. The letter should be brief and formal while at the same time sparking the interest of the prospective employer. Try to give a reason why you should be interviewed for the advertised position. Never prepare a cover form letter for photocopying and submission to numerous firms. Such letters indicate that the sender is lazy and uninterested in taking the time to write personally to a prospective employer.

Preparing for the Interview

Interviewing is stressful to say the least. Everyone who has been on a job interview recognizes that uncomfortable feeling of being put on the spot. You must prepare yourself psychologically for the interview so that you can take control. Think of the interview as an opportunity to emphasize all of your positive professional qualities. At the same time, you must be aware of your weaknesses and know how to defend them or put them in a more positive perspective. In any case, being positive and enthusiastic is the real key to a successful interview.

The first thing you should do is to work on your image. Dress conservatively and professionally in an outfit that you are comfortable with. Women should avoid using heavy makeup or trying a new hairstyle for the interview. Don't do anything that will make you uncomfortable before the interview. Give yourself plenty of time to get there. If you are unsure of the directions, call and confirm them with the receptionist. Find out as much about the company as you can before you go to the interview. If you are dealing with an employment agency, you should be able to glean some of this information from the employment counselor. If you are leaving your present job for a negative reason, do not discuss it with the interviewer. Do not discuss former jobs in any context other than your work experience. Speak confidently and try not to appear nervous or jittery when answering questions.

If the salary range has not been stated in the advertisement, wait for the interviewer to introduce the topic. If you have been sent to the interview by an agency, the employment counselor should have given you an idea of the salary range. Salary negotiations are always handled by the employment agency you have contracted with. If you are asked what your salary requirements are, ask what the salary range for the position is (if you don't know) *before* you answer the question. Keep in mind that you should aim for an increase in salary when you make a job change. Ask questions about the benefits packages, overtime, and the salary and performance review process. If you are going to be reviewed within six months for a salary increase, you may be willing to start at a lower rate than if you will not be reviewed for a year from your starting date with the company.

Job Application Cover Letter

100 School Street
Framingham, MA 01701
February 13, 1984

Ms. Valerie Kaishian
Personnel Manager
Trademark Publications
50 Broad Street
Boston, MA 02110

Dear Ms. Kaishian:

I would be most interested in applying for the position of Editorial Secretary listed in the Boston _Globe_ of February 12, 1984.

As you can see from the attached profile, I have worked in the acquisitions departments of two other publishing companies. I enjoyed the acquisitions support function very much, and I feel that my past experience qualifies me for the Editorial Secretary's position as you have described it in your advertisement.

In addition to handling the manuscript review process, I have communicated with outside authors extensively, relating to meeting deadlines and manuscript production schedules.

I look forward to hearing from you about the possibility of a personal interview. I can be reached during business hours at 295-8326, extension 451.

It would indeed be a challenge to work with the writers and editors at Trademark Publications, a company well known to us for its excellent products.

Thank you for your consideration.

Sincerely yours,

Elizabeth Simms

Elizabeth Simms

Enclosure: Personal Profile

Those difficult interview questions.   Try to prepare yourself in advance for some of the more difficult questions an interviewer might ask. For example:

Dialogue A
Interviewer: Why are you leaving your present job?
Applicant: I've been at my present job for three years now, and although I have had two promotions, I feel that I need to make a move for my professional growth.

You may be asked about your weaknesses, and you should be prepared to answer that question. Try to focus on a weakness that can also be a positive quality in your profession. A conversation about your weaknesses might go as follows:

Dialogue B
Interviewer: We have discussed your strengths, Ms. Clark. What about your weaknesses?
Applicant: I think my biggest weakness is being a perfectionist. Sometimes I take my work too seriously and strive too hard for perfection. I take pride in my work, and if I feel it isn't perfect it really bothers me.

Open questions are always difficult and most of the questions a good interviewer asks require answers that reveal a lot about the job candidate. Another dialogue may go as follows:

Dialogue C
Interviewer: Why do you think you want this job?
Applicant: I think this job would give me the opportunity to use the skills I have to the best of my abilities. I also think I could learn a great deal from working in a successful, established company.

Another open question with a twist is shown in the next hypothetical example. You should answer this question assertively and truthfully, yet without sounding conceited.

Dialogue D
Interviewer: Why should we hire you?
Applicant: From what you have told me about the job specifications, you require a person with *(specify the kind)* educational background, state-of-the-art skills such as *(specify the skills)*, and dependability *(or whatever else)*. I think that I can bring you those attributes.

Try to anticipate as many difficult questions as you can and prepare yourself for them. The key to a good interview is being able to answer questions with intelligent, confident, honest answers.

After the interview.   Always send a thank-you letter to your interviewer. It may be the touch that gets you the job over another equally qualified applicant.

Interview Follow-up Letter

```
                                          100 School Street
                                          Framingham, MA 01701
                                          February 17, 1984


     Mr. Lee C. Costa
     Sponsoring Editor
     Trademark Publications
     50 Broad Street
     Boston, MA 02110

     Dear Mr. Costa:

          Thank you for the opportunity to discuss the editorial secre-
     tarial position at Trademark Publications.  The job as you presented
     it during my interview yesterday sounds very stimulating.  I'm sure
     that the activities involved in the position would challenge me.

          At this time I would like to reiterate my interest in this
     position.  I also would like to thank you for taking the time to
     show me around the company and explain in detail the nature of its
     products.  I look forward to further discussions with you.

          Thank you for your consideration.

                                          Sincerely,

                                          Elizabeth Simms

                                          Elizabeth Simms
```

Professional Support and Assistance

For those of you who are career-oriented and upwardly mobile, it is important to establish the right connections with people who can aid you in furthering your career.

Mentors. If you have been lucky enough to establish a relationship with a professional person whom you consider to be a role model, you might refer to that person as a *mentor*. A mentor has the kind of professional wisdom gained through experience that is invaluable to another person who wants to improve his or her job status. For instance, when you want to make a career move, your mentor can advise you about the viability of the prospective move, explain its positive aspects, and counsel you about its negative aspects. Having made a connection with a person whom you respect and admire, you should nurture the relationship. Counseling and guidance from an experienced person based on trust and mutual admiration is one of the most valuable elements for success in business. Connections often make the difference between a mediocre career and success in reaching your professional goals.

Associations and networks.   Professional networks and associations are also valuable vehicles for career development. Attending meetings with other people in the same profession can do a great deal to expand your professional horizons. Many networks and associations exist today for the professional secretary. Professional Secretaries International, sponsors of the Certified Professional Secretary exam, has long been considered a particularly effective network. As we have said earlier, PSI offers courses and seminars to assist you in upscaling your status. PSI also publishes a quarterly journal entitled *The Secretary.*

Secretaries Network is a Chicago-based association sponsored by Women Employed. It deals with current issues affecting the secretarial community. Secretaries Network publishes a newsletter called *The Secretary's Network Newsletter* and a number of books on career development relevant to current issues like *Technological Change in the Office,* an outgrowth of research done by the Network for the Ford Foundation. The seminars and meetings sponsored by the Network are based in Chicago. The organization also has set up an informal job bank for local companies. You may obtain information on publications and newsletters by writing to The Secretaries Network, c/o Women Employed, 5 S Wabash, Suite 415, Chicago, IL 60603. Other associations, networks, and support groups exist in almost every major city in the country. You can find the names of those that might interest you in the library or in your Yellow Pages under *associations.*

It is sometimes difficult to stay interested in your professional development once you have found a comfortable niche in a company. People often settle for job situations that are less than satisfactory because comfort has become a habit. Involvement in associations and networks helps you to keep your eyes open to continuing educational opportunities and the need for ongoing career development. With the impact of high technology on the business place today, networking, continuing education, and intellectual flexibility will be crucial to you in your ongoing efforts to use technology and the new career opportunities generated by it to your own advantage. This is preferable to your remaining in a static mode and being controlled and used by the technology.

A Word about MBOs

MBO—or Management by Objectives—is a joint supervisor-employee program in which the employee's performance is evaluated in writing as a kind of barometer of productivity, goal achievement, and standard of excellence. While employees are evaluated according to this system at different times dictated by individual company policy, the basic format of the MBO plan is rather consistent across the board.

The first section of an MBO program contribution evaluation sheet usually lists your name, position, department, date of last evaluation, and an enumeration of the pertinent divisional or departmental objectives to which your job generally relates or contributes. The next section lists, in two parallel columns, your personal accountabilities and goals in numbered sequence. The third section is a grid or graph of your performance record (this is the real barometer of how you've performed during the past evaluation period). You can be evaluated goal-by-goal, or a single evaluation can be assigned to each of your accountabilities. A space for supervisor comments is left open so that the evaluations on the grid can be tied in with your list of goals or accountabilities, plus any additional clarifying comments on each. The grid categorizes your performance as, for instance,

Exceptional

Expected High Standard

Not up to Standard

or perhaps

Exceptional

Excellent

Satisfactory

Substandard/Unsatisfactory

A fourth section then evaluates your overall performance, measured by a set of benchmarks identical or similar to the ones listed above. Finally, a summation is given by the supervisor of your overall contribution to the departmental, divisional, or corporate efforts of the past year (or evaluation period).

Ideally, you and your supervisor should sit down and discuss your contribution to the divisional/departmental objectives, your accountabilities, and your goals after the supervisor has prepared a draft of them. In most instances your accountabilities list will reflect your written job description. Your goals are more specific—these show what your real assignments in the office are. After you and your supervisor have discussed these sections, both of you sign the document. You both sign the document a second time after the evaluations have been made and your supervisor has discussed them with you. A space is reserved there for your own comments.

The MBO program, which is used by many small, mid-size, and large companies, is an excellent way of extending the concept of responsibility and team play from the sphere of abstract office procedure into the area of concrete career development and improvement. With the MBO there should be no real surprises: you know what you have to do and you find out in writing at a predetermined time whether management feels that you've done it and done it well. It is a good idea to take the time to reread the objectives, accountabilities, and goals sections from time to time just to remind yourself why you are in the office and what you must do to advance yourself there.

3

Generation of Business Documents: Electronic Typewriting

Richard K. Turner • *Product Manager, Office Systems Marketing, Wang Laboratories, Inc.*

WHY ELECTRONIC TYPEWRITERS?

How Did Electronic Typewriters Become Popular in Offices?

In the mid-1970s secretaries and office managers were looking for an easy-to-use, low-cost machine that could aid the secretary in a variety of typing tasks. Word processors were too expensive at that time and generally needed dedicated operators. Very simply, an electronic typewriter uses a small computer-operated motor to rotate the typewriter's printing element instead of springs and levers attached to the keys. Since these keys now send electronic impulses, it is possible for additional computer logic to "read" those impulses, store them in a memory, and erase them. That is how electronic typewriters perform special functions like line correction, centering, and automatic carriage return.

Electronic typewriters quickly became popular with typewriter manufacturers: they were easier to manufacture than conventional typewriters because there were fewer moving parts, and they were more reliable because they didn't need adjustments. Today, no major typewriter company manufactures standard electric office typewriters—all their new models are electronic.

Less expensive electronic typewriter models cost about the same as the older electric models, so companies are replacing aging electric typewriters with electronic ones. Because the more expensive models have powerful features which save time and can reduce a secretary's workload, many companies are choosing sophisticated electronic typewriters for their secretarial staffs.

Why Should the Secretary Understand the Electronic Typewriter?

In your office career, it is likely that you will have to operate one or more of these electronic typewriters. Because they are treated by the individuals buying them as typewriters, you will be expected to understand how to use an electronic machine. Be sure to locate the basic operating manual or contact the electronic typewriter vendor if the original manual has been misplaced.

Knowing how to get the most from an electronic typewriter can be a great advantage for you. If you're just starting a job, it can allow you to concentrate on

IBM Electronic Typewriter 85

Courtesy of International Business Machines Corporation.

understanding the workflow of your new office and help to reinforce your new employer's confidence in your capabilities. Electronic typewriters take much of the drudgery out of difficult typing situations, and your work can always be letter-perfect if you take advantage of your machine's many features. Electronic typewriters can be a pleasure to use. Revisions can be made without retyping the entire page and standard phrases can be recalled on demand. In short, they can help you become a more valuable member of the office team.

WHAT DO ELECTRONIC TYPEWRITERS MEAN TO THE SECRETARY?

How Do Electronic Typewriters Compare to Standard Electric Typewriters?

The basics of electronic typewriters and standard electrics are the same:

1. standard QWERTY alphabetic typing keyboard
2. similar positioning of format keys: **backspace, tab, margin release, space bar,** and **return**
3. typewriter carriage
4. line spacing is single, one and one-half, double, or triple
5. ability to type in pica (10 characters per inch) or elite (12 characters per inch)

Normal typing is the same: all electronic typewriters can be operated like standard electrics, and it is not necessary to perform any special operations in order to type. If the typewriter has special power-on features like automatic paper insertion, these can usually be disabled by depressing a **typewriter** key that turns off all but the very basic electronics.

There are differences, however. All electronic typewriters contain an automatic **correction** key, usually marked with an "X." Unlike standard electrics, this key will correct the mistake in one keystroke: the typewriter lifts off the last typed character and backspaces. A character memory allows you to remove additional characters simply by depressing the key again. Depending upon the typewriter, as few as eight characters or as much as a page can be removed this way. There are many more automatic features distinguishing them from electrics. These features are covered in detail in subsequent sections.

What Does Learning to Operate an Electronic Typewriter Entail?

Most electronics are designed to assist the operator in general typing chores— their functions are very logical and most special keys are self-explanatory. For those of you not having an instruction manual, we discuss common electronic typewriter functions in this chapter; these guidelines apply to most electronics. You may find it useful to experiment gradually with your new typewriter, trying special functions on work that isn't a rush job or that can be redone if you have problems. You can use more features as you become comfortable with the typewriter, so specialized training usually isn't necessary. The key to getting the most from your new machine is to take your time. Your electronic can work just like the standard electrics you already know, and it will be easy to learn new features if you pace yourself while adjusting to the new machine.

What Sorts of Things Can an Electronic Typewriter Do for a Secretary?

An electronic typewriter is best suited for the following jobs:

1. routine correspondence—letters, brief reports, envelopes, labels, index cards, and forms

2. multiple mailings—identical or similar letters sent to a group of different recipients

3. reports—reports styled in a simple format or brief in length

4. statistical or columnar documents

Since the electronic typewriter is designed to work like an advanced version of a standard electric, there is a close relationship between the work being done and how it looks when printed (or typed) onto paper. How much memory your typewriter has will determine how many characters or lines you can type before you have to proofread your work and then use the automatic correction capabilities. On less advanced models, you should type in a "first-time final" fashion: check your work as you are typing so that you can correct mistakes shortly after having made them. You can go back and successfully remove whole words later but it may require some skill to keep your line endings even.

Because the typewriter will do things such as automatically center headings, underscore words as you type them, and automatically return the carriage to the next typing line, you will be able to type much faster and concentrate on the text being typed. Even the simplest electronics usually have automatic statistical typing features, so you can lay out a simple table and get the numbers all decimally-aligned the first time it is typed. Most electronic typewriters have a feature for automatically filling in forms. You simply store the stop points once in the memory, and the unit will remember these locations as you actually fill in the form. Fine alignment on forms also can be stored by using the horizontal and vertical half-space keys.

ELECTRONIC TYPEWRITERS—HOW TO MAKE THEM WORK FOR YOU

Your Electronic Typewriter's Capabilities

Electronic typewriters borrow a bit of technology perfected in computers: they have a microprocessor and a memory, and they can perform automatic functions on their own. All electronics house a small computer that not only guides the print mechanism but also stores the material you type into it. The electronic could be thought of as memorizing what you type into it and the keys that you depress. This memorization may be limited to twenty characters or may span pages. When you depress the **correction** key, the computer backs up in memory, automatically removes the last keystroke from that memory, and lifts the error off the paper. When you start typing again, it adds new characters to the memory. As you fill this small memory with letters, the earlier letters are dropped off to make room for new ones. If your correction memory is forty characters, for example, the typewriter can remember only the last forty characters typed. Most electronic typewriters can store more than one margin setting. Thus if you need a different setting for internal memos as opposed to outside correspondence you simply recall the appropriate setting. Most of the machines remember the last setting used before the power was turned off.

Keys for special functions like centering are called *function keys*. When you depress the **center** key, for example, you send a command to the computer that the next sequence of characters is to be centered. The computer checks the margins for a center point, or selects a tab stop if you are centering table headings, and moves the print mechanism to the proper center position. Nothing will print until you finish typing the phrase, usually by pressing the **return** or **tab** key. The typewriter then prints out the characters exactly centered between the margins or on either side of the tab stop. Functions such as underlining and bold print can be accomplished by pressing these special function keys or moving slide switches. To turn the function key off, simply press the special function key again or move the slide switch to its original position.

When the typewriter has done something you didn't expect it to do, such as automatically indenting your next paragraph, it is because you have accidentally touched a function key or because a function mode has not yet been canceled or turned off. All typewriters have legends on their keys for the various functions, and also indicators of how to turn them off if the mode can't be logically canceled with the **return** or by pressing the function key again. When you make an error with a function key, the typewriter will emit a warning tone, usually a short beep. The tone may mean that the computer can't perform the function, like setting the right margin in front of the left. Or the tone may be signaling you to turn off a function mode before going on to type something else.

How to Manage Your Work and Get the Most from Your Electronic

First of all, you will need to know just what the machine can and cannot do, since each model is different and some are more powerful than others. If your typewriter is a very simple one, it may not be much different from a standard electric. Your machine will have some memory, so you should determine how many characters it can store.

Since electronics offer you a wide variety of print wheels or elements, you may have several different print styles from which to choose. Some are very similar, so again, it helps to note which print wheel you used when typing different jobs if you change elements frequently. In that way you can edit the work in the correct typeface later on.

You may have keys for adjusting page alignment when positioning paper in the typewriter. Use these keys instead of the platen release whenever possible, since the typewriter will remember positioning keys and will be able to relocate your position if you need to go back and change something.

If you have a large memory feature on your typewriter, use the memory wisely. Don't put short things like index cards or envelopes into the memory unless they are to be retyped very frequently. Save the memory for letters or pages that you think may be changed or edited. That way, you can make your corrections in memory and print out a clean revision of the changed pages.

How to Use Operator Manuals and Training

Every major electronic typewriter is different. Aside from the basic typewriter QWERTY keyboard, there are no true across-the-board standards. Not only are the operations themselves often different, but also different words and abbreviations are used by various manufacturers for similar functions. Familiarity with the operator's manual provided by the manufacturer is a critical part of learning how to use your electronic typewriter's features. If you can't find the manual, call the dealer servicing the machine. If the dealer can't supply a manual, a copy of it usually can be made, or a copy of a manual for a similar machine can be provided. The manual should provide these essential data:

1. the capabilities of your particular machine

2. its theory of operation (the details of how it "thinks")

3. an explanation of the different function keys, their labels, and how they work

4. examples of work requiring special functions

5. a troubleshooting guide for error conditions and service hints

In addition to the operator's manual, most manufacturers provide a quick reference guide in the form of a small booklet, a laminated card, or a series of reference cards. While the quick reference guide can get you through most unfamiliar functions, it is not detailed and shouldn't be used without your reading the operator's manual first.

The best way to get to know your new electronic is to take the operator's manual home with you and read it thoroughly. Do this as soon as possible; if you are getting a new machine or starting a new job, try to get the manual and read it before you use the machine for the first time. At home, you can take your time and familiarize yourself with the manual, the theory behind your machine, and (maybe the most important item) how the manual is organized. Then, you will know where to find specific sections when you need them fast.

Most manuals are very straightforward and have clear illustrations. Many include practice exercises that can help you perform unfamiliar tasks and use the advanced features of the machine. When you have spare time in the office, you should try these exercises for tasks you haven't yet encountered if they have been included in the manual. If the manual is concise and doesn't have exercises, then practice some of the functions from the different chapters. You will quickly master your new unit.

Manufacturers usually don't provide training. Most of those that do will provide only a few hours of instruction to help get you started. Since electronics are very simple and you can always get work out of them without using the advanced features, lengthy training would seem wasteful.

ELECTRONIC TYPEWRITERS—GETTING STARTED

Basic Operations

Familiarize yourself with your typewriter's keyboard, paying careful attention to the location of:

1. **correction** key

2. **tab set/clear** keys

3. **express backspace** (if your machine has one)

4. **index** key

5. **margin release** key

Turn on the unit; the power switch will be a rocker-type switch with a circle on one end and a vertical bar on the other end. This bar is a standard symbol for *power on.* The power switch can be in one of several places:

1. right side of the keyboard (IBM)

2. front edge, underneath the keyboard (Xerox)

3. rear top cover, near the paper release lever (Royal, some Japanese models)

4. rear cover, on lower side toward the back (most Japanese models)

Because of the way electronics are manufactured, it is unusual in machines other than IBM to find the power switch on the keyboard as on standard electrics.

When you turn on the unit, most models run through a quick diagnostic routine: the typewriter's computer checks its circuits to determine if there are any problems before you begin typing. During this brief check (it only lasts a few seconds) the print element may spin, the keyboard indicator lights—if there are any—may flash, and the carriage will move over to the left-hand margin. The machine will beep to signal the end of the test and then you can begin typing.

You will need to determine whether you have **automatic paper insertion.** Some machines, such as the more advanced Adlers and Royals, have no carriage knobs—all paper motion is electronic. You will find an insertion feature in one of three configurations located:

1. as a large lever on the right side of the carriage behind the paper release lever

2. as a key on the keyboard, usually above the **return,** on the right side

3. as a built-in component of the paper bail movement lever on the left side of the carriage

To insert paper, first locate the paper support, usually a flip-up arm or arms toward the back of the typewriter. The flip-up arm(s) may be adjustable to your paper length: set the length if necessary. Setting the length in advance will tell you how much space is left on your page as you reach the bottom of the sheet. Place the paper against the support, letterhead or printing facing away from you, with the top edge of the paper in an upside-down position resting firmly against the platen (roller).

Along the top of the platen, usually behind it, is a horizontal position scale. Center is clearly marked, along with symbols for "portrait" (normal) and "landscape" (sideways) paper orientations, for standard $8\frac{1}{2}'' \times 11''$ paper. It is very important to line up the paper so that the center is in the middle of the page, rather than putting the paper at flush left position like you would do on a standard electric. Since centering and other functions are now computer-controlled, many typewriters need to know where the center point of the paper is, and some will automatically assume that the paper has been centered using the guide. If you don't line up the paper as described earlier, your centered headings and page numbers may be inadvertently offset.

If there is an insertion lever, pull it forward. If there is an insertion key, press it once (but don't hold it down). If the inserter is part of the bail movement lever, pull it firmly forward and then release it. Inserters usually bring you one inch from the top of the paper—line seven in typewriter single spacing. Only about half of the electronics have paper inserters. If there is no electronic feature to insert paper, roll it in using the platen knobs.

To find your typing position, you will see a clear plastic gauge surrounding the print element area. Horizontal lines indicate the bottom of your print line: a single line is designed to rest just along the bottom edge of your line or characters, and pairs of lines are designed to "frame" lowercase characters evenly between

Keyboard on Xerox Memorywriter

Courtesy of Xerox Corporation.

them. A pointer in front of or over the print element indicates the left-most edge where the next character will strike the paper.

Margins and Setup

Electronic typewriters can store several different margins as well as tab settings. The keys used to set left and right margins and tabs are much the same as those on electric typewriters. Most machines with electronic margins have default settings, preset and always remembered. Consult your operator's manual for information on changing these settings if you want the machine to remember a different margin when you turn it on, or "power it up," as the startup procedure is sometimes called.

Tab stops are usually defaulted, also. Since they are often electronic, there may not be a "clear all tabs" feature. Using the **tab** key, move to each tab stop with memory off. If you want to remove the stop, switch on the memory if it is switchable, and depress the **clear tab** key. After you have checked all the existing tabs, you can then set new ones or make additional settings by spacing to the desired positions and depressing the **set tab** key.

Some machines with electronic margins display their settings as a series of small lights called LEDs (light-emitting diodes) on a special margin scale. Others do not display any settings. It is therefore important to move through your margins and tabs with paper in the machine before you begin typing to ensure that your margins have been set exactly as you want them. Move across the line twice, once with the **tab** key to verify the tabs, once with the **space bar** held in repeat position (either held down continuously or using the **repeat** key—a small key marked with "R" or circled "R" to one side of the **space bar**). A beep tone will indicate your right-hand margin. If you have an automatic carrier return, the space procedure should cause the typewriter to return automatically, and advance to the next line. On some machines this feature is automatic; others have a key for autoreturn. On very basic machines this feature may not be available. As you become more familiar with your typewriter this procedure for setting margins won't be necessary, but you will find it useful the first few times that you have to set new margins. Again, consult your operator's manual since each machine is different.

Basic Typing Techniques—on Paper

It is a good practice to make sure you have a ribbon and a correction tape in place in the typewriter before starting work. Also, check your print element for the proper typestyle and pitch (your manual should outline these procedures). Check your line spacing for the proper setting. Line spacing usually will be electronic; the key for setting this spacing is usually on the keyboard. For any key with multiple settings, it usually operates in a cyclical manner: each depression of the key will select a new setting in sequence and will cycle through all available settings.

All electronics offer selectable pitches:

1. 10-pitch (pica)—10 characters per inch, often considered standard type
2. 12-pitch (elite)—12 characters per inch, giving a more compact printout

3. 15-pitch (micro)—15 characters per inch, for very condensed printing and numeric tables

4. proportional spacing (PS)—variable characters per line (closest to elite), making letters such as "M" wider and letters such as "i" and "1" narrow, similar to set type in books and magazines

Some machines, such as the Xerox models, can "read" the print element and set the pitch according to the typestyle. On most electronics, however, it is necessary to match the pitch to the setting given on the print element; otherwise the characters won't be properly spaced. Some typists prefer to use 12-pitch elements in a 10-pitch spacing so as to impart a more formal look to business letters. Certain typestyles, such as Letter Gothic, are designed to be properly spaced in both 10- and 12-pitch.

Proportional Spacing must be used only with proportionally spaced, PS typestyles. Otherwise, the printout will look unbalanced. The same effect will occur with PS print elements printed in 10-, 12-, or 15-pitch: because the spacing is different, some characters will appear crowded or others spaced too far apart. And proportional spacing usually cannot be corrected after the paper has been removed from the typewriter.

Finally, before you begin to type, verify that automatic modes such as **underscore, center,** and **bold-print** are off (usually indicated by LEDs). You can now begin typing. Since you are working on paper in this example, perform all corrections and functions as you encounter them. A description of basic electronic typewriter functions for working on paper is given below.

Carrier return. Electronics count characters near the right margin. Whenever you depress the **space bar** within five to eight spaces of the margin, this signals a break between words, and the typewriter automatically returns to the next line. Characters typed while the carrier is returning are held in memory and are printed as soon as the printhead is positioned on the new line.

Center. To center a phrase, first depress the **center** key and type the characters to be centered. When you depress **return,** it will play out the buffered characters exactly centered and return to the left margin of the next line. An LED usually indicates that you are in the centering mode.

Underline. There may be two ways to underline. The preferred way is to use the automatic underline or underscore (preferred because it can be automatically corrected if you make an error). Before you begin typing the underlined word, depress the **underline** mode key. An LED will indicate that the underscore mode is on. As you type in underscore mode, the machine will type each character and underline it simultaneously. The correction feature will remove both the character and its underline in the underscore mode. Before spacing, turn the underscore mode off when you complete the word. Some electronics, such as IBM models, offer full auto underscore and word underscore. Word underscore will underline only character units (words), leaving spaces between them blank and not underlined. Both modes operate in the same manner.

A second way of underlining is to perform a normal underline, like you would on a standard electric. Type the word, then use the **backspace** to return to the start of the word, and depress **shift** plus **dash/underline** typing key. A note of caution: some electronics don't have a **backspace,** so check the keyboard before trying to underline in this manner.

Bold print.   Because of their electronic mechanisms, most electronics can automatically double-strike characters; i.e., they adjust the spacing in a special way to produce thicker, darker characters called bold-print. Bold-print is a mode controlled either by a **bold** key or a combination bold and underline key. Bold works the same way as underscore does. Remember, you must be in bold mode to correct bold characters.

Expand print.   Many electronics also have the logic to automatically add additional space between characters as you type. This capability, called "expanded print," helps make titles and headings more pronounced. It is a mode, and operates exactly like underscore and bold.

Reverse print.   Some electronics, such as the Olivetti models, offer the ability to print white characters within a solid black background. The machine creates the black background and then lifts off only the character outline, resulting in reversed printing.

Justified print (Justify).   Most electronics offer automatic justification, a mode in which the machine automatically counts the total number of characters and spaces in a full line, and then adds additional space in small increments to stretch out the line to fit exactly within the margin. Justified print will give an even right margin (unjustified print is referred to as having a ragged right margin, since lines end at different points near the right side of the page).

When set in the justify mode, the typewriter usually will not print your line until the margin zone has been reached and autoreturn occurs, or until the **return** key has been depressed as the text nears the right margin. The typewriter will

Royal 5041 Electronic Typewriter

Courtesy of Adler-Royal Business Machines, Inc.

then print the entire line, evenly spacing the words so that they fit exactly between the margins. Using justify with proportional spacing gives letters and documents a very professional, "printed" look.

Correction key.   All electronics use a lift-off correction feature: a special solvent-based sticky correction ribbon is used to dissolve the ribbon ink and lift all traces of the undesired character off the paper. It is very difficult to find the error after it has been removed, and most kinds of paper allow many corrections before the paper surface becomes rough due to the adhesive surface of the correction ribbon. When typing on paper it is best to use the **correction** key as soon as you realize that you may have made an error.

Each depression of the key activates the memory and auto-correction sequence. The typewriter will back up and remove the previous character from the page. Depress this key until all characters up to and including the mistake have been removed. Then simply begin retyping.

Relocation of errors.   Alternately, your unit may offer reverse keys, such as **backspace** and **index/reverse.** Use these keys to go back to errors. Locate the error and retype it if the word is no longer in memory. Then, use the **correction** key; it can remove several layers of characters so that the original error plus the retyped error are removed. Type the proper key; then use the space bar to return to your last typing position.

Some slightly more advanced electronic typewriters offer automatic relocation. These units have sufficient memory to retain at least a page of text. **Backspace** and **index/reverse** keys are used to locate the last character of the mistake. The **correction** key is used to remove the error from both the page and the memory. A special **relocate** key can be used to return to the last typing position and preserve the integrity of the memorized text. Always remember to proofread your work and correct all errors while the paper is still in the typewriter. As mentioned earlier, the electronic computer will be unable to properly align the correction feature after you have removed the paper.

To correct errors after having removed the paper, reinsert it and move to the nearest space before or after the error. Use the paper release lever to align the paper using the markings for alignment on the transparent card guide around the print element. You may wish to type a lowercase letter such as "s" in the space to check the alignment—the test letter should fall exactly between the two words and at the same horizontal height. Then, erase the "s" with the **correction** key. Move to the error, retype it, and use the **correction** key to remove both impressions. These techniques work well on paper, in the direct typing mode. They work equally well when using your system's memory during typing.

Basic Typing Techniques—in Memory

This section, and the one following it, describes basic use of limited memory. Although many modern machines offer displays, their use is simply an extension of the basic memory. Your typewriter's basic memory is always on. If you have a **memory** key, this key controls a larger "page" memory: even when turned off, your typewriter will maintain a running memory of eight to twenty characters or more. This memory's principal use is for correction: think of it as a correction zone that remembers the last few typed characters. Imagine your typing line or paper typing width cut into three equal lengths; your correction memory will be roughly equal to the length of one of these segments from your last typing point back. Some models maintain a page or more of correction memory. Consult your operator's manual for the actual character length of your machine's memory. The correction memory will also remember format keys: **tab, return,** and **index.** Each return or tab, therefore, takes up the space of one character. The correction memory is useful only when combined with paper output: once the paper has been taken out of the typewriter, the correction memory isn't useful for corrections or edits without retyping the errors. There are generally two ways to type into correction memory: direct typing, and delay typing mode.

Direct typing—memory.   The memory feature is used here for corrections. Using the **correction** key, you can remove letters in addition to returns or tabs. Repeated depressions of the **correction** key will remove any tabs or returns encountered in previously typed text. Do not use the **backspace** key to move to previously tabbed positions if you have typed a wrong number of tabs; this will disable the correction memory. Use the **correction** key instead, and retype any characters that you want to keep on the paper.

With regard to memory in mode areas, when you correct into words typed under the underline, bold, or reverse print modes, the typewriter will turn on the mode and apply it to all new characters typed. When correcting into mode areas, observe the typewriter's indicator lights. You will have to turn off the mode as soon as you have completed retyping of words to be underscored, made bold, or reversed. Then, you can resume normal typing.

With regard to memory in centered areas, your typewriter may or may not treat centered areas as modes when correcting. If they are not treated as modes, the typewriter will remove characters but will not automatically recenter new ones. If your correction involves more than one character, you should remove the entire word or words in this case and retype using the **center** key. If center is remembered as a mode, the typewriter will require you to remove the entire centered phrase. It will not allow you to perform any other functions until it reaches the beginning of the center command. Most typewriters that memorize centering will then automatically move to the center point and turn on the center mode. You then can retype your phrase, perfectly centered.

Delay typing—memory.   Many typewriters have either a **delay** key or a delay mode on a cycle key. Delay typing without a display is useful for positioning when you are typing envelopes and forms. During delay typing, the print element will "ghost" your typing: that is, it will space horizontally across at the exact typing position for each letter you type. Nothing will print until you depress the **return,** or, on typewriters with autoreturn, until you have reached the right margin.

In order to view typed phrases before you have completed the line, type one space and depress the **return.** The phrase will print and the print element will return to the next line. To relocate your last position, depress the **correction** key: it will move you back to the previous line and remove the extra space. You can continue typing in this manner to preview all material in delay typing. Use this partial delay technique whenever you think you may have made an error, or whenever you want to check the alignment in complicated forms or on nonstandard envelopes.

All corrections in delay typing work the same way as direct typing, except that you are "blind" to whatever may have been typed because it will not have been printed out yet. Typewriters with a page or more of limited memory can perform very extensive "blind" editing, a matter discussed later in this chapter.

Using Limited Memory/Phrase Memories

One very useful function found on most electronic typewriters is phrase memory. These are usually limited memories allowing you to remember specific phrases by simple address or name schemes, and replaying them into text. A phrase memory allows you to enter sentences, headings, addresses, and other short items into a special memory area. Then, by touching a few keys, you can recall the phrase and have the typewriter automatically type it into your original. Most electronics allow you to enter several phrases into this memory; each one has a unique name, and will be remembered until you enter a new phrase under the same name.

Entering Phrases

For entering a phrase, your typewriter will have either a **phrase** key or a **memory** key. Depress the key before typing your phrase. Often, an LED will indicate that the phrase memory is on. Phrase memories differ with each machine. Be sure to consult your operator's manual for details. In any case, though, phrases usually can be edited in one of the two ways described below.

Memory/store.   These typewriters have a **memory** or **phrase** key and a **store** key. You turn the memory on by depressing either the **memory** or the **phrase** key; sometimes the sequence **shift** or **code** plus **phrase** is used to enter phrases. You can use the **correction** key, and the **tab** and **return** keys can usually be included in the phrase.

After completing the phrase, depress the **store** key. The typewriter will signal you to enter a reference: this is usually a single letter or number or a brief name or title that will become the unique reference for the phrase. After typing in a reference or name, depress either the **return** key or the **store** key again, depending upon your machine. The typewriter will then remember the phrase, and you can reuse it by recalling it, using the unique reference or name that you have assigned to the phrase.

Phrase (no store key).   These machines use only the **phrase** key. The **phrase** key places the typewriter in the phrase mode. The first character(s) or number you type is the reference and won't print on the paper. To enter this reference into memory, depress the **return.** The phrase mode will stay on and the next keys you type will become the phrase. When you finish the phrase, depress the **phrase** key again and the phrase plus reference will be remembered.

Recalling Phrases

In order to recall phrases, you first need to be sure that you have typed up to the exact point where you want the phrase entered on your paper. Then, depress the **recall** key followed by the special reference sequence (which you assigned to the phrase when you typed it into memory), or use the **phrase** key in combination with **shift** or **code** (be sure to consult your manual). As soon as you enter the special reference, which will not be typed on the paper, the typewriter will locate the proper phrase, type it out, and return you to the typing mode. Always remember that phrases will be typed into your current margins; if there are tabs in the phrase, they will cause the print element to move to your current tab settings, which may be different from the margins and tabs originally used when you entered the phrase.

Phrase Directories

Since the typewriter can remember several phrases, most models have the ability to print out a directory or index of all the phrase references that you have used. This directory is designed to give you a printout of everything stored as a phrase in your typewriter. Typewriters with page memories (discussed under advanced features) also have a directory of documents stored in memory. There is usually a difference between these two directories or indexes: a phrase directory will print out both the reference and the complete phrase, while a document directory will only print out the titles. A phrase directory is designed to be printed and then stored in a convenient place at your desk so that you can refer to the printout if you can't remember the reference for a particular phrase.

Format memory.   Most electronics offer a default setting for margins and tabs. Since you can select pitch, most machines will have different default settings for each pitch. Some models can recall changes in formats. These are stored like phrases, and when recalled will change your format at the beginning of the next typing line (unless you have already reached the left margin). If formats are stored in the same memory as phrases, they often can be combined, so that a special format change and a standard phrase can be recalled in one step. Remember that recalling a stored format will change your entire format. Be sure when you store the format that you have chosen all the tab settings you will need and both margins. Most machines will not store just a new tab stop or single (left or right) margin setting.

ADVANCED FEATURES

Using the Printer for Memory Operations

Most of the medium-priced electronics have what is called a "page memory." (An electronic typewriter can have any amount of memory depending upon the model.) A page or document memory is the ability to remember upwards of 2,000 characters as one or more "documents": here, the term *document* refers to any amount of text stored under a specific address or name.

A typical or average page of text contains less than 2,000 characters. Letters and double-spaced text pages are considerably shorter. Some typewriters require you to name each page as a separate document. Most advanced models allow you to specify electronic page markers and will permit multiple pages under a single document name. Regardless of the size of the memory, editing on paper is accomplished in the same manner.

Typing into a page memory is no different except that permanent storage into the typewriter's memory or buffer will require giving the page a name or address. Storing into memory will clear the typewriter for other typing. This is particularly useful when you are submitting the printed page or document for approval and signature, since several hours may elapse before your supervisor returns the original to you for changes and corrections.

Many typewriters store pages using the same buffer as phrases; others have separate buffers. The page store sequence is usually identical to phrase storage, except to indicate whether the segment being stored is text or a phrase. If you can assign a name to the page, choose a short name easily remembered and indicative of the stored text. For example, a report to E. B. Jones might be named "JREPORT," "JRPT," or simply "JONES."

Electronics such as the most basic Adler and Royal models use their memories as large undivided buffers. With these models, the naming procedure is unnecessary but you may have to scan through the memory to find your document (using the display or search techniques discussed later).

Once you have received a marked-up original, or have proofread the page yourself and have made editorial notations, you are ready to make corrections. First, you may have to recall the text into memory, using the recall feature plus the document's name or address. To correct edited material, use the marked-up original as a guide and use the typewriter's memory to print out a new copy as you edit. This technique involves playing out portions of the text and making edits as you go along. The result is a perfectly typed, corrected original. Most corrections in this case will not use the **correction** key. A typewriter with page memory will usually contain the following types of keys:

1. **rewind** or **memory rewind**—will access the beginning of the memory or page (sometimes referred to as **start** or **begin**)

2. **print**—will play out text in memory and print it on paper (sometimes referred to as **forward**)

3. **stop**—will stop the playout (this may also put a stop code in your text, explained later in this chapter)

4. **print character/word/line**—will play out single characters, words, or lines and stop immediately after playout

5. **advance**—will play out single characters, or can be held down for a repeat function to play out larger portions of text

6. **skip character/word/line**—will skip over characters, words, or lines in memory that you don't want played out

7. **delete character/word/line**—will delete characters, words, or lines from the memory

8. **search character/word**—will find a particular word or location, playing out text until the search word or character is reached

Editing in memory while using the printer is quite easy. After you have accessed the beginning of the memory or page, turn the printer on, place paper in the typewriter, and find your first change on the marked-up original. Most models allow you to search for the location of the correction and make the necessary changes in the memory before printing. For those models that do not have this feature it is necessary to print as you correct.

Print all text up to the point of the change using the **print** or **forward** keys combined with **line, word,** or **character** keys, or held down for repeat action:

1. print line—will print the full line of text, return to the beginning of the next line, and stop

2. print word—will print one word plus one space (or punctuation mark) and stop at the beginning of the next word

3. print character—will print one character and stop at the next character position

The editing functions that can be performed in this manner are described below.

Insert.   Simply begin typing inserted material at the proper location; it will be automatically added to the memory. When your insert has been completely typed in, depress the **print** plus amount keys (**line, word,** or **character**) to resume printing the text after the insertion point. Make sure autoreturn is on so that the typewriter can correct your line endings.

Delete.   You can delete characters from memory by using the **delete** key plus amount keys. After deleting the desired characters, resume printing the rest of your page.

Skip.   If you don't want certain words to be printed out, but you do want to keep them in memory for a later revision, many typewriters will allow you to skip over portions of text. **Skip** plus amount keys will advance the memory without printing or deleting. When you have skipped the desired amount of text, continue printing the rest of the page.

Search.   If you want the printout to begin at a specific point, not at the beginning of the page, many machines offer a search capability. To search for a particular word or a group of characters, depress **search,** enter the group of characters (called a *string*) exactly as typed previously, and depress the **search** key again (or the **start** key on some models). Adler and Royal typewriters allow you to depress **relocate** to print out text up to the search word. If the desired search word appears several times in the original, successive depressions of the search activation key (**search, start,** or **relocate**) will advance the memory to successive search words. When you have finished the last change, depress the **print** plus amount (or **remainder, relocate,** or **end**) keys to print the remainder of the page automatically.

Multiple pages.   Automatic pagination is offered on some machines. The typewriter will count the number of lines as it prints them. When the end of the page has been reached (usually a total of fifty or fifty-five lines), the typewriter will signal you to this effect. You can print additional lines if you so desire, or you can change the paper and begin a new page. Consult your operator's manual if you wish to change the page end location. Multiple page documents are discussed in detail further on in this chapter.

Using Displays or Memory "Windows"

Many of the medium-range electronic typewriters and all of the higher-priced models offer some kind of display. Displays are usually from five to forty characters in length, and will display typed or stored text on a partial-line basis. Brief instructions (prompts) and warnings (error messages) also may be displayed.

Some machines, like the Adler and Royal models and certain Japanese units, have a second smaller display for codes referring to instructions or function selections.

There are two types of display: illuminated (LED or electro-fluorescent) and contrast (LCD). Illuminated displays have letters composed of a matrix of light-dots, in red or green, on a dark background. They are easier to read in low-level light but direct sunlight is strong enough in some cases to wash out the light-dots completely. LCD or contrast displays have dark gray crystals, formed into dot-character or bar-character patterns, on a lighter gray crystal background. These displays can be read in the brightest light but lose contrast in low illumination. If you have trouble reading your display, changing the position of the machine may improve its clarity.

A display should be thought of as a "window" through which your text passes in a continuous line. The display will show you the actual characters typed as well as formatting symbols. Since it can't display returns or tabs by position, it will include symbols to indicate tabs, returns, and special functions such as centering. Symbols vary with each machine, but some common ones are:

1. ↵ return

2. → tab

3. ← backspace (*not* **correction** key)

4. ↑ up index (paper moving up)

5. ↓ down index (paper moving down)

6. · space (smaller dot than **period**)

Special functions, such as **center,** are usually displayed as a block containing a number or letter.

Displays are very useful when editing. Some electronic typewriters having displays will permit you to edit using display only; they can't edit on paper. Other machines allow you to turn the display off for straight typing tasks. A display allows you to scan quickly for errors, for the letters move through the display much faster than they can be printed. In addition to the usual paper editing keys, display typewriters usually have **forward character/word/line** keys. These keys move the window forward through your text. **Forward** is used instead of the **print** key when editing. All displays have some kind of pointer, usually five to eight characters from the right-hand side of the display or window boundary. This indicator will point to a position between two characters—this spot is your **cursor position** for insert and delete:

1. insert—any new text will be inserted between the two characters, at the cursor position

2. delete—any deletions or erasures will occur at the character to the right of the cursor position; the **correction** key will remove characters to the left of the cursor position

These two functions—insert and delete—work much the same way as paper typing. The display feature makes them seem very different, only because you are no longer editing during playout. The window or display is dynamic: as you edit your text, the characters displayed in the window change. Since all editing will

Cursor Position on Display, Xerox 620 Memorywriter

Courtesy of Xerox Corporation.

occur around the cursor position, you will always know what will follow your edit and what has preceded it.

Insert.   Simply move text forward until the cursor position is at the desired insert point. The cursor can be thought of as an insert caret for this function. When you have reached the insert position, begin typing. While you type, letters will move left and scroll off the display (i.e., disappear into memory), just as the window boundary is reached. The letters to the right of the cursor position will not move. New letters will appear to the left of the cursor—they will be "inserted" into the window. You can also insert format keys, such as **tab** and **return**; they will be displayed as symbols. When you have completed the insert, use the **forward** key to move to the next change.

Delete.   Move or scroll your text forward until the cursor position is just before the beginning of the text to be deleted. As you depress the **delete** key, characters (or words or lines—defined by the return symbol) will move toward the cursor and disappear at the left side of the cursor position. The remaining text will appear at the cursor position. You will notice return symbols in the display even if you have typed the original using autoreturn: the typewriter automatically puts in temporary returns each time it advances so that it will remember line endings during editing, even if during final printout or playback those line endings change. You also can delete format symbols in display editing. Upon printout, your text will be printed at new tab stops or have new line endings. Be careful when deleting or adding tab symbols because you can't see the format changes until you print the page.

The other editing functions already discussed for editing on paper also work nicely with displays. The search key is very powerful for display editing, since it can find desired word or editing positions almost instantly. Editing using a display is very easy. Once you have used a display to insert and delete or to find text locations, you will probably never edit directly on paper again. Since you can see what is happening in the memory as you edit, you will find that the display is very straightforward. If using a display seems confusing at first, type in a short practice document and experiment with various editing functions. You will quickly master using the display. Your operator's manual also will have useful examples of display editing. Display editing is the simplest and quickest way to correct text.

Special Format Functions, Tables, and Forms

Even most of the simplest electronics have special format functions. These are:

1. indent
2. decimal tab
3. stop code

Indent.   The **indent** key will position text at the next tab stop and will set a temporary left margin at that position. Instead of returning to the left margin for each new line, the typewriter will return to the tab stop. Indent allows you to type indented paragraphs automatically. The indent function is terminated by either the **return** key or an **end-indent** key (frequently the **code** key plus **return**).

Decimal tab.   The **decimal tab** key allows you to align numbers around tab stops for typing tables or columns of numbers. To use the decimal tab feature (or *dec tab*), you will need to set tab stops at the locations where you would like each column of numbers to end. Some machines have a special **dec tab set** key for this function, and require you to set dec tab stops for decimal alignment.

The typewriter will use the decimal point as the alignment position, so that numbers such as hundreds or thousands will align flush right, or so that columns of numbers with decimal points will have all those points aligned in a neat column. Don't worry if your numbers are whole (i.e., numbers without decimal points)—the typewriter will treat the first space following a number as a decimal point.

To type columns of numbers after having set your tab stops, depress the **dec tab** key before typing the first number. The typewriter will move to the tab stop; like the center function, it will move left as you type your number but will not print until you type a period (decimal point), a space, the **return,** or the **dec tab** key again. Then, the number will print out and will either end or align its decimal point at the tab position. Each line of numbers typed using the **dec tab** key will line up under the previous line, resulting in a perfect table. The following is an example of decimal tabulation:

(. . . . . . . tab stop → . . . . tab stop → . . . . tab stop → . . . .)

$ 423.65	22 units	3,425
16.00	3	96
8.65	124	831
.12	–	17

Note that the space following the dollar sign is not treated as a decimal point; most electronic typewriters can recognize dollar, cent, and per cent signs, and will ignore the spaces following them for decimal alignment.

Stop code.   This feature enables you to put marks into a document which will cause the typewriter to stop at the marked position during printout. Stop codes enable you to do the following:

1. type repetitive letters once, using the stop code to insert new variables (address, name, etc.) during each printout
2. mark words that you could not decipher when typing the original, for relocation during editing
3. mark the positions for figures or information deliberately left blank in your original

After typing in material at a stop code, press **print** to resume the playout. Usually the amount of information you can insert at each stop code is unlimited. Be sure to consult your manual about stop codes, since some typewriters won't memorize material typed after stop codes, and others may inadvertently memorize typed-in variable information in a repetitive letter original. Special format features are also available on most machines. These include:

1. flush right typing
2. required space and required return
3. stored formats

Flush right.   This feature allows you to align phrases flush right: the last character of each phrase will align at a tab point or the right margin. This feature is useful when typing programs and itineraries. It works like the center function (it is a mode operation). Some machines offer a flush right tab instead, which operates similarly to a decimal tab.

Required space.   A required space, usually entered as **code** or **shift** plus **space,** will link adjoining words so autoreturn doesn't split them between lines. An example for the use of required space would be the title "Dr. Anderson." A required space between the words "Dr." and "Anderson," instead of a regular space, will cause the typewriter to treat the title as a single word.

Required return.   A required return is useful during justified printing, for it will prevent the typewriter from trying to justify the last line of a paragraph if the end is close to the right margin. It is entered like **required space,** with **space** substituted for **return** in the key sequence.

Stored formats.   Many typewriters can store formats in memory under a name, or in a special format location, for recall into a document. These stored formats include left and right margins and all tab stops; sometimes, pitch also can be included. To store a format, make the desired format changes and depress the **store** or **format store** key as indicated in your manual. Ensure, however, that you are at the left margin when recalling formats into a document; otherwise your current typing line may be affected. A recalled format usually will be displayed in memory as a code, which can be deleted like text.

Tables.   There are two ways to type tables: the first is conventional statistical typing, and the second employs a special table layout function on certain machines. It is easiest to set up a table on paper rather than in memory. To type a table in the conventional manner, type your headings first, while aligning them into columns at the desired positions. Then return to your left-hand margin and clear your tab settings. Space over to the location under each heading where your decimal point (or end point for whole numbers) is to be found and set a tab stop or dec tab stop, depending upon the features of your typewriter. When you have set all the tab stops for your table, you can use **return** or **express** to move back to the left margin, and then begin typing using the **dec tab** key instead of the **tab** key for your numbers. The typewriter will memorize the dec tab codes along with the numbers so that you can edit the original and so that new or changed numbers will decimally align at the original positions.

The second method for tables uses a table layout feature. The purpose of this feature is to set up your format automatically for balanced columns—a format featuring equal amounts of space between each column. To use table layout, return to the left margin and turn on the function (usually a key). Then, *type the longest entry in each column* using the **dec tab** key before each entry. The type element may advance but nothing will print out. When you have typed one full line of your table (an entry for each column), depress the **return** key or the **table layout** key again. The typewriter will calculate the length of each entry and will set the proper tab stops automatically. It will signal when the format is complete and when you can begin typing your table. Most electronic typewriters do not allow you to insert or delete columns in an existing table on a column basis. You usually need a word processor for that function.

Forms.   Many typewriters also have a forms mode, designed to enable you to set up a form once and use the same template or form setup to type multiple revisions of that form. Electronic typewriters also have graduated spacing capabilities. Using the **index/reverse index** keys (up and down arrows for vertical movement) and a **graduated space bar** for horizontal movement, you can move the typing position in small, exact increments to line up forms and compensate for forms that don't line up on a conventional typewriter.

The graduated spacing function may be available in one of two forms. The first is as a **graduated spacing** key, which will be a mode function. Be sure to turn off **graduated spacing** before typing, because your letters will be too crowded if they are typed in graduated spacing. The second is as a special **space bar** key sequence, frequently **code** plus **shift** plus **space**. Some typewriters combine graduated spacing and the forms mode: the typewriter will automatically use graduated spacing between defined fields. If you do not have a forms mode, you can still type forms by using graduated spacing and the delay print function. If you have a page memory, you can use the **tab** key and stop codes to print several versions of the form after having typed the first one.

To use a forms mode, insert your form, set the desired margins, and turn on the forms mode. Use the **space bar** and **return** to move the typing position to the various fields (use graduated spacing if necessary). At the beginning of each field, depress the **tab** key; on some machines, depressing the **return** key will terminate an entry area. When you have set tabs or entry areas for all the fields on the form, depress the **end** key, reinsert your form, and depress the **start** key. Then, at a touch of the **tab** key, the typewriter will move automatically to each field and will allow you to fill in the desired information.

Since the forms modes on different electronic typewriters vary considerably, be sure to consult your operator's manual for details regarding your own machine's forms features.

Advanced Editing Functions

Many electronic typewriters support advanced editing functions for working with multiple-page documents. These features include:

1. search and replace
2. hyphenation
3. pagination
4. block move

An electronic typewriter will generally treat a multiple-page document as a linked series of single-page documents, meaning that you will, in most cases, be editing and printing a single page at a time.

All typewriters have a page-end indicator, usually on a paper support behind the platen. This guide will show you how many lines are left, indicated by the paper's top edge resting against the markings on the support. Remember to leave five or six lines of space at the end of the paper. Some typewriters have a page-end feature that will electronically count the number of lines you have typed and will signal you when a preset number of lines has been reached.

Many typewriters can store several pages but require you to give each page a different name. The "size" of each of these pages is limited to the size of your working memory or page buffer. Short multi-page documents, such as two-page letters, usually can be stored as a single "page" because format keys such as **tab** and **return** don't take much space. The same is true of double spacing. To include several short pages under a single page name, depress the **return,** followed by a stop code, at the bottom of your first page. To facilitate editing and make use of the autoreturn feature, place the stop code at the end of a paragraph. When you print the document, the typewriter will pause at the stop code. You then can insert your second sheet and resume the playout.

If your document is longer than two pages, you will have to store the pages as individual documents. As an aid to recalling the pages in sequence for editing and printing, write down the name or location of each page in the system's memory (using the reference you have assigned to each page). Insert this notation at the top of the first page of the rough copy being typed or the original being edited. That way, you will have a convenient listing of the page locations without having to use the directory or printout feature. Another method is to use similar document names but to include the actual page number within the name, if your typewriter will permit numbers in page references or names. As you reach the end of each page, store it in an appropriate location; for example, the third page of "Report to W. B. Jones" could be stored under "JONES3."

Some typewriters not supporting multi-page document names have pagination features that allow you to adjust page lengths during editing. (Pagination is discussed further on in this section.) Advanced typewriters, including many Japanese models such as the Panasonic and Canon units, permit storage of multi-page documents under a single document name, just like a word processor does. These units usually do not have a way to move directly between pages without scrolling through all the text in the document. The search function is the fastest way to move to particular pages, using these machines. In order to find a particular page using search, you should look for a phrase unique to that page for the quickest access. The "unique" phrase usually can be your page number, typed at the top of the page and stored in memory as part of the page. Depress the **search** key and enter the page number exactly as it has been originally typed. If you have typed "page" or a dash before the numeral, enter that as part of your search string. Otherwise, the typewriter may find other numerals in your text in addition to the page number at the top of the desired page. Depress **search** again or **forward** to activate the search, depending upon the individual machine. When the page is pulled into memory, cancel the search if your typewriter's search function is interactive and begin editing.

Search and replace.   The search and replace feature on some advanced machines will allow you to replace automatically all or selected occurrences of one phrase with another phrase. This feature, for example, lets you change "Smith" to "Williams," or "Jan." to "January," throughout a document. To use the feature, depress the **replace** key and type in the phrase that is to be replaced, such as "Smith." Depress **replace** again and type the phrase that will replace the original phrase, in this case "Williams," and depress **replace** again, or **forward** or **start** (be sure to consult your manual first). Some typewriters will stop at each occurrence: in a case like this, depress the **replace** key again to replace the word, or the **search** or **forward** keys to skip it and find the next one.

Hyphenation.   Hyphenation is offered on many machines: auto-hyphenation will place a special temporary hyphen within a word—a hyphen that will be removed automatically if you edit and change your line endings later. Hyphenation is usually a mode, similar to autoreturn, and will prompt you to insert a temporary hyphen when the margin has been reached. Simply depress the **hyphen** key at the desired break: the temporary hyphen will be typed and the machine will advance to the next line. Certain machines require you to depress the **hyphenate** key (a special function key) when you have reached the word to be broken; use **space** to move to the break point and depress **hyphenate**.

Pagination.   Pagination features allow you to adjust page endings when you have inserted or deleted large amounts of material. On typewriters that don't support multiple-page document names, you can sometimes link one-page documents together. The link feature should be used during editing. Use link to join two pages: move to the point in the text at which you want the expanded page to end and either store it or enter a page-end symbol, depending upon the kind of machine. You will then have to link and subsequently store each following page in the document if you use the link feature so as to ensure that no page is longer than the length you desire.

Manual pagination on printout is a simple method of paginating. For shortened pages, print the entire page and then call the next page into memory without removing your paper. Play out this next page line-by-line until the paper is full (the desired last line is reached on the page end indicator), and insert your next sheet. Play out the remainder of the appended page using the **remainder** key. For pages turning out longer than desired, stop the playout before the paper becomes full, play out line-by-line until the desired length has been reached, and then change the paper. Using the **remainder** key, play out the remainder, bring the next page into memory, and play it out on a line basis so as to append this next page onto your current sheet. For page numbering in manual pagination, simply· type the appropriate number at the top of each page before resuming playout.

Automatic pagination.   This feature is available on most multi-page document-based typewriters. During input, you can usually insert a page break into your text by depressing a **page end** key when the typewriter signals you at the end of the page. During editing, these symbols can be deleted manually and reinserted at the desired end point.

To paginate automatically at printout, begin playing out your document. The typewriter will automatically delete previous breaks and will stop when a preset number of lines has been printed. Some typewriters will stop several lines before the page end to allow you to change page endings, to take care of "widows" or "orphans" (i.e., split paragraphs in which only one line appears on a page). Print-out can be advanced on a line-by-line basis. Depress the **page end** to signal the end of the page, insert a new sheet, and continue playout.

Automatic page numbering.   This feature is available on many machines with automatic pagination. It will be necessary to start from page one the first time the document is printed since the typewriter will count the number of pages printed and will automatically number subsequent pages. On some machines, the page number will be remembered so that individual pages can be printed with numbering at a later point.

Block move.   Some typewriters allow you to move text in memory. Simply locate the part of the text that is to be moved, depress the **move** key, and advance the memory to the end of the phrase to be moved, referred to as the *move string*. Depress **move** again or **return**. Locate your new position and depress **move** (or **insert** or **position**). The text will be moved automatically from the old position to the new one (be sure to consult your manual, for move features differ markedly among various brands of machines).

Using Extended Memory

Many typewriters have very large internal memories capable of holding a variety of phrases, formats, or documents. Typewriters with extended memory usually differentiate between phrase/format memory and document memory. These two memories usually have separate directories, as discussed earlier. Compared with document memory, phrase memory doesn't occupy much memory space. Since your extended memory is inside the machine and can't be removed, and also has a limit, the key to effective use of extended memory is management.

Always keep a printed-out version of your document directory. When you first print the directory, write in the date and a brief description next to each name or document title. Keep this directory close at hand—in your desk or in a binder. At some point near the end of the business day, reprint the directory if you have added documents to the memory. Put short notes after any new documents and place these new directory printouts in a folder with the original. Once a week, compare your directories and, based on the dates and contents, decide if any entries can be deleted. Some typewriters don't have a delete function, but you can recall the old title and delete all text stored under it. Be sure to mark these titles as deleted when you print out the directory. Another way to delete a document is to store a new one under an old name. Once or twice a month, print out a new copy of the directory and note all documents that have been stored for two weeks or longer. If they are no longer needed, delete them. Then print out an updated directory and write notes next to all entries. Old directory copies then can be discarded.

Some typewriters can store over 100 phrases and documents, so it is important to keep track of your memory and its contents. Also, use discretion when storing documents: if a document is very short or unlikely to be reedited, don't store it. After a document has been signed and distributed, delete it unless it can be reedited into a new document later on. Store an envelope address after the body of the letter in the same document, and separate the letter and envelope text with a stop code. That way, envelopes and letters won't get separated. Finally, if you find you are filling your memory to capacity once a week, or you realize that you are typing long documents that don't easily fit into your machine's memory, you may be a candidate for some kind of removable storage attachable to your typewriter. (These options are explained in the last section of this chapter.)

Special Applications

Because electronic typewriters are designed for routine business correspondence, one very important use of the electronic's special features is *merge printing*. It applies to the printing of repetitive letters. An identical or similar letter frequently will be sent to a group of different people, each requiring a new address and salutation. Sometimes variable figures or information are included in the body of the letter, such as the number of owned shares in letters to stockholders, or the amount of payment due sent to past-due accounts. The electronic typewriter will permit you to type the body or repetitive portion of such letters just once, and insert the variable information at printout.

In order to output repetitive letters, you will need to create a master—the body of the letter, specially formatted for insertion of variables on printout. In typing the master letter, take your written copy and circle each item that will change: e.g., address, salutation, variable figures, and so forth. Then input the letter into the typewriter. Type a stop code wherever a variable piece of information will come. When you are through, print your master and proof it, and then ask your supervisor to review it for changes.

When the master is ready to be filled in with addresses and other variables, insert your letterhead and begin playout. The typewriter will stop at each stop code. If the memory is switchable, turn it off and type the required information. Then turn the memory back on and resume playout. When the first letter has been completed, you can rewind the memory and output your next letter. If the memory cannot be turned off you will have to type in the new variable and then delete or erase forward the old variable from memory before continuing. Make sure you have the previous letter handy as a reference if you don't have a display so that you can locate the end of the previous variable when deleting. Using stop codes and this method, you can prepare a series of original letters quickly and in a few simple steps.

Document assembly.   This function can be accomplished in many advanced machines. A document may be assembled by merging stored paragraphs from the phrase memory with a master document or several master documents.

Some typewriters can use a document link feature to combine several documents and phrases into one longer document. Each piece of the document is typed and stored in a separate location when this feature is used. The typewriter is then placed in a special "link" mode, the documents to be linked are specified by name and in exact order, and an assembled document is automatically output by the typewriter. If no new format changes are included in the individual document, the final document will be printed out under the format of the first document in the linked sequence.

Document assembly is a very useful feature for offices using standard paragraphs (called "boilerplate") in general typing and correspondence. Examples of document assembly are property deeds or wills. These contain standard paragraphs used over and over again; but in the case of a property deed, for example, different paragraphs could be required, depending upon whether the property is new or is being resold, the location of the property, etc. Document assembly features allow you to use paragraphs you may have already stored in your memory, and simply type a short linking document to print out automatically a complete deed or other document from the stored paragraphs.

ELECTRONIC TYPEWRITERS—HOW TO KEEP THEM WORKING FOR YOU

Common Problems with Electronic Typewriters

Electronic typewriters are among the most reliable machines in today's sophisticated office. While most problems are related either to the environment or to operator error, computer components are nevertheless susceptible to abrupt changes in temperature or to sudden jarring, and will sometimes fail as a result. Common problems usually involve power, memory, or the printer mechanism. The problems frequently can be avoided, identified, or corrected without a service call. These problems are sometimes related to the location or installation of your typewriter. One of the most common sources of failure is interruption of power: either the electric cord has been inadvertently removed from the wall outlet or the building power has been cut, as sometimes happens after working hours.

Memory failure usually appears as an inability to recall text, make corrections, or, in extreme cases, perform functions. Heat-related problems can cause erratic memory operation: high temperatures will cause partial loss of memory, and temperatures too low for the computer will result in slow, incomplete operations. Some typewriters will check memory status at power-up and will automatically shut themselves down and present a service call code in their display if memory failure is detected by the machine's diagnostic routine. In terms of the printer, common problems are ribbon jams and print element misalignment. Most of these problems can be fixed without assistance. If the typewriter refuses to print an edited or stored document, the problem is often related to memory and not the printer mechanism.

How to Avoid Trouble

Your electronic typewriter is designed to be placed on a desktop and will fit into the space provided for most standard electrics. Make sure *not* to push the unit snug against a back wall, since the electronic circuits need adequate airflow for cooling. Also, be careful not to jar the typewriter because electronic circuits are sensitive. Some very old secretarial desks have a swing-out typewriter stand; the typewriter is bolted to a shelf which then can be pushed back into the desk behind a door when not in use. These desks use spring-loaded arms to move the old-fashioned heavy metal typewriters into position. *Do not install your electronic typewriter into this kind of desk unless the swing-out shelf can be permanently fixed in the typing position.* The sudden jarring motion of the spring-loaded arms when moving an electronic typewriter will cause serious damage to the computer circuits inside the unit.

Extreme heat or cold may adversely affect the operation of your typewriter. Temperatures over 85°F will cause the memory to fail, although permanent damage is unlikely. If the office is colder than 55°F, allow your typewriter to warm up gradually with the rest of the office before typing, since typewriter circuitry doesn't operate well in very cold temperatures.

Make sure your typewriter is securely plugged into a wall outlet, not an extension cord, unless the extension has a fuse and a three-prong outlet. You can plug items without motors, such as lights, into the same outlet, but keep machines like copiers and electric pencil sharpeners plugged into separate outlets. Dictating units have very small transport motors and usually won't bother your typewriter, but other motor-driven machines generate interference on the electrical line that can affect your typewriter's memory. Another less obvious cause of memory problems is static. A buildup of static, usually caused by dry winter heat and nylon-based carpeting, can zap the memory and erase parts of the stored text. Use a static spray if you receive static shocks from metal objects in order to keep the static from affecting the typewriter.

When you leave the office, cover your typewriter to keep dust out of the electronic keyboard. Most printers have protective covers over their openings—these are for operator safety, so you can't get hair or clothing caught in the moving parts—but they also help to keep dust and objects such as paper clips out of the mechanism. Because electronic typewriter mechanisms move faster than conventional typewriters, foreign objects such as strands of hair can bind the mechanism and cause a failure.

Ribbons and print elements also can cause problems. Take special care when changing ribbons and correction tapes: improper installation may cause sticking (the correction tape is adhesive), or ribbon binding. When inserting new print elements, press the daisy wheel (if your unit uses wheels) firmly on the hub, unless the typewriter uses cartridge daisies or self-indexing wheels (such as the ones on Xerox models). If the letters are misaligned or the wheel makes unusual noises, ensure that the wheel is firmly in place. Be careful not to bend the letters or petals. If a petal is broken or looks bent, discard the wheel, since broken daisy wheels can damage the printer mechanism.

How to Keep from Overworking Yourself and Your Electronic Typewriter

An electronic typewriter will work all day, and can keep up with even the heaviest workloads. As was stressed before, managing your work and organizing it around your typewriter will keep both of you from being overworked. Don't use your typewriter as a resting place for papers or books. Heavy items can break the plastic cover over the print mechanism, and paper covering the cooling slots will cause the unit to overheat. If you inadvertently pour something over the keyboard, turn the unit off for a day and allow it to dry out. Coffee and other substances containing sugar may cause keys to stick. And operating a wet keyboard can cause electrical shorting. If you need to use correction fluid on an error, remove the paper first, or roll it well above the typing line. Some correction fluids contain a substance that can dissolve part of the letters on a daisy petal. Line drawing on the paper also should be done outside the unit. If the memory or typewriter "hangs" (i.e., gets stuck in one position or won't clear an error), the condition can sometimes be cleared up by powering down and then starting the typewriter again. However, don't do this too often—you may blow the typewriter's fuse. The following guidelines can help streamline your work:

1. Too many corrections on a page may take more time to correct automatically than retyping the page.

2. It sometimes helps to plan the editing of a heavy load of documents—group together the work that requires similar editing techniques.

3. Type all your forms at a single sitting if possible, since forms typing requires some adjustment from standard typing.

4. Don't save lengthy jobs until the end of the day, since it will take several minutes to play out each page after corrections have been made.

5. Group together work that uses the same print elements—it is tedious to have to change a print wheel with every page.

While some of these guidelines may apply more to the use of word processors than to electronic typewriters, you nevertheless can adapt them to your own work situation and schedule.

Routine Maintenance and Supplies

Since electronic typewriters require fewer adjustments, routine service is not needed. Electronics do not use cloth ribbons and they have permanent dust guards over their printer mechanisms; hence, professional cleaning is not required. Generally, the only time you should require maintenance is in the case of a mechanical failure. If your typewriter won't work properly and you have checked to be sure the problem isn't environmental or an operator error, place a service call to your dealer. Because electronic components are very complex, the cost of service is high, almost as high as that for a computer. For that reason, many people purchase a service contract. For approximately 8–10% of the price of the machine per year, the dealer or manufacturer will repair the machine as often as needed and will replace any defective or worn parts for no additional charge. There is no hard-and-fast rule for whether or not you need a service contract: it boils down to a choice of guaranteed service at a high but fixed cost, or the calculated risk of your typewriter's not requiring more maintenance than the cost of the policy.

Supplies are also an important aspect of keeping your machine running smoothly. Run out of ribbon or break your last print element, and your typewriter will be out of commission. Unlike electric and Selectric typewriters, the variety of ribbons, correction tapes, and print wheels is nearly endless—and every manufacturer is different. The highest quality (and most expensive) ribbons are called single-strike. They allow the typewriter to use each section of ribbon only once. Ribbons are available in black, and often blue, green, and brown. Many offices use colored stationery complemented by a colored ribbon.

A ribbon should last about two weeks. If you use ribbons faster than this, ask your dealer for a high-capacity or multi-strike ribbon. Multi-strike ribbons advance more slowly, so that the typewriter can strike each section of ribbon several times. This ribbon will cost about one and a half times more than a normal ribbon but it should last twice as long. Unlike electric typewriter fabric ribbons, however, both single- and multi-strike ribbons move in only one direction, and when you reach the end the ribbon must be changed. Some typewriters, such as the Adlers and Royals, have a "ribbon-saver" switch that helps to prolong ribbon life. All electronics use cassette ribbons: they are one-piece, with both spools enclosed in a plastic case. They snap into place in the machine, and no threading is required except to place the ribbon between a pair of ribbon guides on either side of the print element.

Buy your ribbons a box at a time (a half dozen are packed in each box). Store the ribbons in a cool dry place, out of direct sunlight. Ribbons tend to dry out, which is why you shouldn't order high-capacity ribbons unless you really need them. Manufacturers usually seal their ribbons in protective plastic pouches. When you have two ribbons left in the box, order a new box. You probably will have to buy ribbons from your dealer or from the manufacturer. Try not to buy the brands that are not authorized by the manufacturer—they may not work with your typewriter's correction system.

Correction tapes last longer than ribbons, i.e., about three to four weeks. Although they too are packed in boxes of six, they are not sealed in plastic because they usually do not dry out. Order correction tapes as you would order ribbons—when you have two tapes left in the box. Ensure that the correction tapes are compatible with your ribbons: some manufacturers (such as IBM) specify different correction tapes for different ribbons (the spools of the ribbon and correction tape are usually color-coded).

Print elements usually cost about $20.00. You will probably use the 10-pitch most frequently, and you can expect your most often used element to last six months. During use, the constant hammering of the letters against the platen will flatten them out. Check the element's clarity every month or so by typing a few lines with the used element and comparing it with the same lines typed on your new spare element. If the letters from the old element look denser and less sharp, discard it. Using a badly worn element risks breaking off petals inside the printer mechanism, a situation possibly requiring a service call. *Never* clean print elements with typewriter cleaner—it may dissolve the plastic in the wheels. Store your extra wheels in a convenient desk drawer, always in their cases. Many office supply dealers sell print element cases capable of holding several elements, storable on a shelf.

Most manufacturers offer specialty wheels or elements for scientific or foreign-language typing. For routine work you will not need these wheels, since most elements already contain ninety-six or more characters instead of the normal eighty-eight. Several companies will also make custom daisy-wheel elements by adding special characters to your favorite print styles. Custom wheels generally cost twice that of normal wheels. If you need a custom daisy wheel, ask your dealer to refer you to a manufacturer such as Camwil in Hawaii. Be sure to order extra custom wheels, since they can take eight weeks or more to receive.

To clean the outside of your typewriter, use a soft cloth and a mild cleaning solution such as window cleaner, or a soap-and-water mixture. Be careful when using strong spray-on cleaners such as Fantastik on the keys or plastic parts, since some plastics may discolor or react negatively. Also be careful not to scratch the display window when cleaning it. If you keep your typewriter covered when not in use, only infrequent cleaning will be required.

BEYOND THE ELECTRONIC TYPEWRITER

Electronic Typewriter Options: External Storage and Communications

Two of the most popular options for electronic typewriters are extended storage and telecommunications. Your unit already may have either or both of these, or you may find that the options might be useful additions for your office.

External storage. External storage is a term describing a removable device that can store documents. A storage module allows you to file documents from the typewriter's memory to some kind of removable, permanent storage medium, and to retrieve the documents when needed later on. There are four popular types of storage media, each coming in a variety of sizes:

1. cassette tapes—similar to audio cassette tapes, except that the typewriter can store documents on them in a "digitized" (i.e., a machine-readable) form

2. cards—small card-shaped pieces of magnetic film that can store one or more pages of text

3. floppy diskettes—flat disks of magnetic material that are 5¼″ in size and can store larger amounts of text than tapes or cards and retrieve it more rapidly

4. microdiskettes—new recording media that are 3″ versions of the floppy diskette

Diskettes are by far the most popular external storage medium: they are inexpensive and can store up to several hundred pages, they are designed to spin rapidly in disk-drive units for fast document access, and they can be indexed automatically so that documents of any size can be stored and new pages can be added to existing documents. Since cards and tapes can't be rapidly scanned and indexed, it is not possible to add new pages to an already-stored document on card or tape. Some diskettes are even compatible with certain computer systems; hence, documents can be transferred between the computer and typewriter through the removable diskette. Diskette drives, and cassettes or cards, operate just like your typewriter's extended memory. A diskette or other medium is placed in a drive unit, located either inside the typewriter or in a separate external box, and the same **store** and **recall** keys are used.

If you find that your typewriter's memory frequently becomes full, or you have a number of letters and documents that are routinely reedited, you may be a candidate for an external storage unit. Many typewriters are designed to allow

Royal 1040 Modular and Expandable
Electronic Typewriter

Courtesy of Adler-Royal Business Machines, Inc.

addition of a disk or tape unit at any time, so your dealer or manufacturer may be able to upgrade your unit, usually right in your office.

Diskettes are thin and susceptible to damage, so be careful not to bend them, write on them, or store them in a flat position. Diskettes should be stored in their protective jackets, standing upright in the boxes provided by the manufacturer. Many office supply dealers carry a variety of convenient disk storage units. Always store a printed copy of the directory or index along with the diskette so that you can quickly locate the documents stored on particular diskettes.

Communications.   Communications, or telecommunications, is another popular option. Telecommunications is a process through which telephone lines are used to send messages or documents electronically between typewriters, computers, and other communicating devices. A special telephone adapter, either an acoustic coupler into which you set the telephone handset, or a modem box that attaches directly to the telephone, is connected to a special communication circuit inside the typewriter or in a separate box.

Communications is useful if you need to send or receive documents between other offices, or if you need to send or receive data routinely with computer systems. Communications links are very specific since each different device may communicate using different standards, called *protocols.* Your dealer or manufacturer must install the communications option and will tailor the specifications for proper communications to the desired receiving system or host computer. The dealer or manufacturer also will supply instructions, and sometimes a brief training course, so that you can utilize the communications option effectively. Like external storage devices, communications can be added to many electronic typewriters.

Electronic Typewriter Add-on Word Processors
At least four independent companies, along with most manufacturers, have developed word processing systems based around electronic typewriters. These devices, called *add-on word processors,* can be attached to nearly any electronic typewriter. An add-on word processing system usually will include one or two

Olympia ETXI Text Editor with Orbit

Courtesy of Olympia USA

diskette drives and a CRT (cathode-ray tube) or monitor, similar to a television screen. Most add-on units use the typewriter's keyboard and printer; some include an auxiliary keypad for functions not found on most typewriters. Add-ons can be attached to any level of electronic typewriter, but a large percentage of them are attached to very basic typewriters. They are an inexpensive way to obtain the benefits of word processing.

Because you have a screen to work with in an add-on unit, the display can now show you the upper or lower portion of a whole page. Editing or reformatting changes show up instantly and you can view a representation of your page on the screen before printing. Add-on word processors also allow you to move and copy text from one page or document to another, a task made simple because you can watch the entire process on the screen.

Facit 8001 Electronic Typewriter

Courtesy of Facit, Inc.

4

Generation of Business Documents: Word Processing

Edward F. Coyman, Jr. • Product Manager, Office Systems Product Group, Wang Laboratories, Inc.

INTRODUCTION TO WORD PROCESSING

"What are word processors anyway?"

"I know what they are! I've seen them in lots of kitchens; they slice and dice and chop and blend and . . . don't they?"

To those of you who are familiar with word processors this hypothetical exchange may sound somewhat gee-whiz in tone. But the comparison between the two very different machines is nevertheless valid, for in both technologies matter is put into a high-speed device, manipulated within the device and/or changed into a different form in a way much faster than could have been accomplished manually, removed from the machine, and used in a specific way for a predetermined purpose.

Word processing, according to *The American Heritage Dictionary*, Second College Edition, is "a system of producing typewritten documents, such as business letters, by use of automated typewriters and electronic text-editing equipment." The subject we want to address specifically in this chapter is the "text-editing equipment" portion of that definition.

To expand on this area and understand why the modern word processor is the way it is, you need to think about the older types of office equipment that a secretary was and, in many firms, still is expected to work with. Try to envision a manual typewriter, correction fluid, carbon paper, walls of filing cabinets, stenographic note pads, etc., etc. Now try to think about working with this equipment. Think about manually typing twenty copies of the same letter for distribution to different recipients because each recipient requires an original. Think about completing your fifth revision to a forty-page document and having your executive make major changes by inserting several new paragraphs throughout the document. Think about using carbon paper to create a duplicate copy and not having all of the characters transfer clearly onto the copy. Think about searching endlessly for a document lost in the filing system. Think about retyping everything because a single character has been left out!

Sound familiar? Most secretaries probably remember working like that at one time or another. It is not only frustrating but also a complete waste of a secretary's time. A solution to the problem is a word processor: a word processor will allow the user to print as many originals as desired, make revisions without having to retype entire documents, combine two documents with only a few keystrokes, merge a letter with a list of varying address headings and automatically create dozens of individual letters for distribution, or automatically search through hundreds of documents to locate the needed one quickly. The list of capabilities goes on and on and is growing every day as newer and faster technology becomes available. The word processor is becoming standard in every office environment and with it comes a generation of secretaries who are expected to understand a word processor's features and capabilities, the concept behind them, and the proper use of the equipment so as to maximize productivity.

Many people are afraid of things they do not understand and as a result are often turned away from new and more sophisticated technology. The introduction of word processing or any other type of office automation equipment sometimes can produce this effect. Some people are convinced that the introduction of word processors will mean layoffs with human beings being replaced by machines, but this is hardly the case. The word processor is used to increase the secretaries' productivity levels, improve performance, and create time for more important management support functions by reducing the amount of time spent at the typewriter. The equipment was never intended to replace the secretaries. By increasing your level of expertise with word processing systems and by broadening your knowledge of modern office technology, you, the secretary, will be better equipped to compete for and fill the more demanding and higher paying positions of today's business place.

WORD PROCESSING EQUIPMENT ARCHITECTURES

Stand-alone Systems

A stand-alone word processor can function in total independence from any other system. A user can operate it in an isolated area and not have to rely on other individuals and machines. The stand-alone is a self-contained system providing the user with all of the essential hardware and software components required to create, edit, store, and print word processing documents. Modern electronic stand-alone system components usually include a single keyboard and screen coupled with a central processor, a storage device, a printer, and possibly a telecommunications interface. The term *stand-alone* should not necessarily lead anyone to believe that this type of system is limited in function, or that it is at the bottom of the scale of system capabilities. A stand-alone system could be a large computer with a single workstation and printer. A system of this sort might be used for inventory control in a warehouse. For instance, it might be used there to help the loading dock manager write activity and inventory reports. Although quite large in capacity, performance, and features, this system is still considered a stand-alone, for it supports a single user and is independent of other systems.

Shared-logic Systems

The principle behind the shared-logic system approach is one that allows for a number of workstations and other peripherals to be attached to a central processing unit, or CPU. This CPU, activated by commands sent from users at their

Wang 01541/50 Word Processing System

Courtesy of Wang Laboratories, Inc.

workstations, will control the handling and manipulation of data in memory, storage devices, printers, workstations, other peripherals, and communications equipment. The advantage of the shared-logic system over the stand-alone approach is that multiple workstations can access and share a common CPU, memory, storage devices, peripherals, and communications, thus reducing the per-workstation cost of the system. The disadvantages of the shared-logic system architecture are primarily performance and the risk of being dependent on a single resource. The performance problem develops because additional workstations and peripherals are added to a system still dependent on a single processor to handle system activities. This problem is experienced by the user in the form of system degradation; that is, slow response time when numerous users are working on the system. The risk of being dependent on a single CPU is obvious: should it fail, the entire system becomes inoperable.

People often refer to a shared-logic system as supporting dumb terminals. This expression comes from the fact that the workstations and peripherals themselves are not required to perform any processing tasks and are only input/output extensions of the central processing unit. The CPU handles all system activity and performs all processing with the peripherals being extensions of the CPU.

Distributed-logic Systems

The distributed-logic system architecture is very similar to the shared-logic system described in the previous section. Although they physically look very similar (that is, both have multiple workstations connected to a CPU), the distributed-logic system utilizes an entirely different approach to the handling and processing of information in the system. This approach provides the workstations, printers, and peripherals with local memory and processing capabilities that do much of the work required of the CPU in the shared-logic architecture. The result of this distribution of the system's logic is increased response time and a much slower rate of degradation as additional workstations and peripherals are added.

The processing done inside the peripherals is handled by a microprocessor. This microprocessor is a miniature computer designed to handle specific processing tasks before and/or after they are handled by the CPU. By doing as much information processing in the workstation as possible before sending the data to the CPU, the microprocessor in the workstation takes much of the burden off of the CPU and increases the system's overall performance level. The printer, like the workstation, also can handle processing tasks for document printing, thus providing the CPU with some additional help.

Timeshare and Mainframe Systems

A timesharing word processing environment consists of one or more workstations linked to a very large computer system, or mainframe, via telecommunications. This mainframe, in addition to providing data processing services for a number of remote users, also provides word processing software. The mainframe supplies the central processing power for the word processor user and allows for the utilization of compatible workstations and output devices perhaps already owned or conveniently located in the office. With this system, the user pays for the use of someone else's CPU and the cost of communicating with it. This type of arrangement may be satisfactory for firms that already have a data processing timesharing relationship with a mainframe and wish to add word processing to it. The drawback to this arrangement is delayed response time in that the user must communicate over relatively slow telephone lines. In addition, the user may have to compete for line time to the CPU with data processing and any other word processing users also utilizing the same mainframe. Timeshare word processing is not encountered very often in an office because it is usually quite costly and would never be an efficient way of doing just word processing.

Personal and Microcomputer-based Word Processing

Personal and microcomputers are typically small stand-alone systems designed for professionals, small businesses, and home users. These small systems are usually limited in their processing power and memory facilities, but are often adequate for the user who wants a simple system to run a small firm's payroll, accounts receivable, or inventory program. Such systems typically include a workstation with keyboard and screen, some internal memory, and interfaces to options such as storage devices, printers, and telecommunications capabilities. The manufacturers of personal or microcomputers and/or firms dealing in software packages may offer word processing software to run on your system. Such word processing software can range greatly in cost and capabilities. For some systems you can obtain software typically providing minimal text-editing capabilities and relying very heavily on command code language oriented more to the computer user than the word processor user. Some software packages are very user friendly; i.e., they are easy to use and provide advanced word processing capabilities with high performance and great flexibility. If the type of word processing software you want is unavailable from one vendor, chances are good that it can be found elsewhere.

Integrated Information Systems

The integrated information system offers the user the processing power and storage capability of a large computer system with the added advantage of having

Wang Professional Computer

Courtesy of Wang Laboratories, Inc.

powerful word processing capabilities. This type of system is usually a mid- to large-size computer supporting a large number of workstations, a variety of printers and peripherals, a multiple number of storage devices, and accommodating the needs of the programmer and word processor user alike. The integrated information system has the advantage of being able to offer advanced word processing capabilities because of its processing power and storage capacity. This capability is provided to the user who requires only word processing as well as to the programmer who may only use it occasionally.

There are many disadvantages to such an integrated system for the organization needing only the word processing features. This type of system is often physically large and quite noisy, typically existing in a computer room environment that requires air conditioning, special wiring, and some sort of soundproofing. The printers, CPU, and storage devices are located in a central area away from the word processor user's desk. This sort of system is often bothersome for the office worker because the equipment cannot be located close at hand, due to its noise and special environmental requirements, thus resulting in numerous trips to the computer room to pick up printouts and to load and unload stored documents.

Office Automation Systems

The office automation (OA) system represents the current high point in systems for today's office worker. The OA system combines advanced word processing capabilities with such sophisticated office applications as calendar management, telephone management, spreadsheet calculations, graphics, voice capabilities, and spelling and document analysis, to name just a few. In addition, the OA system is designed to exist in an office environment, replacing the telephone, calculator, Dictaphone, calendar, and clock as desktop devices.

The OA systems of today are compact, easily installed in the average office, support a number of workstations, and provide the latest in high-quality printing and output devices designed for document generation. Office automation systems typically offer compact storage devices designed to handle relatively large amounts of text and are ergonomically comfortable.

The OA system does not overlook the office worker desiring the capability to write programs: OA systems are frequently available with one or more programming languages such as C or BASIC in addition to their office capabilities. Most word processor manufacturers are concentrating in this area of development. Each manufacturer seems to be claiming that it can solve all of your office needs with just one system. Office automation systems have progressed and have reached levels where voice recognition and speech synthesis will be standard features in the next few years.

THE PARTS OF A WORD PROCESSOR

Keyboards

The keyboard is the primary interface to the word processor. It allows the user to give the system commands, access text and data for editing and creation, and access and control the other devices attached to the word processor. Each manufacturer's keyboard may be of a different design, but the industry standard has become the QWERTY keyboard. The QWERTY, meaning that the first six alphabet keys spell QWERTY, is very similar to the keyboard on a typewriter. In addition to the basic alphabet, numbers, and punctuation-mark keys, some additional keys not required by a typewriter have been added to the word processor keyboard. These keys typically include an **execute** or **command** key, a **cancel** or **stop** key, and direction keys (i.e., keys having arrows pointing up, down, right, and left). The direction keys are used to control the cursor, the little indicator that represents the user's location on the screen. The direction keys control the position of the cursor in relation to the text that the user sees. The **execute** or **command** key is used to signal the system that you are ready to begin a process other than the one you are currently engaged in. The **cancel** or **stop** key is used to indicate that you would like to terminate the current process. The modern word processor keyboard usually incorporates several additional function keys designed to make the system more user friendly. These keys include, for instance, **insert, delete, copy, move, indent, center, previous screen,** and so on. Function keys like these have been designed to save the user time and confusion, in that each key represents a complete and often-used function. For example, by simply pressing the **page** key once, the user could create a new page in the document without any other keystrokes.

Keyboards may be physically attached to the workstation screen by incorporation of both the keyboard and the screen into one workstation unit, or they may be attached with a cable, an arrangement that, in effect, creates a movable keyboard. The movable keyboard is considered more user friendly in that it allows the user to sit back from the screen, thus reducing the chance of eyestrain and providing greater freedom of movement. Mechanically, the keyboard is a simple switching device that sends messages to the system in the form of previously coded numerical values. For example, each time you press the key representing the letter "D" in the alphabet, the key closes a switch that triggers a message to send an eight-digit or 8-bit code to the system. The code looks like this: 01000100. The numerical value for the letter "D" is referred to as ASCII code.

The acronym *ASCII* stands for "American Standard Code for Information Interchange" and is the principal way by which computers and word processing systems represent data in electronic form. Once the data have been translated into the electronic ASCII code, they can be more easily manipulated and stored by the system.

Screens

The most popular type of word processor screen is the cathode-ray tube or CRT display. This type of workstation screen is very similar to the screen in your television set at home. It is a glass tube, the interior surface of which has been coated with the chemical phosphor, and the air inside of which has been pumped out. At the back of the tube is an electron gun that directs a beam of electrons toward the inside surface of the screen, that being the flip side of the viewing surface. The invisible beam is projected onto the inside of the screen and illuminates the phosphor-coated glass tube in the form of the desired characters.

All types of CRT workstation screens are available, some with small displays and some with large ones. Standard CRTs are rated by their diagonal size—that is to say, the distance along the diagonal from one corner to the other corner. The most popular size for CRT workstation screens is a ten- or twelve-inch diagonal display. A CRT of this size will display twenty-four lines of text by eighty characters wide, which is about one third or one half of a page. Some manufacturers provide larger CRTs with their workstations. The larger CRTs will display the equivalent of a standard $8\frac{1}{2}'' \times 11''$ page of text. This type of display, sixty-six lines by eighty characters, is referred to as a full-page screen. Most CRTs provide for the adjustment of contrast and brightness of the image and are available with a light green character display on a black background, a white on black, or an orange on black.

The image of an individual, on-screen character is not that of a single letter but rather the image of a group of tiny illuminated dots. These dots form a matrix arranged in such a fashion as to represent a particular character when illuminated on the screen. The most popular dot matrix for word processing systems is the five-by-seven, which provides enough detail to the character to satisfy most users. The dot matrix making up each character on the screen is only a temporary image. It will last only as long as the phosphor coating stays illuminated, which is a fraction of a second. How then is it possible for the screen to maintain images for an extended period of time? The secret is in a process called *refreshing* or *repainting* the screen. Every sixty seconds the electron gun at the back of the tube paints a stream of electrons line-by-line, starting from the upper left-hand corner of the screen and working its way to the bottom right-hand corner. The process of refreshing the screen happens so fast that the user cannot detect any flicker of the characters.

Most CRT workstations use a moving character referred to as a cursor. The user controls the position of the cursor in relation to the text appearing on the screen. The user can move the cursor's position by using the cursor direction keys on the keyboard. The cursor will take up the space of one character on the screen and may appear as a single blinking or fixed underline mark. Some cursors appear as a block, which, when placed over a character, becomes transparent, thus allowing the user to see the character underneath it. When the user wishes to enter text or edit existing text on the screen, the cursor will show the position

Screen Sample with Highlighted Text

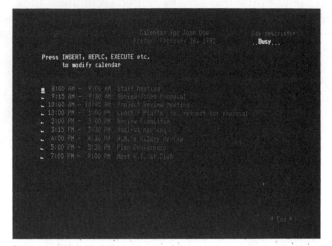

Courtesy of Wang Laboratories, Inc.

in which the user is currently located. The cursor is also utilized to make selections from screen menus, to indicate text for particular commands, and to give the user a focal point on the screen.

Aside from providing the basic capabilities described above, some manufacturers offer additional standard or optional features that can be added onto their CRT workstations. These features include the display of a variety of character fonts and sizes, natural or foreign-language display capabilities, screen graphics (the ability to draw on the screen), reverse video (the ability to have light characters on a dark background or dark characters on a light background), and imaging capabilities (the ability to display actual photographic images on the screen).

EXTERNAL STORAGE DEVICES

Floppy Diskette

The most popular electronic storage medium for word processors is the floppy diskette. The floppy diskette is composed of a round piece of flat, flexible plastic coated with an iron oxide material. This thin disk, enclosed in a plastic or cardboard jacket similar to a 45 RPM record jacket, comes in 8″, 5¼″, and 3½″ sizes. The most popular size used in word processors is the 8″ one, although the 5¼″ (or *minifloppy*) is growing in popularity. The jacket, typically bearing the manufacturer's name, not only protects the magnetic media within but also provides a label useful for filing purposes. The diskette jacket is also equipped with strategically positioned openings so that when the diskette is loaded, the drive mechanism can grasp the diskette and spin it at a high speed—360 RPM for the 8″ and 300 RPM for the minifloppy—with the surrounding jacket remaining motionless. The jacket exerts very little friction on the spinning diskette within it, for it is coated with very smooth plastic.

The holes in the jacket include a spindle hole allowing the tapered spindle or cylinder of the drive mechanism to access the diskette for positioning and spinning purposes. If the user places the diskette in the drive so that it is positioned a little off-center, the tapered cylinder within will ensure that the diskette is on center and properly aligned. A second opening in the diskette jacket is called the head access slot. This opening is positioned as a wide slot running from a point near the center out to one side edge of the jacket. The opening may be on one or both sides of the diskette jacket, depending on whether it is a single- or double-sided diskette. When the diskette is mounted in the drive, the head access slot is located directly beneath the drive's read/write head. The read/write head is the portion of the disk drive that passes information to the diskette in the form of electromagnetic code. The diskette, being coated with an iron oxide compound, is capable of storing this electromagnetic information on its surface. The read/write head is positioned on the end of an arm that moves the head back and forth across the surface of the disk so as to be able to encode information onto one of the many disk tracks passing underneath it. The read/write head floats above the disk on the end of the read/write arm. When the arm is extended for accessing purposes, the distance between the head and the disk is so small that an object as small as a particle of smoke placed between the head and disk surface could cause the head to scratch the disk, resulting in a fatal head crash. The head should never actually touch the surface of the disk but must be placed very close so that it can read or write upon the diskette surface with these electromagnetic pulses.

The third hole in the diskette jacket is the index hole corresponding to at least one similar hole in the actual disk. When the jacket hole lines up with the hole in the disk, it signals the beginning of each track to the system. A small light pointed at the hole and a photo cell trigger on the other side of the hole produce a timing signal to the system that indicates the diskette's tracks. Floppy disks have at least one hole indicating the home position. Hard-sectored disks may have sector holes that also indicate, via the same photoelectric trigger mechanism, the position of each sector as it passes under the read/write head.

Floppy diskettes are equipped with a write protection notch. This notch appears to the user as a small cut in the edge of the diskette jacket. When mounted in the drive, the notch is positioned so that a light source and photo cell trigger contained inside the drive can be used to tell the system if the notch is open or if it is taped shut by a write protection label. The user puts this label over the notch and removes it when desired. The meaning of the open or closed notch depends on the diskette size used and the manufacturer of the drive. When the notch on a minifloppy is covered with a label, the disk is protected from being written on. But when the label is removed, the disk is no longer protected and can be accessed. For the 8″ floppy, the procedure is just the opposite: the notch is covered when it is to be written on but uncovered when it is to be write protected. The diskettes you use will contain information regarding their proper positioning in the drive, e.g., which corner should be up or what side should be facing down. Such information ensures that you load the media properly.

The system you use may contain one or more floppy diskette drives—drives that may be used for archiving purposes (i.e., the filing and removal of documents from the system) or that may act as system drives (i.e., they can store the software required by the system for general operation). Many manufacturers use different approaches and not all floppy diskette drives are used for document archiving. In general the amount of storage available to the user of the various floppy diskettes ranges from 256K up to 1024K, depending on diskette size, number of sides used in encoding, and density. (Incidentally, K = 1000 characters.)

Hard Disks

Some word processing systems, particularly the larger ones supporting multiple users, employ hard disks as storage media. The difference between the hard disk and the diskette is that the hard disk is made of stiff metal and is usually much larger in diameter. This type of disk is often mounted for carrying and storage purposes in a hard plastic case used to seal out dust and dirt instead of being mounted in the flexible plastic or cardboard case used with the floppy. The hard disk is often sold mounted as a single disk or stacked with other hard disks in a single plastic case to form a disk pack. The type of construction and number of actual disks in a disk pack depend on the amount of storage capability the manufacturer is trying to provide for that particular disk drive. These disk packs can store great amounts of text and data and are standard media on the larger systems.

The same read/write head principle used on the diskette applies to the hard disk, but since a disk pack containing many hard disks can be mounted on a single disk-drive spindle, the drive unit requires multiple read/write heads in order to access all of the disk area.

The amount of storage available on a single hard disk drive can range from 5MB up to 640MB for some of the larger drives (MB = megabytes). Some hard disk drives, particularly in the smaller sizes, come with removable disks or disk packs for off-line data storage. Drives are manufactured with the capability for removal of all, some, or none of their disks; each capability variation is determined by the individual manufacturer's design and disk-drive size. Large disk drives produce a considerable amount of noise and heat, therefore making them unpleasant to work near in an office. Consequently, most large disk-drive units are placed in a computer room with the rest of the equipment requiring special environmental considerations.

Winchester Disks

The Winchester drive is a small sealed hard disk-drive and pack assembly offering greater storage capacity and speed than the floppy but without the size, noise, or heat output of the larger hard disk-drive units. The storage capacity of the Winchester drive ranges from 5MB to 100MB or more and the standard speed is 3000 RPM. The primary disadvantage to this type of disk is the expense; although prices are beginning to come down, they are still relatively high. Winchesters are manufactured primarily as fixed disks internal to the system, but they are also available as a removable pack on some systems. Introduction of Winchester disk technology has reopened some of the problem areas that once prevented hard disk storage capabilities from being incorporated into some of the smaller systems. A Winchester disk can now be built into a workstation or CPU to provide stand-alone system users with much greater storage capabilities than possible with just floppies. Besides being small they are very quiet and produce minimal heat, thus allowing their use as part of desktop office equipment.

Video Disks

A new technology for information storage will soon be available to word processor and computer users alike. This technology, referred to as *video disk*, stores images of things on a disk instead of storing an electromagnetic code. A video disk system operates by converting information, let's say a document, into a picture. This picture is then stored by having the image projected and captured onto the surface of a special plastic disk. The picture images are reduced many times in size, thus allowing the video disk to hold hundreds of times the amount of memory that an electrically encoded disk can hold. This sort of technology is currently in use with home entertainment systems that play movies. The difference between office-application video disks and those for home entertainment purposes is that the images creating the motion-picture film have been stamped onto the surface of the plastic disk and can only be played back like a phonograph record, whereas the video disk used by the computer in the office is not mechanically stamped and therefore is capable of information storage, retrieval, and editing just like the electromagnetic disks are.

Magnetic Tape
Magnetic tape storage devices are used with some of the larger word processing systems for bulk storage of infrequently used documentation. This storage is most often associated with large computers and may be used on systems performing both data processing and word processing functions. The most common type of tape drive unit encountered in a large word processing environment is the nine-track tape. The term *nine-track* refers to the number of read/write heads positioned above the surface of the tape. The tape material is similar in design to that of the disk, in that it is covered with an iron oxide coating which holds the electromagnetic coding placed there by the nine heads. The big difference between the tape and disk is that all of the information placed on the tape is linear as opposed to circular in array. A linear data array means that the tape drive must constantly spin hundreds of feet of tape backward or forward in order to position the requested data under the read/write heads. This process is avoided with a disk drive as the approximate location of the data on a disk will pass under the read/write head several hundred times a minute. Compared with disks, tape is a relatively slow way of storing information. For example: a user wishes to retrieve two documents (#A and #Z) from a standard nine-track tape. The user desires to have #Z retrieved first and #A second. Should #Z be located at the far end of the tape and #A located at the beginning, the system would have to spool the entire length of the tape twice to retrieve the two documents.

Magnetic tape is often utilized to back up a system disk for off-line storage of information (i.e., to file unused information onto a removable media). The process of backing up clears the disk of unused information and aids in optimizing the system's performance by providing free disk space. Information filed onto tape can be removed and stored in a file cabinet for safekeeping. The filed information always can be remounted and returned to an active disk if desired.

Magnetic Cards and Cassettes
Some electronic typewriter manufacturers still supply magnetic card- or cassette-based machines, but most modern word processing systems are now floppy disk- or Winchester-based. In the word processing industry the use of magnetic cards and cassettes has been primarily replaced by these faster and easier-to-use storage devices. Magnetic card- and cassette-based systems allowed the user to record and play back text keyed in by the operator. The operator then could make text

corrections by typing over the previously entered material and printing out the new version.

PRINTING DEVICES

Daisy Wheel

As was explained in the previous chapter, the daisy-wheel printer gets its name from the shape of its print element. The print element is that part of the printer containing the character set being used by the printer. The print element of the daisy wheel is shaped like a flower, with the petals containing the type slugs. The slugs are on the end of flexible arms rotating around a hub. The hub is mounted on a spindle contained within the carriage. During operation the wheel spins until the desired character is positioned at the top of the wheel. At this moment a small impact hammer strikes the back of the character, forcing the type against the ribbon and onto the paper, thus creating the desired character image. While this rotation, character alignment, and hammering is going on, the carriage is moving along, creating a line of type on the paper. Some daisy-wheel printers print in one direction only and others are bi-directional (i.e., they print in both carriage directions). Daisy-wheel printers tend to be on the noisy side and, when placed in the middle of an office, can cause considerable problems for the people expected to work next to them. A solution to the noise problem usually lies in the use of a silencing hood or shield to muffle the sound of the printer. These sound-deadening devices are available for most daisy-wheel printers and can be obtained from the printer manufacturer or through third-party suppliers specializing in acoustic office equipment. The daisy-wheel printer is the most popular printer in the word processing industry today. It is reasonably priced with its print considered of typewriter quality. The excellent print quality makes the daisy a standard for business correspondence.

Dot Matrix

The dot matrix printer uses a matrix of tiny moving wire rods contained in the print head to print out its characters. The print wires are bundled together in the print head to form a matrix, usually five-by-nine, which when moved at the right moment will compose each character in the character set. Each little wire has a tiny fast-acting hammer on one end of it, with the other end sticking out of the open end of the print head. The print head is placed very close to the ribbon and paper so that it can easily transfer the individual dots of the matrix through the ribbon onto the paper. Software, coded in for each character in the character set, tells which little hammers are to strike the ends of the wires and when they are to do this, while the print head moves along creating a line of text. Dot matrix printers are usually faster than daisy-wheel printers, but in the past they have not offered the print quality available with the daisy. Traditional applications of matrix printers have been draft printing, computer output, and informal correspondence. A new matrix printer technology increasing the output quality of the type to that of the letter-quality character printer is now available from many manufacturers. This newer approach uses multiple passes of the print head to complete each line of text. By using, for example, two passes instead of a single pass, the print head can double the number of dots used to compose each charac-

35 cps Daisy Wheel Printer

Courtesy of Wang Laboratories, Inc.

ter image. This increase in the number of dots to the matrix creates a much more complete, detailed image. The new approach removes the coarse-looking dot image traditionally associated with the matrix printer and provides the user requiring a letter-quality printer with a faster alternative to the daisy wheel.

Line Printers

Line printers are used for high-volume draft output and are most often associated with larger systems and the computer room environment. The line printer operates with a continuously moving chain or band containing the slugs used to create the individual characters. The chain type is composed of individual links with each link holding a character. The band type of printer uses a plastic ribbon with the character slugs glued onto or molded into it. The chain or band travels

Matrix Printer

Courtesy of Wang Laboratories, Inc.

around two rotating drums, one at each end of the printer. As the chain or band rotates around the drums, one side of the chain passes very close to the paper. A long line of little hammers is located behind this part of the chain, one hammer for each possible character position on the line. Each time a character on the chain or band lines up with the spot where that character should appear on the paper, the little hammer behind it strikes that character slug against the ribbon, which then transfers the image onto the paper. This process happens very fast and many characters are printed on a line simultaneously. It appears to the user that an entire line is being printed at a time; thus, the designation *line printer* evolved.

Ink Jet

The ink-jet printer is similar to the dot matrix printer in that the character images are formed from a matrix of ink dots. The print head of the ink-jet printer is placed very close to the surface of the paper and special quick-drying ink is actually sprayed onto the paper to form the characters. The ink, stored in a reservoir forming part of the print head, is fed to each jet comprising the matrix of the print head. The speed of an ink-jet printer is similar to that of a dot matrix printer. However, the ink jet produces much higher print quality than the matrix printer.

Electrostatic

An electrostatic printer uses the matrix principle of the dot matrix printer to form the desired characters, but employs a different technique to transfer the ink onto the paper. The print head of the electrostatic printer may look very similar to that of the conventional dot matrix type, but instead of having a little hammer to strike the end of the wire rods in the print head, the wires place electrical charges onto the surface of the paper. The paper is then passed under a shower of fine carbon particles that are attracted to the electrically charged areas. These particles, having now formed the desired characters, are then sent through a fixing process that bonds and dries them to the paper.

Laser Printers

A laser printer utilizes laser light as part of the printing process. The laser unit inside the printer shines in a dot matrix pattern onto the surface of an electrically sensitive selenium drum similar to the way in which the electron gun at the back of a CRT workstation paints the screen. This drum is sensitive to laser light and holds the image of the characters on its surface. In a second process, paper is passed over the drum and becomes electrically altered. The areas on the paper where characters are to appear are now charged with current similar to the electrostatic printer described earlier. As in the electrostatic process, the paper is then passed through a toner or under a particle shower that clings to the charged areas and brings out the characters on the paper. To complete the cycle, the paper is sent through a fixing and drying process. A laser printer's quality and speed are very good, and the machine operates extremely quietly. Although the cost of this technology is currently high, it will come down in time.

Thermal

A thermal printer works on the same basic principle as some of the other dot matrix printers, but uses heat-sensitive paper instead of ink or a toner to produce the character images. Within the print head each dot on the matrix contains a small wire rod. This wire rod is heated by electric current and is pressed against the surface of the paper. The heat-sensitive paper changes color the instant the heated wires come in contact with it. Thermal printers offer quiet operation and good print quality. Although they are considered new to the word processing market, they are beginning to gain popularity.

CHARACTER SETS AND FONTS

The font is the element used by the printer, and particularly by impact printers which actually hold the individual characters that are then transferred onto the paper. In an IBM electric typewriter this is represented by the golf ball; in a daisy printer, by the print wheel. Each font contains a character set containing a specific number and style of characters. The set will include an alphabet as well as numbers, symbols, and any special signs. In addition to the style and number of characters contained on the font, the system will allow the user to specify the pitch of the characters. The pitch refers to the spacing between the characters on a single line. Standard pitches are 10, 12, 15, and proportional space. Proportional space is used to adjust the characters on each line so as to create a more even look to the text.

SHEET FEEDERS

Paper to be passed through a printer for printing can be handled in a number of different ways. The first and most obvious is by manually inserting and positioning individual sheets. This method may be acceptable for the occasional one- or two-sheet print job on a letter-quality printer, but it is totally unacceptable for high-speed printers, draft printers, and volume jobs. The methods available for feeding paper into the printer will depend on the individual printer and the type

Sheet Feeder

Courtesy of Wang Laboratories, Inc.

Envelope Feeder

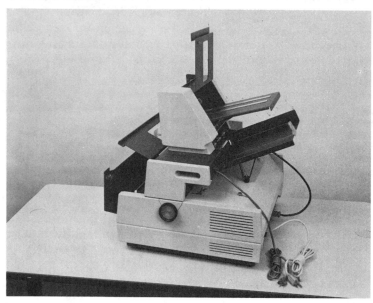

Courtesy of Wang Laboratories, Inc.

of paper used. Continuous-form paper comes equipped with feed holes along both sides, and each sheet is attached to the sheet before it. This paper is standard fare on high-speed and draft printers. It is fed to the printer either on a tractor-feed attachment or via a pin-feed capability on the printer platen. The pin-feed printer will handle paper only as wide as the platen, but the tractor-feed printer, being adjustable, will handle paper of varying widths, thus allowing the use of paper smaller than the platen width. The advantage of this type of paper feed is its continuous unattended operation with no stopping between pages or between print jobs. The disadvantage of using continuous-form paper is the rather poor quality of the paper. In general this type of paper is used for draft output and is popular in the computer room. For business correspondence continuous-form paper must be burst and trimmed into single sheets, but the paper usually retains ragged edges from its perforations and never quite looks professional. The best way to feed letter-quality paper automatically into a printer is by using a sheet feeder. A sheet feeder mounts on top of a letter-quality printer and will automatically load, remove, and stack individual sheets of paper into the printer. Some sheet feeders have multiple bins allowing the user to load different types of paper, e.g., letterhead, plain paper, and so on. The user can then specify what portion of the text is to be printed on what type of paper and the sheet feeder will take care of the rest. After printing, the spent sheets are then stacked in a storage bin until the operator comes to claim them. Most letter-quality printer manufacturers offer automatic sheet feeders as options; if not available directly from the manufacturer, they are usually obtainable from third-party suppliers.

ACOUSTIC HOODS

Many printers, particularly those of the impact type, produce sound that can be annoying. This sound is most disturbing when the printer is located in the middle of an office workspace. A variety of sound hoods are available, which, when placed over the printer, will decrease the sound to more tolerable levels. Acoustic hoods often have their own cooling fans to help dissipate the heat accumulating under them. Acoustic hoods, also custom-fitted to particular printers, provide special access doors for printer controls, sheet feeders, and continuous-form paper. Most manufacturers offer acoustic hoods and/or sound baffling devices for their letter-quality impact printers. Otherwise, these devices are usually available from third-party suppliers.

TELECOMMUNICATIONS TIE-INS

Telecommunications refers to the ability to transfer information over the telephone lines. For the user with a stand-alone word processing system this may mean the ability to act as a terminal to a larger host system located in another building; it may mean that information generated on one system can be sent to a remote printer for printing on another floor; or that documents generated on one system can be sent to another for review. Telecommunications can link devices over any distance ranging from a few feet to around the world.

In order to telecommunicate information from one system to another, both systems must speak the same language. The language component of telecommunications is referred to as the *protocol*. A protocol is one of several standard industry methods by which systems transfer information according to a certain format and procedure, thus ensuring that the information is transmitted and received correctly. In addition to having the software to generate the required protocol, each system must have a device enabling it to connect to the telephone line network—a connecting device referred to as a *modem*. A modem is the box that makes the actual physical connection between the system and the telephone line. Various types of modems are used. A modem may have a receptacle so designed that the telephone handset can be placed on it or it may be so configured that the telephone can be plugged directly into it.

The transmitted and received data is measured in units of bits per second, more commonly referred to as the *baud rate*. Modems are rated by their baud speed and vary greatly in range; a popular size with word processors is 1200 baud.

HUMAN INTERFACE

The terms *human interface* or *user interface* refer to the way in which an operator of a given type of machine is required to provide instructions to the machine and/or receive information from the machine. This section addresses the types of user interface found on most word processing systems.

Pointing Devices and Cursor Manipulation

The system you are using will have some sort of on-screen pointing device. This device may be a character in the shape of an arrow, a dash, a little hand, or one of a dozen or so types of little pointers. For the sake of simplicity, we will refer to all of these pointing characters as *cursors*. The cursor is the movable reference point used to indicate where the operator's current position is on the screen. The movement of the cursor can be controlled by a number of methods, and a word processing manufacturer may provide one or more of these methods with its system.

The most popular and certainly the oldest method of cursor manipulation is the use of directional keys. These keys are usually positioned in a cluster on the keyboard and may consist of **north, south, east, west,** and **home** keys. A directional key will move the cursor in the direction in which it is labeled, this being accomplished in either of two ways. With the first method the user presses the **north** direction key and the cursor moves to the north or top of the screen. With the second method the cursor remains stationary and the text scrolls to the south of the screen, thus positioning the cursor to the north of the text. With the latter method, the cursor remains fixed in a central spot on the screen while the text is moved about in relation to the cursor. The **home** key allows the user to reposition the cursor into its home or starting spot with a single keystroke.

The mouse.   Many manufacturers of word processing equipment offer alternatives to directional cursor keys, the most popular of which is the electronic *mouse.* The mouse is a small movable palm-sized box. The mouse typically has at least one built-in Select or Execute button and is attached to the workstation by a thin wire. The user keeps the mouse on a flat surface next to the workstation. Moving the mouse with the hand will cause the cursor on the screen to move in the same direction. The mouse, often available in conjunction with the standard directional keys, has been designed to make the system easier to use and to increase the user's operating speed. The internal workings of the mouse are of two basic types. The first and oldest involves use of a small roller ball mounted inside the mouse. The ball is rolled across the work surface; its movement is recorded by the electronics inside the mouse. This information is then transferred into commands for cursor movement on the screen. The second method— one very new to the market and not yet available on most systems—involves use of acoustics. As the mouse is moved across the work surface a felt pad at its base makes noise too soft for the user to hear but loud enough for the electronics inside the mouse to detect. This noise is then measured and converted into cursor command messages that are sent to the workstation and are in turn used to manipulate the cursor on the screen. Of the two available types, the mouse with the internal rolling ball is much cheaper, but it is noisy and unsteady in the hand. The felt pad type of mouse is superior in movement and design, but like most superior products, it is more expensive.

Track ball.   The track ball operates on the same principle as the mouse; it is the same size with a roller ball and select button and is attached to the workstation with a wire. The difference between the track ball and the mouse is that the housing for the track ball stays in one place and the user moves the ball by rolling the palm of the hand across the ball's surface. The movement of the cursor corresponds with the movement of the ball.

A new product called a *track pen,* operating on the same principle as the track ball, is now available. Instead of having a large ball mounted in a stationary base, the track pen ball is much smaller and is mounted in the end of a hand-held pen. The cursor manipulation techniques of this product are as superior as those of the track ball.

Joy stick.   The joy stick consists of a small palm-sized box with a short stick or lever attached to its top. The unit is attached to the workstation by a wire and is operated by moving the stick to one side or the other. The cursor will move in the direction in which the stick is moved. The joy stick is intended to increase operator speed and ease of use.

Light pen.   A light pen consists of a pen similar in size to a conventional ink pen but with a photosensitive tip on one end and a wire linked to the workstation on the other end. The light pen allows the user to select on-screen objects by touching the screen with the pen's light-sensitive tip. The light pen also allows the user to draw lines and images on the screen in the same fashion. Although the light pen is limited for word processing use, it is useful with systems offering graphic capabilities.

Electronic sketch pad.   The electronic sketch pad is similar in theory to that of the light pen in that it allows the user to draw images that will appear on the screen. Rather than touching the screen with a light-sensitive pen, the user draws on a special pad kept near the workstation. Both pen and pad are connected to the workstation with wires. The information drawn on the pad is transferred into the system and can be viewed on screen by the user.

Joy disk.   The joy disk is a disk-shaped geometric piece of plastic mounted on the workstation keyboard. The operator manipulates the cursor by moving the disk to one side or the other. The disk "floats" in a hole on the keyboard and can be moved by the user in any direction.

Cursor disk.   A cursor disk, like the joy disk, is mounted on the keyboard and controls the movement of the cursor on the screen. The difference between the two is that instead of floating in a hole on the keyboard, the cursor disk is fixed in place with the operator being required to depress the disk with a pen or finger in order to move the cursor. The cursor will then move in relation to the region on the disk touched by the operator.

Menus

A *menu* on a word processing system is nothing more than a list of options available to the user at a specific point in the system. The menu allows the user to give the system commands and open and close the doors to avenues of travel within the various levels of the software. A menu may physically appear on the screen as a vertical list of items with a small check-off box next to each one, or it may appear as a bar across the top, bottom, or side of the screen with its options printed on the bar. In the first type of menu, the user selects the desired item by moving the cursor or a little character called an *acceptance block* from one check-off box to the next. In the second approach the user either highlights the item on the command bar or indicates the desired item by placing the cursor on it. After the user has indicated the desired menu pick, he or she can select that item by pressing the **execute, select,** or **return** key, depending on the individual system being used.

Command Languages

A system using command language does not have to rely on a menu to receive instructions. Command language allows the operator to give the system direct instructions in the form of a system code. Each code provided by the user will invoke a specific action by the system. An example of this type of command code language might be "$Email;r.jones*". In this case "$" signals the system that a command is being given, "Email;" signals that the user desires to access the system's electronic mail application, "r.jones" signals that the system is to open the mail file of Robert Jones, and "*" indicates that a wild card search is desired of the file and that all items in the file should be displayed on the screen. One can

Menu on Screen

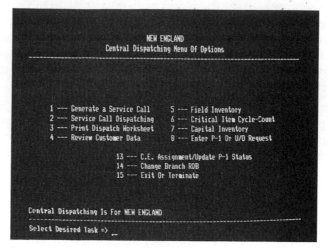

NEW ENGLAND
Central Dispatching Menu Of Options
----

1 --- Generate a Service Call   5 --- Field Inventory
2 --- Service Call Dispatching   6 --- Critical Item Cycle-Count
3 --- Print Dispatch Worksheet   7 --- Capital Inventory
4 --- Review Customer Data   8 --- Enter P-1 Or U/O Request

              13 --- C.E. Assignment/Update P-1 Status
              14 --- Change Branch RDB
              15 --- Exit Or Terminate

Central Dispatching Is For NEW ENGLAND

Select Desired Task =>

Courtesy of Wang Laboratories, Inc.

easily see that command code language allows the user to combine several steps at once, thus saving time and increasing the user's operating speed. Command code language is common with many computer manufacturers but is not considered user friendly in the word processing environment. This type of user interface can be very complicated and requires the operator either to memorize dozens of commands and formulas or to refer to tables and charts listing the desired function and its associated command.

Icons

An icon-based user interface utilizes pictures or images to represent system functions. Icon-based systems frequently feature touch-sensitive screens that allow a user to select an item by touching it on the screen with a finger. For example, a system with an electronic mail application might have a small picture of a mailbox on the screen. By touching the on-screen mailbox or by appropriately positioning the cursor and selecting it, the user would be able to "look into the mailbox" and read the messages sent to that address. The future of user interfaces for office systems looks bright. Manufacturers are now offering touch screens, icon-based menus, mice, and innovative menu designs that are being combined to produce fast and easy-to-use systems requiring minimal operational training.

WORD PROCESSING SOFTWARE

Basic Functions

Vertical and horizontal scrolling. Vertical scrolling is the ability of the workstation screen to move up the text automatically as additional text is entered. This activity can be accomplished in two ways: the first way has the text scroll up one line at a time, and the second has the text move up only when the screen becomes full. Horizontal scrolling allows the system to handle lines of text wider than the width of the screen itself. The workstation screen automatically slides the text to the left as additional text is added to the line.

Word wrap.   Word wrap allows the word processor user to enter text without concern about placing a return at the end of each line. As text is being entered, the word wrap feature will determine automatically whether or not a word can fit at the end of a line and will move it to the start of the next line if space is a problem.

Create.   The create capability refers to the actual creation of a new document on the word processing system. The creation function will automatically place an index entry in the system's document index file and will allow the user to assign information to it such as name, author, operator, date, special instructions, and so forth.

Insert.   The insert function allows the operator to indicate a particular position in the text and automatically enter a new word or words there. The system will automatically adjust the text to accommodate the new entry without requiring that the document be retyped.

Delete.   Delete works on the same principle as insert. Through the delete function, the operator is able to indicate text to be removed from the document. After removal, the document is then automatically adjusted to reflect the change without the operator having to retype the document.

Copy.   The copy function allows the operator to specify any text in a document, and have that text copied to another part of the same document or to another document altogether without having to retype the text.

Move.   Move allows the operator to indicate specific text in a document and have this text moved automatically to another part of the same document or to another document without having to first delete and then retype the text. This capability combines the delete and copy functions described earlier.

Indent.   The indent function allows the operator to indent an entire block of text automatically. It can be used to alter an existing document or it can be used during text input to create an indented block. The indent function is usually terminated during input by typing a return.

Center.   By using the word processor's center function, a user can type in text that will be automatically placed on the center of the line. Like the indent capability, the center function also can be used to edit existing text automatically.

Search.   A word processor's search capability allows the operator to specify a desired text stream and then have the system automatically search through the document for it. After having located the desired text, the operator is free to make any desired changes.

Replace.   The replace function allows the user to specify text for deletion in an existing document and have that text replaced automatically with different text. This feature combines the delete and insert functions described earlier. A global replace function combines the regular replace capability with that of the search feature. Global replace will search through the document, find the desired text, and automatically replace it with new text.

Decimal alignment.   A word processor's decimal alignment capability will automatically line up numbers on their decimal points to allow for creation of numeric columns. Each number in the column will have its decimal point positioned below the one above it.

Text Formatting

Document format.   *Document format* refers to the number of characters to the line, the number and position of tabs, and the document's line spacing.

Format lines and rulers.   The information making up a document format is contained in the format line or ruler of the document. The operator creates the format line, which allows for the positioning of tabs, indication of line length, and line spacing. The information in this line may be modified at any point so that changes in the format are possible within the same document.

Reformatting.   To reformat a document, a user simply changes the format line of an existing document to a new configuration of tab spaces, line length, and line spacing. The new format line then automatically modifies the text associated with it to the new desired format.

Justification.   Text justification is the system's ability to modify the arrangement of the characters on each line in such a way as to make both left- and right-hand margins smooth. This capability makes the document look more professional since the ragged right-hand margin is no longer a problem.

Line spacing.   The system's line spacing capabilities allow the operator a wide range of spacing possibilities. The operator specifies the desired spacing in the format line or ruler. Spacing capabilities usually include zero spacing, quarter, half, single, double, triple, and so on.

Margins.   Document margins are specified by the user, and are usually done so in the format line or ruler. Many word processors have fixed left-hand margins and allow the user to specify the right-hand margin only at the time of document creation. In this type of system, the left-hand margin can then be modified at the time of printing as part of the document print command.

Page Management

Creating pages.   Page creation on most word processors is usually made possible through the use of a **page** key or page command code. The operator can define the end of a page by positioning the cursor at the point where the page break is desired and then by typing the **page** key or code. The system will create the page break, marking the end of the page with a special indicator that appears only on the screen. As the new page indicator appears following the break, a page format line or ruler is brought to the top of the screen. This ruler is a copy of the same ruler used for the previous page.

Page numbering.   To number the pages of a word processing document, the user is required to indicate the desired numbering sequence, the points at which this sequence is to begin and end, and the location of the numbers on the pages. Depending on the system being used, this information may be required at the time of printout, which would take the form of a print menu, or as part of a footer command (discussed in a forthcoming section).

Pagination.   Pagination, the act of placing page breaks in an unpaginated document, can be a manual or an automatic process. In the manual mode the user flips through the document by viewing screen after screen and inserts page breaks in locations where deemed most appropriate. In the automatic mode, the user specifies the number of lines desired on each page and the system flips through the document, placing page breaks at the designated page length. When a page break lands in the middle of a block of text, the system will stop and prompt the user to place the page break manually. This last feature prevents placement of breaks in awkward locations. Automatic page numbering can be carried out at the screen level or upon printout, depending on the system.

Repagination.   Many times a user will paginate a document only to find out that it is necessary to go back and make major edits to the text. These edits often include page deletions and additions. Such changes in the total number and placement of page breaks throw off the original numbering sequence, resulting in a need to repaginate the whole document. Repagination is conducted just like original page numbering. It can be either manual or automatic, with the automatic mode being viewed on the screen or at printout, depending on the system. Numbering during repagination will override the original numbering scheme, thereby creating a new sequence.

Headers and footers.   A *header* on a word processing document is a text entry to be repeated automatically in the top margin of all pages in the document. This text entry could be anything from a single character or number to a more detailed document description with date and reading instructions. Page numbering in a document is often referred to as a header when placed at the top of each page. A footer is similar in characteristics to the page header described above except that it is positioned at the bottom of the page instead of the top. On most word processing systems the creation and attachment of footers to a document is handled in the same fashion as the page header.

Notes.   Many word processing systems allow the operator to insert a special indicator in the margin of the text. This indicator is inserted there to tell the operator or reader using the workstation that there is a comment concerning the text marked by the note indicator. The user can then press a certain key or key sequence and view the comment. The comment and note indicator appear only on the screen and are not printed when the document is sent to print.

Additional Functions

List or record processing.   Most word processor manufacturers provide some sort of list or record processing application with their equipment. If list or record processing is unavailable from a particular manufacturer, it usually can be obtained from a third-party software supplier. List processing, as we shall refer to it in this section, provides the user with a data processing type of capability. In other words, list processing provides an easy way for a user to set up lists or records of information. This information may be in the form of names, dates, places, telephone numbers, part numbers, and the like. The program also helps the user to maintain these lists once they have been set up, to sort through and extract specific pieces of information from the lists, and to generate reports based on them.

List processing uses a database of records or lists. Each record or list contains several pieces of information. As mentioned above, the information can take the form of mailing addresses, names, numbers, and so on. Specific types of data on a record constitute a *field*. For example, a record containing information used for billing purposes would have a field for the amount of payment requested, and a separate field for the name of the person billed. The rest of the information on the record would also be broken up into data fields. The type of field on the record (for example, the telephone number field), is referred to as the *field name*. The information contained in that field is referred to as the *field value*. A group of records all dealing with the same type of data kept together on the system is referred to as a *file*. The file is usually labeled according to the type of information stored in the records. A user may have a customer file for billing, a supplier file for ordering equipment, or a personnel file with employee information.

The real advantage to list processing is what it can do with all of this information. For example, a user can automatically pull all records of overdue accounts, get the names of all employees who have been with the firm for over five years, or create a mailing list of suppliers selling widgets for under one dollar. This information then can be merged into other document forms such as billing letters, order forms, and addressed envelopes, to name just a few.

Sort.   A sort capability on a word processor provides the user with an easy way in which to order documents, records, or lists of information into a variety of hierarchical schemes automatically. Sort capabilities can be applied to multiple fields at one time, and can be ordered in an alphanumeric sequence if lists or columns contain letters and numerals in combination. Sorts can be alphabetical or numeric; and they can operate strictly on uppercase characters, strictly on lowercase characters, or on both upper- and lowercase characters if desired. All sorts can be organized in ascending or descending order.

Glossaries or boilerplate capabilities.   *Glossary* and *boilerplate* are terms used by some word processor manufacturers to describe a special type of document process in which the user can create standard documents by providing only key pieces of information while the system is creating the document. For example, a contracts department may have a glossary designed to generate a document to be distributed to various manufacturers as a request for proposal. The contracts office issues hundreds of requests each month for different types of equipment. While the equipment and details of the request differ, the overall format and bulk of the document remain the same, time after time. A glossary can generate all of the standard portions of the request and can stop and prompt the operator to fill in any portions wherein nonstandard wordage is required. As each nonstandard portion is filled in by the user, the glossary fills in the rest of the standard text until the next area requiring operator attention has been reached. At this point the glossary stops and prompts the user to fill in the details, after which it once again proceeds until the job is complete.

In order to establish this type of convenient document generation, the user is required to create the actual request for proposal in the form of a glossary file and then indicate in it the particular portions requiring user intervention. The glossary document is then called up and processed to generate the new request for proposal containing the variable information inserted by the user.

Math functions.   Many word processors offer complete calculator capability as part of the system software. This capability can range from simple math to complex equation handling. Most manufacturers supply the capabilities of multiplication, division, addition, and subtraction. Many systems have numeric key pads resembling the standard adding-machine key layout. When the user activates the calculator capability, the figures and numeric calculations appear in the form of an on-screen display. This electronic scratch pad—really a "throwaway screen"—is kept separate from any other document the user may have been working on at the time that the calculator was activated. Once the calculations have been completed, the screen can be erased, and word processing per se can resume.

Security.   Word processor security systems vary greatly in range. Many systems come with no security features at all, others come with simple password capabilities, and still others have complex features that track a user and keep a record of that user's activities. For most office purposes, the simple user password system is probably sufficient. This type of system enables the user either to password-protect individual documents or to assign passwords to individual users for access into the system.

The security systems for equipment used in top-secret government work are very complex and costly. Most systems of this type provide for an audit trail capability that tracks users and their activities, requests passwords from the users, scrambles or encrypts all data transmissions, and prohibits the users from looking at data not approved for their particular security levels. This expensive security also requires maintenance by special administrators. To a certain extent, security of this type is now making its way into the commercial sector, particularly in the banking, insurance, medical record, and defense contractor fields.

Advanced Capabilities

Spelling verification.   Spelling verification applications are available from most word processing manufacturers and third-party software suppliers. In its simplest form, a spelling verification feature allows the operator to have a document automatically checked for misspelled words. This can be accomplished in two ways. The simplest way is to run the completed document through a batch process that marks the errors by underlining or highlighting the affected words. The operator then makes corrections to the text or to the error list, depending on the type of program being used. Some verification programs not only will mark the misspelled words but also will provide the operator with a list of suggested corrections for each error. But the best types of verification and correction systems are those operating as part of the word processing editor itself and not functioning as a background or batch process. These interactive types of verifiers and correctors flag errors and suggest corrections while the user is still entering text. They are quick and accurate and are reaching a point where the suggested corrections are 90% right. Soon they will have the capability to insert the corrections automatically into the text without operator intervention.

Electronic dictionary.   The electronic dictionary is designed to function just like a hardbound print-product dictionary. The user is allowed to look up entries and find their definitions. The advantages of an electronic dictionary over a manual one are many. For one thing, the electronic version allows the user to indicate to the system the word requiring a definition either by typing the desired word into a fill-in field, by highlighting an existing word in the text, or by underlining that word. Once the word in question has been indicated, the program will automatically search the dictionary database for the entry and will display the definition on screen in the form of a window or box. In addition, electronic dictionaries use numerous types of databases. These databases can be traditional dictionary databases, specialized industry or trade-specific dictionaries containing medical or legal terms, or user-created dictionaries composed of definitions relating to specific departments, jobs, or individuals—an added advantage.

Electronic thesaurus.   The electronic thesaurus is very similar to the electronic dictionary in that it functions just like its hardbound counterpart. Its approach is also similar to that of the electronic dictionary. The user specifies the word to be checked by highlighting, underlining, or typing that word into a special field. The electronic thesaurus application then finds the word in its database and displays the desired data on screen in a window or box. The difference between the electronic dictionary and the electronic thesaurus is that the thesaurus provides not a definition but rather recommendations for synonym substitution. In the case of the thesaurus, there is usually a direct tie into the word processing editor allowing the user to replace the indicated word in the text with one of the synonyms chosen from the thesaurus display.

Letter generator.   Some word processing systems come with electronic letter generators. An application of this sort allows you to select the type of letter you desire from a menu of several different types. It asks you to supply the name and address of the recipient, the salutation, and the general tone desired. You then will receive a completed business letter ready for final review. Letter generation applications will write letters for bankers, doctors, lawyers, engineers, business managers, collection agencies, personnel departments, and so on. The more advanced letter generation applications can produce many business letters, all treating the same subject but with no two being exactly alike. This capability is derived from the use of a thesaurus database in conjunction with the letter generation application. A letter generator like this eradicates the sometimes ugly image conveyed by a firm through its repeated use of standard form letters that are so obviously identical and impersonal.

Auto-hyphenation.   Most word processing systems have some sort of hyphenation capability. The system may simply flag the words requiring hyphens at the ends of lines. With this method the operator is required to determine the proper location of the hyphenation point in the flagged word. But the best type of hyphenation application is one that automatically flags the word requiring attention and then determines the correct position for the hyphen. This type of hyphenator uses either a lexical database in which the hyphenation location for each word contained therein is shown or a set of rules that determines the proper hyphenation locations. The rule-based hyphenators, relatively new to the industry, are considered to be the most advanced.

Index generation.   Automatic index generation is available on some word processors today. This application operates by taking a completed word processing document and running it through the generator process in a batch mode. After completion, the application provides the user with an index of subjects cross-referenced to the page numbers of the document on which they were found. The completed index either can be generated into a separate document for the user to edit or can be automatically attached to the end of the processed document. The operational principle behind the automatic index generator is very simple. The application looks at each word in the document and, based on a set of rules, places words of certain categories into the index. The types of words placed in the index are usually nouns, words beginning with capital letters and not starting sentences, words in parentheses, biographical names, geographic designations, and so forth.

ERGONOMICS

The term *ergonomics* refers to the incorporation of human factors design into a piece of equipment. The human factors field studies the relationship between the shape, function, and characteristics of the human body and the way in which it can interface with a machine. An ergonomically designed system will be comfortable for the operator to use and will not engender eyestrain, hand fatigue, backache, and hundreds of other possible discomforts. A typical word processing system having been designed with user comfort in mind will be quiet, will not produce unnecessary screen glare, and will have a detachable keyboard. The system also should allow the user to adjust the screen into a variety of positions, it ought to be appealing to use, and it should require only minimal physical effort to operate. As systems become more advanced and offer greater capabilities, they will slowly replace many of the other machines we currently have on our desks today. Workstations now being designed will eventually become the single component required by an office worker to perform any office function. These workstations will replace the telephone; the calculator; the desk calendar; the dictionary, encyclopedia, and thesaurus; the spelling, grammar, and style guides; the clock; the in-basket and out-basket; the mailbox; the file cabinet; the tape, paperclips, and staples; ad infinitum. The office of the future will be paperless, having nothing more in it than a workstation and its user.

As we approach this level of systems functionality, designers and manufacturers realize that an office worker will be spending close to eight hours a day at a workstation. The greater concentration of a person's time in a single location will result in additional stress, especially with regard to eye fatigue; noise pollution; and neck, back, and hand strain. Any successful system must be designed with comfort and modularity in mind—factors allowing the user to modify and reconfigure the hardware to meet his or her own needs, instead of having to adjust the body to the needs of the equipment. In recent years great concern has developed over the amount of radiation that humans become exposed to over an average life span. This is a genuine concern, for many of us do become exposed to radiation every day. Modern word processing terminals produce radiation falling below the government standards for safe radiation levels. And modern ergonomic workstation designs allow operators to sit back from the screen through the use of detached keyboards, further reducing the already minimal radiation exposure.

An Ergonomic Workstation from Wang

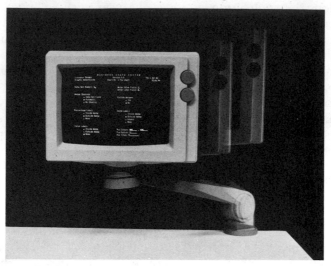

Courtesy of Wang Laboratories, Inc.

HANDLING AND STORAGE OF ELECTRONIC MEDIA

The basic types of electronic storage media that one might encounter in a word processing environment could include floppy disks, hard disks, magnetic tape, and magnetic cards. As described in the section dealing with storage devices, these various media have one thing in common—a thin coating of magnetic material storing the data in magnetic form. This thin coating is an iron oxide holding the magnetic coding that has been placed on it by the disk drive's read/write head. Consequently, it is very important to avoid touching the surface of the magnetic media. Particles from the skin, which are too small for the naked eye to see, can damage the media and cause loss of data and equipment failure. Magnetic media are also very susceptible to variations in temperature and humidity. The ideal storage temperature is between 60°F and 90°F with a relative humidity between 20% and 80%, noncondensing. Storage media must be isolated from intense heat and severe cold; for instance, a diskette left out in a hot car could easily be destroyed by the heat. Care must also be taken to shield the media from strong electromagnetic fields such as those of an airport x-ray machine. Since the essence of the storage media is its ability to be magnetized, any strong magnetic fields near it could cause a change in magnetism possibly resulting in a change or loss of data.

THE WORD PROCESSING EQUIPMENT ENVIRONMENT

Like the magnetic media used with your word processing system, computer equipment is sensitive to the environment in which it is placed. Most systems require environments offering temperatures of 60°F to 90°F with humidity between 20% and 80%, noncondensing. Fortunately, most office environments fall within these ranges. However, it must be pointed out that when a number of word processing systems are placed in a confined area the heat buildup can be significant enough to warrant special air conditioning as well as electrical wiring and sound partitioning. In general, the small system and stand-alone do not cause this sort of problem; the larger systems with their bigger disk drives and volume printers are the real culprits.

Attention to stray electromagnetic fields applies not only to the storage media but also to the entire system. If your work area does not have static-free carpets, it may be necessary to lay down a special antistatic mat or to spray the carpet around the system with a static-free spray. Static charges can interfere with the electronic operation of the equipment and may cause system failure.

5

Generation of Business Documents: Dictation and Transcription

Donna L. Muise • *Executive Assistant, Editorial and Production, Reference Division, Houghton Mifflin Company; formerly Editorial Operations Secretary, Houghton Mifflin Reference Division*

INTRODUCTION

Generation of documents is obviously an important and highly visible means of communication and presentation for companies, executives, and secretaries. A picture may paint a thousand words, but if a color is off by even a single hue, the whole meaning or interpretation may be adversely affected. So, too, it goes with correspondence. We all have our horror stories about documents that created an embarrassment or two. The Post Office was right on target several years ago with its slogan, "Zip Codes move the mail and mail moves the country." Secretaries are the zip in the business sector and without their refined skills in receiving information, transcribing the spoken word to the written word, and producing effective, perfect documents, the circuitry of business would come to a debilitating and expensive halt. Thus, analyzing your job responsibilities, setting high personal standards, and working toward melding the two for the realization of both are essential functions of success for the professional secretary.

DICTATION

Transcribing the spoken words of the dictator to written words is not as easy as it sounds. For example, accents, inflections, individual speech patterns or impediments, and specialized vocabularies all can and do affect what the transcriber hears. As a result, the hard copy generated may or may not accurately reflect the information that the dictator was trying to relay.

All companies have different requirements for processing information. Due to the sophistication of modern business equipment, corporations have available many options from which to choose their dictation systems and thus satisfy their documentation/communication needs. It is imperative that the secretary know how to use the designated equipment correctly, not only for the purposes of dictation and transcription but also in terms of day-to-day maintenance and reliable, expedient repair services. And sooner or later, you may be called out of your department to assist in another department that uses a different kind of machine. Look at this assignment as an opportunity to learn a new skill and thereby add to your repertoire of capabilities instead of as an infringement upon the sanctity of your job description.

Equipment

From the corporate standpoint, one of the most endearing qualities of dictation/transcription equipment is economy. Business letters are expensive to produce, but with the increasing technological advancements in input and output equipment, modern systems help to defray the cost of letters and other documents by reducing the amount of time spent generating copy not only by the transcriptionist but also by the dictator.

Ease of operation and interchangeability are also important considerations. Our time is too precious to be squandered trying to discern what functions are performed by an array of twenty-five multicolored buttons. So, too, a machine does not serve our needs if its recording medium is unique to the machine system. Ideally, it should be adaptable to many different machines. Additionally, the pace of today's business does not always afford executives the convenience of calling secretaries into the office for lengthy dictation sessions. Therefore, alternatives must suit the needs of the employees and allow them more time for tasks equally important as generation of documents. It is for these and other reasons that the science of word processing continues to grow and change with the demands of a spreading worldwide business community that becomes more closely knit as its means for generating documents approaches unprecedented speeds.

Portable machines.   A significant portion of machine dictation is given into lightweight (eight to twenty-five ounces), portable units that can be carried safely and unobtrusively in the pocket or attaché case. These portable machines are versatile units usable on planes, at home, or in cars. They are the next best thing when one does not have access to a telephone or to office personnel; for example, portable units are particularly useful at conferences and in field work.

Many portable units are designed so that the functions of record, playback, fast forward, and rewind can be controlled with one finger. Such simplicity encourages the busy executive to use and rely on the portable model. The recording time offered ranges from fifteen to ninety minutes, depending on whether the medium is a cassette, minicassette, mag belt, or visible belt.

For the executive, portable machines offer several other useful features. First, a pause button allows the dictator to deliver correspondence at his or her desired pace. Second, a digital counter identifies the amount of tape available on the medium in use. This feature is also useful in locating correspondence quickly. Index strips are important tools for both the dictator and the transcriber. These strips identify the number and lengths of dictation segments. Furthermore, they allow you to keep track of your place within a segment of dictation and flag priority transcription or instructions, and they can identify what the dictation is. The notation of confidentiality also can be indicated.

Indexing may be executed in several ways: by using an audible tone on the recording medium; by putting a visible mark on the index strip; or by electronically cueing the tape so that instructions or the ends of documents may be seen on the display panel of the transcribing machine. When the tape is played at high speed, audible signals, or cue tones, can be heard to alert the transcriptionist to instructions and/or priorities.

When it is the practice to use an actual index strip, the procedure is as follows. The strip is inserted into the appropriate slot on the machine. As the dictator's voice is recorded, a needle moves across the strip. Should an instruction be inserted or when an end-of-letter signal is required, the dictator depresses the applicable button and subsequently a mark is made on the strip. When the executive concludes the dictation, he or she simply removes the strip and sends or delivers the tape and index strip to the transcriptionist. As an additional aid to the indexing feature, some transcribing machines will automatically stop at points cued on the system. See the section on transcription for further explanation.

For the transcriptionist, the portable unit can double as a transcribing machine. A headset jack may be inserted directly into the unit. Volume and speed controls allow adjustment of the recorded speaking voice to a comfortable, comprehendible playback speed. The fast forward and reverse functions afford the transcriber the freedom to back up or to fast forward the tape when desired.

Finally, a transcribe module adapter can be used to transfer the recorded information into a centralized endless-loop system. Recorder couplers take pre-recorded dictation and immediately transmit it to the office simply by the dictator's dialing the number of the office. The dictation is re-recorded from the original tape onto a tape in the office, from which point it is ready for transcription. Each of the aforementioned features is available on all, but is not specific to, portable machines. Desktop units are also equipped to handle the demands of complicated dictation and transcription.

Desktop units.   The portable machine does not always meet the needs of offices experiencing heavy loads of dictation. The desktop transcription unit can be a useful, practical companion to the portable machine or it can be used alone for both dictation and transcription. When used as a dictation machine, a microphone must be attached. As a transcription machine, the microphone is replaced with a headset, and a foot pedal is also attached. However, the desktop machine can perform only one of these functions at a time. Therefore, it is important to anticipate times of heavy dictation and to arrange for the availability of compatible units in order to prevent a backlog of work.

As with portable units, the market is moving toward designing compact, attractive units that are easy to use. Many models offer instant-on and automatic-off features, as well as one-button control of major functions (record, rewind, fast forward, etc.). The microphones that accompany desktop models are sometimes shaped like telephone receivers. This attribute is designed to help the user feel less uncomfortable while using the device. All controls are located on the microphone for ease of operation, regardless of whether the medium in use is a standard, mini- or microcassette, or cartridge-loaded magnetic disk.

Desktop models also have the ability to record conferences and telephone conversations. Models with speakers allow groups to listen to recordings at a single time and place. The executive and assistant may use the machine as a means of interoffice communication when unable to confer with each other. The secretary may record telephone calls and messages that occur during the executive's absence. In turn, the executive may record messages, instructions, or assignments for the assistant. On some machines, a feature is included whereby the unit may serve as an intercom between the executive and secretary.

Though desktop units may provide all the features an office with a high level of dictation may require, they are also compatible with portable machines. The secretary and executive may skillfully and expediently utilize these dictation systems to generate documents swiftly through their offices. There is, however, a more advanced technology that carries the conveniences of the aforementioned models one step further; this is the centralized dictation system.

Centralized dictation systems.   Today, many firms are utilizing word processing centers for dictated matter. These centers are designed as work group configurations. The staffing and location of the work group(s) are determined by the size of the company and the dictation demands of its executives. Large firms may employ hundreds of transcriptionists in one configuration in a single, central station. Conversely, small groups can be stationed in satellite, or remote, centers in various places throughout the company.

Within the configuration, a supervisor is responsible for delegating assignments and reviewing the finished products. The supervisor also keeps records of the quality and amount of output from each transcriptionist. Some centralized dictation systems are helpful to supervisors in that they can monitor the amount of work each transcriptionist completes and how much dictation is yet to be transcribed; some models can even calculate the transcriptionists' typing speeds.

The means used to transmit dictation from a remote location—depending on whether the dictator is within the grounds of the firm—is via either a telephone or a specially wired microphone. If an executive uses the system infrequently, provisions can be made for him or her to use a standard telephone. If the dictation is frequent and extensive, it is advisable for the executive to have in the office a phone used exclusively for dictation. This phone, or private wire, is accessed to a cassette recorder. Most centralized systems record data through the use of endless loops (or tanks) or multiple-cassette systems. Endless loops (found in Private Branch Exchanges—PBXs) provide many hours of continuous recording capabilities. The multiple-cassette system uses several cassettes loaded into the system in sequence. When the tape runs out on one cassette, the used tape drops out of the machine and a new, blank cassette is dropped into its place. Or, when one cassette is filled, the system automatically begins recording on the next available cassette.

The most attractive qualities of the centralized system, from either the executive's or the company's point of view, are that they not only can provide many hours of continuous recording but also can receive input 24 hours a day, 7 days a week, 365 days a year. Additionally, the centralized system can be standardized to allow for growth and modification according to the needs of the corporation. (The advantages of standardized equipment in office automation were established at the beginning of this chapter.)

Guidelines for Equipment Purchase

Many factors should be considered when choosing dictation equipment. The decision should not be made in haste and should cover a realm of equipment vendors. You can find a listing of appropriate manufacturers in the Yellow Pages or in the Business-to-Business Book. Your inquiries will be answered with brochures and/or visits from a salesperson. Once you have made your decision and have purchased a dictation system, a representative from the company will come to your office and instruct you in the use of the machine and the scope of its capabilities, should you request this service. Following is a list of factors to consider when looking at equipment. Remember to consider the unique environment of your office as you evaluate them:

1. Amount/frequency of dictation
2. Place of dictation (i.e., does the dictator dictate while traveling or in the office exclusively?)
3. Number of people using the dictation system
4. Amount and complexity of functions
5. Price
6. Standardization capabilities
7. Compatibility with other machines and/or media
8. Size of equipment
9. Space available at the workstation(s)
10. Quality of manufacturing
11. Warranty
12. Guarantees
13. Serviceability (ease and speed of repairs)
14. Quality of voice rendition
15. Ability to provide other communications needs within your office, department, or company

The Workstation

One of the considerations when choosing an appropriate dictation system is the workstation. Implied in this consideration is the office environment and space and the equipment in use. The desktop transcription unit should be located in a spot that is close enough to the typewriter or word processor so that both the manual buttons and foot pedal are operable from the secretary's seat. The unit should be far enough away from the edge of the desk so that it will not be accidentally knocked off the desk. If your work area is noisy or if there are frequent passers-by, you will want to have headphones readily accessible. Always be careful not to place food or beverages on or near the equipment.

The dictation media should be stored in a clean, little-trafficked place. Normally, magnetic media are almost indestructible and indefinitely reusable, but should the media become dust-covered, wipe them with a clean, dry cloth. Should you get or find fingerprints on the media, again, wipe with a clean, dry cloth. (Fingerprints may cause malfunctioning in the record or playback functions of some media.)

The location of your workstation may not be under your control; however, the organization of it is. Arrange your area so that it is efficient, well supplied, and neat. Your workstation should also be functional for your boss(es). After all, the objective is achievement of an office environment where the executive and assistant function as a team; the paperwork is produced swiftly, smoothly, and accurately; and the results proffer not only a job well done and personal satisfaction but also a proper and impressive presentation reflecting the goals of the corporation.

Shorthand

As with any skill, shorthand is a beneficial one to have even at a time when office automation is a trend most businesses are following. Many executives still dictate to stenographers, and the finished product is just as polished and accurate as any accomplished with a machine. The techniques you use to generate a document go far beyond the words-per-minute rate at which you are able to receive dictation. Actually, the techniques involved are developed through education, observation, experience, and, unfortunately, trial and error. The techniques you learn can be universal or specific to your own office situation.

Education.   Following are helpful suggestions for making the dictation session as unstressful as possible for you (see the first illustration):

1. Start each day's dictation on a clean notebook page.

2. Bind off the used portion of your notebook with a rubber band; this way, you can turn directly to the next available sheet without delay.

3. If daily dictation is light to moderate, write the date above the column you will use when dictation first begins; number the pages consecutively (1, 2, 3, 4, etc.) at the top and circle this number on each page. When you begin taking dictation the next session, start with ① again.

4. At the end of a letter or memo—but not the end of the session—draw a single, bold line after the last line of dictation. When the session has ended, draw bold double lines after the last line of the final letter or memo.

5. If dictation is heavy, you should indicate the date on every page to ensure that all material for the session or day remains intact. Follow instruction 4 for marking the end of dictated matter.

6. Use a pen that allows your hand the greatest writing fluency. Usually, a fine-point ink pen is the best, but the choice is personal. Leave the cap of the pen on your desk instead of storing it on the end of the pen while you are taking dictation. This will afford you even greater fluency when every second counts.

7. Use circled letters to mark significant changes (more than a few words) in the notes; i.e., write Ⓐ at the point where the first change occurs. Key the new material with an Ⓐ also. The next change will be marked with a Ⓑ, and so forth. ALTERNATIVE: If the dictator customarily makes many significant changes during the course of a dictation session,

Shorthand techniques: (A) courtesy copy notation, insertion, and underscore; (B) insertion continued, end of letter, and discrepancy; (C) discrepancy continued and end-of-session notation; and (D) next session notation, longhand, and rush indication.

you may find it wiser to take notes in only one column, leaving the other blank for corrigenda.

8. Write in longhand any name, address, or technical term the dictator spells out.

9. Leave a few lines of space between dictation items to insert processing or mailing instructions, courtesy copies, or other notations. Be careful not to overlook instructions.

10. Flag rush items with a clip or by folding back the corner of the page so that it extends outside the trim of the notebook.

11. Draw one line under words to be underscored; two lines under words to be typed all in capitals.

12. Should you notice discrepancies within the dictated material, mark the area with an X. After the dictator has finished speaking, you may question him or her and verify the data.

13. Turn notebook pages efficiently and noiselessly. You can gradually move up the page with the thumb from your free hand as you write and quickly flip the page over when you run out of room. Or, you can begin to grasp the corner of the page when you near the end of the last column. Regardless of the method used, be careful not to snap or rustle the paper loudly so that it distracts the dictator or causes you to miss a word or two.

14. If you are behind and are losing the meaning of the dictation, it is then permissible to interrupt the dictator at an appropriate pause in the dictation. Read back the sentence immediately preceding the place where you lost the flow of the dictation.

15. Transcribe material as soon after the dictation session as possible. This way, much of the information is still fresh in your mind.

Experience.   Though it is usually not a good practice to categorize people, in your work experience you may come across dictators whose styles fall into one or more of the following modes: maundering, roaming, speeding, assuming, and last-minute dictating. Any one of these idiosyncracies can cause the secretary problems either in recording or transcribing the dictation accurately or in delivering perfect final copy. Oftentimes, the dictator may not realize how difficult he or she is making the stenographer's job by subscribing to one of the aforementioned speaking or behavior patterns. Following are some suggestions on how you may deal with any of these situations:

1. For whatever reason, some dictators do not enunciate clearly and thus make it very difficult for the secretary to distinguish many words during the course of a session. If you cannot determine the missing word from the context of the sentence (often even a phrase is slurred), you should interrupt the dictator either at a pause happening soon after the poorly enunciated material or at the end of the letter or memo. Do not wait too

long or after too many missed words (three or four) to ask the dictator for clarification.

2. Some dictators find it helpful to roam around the room while dictating. Under any circumstances, it is difficult to hear what someone is saying when his or her back is turned to you. In the dictating session, this is an annoying situation. Follow the same instructions mentioned in #1. If roaming is a considerable problem and severely impedes the progress of the session, you and your supervisor will have to review the situation and find an agreeable compromise.

3. Some executives are extremely well organized in their correspondence, and, as a result, dictate extremely fast; so fast, in fact, that even the best of stenographers would have trouble catching every word. As long as your shorthand is up to par, it is permissible and advisable to inform the dictator that you are not getting all that is said.

4. Another hazard you may encounter in the course of your working relationship with your supervisor is his or her assuming that you have certain information, when, in fact, you do not. They may think they have told you what course of action they are planning to follow or in what form they wish the dictated document to be presented. Their neglecting to impart this information is not out of inconsideration; more likely, it is simply an oversight due to an overload of work or an eagerness to begin or complete a project. It is best to clarify any doubtful areas at the conclusion of the session and/or before you present the executive with the final document. You will save yourself and the executive valuable time by doing so.

5. Last-minute dictating creates a problem in that it is usually necessary to transcribe and generate a presentable document in a severely restricted amount of time. In this situation, inquire which documents must go out that business day and determine the levels of urgency of the remaining letters and memos. Learning to set priorities is often an arduous skill for secretaries to acquire, but most would agree that it is a vital one. Meanwhile, at a time other than during the dictation session, tactfully discuss the alternatives to the predicament of last-minute dictation.

In the business of generating documents, it is permissible to ask questions whose purposes are to clarify a word, phrase, or situation. Such questions, when posed in a tactful and timely manner, are energy efficient and advantageous to the operation of your office.

The Workstation
Your workstation is an extension of yourself, inasmuch as it is part of your total, on-the-job appearance. Humorous colloquialisms extolling the virtues of a clut-

tered or messy desk as being a sign of genius (or a clean or bare desk as signifying the antithesis) are just that—humorous, and have no basis in fact. In reality, managing the workstation efficiently and sensibly will help you to work effectively with your coworkers, to assist your supervisor(s) competently, and to make your duties proceed more swiftly—if not more easily. In short, keeping your workstation organized will yield subtle benefits day after day.

Supplies.   The best way to attack the workload a hectic business day entails is to be prepared for whatever may happen at any given time. All possibilities are succinctly stated in Murphy's laws:

> Nothing is as easy as it looks.
> Everything takes longer than you think.
> If anything can go wrong, it will.

Once you accept this probability, you can concentrate on being prepared for anything. There are basic supplies every office worker needs, and they are listed here to avoid an act of omission: stapler and staple remover, paper clips of several sizes, pens, pencils, markers, erasers, tape, small notepaper, water bottle, correction tape or fluid, ink pad, and date stamp. The most important tool, however, is your desk. A secretary's desk should be functional, compact, versatile, and, it is hoped, attractive. You have probably noticed that most executive desks have a very large desktop area and two, sometimes three, small drawers. Usually, a matching credenza stores the executive's files and other documents. The desk is basically to work at and remains free of other things that may clutter the area or distract the executive.

The secretary's desk is a horse of a different color. Space is usually limited—making it a valuable commodity—and virtually everything he or she needs during the course of the day should be no more than three to five feet away from the focal point of the workstation. One necessity of a functional desk for the secretary is that from a seated position on a swivel chair, you should be able to swing around from point A, past point B, and end at point C without any barriers or additional maneuvering other than a 90° arc (see the next illustration). The main portion of the desk ideally houses three drawers, but it is not uncommon for it to have only two. The center drawer should be reserved for writing implements, scissors, confidential papers, work in process, manuals, and the like. To the right

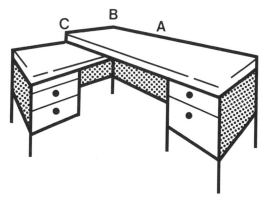

A secretary's desk should be functional, compact, and versatile.

will be a small, regular-size drawer useful for storing other supplies, such as boxes of paper clips, glue, packages of labels, typewriter cleaning brushes, a typewriter cover, masking tape, cassettes, equipment maintenance supplies, and so forth. In short, things used frequently, but that have more space requirements because of their shapes and sizes, are conveniently stored in this drawer. The bottom drawer is for files. Here you should keep the files you or your boss refer to most often or which are current, confidential, or high-priority. It is up to you to devise the most useful and effective filing system for your office. See Chapter Seven for assistance in records management.

To the left and extending at a 90° angle from the main part of the desk is a typing table designed so that your typewriter fits conveniently on the right half. The height of the table is a few inches lower than the main desk, therefore placing the typewriter in such a position that you are comfortable while using it. There is enough surface area to the left of the machine to place at your fingertips a copyholder (if the left is a more comfortable direction for you than the right), sufficient stationery or paper to complete the job, or any additional documentation related to the project at hand. In some desks, the typing table area houses three drawers with dividers for keeping the various office forms and stationery separated—letterhead, second sheets, envelopes, memo paper, scrap paper, special mailing labels and forms, and so on. Other desks have one large drawer that slides out or opens up to several slots serving the same purpose as the three separate drawers. You should remember that this drawer (or drawers) usually cannot be locked as the drawers in the main part of the desk can, so never store any valuables or confidential materials in this section.

The top of your desk ought to be organized for maximum efficiency. Place the phone on the side which is most comfortable for you to answer it. For example, if you are right-handed, place the phone to the left of your body so that you can quickly pick up the receiver with your left hand and begin writing with your right. This plan avoids wasteful switching of hands for taking messages. Always keep a message pad and pen next to the phone.

You will also need some desk organizers to keep your various documents in order and to provide points of reference for your coworkers and your boss(es), who deliver and retrieve materials to or from your workstation. The preferred organizer is a set of stacked trays or grouped vertical racks. Whichever one you choose, the uses can be quite versatile. One tray or rack should be for outgoing mail. Another can be for materials your boss drops at your desk on the way by, and another can be a temporary holding space for documents to be filed later on. However you decide to systematize the flow of work across your desk, the main idea is to make it as suitable as possible for everyone who comes in contact with the system. Label the trays or racks clearly. You would not want your boss to deposit an edited report in the outgoing mail rack or in the filing tray when you were not around to rescue the document from its ill fate. Though you will quickly memorize the proper places for your things, others may not. An ounce of prevention really is worth a pound of cure.

Last but not least in the way of essential supplies are reference materials. You should have easily accessible a current edition of a collegiate-level dictionary or a dictionary specifically designed for the office. As stated earlier in this chapter, office automation, technology, and business science are changing and expanding rapidly. Our language reflects these changes. An outdated dictionary will not tell you how to spell any of these new words, let alone what they mean or in what contexts they are used. Of course, a secretarial handbook is also a valuable asset to your reference library. As with the dictionary, it should cover both the conventional rules of thumb as well as reflect the state of the art. Finally, the other reference materials you will probably gather are an employee's manual, supply catalogs, and telephone books.

Management.   Once you have all the necessary materials, you must be able to pool these resources and make them work effectively for you. With everything in its place and kept in proper working order, you must create a system. (A *system* is a group of related elements that work together toward a common goal.)

Your system of generating documents should be managed in such a way that you are able to receive the information—or data—at a moment's notice, produce a perfect document, and follow through with swift, intact delivery of the document to its correct destination. It is a very simple process: input → output → implementation. The system breaks down when you cannot find your steno book; when the typewriter is unusable because you forgot to call the repair service at the time the machine stopped working properly; or when a document has been misdirected. But when you manage things well, paying attention to details, your office will run smoothly. When Murphy's Law goes into effect, you will be able to redeem the situation simply by fixing the temporary glitch in your system. Remaining organized, knowing what corners not to cut, and managing your time well will help you to achieve your—and your boss's—objectives whatever the situation, whatever the crisis, whatever the document.

Productivity.   High productivity is the natural course of events when you have established a functional workstation (adequately supplied and efficiently managed). When generating a document, establish your guidelines prior to beginning your work. Be aware of any special problems or sensitivities surrounding the material that you are generating and take any necessary precautions. Keep your equipment in good working order—treat it as if you had bought it with your own hard-earned money. With all these components of your system working together, combined with your skills and experience, you will increase your productivity and, furthermore, your worth to your supervisor and your company.

Minutes of Meetings

Many executives spend a significant amount of their time in meetings. Therefore, it is very important that the structure of these meetings be well planned from all aspects. No one likes to spend hours belaboring one or two subjects when they could be settled in a much briefer period, had only one of several things happened prior to the meeting:

1. Ample notice of the meeting given

2. Agendas distributed prior to the day of the meeting

3. Meeting room reserved and prepared properly for the duration of the meeting

The secretary's role in planning and participating in any meeting that involves his or her supervisor(s) is instrumental to ensuring a successful meeting insofar as each of the aforementioned items is concerned.

Preparing for the meeting.   Once your supervisor has instructed you to set up a meeting, you should determine the date and time the meeting is to be held. Often these criteria will depend on the availability of a meeting room, in which case you will be required to shop around for a room, present alternatives to the executive, and proceed with plans derived from his or her decision. Next, you need to know who is to attend the meeting and if any of the attendees is required to bring specific documents or to present a report. You will also need to know what your recourse should be in the event that one or more of the people on the attendance list is unable to attend. Can the meeting take place without that person? Should the meeting be postponed to a time more convenient to that person? Can a substitute sit in for the one unable to attend? Finally, you need to know what, if any, audiovisual equipment will be needed during the course of the meeting.

Once you have done the preliminary work for the meeting, you are ready to inform the participants. Seven to ten business days are considered appropriate notification of a meeting. Depending on the level of formality in your company or the nature of the meeting, you may phone the participants' offices and then confirm the verbal notification in writing by sending a brief letter stating the date, time, location, nature of the meeting along with the agenda, and any special requests of the individual. Phoning first is often a better way to arrange a meeting because you can coordinate the participants' responses and iron out any problems before transmitting written material. Preplanning goes a long way toward saving time for everyone involved. It may not always be possible to transmit a final agenda with the meeting notification. As soon as possible, distribute the agenda so that all participants will have ample time to prepare themselves for the topics of discussion. The agenda will also give them clues as to what documentation they should bring to the meeting. (See the next illustration.)

Taking the minutes.   Arrive at the meeting before everyone else does to ensure that everything is ready. To take the minutes, you should have plenty of materials—whatever the medium—to get you through a lengthy dictation session. When the meeting is called to order, the hard work begins. Make sure you have a copy of the agenda for yourself. Even if it is not followed in exact order, you will need it to key your notes, a process addressed later in this section.

The most difficult part of taking minutes is deciding what information has to be written down verbatim, what can be paraphrased, and what is unessential for the official record. Minutes are meant to be concise, factual, and objective recordings of what has happened during the course of a meeting. You cannot inject personal preferences into your notes. You cannot give more weight to what certain people say and not record the pertinent remarks of others. You must be able to interpret statements for what is truly being said, not what you hear by way of the deliverer's voice inflections, intonations, or mannerisms. It can be very difficult to discriminate from among all the opinions and facts just what should be recorded in the minutes. For example, if the implementation of a new procedure is being discussed and it appears that the motion for its institution will be passed, it is equally important to write down why the Publisher feels the procedure will not work, as it is to record why the editors feel that it will.

You must listen carefully *and* take down information even when more than one person is talking at the same time. You will have to do some quick sorting in your mind in order to record facts accurately without distortion, while at the

Agenda

```
                          AGENDA

                      Editorial Meeting

                      April 16, 19--


     1.  Call to order

     2.  Roll call

     3.  Minutes of previous meeting (corrections, omissions)

     4.  Director's report

     5.  Publisher's report

     6.  Production Manager's report

     7.  Unfinished business

            a.  works in progress

            b.  proposals before the board

            c.  staff

     8.  New business

            a.  budget

            b.  new proposals

     9.  Announcements (including date of next meeting)

    10.  Adjournment
```

Always type the agenda with at least three line spaces between each item.

same time making sure you attribute all statements to their correct sources. In corporate or organizational meetings, it is necessary to record motions and resolutions verbatim as well as the names of those who made them.

Knowing what you are to be aware of during the progress of the meeting, you are ready to record. Here's how you should do it:

1. Write down the date, location, and time the meeting begins.
2. Record the names of those present and absent (if the number is less than twenty). A quorum check is necessary for larger meetings.
3. Label the meeting (regular, weekly, annual, special, or executive).
4. Name the presiding officer.
5. Record the action. When the meeting begins, key your notes to match the activity. That is, if the discussion is "works in progress" and this subject is item "a" under "7. Unfinished Business," then key your notes "7a" and record the discussion. This relieves you of writing "7. Unfinished Business: a, works in progress." When you type your notes, you simply refer to your agenda to transcribe the key "7a."
6. Record the time of adjournment.

See the section on shorthand for suggestions on coding your stenographic notebook for changes, deletions, and additions while taking minutes.

Transcribing the Minutes

Always keep in mind that minutes serve as official records of meetings. Therefore, it is imperative that you objectively record the minutes and conscientiously transcribe them into the final, formal document anticipated by the attendees.

Drafts.　Drafts are like dress rehearsals. Everything is in place, except the audience. If you make a mistake, you can correct it before the audience sees it—and they will never be the wiser. When you sit down at your typewriter, you should have the following materials accessible:

1. the agenda
2. your notes (do not rely on memory)
3. *Robert's Rules of Order* or similar reference books on parliamentary procedure
4. any reports or other documents distributed at the meeting
5. verbatim copies of motions and resolutions
6. the constitution or bylaws of the group (if applicable)

Prepare the draft in the following manner:

1. The draft should be double-spaced so that handwritten corrections may be easily and clearly inserted.
2. Pages should be numbered consecutively.

3. A heading or subheading should not be separated from the first two lines of the summary that follows it when falling at the bottom of a page.

4. Include all materials that will be attached when final, formal minutes are distributed.

It is good practice (and usually required) to present the presiding officer with a typewritten draft of the minutes. If this is not feasible, then you should present the draft to your supervisor before typing the final copy. Either person will be able to weed out any misinterpretations or extremely sensitive material that should not be published.

Final copy. The final copy may be single- or double-spaced. Check copies of previous minutes for your organization's preferred style. The paper used also depends on precedent. Some groups have specially printed stationery for official minutes, while others use white bond paper of second-sheet quality.

When designing your minutes, refrain from using distracting symbols or excessive, heavy lines to mark different topics of discussion or to separate portions of the meeting. Make sure that significant points are easily identifiable in the typewritten minutes, but do not overdo it. Simple, straightforward documents will be much more attractive than pages marred with repetitive asterisks, ellipses, and underscores. Most minutes today are written in a narrative style, compared with the perfunctory outline style once used. Because of this significant change, it is especially important that your summaries of the discussions succinctly express the scope of the conversations. If you have not conveyed what went on during the meeting, your efforts have been for naught. See the next illustration for an example of acceptable official minutes.

The Dictation: A Paradigm

As with any other office procedure, a dictation session should not be entered into without sufficient preparation. You either know now or will learn from experience that when dictation is off the top of the head, the result is usually unsatisfactory and incomplete, meaning that both the dictator and the transcriber must go through the letter at least one more time to get it into its proper form.

Preparing to give dictation. Lest you think the dictator's job is an easy one, think again. It is not easy to compose memos, letters, or reports by dictating your thoughts into a machine or to a stenographer. In fact, several studies conducted by the International Information/Word Processing Association (IWP) reveal that longhand is the preferred method of input (75%). Machine dictation follows at 12%, shorthand at 8%. The remaining 5% of input is comprised of miscellaneous methods of dictation. Though longhand may be the preferred way, it certainly is not the most efficient. And since our goal is to achieve maximum efficiency and quality, you should take the necessary amount of preparatory time to achieve this end:

1. The earlier in the day that you deliver dictation usually means a faster turnaround time.

2. Gather your thoughts and materials prior to the session. Collect any data you may require during the course of your dictation.

Minutes

Editorial Scheduling Meeting
October 16, 19--

The weekly editorial scheduling meeting of Friday, October 16, convened at 10 a.m. in the conference room. The presiding officer was Amanda Billings. Members of the staff present included Robert Desmond, Carl Edwards, Denise Jameson, Martha Nichols, and Philip Thompson. Roger Lochman was unable to attend.

The minutes of the previous meeting, held on Friday, October 9, were read and accepted. There were no corrections or omissions.

Mrs. Billings reported that the Corporation is looking to the office products line to balance the shortfall in sales expected in the Secondary Education Division. She asked that everyone keep this goal in mind when ambitious schedules are established for new projects.

Robert Desmond informed the staff that he is preparing an analysis of the titles in progress in relation to their marketability, production costs, production schedules, and longevity. He requested that each editor submit a summary of costs to date for freelance services.

Carl Edwards reemphasized the need for constant, even workflow so that both editorial and production functions will proceed efficiently. He will be free to meet with any editors who wish to discuss flow of manuscript to composition.

Amanda Billings reminded everyone that they must submit their appropriate sections of the formal publishing plans for the office products line to her by October 23.

The staff voted to reject a manuscript entitled DICTIONARIES: FRIENDS OR FOES? that was circulated among them during September. The vote was unanimous.

Denise Jameson raised the question again as to when a new editor will be hired to replace Tom Westman. Due to the ambitious schedules and shorthanded staff, this situation should be addressed as soon as possible.

Mrs. Billings requested that Mr. Desmond and Mr. Edwards submit a preliminary budget for 1984 to her by December 1.

Mr. Desmond gave Amanda Billings a new manuscript he received this week from a retired linguistics professor. His preliminary reaction to the proposal is that it would be better suited for the College Division. The manuscript will be routed in the normal fashion, and a decision will be made at the December 2 meeting.

The next meeting of the editorial staff will be held on Friday, October 23.

The meeting was adjourned at 11:30 a.m.

3. Outline in your mind or on paper the logical sequence of the presentation of the material. Review the correspondence or documentation being answered to be sure that your dictation will cover all aspects.

4. If you are dictating into a word processing center, identify yourself, your department or location number, and your telephone extension.

5. State that your material will be a letter, memo, or report.

6. State how many copies of the final document you wish to receive.

7. Indicate how you wish your name to be typed, your title, the closing you prefer, and what kind of envelopes (if any) must be submitted with the final document.

8. Indicate the need for confidentiality when applicable. Give instructions for erasing this material from tape or for destroying or storing the written version of the dictation.

9. Give addresses and spell out unfamiliar words or unusual spellings.

10. Speak at a slow, intelligible rate. Be extra careful about dates, names, and figures. Dictate numbers one at a time, e.g., one eight nine five.

11. If you wish to have certain forms of punctuation inserted, you must indicate these as they occur.

Dictation Simulation

Following is a step-by-step simulation of dictation. Though the instructions begin with directions for using a machine for recording, the instructions to the transcriptionist and the actual dictation are conducted in the same manner.

1. Make sure the tone, speed, and volume controls are set appropriately.

2. Insert the minicassette and close the holder. When you have done this, the tape will automatically rewind.

3. Place a fresh index strip into its compartment.

4. Take the microphone from its holder—this causes the machine to be activated. Hold the microphone three to four inches away from your mouth. Speak across the face of the instrument rather than directly into it.

5. Depress the dictate switch and the light will come on. Slide the start/stop switch downward when you begin dictating.

6. To give instructions to the transcriber, slide the designated switch up, and the index strip or electronic cueing system will be marked.

Instructions

This is Amanda Billings, Director of the Elementary Education Division. I will dictate a memo to Robert Desmond. I would like a copy to go to Carl Edwards and two copies to my office. Use single spacing with two lines between paragraphs. Do not indent each new paragraph—I would like everything flush left on the margin.

Dictation

Subject (all capitals) staff requirements for one nine eight four (triple space) (capital A) at our (capital O) october one six weekly meeting (comma) the question was raised as to when manage-ment would be interviewing candidates for the editor's position that was vacated (correction, left empty) when (capital T) tom (capital W) westman relocated (period) (capital T) the position has been vacant since (capital A) august (period) I know that you have been busy with several other projects (correction, time hyphen consuming projects) during the last few months (comma) but I do feel that we should address the situation at this time (period) (new paragraph) (capital P) please submit by (capital T) thursday morn-ing a brief job description to be used on the internal job postings (period) (capital A) as you know (comma) I must have the copy to the (capital P) personnel (capital D) department by 2 pm (capital T) thursday in order for the job to be listed on next (capital M) monday's (that's apostrophe s) postings (period) (new paragraph) (capital Y) your description should include requirements such as previous experience (comma) educational background (comma) and specific skills (comma) duties (comma) and responsibilities (period) (correction: transpose educational background to precede previous experience) (capital Y) you may want to retrieve a copy of (capital T) tom's job description to help you with this task (period) (end memo)

If you are dictating to a stenographer, be aware of who your stenographer is. By this I mean if you know the secretary is not especially adept at comma rules, paragraph breaks, or discerning the ends of some sentences, by all means put these instructions into your dictation. However, if the secretary has a firm com-mand of grammar, there is no need for you to do this. Before I was promoted to my present position, there were only a few occasions that my supervisor had to give dictation to anyone other than me. Without fail when I came back to take dictation, she had been forced into the time-consuming habit of dictating all the commas and periods and so forth. I would let her do it for a few sentences before indicating with a look or smile that I really did not need to be told when to put a question mark and where to place a comma. She knew this, of course; it was just a matter of getting reacclimated to the person who was holding the steno book. My supervisor and I joke about this situation, but somebody you might find yourself dictating to may not find the situation so humorous.

TRANSCRIPTION

A flawless document is the just reward of transcribing dictation well. But do not expect transcription to be perfect every time (only Minute Rice is perfect every time). The point is that in order to aim toward perfection, you must develop the techniques that work for you, the ones that help you get the job done accurately and swiftly. Following are techniques essential to the process of transcription.

Transcribing from a Machine
If you were to transcribe the dictation given in the previous dictation simulation, you would first need to prepare your workstation and equipment for the job.

1. Put the recorded medium into your machine.

2. Connect the headset or earpiece.

3. Adjust the foot pedal or the thumb control panel.

4. Check the start button, tone, volume, and speed control levers for correct positions.

5. Insert the index strip.

6. Move the scanner to the first priority item.

7. Determine the length of the item by reading the index strip.

8. Set your margins and tabs and insert the paper to the correct depth for the length of the item.

9. Activate the machine.

10. Listen to any instructions before beginning to type.

11. Reposition the scanner at the beginning of the item you are about to transcribe.

12. Depress the foot pedal or thumb control and listen to the first thought unit.

13. Type the first thought unit.

14. Listen to the second thought unit as you are finishing typing the first.

15. Establish a rhythm of listening and typing as described in items 13 and 14.

Transcription

Memorandum

TO   Robert Desmond   FROM   Amanda Billings   *Amanda*   DATE 10/19/--

SUBJECT   STAFF REQUIREMENTS FOR 1984

At our October 16 weekly meeting, the question was raised as to when management would be interviewing candidates for the editor's position that was left empty when Tom Westman relocated. The position has been vacant since August. I know that you have been busy with several other time-consuming projects during the last few months, but I do feel that we should address the situation at this time.

Please submit by Thursday morning a brief job description to be used on the internal job postings. As you know, I must have the copy to the Personnel Department by 2 pm Thursday in order for the job to be listed on next Monday's postings.

Your description should include requirements such as educational background, previous experience, and specific skills, duties, and responsibilities. You may want to retrieve a copy of Tom's job description to help you with this task.

cc: C Edwards

dlm

Index Strip

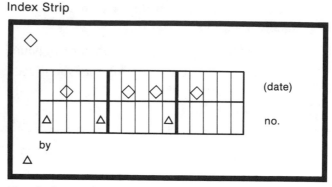

The index strip provides the transcriber with useful information.

Index strips. The index strip illustrated here has fifteen calibrations. Each calibration is representative of one minute of recorded dictation. The diamond symbol is used to indicate the end of a letter and the triangle symbolizes the location of an instruction or correction. The index strip shown here gives the transcriber the following information: the first item is 25 lines long; the second, 45; the third, 20; and the fourth, 30. There are instructions for items one, two, and four.

Transcribing from Shorthand

Transcribing from shorthand comes with its own set of procedures. The main thrust of your concentration switches from using your ears to using your eyes. However, you still need to establish a routine, or rhythm that gives you the best working conditions and the desired finished document.

1. Place your notebook on a copyholder positioned at the most comfortable angle for you.
2. Review any priority items that may be flagged.
3. Look over your notes for insertions or other notations so that you are aware of their places in the document.
4. Estimate the length of the letter and set your margins and tabs accordingly.
5. Insert the paper to the appropriate depth.
6. Aim to establish a rhythm between reading and typing.
7. Double-check your typewritten document against your notes to verify that all the material has been incorporated correctly.
8. Draw a single vertical line through the document in your notes to show that you have transcribed the material.

Transcribing from a Shorthand Machine

Transcribing from a shorthand machine involves its own processes. The following list gives a breakdown of the basic steps.

1. Remove the notes from the platen.

2. Insert the tape into a transcription box. Make sure that two lengths of the tape are visible at any given time.

3. Check for priority or rush items.

4. With a colored pencil, edit the notes for corrections, insertions, or deletions. Flag changes in copy with three asterisks, stacked vertically before and after the change. Begin the new copy with the number 2 and record the new material.

5. Estimate the length of the document. This can be done by estimating the number of words in one fold of the tape. Multiply this figure by the number of folded sections of tape for the complete document. The result is an estimated word count.

6. Set margins and tabs accordingly on your typewriter.

7. Establish a rhythm between reading and typing phrases.

8. Remove the finished tape from the transcription box and store it properly.

The importance of developing the proper dictation and transcription techniques cannot be stressed enough. A secretarial job is one position in which the incumbent truly needs to achieve maximum speed and efficiency as quickly as possible (which translates to *immediately*). Once you have mastered all the equipment in your office and interfaced successfully with your supervisor and your coworkers involved in generating documents from your office, you must produce a final document that is attractively presented, error free, and in acceptable business form. The next chapter provides written and visual guidance toward this end.

Table 1. **Letter Placement***

Stationery	Top Margin	Side Margins	Bottom Margin
Standard	Begin date on line 15	20 and 85 (elite) 25 and 80 (pica)	If it's the end of a letter, leave at least 6 lines; if the letter is continued, you may leave up to 12 lines.
Monarch	Begin date on line 14	20 and 85 (elite) 25 and 80 (pica)	Same as above.
Baronial	Begin date on line 12	25 and 80 (elite) 30 and 75 (pica)	Same as above.

*If you need to lengthen or shorten a letter, you can adjust the date line to fall higher or lower; also you may add or decrease line spaces around the inside address, salutation, closing, reference initials, or the indicators for any courtesy copies or enclosures.

6

Generation of Business Documents: Conventional Procedures

Anne H. Soukhanov • *Senior Editor, Reference, Houghton Mifflin Company, Reference Division*

INTRODUCTION TO THE FORMATTING OF BUSINESS DOCUMENTS

In the Introduction to their book *In Search of Excellence: Lessons from America's Best-Run Companies*, Thomas J. Peters and Robert H. Waterman, Jr. inform us that "one of the main clues to corporate excellence has come to be . . . incidents of unusual effort on the part of apparently ordinary employees. When we found not one but a host of such incidents, we were pretty certain that we were on the track of an exceptional situation. What's more, we were fairly sure we would find sustained financial performance that was as exceptional as the employees' performance." (New York: Harper & Row, 1982, p. xvii.)

Product quality and reliability, service to the consumer, and in Peters and Waterman's words, "productivity through people" are the linchpins of corporate success and of individual success within the corporate entity. Since the secretary and the executive work in close cooperation to achieve corporate and individual goals in business, the remarks made by Peters and Waterman are clearly pertinent to your overall function. But what does all of this have to do with a routine daily activity such as the preparation of executive-generated documents? First of all, it is a well-known fact that paperwork and meetings consume the greater part of an executive's day. As a result of the first activity, you are called on to spend much of your own time typewriting or keyboarding the executive's letters, memorandums, and reports. This expenditure of time costs the company money: it has been estimated that the cost of one business letter is now over $7.00, including managerial and secretarial time, supplies, and postage fees. And costs are expected to climb every year. (For example, in 1979 the cost of a single letter was a little over $5.00, while in 1974 it was only about $3.00.) Multiply the current cost of $7.00 by the total number of letters generated in your office alone in one year and you're into Big Money.

Secondly, the appearance of your outgoing documents has a direct impact on the recipients' perception of your company's product quality and reliability, not to mention the caliber of its personnel. How can one presume that a company's products are excellent and its employees competent if its routine business communications are improperly formatted, error-filled, or sloppily corrected? In short, an unacceptable written communication reflects adversely on you, the executive for whom you work, and the corporation. Keeping these things in mind, you have a daily opportunity to exhibit in your typewritten documents exceptional concern for quality, neatness, and accuracy—tangible indicators of your company's style and substance. With every outgoing letter, memorandum, press release, or report you should show the recipients that yours is a top-of-the-line corporation. The forthcoming sections of this chapter are intended to assist you in translating dictated or handwritten material into a keyboarded format that will convey a visual, as well as a written message to the reader. The visual message—indicated by correct format, total neatness, absence of errors, and irreproachable grammar—is this: our company and all of its employees from the chief executive officer to the lowest-ranking worker are quality-conscious, and our concern for quality ranges from our most sophisticated product to our most routine piece of outgoing business mail.

BUSINESS LETTERS

The following styles are most often used in modern corporate correspondence: the Block Letter, the separate elements of which are positioned flush with the left margin; the Simplified Letter, also flush left in format but lacking a salutation and a complimentary close; the Modified Block Letter and the Modified Semi-block Letter, some elements of which are indented or are placed near or to the right; and the Executive Letter, the inside address of which appears flush left after the complimentary close and the signature space. The Hanging-indented Letter, also discussed herein, is most often used in direct-mail sales, advertising, and product promotion. The half-sheet is used for very brief notes. All of these are illustrated in full-page facsimile form on pages 154–161.

Major Parts of Business Letters

The major parts of most business letters are the date line, the inside address, the salutation, the message, the complimentary close, and the signature block. Ancillary elements included when needed or according to corporate policy include a reference line, special mailing instructions, special handling instructions, an attention line, a subject line, writer/typist initials, an enclosure notation, a copy notation, and a postscript. These elements are discussed in a separate subsection following this one.

Date line.   The date line includes the month written out in full (i.e., it is neither abbreviated nor styled in Arabic numerals), the day in Arabic numerals, a comma, and the full year also in numerals: January 15, 1984. You may position the date two to six lines beneath the last line of the printed corporate letterhead, depending on the estimated length of the letter or on the guidelines in your company's correspondence manual. Three-line spacing is the most flexible choice, with extra space added between the date and the first line of the inside address if the letter is rather short. The date is positioned flush to the left in the Block and Simplified Letters; about five spaces to the right of center, in the exact center, or flush right in the Modified Block and the Modified Semi-block Letters; and flush right in the Executive and Hanging-indented Letters.

Inside address. The inside address, the second essential letter element, includes the recipient's courtesy title (such as *Ms., Dr.,* or *Mr.*) or honorific (such as *Esq.,* with which one never uses *Mr., Ms., Miss,* or *Mrs.*), and his or her full name on line one; the recipient's corporate title (such as *Vice President, Marketing*), if required, on the next line; the recipient's official corporate affiliation (such as *National Broadcasting Corporation*) on the next line; the street address on another line; and the city, state, and Zip Code on the last line. Include suite, apartment, or room numbers on the street address line if necessary. If the address includes an intracompany mail stop number such as MS 2B 31A, do not include that number on the address line; instead, put it after the company name with at least two spaces intervening. If the letter is addressed to a corporation rather than to an individual, the full corporate name appears on line one followed by a departmental designation (if required) on the next line, and the full address on subsequent lines. In all letter styles, the inside address is positioned flush left in blocked, single-spaced format. In all letter styles except the Executive, the inside address is the second element after the date line. (In the Executive Letter, the inside address appears at the bottom left after the complimentary close and signature space.) You may position the inside address from eight to twelve lines beneath the line on which the date appears, except in the Simplified Letter in which you must place the inside address exactly three lines below the date. Examples of the wording of typical inside addresses are:

Ms. Joan Goodwin
Vice President, Sales
CCC Corporation   MS 2A 341C
1234 Matthews Street   Suite 34
City, US 98765

Dr. Joan Goodwin
Chief, Emergency Department
City Hospital
44 Hospital Drive
City, US 98765

Joan Goodwin, Esq.
Goodwin, Talbot & Kendall
One Court Street
City, US 98765

Ms. Joan Goodwin
Vice President, Research
  and Development
CCC Chemicals
One Industrial Drive
City, US 98765

Salutation. The salutation, used with all letter styles except the Simplified, appears two lines below the last line of the inside address, flush with the left margin. In the Executive Letter the salutation appears from two to six lines below the line on which the date has been typed, depending on the length of the message. The first word of the salutation as well as the first word of a proper name or title is capitalized:

Dear Dr. Lee:

Dear John:

My dear Dr. Lee:

Gentlemen:

Your Excellency:

Dear Engineering Department:

Most Reverend Sir:

A colon typically punctuates the salutation. However, if you are using a minimal punctuation system (the so-called "open punctuation system") in order to reduce keystrokes, you may leave the salutation unpunctuated. Remember, though, that when you leave the salutation unpunctuated you also must leave the complimentary close and any enclosure or copy notations unpunctuated.

Table 1.   Inside Addresses: Questions and Answers

Question	Answer
How do I style the addressee's name and business title?	Check the letterhead or the signature block of previous correspondence for correct spelling, or check with the writer. If all else fails, call the recipient's secretary for spelling verification. An incorrect title or a misspelled name creates a very negative impression on a recipient of a letter.
When may I use abbreviations in an inside address?	You may use abbreviated courtesy titles and honorifics such as *Mr., Ms., Mrs., Dr.,* and *Esq.* Do not abbreviate company names, departmental designations, or corporate titles. You may, however, use abbreviations such as *Co., Inc.,* or *Ltd.* if they have been so used on the printed letterhead and form part of the official company name. Words such as *Street* may be abbreviated to *St.* If you are addressing large numbers of letters for automated sorting, use the capitalized, unpunctuated abbreviations recommended by the U.S. Postal Service. See the section on addressing envelopes for automated mail sorting in this chapter. In all cases, however, you should use the capitalized, unpunctuated two-letter state abbreviations recommended by the Postal Service.
How do I handle overly long lines in an inside address?	When an addressee's title (such as *Vice-president, Research and Development*) overruns the center of the page, carry over part of the title to another line and indent it by two spaces, as: Vice-president, Research and Development
How many lines should an inside address have?	The inside address should not exceed 5 full lines (runovers excepted).
How do I style addresses involving street numbers under *three*?	Write out in full numbers up to *three*: One Court Street; Two Park Street. Use Arabic numerals for *three* and above: 3 Marlborough Street; 8 Carson Terrace.

Table 1.   (*continued*)

Question	Answer
How do I style numbered streets such as *42nd Street*?	You may use ordinals or you may write out the number in full: 500 42nd Street *or* 500 Forty-second Street; 200 5th Ave. *or* 200 Fifth Avenue; 1234 19th St., NW *or* 1234 Nineteenth Street, NW.
Where do I position suite numbers, mail stops, and so forth?	Put suite, room, and apartment numbers on the street address line, two spaces after the last word on the line, as:
	500 Fifth Avenue Suite 44V
	Mail stop indicators, however, appear two spaces after the last word on the corporate name line:
	CCC Corporation MS 12Z 45I
How do I style an inside address involving two or more recipients having different addresses?	Type two (or more) complete sets of names and addresses, one after the other in alphabetical order or in order of importance, with double spacing separating the units one from another. Single-space each unit internally. If you are using a word processor, command the machine to print out two originals, one for each addressee. If you are using a conventional typewriter, make a photocopy of the original for each recipient and keep the original as a file copy. Ensure that the photocopies are clear and sharp. Use separate envelopes for the letters, of course, and include only one name and address thereon.

Message.   The message begins two lines below the salutation in all letter styles except the Simplified, in which it begins three lines below the subject line. (See the subsection on subject lines and the full-page Simplified Letter facsimile for details.) Paragraphs in conventional business letters are usually single-spaced themselves, with double spacing separating them one from another. Only in very short letters on half-sheet stationery is double spacing used today. If the message of a very short letter is double-spaced, you must indent the first line of each paragraph by six spaces. Paragraphs in the Block, Simplified, and Modified Block Letters are typed flush with the left margin. The first line of each paragraph in the Executive Letter may be blocked flush left or indented, depending on the preference of the writer or the typist. In the Modified Semi-block Letter, the first line of a paragraph is indented about five or six spaces. In the Hanging-indented Letter

Table 2. Salutations: Questions and Answers

Question	Answer
What's the current usage status of *Dear Sir* and *Dear Madam*?	*Dear Sir* is passé in general business correspondence: it is now used only in form letters and in letters to important personages such as a President-elect of the United States. The same goes for *Dear Madam* (in addition, some women find its use offensive). See the forms of address section in this chapter for detailed guidelines regarding the use of these two salutations.
What do I do when I can't determine the sex of the recipient from the written or typed signature on previous correspondence?	You can simply omit the courtesy title *Mr., Ms., Mrs.,* or *Miss* and say: Dear Lee Lawson. Or you can use the neuter abbreviation *M.* before the person's surname: Dear M. Lawson.
How do I address a mixed-gender group?	Style the salutation collectively, as: Dear S&S Engineers, Dear Engineering Managers, Dear Management, Dear Chemists, Ladies and Gentlemen, and so on.
Are people really using the nonsexist alternatives to *Gentlemen*?	Yes, and some of them (aside from the patterns shown above) are: Dear People, Dear Roth Corporation (or whatever the company name is), Dear Salespeople, and so on.

the first line of each paragraph is positioned flush left with subsequent lines block indented by five or six spaces, thus creating a stylish visual effect.

If the message contains an enumerated list you should block and center the listed matter by five or six more spaces, right and left. Single-space the individual units in the list but allow two spaces between each unit. Tables also should be centered on the page. Long quoted matter (i.e., a quotation exceeding six typed lines) must be centered on the page and single-spaced internally. No quotation marks are used unless there is a quotation within a quotation (see the rules for the use of quotation marks in Chapter Eleven, herein). Use double spacing above and below lists, tables, and long quotations to set the material off from the rest of the message.

If the message exceeds one page, use a blank continuation sheet matching the letterhead sheet in size, color, texture, and weight. At least three lines of the message must be carried over to the continuation sheet: at no time should the complimentary close and signature block stand alone there. The margin settings used on subsequent sheets should match those chosen for the letterhead sheet. Allow at least six blank lines from the top edge of the sheet before typing the heading which includes the name of the recipient (courtesy title + first name and surname or courtesy title + surname only), page number, and date. The continuation sheet heading may be single-spaced and blocked flush with the left margin:

Page 2
Ms. Jean McGhee
June 24, 19—

or, it may be spread across the top of the page, beginning flush left, and ending flush right:

Ms. Jean McGhee   –2–   June 24, 19—

The flush left block style is required with the Block and Simplified Letters. The spread is used with the Modified Block, Modified Semi-block, Executive, and Hanging-indented Letters. With the spread, the page number is centered and enclosed with two hyphens, either set tight with the numeral as shown above or spaced: – 2 –. Never abbreviate the date on a continuation sheet.

Complimentary close.   The complimentary close is used in all letters except the Simplified. The complimentary close is typewritten two lines beneath the last message line. The first word of the complimentary close is capitalized:

Very truly yours,	Sincerely yours,	Regards,
Yours very truly,	Yours sincerely,	Best regards,

A comma typically punctuates a complimentary close. If, however, you are using a minimal punctuation system, you may omit the comma. Remember, though, that when the comma is omitted here, the colon also must be dropped in the salutation, and ancillary notations such as enclosure notations and copy notations must go unpunctuated. Placement of the complimentary close varies with the style of letter chosen. Table 3 lists choices of letter styles and provides indicators of complimentary close page placement for each style.

You should use the complimentary close indicated by the writer because the chosen wording often reflects the nature of the relationship between writer and recipient. For instance, "Very truly yours" is rather neutral though somewhat formal in tone, while "Respectfully yours" indicates the high degree of formality often required in letters to heads of state or high-ranking clerics. "Sincerely" is much more informal, and wording such as "Best ever" or "Cheers" indicates

Table 3. Complimentary Close Positions

Letter Style	Complimentary Close Position
Block	flush left
Simplified	none
Modified Block Modified Semi-block Hanging-indented	center page aligned with date *or* 5 spaces to right of center page; aligned with date *or* flush right aligned with date; position of date dictates placement of complimentary close
Executive	flush right aligned with date

Table 4. **Complimentary Close Wording**

Tone	Example
most informal: indicates close personal relationship between writer and recipient	Cheers Regards Best regards Best ever As ever Kindest regards Kindest wishes
informal and friendly: indicates personal relationship between writer and recipient who may or may not be on a first-name basis	Yours Cordially Most cordially Cordially yours
friendly but rather neutral: appropriate to all but the most formal letters	Sincerely Sincerely yours Very sincerely Most sincerely Very sincerely yours Most sincerely yours Yours sincerely
polite, neutral, and somewhat formal: often used in law office correspondence as well as in general business correspondence	Very truly yours Yours very truly Yours truly
highly formal: indicates that the recipient outranks the writer; often used in high-level diplomatic, governmental, or ecclesiastical correspondence	Respectfully Respectfully yours Yours respectfully Most respectfully Very respectfully

particularly friendly, close relations between the writer and the recipient. Table 4 lists and discusses a number of frequently used complimentary closes.

Sometimes the relationship between the writer and the recipient may change from close to distant, or from friendly to hostile. The tone of the message may indicate such a change, but you cannot always be sure. This is yet another reason for you always to use the closing designated by the writer.

Signature block. The signature block indicates the writer's name and possibly his or her corporate title, if the title does not already appear in the printed letterhead. With the Block, Modified Block, and Modified Semi-block Letters, this matter is aligned vertically with at least four or five blank spaces intervening between the complimentary close and the first line of the typed signature block to allow for the written signature. Leave even more space here if your executive's signature tends toward the flamboyant. With the Hanging-indented and Executive Letters, the typewritten signature block is often omitted, with space left for a written signature. The Simplified Letter features a typed signature block positioned flush with the left margin, at least five lines below the last line of the message. The writer signs in the space allotted. The executive's name and corporate title are typed in capital letters with a spaced hyphen separating them.

A rather infrequently used signature block is the one in which the company name appears after the complimentary close, with the writer's name and title

Table 5. Signature Block Spacing and Position According to Letter Style

Letter Style	Vertical Spacing from Last Message Line	Page Placement	Placement of Writer's Name and Corporate Title within Typed Signature Block
Block	2 lines	flush left	writer's name (line 1) writer's title (line 2)
Simplified	at least 5 lines	flush left	writer's name and title all on line 1
Modified Block, Modified Semi-block	2 lines	aligned with date and complimentary close: center, right of center, or flush right	writer's name (line 1) writer's title (line 2)
Executive, Hanging-indented	2 lines	flush right	written signature only if writer's name forms part of the printed letterhead

appearing after the written signature. This style is used primarily with small business direct-mail advertising and in some contracts. Skip two lines between the complimentary close and the company name. Type the company name in capital letters. Skip five lines for the written signature and then type the writer's name in capital and lowercase letters followed on the last line by the writer's title:

```
Very truly yours,

HOWARD PLUMBING CONTRACTORS, INC.



John R. Howard
President
```

Table 5 explains the page placement of typed signature blocks with respect to the chosen letter style. The full-page letter facsimiles on pages 154–161 illustrate various letter styles and the placement of the complimentary close and signature block in them.

Ancillary Elements in Business Letters

The following elements are optional in a business letter, with inclusion or omission dependent upon the nature of the letter or the writer's wishes: a reference line, special mailing instructions, special handling instructions, an attention line, a subject line, writer/typist initials, a copy indicator, an enclosure notation, and a postscript. Forthcoming subsections discuss and illustrate the page placement and styling of these elements.

Reference line.   This notation, including data such as a file, policy, invoice, or order number, may be included if the recipient has requested it or if the writer

Reference Line: Modified Block or Modified Semi-block Letter

Houghton Mifflin Company

Two Park Street, Boston, Massachusetts 02108   Reference Division
(617) 725-5000   Cable HOUGHTON

                                        September 20, 19--
                                        Reference 12A 90C 17D

          Ms. Linda Martinez
          Production Manager
          E-Z Typesetters Inc.
          1200 Simpson Street
          City, US 98765

          Dear Ms. Martinez:

---

knows that its inclusion will facilitate the filing of correspondence. The reference line may be centered on the page between one and four lines under the date line. However, with the Block and Simplified Letters the reference line is always aligned flush left, one line below the date. (See the facsimile.) If you include a reference line on the letterhead sheet you also must insert it on every continuation sheet. When using the Block style, place the reference line on line four of the continuation sheet heading:

Page 2
Ms. Laura LaValle
March 15, 19—
Z–123–456–7

When using the Modified Block or the Modified Semi-block Letters, include the reference line one space below the date:

Ms. Laura LaValle   –2–   March 15, 19—
                                                               Z–123–456–7

Avoid using the Simplified, Executive, or Hanging-indented Letters with material requiring the inclusion of reference lines.

Special mailing instructions.   Indicate on the letter itself as well as on the envelope any special mailing instructions designated by the writer. These include certification, registration, special delivery, or overseas air mail. Such instructions are typed in capital letters, flush left, about four line spaces below the line on which the date appears and about two lines above the first line of the inside address. Vertical line spacing between the date and the special mailing instructions may vary slightly, depending on the length of the message and page space available.

Special handling instructions.   Sometimes a writer generates a letter requiring either a PERSONAL or a CONFIDENTIAL indicator. These instructions are typewritten in capital letters on the envelope and on the letter itself. The designation PERSONAL means that the letter is an eyes-only communication for the

Special Mailing Instructions

Houghton Mifflin Company

Two Park Street, Boston, Massachusetts 02108
(617) 725-5000   Cable HOUGHTON

Reference Division

6 lines (variable)

January 4, 19--

4 lines (variable)

REGISTERED MAIL ⎤ 2 lines

Mr. John M. Lindley
Treasurer
Bay City Bank Corporation
City, US 98765 ⎤ 2 lines

Dear Mr. Lindley:

---

recipient. CONFIDENTIAL means that the recipient and any other persons so authorized may open and read the letter. Special handling notations are placed about four lines below the date and from two to four lines above the first line of the inside address. If the message is quite brief, you may place the notation as many as six lines below the date. PERSONAL and CONFIDENTIAL notations are always positioned flush with the left margin. If a special mailing instruction such as CERTIFIED MAIL has been included too, put the special handling instruction below it and block both of them flush with the left margin as shown in the next facsimile.

Special Handling Instructions

Houghton Mifflin Company

Two Park Street, Boston, Massachusetts 02108
(617) 725-5000   Cable HOUGHTON

Reference Division

4 lines (variable)

November 14, 19--

3 lines (variable)

CERTIFIED MAIL ⎤ 1 line
CONFIDENTIAL ⎤ 2 lines

Ms. Anne D. Raymond
Vice-president
Deever Corporation
P.O. Box 4459
City, US 98765 ⎤ 2 lines

Dear Ms. Raymond:

Attention Line: Block Letter with Mixed-gender Salutation

Houghton Mifflin Company

Two Park Street, Boston, Massachusetts 02108   Reference Division
(617) 725-5000   Cable HOUGHTON

6 lines (variable)

August 13, 19--

4 lines (variable)

E-Z Typesetters Inc.
1200 Simpson Street
City, US 98765 ⎤ 2 lines
Attention Linda Martinez ⎤ 2 lines

Ladies and Gentlemen

Attention line.   Letters addressed to a corporation, department, or organization collectively but at the same time routed to the attention of a specific person within the group require insertion of an attention line. Block this line flush left in all letter styles except in the Modified Semi-block Letter where the line is centered. Position the attention line two lines below the inside address and two lines above the salutation. Never underscore an attention line. Use capital letters for the *A* in *Attention* and for the first letters of the proper name that follows. Never abbreviate *Attention*. Use a colon after *Attention*, or if you are using a minimal punctuation system, drop the colon. Examples:

Attention: John Hodges

or with minimal punctuation:

Attention John Hodges

Never insert a period after an attention line. The salutation that follows must be a collective one, for the letter is directed to a collective readership. Use a salutation such as *Gentlemen, Ladies and Gentlemen,* or *Dear CCC Company.*

Subject line.   The subject line, an ancillary element in all letter stylings except the Simplified in which it is required, presents the main thrust of the message in as few words as possible. Typewritten in capital letters, it appears three lines below the last line of the inside address and three lines above the first line of the message in the Simplified Letter. In all other letter styles the subject line appears two lines below the salutation and two lines above the first line of the message. The subject line in all styles except the Simplified may be introduced by the word *Subject* styled in any one of the following ways, or the word may be omitted:

Subject: Pretrial Conference with Judge Baxter
SUBJECT: Pretrial Conference with Judge Baxter
SUBJECT: PRETRIAL CONFERENCE WITH JUDGE BAXTER

Subject Line: Block Letter

Houghton Mifflin Company

Two Park Street, Boston, Massachusetts 02108
(617) 725-5000   Cable HOUGHTON

Reference Division

4 lines (variable)

March 15, 19--

3 lines (variable)

Mr. Alexander I. Dalgish
Senior Product Manager
Kaycee Systems, Incorporated
4590 Sixteenth Street
City, US 98765

2 lines

Dear Mr. Dalgish:

2 lines

Subject: Research & Development of Product X - Progress Reports

2 lines

At our meeting on February 20, 19-- we agreed that a joint effort in producing
progress reports regarding Product X is called for. With this in mind we have

---

In the Simplified Letter, you may not use the word *Subject.* Simply state the subject in capital letters:

PRETRIAL CONFERENCE WITH JUDGE BAXTER

In some law office correspondence, subject lines are introduced by the terms *In re:* or *Re:* but these terms are not used in modern general correspondence. Avoid insertion of a period after a subject line, and avoid using the Executive or Hanging-indented Letters in correspondence requiring this line.

Subject Line: Simplified Letter

Houghton Mifflin Company

Two Park Street, Boston, Massachusetts 02108
(617) 725-5000   Cable HOUGHTON

Reference Division

March 15, 19--

6 lines (variable)

Softsell, Incorporated
34 State Street Suite 34
City, US 98765

3 lines

NEW SOFTWARE PRODUCT ANNOUNCEMENT

3 lines

Senior Buyers of Softsell, we are proud to announce the forthcoming launch of a new
series of lexical software that is expected to revolutionize the field of spelling

Writer/typist initials.   The initials of the writer and/or typist are positioned flush left with the left margin two lines below the last line of the signature block in all letter styles. Most companies use two or three capitalized letters for the writer's name and two or three lowercase letters for the typist's name. Modern trends indicate omission of these initials unless someone other than the writer signs the letter or unless their inclusion is necessary for filing or output control purposes. In the Simplified Letter only the typist's initials appear. Examples:

MAR:ahs	MAR/as	MAR:AS	Michael A. Roberts: AS
MAR:as	MAR/ahs	MAR:AHS	Michael A. Roberts
mar:ahs	MR/as	MR:AS	AS

A letter to be signed by one person (such as a chief executive) but written or dictated by another (such as an executive assistant) and typed by the secretary bears three sets of initials styled as follows:

HTM:PTK:lc

Here, HTM stands for the chief executive, PTK stands for the executive assistant, and lc stands for the typist/secretary.

Enclosure notation.   If a letter contains an enclosure or enclosures, type a notation to this effect flush with the left margin two lines below the writer/typist initials or two lines below the signature block if no such initials have been included. Use any one of these styles:

conventional punctuation	**minimal punctuation**
Enclosures: 3	3 Enclosures
Enclosures (3)	Enclosure
3 encs.	3 encs
Enc. 3	encl
encl.	enc
enc.	encs
encs.	

Particularly important enclosures ought to be listed numerically and described. Block and single-space such material:

encs: 1.   Proxy Statement
       2.   P & L Statement, 1983–1984

If the enclosures themselves have not been clearly labeled as to subject and content, affix to the material a self-adhesive sticker identifying each one. To avoid confusion, use on the stickers the same descriptors used in the typed enclosure notation. If materials referred to in the letter are to be mailed under separate cover, indicate this fact:

Separate Mailing: Press Kit
                Media Reception Schedule

Copy notation.   Since photocopiers have all but replaced carbons, the abbreviation *cc* is now referred to as a *copy notation* or a *courtesy copy*. If included in a letter, this notation should be typed flush with the left margin, two lines below the signature block or two lines below any other notation preceding it. If used with writer/typist initials or enclosure notations, the copy notation appears last. Use any one of these styles:

conventional punctuation	**minimal punctuation**
cc: Harold T. Martin	cc Harold T. Martin
CC: Harold T. Martin	CC Harold T. Martin
cc: Mr. Martin	cc Mr. Martin
Mr. Peters	Mr. Peters
Mr. Smith	Mr. Smith
CC: Ms. Taylor	CC Ms. Taylor
Ms. Uhlander	Ms. Uhlander
Ms. Vest	Ms. Vest
cc: HTM	cc HTM
RWY	RWY
MCZ	MCZ

Multiple recipients are listed in alphabetical order according to full name or initials as shown above. If the writer so desires, give the copy recipient's full name and address:

single copy recipient

cc: Gene D. Dawson, Esq. (1 copy, Medical Claim)

several copy recipients

cc: Gene D. Dawson, Esq. (1 copy, Medical Claim)
    One Court Street   Suite 14
    City, US 98765

    Albert T. Goldberg, MD (1 copy, Discovery)
    Two Hospital Drive
    City, US 98765

Signature Block, Typist Initials, and Enclosure
and Copy Indicators: Modified Semi-block Letter

and so we will expect to receive the final page proofs on January 19, 19--. Many thanks for your adherence to our schedules.

2 lines

Sincerely yours,

4 lines

Christopher I. Kendall
Production Manager   1 line

2 lines

CIK:ahs   2 lines

enclosures: 4   2 lines

cc: Janet T. Booker
    Mary Y. Miller   1 line

Atlanta / Dallas / Geneva, Illinois / Hopewell, New Jersey / Palo Alto / London

Notice that double spacing separates each unit from the other, although the units are themselves single-spaced. If the writer wishes to send enclosures to the copy recipients, the enclosures are listed next to the names of the recipients.

A writer may wish that copies of a letter be distributed to others without that fact being revealed on the original. In this case, use *bcc* or *bcc:* before the names or initials of the recipients. The notation stands for *blind copy* or *blind courtesy copy* and appears only on the copies, either in the same position as the regular copy notation or in the top left corner of the letterhead sheet.

Postscript. If a postscript must be appended to a letter, it is typed from two to four lines below the last notation. In the Block and Modified Block Letters the postscript is set flush left. In other letter styles involving indented paragraphs, the postscript is indented exactly as the body paragraphs are. All postscripts are single-spaced, with margins matching those in the rest of the letter. In modern practice, it is now customary to omit the heading *P.S.* Have the writer initial all postscripts.

The Look of the Letter

Having discussed in detail all of the elements making up business letters, let us now turn to the matter of total visual impact. As soon as one opens a letter, one is immediately struck by its overall appearance on the page. Are the margins equal? Are the margins sufficient on right and left and at the top and bottom? One also notices and responds to the color and texture of the paper when holding the letter. Has the stationery been neatly folded and inserted into the envelope, or has it been untidily creased? Is the paper smudged or torn? Is the paper heavy enough to have withstood the impact of keystrokes, the ink of the printed letterhead, and the often rough handling of the mail system? Then, when one reads the letter, one immediately notices spelling and typographical errors, unsightly corrections, and ugly strikeovers, should they be present. As we have said before, the total letter is a product of your company. It is also a product of your skills as a secretary, and its look and feel should project a positive corporate image. This section discusses various ways by which you can enhance both product and image.

Margins and letter symmetry. To achieve maximum balance and symmetry on the page, follow these rules:

1. Try to estimate the length of the letter before touching the keyboard. Read through the executive's handwritten notes, reread your shorthand notes, or listen to the electronically stored dictation to get a ballpark estimate of the word count.

2. Consider the inclusion of any long quotations, tables, or lists to be displayed within the running text. Inclusion of such material will affect your total format and will add to the amount of tabbing you must do.

3. Determine if any special characters such as Greek letters or scientific symbols and mathematical/chemical formulas are to be included.

4. Set your margins after you have completed steps 1 through 3. Use these guidelines: 1″ margins for lengthy letters of over 300

words or over 2 pages; $1\frac{1}{2}''$ margins for medium-length letters of about 100–250 words; and 2″ margins for short letters of 100 words or less. Note that the $1\frac{1}{2}''$ margin is the most commonly used setting.

5. Be sure to take into account the fact that the closing section of a letter usually encompasses 2″ of vertical page space or 10–12 lines plus the bottom margin. Thus, you ought to reserve at least 1″ (or 6 vertical line spaces) for the bottom margin, especially if printed matter has been included there as part of the letterhead. Letters overrunning the bottom margin indicate amateurish work.

6. Develop your own system for warning yourself that the bottom margin is near. With conventional machines, the simplest method is to keep an eye on the machine's page end indicator. Another method is to mark lightly a 1″ bottom margin in pencil on the left or right side of the page. This can be easily erased. Still another method is the use of a backing sheet set somewhat to the right or left of the stationery. You will have marked the 1″ margin ending on that sheet with a bright marker. You also can include an early warning marker about 4″ above the final mark. Guide sheets for standard, Executive, and half-sheet stationery can be made up in advance. Finally, you can use the old-fashioned numbered guide sheet positioned slightly to the right of the stationery. Having pasted an $8\frac{1}{2}'' \times 11''$ blank sheet onto a larger sheet, you then begin numbering the available vertical line spaces in the far right margin, starting with 1 and ending with 66. On line 63 type E next to the numeral to indicate the end of an Executive sheet. On line 56 type HS to indicate the end of a half-sheet. One inch above 66, 63, and 56 respectively, add end-of-page indicators in different colors marked with the letters S (for standard), E, and HS. In this way, one guide sheet will suffice for three stationery sizes.

Be sure that the marginal settings on the continuation sheet match those on the letterhead. Avoid setting the stops to the inflexible six-inch typed line: every letter differs in content, length, and purpose so you must be flexible enough in your own formatting to accommodate these differences. A rigid line length setting is useful only in printing out multiple form letters, the content and length of which will remain relatively constant once the prototype has been input into memory.

Paper.   Top quality stationery is an indicator of the company's concern about its public image. Factors to consider when purchasing business papers include weight, texture, and color. The paper ought to be heavy enough to withstand corrections without tearing, buckling, or disintegrating. Likewise, it should withstand the pressure of keystrokes without pitting. At the same time it should be readily foldable without cracking. The ink from the printed letterhead must not bleed through onto the obverse side. The texture should be such that the typed

Table 6. Business Papers and Their Weights

Business Paper	Application	Weight
standard	correspondence	24 or 20
executive (Monarch)	CEO and other top management correspondence	24 or 20
half-sheets	very short letters	20 or 24
professional	short letters	24 or 20
bill	invoices, billings	24 or 20
manifold or onionskin	overseas air or carbon copies	13 or 9
memorandum	interoffice communications	20 or 16
continuation sheets	communications exceeding one page	weight must match that of the first sheet

characters are clear and undistorted and the written signatures and any handwritten symbols or signs appear smooth and even without blotching. If colored stationery is selected, its dye should be fast so that the paper will remain in good condition over time without fading.

The letterhead is printed on the felt side of the paper—i.e., the side from which you can read the watermark. In this connection, remember that you should type on the felt side of the continuation sheet. As we have said before, all continuation sheets and envelopes should match the letterhead in color, texture, and weight. Paper weight equals the weight in pounds of one ream cut to standard size. The heaviest paper weight is 24 for business correspondence, and the lightest is 9. Weights differ according to application in the office as shown in Table 6.

Prices of paper vary according to weight and composition. Prices also fluctuate widely from time to time. The one constant is that paper prices seem to rise from year to year. Hence, you should protect your supplies for the sake of cost-effectiveness. Store your stationery in the original boxes with the tops on. Store only a small supply in your desk stationery drawer; otherwise, you can expect deterioration and soiling over time.

Letter Facsimiles

The following subsection of the chapter contains full-page facsimiles of the traditionally used business letters. The illustrations are shown in this sequence: the Simplified Letter, the Block Letter, the Modified Block Letter, the Modified Semiblock Letter, the Executive Letter, the Hanging-indented Letter, and the Half-sheet Letter. Within each illustration you will find detailed guidelines regarding the proper margin settings, the type of spacing used within and between paragraphs, and the positioning of the essential and ancillary elements of the letters.

Following the letter facsimiles is detailed discussion of envelope addressing procedures, envelope sizes according to business application, computerized mail handling as it affects envelope addressing techniques, and abbreviations recommended for use by heavy commercial mailers to facilitate fast sorts and delivery.

The Simplified Letter

Houghton Mifflin Company

Two Park Street, Boston, Massachusetts 02108
(617) 725-5000   Cable HOUGHTON

Reference Division

January 4, 19--

Ms. Barbara C. Mackie
HCI Corporation   MS 34A 78N
One State Street
City, US 98765

ADMINISTRATIVE MANAGEMENT SOCIETY'S SIMPLIFIED LETTER

Ms. Mackie, this is a facsimile of the Simplified Letter recommended for many
years by the Administrative Management Society. It is a lean, clean format that
saves you time through fewer keystrokes and less typewriter movement, saves money,
boosts productivity, and enhances the look of the outgoing product.

The date is flush with the left margin from three to six lines beneath the letterhead. The inside address, also flush left, is typed three lines below the date
to facilitate the use of window envelopes. There is no salutation; this solves
the gender question in letters to correspondents who have signed previous letters
with their initials and a surname only. (In the inside address of a letter to
such a correspondent, you too can omit the courtesy title and type the person's
initials plus the surname.)

Type a capitalized subject line three vertical line spaces below the last line of
the inside address. Position the subject line flush with the left margin and omit
the words Subject or Re. The subject line encapsulates the main topic of the
message and should be brief and to the point. It is also a convenient filing
tool.

The message begins three lines below the subject line. All paragraphs are set
flush left. Paragraphs are single-spaced internally. Double spacing separates
one paragraph from another. The first paragraph opens with use of the recipient's
name in direct address as shown here--a polite way of engaging the recipient's
interest at the outset.

Enumerated lists and tabular data, if included, are set flush left with double
spacing separating one item from another. Items are single-spaced internally.
Long quotations are block indented by six character spaces. Such quoted matter
is single-spaced internally, with double spacing separating it top and bottom
from the rest of the message.

If the letter exceeds one page, use a continuation sheet matching the letterhead
in size, color, texture, and weight. Begin the heading at least six vertical

Atlanta / Dallas / Geneva, Illinois / Hopewell, New Jersey / Palo Alto / London

Ms. Mackie
Page 2
January 4, 19--

lines below the top left edge of the page. The flush-left heading includes
the recipient's name on line one, the page number on line two, and the full
date on line three. Maintain continuation sheet margins and paragraph style
as described for the first sheet. At least three message lines must be
carried over to the continuation sheet: at no time should the signature block
stand alone there.

The Simplified Letter has no complimentary close. This feature saves keystrokes. Type the writer's name and corporate title in capital letters at
least five or six lines below the last line of the message, and flush with the
left margin. A spaced hyphen separates the writer's name and title. The
writer then signs the letter in the space allowed.

Skip two spaces and typewrite your own initials flush with the left margin.
There is no need to include the writer's initials in this notation. If a
courtesy copy or enclosure notation is required, enter the material two lines
beneath your initials.

The Administrative Management Society tells us that "the Simplified Letter
stresses real economy of motion for secretaries. Its use results in better
looking letters with less effort. It will give them the pride of producing
more effective letters, and will result in increased productivity of a company's secretarial force--which ultimately saves money."

We recommend the Simplified Letter to all of our readers, and especially to
those who produce high volumes of correspondence.

Jane M. Doe

JANE M. DOE - SENIOR EDITOR

ahs

cc   Marietta K. Lowe
     Roberta Y. Peterson
     Candice S. Taylor

enclosures (7)

The Block Letter

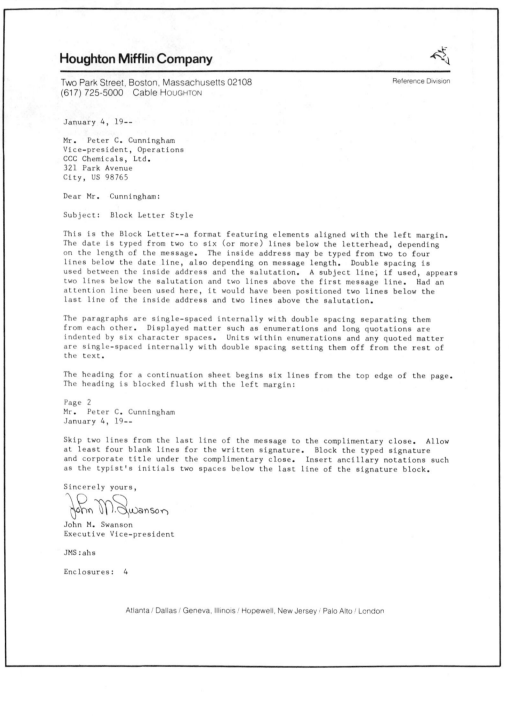

Houghton Mifflin Company

Two Park Street, Boston, Massachusetts 02108   Reference Division
(617) 725-5000   Cable HOUGHTON

January 4, 19--

Mr. Peter C. Cunningham
Vice-president, Operations
CCC Chemicals, Ltd.
321 Park Avenue
City, US 98765

Dear Mr. Cunningham:

Subject: Block Letter Style

This is the Block Letter--a format featuring elements aligned with the left margin. The date is typed from two to six (or more) lines below the letterhead, depending on the length of the message. The inside address may be typed from two to four lines below the date line, also depending on message length. Double spacing is used between the inside address and the salutation. A subject line, if used, appears two lines below the salutation and two lines above the first message line. Had an attention line been used here, it would have been positioned two lines below the last line of the inside address and two lines above the salutation.

The paragraphs are single-spaced internally with double spacing separating them from each other. Displayed matter such as enumerations and long quotations are indented by six character spaces. Units within enumerations and any quoted matter are single-spaced internally with double spacing setting them off from the rest of the text.

The heading for a continuation sheet begins six lines from the top edge of the page. The heading is blocked flush with the left margin:

Page 2
Mr. Peter C. Cunningham
January 4, 19--

Skip two lines from the last line of the message to the complimentary close. Allow at least four blank lines for the written signature. Block the typed signature and corporate title under the complimentary close. Insert ancillary notations such as the typist's initials two spaces below the last line of the signature block.

Sincerely yours,

John M. Swanson

John M. Swanson
Executive Vice-president

JMS:ahs

Enclosures: 4

Atlanta / Dallas / Geneva, Illinois / Hopewell, New Jersey / Palo Alto / London

The Modified Block Letter

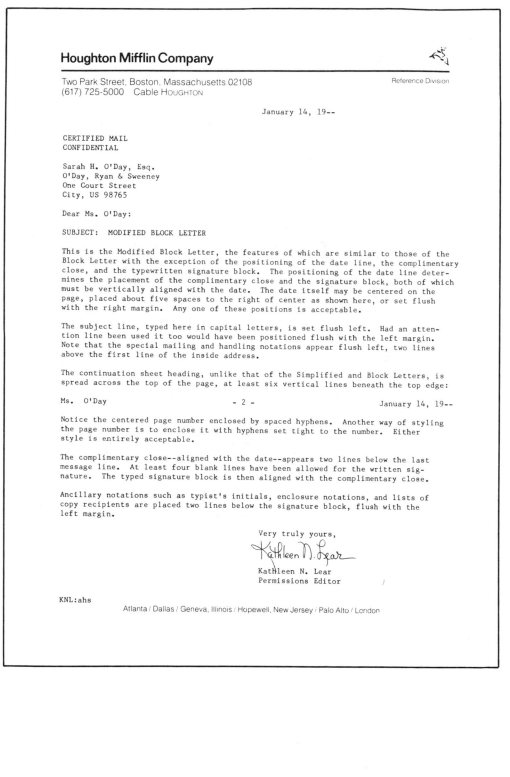

Houghton Mifflin Company

Two Park Street, Boston, Massachusetts 02108
(617) 725-5000   Cable HOUGHTON

Reference Division

January 14, 19--

CERTIFIED MAIL
CONFIDENTIAL

Sarah H. O'Day, Esq.
O'Day, Ryan & Sweeney
One Court Street
City, US 98765

Dear Ms. O'Day:

SUBJECT: MODIFIED BLOCK LETTER

This is the Modified Block Letter, the features of which are similar to those of the Block Letter with the exception of the positioning of the date line, the complimentary close, and the typewritten signature block. The positioning of the date line determines the placement of the complimentary close and the signature block, both of which must be vertically aligned with the date. The date itself may be centered on the page, placed about five spaces to the right of center as shown here, or set flush with the right margin. Any one of these positions is acceptable.

The subject line, typed here in capital letters, is set flush left. Had an attention line been used it too would have been positioned flush with the left margin. Note that the special mailing and handling notations appear flush left, two lines above the first line of the inside address.

The continuation sheet heading, unlike that of the Simplified and Block Letters, is spread across the top of the page, at least six vertical lines beneath the top edge:

Ms. O'Day   - 2 -   January 14, 19--

Notice the centered page number enclosed by spaced hyphens. Another way of styling the page number is to enclose it with hyphens set tight to the number. Either style is entirely acceptable.

The complimentary close--aligned with the date--appears two lines below the last message line. At least four blank lines have been allowed for the written signature. The typed signature block is then aligned with the complimentary close.

Ancillary notations such as typist's initials, enclosure notations, and lists of copy recipients are placed two lines below the signature block, flush with the left margin.

                                        Very truly yours,

                                        Kathleen N. Lear
                                        Permissions Editor

KNL:ahs

Atlanta / Dallas / Geneva, Illinois / Hopewell, New Jersey / Palo Alto / London

The Modified Semi-block Letter

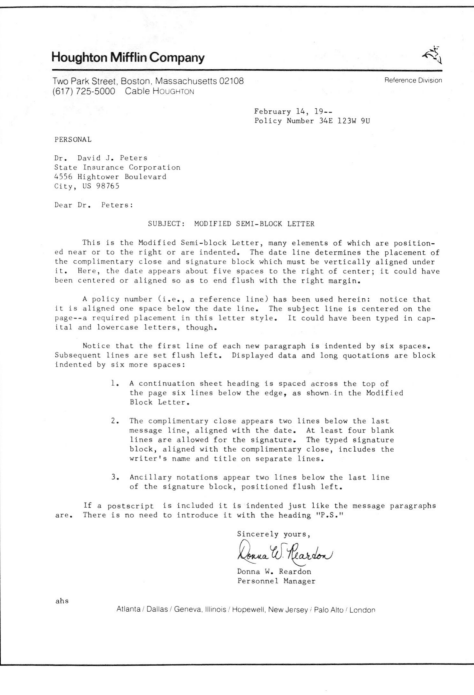

Houghton Mifflin Company

Two Park Street, Boston, Massachusetts 02108   Reference Division
(617) 725-5000   Cable HOUGHTON

                              February 14, 19--
                              Policy Number 34E 123W 9U

PERSONAL

Dr. David J. Peters
State Insurance Corporation
4556 Hightower Boulevard
City, US 98765

Dear Dr. Peters:

                SUBJECT: MODIFIED SEMI-BLOCK LETTER

        This is the Modified Semi-block Letter, many elements of which are position-
ed near or to the right or are indented. The date line determines the placement of
the complimentary close and signature block which must be vertically aligned under
it. Here, the date appears about five spaces to the right of center; it could have
been centered or aligned so as to end flush with the right margin.

        A policy number (i.e., a reference line) has been used herein: notice that
it is aligned one space below the date line. The subject line is centered on the
page--a required placement in this letter style. It could have been typed in capital and lowercase letters, though.

        Notice that the first line of each new paragraph is indented by six spaces.
Subsequent lines are set flush left. Displayed data and long quotations are block
indented by six more spaces:

        1. A continuation sheet heading is spaced across the top of
            the page six lines below the edge, as shown in the Modified
            Block Letter.

        2. The complimentary close appears two lines below the last
            message line, aligned with the date. At least four blank
            lines are allowed for the signature. The typed signature
            block, aligned with the complimentary close, includes the
            writer's name and title on separate lines.

        3. Ancillary notations appear two lines below the last line
            of the signature block, positioned flush left.

        If a postscript is included it is indented just like the message paragraphs
are. There is no need to introduce it with the heading "P.S."

                              Sincerely yours,

                              Donna W. Reardon
                              Personnel Manager

ahs

        Atlanta / Dallas / Geneva, Illinois / Hopewell, New Jersey / Palo Alto / London

The Executive Letter

Houghton Mifflin Company

Two Park Street, Boston, Massachusetts 02108   Reference Division
(617) 725-5000   Cable HOUGHTON

                                        October 14, 19--

Dear Mr. Fitzpatrick:

      This is the Executive Letter. In this styling, the inside address
appears from two to five lines below the last line of the signature space,
depending on the length of the message. It is aligned tight with the left
margin.

      The Executive Letter is commonly used by secretaries to chief execu-
tive officers, especially in correspondence with their personal friends
and corporate associates. The letterhead usually contains the writer's
name and corporate title; hence this information need not be included in
the typewritten signature block.

      The date appears flush with the right margin. The paragraphs are in-
dented from five to ten spaces. Carried-over lines are typed flush left.
Paragraphs are single-spaced internally. Double spacing separates the
paragraphs one from another.

      The complimentary close is vertically aligned under the date line,
i.e., flush with the right margin. Here, the typewritten signature block
is included four lines below the complimentary close because the writer's
name and title do not appear on the printed letterhead.

      If the typist's initials or another notation is included, it appears
two lines beneath the last line of the inside address, also blocked flush
with the left margin.

                                        Sincerely yours,

                                        M A Robinson

                                        Michael A. Robinson
                                        Vice President

John R. Fitzpatrick, Esq.
Fitzpatrick, Sweeney & Connon
Two Court Street
City, US 98765

MAR:ahs

Enclosure

        Atlanta / Dallas / Geneva, Illinois / Hopewell, New Jersey / Palo Alto / London

The Hanging-indented Letter

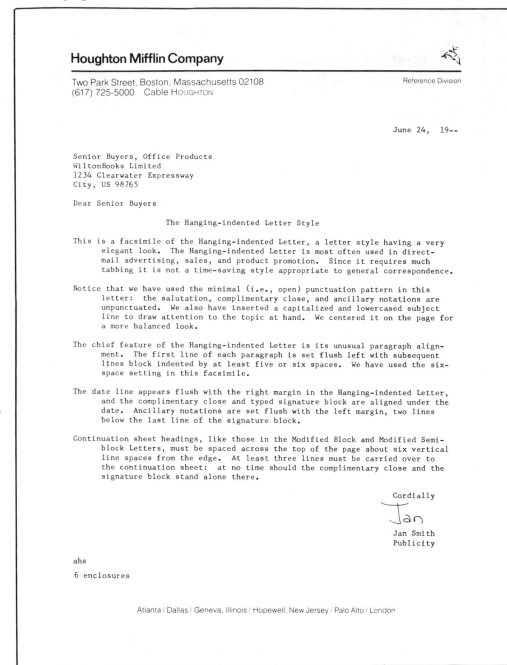

Houghton Mifflin Company

Two Park Street, Boston, Massachusetts 02108   Reference Division
(617) 725-5000   Cable HOUGHTON

June 24,   19--

Senior Buyers, Office Products
WiltonBooks Limited
1234 Clearwater Expressway
City, US 98765

Dear Senior Buyers

The Hanging-indented Letter Style

This is a facsimile of the Hanging-indented Letter, a letter style having a very
    elegant look. The Hanging-indented Letter is most often used in direct-
    mail advertising, sales, and product promotion. Since it requires much
    tabbing it is not a time-saving style appropriate to general correspondence.

Notice that we have used the minimal (i.e., open) punctuation pattern in this
    letter: the salutation, complimentary close, and ancillary notations are
    unpunctuated. We also have inserted a capitalized and lowercased subject
    line to draw attention to the topic at hand. We centered it on the page for
    a more balanced look.

The chief feature of the Hanging-indented Letter is its unusual paragraph align-
    ment. The first line of each paragraph is set flush left with subsequent
    lines block indented by at least five or six spaces. We have used the six-
    space setting in this facsimile.

The date line appears flush with the right margin in the Hanging-indented Letter,
    and the complimentary close and typed signature block are aligned under the
    date. Ancillary notations are set flush with the left margin, two lines
    below the last line of the signature block.

Continuation sheet headings, like those in the Modified Block and Modified Semi-
    block Letters, must be spaced across the top of the page about six vertical
    line spaces from the edge. At least three lines must be carried over to
    the continuation sheet: at no time should the complimentary close and the
    signature block stand alone there.

Cordially

Jan

Jan Smith
Publicity

ahs

6 enclosures

Atlanta / Dallas / Geneva, Illinois / Hopewell, New Jersey / Palo Alto / London

The Half-sheet

Houghton Mifflin Company

Two Park Street, Boston, Massachusetts 02108
(617) 725-5000   Cable HOUGHTON

Michael A. Rybarski
Vice President and
Director, Reference Division

January 15, 19--

Mr. Lee Martin
123 Salem Turnpike
City, US 98765

Dear Lee:

This is an example of a very short note typed on
half-sheet stationery. The half-sheet is often used
for one- or two-paragraph communications such as informal corporate invitations, letters of appreciation,
or letters of congratulation.

Notice the narrow margins set to align with the
right and left edges of the printed letterhead. We
have chosen the Modified Semi-block Letter style here,
but you may use the Block, Modified Block, or Executive Letters also.

Since the writer's name and title have been included in the printed letterhead there is no need to
include it in the signature block.

Sincerely yours,

Executive Signature

ahs

enclosure: check

Envelopes

Envelopes must match the letterhead and continuation sheets in color, texture, and weight. The standard $8\frac{1}{2}'' \times 11''$ stationery will fit the Numbers $6\frac{3}{4}$, 9, and 10 commercial, window, or overseas air envelopes. Executive stationery fits the Monarch envelope. Half-sheet paper fits the Baronial, or $3\frac{5}{8}'' \times 6\frac{1}{2}''$ envelope. Table 7 provides standard envelope configurations and sizes.

Envelope addresses must include these data:

addressee	**sender**
full name	full name
street address	street address
city, state, Zip Code	city, state, Zip Code

Optional data, included as required by the circumstances, are suite/room/apartment numbers, special mailing instructions (such as certification, registration, special delivery, or overseas air mail), special handling instructions (such as CONFIDENTIAL or PERSONAL), and attention indicators (such as Attention: Joseph Stone).

Table 7. **Envelopes**

Type of Envelope	Number	Measurements
Commercial		
	$6\frac{1}{4}$	$3\frac{1}{2}'' \times 6''$
	$6\frac{3}{4}$	$3\frac{5}{8}'' \times 6\frac{1}{2}''$
	7	$3\frac{3}{4}'' \times 6\frac{3}{4}''$
	$7\frac{3}{4}$	$3\frac{7}{8}'' \times 7\frac{1}{2}''$
	Monarch	$3\frac{7}{8}'' \times 7\frac{1}{2}''$
	Check $8\frac{5}{8}$	$3\frac{5}{8}'' \times 8\frac{5}{8}''$
	9	$3\frac{7}{8}'' \times 8\frac{7}{8}''$
	10	$4\frac{1}{8}'' \times 9\frac{1}{2}''$
	11	$4\frac{1}{2}'' \times 10\frac{3}{8}''$
	12	$4\frac{3}{4}'' \times 11''$
	14	$5'' \times 11\frac{1}{2}''$

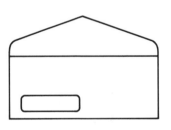

Window
Standard window size and position is $1\frac{1}{8}'' \times 4\frac{1}{2}''$, $\frac{7}{8}''$ left, $\frac{1}{2}''$ bottom.

$6\frac{1}{4}$*		$3\frac{1}{2}'' \times 6''$
$6\frac{3}{4}$		$3\frac{5}{8}'' \times 6\frac{1}{2}''$
7		$3\frac{3}{4}'' \times 6\frac{3}{4}''$
$7\frac{3}{4}$		$3\frac{7}{8}'' \times 7\frac{1}{2}''$
Monarch		$3\frac{7}{8}'' \times 8\frac{5}{8}''$
Check $8\frac{5}{8}$**		$3\frac{5}{8}'' \times 8\frac{7}{8}''$
9		$3\frac{7}{8}'' \times 8\frac{7}{8}''$
10		$4\frac{1}{8}'' \times 9\frac{1}{2}''$
11		$4\frac{1}{2}'' \times 10\frac{3}{8}''$
12		$4\frac{3}{4}'' \times 11''$
14		$5'' \times 11\frac{1}{2}''$

*Window position is $\frac{3}{4}''$ left, $\frac{1}{2}''$ bottom.
**Window size is $1\frac{1}{4}'' \times 3\frac{3}{4}''$; three positions, including $\frac{3}{4}''$ left, $1\frac{3}{16}''$ bottom.

Guidelines for addressing envelopes. Follow these suggestions based on the latest United States Postal Service regulations when addressing envelopes:

Envelope Size and Color

1. Use rectangular envelopes measuring no smaller than $3\frac{1}{2}'' \times 5''$ and no larger than $6\frac{1}{8}'' \times 11\frac{1}{2}''$.

2. Ensure that color contrast between paper and typescript is sharp.

Styling of the Address Block

1. Single-space the address block; do not use double or triple spacing and never use a slanted format.

2. Type the address block about 5 spaces to the left of center.

Table 7. (*continued*)

Monarch Window

Monarch $3\frac{7}{8}'' \times 7\frac{1}{2}''$

Standard with Special Window
Positions

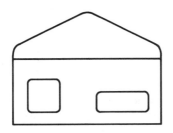

$6\frac{1}{4}$	$3\frac{1}{2}'' \times 6''$
$6\frac{3}{4}$	$3\frac{5}{8}'' \times 6\frac{1}{2}''$
7	$3\frac{3}{4}'' \times 6\frac{3}{4}''$
$7\frac{3}{4}$	$3\frac{7}{8}'' \times 7\frac{1}{2}''$
Monarch	$3\frac{7}{8}'' \times 7\frac{1}{2}''$
Check $8\frac{5}{8}$	$3\frac{5}{8}'' \times 8\frac{5}{8}''$
9	$3\frac{7}{8}'' \times 8\frac{7}{8}''$
10	$4\frac{1}{8}'' \times 9\frac{1}{2}''$
11	$4\frac{1}{2}'' \times 10\frac{3}{8}''$
12	$4\frac{3}{4}'' \times 11''$
14	$5'' \times 11\frac{1}{2}$

Continuous

Mounted on computer carrier
strip. Available in many styles
and sizes. Plain or printed.

Courtesy of Boston Envelope, 150 Royall St., Canton, MA 02021.

3. The address block should fill no more than $1\frac{1}{2}'' \times 3\frac{3}{4}''$ of line
   space. At least $\frac{5}{8}''$ of blank space should be allowed from the
   last line of the address to the bottom of the envelope.

4. With window envelopes, ensure that the inside address on the
   letterhead has been positioned so that all elements are clearly
   visible through the window (this includes checking to see that
   the letter has been properly folded). You should have maintained margins of at least $\frac{1}{4}''$ between the top, bottom, left, and

right edges of the inside address block and the top, bottom, left, and right edges of the window space.

5. Nothing should be printed or typed in the space extending from the right and left bottom edges of the address block to the right and left bottom edges of the envelope. Likewise, the space extending below the center of the address block to the bottom center edge of the envelope should be blank.

Conventional address block styles.   If addressing a letter to an individual, follow the patterns shown earlier in this chapter. If addressing a letter to a corporation, follow this pattern:

CCC Corporation
987 Industrial Drive
P. O. Box 444
Keystone, US 12345

Remember, though, that if both a street and a box number are used, the location on the line just above the line on which the city, state, and Zip Code appear is the destination of the letter. Therefore, if you wish the letter to go to the street address and not to the post office box (which may involve another Zip Code), put the street address last before the city, state, and Zip Code. If using an attention line, follow this pattern:

CCC CORPORATION
Attention John Hodges
987 Industrial Drive
Keystone, US 12345

Special mailing instructions are typed in capital letters below the space for the postage (i.e., approximately nine vertical line spaces from the right top edge of the envelope and not overrunning a $\frac{1}{2}$" margin). Special handling instructions are also typed in capital letters and are positioned to the upper left of the address block about nine vertical line spaces below the left top edge of the envelope. Any other such notations should be styled in underscored capital and lowercase letters, as Please Forward or Please Hold for Arrival, and should be typed about nine vertical line spaces from the left top edge of the envelope.

Addressing Envelopes for Computerized Sorting

Large-volume mailers are urged to address their envelopes in such a way as to expedite and not obstruct the Postal Service's electronic mail sorting system. (This topic is also discussed in Chapter Nine.) The Postal Service recommends that you use any of seven basic address formats, all employing capital letters, abbreviations, and minimal punctuation. These formats—designed to facilitate automated mail handling—also save you unnecessary keystrokes and thereby increase your own output. The seven formats are: (1) Post Office Box, (2) Rural Route, (3) Building/Business/Personal Name, (4) Standard Street Address/

Standard Envelope

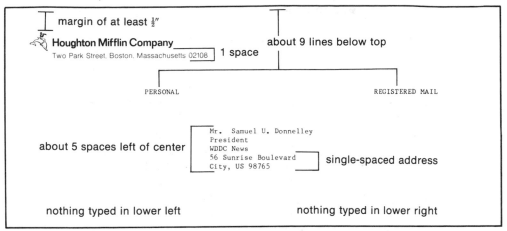

Numeric, (5) Standard Street Address/Alphabetic, (6) Community Identity, and (7) Dual Address. Examples:

Post Office Box

MS SARAH SMITH
PO BOX 123
CITY, US 98765

Rural Route

MR JG LOUGHRY
RR 5 BOX 94–C
RURAL LOCALE, US 12345

Building/Business/Personal Name

EZ CREDIT CORP
ATTN JAY MORTMAIN
CITY INDUSTRIAL PK
123 E INDUSTRIAL DR
CITY, US 98765

Standard Street Address/Numeric

MS JANE DOE
123 E 53RD ST APT 221
CITY, US 98765

Standard Street Address/Alphabetic

MS JANE DOE
603 FIRST ST APT 80
CITY, US 98765

Community Identity

MR JOHN T WATSON
HILLENDALE
13 FRANKLIN ST
CITY, US 98765

Dual Address

RRR CORP
123 E PARK AVE
PO BOX 100
CITY, US 98765
or
RRR CORP
PO BOX 100
123 E PARK AVE
CITY, US 98765

Remember that the address to which you want delivery to be made must appear on the last line above the city, state, and Zip Code. In the first example under Dual Address, delivery will be made to the post office box, but in the second example, delivery will be made to the street address.

Zip + 4. The Postal Service currently offers a voluntary Zip + 4 coding program for extra high-speed automated sorts. This program is particularly useful to high-volume business mailers. Rate incentives have been proposed to make the program even more attractive to commercial mailers. With Zip + 4, optical character readers (OCRs) in the originating post office can read the city, state, and Zip Code. Special printers apply a bar code on letter-size mail. The bar code—a series of vertical bars and half-bars—corresponds to Zip + 4 and allows all subsequent

Table 8.   **Two-letter Abbreviations for U.S. States and Dependencies**

State	Abbreviation	State	Abbreviation
Alabama	AL	Montana	MT
Alaska	AK	Nebraska	NE
Arizona	AZ	Nevada	NV
Arkansas	AR	New Hampshire	NH
California	CA	New Jersey	NJ
Canal Zone	CZ	New Mexico	NM
Colorado	CO	New York	NY
Connecticut	CT	North Carolina	NC
Delaware	DE	North Dakota	ND
District of Columbia	DC	Ohio	OH
Florida	FL	Oklahoma	OK
Georgia	GA	Oregon	OR
Guam	GU	Pennsylvania	PA
Hawaii	HI	Puerto Rico	PR
Idaho	ID	Rhode Island	RI
Illinois	IL	South Carolina	SC
Indiana	IN	South Dakota	SD
Iowa	IA	Tennessee	TN
Kansas	KS	Texas	TX
Kentucky	KY	Utah	UT
Louisiana	LA	Vermont	VT
Maine	ME	Virginia	VA
Maryland	MD	Virgin Islands	VI
Massachusetts	MA	Washington	WA
Michigan	MI	West Virginia	WV
Minnesota	MN	Wisconsin	WI
Mississippi	MS	Wyoming	WY
Missouri	MO		

sorts to be done on low-cost, high-speed bar code readers (BCRs). The equipment reads Zip + 4 and then sorts the mail according to sector or segment. This process, in effect, separates the mail and routes it to a box number, a firm, a building, or the carrier assigned to a particular locale. Zip + 4 looks like this: 01075–1234 where the traditional five-digit Zip Code 01075 is followed by a hyphen and four more figures: 1234, in this hypothetical example. The digits 01075 represent the major geographic location (in this case, a town in Massachusetts). The numbers 1 and 2 in 1234 represent a sector within the major geographic location. The sector might include several selected blocks, a group of streets, a large building, or another smaller geographic location within the major one. The numbers 3 and 4 represent a segment within the "12" sector. The segment might be one side of a block, two sides of a street, one floor in a large building, a cluster of mailboxes, or one post office box in a cluster. It is expected that Zip + 4 will be in full operation by the late 1980s and that by 1987 at least 50% of all high-volume commercial mailers will be using the system routinely. Eventually, Zip + 4 will eliminate all hand sorting.

Table 9.   Abbreviations for Streets and Words Often Appearing in Place Names

Street/Place Name	Abbreviation	Street/Place Name	Abbreviation
Academy	ACAD	Dale	DL
Agency	AGNCY	Dam	DM
Air Force Base	AFB	Depot	DPO
Airport	ARPRT	Divide	DV
Alley	ALY	Drive	DR
Annex	ANX	East	E
Arcade	ARC	Estates	EST
Arsenal	ARSL	Expressway	EXPY
Avenue	AVE	Extended	EXT
Bayou	BYU	Extension	EXT
Beach	BCH	Fall	FL
Bend	BND	Falls	FLS
Big	BG	Farms	FRMS
Black	BLK	Ferry	FRY
Bluff	BLF	Field	FLD
Bottom	BTM	Fields	FLDS
Boulevard	BLVD	Flats	FLT
Branch	BR	Ford	FRD
Bridge	BRG	Forest	FRST
Brook	BRK	Forge	FRG
Burg	BG	Fork	FRK
Bypass	BYP	Forks	FRKS
Camp	CP	Fort	FT
Canyon	CYN	Fountain	FTN
Cape	CPE	Freeway	FWY
Causeway	CSWY	Furnace	FURN
Center	CTR	Gardens	GDNS
Central	CTL	Gateway	GTWY
Church	CHR	Glen	GLN
Churches	CHRS	Grand	GRND
Circle	CIR	Great	GR
City	CY	Green	GRN
Clear	CLR	Ground	GRD
Cliffs	CLFS	Grove	GRV
Club	CLB	Harbor	HBR
College	CLG	Haven	HVN
Common	CMM	Heights	HTS
Corner	COR	High	HI
Corners	CORS	Highlands	HGLDS
Course	CRSE	Highway	HWY
Court	CT	Hill	HL
Courts	CTS	Hills	HLS
Cove	CV	Hollow	HOLW
Creek	CRK	Hospital	HOSP
Crescent	CRES	Hot	H
Crossing	XING	House	HSE

Table 9.   *(continued)*

Street/Place Name	Abbreviation	Street/Place Name	Abbreviation
Inlet	INLT	Pillar	PLR
Institute	INST	Pines	PNES
Island	IS	Place	PL
Islands	IS	Plain	PLN
Isle	IS	Plains	PLNS
Junction	JCT	Plaza	PLZ
Key	KY	Point	PT
Knolls	KNLS	Port	PRT
Lake	LK	Prairie	PR
Lakes	LKS	Radial	RADL
Landing	LNDG	Ranch	RNCH
Lane	LN	Ranches	RNCHS
Light	LGT	Rapids	RPDS
Little	LTL	Resort	RESRT
Loaf	LF	Rest	RST
Locks	LCKS	Ridge	RDG
Lodge	LDG	River	RIV
Loop	LOOP	Road	RD
Lower	LWR	Rock	RK
Mall	MALL	Row	ROW
Manor	MNR	Run	RUN
Meadows	MDWS	Rural	R
Meeting	MTG	Saint	ST
Memorial	MEM	Sainte	ST
Middle	MDL	San	SN
Mile	MLE	Santa	SN
Mill	ML	Santo	SN
Mills	MLS	School	SCH
Mines	MNS	Seminary	SMNRY
Mission	MSN	Shoal	SHL
Mound	MND	Shoals	SHLS
Mount	MT	Shode	SDHD
Mountain	MTN	Shore	SHR
National	NAT	Shores	SHRS
Naval Air Station	NAS	Siding	SDG
Neck	NCK	South	S
New	NW	Space Flight	SFC
North	N	Center	
Orchard	ORCH	Speedway	SPDWY
Oval	OVAL	Spring	SPG
Palms	PLMS	Springs	SPGS
Park	PARK	Spur	SPUR
Parkway	PKY	Square	SQ
Pass	PASS	State	ST
Path	PATH	Station	STA
Pike	PIKE	Stream	STRM

Table 9.   *(continued)*

Street/Place Name	Abbreviation	Street/Place Name	Abbreviation
Street	ST	Union	UN
Sulphur	SLPHR	University	UNIV
Summit	SMT	Valley	VLY
Switch	SWCH	Viaduct	VIA
Tannery	TNRY	View	VW
Tavern	TVRN	Village	VLG
Terminal	TERM	Ville	VL
Terrace	TER	Vista	VIS
Ton	TN	Walk	WALK
Tower	TWR	Water	WTR
Town	TWN	Way	WAY
Trace	TRCE	Wells	WLS
Track	TRAK	West	W
Trail	TRL	White	WHT
Trailer	TRLR	Works	WKS
Tunnel	TUNL	Yards	YDS
Turnpike	TPKE		

Address formats for military mail.   The Postal Service recommends that you use the format shown in this section for mail addressed to United States military personnel using Air Force, Army, and Fleet Post Offices. For Army and Air Force addressees, enter the addressee's name on line one, followed on line two by the addressee's unit and PSC number, followed on line three by the organization to which the addressee is assigned, followed on the last line by the APO:

PVT GG DOE
COMPANY F, PSC 3250
167TH INFANTRY REGT
APO, NY 09801

With mail addressed to members of the United States Navy and Marine Corps, type the addressee's name on line one, followed on line two by the name of the addressee's shore-based organization, mobile unit, or the name of the addressee's ship. On the last line type the Fleet Post Office and its number:

JOHN M DOE QMSN USN
USS SEA SQUIRT (DD 729)
FPO SAN FRANCISCO 96601

Addressing mail to Canada.   Follow the format recommended by Canada Post to expedite automated handling: use capital and lowercase letters with the addressee's name (line one), the firm name if included (line two), and the street address (lines two or three). On a subsequent line, enter the city name in capital letters followed on the same line by the name of the province styled either in written-out or abbreviated form as shown in Table 10. The six-character Canadian Postal Code is typed on another line. Remember that one character space separates the first three numbers and letters from the last three in the Postal

Table 10.   **Abbreviations for Canadian Provinces**

Province	Abbreviation
Alberta	AB
British Columbia	BC
Labrador	LB
Manitoba	MB
New Brunswick	NB
Newfoundland	NF
Northwest Territories	NT
Nova Scotia	NS
Ontario	ON
Prince Edward Island	PE
Quebec	PQ
Saskatchewan	SK
Yukon	YT

Code. Conclude the address block with the capitalized word CANADA if you are mailing the letter from outside Canada. Example:

Ms. Ann FitzGerald
FitzGerald and McHenry
123 Queen Street
OTTAWA ON
K1A 0B3
CANADA

Forms of Address

Business etiquette requires the proper use of forms of address in correspondence. Use of the right form of address applies to the inside address, the salutation, and the envelope address block. Forms of address include courtesy titles such as *Ms.* or *Dr.*, honorifics such as *Esq.* or *The Honorable*, military rank designations such as *Lt.* or *GySgt*, and titles such as *His Holiness, Senator*, or *The Right Reverend* for high-ranking personages. The next few subsections discuss particularly problematic usages of honorifics and courtesy titles. A complete forms of address table giving the proper forms of address for various academic, clerical, consular, diplomatic, governmental, military, and professional title holders concludes this section.

Esq.   This abbreviation stands for *Esquire*, which often follows the surnames of men and women in the American bar and in the consular corps. It is used in the inside address, on the envelope, and in the typed signature block but it is never used in the salutation. It is never used in conjunction with courtesy or professional titles such as *Ms.* or *Dr.* preceding a name. Likewise, it is never used in conjunction with another honorific such as *The Honorable*. Its plural form is

Esqs., used when referring to multiple addressees holding the title. In highly formal diplomatic correspondence, *Esquire* may be written out in full, but most recent evidence indicates that the United States Department of State is discouraging use of the term altogether. In Great Britain, *Esq.* is routinely used with the names of chief executive officers, prominent professionals in law and medicine, and high-ranking diplomats. Examples of the proper use of *Esq.* in American business correspondence are:

Janet L. Wills, Esq. Attorney-at-Law	Dear Ms. Wills:
John L. Wills, Esq. American Consul	Dear Mr. Wills:
Norton L. Levin, Esq. Samuel I. Gold, Esq. Attorneys-at-Law	Dear Mr. Levin and Mr. Gold: Dear Messrs. Levin and Gold:
Levin & Gold, Esqs. Attorneys-at-Law	Dear Messrs. Levin and Gold: Dear Mr. Levin and Mr. Gold:

Honorable.   *The Honorable* or its abbreviated form *The Hon.* is used in the United States with the names of certain high-ranking appointed or elected officials, as judges, clerks of courts, representatives, senators, governors, and the President and Vice President. It may be used in the inside address and on the envelope of a letter destined for the holder of the title, but it is never used by the holder in written or typed signatures, on letterhead or business cards, or in invitations.

Never use *The Honorable* with a surname only (i.e., "The Honorable Smith" is incorrect); a first name, an initial or initials, or a courtesy title must intervene (as in *The Honorable John Sweeney; The Honorable J.M. Sweeney; The Honorable Mr. Sweeney*). As with *Esq.*, *The Honorable* or *The Hon.* may be used with the name of a high-ranking woman official. Examples:

The Honorable Lee Whalen
The Honorable L.B. Whalen
The Honorable L. Brantley Whalen

The Honorable Mr./Ms. Whalen
The Honorable Dr. Whalen

In addressing correspondence to a married couple, one of whom is the title holder, follow these patterns:

if husband holds the title

The Honorable John M. Sweeney and
   Mrs. Sweeney
The Honorable and Mrs. John M.
   Sweeney
The Hon. and Mrs. J.M. Sweeney
	Dear Mr./Judge, etc., and Mrs.
	   Sweeney:

if wife holds the title/business correspondence

The Honorable Elizabeth Lee and
   Mr. Lee
The Hon. Elizabeth Lee and Mr. Lee
	Dear Judge, Senator, etc., Lee and
	   Mr. Lee:

if wife holds the title/social correspondence

Mr. and Mrs. Albert A. Lee   Dear Mr. and Mrs. Lee:

if wife holds the title and has retained maiden name/business correspondence

The Honorable Ann Stone and   Dear Judge, Senator, etc., Stone and Mr.
  Mr. Allen Wheeler   Wheeler:
The Hon. Ann Stone and Mr. Allen
  Wheeler

if wife holds the title and has retained maiden name/social correspondence

Ms. Ann Stone and Mr. Allen Wheeler   Dear Ms. Stone and Mr. Wheeler:

In limited address space *The Honorable* may appear by itself on line one with the addressee's name on line two.

Madam/Madame.   Use *Madam* only in letters to high-level women diplomats or government officials, such as the United States Ambassador to the United Nations or a woman justice of the Supreme Court. The term is used only in salutations:

Dear Madam:
Dear Madam Justice:

Madame, on the other hand, is used in salutations of letters destined for foreign heads of state and diplomats:

if woman holds the office

Dear Madame Ambassador:
Dear Madame Prime Minister:

Madame is also used with the names of the wives of high-ranking foreign diplomats and with the names of the wives of foreign heads of state:

if husband holds the title

Excellency and Madame Cortez:

Mesdames.   This word is the plural of *Mrs., Madam,* and *Madame.* It is the equivalent to *Messrs.* in business usage and may appear before the names of two or more women (married or single) associated together in a firm. It is used in the inside address, on the envelope, and in the salutation:

Mesdames Sarah Walker and   Dear Mesdames Walker and
  Laura Phelps   Phelps:
Mesdames Walker and Phelps   Mesdames:

If the two women share the same surname, follow these patterns:

Mesdames A.L. and L.T. Phelps   Dear Mesdames Phelps:
The Mesdames Phelps   Mesdames:

Never pluralize the surname in instances like this.

Messrs.   This term is the plural abbreviated form of *Mr.,* and, like *Mesdames,* it is used with the names of two or more men associated together in a firm. *Messrs.* is used in the inside address, on the envelope, and in the salutation:

Messrs. Dabney, Langhorne, and Lee   Dear Messrs. Dabney, Langhorne,
                                                        and Lee:

If two men share the same surname, follow these patterns:

| Messrs. C.D. and R.R. Langhorne | Dear Messrs. Langhorne: |
| | Gentlemen: |

Never pluralize the surname in an instance like this.

Misses.   This is the plural of *Miss* and its use parallels that of *Messrs.*:

Misses Carleton and East	Dear Misses Carleton and East:
	Ladies:
Misses A.Y. Carleton and D.C. East	Dear Miss Carleton and Miss East:
Misses Maureen and Mary O'Day	Dear Misses O'Day:
The Misses O'Day	Ladies:

Ms.   *Ms.*, like *Mr.*, indicates nothing with regard to a person's marital status. *Ms.* may be used in the inside address, on the envelope, in the salutation, and in the typed signature block of a letter. Never use *Ms.* with a woman's married name (i.e., "Ms. Robert A. Keith" is incorrect). The plural form is either *Mses.* or *Mss.* and its use parallels that of *Misses.* Examples:

Mses. (*or* Mss.) Grey and Holt	Dear Mses. (*or* Mss.) Grey and Holt:
Mses. (*or* Mss.) C.C. Grey and	Dear Ms. Grey and Ms. Holt:
D.D. Holt	
Mses. (*or* Mss.) Nan and Pam	Dear Mses. (*or* Mss.) Lee:
Lee	
The Mses. (*or* Mss.) Lee	Dear Nan and Pam Lee:

Professor.   Avoid abbreviating *Professor* to *Prof.* in instances where it appears only with a surname (i.e., "Dear Prof. Webber" is incorrect). Avoid wording salutations to professors as just "Dear Professor" and never say "Dear Prof. Smith." Correct patterns are given below:

Professor (*or* Prof.) Lee O'Brien	Dear Professor O'Brien:
	Dear Dr. O'Brien:
	Dear Ms./Mr./Miss/Mrs. O'Brien:

In addressing correspondence to a married couple, one spouse of which is a professor and the other is not, follow these patterns:

if husband is a professor

Professor and Mrs. Lee O'Brien	Dear Professor and Mrs. O'Brien:
	Dear Dr. and Mrs. O'Brien:
	Dear Mr. and Mrs. O'Brien:

if wife is a professor/business correspondence

| Professor Diana O'Brien and | Dear Professor O'Brien and Mr. O'Brien: |
| Mr. O'Brien | Dear Dr. O'Brien and Mr. O'Brien: |

if wife is a professor/social correspondence

| Mr. and Mrs. Lee O'Brien | Dear Mr. and Mrs. O'Brien: |

If the woman has retained her maiden name, follow these patterns in social and business correspondence:

Professor Diana Quirk	Dear Professor Quirk and Mr. O'Brien:
Mr. Lee O'Brien	Dear Dr. Quirk and Mr. O'Brien:
	Dear Ms. Quirk and Mr. O'Brien:

Letters addressed to multiple recipients, all of whom are professors, are styled as follows:

Professors B.B. Doe and C.C. Roe	Dear Professors Doe and Roe:
	Dear Drs. Doe and Roe:
	Dear Mr. Doe and Mr. Roe:
	Dear Messrs. Doe and Roe:
	Gentlemen:
Professors C.L. Jones and D.C. Lawton	Dear Professors Jones and Lawton:
	Dear Ms. Jones and Mr. Lawton:
	Dear Drs. Jones and Lawton:
Professors T.A. and A.Y. Lee	Dear Professors Lee:
The Professors Lee	Dear Drs. Lee:
	or if men
	Gentlemen:
	or if women
	Mesdames:
	or if wed
	Dear Professors Lee:
	Dear Drs. Lee:
	Dear Mr. and Ms. (*or* Mrs.) Lee:

Reverend.   This title is the one most misused in business correspondence: few people seem able to remember that it ought to be preceded by *The.* Never use *The Reverend* or its abbreviated form *The Rev.* with a surname only (i.e., "The Reverend Smith" is incorrect). *The Reverend* or *The Rev.* is used on the envelope, in the inside address, and in the signature block but never in the salutation (i.e., "Dear Reverend Smith" is incorrect). Follow these patterns:

The Reverend John M. Mills

The Rev. John M. Mills

The Reverend Dr. John M. Mills

The Rev. Dr. John M. Mills

The Reverend, like *The Honorable,* may be used with a surname only if a courtesy title such as *Mr., Dr.,* or *Ms.* intervenes:

The Reverend Ms. Kendall

The Rev. Dr. King

The Reverend Professor O'Neill

When addressing a letter to a minister and the minister's spouse, follow these patterns:

if husband is a minister

The Reverend and Mrs. A.A. Lee	Dear Mr./Dr. and Mrs. Lee:
The Rev. and Mrs. A.A. Lee	*or, depending on denomination*
	Dear Father Lee and Mrs. Lee:
	Dear Father Andrew and Mrs. Lee:

if wife is a minister

The Reverend Ann T. Lee and Mr. Lee	Dear Mrs./Dr. Lee and Mr. Lee:
The Rev. Ann T. Lee and Mr. Lee	

Two or more ministers may be addressed as *The Reverends, The Revs., The Reverend* (or *The Rev.*) *Messrs.*, and *The Reverend* (or *The Rev.*) *Drs.* plus their names. You also might wish to repeat *The Reverend* or *The Rev.* before each name instead of pluralizing the title:

The Reverends P.X. and F.I. Connon	Gentlemen:
The Revs. P.X. and F.I. Connon	*or, depending on denomination*
The Rev. Messrs. P.X. and F.I. Connon	Dear Father Patrick and Father Francis:
The Rev. Messrs. Connon	Dear Fathers:
The Reverend Messrs. Connon	
The Rev. P.X. Connon and The Rev. F.I. Connon	

If the clerics have different surnames, these patterns are appropriate:

The Rev. Messrs. P.X. Connon and F.I. O'Brien	Gentlemen:
	Dear Mr./Dr. Connon and O'Brien:
The Reverend P.X. Connon	*or, depending on denomination*
The Reverend F.I. O'Brien	
The Revs. Connon and O'Brien	Dear Father Patrick and Father Francis:
	Dear Fathers:

Table 11. **Forms of Address**

Academics	Form of Address	Salutation
assistant professor	Professor Joseph/Jane Stone Mr./Ms./Dr. Joseph/Jane Stone	Dear Professor Stone: Dear Mr./Ms. Stone: Dear Dr. Stone:
associate professor	Professor Joseph/Jane Stone Mr./Ms./Dr. Joseph/Jane Stone	Dear Professor Stone: Dear Mr./Ms. Stone: Dear Dr. Stone:
chancellor, university	Dr./Mr./Ms. Joseph/Jane Stone	Dear Chancellor Stone:
chaplain	The Reverend Joseph/Jane Stone	Dear Chaplain Stone: Dear/Mr./Ms. Stone: Dear Father Stone:
dean, college or university	Dear Joseph/Jane Stone *or* Dr./Mr./Ms. Joseph/Jane Stone Dean, School of _____	Dear Dean Stone: Dear Dr./Mr./Ms. Stone:
instructor	Mr./Ms./Dr. Joseph/Jane Stone	Dear Mr./Ms./Dr. Stone:
president	President Joseph/Jane Stone *or* Dr./Mr./Ms. Joseph/Jane Stone	Dear President Stone: *or* Dear Dr./Mr./Ms. Stone:
president/priest	The Reverend Joseph Stone, S.J. President of _____	Sir: Dear Father Stone:
professor, college or university	Professor Joseph/Jane Stone *or* Dr./Mr./Ms. Joseph/Jane Stone	Dear Professor Stone: *or* Dear Dr./Mr./Ms. Stone:

Table 11.   (continued)

Clerical and Religious Orders	Form of Address	Salutation
abbot, Roman Catholic	The Right Reverend Joseph Stone, O.S.B. Abbot of _____	Right Reverend Abbot: Dear Father Abbot:
apostolic delegate	His Excellency The Most Reverend Joseph Stone Archbishop of _____ The Apostolic Delegate	Your Excellency: My dear Archbishop:
archbishop, Armenian Church	His Eminence the Archbishop of _____	Your Eminence: Your Excellency:
archbishop, Greek Orthodox	The Most Reverend Joseph Archbishop of _____	Your Eminence:
archbishop, Roman Catholic	The Most Reverend Joseph Stone Archbishop of _____	Your Excellency:
archbishop, Russian Orthodox	The Most Reverend Joseph Archbishop of _____	Your Eminence:
archdeacon, Episcopal	The Venerable Joseph Stone Archdeacon of _____	Venerable Sir: Dear Archdeacon Stone:
archimandrite, Greek Orthodox	The Very Reverend Joseph Stone	Reverend Sir: Dear Father Joseph:
archimandrite, Russian Orthodox	The Right Reverend Joseph Stone	Reverend Sir: Dear Father Joseph:
archpriest, Greek Orthodox	The Reverend Joseph Stone	Dear Father Joseph:
archpriest, Russian Orthodox	The Very Reverend Joseph Stone	Dear Father Joseph:
bishop, Episcopal	The Right Reverend Joseph Stone Bishop of _____	Right Reverend Sir: Dear Bishop Stone:
bishop, Greek Orthodox	The Right Reverend Joseph Bishop of _____	Your Grace:
bishop, Methodist	The Reverend Joseph Stone Methodist Bishop	Dear Bishop Stone:
bishop, Roman Catholic	The Most Reverend Joseph Stone Bishop of _____	Your Excellency: Dear Bishop Stone:
bishop, Russian Orthodox	The Most Reverend Joseph Bishop of _____	Your Grace:
brotherhood, Roman Catholic, member of	Brother Joseph Stone, C.F.C.	Dear Brother: Dear Brother Joseph:
brotherhood, Roman Catholic, superior of	Brother Joseph, C.F.C. Superior	Dear Brother Joseph:
canon, Episcopal	The Reverend Canon Joseph Stone	Dear Canon Stone:
cantor (man)	Cantor Joseph Stone	Dear Cantor Stone:
cantor (woman)	Cantor Jane Stone	Dear Cantor Stone:

Table 11.   (*continued*)

Clerical and Religious Orders	Form of Address	Salutation
cardinal	His Eminence Joseph Cardinal Stone	Your Eminence:
clergyman, Protestant	The Reverend Joseph Stone *or* The Reverend Joseph Stone, D.D.	Dear Mr. Stone: *or* Dear Dr. Stone:
clergywoman, Protestant	The Reverend Jane Stone *or* The Reverend Jane Stone, D.D.	Dear Ms. Stone: *or* Dear Dr. Stone:
elder, Presbyterian	Elder Joseph/Jane Stone	Dear Elder Stone:
dean of a cathedral, Episcopal	The Very Reverend Joseph Stone Dean of _____	Dear Dean Stone:
metropolitan, Russian Orthodox	His Beatitude Joseph Metropolitan of _____	Your Beatitude:
moderator, Presbyterian	The Moderator of _____ *or* The Reverend Joseph Stone *or* Dr. Joseph Stone	Reverend Sir: My dear Sir: Dear Mr. Moderator: *or* My dear Dr. Stone:
monsignor, Roman Catholic (domestic prelate)	The Right Reverend Monsignor Joseph Stone	Right Reverend Monsignor: Dear Monsignor: Dear Monsignor Stone:
papal chamberlain	The Very Reverend Monsignor Joseph Stone	Very Reverend and Dear Monsignor Stone: Dear Monsignor Stone:
patriarch, Armenian Church	His Beatitude Patriarch of _____	Your Beatitude:
patriarch, Greek Orthodox	His All Holiness Patriarch Joseph	Your All Holiness:
patriarch, Russian Orthodox	His Holiness the Patriarch of _____	Your Holiness:
pope	His Holiness The Pope	Your Holiness: Most Holy Father:
president, Mormon Church	President Joseph Stone Church of Jesus Christ of Latter-Day Saints	Dear President Stone:
priest, Episcopal	The Reverend Joseph/Jane Stone The Rev. Dr. Joseph/Jane Stone	Dear Mr./Ms. Stone: Dear Dr. Stone:
priest, Greek Orthodox	The Reverend Joseph Stone	Dear Father Joseph:
priest, Roman Catholic	The Reverend Joseph Stone, S.J.	Dear Reverend Father: Dear Father: Dear Father Stone:
priest, Russian Orthodox	The Reverend Joseph Stone	Dear Father Joseph:

Table 11.   (*continued*)

Clerical and Religious Orders	Form of Address	Salutation
rabbi (man)	Rabbi Joseph Stone *or* Joseph Stone, D.D.	Dear Rabbi Stone: *or* Dear Dr. Stone:
rabbi (woman)	Rabbi Jane Stone *or* Jane Stone, D.D.	Dear Rabbi Stone: *or* Dear Dr. Stone:
sisterhood, Roman Catholic, member of	Sister Mary Viventia, C.S.J.	Dear Sister: Dear Sister Viventia: Dear Sister Mary:
sisterhood, Roman Catholic, superior of	The Reverend Mother Superior, S.C.	Reverend Mother: Dear Reverend Mother:
supreme patriarch, Armenian Church	His Holiness the Supreme Patriarch and Catholicos of All Armenians	Your Holiness:

Diplomats		
ambassador, U.S.	The Honorable Joseph/Jane Stone The Ambassador of the United States	Sir/Madam: Dear Mr./Madam Ambassador:
ambassador to the U.S.	His/Her Excellency Joseph/Jane Stone The Ambassador of _____	Excellency: Dear Mr./Madame Ambassador:
chargé d'affaires, U.S.	The Honorable Joseph/Jane Stone United States Chargé d'Affaires	Dear Mr./Ms. Stone:
chargé d'affaires to the U.S.	Joseph/Jane Stone, Esq. Chargé d'Affaires of _____	Dear Sir/Madame:
consul, U.S.	Joseph/Jane Stone, Esq. United States Consul	Dear Mr./Ms. Stone:
consul, to the U.S.	The Honorable Joseph/Jane Stone Consul of _____	Dear Mr./Ms. Stone:
minister, U.S.	The Honorable Joseph/Jane Stone The Minister of the United States	Sir/Madam: Dear Mr./Madam Minister:
minister to the U.S.	The Honorable Joseph/Jane Stone The Minister of _____	Sir/Madame: Dear Mr./Madame Minister:
representative (foreign), to the United Nations (with rank of ambassador)	His/Her Excellency Joseph/Jane Stone Representative of _____ to the United Nations	Excellency: My dear Mr./Madame Stone: Dear Mr./Madame Ambassador:
secretary general, United Nations	His/Her Excellency Joseph/Jane Stone Secretary General of the United Nations	Dear Mr./Madam/Madame Secretary General:

Table 11.   *(continued)*

Diplomats	Form of Address	Salutation
undersecretary to the United Nations	The Honorable Joseph/Jane Stone Undersecretary of the United Nations	Sir:/Madam: (if American) Sir:/Madame: (if foreign) My dear Mr./Ms. Stone: Dear Mr./Ms. Stone:
U.S. representative to the United Nations	The Honorable Joseph/Jane Stone United States Representative to the United Nations	Sir/Madam: Dear Mr./Ms. Stone:
Federal, State, and Local Government Officials		
alderman	The Honorable Joseph/Jane Stone	Dear Mr./Ms. Stone:
assistant to the President	Mr./Ms. Joseph/Jane Stone	Dear Mr./Ms. Stone:
attorney general, U.S.	The Honorable Joseph/Jane Stone Attorney General of the United States	Dear Mr./Madam Attorney General:
attorney general, state	The Honorable Joseph/Jane Stone Attorney General State of _____	Dear Mr./Madam Attorney General:
assemblyman, state	The Honorable Joseph/Jane Stone	Dear Mr./Ms. Stone:
cabinet member	The Honorable Joseph/Jane Stone Secretary of _____	Sir/Madam: Dear Mr./Madam Secretary:
cabinet member, former	The Honorable Joseph/Jane Stone	Dear Mr./Ms. Stone:
chairman, congressional committee	The Honorable Joseph/Jane Stone Chairman, Committee on _____	Dear Mr./Madam Chairman:
chief justice, U.S. Supreme Court	The Chief Justice of the United States	Dear Mr. Chief Justice: Sir:
associate justice, U.S. Supreme Court	Mr./Madam Justice Stone	Dear Mr./Madam Justice: Sir/Madam:
associate/chief justice, Supreme Court, former	The Honorable Joseph/Jane Stone	Dear Mr./Ms. Stone: Dear Mr./Madam Justice Stone:
clerk, county	The Honorable Joseph/Jane Stone	Dear Mr./Ms. Stone:
clerk, of a court	Joseph/Jane Stone, Esq. Clerk of the Court of _____	Dear Mr./Ms. Stone:
commissioner (federal, state, local)	The Honorable Joseph/Jane Stone	Dear Mr./Ms. Stone:
delegate, state	**—See assemblyman, state**	
director, federal agency	The Honorable Joseph/Jane Stone Director _____ Agency	Dear Mr./Ms. Stone:
district attorney	The Honorable Joseph/Jane Stone District Attorney	Dear Mr./Ms. Stone:

Table 11. (*continued*)

Federal, State, and Local Government Officials	Form of Address	Salutation
governor	The Honorable Joseph/Jane Stone Governor of _____	Dear Governor Stone:
governor-elect	The Honorable Joseph/Jane Stone Governor-elect of _____	Dear Mr./Ms. Stone:
governor, former	The Honorable Joseph/Jane Stone	Dear Governor Stone: Dear Mr./Ms. Stone:
judge, federal	The Honorable Joseph/Jane Stone Judge of the United States District Court for the _____ District of _____	Sir/Madam: Dear Judge Stone:
judge, state or local	The Honorable Joseph/Jane Stone Judge of the Court of _____	Dear Judge Stone:
justice, Supreme Court, associate, chief, and former	**—See chief justice, supreme court** and subentries thereto	
librarian of congress	The Honorable Joseph/Jane Stone The Librarian of Congress	Sir/Madam: Dear Mr./Ms./Dr. Stone:
lieutenant governor	The Honorable Joseph/Jane Stone Lieutenant Governor of _____	Dear Mr./Ms. Stone:
mayor	The Honorable Joseph/Jane Stone Mayor of _____	Dear Mayor Stone:
postmaster general	The Honorable Joseph/Jane Stone Postmaster General United States Postal Service	Dear Mr./Madam Postmaster General:
president, U.S.	The President The White House	Dear Mr. President:
president-elect, U.S.	The Honorable Joseph Stone The President-elect of the United States	Dear Sir: Dear Mr. Stone:
president, U.S., former	The Honorable Joseph Stone	Dear Mr. Stone: Dear Mr. President: Dear President Stone:
press secretary, to the President	Mr./Ms. Joseph/Jane Stone Press Secretary to the President	Dear Mr./Ms. Stone:
representative, state	**—See assemblyman, state**	
representative, U.S.	The Honorable Joseph/Jane Stone United States House of Representatives	Dear Mr./Ms. Stone:
secretary of state, for a state	The Honorable Joseph/Jane Stone Secretary of State State Capitol	Dear Mr./Madam Secretary:

Table 11. *(continued)*

Federal, State, and Local Government Officials	Form of Address	Salutation
senator, former (state or U.S.)	The Honorable Joseph/Jane Stone	Dear Senator Stone: Dear Mr./Ms. Stone:
senator, state	The Honorable Joseph/Jane Stone The State Senate State Capitol	Dear Senator Stone:
senator, U.S.	The Honorable Joseph/Jane Stone United States Senate	Dear Senator Stone:
speaker, U.S. House of Representatives	The Honorable Joseph/Jane Stone Speaker of the House of Representatives	Dear Mr./Madam Speaker:
territorial delegate to the U.S. House of Representatives	The Honorable Joseph/Jane Stone Delegate of _____ United States House of Representatives	Dear Mr./Ms. Stone:
undersecretary, of cabinet department (applies to deputy and assistant secretaries also)	The Honorable Joseph/Jane Stone Undersecretary of the Department of _____	Dear Mr./Ms. Stone:
vice president, U.S.	The Vice President of the United States *or* The Honorable Joseph Stone Vice President of the United States	Sir: My dear Mr. Vice President: Dear Mr. Vice President: *or* Dear Mr. Vice President:

Military Ranks*	Branch of Service	Form of Address	Salutation
admiral	USCG/USN	ADM Lee Stone, USCG/USN	Dear Admiral Stone:
brigadier general	USAF USA USMC	Brig Gen Lee Stone, USAF BG Lee Stone, USA BGen Lee Stone, USMC	Dear General Stone: Dear General Stone: Dear General Stone:
captain	USAF/USMC USA USCG/USN	Capt Lee Stone, USAF/USMC CPT Lee Stone, USA CAPT Lee Stone, USCG/USN	Dear Captain Stone: Dear Captain Stone: Dear Captain Stone:
chief warrant officer	USAF/USA	CWO Lee Stone, USAF/USA	Dear Mr./Ms. Stone:

*These military ranks and their abbreviations are used with the names of military officers. The abbreviated rank is followed by the full name, a comma, and the appropriate abbreviation of the person's branch of service (USAF for United States Air Force, USA for United States Army, USCG for United States Coast Guard, USMC for United States Marine Corps, or USN for United States Navy). Example: ADM Lee Stone, USN. These forms of address apply to men and women, and the first name *Lee* is meant to cover both sexes. Subsequent pages give cadet/midshipman and enlisted ranks.

Table 11.   (*continued*)

Ranks	Branch of Service	Form of Address	Salutation
colonel	USAF/USMC	Col Lee Stone, USAF/USMC	Dear Colonel Stone:
	USA	COL Lee Stone, USA	Dear Colonel Stone:
commander	USCG/USN	CDR Lee Stone, USCG/USN	Dear Commander Stone:
ensign	USCG/USN	ENS Lee Stone, USCG/USN	Dear Ensign Stone: Dear Mr./Ms. Stone:
first lieutenant	USAF	1st Lt Lee Stone, USAF	Dear Lt. Stone:
	USA	1LT Lee Stone, USA	Dear Lt. Stone:
	USMC	1stLt Lee Stone, USMC	Dear Lt. Stone:
general	USAF/USMC	Gen Lee Stone, USAF/USMC	Dear General Stone:
	USA	GEN Lee Stone, USA	Dear General Stone:
lieutenant	USCG/USN	LT Lee Stone, USCG/USN	Dear Lt. Stone: Dear Mr./Ms. Stone:
lieutenant colonel	USAF	Lt Col Lee Stone, USAF	Dear Colonel Stone:
	USA	LTC Lee Stone, USA	Dear Colonel Stone:
	USMC	LtCol Lee Stone, USMC	Dear Colonel Stone:
lieutenant commander	USCG/USN	LCDR Lee Stone, USCG/USN	Dear Commander Stone:
lieutenant general	USAF	Lt Gen Lee Stone, USAF	Dear General Stone:
	USA	LTG Lee Stone, USA	Dear General Stone:
	USMC	LtGen Lee Stone, USMC	Dear General Stone:
lieutenant (junior grade)	USCG/USN	LTJG Lee Stone, USCG/USN	Dear Lt. Stone: Dear Mr./Ms. Stone:
major	USAF/USMC	Maj Lee Stone, USAF/USMC	Dear Major Stone:
	USA	MAJ Lee Stone, USA	Dear Major Stone:
major general	USAF	Maj Gen Lee Stone, USAF	Dear General Stone:
	USA	MG Lee Stone, USA	Dear General Stone:
	USMC	MajGen Lee Stone, USMC	Dear General Stone:
rear admiral	USCG/USN	RADM Lee Stone, USCG/USN	Dear Admiral Stone:
second lieutenant	USAF	2d Lt Lee Stone, USAF	Dear Lt. Stone:
	USA	2LT Lee Stone, USA	Dear Lt. Stone:
	USMC	2dLt Lee Stone, USMC	Dear Lt. Stone:
vice admiral	USCG/USN	VADM Lee Stone, USCG/USN	Dear Admiral Stone:
warrant officer	USAF/USA	WO Lee Stone, USAF/USA	Dear Mr./Ms. Stone:

Cadets and Midshipmen

cadet		Cadet Lee Stone	Dear Cadet Stone: Dear Mr./Ms. Stone:
midshipman		Midshipman Lee Stone	Dear Midshipman Stone: Dear Mr./Ms. Stone:

Table 11.   (*continued*)

Ranks	Branch of Service	Form of Address	Salutation
Enlisted Personnel: A Representative Listing			
airman	USAF	AMN Lee Stone, USAF	Dear Airman Stone:
airman basic	USAF	AB Lee Stone, USAF	Dear Airman Stone:
airman first class	USAF	AlC Lee Stone, USAF	Dear Airman Stone:
chief petty officer	USCG/USN	CPO Lee Stone, USCG/USN	Dear Mr./Ms. Stone:
corporal	USA	CPL Lee Stone, USA	Dear Corporal Stone:
gunnery sergeant	USMC	GySgt Lee Stone, USMC	Dear Sergeant Stone:
lance corporal	USMC	L/Cpl Lee Stone, USMC	Dear Corporal Stone:
master sergeant	USAF USA	MSGT Lee Stone, USAF MSG Lee Stone, USA	Dear Sergeant Stone: Dear Sergeant Stone:
petty officer	USCG/USN	PO Lee Stone, USCG/USN	Dear Mr./Ms. Stone:
private	USA USMC	PVT Lee Stone, USA Pvt Lee Stone, USMC	Dear Private Stone: Dear Private Stone:
private first class	USA	PFC Lee Stone, USA	Dear Private Stone:
seaman	USCG/USN	SMN Lee Stone, USCG/USN	Dear Seaman Stone:
seaman first class	USCG/USN	S1C Lee Stone, USCG/USN	Dear Seaman Stone:
senior master sergeant	USAF	SMSGT Lee Stone, USAF	Dear Sergeant Stone:
sergeant	USAF USA	SGT Lee Stone, USAF SG Lee Stone, USA	Dear Sergeant Stone: Dear Sergeant Stone:
sergeant major (a title not a rank)	USA/USMC	SGM/Sgt.Maj. Lee Stone, USA/USMC	Dear Sergeant Major Stone:
specialist (as specialist 4th class)	USA	S4 Lee Stone, USA	Dear Specialist Stone:
staff sergeant	USAF USA	SSGT Lee Stone, USAF SSG Lee Stone, USA	Dear Sergeant Stone: Dear Sergeant Stone:
technical sergeant	USAF	TSGT Lee Stone, USAF	Dear Sergeant Stone:

Table 11.   (*continued*)

Professions	Form of Address	Salutation
attorney	Mr./Ms. Joseph/Jane Stone Attorney-at-Law *or* Joseph/Jane Stone, Esq.	Dear Mr./Ms. Stone:
dentist	Joseph/Jane Stone, DDS	Dear Dr. Stone:
physician	Joseph/Jane Stone, MD	Dear Dr. Stone:
veterinarian	Joseph/Jane Stone, DVM	Dear Dr. Stone:

Titles and honorifics in signature blocks.   The only courtesy titles used before a writer's name in the typed signature block are *Ms., Miss,* and *Mrs.* With a single exception (i.e., *Mrs.* plus the writer's husband's name), these courtesy titles, if used, must be enclosed in parentheses. They are never used in the written signature. Remember that *Mr.* is never used in the typed or written signature.

Typewritten signature	**Written signature**
(Ms.) Jane Doe	Jane Doe
(Miss) Jane Doe	Jane Doe
(Mrs.) Jane Doe	Jane Doe
Mrs. John M. Doe	Jane Doe

If the writer holds an advanced degree such as *MD, PhD, DVM,* or *DDS,* the abbreviated form of the degree may be used in the typed and written signatures following the surname. The writer never uses *Professor* or *Doctor/Dr.* preceding the name.

Typewritten signature	**Written signature**
J. Robinson Smith, MD Chief of Surgery	J. Robinson Smith, MD
Nancy Y. Hanks, PhD Professor of Molecular Physics	Nancy Y. Hanks, PhD

Holders of *Esq.* may use it in the typewritten signature block but not in the written signature:

Typewritten signature	**Written signature**
Jane L. Smith, Esq.	Jane L. Smith

Holders of *The Honorable* never use the term themselves:

Typewritten signature	**Written signature**
John M. Sweeney Associate Justice	John M. Sweeney

Ministers may choose to use *The Reverend/The Rev.* before their names in the typewritten signature block; however, they never use it in the written signature:

Typewritten signature	Written signature
Francis S. O'Leary, SJ	Francis S. O'Leary, SJ
Jonathan K. Stein, DD	Jonathan K. Stein, DD
Eric C. Swenson Pastor	Eric C. Swenson
The Very Rev. Alexis I. Ivanov Rector	Alexis I. Ivanov

Government officials and military personnel never put their titles or rank designations before their full names in typed or written signatures. Titles and indicators of rank appear only in the typed portion of the block, one line below the writer's name:

Typewritten signature	Written signature
Edward M. Keene United States Senator	Edward M. Keene
Elizabeth A. Meaney United States Ambassador	Elizabeth A. Meaney
Lee A. Lawson Captain, USA	Lee A. Lawson

MEMORANDUM FORMAT

An interoffice memorandum, like a business letter, is a means of transmitting written information from one person, group, or office to another or others. Unlike a letter, however, a memorandum lacks an inside address, a salutation, and a complimentary close. Instead, a memorandum has the following headings: a "To" line on which you list the recipient or recipients; a "From" line on which you list the writer or writers; a date line on which you include the month, day, and year when the communication was written; and a subject line on which you type the main thrust of the message. The headings for these lines are printed at the top of the memorandum sheet. Ancillary data such as a telephone extension, a department name, or a "Copies to" indicator also may be included in the printed headings, depending on the policy of your company. The rest of the page is designated for the message. The typist's initials, lists of courtesy copy recipients, distribution lists, or attachment notations appear at the end of the message, if necessary. Should the memorandum contain sensitive material, the notation CONFIDENTIAL is typed in capital letters at the very top of the sheet above the main printed heading *Memorandum*.

Paper size and the appearance of the memorandum.   The most usual paper size is $8\frac{1}{2}'' \times 11''$; however, the half size measuring $8\frac{1}{2}'' \times 5\frac{1}{2}''$ may be used for very brief messages. Memos also may be typed on plain bond paper, but if this method is used you must head the sheet with the capitalized term MEMORANDUM followed on subsequent lines by capitalized TO, FROM, DATE, and SUBJECT headings punctuated by colons.

Since the weight of memorandum paper is generally lighter than that of letterhead, you should use a heavy backing sheet while typing to cushion the paper and protect it against pitting from keystroke impact. Memorandum carbon packs are still available for cost-effective single-copy applications, but the current trend in business is overwhelmingly toward the use of photocopiers. Some companies use colored memo paper especially for interoffice communications generated by chief executive and chief operating officers. Color choice, weight, size, and design of memorandum paper vary according to company policy.

Maintain appropriate margins so that the memorandum is balanced attractively on the page. One-inch margins are best for long memos, while 1½″ margins work well with medium-length and shorter memos. Align your heading fill-ins so that they look neat and consistent. Some printed headings are themselves aligned to the right in order to facilitate typing the fill-ins:

        TO: Marketing Division
     FROM: Office of the President
     DATE: 12/13/83
 SUBJECT: Dictionary Advertising Campaign

If the printed headings have been so aligned, skip two spaces before typing the fill-ins. If the headings are aligned to the left instead, begin typing the fill-ins two spaces to the right of the longest heading (usually the subject heading) and block all other fill-ins with it:

TO: Marketing Division

FROM: Office of the President

DATE: 12/13/83

SUBJECT: Dictionary Advertising Campaign

Regardless of the positioning of the printed heads, however, you must skip two spaces before beginning the fill-ins. Ensure that your fill-ins are aligned with the printed headings: they should appear neither above nor below the headings. Use your variable line spacer or ratchet release to achieve proper horizontal alignment.

The appearance of an interoffice memorandum is a tangible indicator of your skills and your attitude toward the company. Memos with ugly strikeovers, penned-in corrections, marginal runovers, poor spelling, bad grammar, unaligned headings, and crumpled paper edges reflect badly on you, your executive, and your entire department. Remember also to store your memo paper in its original container. Keep only a small quantity in your desk drawer; otherwise, the paper will deteriorate from exposure to dust and also may become crumpled along the edges.

The "To" line: content and styling.   The "To" line may contain a single name or several names. It also might include a departmental name or the collective designation "All Desks" with material to be distributed companywide. A courtesy title such as *Mr.*, *Ms.*, or *Dr.* is generally omitted unless the recipient outranks the writer. If the memo has been addressed to several recipients one of whom requires use of a courtesy title, similar titles must be used with the names of the other recipients. You may use full names or initials and surnames in the "To" block. For instance, you might say *Jane C. King* or *J.C. King*. Follow the style dictated by the writer. The recipient's departmental affiliation may be included on a line under the name, depending on the size of the company and its policy:

TO: Frank R. Richardson
      Polymer Research Division

With a memorandum directed to many individuals, type the asterisked word *Distribution** in the "To" line space. At the end of the message, skip two lines, repeat the word *Distribution**, skip two more lines, and list the recipients in a single-spaced flush left block, one name to a line, in alphabetical order by surname or in order of corporate rank. Use the latter order only when the memorandum has been directed to a group of high corporate officers. In a case like this, the chief executive officer's name would appear first on the list followed by the names of various vice presidents in order of rank within the company.

The "From" line: content and styling.   The "From" line may contain a single name or multiple names. It may indicate that the memo is from a particular office or department. The "From" line is styled just like the "To" line, except for the omission of a courtesy title with the writer's name: the writer's name may appear as a full form (John L. Lee) or in abbreviated form (J.L. Lee), but a courtesy title (such as "Mr. John L. Lee") is never used.

The date line.   You may abbreviate dates in memos to the all-numeric form such as 12/13/83 where 12 means December, 13 means the thirteenth day of the month, and 83 means 1983. The full form—December 13, 1983—is also correct. Use the style that the writer prefers.

The subject line.   The gist of the letter is encapsulated in the subject line, which should be short (one-liners are preferable from the reader's standpoint, and for subsequent filing purposes). The writer should dictate the subject line. Key words within the subject line may be capitalized initially or the entire line may be capitalized. Do not underscore the subject matter and do not punctuate the line with a period.

The message.   Skip three vertical line spaces from the last heading and its fill-in before beginning the message. Paragraphs may be blocked flush with the left margin or indented to the right by five or six spaces. Single-space the paragraphs internally, and use double spacing to separate the paragraphs from each other. (With very short memos you may double-space the entire message; however, you must indent the paragraphs by at least six spaces to set them off one from another.) Maintain adequate margins to the right, left, and bottom of the page. Some writers prefer to enumerate their paragraphs with Arabic or Roman numerals or with letters. Follow the style indicated by the writer. Displayed data such as long quotations, numerical lists within paragraphs, and tables should be set off from the body of the message by block indentations and double spacing at the top and the bottom of the displayed matter. Displayed quotations and lists should be single-spaced internally. Skip two lines between each unit of an enumeration.

With a message exceeding one page, use a plain continuation sheet matching the printed memorandum page in color, texture, weight, and size. Margin settings and paragraph alignment must match the format on the first page. Skip at least six vertical line spaces from the top edge of the sheet before typing the heading. Either block the heading flush with the left margin or spread it across the page. If the heading on the first sheet reads "Distribution*" use the flush left format, and

Full-page Memorandum

Memorandum

TO Janis Wilcox   FROM Arthur R. Lee   .   DATE 12/13/83

SUBJECT Memorandum Format

This is an example of a properly formatted full-page company memorandum featuring printed headings. Notice that the fill-ins have been horizontally aligned with the heads and that two spaces have been left between the last letter of each head and the first letter of each typewritten fill-in.

Since this is a rather long memo, we have set our margins at one inch. Had the memo been short, we might have chosen a 1½-inch or a 2-inch margin setting with double-spaced, indented paragraphs.

You ought to skip at least three vertical lines from the last heading to the first line of the message. This space may be increased with extremely short memos.

Handle displayed enumerations like this:

1. Skip two vertical lines between the text and the first item in the enumeration.

2. Block and indent the entire enumeration as we have done here.

3. Skip two lines between each item in the list, but maintain single spacing within each unit.

4. Skip two vertical lines between the last line of the last enumerated item and the first line of the continuing text so that the displayed material will be clearly set off from the rest of the message.

Use a blank continuation sheet matching the memorandum paper in size, weight, color, and texture if the message exceeds one page in length. Construct a heading for the continuation sheet or sheets that includes the name of the recipient, the page number, and the date styled as you have typed it on the first sheet.

Paragraphs in memoranda may be indented by five or six lines or they may be set flush with the left margin as we have done here. The flush left format is the easiest.

Include your initials at the end of the message, two vertical line spaces below the last line of text, if you wish. Copy recipients should be listed two lines below your initials or two lines below the last line of the message if no initials appear on the page.

Attachments are listed separately below the other notations or two lines below the last message line if no other notations appear on the page.

cc: Mary Allen
     Sandra Kendall

Attachment: Style Manual

---

include only the page number and the date on the continuation sheet. If you have styled the date in numerals on the first sheet, use that styling on the continuation sheet. If you have written out the date on the first sheet, write it out on the continuation sheet.

Half-sheet Memorandum

Memorandum

TO Editors   FROM Mary Roe *Mary*   DATE 12/13/83

SUBJECT Editorial Department Meeting - New Product Development

There will be a meeting of all editors in my office on Monday, December 19
at 10:30 a.m. for the purpose of proposing and discussing new electronic
and print products for the Reference Division in the coming year. Please
come prepared to discuss your ideas in detail and defend them if necessary.
A detailed agenda will be issued to you before the meeting.

Memorandum on Blank Sheet

MEMORANDUM

TO: All Desks - All Locations   FROM: John R. Doe

SUBJECT: Jean Roe   DATE: 12/13/83

I am pleased to announce the appointment of Jean D. Roe as Assistant
Business Manager for the Reference Division. She will be responsible for
many of the budget-related financial systems in place and for the development of new systems for project and quality control in print and electronic
media. She will provide assistance in coordinating Reference Division data
processing projects and other administrative services.

Jean has been an auditor with the Internal Audit Department of Houghton
Mifflin Company since June, 1982, and has participated in audit programs for
the School and Reference Divisions in Boston and in various regional offices.
She brings to Houghton Mifflin her experience as a project manager in the
Social Services Department for the Commonwealth of Massachusetts and three
years' experience as a Senior Auditor and Senior Consultant for Arthur Young
& Company. She has also worked as an accountant in the Boston office of Dun
& Bradstreet.

Jean is a Certified Public Accountant in the Commonwealth of Massachusetts. She earned her B.A. in economics from Boston College and her M.B.A.
from Harvard. She and her family reside in Wellesley.

I am sure that all of you will extend a most enthusiastic welcome to
Jean as she joins the Reference Division at this very exciting time.

Typist's initials.   Typist's initials, if included, are positioned two vertical line spaces beneath the last message line, flush with the left margin. Inclusion of these initials depends on company policy, the writer's wishes, and/or the typist's own preferences.

Copy recipients and distribution lists.   Copy recipients' names appear two vertical line spaces below the typist's initials (if included) or two lines below the last line of the message:

cc: Kathryn K. Overton
      Michael I. Simms
      Theodore R. Thomas
      Laverne T. Udall

A distribution list for many recipients of copies is set up in much the same manner, with two spaces separating the distribution notation from the list itself:

Distribution*

Mary A. Brown
Alice V. Collins
Franklin B. Fields
James W. Hay
Leo V. Isaacson
Mary W. Kay

With a memo destined for a single recipient, the writer usually retains a copy and sends the original to the intended recipient. With memos to multiple recipients, the writer usually retains the original and sends copies to all of the recipients. (Put a check by the name of each recipient before putting the memo in the envelope.)

Attachment notations.   If attachments accompany the memo, put a notation to this effect two lines below the last notation on the page or, if there are no other notations, put the attachment notation two lines below the last message line. Don't forget to staple or clip the attachments to the memorandum.

Attachments: P & L Statement 1984
               OP Sales Estimates 1985

Envelopes.   Memorandums are generally routed to their recipients via unsealed, string-tied interoffice mailers. These envelopes have lines on which you write the recipient's name and intracompany location. With confidential memos, use a sealable manila envelope or a regular letterhead envelope with the word CONFIDENTIAL typed or hand-lettered in the top left corner, the recipient's name in the center, and the notation "Company Mail" or "Interoffice Mail" lettered or typed in the space where the postage ordinarily would have been affixed. Another way of indicating that the envelope is for interoffice delivery is to place an inked-in "X" mark where the postage ordinarily goes.

PRESS RELEASES

Companies issue press releases chiefly to help maintain a high public profile and thereby increase sales. For example, a press release might be issued to promote the launch of a new product or to announce markedly increased revenues, stock splits, or bigger dividends. Other stories might announce the appointment of a new chief executive officer or the installation of new members of the board of directors. The press release—just one component of a comprehensive public relations, advertising, and sales campaign—is a highly visible indicator of corporate style and substance, and as such it must be devoid of all errors, especially factual ones. Since you are often called upon to type and proofread press releases, your role in maintaining your company's public image is quite important. Let your company's outgoing publicity be a credit and not a deficit to its reputation.

Since a press release is really a news story, the writer constructs it with a view to immediate newsworthiness. That is, the writer follows journalistic style by putting the most important data in the first paragraph: Who did What? When was it done and Where? And Why was it done? Supporting data are then included in subsequent paragraphs arranged in order from the most important to the least important. In this way, the writer makes the news editor's life much easier, for the story can be pruned from the bottom depending on the space available in the publication in which it will appear, without inadvertent deletion of crucial facts. Similarly, a broadcast editor can cut all but the most salient facts for inclusion in a television or radio newscast.

Paper and format.   A press release is usually typewritten on a special printed form headed *Press Release, News Release,* or *News from* (company). The company's full name, address, and telephone/Telex number(s) are usually printed on the form as part of the heading along with memorandum-style subheadings such as

From: Sandee Martin
Contact: Laura Mason

in which the writer's name appears first followed by the public affairs person whom the editor might wish to contact for further information should a major story develop. These subheadings may be positioned in the top right or left corners of the first page. If the material is to be published or broadcast immediately, the phrase FOR IMMEDIATE RELEASE should be typed near the top edge of the first page in a conspicuous position relative to the heading and subheads.

The paper itself may be $8\frac{1}{2}'' \times 11''$ or it may be $8\frac{1}{2}'' \times 14''$ (legal). Double-space the text for easier editing later on. Allow right and left margins measuring 1" and a bottom margin of about $1\frac{1}{2}''$ to accommodate insertion of the continuation indicator *more.* Leave $2–2\frac{1}{2}''$ of white space from the bottom of the printed heading to the typewritten headline of the first page.

The headline.   The headline—a sentence or phrase focusing on the most important point of the story—is typed in capital letters centered on the page below the printed heading. Skip at least three and possibly four vertical line spaces from the headline to the first line of the story itself.

The story.   Begin the story with a flush left or indented date line (such as BOSTON, December 13—) in which the city name appears in capital letters followed by a comma, the month and the day, followed by a dash set tight or spaced with the day. Do not give the state's name unless your city's name is the same as those of several other cities. Begin typing the story right after the dash, on the same line, with no space or one space intervening between the dash and the first word of the running text:

Press Release

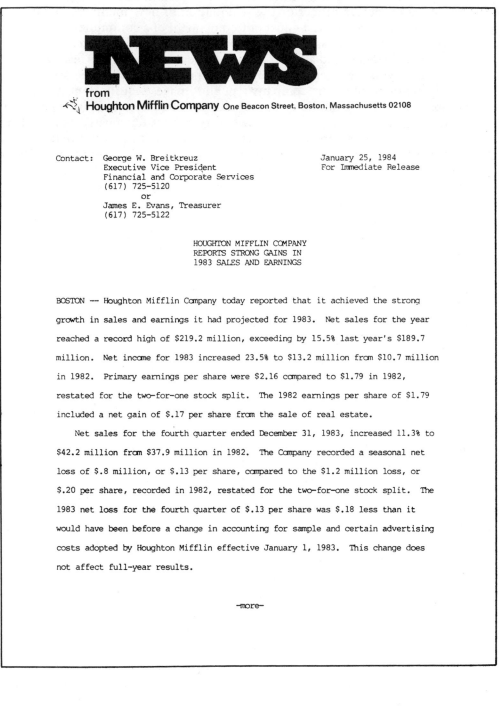

NEWS

from
Houghton Mifflin Company One Beacon Street, Boston, Massachusetts 02108

Contact: George W. Breitkreuz   January 25, 1984
           Executive Vice President   For Immediate Release
           Financial and Corporate Services
           (617) 725-5120
                 or
           James E. Evans, Treasurer
           (617) 725-5122

                      HOUGHTON MIFFLIN COMPANY
                      REPORTS STRONG GAINS IN
                      1983 SALES AND EARNINGS

BOSTON -- Houghton Mifflin Company today reported that it achieved the strong
growth in sales and earnings it had projected for 1983. Net sales for the year
reached a record high of $219.2 million, exceeding by 15.5% last year's $189.7
million. Net income for 1983 increased 23.5% to $13.2 million from $10.7 million
in 1982. Primary earnings per share were $2.16 compared to $1.79 in 1982,
restated for the two-for-one stock split. The 1982 earnings per share of $1.79
included a net gain of $.17 per share from the sale of real estate.

   Net sales for the fourth quarter ended December 31, 1983, increased 11.3% to
$42.2 million from $37.9 million in 1982. The Company recorded a seasonal net
loss of $.8 million, or $.13 per share, compared to the $1.2 million loss, or
$.20 per share, recorded in 1982, restated for the two-for-one stock split. The
1983 net loss for the fourth quarter of $.13 per share was $.18 less than it
would have been before a change in accounting for sample and certain advertising
costs adopted by Houghton Mifflin effective January 1, 1983. This change does
not affect full-year results.

                              -more-

-2-

Harold T. Miller, Chairman and Chief Executive Officer, said, "Educational publishing sales for the fourth quarter rose 18% led by strong performances by both the School and College Divisions. General publishing sales in the fourth quarter approximated those of a year ago with strong increases in the Reference Division's lexical software licensing activities offsetting lower Trade Publishing sales.

"It is important to note that the Company achieved these 1983 results while continuing to make major investments in print and software programs that will help contribute to the future growth of the Company," Miller said.

At its January meeting, the Board of Directors voted a quarterly dividend of S.22 per share, payable February 22, 1984, to shareholders of record on February 8, 1984.

###

```
BOSTON, December 13—John N. Kennedy, Chairman and President of FFF Air
Lines, has announced a new super-saver fare structure, effective immedi-
ately.  Passengers will realize savings of up to 30% on tickets. . . .
```

Indent each subsequent paragraph by at least five or six spaces to set it off from the next one. If the story exceeds one page, type the word *more* in lowercase letters at the bottom of the page, centered within the bottom margin space. Style this continuation indicator as -more- or (more), using hyphens or parentheses. Use blank continuation sheets matching the first sheet in size, color, texture, and weight. Maintain margins on the continuation sheet that match those on the first sheet, except at the top of the page. The heading of the continuation sheet should begin from four to six lines below the top edge. Number and caption the continuation sheet(s) as directed by the writer. The capitalized caption will contain a key word or words derived from the substance of the headline, followed by a dash and the page number set tight on one line, as FFF SUPER-SAVER—2.

The end.   Signal the end of the story by typing one of the following devices in the center of the last page about two or three vertical line spaces from the last line:

 # # # # or #### or ### or –30– or –end– or (END)

Proofreading.   Proofread the entire document line-for-line against the original. Check for typographical, grammatical, and factual errors. Query the executive if a fact appears to be inconsistent with other data or if you think it might be wrong. Then read the document again from beginning to end without looking at the original. Use the team proofreading approach for one last check: have a colleague read the original aloud while you read the final document.

CORPORATE REPORTS

Several kinds of reports are generated in business: memorandum reports, letter reports, and megareports (i.e., long complex documents sometimes encompassing hundreds of pages). These documents serve many needs and are directed to various readership levels inside and outside the company. A report might introduce and then analyze in detail a given market; discuss a particular business problem in depth and then offer a solution; lay out an annual or multiyear strategic plan; delve into a highly complicated legal or financial question; provide impetus for the research, development, and launch of a new product; or offer a stock/investment prospectus. Reports may be destined for staff, line management, top management, or outside clients. Some reports are general in content while others are highly technical. Your task is to organize and keyboard the draft materials into a logically ordered, consistently and neatly typed final product devoid of typographical and factual errors. You also may be requested to assist in producing tabular and graphic exhibits called *visual aids*. And of course the responsibility for proofreading, fact checking, duplication/printing, collation, binding, and distribution to the designated readership probably will be yours.

Although shorter reports are often dictated as memorandums, the longer ones are usually handwritten or typed as annotated drafts. In many cases a long report represents the input of a number of other executives besides yours. For instance, the summary in a new product report might have been written by your executive while the sales forecast might have been prepared by the sales director. The manufacturing cost estimates and production schedule might have been worked out by a manufacturing manager. The financials might have been prepared by a business manager or an accountant, with the advertising/promotion strategy having been developed by an advertising manager or an outside agency. Assuming that your executive is in charge of the entire document, you should be aware of some common pitfalls. Multiauthor reports usually abound in stylistic, spelling, and factual inconsistencies; hence, you should read the entire document from beginning to end and note all inconsistencies, errors, and unclear points before touching the keyboard. Tab them with self-sticking notes and then query the writer or writers responsible for the problematic points or sections. Check all major and subsidiary headings in the text to ensure consistency of style. Find out where the displayed tables and graphics are to appear: will they be scattered throughout the text (if so, room must be left for them) or will they be clustered together in an appendix? If possible, input the report into a word processor and store it on memory for easier final editing/correction.

The Memorandum Report

For a short (i.e., a two- to three-page) report intended for in-house distribution, use the company's printed memo paper and continuation sheets. Put the report title in the subject block and then follow the guidelines in this chapter regarding memorandum format. A typical memorandum report might be a monthly sales analysis for a product line in a given region or territory or a monthly departmental progress report with respect to on-line projects.

The Letter Report

A letter report might be used to convey information to various off-site managers or to the members of a board of directors. A letter report is just what the designation indicates: a letter to the recipient(s) that has been modified stylistically to include various headings and subheadings. The letter report is typed on corporate letterhead and continuation sheets matching the letterhead. We recommend the Block or the Modified Block Letter styles for such a report. These two styles lend themselves readily to graceful, balanced presentation of information, whether it be running text or displayed matter. In most cases the letter will be duplicated for many recipients. We therefore recommend that you save extra white space in the inside address block to accommodate inclusion of names and addresses varying markedly in length.

The following guidelines have been developed to assist you in typing the typically occurring heads and subheads in letter reports. Read the guidelines and then refer to the two-page Block facsimile of a letter report at the end of this subsection (pages 198–199).

REPORT TITLE STYLED AS SUBJECT LINE

position: 3 vertical line spaces below salutation
            3 vertical line spaces above text or first main heading
            flush left
styling: capitalized
            underscored

MAIN HEADING

position: 3 vertical line spaces below what has gone before (i.e., title or text)
            3 vertical line spaces above what follows (i.e., text or another head)
            flush left

styling: capitalized

First-level Subhead

position: 3 vertical line spaces below what has gone before (i.e., text)
            3 vertical line spaces above what follows (i.e., text or another head)
            flush left

styling: capital and lowercased letters
           underscored

Sideheads.   position: flush left, run in with the text
             styling: initially capitalized and then lowercased
                         underscored
                         punctuated with period (optional)

If the Modified Block Letter style is used, the secretary positions the title/subject line, the main headings, and the first-level subheads in the center of the page while maintaining the same vertical spacing as that shown with the Block Letter. The sideheads are run in with the text.

Table 12. Corporate Report Typewriting Guide

Margins

location	machine setting: unbound & top-bound
top/p.1	12 lines
top/p. 2 ff.	6 lines
bottom/all pp.	6 lines
left & right/all pp.	12 spaces/elite 10 spaces/pica
	machine setting: sidebound
left/all pp.	18 spaces/elite 15 spaces/pica

Spacing

element of report	machine setting: unbound, top-bound, & sidebound
body of report	single or double
between paragraphs	if single-spaced paragraphs,

Table 12.   *(continued)*

	double spacing to separate them; if double-spaced paragraphs, triple spacing to separate them
long quoted matter, displayed	single
enumerations, tables	single within units; double between units
footnotes	single
bibliography	single

Indention

element of report	machine setting: unbound, top-bound, sidebound
paragraphs	indented format: 5–6 spaces block format: no indents
long quoted matter, tables, lists	blocked 5–6 spaces right and left
footnotes	2–5 spaces, first line only
bibliography	no indent on first line; 2–5 spaces, runover lines

Pagination: unbound & top-bound—numerals 3–6 lines from bottom center, each page; sidebound—numerals 3–6 lines from top of page or 3–6 lines from bottom and $\frac{1}{2}''$ to the right of center

element of report	kind of number
flyleaves	no pagination
title fly	lowercase Roman numeral i
title page	lowercase Roman numeral ii
front matter (i.e., letters of authorization/transmittal, acknowledgments, table of contents, lists of tables and graphics, preface, foreword, executive summary)	lowercase Roman numeral iii
first text page	Arabic numeral 1
subsequent text pages (i.e., body of report, appendix, footnotes listed separately, bibliography, index)	Arabic numeral 2 ff.

Letter Report Format

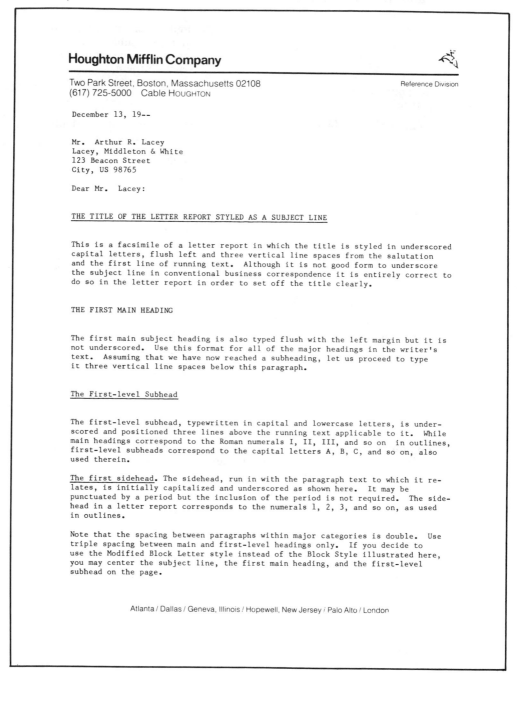

Houghton Mifflin Company

Two Park Street, Boston, Massachusetts 02108   Reference Division
(617) 725-5000   Cable HOUGHTON

December 13, 19--

Mr. Arthur R. Lacey
Lacey, Middleton & White
123 Beacon Street
City, US 98765

Dear Mr. Lacey:

THE TITLE OF THE LETTER REPORT STYLED AS A SUBJECT LINE

This is a facsimile of a letter report in which the title is styled in underscored
capital letters, flush left and three vertical line spaces from the salutation
and the first line of running text. Although it is not good form to underscore
the subject line in conventional business correspondence it is entirely correct to
do so in the letter report in order to set off the title clearly.

THE FIRST MAIN HEADING

The first main subject heading is also typed flush with the left margin but it is
not underscored. Use this format for all of the major headings in the writer's
text. Assuming that we have now reached a subheading, let us proceed to type
it three vertical line spaces below this paragraph.

The First-level Subhead

The first-level subhead, typewritten in capital and lowercase letters, is underscored and positioned three lines above the running text applicable to it. While
main headings correspond to the Roman numerals I, II, III, and so on in outlines,
first-level subheads correspond to the capital letters A, B, C, and so on, also
used therein.

The first sidehead. The sidehead, run in with the paragraph text to which it relates, is initially capitalized and underscored as shown here. It may be
punctuated by a period but the inclusion of the period is not required. The sidehead in a letter report corresponds to the numerals 1, 2, 3, and so on, as used
in outlines.

Note that the spacing between paragraphs within major categories is double. Use
triple spacing between main and first-level headings only. If you decide to
use the Modified Block Letter style instead of the Block Style illustrated here,
you may center the subject line, the first main heading, and the first-level
subhead on the page.

Atlanta / Dallas / Geneva, Illinois / Hopewell, New Jersey / Palo Alto / London

Page 2
Mr. Arthur R. Lacey
December 13, 19--

Since most letter reports will exceed one page, you should plan on using continuation sheets matching the letterhead in size, color, texture, and weight.
Of course, your margins on all subsequent sheets must match the ones you have
maintained on the letterhead.

THE SECOND MAIN HEADING

Many reports contain an Executive Summary (also called an Abstract) and lists
of conclusions and/or recommendations. Consider these sections important
enough to rate main headings as shown just above. The Executive Summary may
appear at the very beginning or at the end. The conclusions and/or recommendations almost always come at the end.

Another First-level Subhead

Displayed data such as tables or lists may be set within the running text or
grouped together in an Appendix. If the material is to be incorporated within the text, follow the guidelines given in the business correspondence section of this chapter for block indention of displayed data.

A second sidehead. The letter report concludes with a complimentary close and
a typewritten signature block, just as a conventional business letter does.
Follow the guidelines given in the business correspondence section of this
chapter.

If enclosures are to be included along with the report, annotate the report to
this effect as we have shown below.

Very truly yours,

Robin N. Brown
Corporate Counsel

RNB:ahs

Enclosures: Proxy Statement
             Agenda, Stockholders' Meeting
             Board of Directors' Meeting Schedule
             Agenda, Board of Directors' Meeting

The Megareport

By *megareport* we mean a lengthy, complex, formal document on a given subject or subjects intended for internal distribution or for an outside client. Its essential elements include a title page, an executive summary (also called an abstract), and pages of running text. Ancillary elements included or omitted depending on the content and purpose of the document, the writer's wishes, and/or company policy, are: a cover, a flyleaf or flyleaves, a title fly, letters of authorization/transmittal, a foreword, a preface, acknowledgments, a list of graphics and tables, a list of conclusions or recommendations, an appendix, footnotes, and a bibliography. Sometimes an index is included.

The report is typewritten on $8\frac{1}{2}'' \times 11''$ white bond paper that will withstand repeated handling. The pages should be typed with a view toward the planned method of binding: will it be stapled at the top left (a good method for shorter reports), or will it be sidebound (preferable for extremely long reports)? The prefatory sections (i.e., the letters of authorization/transmittal, the acknowledgments, the table of contents, the list of graphics and/or tables, the foreword and/or preface, and the executive summary) are paginated sequentially in lowercase Roman numerals (e.g., i, ii, iii, iv, v, and so on) centered on the page about three to six vertical line spaces from the bottom edge of the sheet. The body of the report and all appended materials are paginated sequentially in Arabic numerals positioned at the top right margin about one inch from the top edge of the sheet or about one inch from the bottom edge of the sheet flush with the right margin. The first page of the body of the report is unpaginated.

Select a cover for the report that will protect it over the long term and one that is appropriate for the overall length of it. A ring binder, for example, is particularly appropriate for a five-year plan running hundreds of pages in length. The cover ought to contain a gummed label bearing the title and perhaps the writer's name or the name of the company. The label should be neatly and clearly typed.

The flyleaf, title fly, and title page. Formal reports often have a flyleaf—a blank page appearing at the very beginning. Sometimes a report may have two of these, one at the beginning and another at the end. Flyleaves protect the rest of the document and allow space for readers' comments. The title fly contains the capitalized title of the report, centered neatly on the page. The title page, on the other hand, contains the title plus the subtitle if there is one, the writer's name and corporate title, the writer's departmental affiliation, and the name of the firm. In a multiauthor report, the names of all the writers together with their corporate titles and departmental affiliations may be included on this page. If the report has been prepared for an outside client, the client's name and address also appear on the title page. Job numbers, purchase orders, or contract numbers are included as required by the individual company. The date on which the report was prepared must appear on the title page. If the report is a revision of an older work, that fact should be noted too, as "Revision A – 1983" or whatever. Sometimes key words reflecting the main topics discussed in the body of the report are appended to the title page for use in subject-coded computerized information retrieval systems. Type and spell the key words exactly as the author has written them.

Type the title in capital letters and the subtitle (if any) in capital and lowercase letters. Double-space the title and center it in the top third of the page. Add the writer's name and/or the name of the client plus any other necessary data in the bottom third of the page, positioned in such a way as to be attractively balanced. Use capital and lowercase letters for this material.

Letters of authorization and/or transmittal.   If official written authorization has been given to do a study (such as a market research survey or an engineering proposal for an outside client), the writer often includes a photocopy of that document in the front matter of the study. The photocopy should be clean with sharp contrast between typescript and paper. A letter of transmittal encapsulating the purpose, scope, and content of the study may be included if the report has been commissioned by an outside source. In effect, the letter of transmittal replies to the letter of authorization and says, "Here is what you asked for." This letter should be typed on company letterhead and signed by the writer or the person having overall responsibility for the project. Ensure that the left margin of the letter is wide enough to accommodate side binding (i.e., allow a margin of $2\frac{1}{2}''$ on the left side in documents to be sidebound).

Acknowledgments page.   When other people have assisted the writer in preparing the report, a brief notation acknowledging their help, support, and work is the right way of showing one's appreciation and crediting their efforts. Acknowledgments of this type are included on a separate page, usually styled in one or two short, single-spaced paragraphs. The word ACKNOWLEDGMENTS is typed in capital letters three lines above the text. The text paragraphs are separated by double spacing. All of this material should be centered and balanced on the page.

Table of contents.   The table of contents presents at a glance an outline of the major and subsidiary topics covered in the report together with appropriate pagination. When compiling the table of contents, you should use the major and subsidiary headings found in the body of the report. If the writer has used Roman numerals and letters to introduce the headings, include them in the table of contents. If the writer has used an all-numeric system of signaling heads in the text, use these numbers in the table of contents. Word the headings in the table of contents exactly as they are worded in the text.

The table of contents is centered on the page with ample margins all around. Double-space between headings and subheads; single-space runover lines within these headings. Headings and page numbers must be horizontally and vertically aligned. Numbers, letters, or other devices introducing heads also must be so aligned. Use a continuation sheet for a table of contents exceeding one page, and head the continuation sheet "Table of Contents – Continued", or a variation thereof. This heading should be centered and typed in capital and lowercase letters near the top of the page. Remember, however, that the title for the first contents page must be styled in capital letters, as: TABLE OF CONTENTS. The use of leaders (horizontally typed periods) to link headings with their page numbers is optional. Leaders may be set tight (i.e., typed consecutively in a line with no intervening spaces) or spaced (i.e., typed consecutively in a line with one space between each period). Leaders must align vertically as illustrated in the table of contents facsimile on pages 204–205.

Don't try to type the table of contents until the body of the report has been typed in final form and approved by the writer or writers, because last-minute changes in the text affecting pagination may render your earlier efforts fruitless.

Before typing the contents page you should check and recheck pagination, heading titles, and numerals. After the contents page has been typed, you should repeat this procedure. Have the writer check the material at least once before you release the document for duplication, printing, binding, and distribution.

Lists of graphics and tables.   The table of contents of a report containing few graphics and tables can be augmented with a short list of these features appearing at the end of the contents section. List the graphics in one section and the tables in another. Head the lists: LIST OF GRAPHICS and LIST OF TABLES. Include figure and table numbers, titles, and pagination. Reports incorporating many graphics and tables must include complete lists that are typed on separate pages and styled as above for both of these features. The format of these lists should match that of the contents page.

Foreword and/or preface.   A foreword or a preface or both may be included in a report. The foreword—written by someone other than the writer of the report itself—tells why the report was written. The preface—written by the author of the report itself—is a short statement regarding the scope and content of the study. These sections should be single-spaced on one page apiece, headed FOREWORD and PREFACE, respectively.

Executive summary.   An executive summary, sometimes called an abstract, appears on one page in the front matter. Composed of about 150 words, the executive summary encapsulates for busy readers the major issues, conclusions, and recommendations contained in the body of the report. It is also a useful device in constructing computerized report files. Type the heading EXECUTIVE SUMMARY near the top of the page. Skip three lines and begin the summary. Single-space the paragraphs of the summary, but leave two spaces between each paragraph.

The text.   The text of the report may be double- or single-spaced. Follow the writer's instructions, or, if none are forthcoming, follow your company's typing guidelines. (Many companies prefer that reports be double-spaced so that readers can add comments more easily.) Maintain even, ample margins all around. For sidebound reports maintain a left margin of 2–2½″. (See Table 12, Corporate Report Typewriting Guide, on page 196 of this subsection.) Ensure that the heads and subheads in the text have been typed exactly as the writer has indicated. Three heading systems are in common use today: freestanding headings, all-numeric headings, and Roman numeral/alphabet headings. Freestanding headings are those recommended for inclusion in the letter report:

MAIN HEADING IN CAPITAL LETTERS

<u>First-level Subhead in Underscored Capitals and Lowercase</u>

<u>Run-in subhead underscored and initially capitalized.</u>

Freestanding headings may be aligned flush with the left margin or centered on the page as explained in the section on letter reports. (Run-in tertiary heads are always set flush left.)

The all-numeric system, often employed in technical reports and proposals, features the use of decimals to signal the levels of the headings. Follow the company guidelines with regard to use of all-numeric headings.

1.0   FIRST MAIN SECTION
    1.1   FIRST MAIN SUBSECTION
    1.2   SECOND MAIN SUBSECTION
    1.3   THIRD MAIN SUBSECTION
        1.3.1   FIRST SUBUNIT
        1.3.2   SECOND SUBUNIT
        1.3.3   THIRD SUBUNIT
    1.4   FOURTH MAIN SUBSECTION
2.0   SECOND MAIN SECTION

The combined Roman numeral/alphabet system is basically the same as the general outline system followed by students when writing term papers:

I.   MAIN HEADING
    A.   Subheading
        1.   Sub-subheading
        2.   Sub-subheading
    B.   Subheading
        1.   Sub-subheading
            (a.)   Most limited subcategory
            (b.)   Most limited subcategory
        2.   Sub-subheading
II.   MAIN HEADING

Follow carefully the writer's directions when using this format. Remember that if you have a heading labeled A., 1., or (a.), you must have at least one other heading in the same set, as B., 2., or (b.). A heading in one set should never stand alone.

Some reports are really technical job proposals for outside clients. The body of a proposal usually includes some headings and subheadings excluded from non-technical business studies. They deserve brief mention here. The proposal begins with an introductory section in which the problem to be solved is defined, the objectives of the study are set forth, the proposed solution to the problem is described in steps or work phases, the resultant benefits to the client are given, and the capabilities of the contracting company are delineated. The introduction is followed by a technical operations plan—a detailed section explaining how the goals and objectives will be met and how the total program will be implemented step-by-step. Next comes the management plan detailing the project's organization—i.e., the number of personnel required, the on-going documentation to be generated (e.g., progress reports), and the quality control procedures to be maintained throughout the program. The report often concludes with the financials, a section outlining the forecast costs and fees. This basic format is augmented when necessary by other sections and subsections.

Many reports—technical and general—end with a list of conclusions and/or recommendations. These items should be listed in enumerated format. They should be block indented, single-spaced internally, and double-spaced between each other.

Table of Contents

(i)

TABLE OF CONTENTS - Continued

SECTION IV

EXHIBIT A

The First Text Page of a Lengthy Report

<u>AVAILABLE INFORMATION</u>

The Corporation is subject to the informational requirements of the Securities Exchange Act of 1934 and in accordance therewith files reports, proxy statements, and other information with the Securities and Exchange Commission (the "Commission"). Such reports, proxy statements, and other information filed by the Company can be inspected and copied at the public reference facilities maintained by the Commission at Room 1024, 450 Fifth Street, N.W., Washington, D.C. 20549 and at the Commission's regional offices at the following locations: Room 1028, 26 Federal Plaza, New York, New York 10278; Room 1228, Everett McKinley Dirkson Building, 219 South Dearborn Street, Chicago, Illinois 60604; and Suite 500, 5757 Wilshire Boulevard, Los Angeles, California 90036. Certain information filed by the Corporation with the Commission can be inspected at the Commission's regional office located at 150 Causeway Street, Boston, Massachusetts 02114. Copies of all the above-mentioned material can be obtained from the Public Reference Section of the Commission, Washington, D.C. 20549 at prescribed rates. In addition, such reports, proxy statements, and other information concerning the Corporation are available at the offices of the New York Stock Exchange, 1 Wall Street, New York, New York 10005. Additional updating information with respect to the securities covered hereby may be provided in the future to members of the Plan by means of appendices to the Prospectus.

<u>INCORPORATION OF CERTAIN DOCUMENTS BY REFERENCE</u>

Each of the following documents is incorporated by reference into this Prospectus:

(a)   The Corporation's Annual Report on Form 10-K for the year ended December 31, 19-- filed pursuant to Section 13 or 15(d) of the Securities Exchange Act of 1934.

(b)   The Plan's Annual Report on Form 11-K for the year ended December 31, 19-- filed pursuant to Section 13 or 15(d) of the Securities Exchange Act of 1934.

(c)   All other reports filed pursuant to Section 13 or 15(d) of the Securities Exchange Act of 1934 with respect to the Corporation and the Plan since the end of the fiscal year covered by the annual reports referred to in (a) and (b) above.

(d)   The Corporation's definitive Proxy Statement filed pursuant to Section 14 of the Securities Exchange Act of 1934 in connection with the latest Annual Meeting of Stock-holders of the Corporation and any definitive proxy state-ment so filed in connection with any subsequent Special Meeting of Stockholders.

The First Main Section of a Lengthy Report with Flush-left Paragraphs

SECTION I

XYZ CORPORATION
EMPLOYEES' SAVINGS AND THRIFT PLAN

1. <u>General</u>

The "XYZ Corporation Employees' Savings and Thrift Plan" (the "Plan")
has been established to encourage retirement savings by participating
employees ("Members") of the Corporation and of designated
subsidiaries and affiliates of the Corporation. Commencing January 1,
1984, such savings shall be effected by means of pre-tax salary
adjustment arrangements. The Corporation will also make matching
contributions to the Plan in an amount based upon certain savings by
Members. The Corporation also expects to make an additional
contribution to the Plan on behalf of each eligible Member based upon
its employee stock ownership tax credit. The amount of this
additional ESOP contribution is based upon the total combined
compensation of all eligible Members of the year. All of the
Corporation's matching and ESOP contributions will be invested in
Common Stock of the Corporation, and all or part of Members' savings
may be so invested. All contributions and savings will be held in
trust and invested by Bank of New England, N.A., Trustee of the Plan.
An "Employees' Savings and Thrift Plan Committee" (the "Committee"),
appointed by the Board of Directors of the Corporation, will supervise
and administer the Plan.

The Plan will form part of the Corporation's program for providing
competitive benefits for its employees. The operation of the Plan is
expected to encourage employees to make added provision, through
savings on a pre-tax basis, for their retirement income. It will also
encourage employees to participate in ownership of the Corporation's
Common Stock. The Board of Directors believes that the Plan will
provide an additional incentive to employees to contribute to the
continued success of the Corporation and will be in the best interests
of the Corporation and its stockholders.

The Plan is subject to the provisions of the Employee Retirement
Income Security Act of 1974, as amended ("ERISA"), including reporting
and disclosure obligations to Plan participants, fiduciary obligations
of Plan administrators, and minimum participation and vesting
requirements. The benefit insurance coverage established by Title IV
of ERISA does not provide protection for benefits payable under the
Plan, and the funding requirement under Title I or ERISA are also
inapplicable.

A summary of the Plan's provisions follows. This summary is qualified
in its entirety by reference to the text of the Plan which is appended
as Exhibit A hereto.

3

Headings and Subheadings in a Lengthy Report

15.   <u>Tax Consequences</u>

The Internal Revenue Service has ruled that the Plan qualifies as a
profit sharing plan under Section 401(a) of the Code. The Corporation
will submit the Plan, as amended, to the Internal Revenue Service to
obtain a determination as to whether the Plan, as amended, continues
to qualify under Section 401(a) of the Code, whether the provisions of
the Plan relating to salary adjustment contributions qualify under
Section 401(k) of the Code and whether the provisions of the Plan
relating to the employee stock ownership credit qualify under Section
409A of the Code. So long as the Plan so qualifies under the Code,
the Federal tax consequences to Members under present laws as
understood by the Corporation may be summarized as follows:

(a)   Contributions made to the Plan by the Corporation on your
behalf pursuant to your salary adjustment election, and
any earnings on such amounts, are not includable in
your taxable income until such amounts are returned to
you either as a withdrawal or distribution. At that
time, the entire amount of your distribution in excess
of your pre-19-- after-tax contributions to the Plan is
subject to Federal income tax because none of this
money was previously taxed.

(b)   Any earnings on your pre-19-- after-tax contributions
to the Plan are not taxable to you until returned to
you either as a withdrawal or distribution. Since your
after-tax contributions were subject to Federal
income tax when made, such contributions are not
subject to Federal income tax when distributed or
withdrawn.

(c)   Corporation matching contributions and Corporation ESOP
contributions, and any earnings on such amounts, are not
taxable to you until distributed or withdrawn.

The tax deferral aspect of the Plan can result in some
important tax advantages for you.

(1)   If you wait until you retire to receive funds out
of the Plan, your tax rate may be lower. Retired
persons generally--though not always--have lower
incomes than they had while working, so their tax
rates tend to be lower.

(2)   If, upon retirement or other termination of
employment, you (or your beneficiary) receive a
lump sum distribution from the Plan and part or
all of such distribution is in the form of shares
of Common Stock instead of cash, a portion of the
tax (on net unrealized appreciation) may be
postponed until these shares are actually sold and

11

Appendix Format

SECTION IV

APPENDIX

The information in this Appendix will be updated from time
to time. Be sure to refer to the most current Appendix.

1. Current Administrative Information

The present members of the Employees' Savings and Thrift Plan
Committee are John M. Roe, Jane T. Smith, Martin I. Miller, Joseph L.
Edge, Sally A. Harris, Leila B. Summers, and John T. Williams.

Harry B. Selkirk and Lewis K. Callahan, Directors of the Corporation, are also directors of Bank of New England Corporation, the
parent company of Bank of New England, N. A., Trustee of the Plan.

2. Members of the Plan

As of December 31, 19--, there were 999 employees participating in the Plan, out of a total number of approximately 1,600
employees eligible to participate. As of July 1, 19--, there
were 981 employees participating out of 1,500 eligible.

3. Fund A Minimum Rates

The present minimum rates of interest for contributions to
Fund A during the following years are set forth below. These
rates are in each case guaranteed for five years:

19--	11.5%
19--	10.75%
19--	10%

4. Investment Performance

(a) The table below shows values for shares of the Corporation's Common Stock in Fund B as of the indicated dates, which
are based upon the quoted New York Stock Exchange closing prices
for such shares at the indicated dates.

Valuation Date	Fund B Price per Share of Common Stock of the Corporation *
December 31, 19--	$11.750
December 31, 19--	$19.375
August 31, 19--	$22.500

*Adjusted for 2-for-1 split on July 3, 19--

18

Appendix.   An appendix containing ancillary charts, graphs, illustrations, and tables may be included in the report. The appendix appears before any other back matter sections such as footnotes, a bibliography, a glossary, or an index. Introduce the appendix in capital letters; for example, a centered format:

APPENDIX

TRADE DIVISION FORECAST

VOLUME BY TITLE

1984–1985

The material appears on a separate page as shown above. Multiple appendices should be separately listed on a page as APPENDIX A, APPENDIX B, and so on. Some companies call this section a LIST OF EXHIBITS instead.

Footnotes and bibliographies.   Chapter Eleven provides detailed guidelines to the proper styling of footnotes and bibliographies. Hence, the forthcoming paragraphs concentrate only on mechanical typewriting conventions for reference sources in a report. Keep in mind these general points when preparing footnotes to a long report:

1. Footnotes may appear at the bottom of the pages on which the quoted passages occur or they may be listed separately at the end of the report. Separate listing is the easiest from the typist's standpoint.

2. Footnotes are signaled within the running text by raised Arabic numerals positioned just after the quoted passage with no space intervening. Type the raised numeral after the final quotation mark:

   ```
   ''. . . indicates an instability in an otherwise
   static market.''10
   ```

3. Number the footnotes consecutively throughout the report if they are to be listed together at the end. If the report is particularly long with many major sections in which the notes have been listed on the pages where the quoted matter is found, renumber them with the start of each new section. Be sure to check and recheck the numerals for proper sequence.

4. The first line of a footnote is indented from three to six lines and runover lines are aligned flush with the left margin. The footnote is introduced by a raised numeral keyed to the appropriate quoted text passage with one space intervening, or it may be introduced by the numeral and a period all aligned on the same line as the note itself. The latter method makes for easier typing. Footnotes may be single-spaced internally, with double spacing separating them from one another. They should be double-spaced internally with triple spacing separat-

ing them from one another if the report is to be published in typeset form. Examples:

> [10] Thomas J. Peters and Robert H. Waterman, Jr., *In Search of Excellence: Lessons from America's Best-Run Companies* (New York: Harper & Row, 1982), p. 8.

or with aligned numerals:

> 10. Thomas J. Peters and Robert H. Waterman, Jr., *In Search of Excellence: Lessons from America's Best-Run Companies* (New York: Harper & Row, 1982), p. 8.

The bibliography lists alphabetically the sources used by the writer. Chapter Eleven provides specific style guidelines for bibliographies from the standpoint of business English. The forthcoming paragraphs focus solely on points of typing style. Remember these points when typing a bibliography (note that the entries are ordered alphabetically by author surname):

1. The bibliography, entitled WORKS CITED or BIBLIOGRA-PHY, appears on a separate page in the back matter.

2. The bibliography is hanging-indented: the first line of each entry is set flush left with runovers indented by five or six spaces.

3. Bibliography entries, like footnotes, are unnumbered.

4. Bibliography entries, like footnotes, may be single-spaced internally with double spacing separating them from one another, or they may be double-spaced internally with triple spacing separating them from one another. Use the latter approach if the report is to be typeset for outside publication. Examples:

> Katzan, Harry Jr. *Office Automation: A Manager's Guide.* New York: AMACOM, 1982.
>
> Peters, Thomas J. and Robert H. Waterman, Jr. *In Search of Excellence: Lessons from America's Best-Run Companies.* New York: Harper & Row, 1982.

Index. You may be asked to type an index for a very long, detailed study. The index lists alphabetically all major and subsidiary topics covered in the report along with applicable page numbers. An index is developed by reading through the text and circling all major and subsidiary headings plus all key words in the report. Each circled item is written on a 3" × 5" card together with the page number. The cards are ordered alphabetically and the page numbers and subjects rechecked. The writer then constructs from the cards a draft index.

The main components of an index are main entries, subentries, sub-subentries, and cross-entries. A main entry is a prime subject category usually corresponding to a main heading in the text. A main entry includes a heading and often (but not always) a page number. It is typed flush with the left margin:

Input systems
  for computers, 22, 53–63
  optical character recognition
    for, 16
Input/output units, 53–63

In the example, *Input systems* and *Input/output units* are main entries. Note that the first word of the main entry is initially capitalized, while the other words are lowercased unless they are proper nouns, proper adjectives, or trademarks. Main entries are alphabetically ordered by the first key word.

A subentry represents a topic of secondary importance. It appears under the main entry with which it is associated. Subentries, ordered alphabetically by the first key word, are indented by three spaces. Subentries, like main entries, are composed of headings and page numbers. Subentries are lowercased throughout unless they contain proper nouns, proper adjectives, or trademarks. In the previously shown example, *for computers* and *optical character recognition for* are subentries.

A sub-subentry is a topic of tertiary importance. It appears under the subentry with which it is associated:

Communications, 80–108
  electronic mail systems for, 80–90,
    100–101
      Telex in, 91–92

In the example, *Telex* (a proper noun) is the sub-subentry under *electronic mail systems.* The alphabetically ordered sub-subentries, indented by three spaces, are usually lowercased unless they contain proper nouns, proper adjectives, or trademarks.

Cross-entries direct the reader from one point in the index to another related point where more information is to be found:

Diskettes. <u>See also</u> Floppy disks.
  in word processing systems, 42–81.

In the example, <u>See also</u> Floppy disks is a cross-entry. When the reader turns to the main entry *Floppy disks,* more information is at hand:

Floppy disks (diskettes), 22–32
  microdiskette, 25–32
  minidiskette, 23–24
  standard, 22

Cross-entries are introduced by the underscored and initially capitalized words <u>See also</u> followed by the main entry to which the reader is referred in initial capital letters (i.e., Floppy disks), followed by a period.

Two commonly used index formats are the indented and the run-in. The writer should indicate which of the two indexing formats is to be used. The indented format (used in our earlier examples) is preferable, for it provides quicker information retrieval. Note that each entry is typed on a separate line:

Disk storage media, 85–95
  operating systems on, 96
  software on, 94
  in word processing systems, 42, 82–90

The run-in format occupies less page space but is more difficult for the reader to use since all subentries are run in together:

Disk storage media: 85–95;
  operating systems on, 96;
  software on, 94; in word
  processing systems, 42,
  82–90

An index features minimal punctuation. Follow these guidelines for punctuating index entries:

1. Use a comma between an entry and any term(s) modifying it and between an entry and the page number relating to it:

    Disk storage media, 85–95
      in word processing systems, 42, 82–90
    Disks, standard, 22–24

2. Use a semicolon to separate entries only in the run-in index:

    Disk storage media: 85–95;
      operating systems on, 96;
      . . . .

3. Use a colon after a main entry just before its pagination only in the run-in index:

    Disk storage media: 85–95;
      . . . .

4. Terminate a cross-entry with a period; do not use periods elsewhere:

    See also CRT.

Tables, graphics, and other visual aids.   All visual aids should be titled either in capital letters or in capital and lowercase letters, and sequentially numbered: FIGURE 1, FIGURE 2; TABLE 1, TABLE 2, and so on. Titles may be centered or positioned flush left. Select one style and stick to it for the sake of consistency.

Word processors with graphics capabilities have alleviated most of the drudgery in preparing tabular and graphic exhibits. However, you must have a feel for the length of the table as it will appear in typewritten form and the approximate number of character spaces to be allowed between columns so that you can instruct the machine properly. In general, six character spaces are allowed between columns, especially in tables that are to be typed horizontally. Tables involving more than four columns are generally set up horizontally—that is, the standard page is flipped on its side. The title of the table should appear at the top (i.e., along what used to be the left margin of the vertical sheet) and the end of the table should appear at the bottom (i.e., along what used to be the right margin of the vertical sheet). In this way, the tabular data will face outside and not toward the gutter of the bound report.

Tabular entries and subentries can be capitalized in their entirety, capitalized and lowercased by key word, initially capitalized, or lowercased in their entirety. Main headings are usually capitalized in their entirety as shown in the next example. Once you have selected a style, stick to it throughout all of the tables for the sake of consistency:

TOTAL NET SALES
MANUFACTURING COSTS
ROYALTY EXPENSES
TOTAL COST OF SALES
  % of net
EXPENSES
  Editorial
  Plate
  Sales
  Advertising
  Fulfillment
  Administration

In the previous example, the capitalized items are considered main entries and the indented, capitalized and lowercased entries are considered secondary to the main entries. Secondary entries can be indented as shown here or set flush with the left margin. Choose one style and adhere to it.

Numerical data in tables must be aligned to the right, as:

UNIT SALES TO DATE
12,700
34,000
 6,000
   765

Tabular entries consisting of numerals and symbols such as plus and minus signs, percentage signs, or dollar signs must be aligned vertically. Decimal points also must be so aligned:

$800,000.00	− 14 points	45.9%
4,000.98	− 12 points	6.4%
55,896.00	− 33 points	28.0%
564.34	+ 12 points	60.2%

Avoid the use of vertical and horizontal rules in tables constructed on conventional machines: while the horizontal rules can be done easily on the machine, the vertical ones will have to be drawn in by hand, and hand-drawn rules often look messy.

If the table exceeds one page in length, type a continued heading in capital and lowercase letters, as: "Table 3, continued" and center it on the page. Continue typing the tabular data, using the same tabbing and margins as those on the first sheet. Maintain consistent entry and subentry style.

Displayed lists are useful especially in executive summaries and in sections detailing conclusions and/or recommendations, for the displayed matter is clearly visible to the busy reader. Use of the lowercase o followed by one space and the text is a neat way of presenting important data (a spaced period also can be used in this manner to highlight significant data):

∘ Generating business information
∘ Analyzing business information
∘ Transmitting/distributing business information

Sometimes the writer will include pie charts and graphs to illustrate points made in the body of the report. These should be roughed out by the writer and then submitted to the company's special media department for professional production. In a company lacking such a support department you may be called on to assist the writer in preparing these visual aids. If so, you'll need the following materials: press-on or contact tone sheets, rules, and letters (available in a graphic arts supply store); T-square, ruler, and compass; nonrepro blue pencil or pen; designer's fine-line black pen; rubber cement or a glue stick; art gum; scissors; artist's knife (sharp, triangular blade); graph paper; and hard-finish drawing paper. Graphs are usually laid out as rectangles on an average scale of 4:3 or 7:4. The title may appear at the top or bottom entirely in capitals or in capital and lowercase letters. Choose one style and stick to it. Position the labels and key lines horizontally on the page for easy reading. You can typewrite the title, labels, and key lines or you can use the press-on letters available in art supply houses. If you use the press-on letters (or numbers) be sure to choose a size compatible with the overall size of the graph. Letters that are too large look horsey and detract from the visual impact of the illustration. With line graphs you can ink in the lines by hand or you can use the press-on rules available in art stores. The press-on rules come on rolls. Using the nonrepro blue pencil or pen and a ruler, draw in the lines of the graph. Using the artist's knife, cut the press-on rules to fit the outline of the graphed matter. Pull off the backing and affix the rules where appropriate. With bar graphs, you will need press-on tone sheets showing, for instance, dark areas, striped areas, or dotted areas. Many different styles and designs are available. Using the nonrepro pencil or pen and a ruler, measure and construct the various bars called for. Using the artist's knife and the ruler, cut the tone sheets to fit the various bars, peel off the backing, and affix the tones to the graph. You also can shade the bars by hand, but hand shading does not look as professional as the tone-sheet shading. Ensure that there is a color/tone separation of at least 30% between different shadings and tints in the graph; otherwise the shadings and tints will all look alike when reproduced in black-and-white. The press-on sheets usually contain color separation percentages.

The pie (or circle) chart is a useful way of depicting percentages, say, of corporate growth or market shares. Use a compass fitted with a nonrepro blue pencil to construct the circle. Then use the compass to mark off sectors in degrees corresponding to the desired percentages. Typically used percentage values of a circle are these:

360°	=	100%
180°	=	50%
90°	=	25%
36°	=	10%
18°	=	5%
3.6°	=	1%

Cut the press-on tone sheets to fit the marked-off sectors of the circle and then affix them to the chart. Use press-on letters and numbers to label the sectors. If the color/tone contrast between the parts of the circle and the labels is adequate you can insert the labels within the circle itself. But if the contrast is inadequate or if space is tight, you should put the labels outside the circle and use press-on key lines or arrows to connect the labels with the applicable sectors of the circle.

How to make an overhead.   Before attempting to make an overhead audiovisual, also called a *transparency*, make sure that the brand you plan to use is appropriate for the copying machine you have at hand. The packaging for the transparencies will list the machines and model numbers in which that brand of transparency can be used. For example, some copiers require transparencies to bear a white sensing strip. Additionally, you must determine which way the white strip should face when you load the tray; loading the transparencies the wrong way may result in the machine becoming jammed.

Once you have read the instructions for the brand of transparency you are using, you are ready to begin. Follow these procedures:

1. Load the transparencies properly on top of a moderate base of paper in the paper tray.

2. Secure the paper tray.

3. Set the machine for one copy.

4. Place the document that is to be made into a transparency on the glass in the correct image area for $8\frac{1}{2}" \times 11"$ paper.

5. Close the cover.

6. Activate the machine.

7. Always allow for one transparency to be processed through the copier and dropped into the output tray before activating the machine again.

8. Delete imaged areas with perchloroethylene (tetrachloroethylene) or the suggested solution for the particular brand if corrections must be made. New data may be added with a grease pencil or solvent marker.

Transparencies are made of plastic film, and therefore will not perform with the same high reliability as plain paper. The toner image cannot penetrate into the transparent film, so be careful not to scratch the finished transparency. If the copier jams more than twice during a single job, the problem is probably with the machine. In these cases, a repairperson should be called. Should the copier become jammed, find the defective transparency (look carefully on the drum if it is nowhere else to be found) and remove it. If you cannot find the transparency, *do not operate the copier* until a repairperson has serviced the machine.

You may notice a thin oily coating on the transparency. This is normal and will eventually wear off. You can remove it by gently wiping both sides of the transparency with a dry tissue or by moistening the tissue with rubbing alcohol. You should note that this oily coating contains silicone which can cause irritation to your eyes if contact is made. Should this happen, flush your eyes thoroughly with clean water.

One other point: before attempting to make the transparency you should ensure that the chart, table, or other information to be displayed has been typed or drawn in such a way as to fit the screen size of the audiovisual machine (overhead projector) to be used. Cardboard mats similar to the ones used in picture frames are available in various sizes keyed to the projectors; a common size is $7\frac{1}{2}" \times 10"$. Using a nonrepro blue pencil, you can draw this measure around the material to be reproduced, thus ensuring inclusion of all data.

MAKING INVISIBLE CORRECTIONS IN YOUR DOCUMENTS

All of us make occasional typographical errors, and writers often wish to reword their communications after seeing them in typewritten form. Minor errors are easily corrected in most instances but rewordings often require complete retypes. Documents input into word processing memory are easily edited and corrected with no sign of the changes visible on the final printouts, but this is not necessarily the case with material typed on conventional equipment. The truly professional typist knows how to get the most out of the correction products currently available so as to produce perfect documents.

In the 1980s it would be ridiculous to include in a discussion of correction products the use of the knife and the eraser when so many better materials are on the market. The knife pits and cuts the paper and the eraser digs into the surface of the paper, damaging its texture and resulting in distorted retyped characters. Smudges also can occur due to the effort generated in attempting such corrections. Secretaries now rely on correction fluid, correction strips, tabs, and tapes; and self-correcting typewriter ribbons. A brief summary of these materials follows.

Correction fluid employs fast-drying enamel in white or in blended color tones that is gently brushed over an error to render it invisible. Shake the bottle vigorously before attempting to apply the fluid. Test the consistency of the fluid by putting a tiny dot of it onto a piece of scratch paper. If the liquid is too thick, add some thinner and reshake. You also might consider cleaning the little brush with thinner to remove globs of thick, partially dried fluid. Test the fluid consistency again. Thick application of correcting fluid results in distorted characters, obliterations, peel-off characters, damaged paper, and, over time, a build-up of dried shards within the workings of your typewriter. When making the correction, roll the paper bail forward and the carriage to the far left or right for easier access to the error. Put a tiny dot of fluid onto each incorrect character. Correct each character one at a time for best results. Do not attack an entire word, a whole line, or several characters all at once like a floor painter. Allow the fluid to dry for 8–10 seconds before retyping. Typing onto wet fluid will cause very dark distorted characters. Special correction fluid for use on photocopies is also available.

Tackless lift-off correction tabs are particularly desirable with film typewriter ribbons. When an error has been made you simply backspace to it, insert the correction tab with the coated side placed down directly onto the error, retype the incorrect character, and then remove the tab. The error has been "lifted off." You then backspace and type the correct character. The correction is invisible.

Self-correcting film typewriter ribbons work on the same principle as the lift-off tabs, but you must depress a special correction key in order to backspace to the error. You restrike the last incorrect character to delete it. The self-correcting film ribbon with a lift-off tape removes the error. You then proceed to type the correct character. The correction is invisible.

Chalk-coated correction papers are also handy, but the corrections that they make are not permanent. After a certain period of time the chalk will flake off, the original error will show up, and the correction site will look like a strikeover. Chalk-coated correction papers can be used for drafts and documents having short-term shelf lives. You backspace to the error, insert the paper chalk-side down onto the error, restrike the error, remove the paper, backspace, and type the correct character.

Self-adhesive correction tapes are available in one- and two-line widths. You pull off the desired length of tape, cut it, remove the backing strip, and affix the tape to the page, thereby covering the error or errors. The tape is useful only in documents destined for typesetters. Avoid using it on documents to be photocopied, for the stripping marks will show through on the photocopies. Never use the tape on an outgoing original.

7

Records Management in Conventional and Automated Settings

William Saffady, PhD • *Associate Professor, Department of Library and Information Science, Peabody College, Vanderbilt University; Editor,* Micrographics Equipment Review, Computer Equipment Review, *and* The International File of Micrographics Equipment and Accessories; *Author,* The Automated Office: An Introduction to the Technology, *and* Video-based Information Systems

INTRODUCTION

Definitions

Records management is that field of information management which is concerned with the systematic analysis and control of the operating records created or maintained by businesses, government agencies, nonprofit institutions, and other organizations. As used in this context, the term *records* denotes a wide variety of information carriers. Since its inception in the late 1940s and early 1950s, records management has emphasized the analysis and control of paper documents ranging from 3″ × 5″ index cards to engineering drawings and charts measuring 3′ × 4′ or larger. In the United States, the vast majority of office documents are letter-size (8½″ × 11″), legal-size (8½″ × 14″) or, increasingly, computer printout size (11″ × 14″). These records can be a valuable resource and a source of problems at the same time. They contain information essential to decision-making and daily work routines, but their maintenance in paper form can require large numbers of filing cabinets and significant amounts of expensive floor space. In addition, the organization of paper files for effective retrieval by subjects or other parameters is a complex task. Finally, records in any form are vulnerable to loss resulting from disaster, inadvertent destruction, theft, misfiling, or mishandling. The records management methodologies discussed in this chapter are designed to address these problems.

While paper documents remain its primary focus, records management is increasingly concerned with problems of information storage and handling posed by nonpaper records. Such nonpaper records include photographic negatives and prints, microforms, and videotapes. Similarly, the floppy disks, tape cassettes, and other machine-readable magnetic media created by word processors, microcomputers, and other automated office systems constitute an increasingly important records category. Large quantities of machine-readable records, in the form of magnetic disks and tapes, are likewise maintained by centralized computing facilities, and such records account for a rapidly growing percentage of most organizations' information resources. Like their paper counterparts, photographic and machine-readable records require appropriate storage facilities, must be carefully organized for effective retrieval, and must be protected from inadvertent damage or destruction. On the positive side, however, they permit the development and implementation of paperless information systems that can minimize or eliminate many traditional records management problems. Examples of such systems are discussed in later sections of this chapter.

The Secretary's Role

As mentioned above, interest in records management as a formal discipline dates from the late 1940s and has steadily intensified as expanded business and government activities—combined with the widespread use of copiers, computers, word processors, and other information processing machines—have increased the volume of record production and the complexity of record-keeping activities. Today, records management is a multifaceted discipline drawing on methodologies and technologies developed in a variety of related fields, including data processing, information science, industrial engineering, library science, and business administration. Consequently, a records management program can include many elements, and it is often difficult to separate clearly records management from other information processing activities. In many organizations, records managers supervise duplicating services, the mail room, word processing centers, or related administrative services—the rationale being that such activities create, receive, and/or distribute records which eventually become a records management responsibility.

The structure of records management programs is likewise varied. Some mid- to large-sized corporations, government agencies, or other organizations have formal centralized records management programs staffed by one or more full-time professionals. In such organizations, departmental secretaries typically serve as liaison persons who provide the records management staff with essential information about departmental files and record-keeping requirements. They assist in the preparation of records inventories, implement record retention schedules, prepare records for transmittal to off-site storage, identify potential microfilming applications, and assist in the selection of filing equipment and the development of filing systems. In most departments, the secretary is the person most familiar with record-keeping practices, and the liaison role is critical to the success of a records management program. In many smaller organizations—and some larger ones—there is no formal records management program. Consequently, the individual secretaries must assume full responsibility for records management activities in their departments. While some aspects of records management require specialized technical expertise, many records management concepts are based on common sense and an orderly approach to problem solving characteristic of much of the professional secretary's work. The following sections explain the major facets of a records management program and provide guidelines for their implementation by secretaries working in a broad range of office environments.

MANAGING INACTIVE RECORDS

The Problem of Inactive Records

Most records management programs include a combination of elements designed to address the problems of both active and inactive records. Used in this context, activity and inactivity are determined—in admittedly imprecise fashion—by the frequency with which given groups of records are referenced. While some documents may be referenced on a daily basis, most records are actively referenced only for a brief initial period of time. As an example, correspondence, memorandums, and other routine office documents are usually referenced once or twice shortly after creation but may never be consulted again. Similarly, legal case records, insurance claim files, medical history files, technical project files, and other such documents may remain unused for months or years after the termination of a given transaction or activity, but later may be referenced frequently if and when the matters to which they pertain require further action.

But while they are not needed to support daily operations, many inactive records must be retained for some period of time to meet legal requirements, in anticipation of possible future reference, or—in some cases—because of their historical or research significance. Too often, however, these inactive records accumulate in office work areas or central file rooms where they are stored along with active records in expensive filing cabinets occupying valuable floor space. Department heads and other managers are too often unaware of the economic implications of such practices, but the facts are clear: in early 1984, prices for ordinary, four-drawer, vertical-style, letter-size file cabinets ranged from $200.00 to $400.00, depending on cabinet depth, quality of construction, and appearance. Prices for larger cabinets, lateral-style cabinets, or fireproof models are much higher. A single letter-size file cabinet occupies 7 to 8 square feet of office floor space at $15.00 to $60.00 per square foot, depending on office type and geographic location. Larger cabinets require proportionally greater amounts of space. Depending on document thickness, the number and type of folders and guides utilized, and the amount of working space allotted per drawer, the typical four-drawer, vertical-style filing cabinet can accommodate 8,000 to 14,000 sheets of paper. To put this storage capacity in perspective, the typical medium-volume office copier generates enough paper in one month to fill two such cabinets, and the output of some high-speed computer printers will fill two such cabinets per half day.

To complicate matters further, file cabinets crowded with large quantities of inactive records can prove difficult to use. It is much easier, for example, to misfile papers in crowded cabinets and more difficult to find lost items. It is likewise more difficult to establish and maintain well-organized filing systems in crowded cabinets, and the resulting wasted clerical time and effort can significantly increase the expense of office operations.

The Records Inventory

Even though inactive records are not frequently referenced, they may contain important information that must be retained and protected. While it is difficult to justify the expense of filing inactive records in expensive cabinets occupying valuable floor space, they cannot simply be piled up in closets or basements where they are inaccessible and vulnerable to inadvertent destruction. To reduce existing floor space requirements and/or provide space for future file growth without corresponding increases in file cabinet purchases and floor space consumption, useless inactive records must be identified and discarded. Inactive records of continuing value can be microfilmed or transferred to economical off-site storage for appropriate periods of time. A systematic records inventory is the essential first step in the implementation of such procedures. The purpose of a records inventory is to identify and determine the extent of an organization's inactive records. As discussed in the following section, information acquired during the inventory will be used in the preparation of record retention and disposal schedules.

In organizations with formal centralized records management programs, individual departmental secretaries are typically asked to complete inventory worksheets specifically designed to gather essential data about the department's records. In some cases, the records management staff will also interview secretaries and other department members. In the absence of a centralized records management program, individual secretaries must prepare their own survey instruments and conduct their own inventories. In either case, records are commonly inventoried at the series level, where a record series is a group of related documents supporting a common activity and, in most cases, having a common name. Examples of widely encountered record series include general correspondence, budget reports, purchase orders, and personnel files, but every department will have some series that are unique to it and reflect its special mission. For each series, the following information is commonly collected:

1. the name by which the series is known to department members and other users

2. the form name and number if the series consists of standardized forms

3. a brief description and statement of purpose, indicating the functions that the series supports

4. physical location—that is, the address of the office or other facility where the records are stored

5. inclusive dates

6. physical format: paper, microfilm, videotape, floppy disks, etc.

7. the arrangement of documents or other records within the series—for example, alphabetical by patient name for a medical record series or numeric by claim number for a series of insurance files

8. series volume, expressed in terms of the number, type, and condition of the file cabinets or storage containers occupied by the records

9. annual growth rate, typically estimated by comparing file segments for different years or, if necessary, by counting documents from a representative sample of the series

10. physical attributes, such as the size of documents or other media, condition, color, and texture

11. frequency of reference and names of user departments

In most cases, this information can be determined by carefully examining the records themselves and/or interviewing department members or other users. If desired, inventory results can be summarized on a tabular worksheet listing individual series in rows and containing the categories of information in columns.

Records Scheduling

As indicated above, the records inventory provides information used in the formulation of record retention and disposal schedules. A retention and disposal schedule is a listing that specifies the periods of time for which given record series are to be retained and, if appropriate, the storage location and format. For records to be discarded, it further specifies the date, and, where special security precautions are required, the mode of destruction.

A retention and disposal schedule is a procedural document recognizing that the records created and/or maintained by an organization are its property and are not to be discarded without proper authorization. Properly formulated, retention and disposal schedules will ensure the retention of useful records for appropriate periods of time while preventing the unwarranted accumulation of obsolete records. Retention and disposal schedules are an essential element in any space conservation program and can yield significant reductions in future filing cabinet purchases. When applied to machine-readable records, they also can facilitate the recycling of floppy disks and other magnetic media. By specifying storage locations and formats, retention and disposal schedules provide a framework for the systematic use of off-site storage facilities and microfilm technology.

Organizations with formal centralized records management programs sometimes utilize "document-oriented" or general retention and disposal schedules that list documents by name or type without regard to the specific departments or offices in which they are maintained. These general schedules provide broad retention guidelines for correspondence, purchase orders, travel expense reports, and similar widely used documents. They can be particularly effective for the standardized business forms used throughout an organization, but they cannot accommodate variations in retention requirements among different offices and do not include those record series unique to individual departments. As a supplement or alternative, "activity-oriented" retention and disposal schedules are specifically designed for individual departments or offices and list the records maintained by only that department or office. Such activity-oriented schedules are necessarily more time-consuming to prepare than document-oriented schedules, but they usually result in more comprehensive and effective retention parameters.

Whether general or activity-oriented schedules are employed, each record series or document type is subject to one of three broad groups of retention parameters:

1. Short-term retention: Many records are needed for a brief period but have little continuing utility and will be discarded a short time—perhaps several months to two years—after their creation or receipt. Such records are typically retained in office locations until discarded.

2. Medium-term retention: Other records must be retained for a specified period of time—perhaps for one to ten years—but eventually will be discarded. Such records are often retained in office locations during a relatively brief initial period of active reference and, when reference activity subsides, are transferred to lower-cost, off-site storage facilities from which they are eventually discarded.

3. Long-term retention: A final, often large, group of records must be retained indefinitely. In many cases, such records are microfilmed to save space and the original paper documents discarded. The microfilm versions may be stored in office locations or off-site, depending on anticipated reference activity.

Three broad groups of criteria—legal/fiscal, administrative, and research—are utilized to assign specific record series to one of the above retention parameters. While legal/fiscal criteria receive much publicity, only a small percentage of federal, state, and local laws and regulations specify retention periods for particular types of records, and relevant record retention laws are often difficult to identify and interpret. Legally mandated retention periods are most commonly encountered in industries such as banking or pharmaceuticals, and in activities such as waste disposal or pension fund management, all of which are subject to government regulation. For federal record retention regulations, the most comprehensive source of information is the *Code of Federal Regulations (CFR)*, published by the National Archives and Records Service and updated in weekly issues of the *Federal Register*. In some cases, government contracts awarded to businesses, universities, or other organizations also contain specific record retention provisions. At the state level, record retention requirements are implied by statutes of limitations specifying maximum time periods for legal actions. These statutes vary considerably from state to state. The *Uniform Commercial Code*, which is accepted by most states, likewise places limitations on breach of contract actions and on the legal utility of records retained in support of such actions.

In the absence of specific legal mandates, most record retention decisions are based on anticipated administrative reference requirements to support both daily operations and long-term goals. Even where laws or regulations mandating retention exist, administrative requirements may prove more stringent and warrant longer retention for specific record series. The most effective administrative retention decisions are based on previous reference experience with particular record series. In some cases, the continuing administrative utility of specific records can be established with confidence. Too often, however, records are retained by default. In the absence of reliable information about previous reference activity, their anticipated reference value cannot be assessed, and the organization is reluctant to discard them. Since record destruction is irreversible, many records managers prefer such a conservative approach. In some organizations, a small percentage of records are retained for their historical or other research significance. Such records typically document important programs or events, the activities of important persons, or the formulation of significant public or business policies.

Where a formal records management program exists, individual departmental secretaries can provide valuable information about reference activity and anticipated administrative value to assist the records management staff in the formulation of appropriate retention periods for various record series. In some organizations, secretaries are asked to draft preliminary retention and disposal schedules for discussion, modification, and eventual approval by the records management unit, department heads, and other appropriate persons. In the absence of a formal records management program, the secretaries must prepare retention schedules for their own departments. Records management textbooks available at bookstores and libraries often include retention recommendations for commonly encountered records and summarize federal and state regulations pertaining to record retention. Publications dealing with record retention and related records management concerns are likewise available from the Association of Records Managers and Administrators (ARMA), the Association for Information and Image Management (AIIM), and other professional groups. By attending the meetings of local ARMA or AIIM chapters, secretaries can make valuable contacts with records managers in other companies and often can obtain useful advice about their common record retention problems. In most cases, the determination of research value requires special training, and some organizations employ archivists or other persons with appropriate scholarly backgrounds for this purpose.

Once formulated, retention and disposal schedules must be revised periodically as new records series are created and experience warrants modification of previously established retention periods. The annual review of retention schedules is strongly recommended. The actual implementation of retention schedules is typically the secretary's responsibility. Some secretaries prefer to allot a specific period of time during the summer or other slack periods for this purpose. In some organizations, the records management unit performs compliance audits to determine that retention schedules are being appropriately implemented.

Record Centers

As mentioned in the foregoing discussion of retention parameters, most organizations maintain some medium-term records needing to be retained for a specified period of time, but not needing to be retained in valuable office space. Assuming that reference to them is minimal, such records can be transferred to lower-cost, off-site storage facilities. A record center is a warehouse-type facility designed specifically for the economical storage of inactive, medium-term records pending their eventual destruction. Records are transferred to the center as indicated in retention and disposal schedules. In most cases, the center will not accept records lacking a specific destruction date. In this respect, a record center differs from archives providing permanent storage for records of enduring value. Although some record centers do provide vaults or other special facilities for the long-term storage of microfilm or machine-readable records, the vast majority of records transferred to a record center will be destroyed after a specified period of time, thereby making room for the receipt of additional items.

Record center storage economies are based on a combination of location and density. In urban areas, record centers are often located in basements or other relatively inexpensive space unsuitable for general office use. As an alternative, a record center may occupy a separate building located in suburban or rural areas at some distance from offices where active records are maintained. Rather than constructing or refurbishing their own record center buildings, some organizations rent space within an existing commercial warehouse facility and install shelving to meet record storage requirements. Commercial record centers, located in many medium-sized to large metropolitan areas, are equipped with appropriate shelving and other facilities that are rented on an as-needed basis.

Within a record center itself, storage density is maximized by combining floor-to-ceiling shelving with standardized cardboard containers. The most widely used record center container has interior dimensions of $10'' \times 12'' \times 15''$ and can store approximately one cubic foot of records (the equivalent of about one third to one half of a file cabinet drawer). This container, routinely available from a number of manufacturers and office supply houses, is suitable for the storage of the three most commonly encountered sizes of office records: letter-size, legal-size, and computer printout size. It can also store index cards and other small documents. Special containers are available for larger documents. To maximize storage density by eliminating aisles, containers are sometimes stored in a two- or three-deep configuration per shelf. The resulting cubic foot to square foot ratio—an important indicator of storage economy in records management work—far exceeds that obtainable in offices where wide aisles are required to accommodate extended file drawers and the air space above filing cabinets is wasted.

If the record center is operated by a formal records management department, it will supply standardized containers to departments preparing inactive records for transfer, along with instructions for packing, labeling, and inventorying. The records inventory, often prepared on a special form, lists the contents of each container in a given shipment and is essential for later retrieval of the records. Depth of inventorying varies. Some record centers request only a general description of the contents of each container, while others require a detailed listing of individual folder titles.

As discussed above, records sent to a record center are presumably inactive and should experience minimal reference activity. Some items, however, will occasionally be needed by the transmitting department. Specific reference arrangements vary considerably. In the absence of a formal records management program, a record center may be shared by several departments, each of which services its own records. Where a formal records management program exists, the record center is usually operated by a small staff. In such organizations, the record center functions as a custodial agency rather than a generally accessible reference library. Record center storage is an extension of the transmitting department's own filing space, and the department controls access to the transmitted records just as if they had never left its own offices. Reference requests generally require departmental approval. Prior to contacting the record center, the department will consult its copies of the records inventory sheets to determine the shipment number and container location of the desired records. The record center typically responds to reference requests by returning the requested containers or file folders to the transmitting office. If only a few items are involved, some record centers will provide photocopies.

MICROGRAPHICS AND RECORDS MANAGEMENT

Basic Concepts

As discussed in the preceding section, a record center provides economical temporary storage for inactive records pending destruction. It is generally best suited to medium-term records that will be retained for ten years or less. Document miniaturization through micrographics is the preferred alternative for records designated for long-term retention, and an understanding of micrographics technology is essential to records management work.

Micrographics is that field of information management which is concerned with the production and use of microforms—photographic storage media containing images too small to be read with the unaided eye. The reduced images, properly called *microimages*, may contain either textual or graphic information. In source document microphotography, the oldest and most prevalent approach to microform production, special cameras are used to film paper documents. Microforms also can be produced directly from machine-readable, computer processed data using a technology called computer-output microfilm (COM). In either case, reduction is a measure of the relationship between a given linear dimension of a document, and the corresponding linear dimension of a microimage made from that document. This measure is expressed as $24\times$, $32\times$, $42\times$, and so on, where the reduced linear dimension is $\frac{1}{24}$, $\frac{1}{32}$, or $\frac{1}{42}$ the length of its full-size counterpart. In most business applications, source documents are reduced $24\times$ to $32\times$. COM-generated microforms typically utilize reductions of $42\times$ or $48\times$, although some systems employ reductions as high as $72\times$.

Introduced in the 1920s, the earliest business applications of micrographics technology emphasized the long-term storage of inactive records. In such applications, microfilming can yield very dramatic space savings. As an example, the contents of a four-drawer, vertical-style, letter-size file cabinet can be reduced to four rolls of 16mm microfilm and stored in a space measuring just 4″ wide by 4″ high by 4″ deep. While reduction in the cabinet and floor space required for the storage of inactive records remains an important motive, many organizations now use micrographics to facilitate the management of active records as well. By miniaturizing records, micrographics can make them more accessible and easier to handle. The most sophisticated of these active micrographics systems, described in a later section of this chapter, combine microform storage with computerized indexing. This section reviews the records management applications of the basic types of microforms and describes equipment for the production and use of microforms.

Types of Microforms

Available microforms can be divided, by physical appearance, into two broad groups: roll and flat. The majority of roll microform applications utilize film measuring 16mm wide by either 100 or 215 feet long. One-hundred-foot lengths of 35mm microfilm are used for engineering drawings, charts, maps, and other large documents. In either width, the film can be wound on a plastic or metal reel. As noted above, the capacity of a single 100-foot reel of 16mm microfilm ranges from 2,500 to 3,000 letter-size source documents—the approximate equivalent of one file drawer of records. Roll microforms are well suited to a wide range of documents, offer considerable flexibility in reduction and image positioning, and are the least expensive microforms to produce. Their high capacity makes them a good choice for the long-term storage of inactive records, but the viewing of desired images requires considerable manual film handling. The reel must be removed from its box or other container, mounted on an appropriate reader, threaded through an optical system, and advanced to the desired frame.

With 16mm roll microforms, active reference requirements are better served by self-threading cartridges or cassettes that eliminate manual film handling. A cartridge is a plastic, single-core microfilm container. When mounted on an appropriate reader, microfilm from the cartridge is automatically threaded onto a take-up spool built into the reader itself. The microfilm passes out of the cartridge during use and must be rewound prior to removal of the cartridge from the reader. A cassette is a plastic, double-core microfilm container that encloses both a supply and a take-up spool in a single housing. When used with an appropriate reader, cassettes require no film threading and can be removed at any time without rewinding.

Flat microforms, as the name suggests, consist of sheets of film containing one or more microimages. A microfiche, the best known of the flat microforms, is a 105mm by 148mm sheet of film containing multiple microimages arranged in a two-dimensional grid of rows and columns. Image capacity varies with the grid pattern utilized. In source document applications involving letter-size documents, the most common microfiche format provides 7 rows and 14 columns for a total of 98 images with a reduction of 24×. This format is well suited to case files, medical records, technical reports, and similar documents where unitization is desired. As used in this context, *unitization* denotes the storage of related records on a single microform with no unrelated records. Given their high image capacity, roll microforms typically do not permit such unitization.

Most COM-generated microfiche are based on computer printout size documents and feature both higher reductions and image capacities. The most common format can store the equivalent of 270 printout pages at 48× reduction. A widely encountered alternative stores the equivalent of 208 pages at 42× reduction, while high reduction, COM-generated fiche can store over 600 pages at 72×. Whether produced from computer output or source documents, the top row on a given fiche is typically reserved for eye-legible titling or other information. It is comparable to the tab area of a file folder, and it can be color-coded for easier filing and retrieval.

Widespread adherence to a small number of standardized microfiche formats has enabled equipment manufacturers to build readers and reader/printers that are much less expensive than their roll film counterparts. As described in the next section, available equipment also permits the rapid, on-demand duplication of microfiche in office applications. Many users find microfiche more convenient to handle than roll microfilm, and the lower image capacity facilitates the location of desired documents—an additional advantage in active records management applications.

As a potentially significant limitation, conventional microfiche—like its roll film counterpart—is produced from silver gelatin photographic film that loses its sensitivity once exposed and developed. As a result, new images cannot be added to a previously created silver gelatin fiche, even though empty spaces may remain on the fiche itself. This restricts the use of conventional microfiche to those records management applications involving closed files. Updatable microfiche systems overcome this limitation by using nonsilver photographic technologies permitting the addition of images to previously exposed fiche. As an example, one such system uses electrostatic charges and toner to create images. A copier-like camera permits the addition of new images to blank areas of a previously created fiche, although master fiche must be maintained under special conditions to preserve their updatability.

An alternate approach to the miniaturization of expanding files is the microfilm jacket—an acetate or polyester carrier with sleeves or channels for insertion of strips of 16mm and/or 35mm microfilm. Jackets are available in a variety of sizes and formats. The most widely used example measures 4" × 6" and provides 5 channels for 16mm microfilm strips containing 12 images each. In most cases, the strips are cut from rolls, using a specially designed jacket inserter. Recently, however, several manufacturers have introduced special cameras that produce fully developed precut strips of 16mm microfilm ready for insertion into jackets.

Like microfiche, all microfilm jackets include a title area for eye-legible identification. This area can be color-coded, notched, or otherwise marked for easier filing and retrieval. A variant form of microfilm jacket, called a *card jacket*, combines an index card with embedded channels for the insertion of a few short strips of microfilm. The card jacket is especially useful for credit files, medical history files, student records, and other active records management applications where less than twenty documents must be combined with substantial amounts of eye-legible information.

Aperture cards, the most widely used microforms in engineering applications, combine a tabulating-size card with a hole or aperture containing one frame of 35mm microfilm. The frame typically contains the miniaturized image of one engineering drawing, chart, map, or other large document. The face and back of the card can be designed to meet user requirements. If desired, aperture cards can be keypunched and machine sorted. In most cases, aperture cards are created in two steps. Documents are first recorded on 35mm roll microfilm, from which individual frames are subsequently cut for insertion by a special aperture card mounter. Some other cameras utilize special aperture cards that are premounted with unexposed microfilm. These cameras can produce fully developed aperture cards in less than one minute.

Source Document Microfilming

As noted above, microforms can be produced from paper documents—called *source documents*—or from computer-processed data. Organizations with formal records management programs often have centralized microfilm production facilities equipped with source document and/or computer-output microfilm production equipment. In such organizations, secretaries assist records managers in the identification of potential micrographics applications. Where the volume of microfilming activity is high, microfilm cameras and related source document production equipment may be installed in individual departments. Equipment and techniques for the microfilming of source documents have been greatly improved and simplified since their introduction in the 1920s. While older models were designed for laboratory operation by trained technicians, most newer microfilm cameras and related production equipment are intended for office installations where they will be operated by secretarial personnel. Focus, exposure control, film advance, image spacing, and other operations are performed automatically. In some departments, the microfilming of source documents—the miniaturized counterpart of copying—is a secretarial responsibility. In others, the secretary supervises microfilming operations performed by other employees. In the absence of a centralized records management program, the secretary may be responsible for the establishment of a microfilming program, the selection of cameras and other equipment, and the organization of workflow.

In any case, microfilm production begins with the careful preparation of source documents for filming. Staples, paper clips, or other fasteners must be removed; documents unfolded; torn documents mended; misfiled documents returned to their proper locations; and all documents stacked neatly in the order in which they are to be recorded on film. These work steps usually can be performed at rates ranging from 500 to 1,000 pages per hour. In some applications, files are purged or otherwise reorganized prior to filming, but such time-consuming work steps cannot be recommended for inactive records seldom to be referenced. In most cases, it will prove less expensive to microfilm all inactive records than to weed files selectively. Purging should be limited to readily identifiable duplicates or other obviously unneeded documents.

Once prepared, source documents are microfilmed by specially designed cameras. The majority of available microfilm cameras can be divided into two broad groups: those that produce roll microfilm and those that produce microfiche. As mentioned earlier, cameras are available for the production of microfilm strips or aperture cards, but such devices are relatively few in number and are intended for special applications. Roll microfilm cameras themselves can be divided into two broad groups: rotary and planetary. With rotary cameras, documents inserted into a slit-type opening are rapidly transported past a lens and light source where they are recorded on 16mm microfilm. Automatic feeders can speed the insertion of index cards, checks, or other small documents. Letter-size or larger documents are most often inserted manually. In either instance, rotary cameras are preferred in cases when work throughput and reduced labor costs are the primary considerations. With manual document feeding, most rotary camera operators can average 1,000 pages per hour and will produce about 4 rolls of 16mm microfilm per work day. But because documents are filmed while they are moving, rotary cameras produce images of only fair quality, although rotary camera output is acceptable for many business applications. For maximum versatility where several documents will share a rotary camera, some models support interchangeable lenses, document imprinters, endorsers, and similar attachments as optional accessories.

Planetary cameras are designed for applications requiring higher image quality. The typical planetary camera consists of a lens and film supply mounted on a vertical column perpendicular to a flat copyboard. Individual source documents are positioned face up on the copyboard for filming by the overhead camera. In an alternate design, the planetary camera is styled like a copier and the documents

Micro Auto 16 Planetary Camera

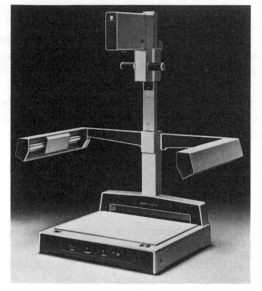

Courtesy of Minolta Corporation.

are placed face down on a glass platen. Reduction varies with the lens in use, and most models support interchangeable lenses. Some models even feature two camera heads for the simultaneous production of a working copy and a security roll. Regardless of design, most planetary cameras require manual document positioning. As a result, typical filming rates will seldom exceed 500 pages per hour. But because the documents remain stationary during exposure, the microfilm images are much sharper than those produced by rotary cameras. As a compromise in those applications requiring both high image quality and high work throughput rates, several companies have recently introduced automatic-feed planetary cameras that transport source documents to a recording surface where they are stopped momentarily for filming and are subsequently ejected. Whether they are manual or automatic-feeding, most planetary cameras produce the 16mm roll film suited to a broad range of business applications. Models capable of producing 35mm roll film are available for engineering and library applications.

Step-and-repeat cameras are a variant form of the planetary cameras designed specifically for microfiche production. Depending on the model, they accept 105mm microfilm in rolls or precut sheets. Documents are recorded in the row and column format characteristic of microfiche. As noted above, fiche formats vary, and the simplest step-and-repeat cameras will record documents in one format and one reduction only—with the 98-frame, 24× format being the most common. More sophisticated models support multiple formats and reductions. Most step-and-repeat cameras require manual document positioning, although some models are equipped with automatic document feeders for improved work throughput.

A special group of planetary and step-and-repeat cameras—called *camera/ processors*—can expose and develop microfilm as one continuous sequence of work steps. Such devices are especially convenient and useful when rapid turnaround time is required, but they sometimes use special film stocks that may prove inappropriate for a broad range of applications. The majority of rotary, planetary, and step-and-repeat cameras expose conventional silver gelatin microfilm requiring external development in a separate processor. While several companies sell relatively simple desktop microfilm processors suitable for office installations, processing can require more technical knowledge and decision-making than other microfilm production work steps. In addition to the processing itself, the developed film must be inspected for image sharpness, contrast, and stability—all of which require some special equipment and training. Where volume is sufficiently high, the centralized microfilm production facilities operated by some formal records management programs may include microfilm processors and related inspection equipment. Inexperienced users, however, are well advised to use a photographic laboratory or service bureau for microfilm processing. Most manufacturers will sell microfilm with processing prepaid. Film also can be purchased from one source and processing services from another. After a roll has been exposed and removed from the camera, it is mailed or otherwise delivered to the designated processing site for development and follow-up inspections. In some large cities, the processed film may be returned the following day.

Processed microfilm is usually duplicated to produce a security copy and/or additional working copies. Such duplication requires special equipment and, if desired, can be performed by the laboratory or service bureau from which the processing services have been obtained. A variety of highly automated microform duplicators are available for this purpose. For low-volume office installations, a number of manufacturers also offer inexpensive desktop duplicators for microfiche, microfilm jackets, or aperture cards. Such units resemble photocopiers in design and operation. Most models use diazo technology in which the original microform and a sheet of duplicating film are exposed to ultraviolet light. The sheet of duplicating film is then exposed to ammonia fumes.

Finally, processed rolls of microfilm or duplicates made from them may be inserted into microfilm cartridges or cut into strips or frames for insertion into microfilm jackets or aperture cards.

Computer-output Microfilm

Computers and other forms of information processing technology have dramatically increased our ability to produce records. These records contain information important to business operations, but they can pose significant problems. As mentioned earlier in this chapter, a single high-speed computer printer can produce enough records in one day to fill four file cabinets. To minimize space consumption and file cabinet purchases associated with computer-generated documents, COM converts computer-processed, machine-readable data directly to microfilm or microfiche without creating an intervening paper copy. A computer-output microfilmer, or COM recorder, is a variant form of computer printer that produces miniaturized output. Most COM recorders are installed in data processing centers or microfilm production facilities where they are operated by trained technicians. But rather than operating their own COM equipment, some organizations retain service bureaus for this purpose.

Secretaries can play an important role in the identification of potential COM applications. Special attention should be given to lengthy computer-generated reports that are printed frequently. The volume of such reports in paper form can quickly mount, and many offices have little available floor space or filing equipment with which to store them. Using computer-output microfilm, a 270-page report can be recorded onto a single microfiche, and a compact desktop index card file can store the equivalent of several tall stacks of computer printouts. Compact fiche reports often prove easier to handle than their bulky paper counterparts, and retrieval is correspondingly facilitated.

Display and Printing Equipment

By definition, microforms contain miniaturized information requiring magnification to be viewed. Microform readers are projection devices that display magnified document images on an integral screen. Most microform readers are designed for desktop installations and are common fixtures in medium-sized and large organizations. Portable models are available for use away from the office. While all microform readers are straightforward, easily operated devices, individual models differ in features such as the microforms accepted, the magnifications supported, and the screen size. Some readers are specifically designed for one type of microform. Others will accept various combinations of roll film, microfiche, microfilm jackets, and aperture cards. Most roll film models feature motorized transport mechanisms to advance the film at high speed. Readers for flat microforms typically feature manually operated carrier mechanisms in which the microform is inserted between two pieces of glass. The most suitable readers for the majority of office applications feature screen sizes ranging from 11" × 11" to 11" × 14". Such devices can display both source documents and COM-generated microforms. For the display of microforms produced at various reductions, most newer readers are equipped with interchangeable lens systems. Individual lenses can be easily removed and replaced to meet particular job requirements. Some models feature dual or triple lens systems for convenient, rapid magnification changes.

As its name suggests, a reader/printer not only can display magnified document images on a screen but also can produce paper enlargements. The operator merely inserts a microform, locates the desired image, positions it on the display screen, and presses the print button. Copies are typically produced within ten seconds. Reader/printers are essential items of equipment when paper copies of microfilmed documents are required for reference, mailing, or other purposes. Available models utilize any of three print processes. Some reader/printers use dry silver copy papers that are exposed to light and developed by heat without additional chemicals. Others resemble photocopiers in their use of the electrostatic process relying on coated paper and liquid or powdered toner. Several companies also offer xerographic reader/printers that can create plain paper copies indistinguishable from those produced by office copiers. Such plain paper printers are typically preferred by microform users, but they can defeat the purpose of microfilming by encouraging the production of paper copies.

Where large quantities of paper copies must be produced or entire microforms must be reconstituted as paper documents, enlarger/printers offer high-speed printing capabilities. Available enlarger/printers are relatively expensive, highly automated xerographic devices which will make single or multiple paper enlargements from specified microform images. While many organizations have no continuing need for them, occasional access to enlarger/printers is offered by microfilm service bureaus and other reprographic service companies.

A Microfiche Reader/Printer,
Model DC–580–AE

Courtesy of Micro Design, a Bell &
Howell Division.

Although they occupy far less space than paper records, microforms do require special file cabinets or other storage containers. Drawer-type files are available for both roll and flat microforms, and such units offer the greatest storage density. As an example, a six-drawer unit approximately the size of a conventional vertical filing cabinet can store up to 780 16mm reels or cartridges. When more frequent retrieval is anticipated, open storage racks with compartments for individual reels or cartridges can be used. Such units are often sold as modular components that can be expanded as the number of microforms increases. They may be mounted on turntables or casters for easier use.

Drawer-type file cabinets can store upwards of 15,000 microfiche, microfilm jackets, and aperture cards. As with paper files, groups of fiche can be separated by tabbed dividers. Smaller tray-type files are available for the desktop storage of flat microforms. Regardless of file capacity, however, the user must flip through individual microforms, examining heading areas until the desired item has been located. For active microfiche and jacket files, panel-type storage units can eliminate much time-consuming microform handling. Panel-type files consist of a paper or plastic housing with pockets into which individual fiche or jackets are inserted upright with their titles visible. By scanning the panels, one can quickly locate the desired microforms. Empty pockets indicate refiling locations. Typical panel capacities range from five to eighty fiche, depending on size and pocket spacing. Similar panels are available for floppy disks in word processing and microcomputer applications. To create high capacity storage systems, individual panels can be stored in binders or mounted on desk stands, rotary carousels, or wall racks.

Working copies of microforms require no special storage environment, but security copies intended for permanent retention must be maintained under tightly controlled conditions. When properly manufactured, processed, and stored, silver gelatin microfilms—the type used by the majority of microfilm cameras—are known to have archival potential compatible with permanent information retention requirements. Used in this context, the term *archival potential* means that the quality, appearance, and content of silver gelatin microfilm images will not change over time. All silver gelatin microfilm sold in the United

States is manufactured to archival specifications, and archival quality processing is within the capabilities of most in-house installations, photographic laboratories, and service bureaus. The establishment of archival storage conditions is left to the end user, however, and in many organizations the secretary must assume such responsibility. To be considered archival, processed microfilm must be packaged and stored under conditions explained in American National Standard PH 1.43–1979, entitled *Practice for Storage of Processed Safety Photographic Film*. Copies of the standard can be purchased from the American National Standards Institute in New York City or from the Association for Information and Image Management in Silver Spring, Maryland. The standard specifies storage in a controlled environment where temperatures do not exceed 70°F and the relative humidity ranges between 15% and 40% for acetate film and between 30% and 40% for polyester film. Such environmental conditions are rarely encountered in offices, but many organizations maintain vault areas that may prove suitable for microfilm storage. The tightly controlled environment of an organization's computer center might provide alternate storage facilities. In cases when in-house facilities are unavailable, archival storage space usually can be rented from companies operating commercial record centers.

FILING SYSTEMS FOR ACTIVE RECORDS

The Official File Concept

The organization of files for later retrieval is the primary concern of active records management. Conservation of space and filing equipment, while important considerations, are of secondary significance, although micrographics technology—as described in the preceding sections—can be applied to active as well as to inactive records. Microfilm jackets, for example, can be used to miniaturize paper files regardless of their level of reference activity or the need to add new documents at a later time.

Despite recent emphasis on paperless information systems, the design of filing systems for paper documents remains the central focus of most active records management programs. In too many organizations, however, filing is considered a mundane activity of minor significance. The difficulties of filing system design and implementation are seldom recognized, and the importance of effective retrieval systems for paper documents only attracts attention when a manager or other executive cannot find documents required for an important meeting or business transaction. Filing is typically the least esteemed of secretarial work routines, and secretaries—reflecting the priorities of their superiors—seldom allot a specific time for it. Instead, documents are filed after the demands of dictation, typing, telephone answering, and other presumably more important tasks have been carried out.

The establishment and maintenance of effective filing systems is one of the most challenging records management responsibilities. It involves major decisions about file scope, location, and arrangement; the establishment of procedures for the routing of documents to the file; and the evaluation and selection of appropriate cabinets and related storage equipment. Many records managers believe that a comprehensive file management program must begin with the establishment of an official file as the sole, complete, and authoritative accumulation of records created or maintained by a given activity. Official files are common in insurance claims processing, accounts receivable, purchasing, and other transaction-oriented activities where work is performed in readily identifiable stages by office employees, each of whom contributes information to the file. Official files are less frequently encountered in scientific research, engineering, architecture, law, and similar project-oriented activities where the work is performed in a discretionary manner by professional employees.

In such work settings, individual employees often maintain so-called "personal" files. These files, storable in individual offices or in adjacent secretarial work areas, offer the convenience associated with close proximity, but they can vary greatly in scope and content. Too often, personal files are incomplete. They may be arranged in a manner that only their creator can comprehend, and are consequently inaccessible to other workers who may need to retrieve information when the creator of the filing system is out of the office. If the creator of a personal file leaves the organization prior to completion of a project or other activity, the record of work accomplished can be very difficult to reconstruct.

These problems can be addressed successfully through the implementation of a procedure stating that participants in project-related activities must route all documents to an official file. This file then serves as a complete and authoritative point of reference for questions that can be answered from project-related documents. The existence of an official file will eliminate time-consuming searches in multiple personal files, and the completeness of the file will increase the likelihood of retrieving the accurate information required for effective decision-making. While adoption of the official file will not necessarily eliminate personal files, it nevertheless does show them up as a mere convenience for individual workers. Workers will remain free to make copies of documents needed in their own offices, but such personal files should include no documents not also contained in the official file. To restrict the growth of personal files, some organizations limit the amount of personal filing space to one cabinet or less per person.

In terms of physical location, an official file may be centralized or decentralized. Centralization typically occurs at the department or division level, with a common pattern being the establishment of a centralized repository for the official files of all projects undertaken by a given department. Complete centralization of all files at the organizational level is rare. But regardless of the level, centralization can facilitate the development of filing systems and the standardization of filing practices. Staff training is simplified and work performance is enhanced, largely because personnel can give their full attention to filing work rather than dividing their time among a variety of clerical tasks. When compared to an equivalent quantity of scattered files, centralization usually requires fewer file maintenance people. In addition, file control and security are usually improved. As potential disadvantages, the distance between workers and the central file area often necessitates some delay in retrieval, and document routing procedures must be strictly enforced if the central file is to have the completeness essential to user confidence.

Alphabetical Files

Whether centralized or decentralized, files can be arranged in any of six ways: alphabetically, numerically, chronologically (a variant form of the numeric arrangement), geographically, phonetically, and hierarchically (a complex system used for subject files). A widely cited records management aphorism advises the filing system designer to select the arrangement that corresponds to the way in which the records will be requested. The aphorism is oversimplified but can be applied effectively to medical records, customer correspondence, organization files, and other name files often arranged alphabetically. Alphabetical arrangements also can be used for subject-oriented filing systems in which individual folders contain topical headings, but complex subject filing requirements are best addressed by the hierarchical systems described below.

Alphabetical arrangements are widely used for file folders, index cards, and many other types of records in which the filing unit consists of a name, subject heading, or similar character string. While basic alphabetical concepts are familiar to all literate people, special rules must be implemented for certain situations. Personal names, for example, are typically inverted for filing in surname, forename, and middle initial sequence. Surnames beginning with *De, Des, La, Les, Van, Von,* or similar prefixes are treated as single filing units. Following widely accepted library practice, some systems equate *Mc* with *Mac* for filing purposes. Others retain the conventional filing sequence. Acronyms and initialed names are typically filed at the beginning of the appropriate alphabetical section, before any filing units consisting of complete words. Abbreviations are spelled out for filing as a full word. Cross-reference cards or sheets, placed in the alphabetical location appropriate to the abbreviation, direct the user to the fuller form of the name.

As secretaries who have used computer-generated listings are aware, there may be considerable variation in the sorting of spaces, hyphens, numeric digits, and other non-alphabetical characters found in names and subject headings. Some alphabetical filing systems employ letter-by-letter sorting in which embedded spaces are disregarded and names or other filing units are treated as a continuous string of characters. More commonly, the word-by-word sorting method treats embedded blank spaces as sortable characters to be alphabetized after the *z*. In the word-by-word approach, articles and nonessential words may be disregarded for filing purposes.

In terms of physical file organization, alphabetical filing is compatible with both the drawer- and the shelf-type filing equipment discussed in a later section. The name or other filing unit to be alphabetized commonly appears on the tab of a file folder or, in the case of card files, at the top of an index card. Guides or other dividers, marked with single- or double-letter alphabetical designations, separate groups of individual folders and draw the user's eye to the desired alphabetical section of the file. While these guides can be prepared by the secretary, several companies sell preprinted alphabetical guides based on statistical analyses of character frequencies encountered in name files of various sizes. They are designed to promote balanced file growth with approximately the same number of folders in each file subdivision. Alphabetical filing systems also can employ color coding for misfile detection, and a number of companies offer special folders for this purpose.

Numeric Files
As the name suggests, numeric arrangements are widely used for case files, transaction files, financial records, and similar applications in which documents are numbered and requested by an identifying number. In some cases, name files or

other alphabetical files are converted to numeric codes to ensure privacy or to decrease filing labor. Compared with alphabetical arrangements, numeric systems require fewer rules to cover special situations, although a name-to-file number index must be maintained in most instances.

Sequential numeric filing is the simplest and most widely encountered type of numeric arrangement. It features the consecutive arrangement of numbered folders, with the highest numbers being added to the end of the file. Like alphabetical arrangements, sequential numeric systems are compatible with drawer- and shelf-type filing equipment. Preprinted or customized guides can be used to subdivide the file into readily identifiable segments, and color-coded ones are available to simplify misfile detection. Sequential numeric filing systems are easily learned and implemented, but several significant disadvantages limit their utility in certain situations. For one thing, in transaction processing and similar applications in which numbers are sequentially assigned to newly created folders, the most active records will be clustered at the end of the file. In large centralized filing situations, considerable contention for those portions of the file can occur as clerical workers stand in line to file or retrieve documents. A related limitation is the inequitable distribution of reference and other file maintenance activity prohibiting the assignment of given portions of a file to specific clerical workers—a technique that fixes responsibility for file maintenance and often results in enhanced work performance. A further limitation is that sequential numeric systems typically require the time-consuming movement or "backshifting" of folders to make room at the end of the file for newly created records as older records are purged.

Terminal digit filing techniques address these limitations. While they may seem confusing initially, terminal digit systems are well suited to large centralized records management applications where reference activity must be distributed throughout a file and responsibility for particular file segments will be assigned to specific people. Terminal digit techniques are especially useful in accounts payable, accounts receivable, insurance claims adjustment, and similar transaction-processing applications. They are also widely used in medical records management.

The terminal digit approach requires a folder or other record identifier of six digits or longer. When shorter record numbers are involved, the number sequences can be padded with zeros to attain the required length. For filing purposes, the folder number is rewritten as three pairs of two digits each, with the resulting pairs being separated by hyphens. Thus, the number "365461" would be subdivided as "36–54–61," where "61" is described as the primary pair of digits, "54" as the secondary pair, and "36" as the tertiary pair. The digit pairs are rearranged accordingly, and the resulting number is filed as if it were "615436." It will be physically adjacent to folders numbered "355461" and "375461." Folder number "365462," which would normally follow "365461" in a conventional sequential numeric system, will be filed as "625436" and will be located in a different part of the file between folders numbered "355462" and "375462." The resultant scattering of sequentially numbered folders allows a more equitable distribution of filing, reference, purging, and other file maintenance activity. Furthermore, the backshifting of folders following purging is eliminated.

Generally, the original transaction number, case number, or other identifier is not changed on the folder itself. The required transpositions are made by clerical workers at the time the folders are to be filed or retrieved. Initial clerical orientation may be slightly longer than with sequential numeric systems, but terminal digit techniques are soon learned. As with sequential numeric arrangements, terminal digit systems commonly employ preprinted or customized numeric guides to divide the file into easily recognizable segments. Color-coded folders also can be used.

Middle digit arrangement, a variant form of nonsequential numeric filing, likewise requires a six-digit record identifier divided into three pairs of two digits each. But unlike the terminal digit approach, the middle pair of digits is considered the primary pair, the first pair of digits is considered the secondary pair, and the third pair of digits is considered the tertiary pair. Thus, folder number "365461" would be filed as "543661." As with terminal digit filing, preprinted or customized guides and color-coded folders can be used. In large centralized applications where even distribution of filing activity is desired, a middle digit arrangement results in a scattering effect similar to but somewhat less radical than that achieved by terminal digit filing. In certain situations, however, conversion from sequential numeric to middle digit filing can prove simpler than conversion to terminal digit filing, since groups of 100 consecutively numbered folders can be moved at one time.

Two additional variations of numeric filing are widely encountered but require only a brief mention. Chronological filing, as previously noted, arranges records by date. It is commonly used for correspondence and transaction files. Alphanumeric systems, in which the folder identifier contains a mixture of alphabetical characters and numeric digits, combine alphabetical and sequential numeric filing techniques. Depending on the procedure used, numerals may be sorted before or after alphabetical characters.

Phonetic Filing

Phonetic filing is designed for large name files in which surnames may sound alike but are subject to variant spellings or frequent misspellings. In a primitive form of phonetic filing, one of the possible spellings of a given surname is selected for use, and all variant spellings of that surname are filed under that form. Cross-references are placed in the file to direct the user to the right spelling.

The Soundex method, a more sophisticated approach to phonetic filing, was developed by Remington Rand in the 1940s. It converts surnames to a four-character alphanumeric code that generally results in the identical filing of similar sounding names of different spellings. In Soundex coding, the first letter of the surname becomes the first alphanumeric code character. All vowels and the consonants *h*, *w*, and *y* are then dropped, and the first three remaining characters are converted to numeric digits using the following table:

Letters	Code Number
B,F,P,V	1
C,G,J,K,Q,S,X,Z	2
D,T	3
L	4
M,N	5
R	6

Thus, the surname "Johnson" would be coded as "J525" as would "Jahnsen." If a name lacks a sufficient number of consonants, the code is completed with zeros. Double letters are treated as a single character as are those adjacent characters with an equivalent numeric value in the Soundex table. Soundex codes are filed according to rules for alphanumeric arrangements.

Geographic Files

Geographic arrangement—a variant form of alphabetical filing—is widely used in sales offices, distribution outlets, and similar organizations. The typical geographic file is initially subdivided by state or other territorial grouping, and is arranged alphabetically. Each state then may be subdivided into cities or regions, again arranged alphabetically. Within each of these subdivisions, folders for correspondents or customers are arranged alphabetically. The purpose of geographic files is to cluster together the records pertaining to particular sales or distribution territories.

Hierarchical Subject Files

As noted in a preceding section, subject files can consist of folders bearing topical headings arranged in alphabetical sequence. As an example of this approach, consider a hypothetical subject filing system used by the marketing department of an electronics company. This subject file contains product literature and published articles pertaining to various microcomputer products and components. A typical section of such a file might include folders with these headings:

Anadex printers	magnetic tape cassette drives
application software	microprocessors
BASIC interpreters	Microsoft BASIC interpreter
central processing units	minifloppy disk drives
compilers and interpreters	operating systems
Diablo printers	read-only memories
display terminals	typewriter-quality printers
dot matrix printers	Winchester disk drives
hard disk drives	Zilog Z80 microprocessor
Hazeltine display terminals	

This folder listing contains a mixture of general and specific headings. Material on related subjects—the various types of printers, for example—is scattered among several folders. None of the general headings are subdivided to reflect specialized facets of a given topic, and there is no broad framework for the establishment of new headings. In actual practice, some folders will likely contain many documents while others will contain only a few pages.

Hierarchical subject filing systems—sometimes called *classification systems*—are designed to address these problems. Rather than utilizing topical headings in conventional alphabetical sequence, hierarchical files arrange documents in a network of logically interrelated subdivisions representing general and specific facets of a given subject or activity. Many secretaries are familiar with the hierarchical classification systems developed for library applications—especially the Dewey Decimal and Library of Congress classification systems employed by most public and academic libraries. Designed specifically for the organization of published information in a wide range of fields, these library-oriented systems are inapplicable to ordinary office files, but hierarchical subject filing systems can be custom-developed for specific business applications.

The first step in the design of a customized hierarchical subject file is the subdivision of all records into very broad groups called *series*. In the microcomputer information file example described previously, a hierarchical subject file might include the following series:

> Central Processing Units
>
> Input Peripherals
>
> Output Peripherals
>
> Auxiliary Storage Devices
>
> System Software
>
> Application Software

Each of these series might be subdivided into two or more primary categories. For example:

> Input Peripherals
> > Keyboard Devices
> > Optical Recognition Equipment
>
> Output Peripherals
> > Paper Printers
> > Display Terminals
>
> Auxiliary Storage
> > Disk Drives
> > Magnetic Tape Drives

These primary categories may be further subdivided into secondary categories as follows:

> Input Peripherals
> > Keyboard Devices
> > > Key-to-disk Units
> > > Key-to-tape Units
> >
> > Optical Recognition Equipment
> > > Optical Character Recognition Readers
> > > Bar Coded Label Readers
>
> Output Peripherals
> > Paper Printers
> > > Dot Matrix Printers
> > > Typewriter-quality Printers
> > > Line Printers
> > > Display Terminals

CRT Displays
Flat Panel Displays

Secondary categories may be further subdivided as required. For example:

Output Peripherals

Paper Printers

Dot Matrix Printers

Impact-type
Thermal Printers

Typewriter-quality Printers

Selectric Type
Daisy-wheel Type
Print Thimble Type

Line Printers

Low-speed
Medium-speed
High-speed

Additional subdivision is possible within secondary categories. For example:

Dot Matrix Printers

Impact-type

Single-pass Printers
Multipass Printers

Thermal Printers

In some hierarchical filing systems, individual series are assigned a numeric or alphanumeric designation. For example:

100   Central Processing Units

200   Input Peripherals

300   Output Peripherals

400   Auxiliary Storage Devices

500   System Software

600   Application Software

The hierarchical nature of such systems can be reflected in decimal subdivisions indicating the logical subordination of categories to one another and primary categories to series. For example:

300   Output Peripherals

301   Paper Printers

301.01   Dot Matrix Printers

301.0101   Impact-type
301.010101   Single-pass
301.010102   Multipass
301.0102   Thermal Printers

301.02   Typewriter-quality Printers
 301.0201   Selectric Type
 301.0202   Daisy-wheel Type
 301.0203   Print Thimble Type

301.03   Line Printers
 301.0301   Low-speed
 301.0302   Medium-speed
 301.0303   High-speed

302   Display Terminals
 302.01   CRT Displays
 302.02   Flat Panel Displays
 302.0201   LCD Displays
 302.0202   Electroluminescent Displays

The hierarchical approach is truly systematic, for it reflects the structure of the activity through which the documents themselves were created. Hierarchical systems are well suited to browsing since related documents are grouped together in the file. Hierarchical systems likewise permit the retrieval of documents at varying levels of specificity. In the previous example, all information about microcomputer output devices can be obtained by retrieving the entire 300 Series. And all information about paper printers can be retrieved via the entire 301 category. A more narrow requirement for information about only dot matrix printers can be satisfied by examining documents in the 301.01 category, while examination of the 301.0101 subdivision will retrieve only those documents dealing with impact-type dot matrix printers.

On the negative side, hierarchical filing systems are time-consuming to construct and typically require a comprehensive understanding of the activity by which the to-be-filed documents were created. Thus, in order to design a hierarchical subject file for a marketing department that maintains information about microcomputers, it is necessary to know quite a bit about the microcomputer industry. A secretary may lack the time and/or the background required to design such systems, although a system like this might be initially designed by a records manager or other trained specialist with the departmental secretary's assistance. Once the system has been designed, the secretary can maintain and, if necessary, modify it.

As a further limitation, classification systems provide only one place for the filing of a given document, even though the document's contents may reflect several different subjects or several facets of the same subject. This limitation can be addressed by duplicating documents for filing in multiple locations, or by creating a relative index. Neither method is entirely satisfactory, however. The obvious shortcoming of filing duplicate copies is that they substantially increase the load of filing labor and the size of the file. A relative index can provide a means of accessing documents by subjects other than the one under which the document is filed, but such indexes can prove time-consuming to maintain. If indexing is to be performed, the computer-assisted filing systems described in the next section offer substantial advantages over hierarchical approaches.

Computer-assisted Document Indexing
As noted above, a relative index can be used to supplement a hierarchical filing system, thus providing access to documents in ways that are not successfully

addressed by a hierarchical framework. For example, correspondence may be filed under appropriate subject categories while a separate index lists the names of correspondents and the file locations of the documents they have written. In a radically different approach to filing system design, computer-assisted document indexing replaces hierarchical or other arrangements with a straightforward indexing procedure. Broadly defined, computer-assisted document indexing uses computer hardware and software to establish, maintain, and search an index keyed to paper documents stored, by sequentially assigned numerical identifiers, in a separate file. To locate documents pertinent to a specific information requirement, the user first searches a computer-maintained index—usually via an on-line terminal, although some systems utilize computer-printed indexes. In the on-line mode, the search is interactive. Computer software guides the user in the selection and narrowing of appropriate index terms. If the search is successful, the user is instructed to remove specific numbered documents from a paper file.

The required computer hardware configuration will vary with the application but typically includes the following: a large-scale, mini-, or microcomputer; one or more video terminals or equivalent input devices to be used for the entry of index data; one or more video displays and/or printers to be used in retrieval operations; and magnetic disks or other media for the storage of the index data. Indexing may rely on custom-developed programs or on one of the prewritten data management software packages that are becoming increasingly available for computers of all types and sizes. Of special interest for office applications are data management packages designed for microcomputers or word processors. Regardless of source, though, the indexing software must permit the entry of index data pertinent to specific documents; the addition, deletion, or other modification of previously entered index data; and the identification of documents pertinent to particular retrieval requirements.

Unlike hierarchical filing arrangements relying on the pre-established framework of series and categories described above, the design of computer-assisted document indexing systems begins with the identification of indexing parameters. An *indexing parameter* is a category of information by which a document will be retrieved. While specific parameters will necessarily vary with the application, the following list is suitable for a broad range of document indexing requirements:

1. document accession number: a sequentially assigned identifier. In applications where a given indexing system supports several departments or activities, alphabetical or alphanumeric prefixes may be used to identify documents by originating department, project name, or other broad grouping. In any case, multipage documents are assigned a single identifier.

2. document type: letter, memorandum, report, Telex, etc. In many applications, document types are abbreviated by a simple two-character identifier.

3. document originator: the name of the person who created and/or signed the document.

4. originator affiliation: the name of the internal department or outside organization with which the document originator is associated.

5. document recipient: the name of the addressee or other recipient of the document.

6. recipient affiliation: the name of the internal department or outside organization to which the document is addressed.

7. document date: month, day, and year as appropriate.

8. subject(s): single-term key words or multiterm key phrases indicating the document's subject content. Most systems permit the assignment of three to six subjects to a single document, thereby providing coverage of major and minor points and addressing a previously discussed limitation of hierarchical arrangements. Depending on the procedure established at the time the system is designed, subject terms may be selected by the document's creator or recipient. As an alternative, secretaries or other persons may perform subject indexing. In most cases, indexers are free to select the subject terms that they consider appropriate to the document. In some systems, however, subject terms must be selected from an approved list called a *thesaurus*. While a thesaurus can improve precision in retrieval operations, most users do not want to spend the time required for thesaurus development, and many applications do not require it.

9. an abstract: a brief summary of document content. While it is not provided in every application, an abstract serves at least two useful purposes: when retrieved on-line, it provides information that might satisfy the user in place of the entire document; it also enables the user to determine that particular documents are not relevant and need not be removed from the document file.

In a typical computer-assisted indexing system, documents are routed to a central file area or other indexing point where sequential accession numbers are stamped or otherwise inscribed on them. Index parameters are then entered at a computer terminal or other input device for on-line storage on magnetic disks. The best indexing software displays a formatted screen with labeled areas and adjacent blank spaces corresponding to index parameters. The terminal operator fills in the blank spaces with the index terms relevant to a given document. Following indexing, the documents are placed in file cabinets in accession number sequence. This arrangement constitutes the major physical difference between computer-assisted document indexing and conventional filing systems where logically related documents are physically grouped within a file. In computer-assisted indexing systems, documents stored in the same portion of a file are seldom related to one another. Logical relationships among documents are maintained in the index; related documents can be retrieved through index searches.

To retrieve documents, a combination of index terms and search commands is entered at an on-line terminal. Computer-assisted document indexing systems are particularly effective in complicated retrieval operations involving multiple

Bell & Howell Data Search System—Series 30

Courtesy of Bell & Howell.

indexing parameters—all of the correspondence received by a particular person on a given subject between specified dates, for example. Because the index is searched electronically, the total transaction time will prove shorter than that associated with conventional filing systems. A successful search results in the display of one or more accession numbers for documents indexed with the stated parameters. These documents are then removed from their locations in the sequentially-ordered paper file. Following examination, the documents must be returned to their proper file locations. Multiple documents usually will be scattered throughout the paper file, but the superior retrieval performance of the computer-assisted indexing approach makes this a minor inconvenience. Unlike manual filing systems that retrieve groups of documents which must be scanned for relevance, computer-assisted indexing produces lists of documents that have been preselected for relevance. As previously mentioned, abstracts can be added to index data to facilitate judgments as to relevance.

While the formulation of an elaborate network of series and categories is not involved, the secretary implementing a computer-assisted document indexing system will require some technical assistance in the selection of computer hardware and indexing software, the calculation of index storage requirements, and the establishment of indexing categories and procedures. Internal systems analysts or external consultants often prove helpful in this respect. Once the computer-assisted document indexing systems have been established, many secretaries find them much easier to maintain and use than conventional filing systems. The computer-assisted systems are compatible with a variety of centralized and decentralized file configurations. If desired, both index and document storage can be centralized. Or, the physical storage of documents can be decentralized within individual departments while an on-line index resides on a centralized computer system. In a completely decentralized approach, both documents and index data can be maintained at the department level, with the latter residing on a microcomputer located in the file area.

An additional advantage of computer-assisted document indexing is its compatibility with nonpaper storage. In a variant approach called computer-assisted retrieval (CAR), documents are recorded on 16mm microfilm or microfiche and their microform addresses are indexed in the manner described above. At retrieval time, the user is instructed to consult a particular film and frame location. Various automated microfilm and microfiche retrieval units are available for this purpose. In the most prevalent approach, the operator loads an indicated 16mm cartridge on a reader/printer and enters the number of the desired frame at an attached keypad. The reader/printer automatically advances the film to display the requested frame for viewing or printing. More advanced reader/printers can operate on-line to a computer, thereby eliminating the need to enter frame numbers once the appropriate cartridge has been loaded. A number of companies market complete turnkey CAR systems consisting of a preselected, self-contained configuration of computer hardware, indexing software, and micrographics equipment. Designed for the rapid implementation of computer-assisted document indexing, these turnkey systems require neither customized hardware selection nor software development. In the future, it is expected that similar systems will combine computer-assisted indexing with optical video disks for document storage.

Electronic Filing Systems

With computer-assisted document indexing, index data is stored and processed electronically, but the documents themselves remain in paper or microform. True electronic filing systems store entire documents in machine-readable computer-processible form on magnetic disks or other media. A few systems convert document images to digital form for this purpose. More commonly, however, electronic filing systems store the actual content of textual documents converted to machine-readable form on a character-by-character basis.

Reflecting the increased tendency toward multifunctionality in automated office systems, electronic filing is an increasingly common component in word processing and electronic mail systems. Following the creation of documents, the operator can enter subjects or other indexing terms as discussed earlier. Rather than printing out a copy for storage in paper files or microfilming, the document is retained on a disk for later retrieval. This technique is particularly effective in multiterminal installations where documents can be accessed from remote workstations. The storage of documents in computer-processible form results in some space consolidation when compared with paper filing systems, and retrieval occurs at high speeds. Compared with computer-assisted indexing of paper or microform documents, electronic filing offers a single-step retrieval procedure in which index data and entire documents can be displayed at the same workstation. If desired, the retrieved documents can be routed to printers for paper output. A further advantage is afforded by some systems which include sophisticated software that can search the entire text of documents for the occurrence of specified words or phrases, thereby significantly expanding retrieval capabilities.

While the concept of electronic filing is very attractive, the available systems still have significant limitations. Data stored on computer-processible magnetic media are not stable and therefore must be recopied periodically to prevent deterioration. Likewise, data generated by one word processing system are often incompatible with other systems, thereby prohibiting the electronic transfer of

The Xerox 8010 Star Information System

Courtesy of Xerox Corporation.

documents. More significantly, the storage space provided by most word processors can only accommodate a relatively small number of documents—perhaps the equivalent of one or two file drawers. Even large multiterminal word processing systems can rarely store the equivalent of several dozen file cabinets. While such systems may be able to store a substantial portion of a single department's files, they are hardly suited to the wholesale replacement of an entire organization's operating records. Word processing and electronic mail systems implemented on large centralized computers offer additional storage facilities, but disk storage—like the office space required for paper records—is invariably a finite resource. As available disk space becomes full, older records must be transferred to magnetic tape for off-line storage. We have pointed out that COM technology can be used to record computer-stored documents on microfilm or microfiche. Continuing improvements in magnetic recording technologies and the introduction of optical recording media should provide additional disk storage densities at attractive costs, thereby enhancing the potential of electronic filing systems by allowing more documents to remain on-line for a longer period of time.

FILING EQUIPMENT

Manual Filing Equipment

While some vendors offer interlocking cardboard containers with pullout drawers, most active records are stored in metal filing cabinets. Such cabinets can be divided into two broad groups: drawer-type and shelf-type. Vertical-style drawer-type filing cabinets are the most widely used record storage containers in general office installations. They are available in models appropriate to letter-size, legal-size, or printout size documents. Legal-size cabinets are more expensive and require more floor space than their letter-size counterparts. As a result, most records managers strongly discourage the routine use of legal-size documents in offices.

Special vertical file configurations permit the storage of small records such as index cards and microforms, or large records such as engineering drawings or maps. Insulated models provide fire protection at substantial extra cost. Various conventional or combination locks can prevent unauthorized access to confidential documents.

Documents are filed from front to back inside each drawer. Conventional or suspended folders can be used. Guides indicate major file sections, while top-mounted folder tabs indicate file contents. The typical vertical-style drawer provides about twenty-five inches of filing space. The number of drawers ranges from two to six. The four-drawer model is most commonly encountered, but five-drawer cabinets are generally preferred for their improved storage density. While the six-drawer configuration offers even greater storage density, its increased height can make the top drawer very difficult to access. While their top surfaces can be used for sorting or other file maintenance routines, the two- and three-drawer configurations waste floor space and are seldom recommended.

Typical lateral-style, drawer-type cabinets measure fifteen inches deep by thirty, thirty-six, or forty-two inches wide and are suited either to letter- or legal-size documents. Inside each drawer, documents can be filed from side to side or, when dividers are used, from front to back. Conventional or suspended file folders can be used. Cabinet height varies with the number of drawers. The four- and five-drawer, lateral-style models provide slightly greater storage density than their vertical-style counterparts. The typical thirty-inch, five-drawer, lateral-style configuration requires 9 square feet of floor space and provides 150 inches of filing space. A five-drawer, letter-size, vertical-style cabinet requires 8 square feet of floor space and provides 125 inches of filing space. Many interior designers prefer lateral cabinets for aesthetic rather than functional reasons, and they often select the two- or three-drawer models to achieve unobstructed visibility in open-plan offices. Appearance aside, such cabinets waste floor space.

Whether vertical or lateral in design, drawer-type files are not suited to very active, high-volume file installations. Time and effort are required to pull out and replace drawers, and only one person can conveniently access a given cabinet at a time. Shelf-type filing cabinets address these limitations. Often considered as variant forms of lateral-style cabinets, they consist of book-type shelving units on which folders are arranged in rows. Side-tab folders are preferred for visibility. The shelves themselves may be fixed or adjustable. Some units feature front panels that can be closed over the shelves for improved security and/or appearance. With some configurations, the shelves may slide forward in the manner of lateral-style, drawer-type cabinets. Special shelf-type cabinets are available for computer printouts and magnetic media. The most versatile shelf-type systems can combine paper and nonpaper media to suit particular requirements.

Shelf-type cabinets are well suited to applications requiring rapid file access by numerous users, and they are most often the filing equipment of choice in centralized file rooms or other large, active records management installations. Because they are usually taller than drawer-type files and do not require wide aisles for extended drawers, shelf-type cabinets offer much greater storage density. Special "compacted" shelf-type units without intervening aisles are mounted on

Lateral Files

Courtesy of TAB Products Co.

tracks for storage. To access a given shelving unit, the adjacent units are moved aside manually or by use of motorized controls. While compacted shelving is expensive, it does offer high density storage in installations where space is at a premium. Whether conventional or compacted, shelf-type filing equipment can be used with alphabetical and numeric file arrangements, and is the only equipment suitable for terminal digit filing. Shelf-type filing cabinets are likewise compatible with color coding or other techniques for visual detection of misfiles.

Motorized Files

As their name implies, motorized filing devices employ mechanical and/or electronic components to deliver documents or folders to users. With manual filing equipment, by way of contrast, the user must walk to the file. Motorized files are designed to save labor and to speed retrieval. Vertical motorized files, the most common variety, were first introduced in the early 1960s. They consist of shelves mounted on a revolving transport mechanism inside a large cabinet. The shelves may store letter-size, legal-size, or computer printout size documents or folders. Special models for storing index cards, microforms, and other small records are also available. To retrieve a given document or file folder, the operator consults an external index to determine its shelf location. This index can be computer-maintained or manually prepared. In either case, the operator enters the shelf number at a calculator-style keypad. The transport mechanism then moves the indicated shelf to an access port, thereby allowing the operator to remove the desired document or folder.

Significant advantages of the vertical motorized files are rapid retrieval, effective security against unauthorized access, and good storage density. A given quantity of records can be stored in approximately one-third the space required by conventional drawer-type filing cabinets. On the negative side, vertical motorized files—like all mechanized filing devices—cost substantially more

Minitrieve® Automated Filing System

Courtesy of Supreme Equipment & Systems Corporation,
New York.

than manual filing cabinets of comparable capacity. The vertical motorized file's high storage density may necessitate floor reinforcement or other site preparation—resulting in significant expense. Once installed, vertical motorized files cannot be moved easily, thus making them a poor choice for departments that change locations frequently. While available devices are quite reliable, downtime is always possible and an equipment malfunction can render documents completely inaccessible. A final, often overlooked limitation is that vertical motorized files work best with a dedicated operator who handles all retrieval requests. Vertical motorized files perform poorly in environments where many people must wait in line to use the equipment.

Horizontal motorized files store documents in shelf-type filing units that revolve on tracks to bring a desired section to a seated operator. They are the records management counterpart of the garment conveyors widely used in the dry-cleaning industry. The typical horizontal motorized shelf file consists of a storage module with shelves or racks for paper documents, index cards, microforms, or other media; floor mounted tracks, around which the shelves revolve; and a control unit that initiates shelf movement. Available units are modular and expandable, although the relocation of previously installed units can pose problems. Like all mechanized filing equipment, horizontal motorized files eliminate the necessary walking associated with the use of manual file installations. They are particularly well suited to situations in which requests for information from files are received at a service counter or by telephone. Horizontal motorized files, like their vertical motorized counterparts, work best with a dedicated operator having a fixed responsibility for the files. This, in turn, results in improved security and control.

Container-oriented document retrievers are the most sophisticated of the mechanized files. Container-oriented retrievers utilize special metal containers for folders or individual documents. Containers are available for letter-size, legal-size, and printout size documents. Smaller models can store index cards or microforms. The containers are arranged on shelves in a row and column pattern, regardless of their size. The typical configuration is a relatively large enclosed unit consisting of two facing sets of shelves separated by an aisle containing a transport/extractor mechanism mounted on a track. To retrieve a given document or folder, the user first consults an external index to determine its container number. As with other types of mechanized files, this index can be computer-maintained or it can be prepared manually. The container number, once determined, is typed at a calculator-style keypad located at an operator workstation forming an integral part of the filing unit. The system is controlled by a microprocessor that directs the extraction mechanism to remove the indicated container from its shelf position and deliver it to the operator workstation. The workstation may be located at the front or side of the file, depending on its configuration. Special configurations can support multiple or remote workstations. Container-oriented document retrievers are versatile units suited to a wide range of documents. They minimize the time and effort associated with manual document retrieval and can significantly improve retrieval time. In some applications, personnel requirements can be correspondingly reduced. Container-oriented document retrievers offer very high storage density in offices with limited space. For maximum flexibility, they can be interfaced with computers and can serve as a component in sophisticated document storage, retrieval, and control systems in which index searches will culminate in the automatic selection and delivery of containers with desired documents. The primary disadvantage of container-oriented document retrievers is their high cost. A substantial initial capital investment is required, and expensive site modifications may be necessary.

8

Telecommunications: Telephone Technology and Usage

Lamont Wood • *Professional Writer; formerly Public Relations Writer, Datapoint Corporation ("Telephone Technology" Section of this Chapter)*

Melissa Ludlum • *Executive Secretary to M.S. Rukeyser, Jr., Executive Vice President, Corporate Communications, National Broadcasting Company, Inc. ("Telephone Techniques" Section of this Chapter)*

TELEPHONE TECHNOLOGY

BASIC TELEPHONE TECHNOLOGY

An enormous proportion of any modern organization's business is conducted over the telephone. Effective use of the telephone depends on an understanding of the functioning and capabilities of the hardware and an awareness of proper telephone techniques. The first part of this chapter provides an overview of the hardware, while the second part deals with the correct ways in which you should use the telephone.

The mouthpiece of a standard telephone contains a microphone packed with carbon granules through which flows a certain amount of direct current voltage. As you speak, the sound waves compress the carbon granules, varying the resistance to the current and causing the modulations of the current to mimic the sound wave. The earpiece consists of a diaphragm that vibrates in response to the modulations of the current, reproducing the original sound. But the earpiece also works in reverse—vibrations of the diaphragm caused by incoming sound induce a current in the wire rather than modulate an existing current, as the mouthpiece does. The transmitted sound is about 40 decibels less than the original sound: this means that even with the mouthpiece covered, the other party can still faintly hear you. With some systems this is true even after you've pushed the hold button.

The DC current used by the telephone is produced by batteries at the local telephone company headquarters. Therefore, in case of a power failure your home telephone should continue to function. The behavior of a multitelephone office system during a power failure depends on the details of its design, since it may use house current to ring the bells and light the buttons. Some have their own emergency power supplies. Most telephone company central office switching mechanisms serve more lines than they can switch. If you pick up the telephone and do not get a dial tone, your telephone company central office is probably overloaded. The mechanism will give you a dial tone the moment a switching path has become available. Significant delays are rare in the United States, but are common in some other locales.

Telephones use rotary or pushbutton dial mechanisms. If you have a rotary telephone subscription with the telephone company, you can only use a rotary telephone. If you have a pushbutton subscription, you should be able to use either. Rotary telephones trigger the telephone company switching mechanisms by sending pulses of electricity, and you may be able to dial a rotary telephone by tapping out the numbers on the switch-hook. Pushbutton telephones send musical tones to the switching mechanisms. You must push each button for at least two tenths of a second to be sure of producing the right tone. A pulse-dialing telephone has pushbuttons, but produces the same dial pulses as those emitted by a rotary telephone.

OFFICE TELEPHONE SYSTEMS

Office telephone systems can be generally divided into key systems and PBXs. Continuing technical advances have, however, blurred the distinction between the two types. With computerization, functions once performed by add-on devices can now be built into the system.

Key Systems

In telephone jargon, a *key* is a pushbutton. A key system is a group of pushbutton desk telephones interconnected so that they all can be used to share a group of outside lines, plus make intercom calls to each other. The basic unit is the key telephone. The most common size has six buttons, one of which is the hold button. (See the first illustration.) The switching gear for the system is contained in a cabinet called the *key service unit*. (See the second illustration.) Large systems also have panels of connectors called *terminal blocks* hidden away somewhere.

With smaller systems it is common for all the telephones to ring when there is an incoming call, introducing the risk that no one or everybody will answer. Larger systems should have a receptionist's station, which can be the only telephone that rings for incoming calls. The receptionist then uses the intercom line to alert the appropriate party that a caller is waiting on a specific line. Modern key systems often use digital (computer) technology, but the chief difference to the user is the smaller size of digital equipment, the wider range of features it can offer, and the fact that the telephones are connected with thin wires instead of thick cables. Today it is not uncommon to find systems with thick instruction folders, dozens of instruction codes to invoke various features, and a dozen or more beeps, tones, and rings to indicate what the system is doing. The following is a description of some of the features you may encounter.

Intercom calls.   On small systems such as one linking a secretary and an executive, a button is pushed to alert the person being called, who then pushes the intercom button, lifts the handset, and speaks. The buzzer buttons are usually in

The Maxiplus™ 5-line Key Telephone

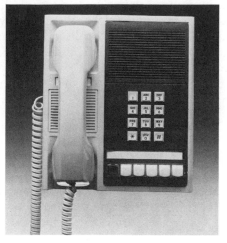

An electronic pushbutton version of a
standard six-button key telephone system.
Courtesy of Comdial Corporation.

a separate box attached to the telephone. With a dial-selective intercom, you
push the intercom button and then dial one, two, or three digits to reach another
person. Such a system may have a direct station selector (DSS)—a console with a
pushbutton for each user. (See the next page.) To make a call, you just press the
button assigned to the person you wish to reach. In large systems the only person
with a DSS will be the receptionist. (A similar console that only shows which
telephones are in use is called a *busy lamp field*, or a BLF.) A call announcing
system allows you to alert the called party via a speakerphone, and usually
permits you to hear the other person's response. Paging through the system's
speakerphones to the whole office or to groups of numbers also may be allowed.

Hold. Any key system worthy of the name will allow you to put a call on hold.
Options include a periodic tone (so that the caller will not think the line has gone
dead) or music or a taped message. *Exclusive hold* means that only the person

Maxkey™ Electronic Key System

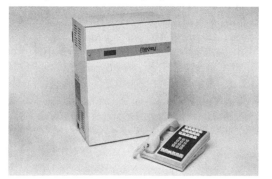

A key service unit with one of the key telephones
it supports.
Courtesy of Comdial Corporation.

ULTRACOM V

A key telephone unit with direct station selector (DSS).
Courtesy of TIE/Communications, Inc.

who put the call on hold can take it off hold. *Recall from hold* means that after a set period on hold the telephone will start buzzing.

Call transferring.   This feature allows you to transfer a call to another telephone number either by dialing a special code or by momentarily depressing the switch-hook and then dialing the new number.

Automatic dialing.   Also called *speed dialing, memory dialing,* or *abbreviated dialing,* this feature allows you to program a list of telephone numbers (intercom or outside) into your desk telephone. Depending on the system, a programmed number can be reached, either by pushing a button or by dialing code numbers.

Last number redial.   Last number redial is like automatic dialing, except that the number in the memory unit is the last number you dialed, which in most systems can be redialed by pressing the # button. This feature is useful when making attempts to get through to a busy number.

Remote station answering.   With remote station answering, you can answer someone else's telephone from your own telephone by dialing a special code or pushing a specific button. A similar feature is night answering, which allows all calls to be routed to a single telephone.

Message waiting.   With message waiting, a special light or tone on your telephone is activated to show that the receptionist has a message for you. Some companies have message centers to which all calls are routed if not answered after three rings. Most modern systems can be programmed to route an unanswered call back to the receptionist.

Privacy.   This feature prevents other people from accessing a line already in use. It is also possible to get an override feature so that an executive can still break into a conversation, but in most cases only after a warning tone has announced the override.

Do not disturb.   Using the do not disturb feature prevents calls from arriving on your line. Depending on the system, the caller may get a busy signal, or the call may be routed to another number. This feature is particularly useful in the office of a very busy executive, especially when both executive and secretary are unable to answer the telephone.

Conferencing. With call conferencing you can be connected to several outside lines at once. All the parties can talk and hear each other. While conferencing is often limited to three lines, it can be expanded further to as many as six or perhaps more.

Camp on. If your line is busy, the attendant can use camp on to attach a call to your line, and the call will go through as soon as you have hung up.

Dial restrictions. A dial restrictions device prevents unauthorized people from dialing restricted outside numbers, exchanges, Area Codes, any long-distance numbers, or any outside numbers at all. Such systems are usually not as sophisticated as PBX long-distance control systems.

PBX Systems

PBX stands for Private Branch Exchange. You also may see the initials PABX (Private Automatic Branch Exchange) or CBX (Computerized Branch Exchange) or other variants. But PBX is the generic name for the office switchboard and its descendants—a system allowing inside telephones to call each other and share a limited number of outside lines. Key systems often exist within PBX networks. The principal difference between a PBX and a key system is that all of a PBX's switching takes place within a central mechanism, triggered by dialing code numbers instead of pushing buttons. For instance, instead of pushing a line button to make an outgoing call, you usually dial "9." Incoming calls go through an attendant unless a Direct Inward Dial system is in use. A PBX can support far more telephones than a key system can, while providing similar features. Features that you may encounter on a PBX or on peripheral equipment attached to one over and above those found on a key system are explained in the next few paragraphs.

Least cost routing. When you make a long-distance call, the system tries to find the cheapest way of placing your call. This usually means waiting a preset period for a WATS line or other discount transmission facility to become available. If none becomes available, your call is placed via direct-distance dialing (DDD). How long you have to wait usually depends on the priority assigned to your telephone—executives might get through immediately, for example.

Long-distance control system. Often offered with least cost routing, a long-distance control system (LDCS) requires that you dial in special access codes before you are allowed to make a long-distance call. For instance, you may be required to dial "88" to reach the controller, followed by your personal code number and the number you wish to reach; then you wait for the least cost router to find an unused WATS line. Depending on the limitations put on your code number, you may be prohibited from making international calls, calls to certain areas, or any outside calls at all.

Station message detail recorder. The obvious enhancement of an LDCS, a station message detail recorder (SMDR) keeps track of all the calls you make, what numbers they went to, how long they lasted, how much they cost, and so on. Most SMDRs can produce management reports breaking the call traffic down into categories such as department, caller, or time of day.

Call detail recorder.   A call detail recorder is basically a simplified SMDR. It logs outgoing calls, their length, destination, and cost, but it has no way of identifying who made the calls.

WATS extender.   A WATS extender attached to a PBX allows you to call the PBX from another telephone and use the system's WATS line. The procedure is often the same as making a call through an Other Common Carrier (OCC).

Digital transmission.   Some modern PBX systems use not only computerized switching mechanisms but also computerized telephone instruments. The telephone encodes your voice as a high-speed digital bit stream. Since computers also use digital transmission techniques, it may be possible to connect computer equipment directly to the office telephone network and transmit at speeds as high as 56,000 baud. This advantage does not extend to outside (nondigital) lines. Fancier digital telephones often include a one-line alphanumeric readout that can give the number of the calling party (for intercom calls only), show the cost of your call while still in progress, and other information, while at the same time doubling as a digital clock. (See the next illustration.)

Direct Inward Dial Systems
Direct Inward Dial (DID) systems allow telephone numbers within a company to be reached by dialing them directly from the outside. However, outgoing calls are subject to the office's PBX or key system. Calls between numbers within the DID system can be placed as conference calls by dialing the last four digits. The DID system may be installed in addition to the PBX, it may be a feature of the PBX, or it may be embodied in special wiring at the telephone company's facilities. This last variant is often called a *Centrex system.*

ULTRACOM CX Display Phone

An electronic key telephone with digital readout.
Courtesy of TIE/Communications, Inc.

Other Equipment

Automatic call distributors.   Organizations such as airline reservation offices experiencing a lot of incoming calls will usually set up a department of call takers served by an automatic call distributor (ACD). The ACD distributes incoming calls to the call takers and calls that cannot be answered are put on hold with music and a reassuring message. Sophisticated ACDs can gather statistics on how many calls were abandoned or how many busied out, can break down the traffic by time of day, and can monitor the productivity of the individual call takers such as airline ticket agents.

Speakerphones.   These devices allow you to speak on the telephone without lifting the receiver. They can be built into some of the fancier telephones. Due to small echoes in the room, the person at the other end may think he or she is listening to you through a rain pipe. This problem can be alleviated to some extent by experimenting with the placement of the microphone or by installing sound-absorbing curtains or carpet. Speaker telephones that suppress or avoid the echoes are also available.

Answering machines.   These devices answer the telephone with a recording and then record whatever message the caller cares to leave. Advanced features include a remote key allowing you to call in from another telephone and listen to whatever messages have been left. Units with a speaker can be used for call screening: you leave the machine on, and if you hear someone whom you want to talk to leaving a message, you can then break in and speak to that caller.

Pocket beepers.   A beeper is a pocket-sized paging device that alerts the bearer that a telephone message has been received. Beepers are worn by people such as physicians or news photographers who must always remain accessible to their offices. To alert a beeper user, you call the telephone number associated with that person's beeper and leave a message. The pager company then sends out a radio signal triggering the beeper's alarm mechanism. Some systems also will broadcast your recorded message, and some other beepers with digital readouts will display the telephone number the user is supposed to call.

Security.   Scrambler telephones, such as those used by the military, are available on the civilian market. They range from inexpensive devices whose encoded output may still be understood by the practiced ear, to sophisticated devices intended to thwart professional cryptanalysts. But an unused telephone also can be a security threat. A device called an *infinity transmitter* can be installed in your telephone allowing someone to call it, keep it from ringing, and then listen to everything being said in your office. Therefore, if you're in a sensitive business, you should always greet unexpected "telephone repair people" with skepticism.

THE AMERICAN TELEPHONE INDUSTRY

In many countries the telephone system is owned by the government and run by government ministries called PTTs (Post, Telegraph, and Telephone). In the United States, the telephone system is owned by corporations acting under governmental regulation. The descendants of AT&T's Bell System provide about 85% of the telephone service in the United States. About 1,500 independent telephone companies service the rest of the nation, usually in rural areas. A call

Table 1. **Bell Operating Companies**

Company	Bell Antecedents
Nynex Corporation	New York Telephone New England Telephone
Bell Atlantic Corporation	Bell of Pennsylvania Diamond State (Delaware) Telephone Chesapeake & Potomac Telephone of Washington, DC Chesapeake & Potomac Telephone of Maryland Chesapeake & Potomac Telephone of Virginia Chesapeake & Potomac Telephone of West Virginia New Jersey Bell
Ameritech	Illinois Bell Indiana Bell Michigan Bell Ohio Bell Wisconsin Telephone
BellSouth Corporation	Southern Bell SouthCentral Bell
Southwestern Bell Corporation	Southwestern Bell Telephone Co.
U.S. West Inc.	Northwestern Bell Mountain Bell Pacific Northwest Bell
Pacific Telesis Group	Pacific Telephone Nevada Telephone

from any telephone company can be completed to any other telephone company. With court-ordered divestiture of AT&T at the start of 1984, the twenty-two local operating companies of the Bell System were combined into seven independent regional operating companies. The new companies and their antecedents are discussed in Table 1. Under the new arrangement, the Bell Operating Companies provide the actual telephone network, your connection to it, and all the customer services involved, much like a utility company supplies electricity. You can get your telephone instruments from any vendor you choose. The vendor from which you bought your telephone is also the one that maintains it, but you should still go to the telephone company to get line problems fixed. At this time, the full impact of the breakup of the Bell System is still a matter of conjecture. The old AT&T motto of "One policy, one system, universal service" no longer applies, and you can probably expect to see diversity arise among the offerings of the seven operating companies. This diversity should allow you to take advantage of many new products and services.

Other Common Carriers

Other Common Carriers, also called *Specialized Common Carriers*, are non-Bell long-distance telephone companies to which you can subscribe. Some have their own intercity microwave and cable networks, while others, called *resellers*, lease circuits or WATS lines from telephone companies. The discount you can expect varies from almost none to 40% or more, often depending on the destination of your call. To use an OCC, you dial its computer switch through a local number, wait for the second dial tone, dial your authorization code, and then dial the number you wish to reach, omitting the initial "1" digit. (Some systems may require you to dial your authorization code *after* the number being called.)

Most OCCs require use of a pushbutton telephone. However, hand-held devices that generate dialing tones are available so that you can still use a rotary telephone to dial the OCC, and then use the device to dial the rest of the numbers. Tone generators that can be screwed into the telephone's mouthpiece (replacing the original microphone) are also available but not all telephones—especially pay telephones—can be dismantled in this fashion. Since OCCs do not have access to the telephone company's switching mechanisms they must use noise sampling techniques to tell if your call has been answered. Stray noises on the line may cause you to be billed even if no one answers. To avoid this problem, many OCCs do not bill you for very short calls. Most OCCs do not have operators on duty, thus making it difficult for you to get credit for wrong numbers. For time and charges, you may be able to time your call and then call the OCC's customer service department and have them figure the cost. Some OCCs offer private lines, speed dialing, account codes for calls billable to your clients, and a service equivalent to 800-number In-WATS service. The billing increment for calls may be less than a full minute. With the breakup of AT&T, some local telephone companies are expected to begin offering direct-distance dialing via OCCs. Instead of dialing "1" prior to a long-distance number, you would dial some other digit or combination of digits indicating the long-distance company you wish to use.

TRANSMISSION FACILITIES

The ten-digit telephone number (such as 311–555–6611) is standard in the United States and Canada. The first three digits (311 in this example) designate your Area Code, or *numbering plan area* in telephone jargon. The next three digits (555) designate the central office or exchange to which your line is attached. The last four digits (6611) designate your line. In many areas, long-distance numbers must be preceded by the digit "1." If you are in the same Area Code as the party you are trying to reach, you do not need to dial the Area Code. In some rural areas you do not have to dial the exchange number if you and the person you are calling are both in the same exchange.

All telephones are connected to a central office where the switching takes place. Calls between numbers of the same prefix are handled within the central office. Calls to numbers with a different prefix must be routed over interoffice trunk lines. In large cities with many central offices, interoffice calls are routed through tandem offices. Calls to another Area Code are routed through your central office's associated toll center. The call may be routed through various other switching centers, depending on destination and line traffic, until the connection has been completed. Even if you call the same long-distance number many times, the routing could be different each time. Many long-distance calls are routed through microwave relay links, using a signal subdivided into smaller bandwidths, with one conversation on each band. If you should hear crosstalk, that means your band has overlapped with another.

Each telephone line requires at least two wires and is referred to as the *customer loop*. In a single-line telephone cable the green and red wires (also called *tip and ring*) are the ones needed to operate your telephone. There may be others (such as the black and yellow ones) but they either are spares or are used for a specialized purpose. Multiline cables use a more complicated color scheme.

TELEPHONE COMPANY SERVICES

With the breakup of the Bell System, it soon may be no longer possible to speak in specific terms about the services you can expect from your telephone company. But the following general points should remain valid for some time.

Message Telecommunications Service

Message Telecommunications Service is also called POTS (Plain Old Telephone Service) and is exemplified by the service used by most residences. In most places, your base monthly bill allows you to make unlimited free local calls. In some areas you are charged for local calls. Local charges may be based on a flat charge per call or on a complex scheme taking into account the length of the call, the distance, and the time of day.

Direct-distance Dialing

Direct-distance dialing (DDD) involves ordinary long-distance calls that you dial yourself. You can dial directly to any number in the United States, Canada, Northwest Mexico, and Mexico City.

Wherever you are, there are two different rate structures—interstate and intrastate. Calls are billed by the minute, figured to the next highest minute, so that sixty-one seconds is billed as two minutes. The first minute is billed at a higher rate than the subsequent minutes. Calls that cover more distance cost more, but not in a proportional way—a 2,000-mile call may cost only twice as much as a twenty-mile call. Interstate calls made in the evening (5:00 p.m. to 11:00 p.m.) are 40% cheaper, while night calls (11:00 p.m. to 8:00 a.m.) are 60% cheaper. (Intrastate discounts may differ.) While you once could call someone at 7:59 a.m. and talk all day at the night rate, this is no longer the case: every minute after 8:00 a.m. will be charged at the day rate, at least for interstate calls.

International Calls

Numbers in Canada and parts of Mexico can be dialed directly using the ten-digit system previously described. Numbers in many other nations can be reached via direct dialing using international access codes. There are four steps involved in international dialing:

1. Dial the international access code—011.
2. Dial the country code (two or three digits).
3. Dial the city code (one to four digits—none in small countries).
4. Dial the local telephone number.

After dialing all the numbers you should then push the # button if you have a pushbutton telephone. This is supposed to speed up the processing of the call, which can take forty-five seconds. To make an operator-assisted international call (such as a collect, credit card, or person-to-person call) use "01" as the international access code. Country codes and some city codes for places that can be reached by direct dialing should be listed in your telephone directory. You will have to call the operator to place calls to other countries not listed there. Country codes are also listed in Chapter Fourteen of this book in the Global Travel and Holidays Chart. See also Table 2, pages 272–273. For questions about international dialing, you can call 800–874–4000.

Marine Radiotelephone

Ships in port or near a coastal city can be reached through the marine operator in that city, obtainable through your local operator. Your call is patched through a shortwave radio link to the ship's radio room. You cannot reach ships at sea this way. Properly equipped ships at sea can be reached through the maritime satellite network (INMARSAT) with the same procedure used for international calls. You just have to know what ocean the ship is in and the ship's telephone number. You dial the international access code (011), the ocean code, the ship's seven-digit number, and the # button if you have a pushbutton telephone. Ocean codes are 871 for the Atlantic, 872 for the Pacific, and 873 for the Indian. INMARSAT calls cost about $10.00 per minute, and if it is long-distance to the satellite uplink facility, you're billed for that, too.

WATS

Wide Area Telephone Service (WATS) is a special telephone line installed at your office that allows outgoing long-distance calls under a billing arrangement that *may* result in lower telephone costs. (WATS lines cannot be used for incoming calls.) There is a widespread myth that WATS calls are free—a myth that can prove costly to those who believe it. The cost of an interstate WATS line is based on usage, just like the cost of using a regular telephone line. The advantage of WATS is that the rates are lower than those for regular telephone calls, and the calls are timed by the second rather than to the next full minute. If you make no calls, all you pay is a basic service fee. The myth of free WATS arose from the rate structure existing before 1981. WATS time was essentially long-distance telephone time bought in advance at a discount, with a large minimum commitment. Businesses whose WATS usage was less than the minimum commitment might let their employees make some personal calls since the overall cost would not be affected. Such businesses might have been smarter not to get WATS lines to begin with.

Inward WATS

Inward WATS lines use the 800 Area Code and are toll-free to the caller. The calls are automatically paid for by the receiver. Printing 800 numbers in advertisements is said to raise the response rate by 20% or more, an important factor to consider in marketing. At one time you had to get separate 800 numbers for intrastate and out-of-state callers, but now this procedure is unnecessary. Other recent enhancements include customized call routing so that calls from different areas of the country will be routed to different offices, and variable call routing so that after-hours calls will be routed to a separate office. The Information operator for toll-free numbers can be reached at 800–555–1212.

Operator-assisted Calls

Operator-assisted calls can be made by dialing "0" and then the number you are trying to reach. The operator will come on before the call goes through. Operator-assisted calls cost more than regular calls except when they are used to overcome a line problem. The surcharge varies. It is usually considered onerous on short calls but less significant on long calls.

Collect calls.   When the operator comes on, you give your name and explain that you are making a collect call. When the call is answered the operator asks if the call recipient will accept the charges. If you ask to speak to a specific person, the call becomes a person-to-person collect call, whether you realize it or not, and the cost is increased.

Third-party calls.   You can call from one number to another number and charge it to a third number, presumably your home or office telephone. The operator may call that number and see if you are authorized to charge calls to it. In some places you might not be allowed to make third-party calls at all from a pay telephone.

Credit card calls.   You give the operator your telephone company credit card number, assuming you've been issued one. In some cases you will be turned over to a recording that will ask you to dial in your credit card number.

Time and charges.   You tell the operator you want time and charges, and then you stay on the line after the call is completed. The operator or a recording will come on and tell you the length of the call and its cost. If you forget and hang up at the end of the call, the operator should call you back immediately and give you the time and charges.

Person-to-person.   You tell the operator the name of the party you are trying to reach, the operator stays on the line until you speak to that person, and charging begins only at that moment. While this may take the risk out of making a long-distance call to someone who might not be in, the surcharge is as much as you might pay for a half dozen short calls. Also, if your party is not there and the operator asks if you want to talk to someone else and you agree, you'll have made an ordinary call for the price of a person-to-person call.

Conference calls.   You should call the operator direct and announce your plans, giving the names and numbers of the people you want to talk to. You should schedule the call with the conferees well in advance.

Foreign Exchanges and Tie Lines

If your office makes a lot of calls to a specific city, you can get a foreign exchange (FX) to that city. An FX is essentially a direct line. When you lift the handset of an FX telephone, you are getting a dial tone from the city it is connected to. There is no usage fee—only the monthly lease for the line. A tie line is a similar leased line between two PBXs in distant cities.

Custom Calling

For an extra fee your local telephone company may be able to provide ordinary telephones with features similar to some of those built into office telephone systems. These features include speed dialing, call waiting, call forwarding, automated answering services, and three-way calling.

ADVANCED BUSINESS TELECOMMUNICATIONS

Videoconferencing

While some organizations may have Picturephones linking various offices or individuals, the use of televised communication has come to mean video teleconferencing between groups of people in specially equipped rooms. Several hotel chains offer such facilities. A firm can build its own videoconferencing system using transmission facilities provided by any of several companies. Videoconferencing can involve one-way or two-way television transmission. One-way transmissions are essentially private TV transmissions to a select audience, and are used for activities such as announcing new policies to a company's national sales force. (See the next illustration.) The salespeople meet in a videoconferencing room in their city and watch corporate management's televised presentation. Questions can be fielded through a telephone hookup. The advantages to videoconferencing are that everyone gets the message at the same time, and executives are not tied up for weeks putting on traveling road shows to educate a sales force.

Two-way videoconferencing involves smaller, more elaborate facilities. The standard configuration is a soundproofed room with a conference table and one or more wide-screen TV monitors on a wall at one end of the table. Two cameras are often used, either to provide coverage from different angles or to project charts or other written material on the screen. Fax machines also may be included. The cost of two-way videoconferencing can be several thousand dollars per session but its advantage is its cost-effectiveness over executive travel time to an off-site location.

Videoconferencing

One-way videoconferencing at a hotel videoconferencing facility.
Courtesy of Hilton Hotels Corporation.

Cellular Radio

Cellular radios are modernized versions of the old mobile car radiotelephones. The old method requires one channel for each conversation; therefore, in metropolitan areas not enough channels are available for everyone wanting to talk. Car radios are reached through the mobile telephone operator in your city. To make a call from a car you first have to find a vacant channel and then you have the mobile operator connect you with the number you want. Cities with cellular radio systems are divided into circular cells, with each cell being perhaps a mile in diameter and served by a small low-power transmitter constantly emitting a special carrier signal. Your cellular radiotelephone constantly tunes itself to the closest and strongest transmitter. When it hears its own number being broadcast, it responds, tunes to a voice channel indicated by the controlling transmitter, and rings your telephone. As you drive from one cell to the next you are handed off to the transmitter in the next cell without your being aware of it. Using a cellular radio is much like using an ordinary pushbutton telephone. You make calls from it by dialing the telephone number and people reach you by dialing your car's telephone number. A red indicator light shows that your telephone is tuned to a cellular transmitter. It is expected that most of the country will be served by cellular radios by the end of the decade, with perhaps three million customers availing themselves of the systems.

Voice Mail

Voice mail involves automated delivery of telephone messages through computerized processing of the speaker's voice. A voice mail system is usually attached to an office telephone system as a peripheral device but it also may be a telephone company service. By using the buttons of a pushbutton telephone, a user can invoke the voice mail system, input the telephone number of the recipient and any special commands (such as delivery at a designated hour), and speak the message. (See the next illustration.) The message is digitalized and stored within the computer. The computer then calls the recipient—either immediately or at a designated time—and plays the message. If the recipient's telephone is busy or no one answers, the computer can keep trying until it gets through. Voice mail is usually used for short messages, with the advantage being that you do not

Voice Message Exchange™ System

Template for the face of a pushbutton telephone when used as a Voice Message℠ terminal with the Voice Message Exchange™ System of VMX, Inc.

Courtesy of VMX, Inc.

have to waste time trying to reach your recipient—your messages will get through on their own, so to speak. Possible options include access to and from outside telephones, the ability to edit messages, audio message headers stating who sent the message and when, delivery verification, message filing, and delivery to multiple recipients.

TELEPHONE COST CONTROL

In firms where no effort is made to control telephone costs, as much as a third of the telephone bill may result from call abuse—i.e., employees using the office telephones to make personal long-distance calls. If you have been given the job of combating call abuse, your best tool may be simple psychology: remind everyone that long-distance calls are not a salary perk and announce that a campaign has been launched against telephone abusers, who can expect to be caught. Pressure also can be brought to bear on them by circulating a copy of the telephone bill and requiring each person to read and sign it, or by simply posting the bill on the bulletin board. You may see the telephone bill drop even if you take no further action. A station message detail recorder also could help identify the call abusers, but nothing will be of much help unless management demonstrates its continuing resolve to take action against phone abusers.

Proper training is important in cost control, especially when you realize that one way of making a phone call can be ten times more expensive than another (an example being a one-minute call made through an OCC compared with the same call placed person-to-person through an operator). Employees should be warned against making person-to-person calls and repeatedly reminded that WATS calls are not free. You also may wish to check inventory and ensure that all the lines and equipment you are being billed for have in fact been installed. In large organizations undergoing constant change there is a good chance that an expensive mistake has been made. Telephone system management is a broad subject requiring specialized knowledge, especially now that the market has been opened to broader competition. Any information supplied by an account representative or equipment salesperson should be taken with the realization that he or she has a financial interest in your decisions. Books and literature on telephone system management are available through the Telecom Library, 205 West 19th Street, New York, NY 10011.

TELEPHONE TECHNIQUES

INCOMING CALLS

Projecting a positive corporate image is something we all hear about and hope to do, but what exactly does it mean? A secretary's role can be particularly important because he or she is often the first voice—and sometimes the only voice—a caller will hear. We all have bad moods or off days, but that's not the caller's fault. Your attitude, your inflection, and your manner will help a caller form an opinion about you and about your company. In my job as secretary to the head of corporate communications for NBC, I spend most of my day on the telephone with a wide variety of people—viewers, TV and radio critics from all around the country, employees of other companies, and other NBC employees. Whether I'm speaking with the chairman of the board or a clerk in the Research Department or a viewer who has a complaint about last night's episode of "Hill Street Blues," I try to be as polite and helpful as possible.

All of us have encountered rude or nasty people on the telephone. If, for instance, you have a billing problem with a department store and the person in the credit department is rude and not particularly helpful, you might hang up the phone in frustration and declare that you will never shop in that store again. That's not saying much for that particular company's corporate image in your eyes. Occasionally, a call might come in from someone who has a question or is seeking information about your company and has been transferred from office to office to office, hearing only "You're on the wrong line" or "I can't help you." By the time the caller gets to your office, he or she is angry and frustrated. Having been through similar experiences, I can sympathize with those callers. When I answer calls like that, I try to avoid having to transfer them once again unless I can be sure the person they're being switched to can definitely provide the correct information. Rather than passing the buck, it's sometimes necessary to find out exactly what it is they want, take down their names and numbers and, when you have ascertained the information, get back to them as soon as possible, or have someone in the appropriate division or department return the calls.

Any incoming call should be answered on the second ring, if possible. How the phone is answered might depend on the preference of the executive. For example, if you work with just one person, you might answer by using his or her name, as "Good morning, Mr. London's office." If your work is more general—for a department rather than for a particular person—it is probably better to answer by identifying the department, as, for instance "Good afternoon, Personnel Benefits." The way in which you answer the phone indicates your attitude toward the caller and toward your job. A friendly and helpful attitude will help project good will for you and for your company.

Correct Hold Procedures

No one likes to be put on hold, but of course it's inevitable in a business office. Being on hold is especially annoying when a caller is left in limbo with no explanation. It's always a good idea to go back on the line with the callers and let them know how long they can expect to continue holding—if that's their preference—or to suggest that they might want to have their calls returned. For instance, if the executive is on another line and the caller wants to hold, check in again after about thirty to sixty seconds and say, "Ms. Slocum is still on the other line. Would you like to continue to hold?"

If the caller does want to hold, it's a good idea to check in again by saying, "I'm sorry, but I think she's going to be on a while longer. May I have her call you back?" Or, if you can get an idea of how long the executive will be on the first call, you might say, "Ms. Slocum knows you're holding and will be with you in just a minute." I try not to keep people holding more than a minute or two, unless they choose to. One thing to remember is that when one person is on one line and someone else is holding on another, it is impossible for others to reach you. So it might be best to suggest a callback.

Occasionally, it's necessary to answer the executive's line by immediately putting a caller on hold. I try to avoid doing that, but sometimes there's no choice—with two or three lines ringing at the same time, I'll answer by saying, "Mr. Rukeyser's office, please hold a moment," and then get back on the line as soon as I can.

Answering Someone Else's Phone and Having a Coworker Answer Your Phone

A ringing phone should never go unanswered. Whether you are assigned to answer someone else's phone, or you just happen to walk by another office where the phone is ringing, you should be as helpful as possible. It might be necessary to explain to the caller that it's not your office, and rather than saying, "I don't know" or "I can't help you," there's nothing wrong with saying, "I'm afraid there's no one in the office right now. May I have Mr. London or his secretary get back to you?"

Don't give out unnecessary or possibly confidential information. When taking a message, get all of the pertinent data—time, name of caller, title and company, phone number, including extension, and any message the caller might want to leave. On the floor where I work, we have a receptionist who will answer our phones while we're out—for a few minutes or during the lunch hour—so that coverage is not a problem, and rarely is it necessary to answer someone else's phone. In many offices, however, arrangements have to be made to have phones answered in the secretary's absence. In one of the executive office suites here at NBC there are six executives and six secretaries. All of the secretaries have each other's extensions on their phones. Each month they make up a schedule of lunch coverage, so that each secretary handles the phones once every six working days. This arrangement provides flexibility for switching days when necessary.

If you ask a coworker to answer your phone, it is your responsibility to explain how the phone should be answered, what calls might be expected by the executive, where the executive can be reached if necessary, and any other pertinent information. Be sure to alert your coworker if the executive is expecting a particular call or, as sometimes happens, if the executive does not want to accept certain calls. Explain how the executive prefers to have the phone answered. You might call the executive by a nickname, but it doesn't necessarily mean that he or she wants the phone answered that way. *Charles* London might be preferable to *Chuck* London.

Correct Call Transfer Procedures

If it's necessary to transfer a call—whether because it came in on the wrong line or because the executive wants to take the call in another office—explain to the caller what you're doing. Don't just say "Hold on." On most office phone systems the correct way to transfer a call is to depress the switch-hook or cradle once and release it immediately. When a steady dial tone comes on, dial the desired extension and, when answered, announce the call and hang up.

If the call does come in on the wrong line, handle it this way: "I'm sorry, Ms. Slocum is not on this extension. If you'll hold a moment, I'll transfer you to the correct line." It's a good idea to give the correct extension to the caller in case he or she gets cut off or wants to call back later.

If the executive wants to take the call on another extension, you can say, "Mr. London is in another office right now but would like to speak with you. Please hold on and I'll transfer you." Stay on the line, and when someone answers the second extension, explain that you're transferring a call and who it's for.

Screening Calls

When a secretary has been working with an executive for a while, he or she has some idea of whom the executive does or does not want to speak with. I am familiar with most of the people who call our office and am able to screen them to my supervisor's satisfaction. If he's in a meeting and comes back to ten messages, he usually leaves it up to me to determine the order in which they should be returned. My manager is very open and willing to speak with almost anyone. We'll often get calls from viewers who want to comment—pro or con—on something they saw on NBC, and he invariably makes himself available. But there are always a few annoying or persistent callers and, after more than two years, I pretty much know who they are and do my best to head them off.

You should never give the impression that the executive doesn't want to speak with the caller, and it's rude to ask "Who's calling?" before indicating whether the executive is in or out. It sounds too much like you're screening the call, which is, of course, exactly what you are doing. An example of how *not* to answer a call is shown in Dialogue A:

Dialogue A

Secretary: Good afternoon. Mr. London's office.
Caller: Is Mr. London in?
Secretary: Who's calling?
Caller: Ed McGuire from UBC.
Secretary: Mr. London is in a meeting now. Would you like to leave a message?

This may give the caller the impression that Mr. London might be in—but not for Mr. McGuire.

It's always helpful if the caller gives identification at the beginning of the conversation. If no identification is forthcoming, you can still handle the situation tactfully as shown in Dialogue B:

Dialogue B

Secretary: Good morning. Ms. Slocum's office.
Caller: Hello. Is Ms. Slocum there?
Secretary: Not at the moment. May I ask who's calling?

My supervisor doesn't like to take calls from people who won't tell me why they're calling. If you are unsure who is on the line, there is nothing wrong with asking, "May I tell him what this is in reference to?"

Annoying calls. Rude or persistent callers can try anyone's patience, and there may not necessarily be a general rule of thumb for dealing with them. The expression, "You can catch more flies with honey than with vinegar" may well be true. One professional secretary whom I know deals with rude people in just that way—the nicer she is to someone who is barking at her, the more flustered the other person becomes, and little by little that person's rudeness evaporates to stunned politeness.

But for some people, dealing with rude callers is in fact annoying, and all the sweetness in the world won't work. In that case patience should prevail, as difficult as it may be. Recently, my patience was tested when an incredibly rude person insisted on making an appointment with my supervisor, who, having had past dealings with the man, made it clear that he did not want to see him. When I indicated to the caller that my supervisor would not be available for several weeks, he became abusive and said he wasn't going to deal "with someone who is just a secretary," and vowed to call me every day until my supervisor would see him. He kept that vow and called me every day for two weeks. I was getting rather testy by then and began to dread answering the phone. Then one day I guess he gave up, because I haven't heard from him since. There's not much to do if a caller insists on calling over and over again. You can always assure the person that you will give the message to the executive. If a caller is profane or insulting, hang up.

Message-taking Procedures

For every message taken, general information is to be recorded: the time of the call, the name of the caller, his or her title and company, the phone number—including Area Code and extension—and the reason for the call. It's a good idea to repeat the number to the caller in order to verify it. It can be rather embarrassing to return a call for the executive—or for the executive to return the call—and have the wrong number. At NBC, we have two forms for messages. One is a telephone message pad with spaces for all the information provided by the caller. The other is a long sheet called a Telephone Message Register. Some executives prefer this one because it enables them to have all of their messages on a single sheet, rather than on five or ten separate message sheets.

In many cases, callers will be known to the secretary but if not, it's a good idea to ask what the call is about. If the executive is unavailable, there's always a chance that someone else can help the caller or that the caller is talking with the wrong office anyway.

Occasionally, you will end up playing "telephone tag" with callers—i.e., someone calls the executive in your office, who isn't in, and when you return the

Telephone Message Slip

Courtesy of National Broadcasting Company, Inc.

Telephone Message Register

**NBC Telephone
Message Register**

Date: March 1, 1984

Time	Name	Telephone	Subject and Action	
9³⁰ a.m	John O'Reilly	(123) 444-5555	Affiliates Meeting	returned
10³⁰ a.m	Loretta Davis	(231) 555-4444	Luncheon Friday	to call back
10⁴⁵ a.m	Martin Green	(222) 666-1111	Talk Show writers	to call back
10⁵⁰ a.m.	Nancy Maginness	(765) 432-1234	News Broadcast subject	returned
11⁰⁰ a.m.	Tobias Quinn	ext. 2310	PR/Election Coverage	
11¹⁵ a.m.	Joe Montague	ext. 6870	Contract for John Doe	
11²⁰ a.m.	Lilly De Garve	(711) 987-6543	TV News Publicity	
1⁰⁰ p.m.	Barbara Torham	ext. 0123	Mary Roberts' contract	returned
1³⁰ p.m.	Bill Bertram	(803) 222-3434	Sales Meeting Presentation	returned
1⁴⁵ pm	Sidney Diamond	(315) 678-9101	8 m. news query	
2⁰⁰ p.m.	Carole Smith	(987) 655-1238	news analysis query	
2¹⁵ p.m.	Lee Lohman	ext. 4444	News Dept. Meeting	returned
3⁰⁰ p.m.	Naomi Walters	ext. 6789	'ection '84 Meeting	returned
3¹⁵ p.m.	Peter Grayson	ext. 7654	Dinner ³/₁₀/84 - reminder	
3³⁰ p.m.	Allen Camp	ext. 9988	Meeting re Primaries	returned
4⁰⁰ p.m.	William Smith	ext. 6654	no message - please call back ASAP	
4³⁰ p.m.	Rachel Lee	(832) 223-3434	query - election news	
5⁰⁰ p.m.	Sally Benson	(983) 456-8348	query - election coverage	
5¹⁵ p.m.	Peter Martini	684-3232	reminder - golf date ³/₁₁/84	

GE-1005 (5/83)

Courtesy of National Broadcasting Company, Inc.

call, the caller isn't in. It gets rather silly after a while. I know of one instance where it literally took two weeks for the two callers to get together, and by the time they did the original caller had forgotten why he had called in the first place!

Diplomatic Termination of Calls
Some callers tend to ramble on as though you have nothing better to do than spend time on the phone with them. These calls can be time-consuming and

Table 2. International Dialing: Codes and Time Differences for Many Countries

To determine the time in the countries listed below, add the number of hours shown under your own time zone to your local time (or subtract, if preceded by a minus sign). Time differences are based on Standard Time, observed in the U.S. (in most states) from the last Sunday in October until the last Sunday in April. This may vary in some countries. Several countries have more than one time zone. The time differences for these countries are based on the following cities: Sydney, Australia; Rio de Janeiro, Brazil; Jakarta, Indonesia; Kuala Lumpur, Malaysia; and Moscow, U.S.S.R.

Country Codes		City Codes	Time Difference U.S. Time Zones			
			EST	CST	MST	PST
Andorra	33	All Points 078	6	7	8	9
Argentina	54	Buenos Aires 1, Cordoba 51, Rosario 41	2	3	4	5
Australia	61	Canberra 62, Melbourne 3, Sydney 2	16	17	18	19
Austria	43	Graz 316, Linz 732, Vienna 222	6	7	8	9
Bahrain	973	*	8	9	10	11
Belgium	32	Antwerp 31, Brussels 2, Ghent 91, Liege 41	6	7	8	9
Belize	501	Belize City*, Belmopan 08, Corozal Town 04	−1	0	1	2
Bolivia	591	Cochabamba 42, La Paz 2, Santa Cruz 33	1	2	3	4
Brazil	55	Belo Horizonte 31, Brasilia 61, Sao Paulo 11	2	3	4	5
Chile	56	Concepcion 42, Santiago 2, Valparaiso 31	2	3	4	5
Colombia	57	Bogota*, Cali 3, Medellin 4	0	1	2	3
Costa Rica	506	*	−1	0	1	2
Cyprus	357	Limassol 51, Nicosia 21, Paphos 61	7	8	9	10
Denmark	45	Aarhus 6, Copenhagen 1 or 2, Odense 9	6	7	8	9
East Germany	37	Berlin 2, Dresden 51, Leipzig 41	6	7	8	9
Ecuador	593	Ambato 2, Cuenca 4, Guayaquil 4, Quito 2	0	1	2	3
El Salvador	503	*	−1	0	1	2
Fiji	679	*	17	18	19	20
Finland	358	Helsinki 0, Tampere 31, Turku-Abo 21	7	8	9	10
France	33	Bordeaux 56, Lille 20, Lyon 7, Marseille 91, Nice 93, Paris 1, Strasbourg 88, Toulouse 61	6	7	8	9
Great Britain	44	Belfast 232, Birmingham 21, Cardiff 222, Edinburgh 31, Glasgow 41, Leeds 532, Liverpool 51, London 1, Sheffield 742	5	6	7	8
Greece	30	Athens 1, Iraklion 81, Kavala 51, Larissa 41, Patrai 61, Piraeus 1, Thessaloniki 31, Volos 421	7	8	9	10
Guadeloupe	596	*	1	2	3	4
Guatemala	502	Guatemala City 2, Quezaltenango*	−1	0	1	2
Guyana	592	Bartica 05, Georgetown 02	2	3	4	5
Haiti	509	Cap Hatien 3, Gonaive 2, Port Au Prince 1	0	1	2	3
Honduras	504	*	−1	0	1	2
Hong Kong	852	Hong Kong 5, Kowloon 3, Sha Tin 0	13	14	15	16
Indonesia	62	Jakarta 21, Medan 61, Semarang 24	12	13	14	15
Iran	98	Esfahan 31, Mashad 51, Tabriz 41, Teheran 21	8½	9½	10½	11½
Iraq	964	Baghdad 1, Basra 40, Hilla 30, Mosul 60	8	9	10	11
Ireland	353	Cork 21, Dublin 1, Galway 91, Limerick 61	5	6	7	8
Israel	972	Haifa 4, Jerusalem 2, Ramat Gan 3, Tel Aviv 3	7	8	9	10

Table 2. (continued)

Country Codes		City Codes	Time Difference U.S. Time Zones			
			EST	CST	MST	PST
Italy	39	Bari 80, Bologna 51, Florence 55, Genoa 10, Milan 2, Naples 81, Palermo 91, Rome 6, Turin 11	6	7	8	9
Ivory Coast	225	*	5	6	7	8
Japan	81	Kitakyushu 93, Kobe 78, Kyoto 75, Nagoya 52, Osaka 6, Sapporo 11, Tokyo 3, Yokohama 45	14	15	16	17
Kenya	254	Mombasa 11, Nairobi 2, Nakuru 37	8	9	10	11
Kuwait	965	*	8	9	10	11
Liberia	231	*	5	6	7	8
Libya	218	Benghazi 61, Misuratha 51, Tripoli 21	7	8	9	10
Liechtenstein	41	All points 75	6	7	8	9
Luxembourg	352	*	6	7	8	9
Malaysia	60	Ipoh 5, Kelang 3, Kuala Lumpur 3	12½	13½	14½	15½
Martinique	596	*	1	2	3	4
Monaco	33	All points 93	6	7	8	9
Netherlands	31	Amsterdam 20, Rotterdam 10	6	7	8	9
Netherlands Antilles	599	Aruba 8, Curacao 9	1	2	3	4
New Zealand	64	Auckland 9, Wellington 4	18	19	20	21
Nicaragua	505	Chinandega 341, Leon 31, Managua 2	−1	0	1	2
Nigeria	234	Ibadan 22, Kano 64, Lagos 1	6	7	8	9
Norway	47	Bergen 5, Oslo 2, Trondheim 75	6	7	8	9
Panama	507	*	0	1	2	3
Papua New Guinea	675	*	15	16	17	18
Paraguay	595	Asuncion 21, Concepcion 31	2	3	4	5
Peru	51	Arequipa 54, Callao 14, Lima 14, Trujillo 44	0	1	2	3
Philippines	63	Cebu 32, Davao 35, Iloilo 33, Manila 2	13	14	15	16
Portugal	351	Coimbra 39, Lisbon 19, Porto 29	5	6	7	8
Qatar	974	*	8	9	10	11
Rumania	40	Bucharest 0, Cluj 51, Constanta 16	7	8	9	10
San Marino	39	All points 541	6	7	8	9
Saudi Arabia	966	Jeddah 2, Mecca 2, Riyadh 1	8	9	10	11
Senegal	221	*	5	6	7	8
Singapore	65	*	12½	13½	14½	15½
South Africa	27	Cape Town 21, Johannesburg 11	7	8	9	10
South Korea	82	Pusan 51, Seoul 2, Taegu 53	14	15	16	17
Soviet Union	7	Kiev 044, Leningrad 812, Minsk 017, Moscow 095, Tallinn 0142	8	9	10	11
Spain	34	Barcelona 3, Madrid 1, Seville 54, Valencia 6	6	7	8	9
Sri Lanka	94	Colombo 1, Kandy 8, Moratuwa 72	10½	11½	12½	13½
Surinam	597	*	1½	2½	3½	4½
Sweden	46	Goteborg 31, Malmo 40, Stockholm 8	6	7	8	9
Switzerland	41	Basel 61, Berne 31, Geneva 22, St. Moritz 82, Zurich 1	6	7	8	9
Tahiti	689	*	−5	−4	−3	−2
Taiwan	886	Kaohsiung 7, Tainan 62, Taipei 2	13	14	15	16
Thailand	66	Bangkok 2	12	13	14	15
Tunisia	216	Menzel Bourguiba 2, Tunis 1	6	7	8	9
Turkey	90	Adana 711, Ankara 41, Istanbul 11, Izmir 51	7	8	9	10
United Arab Emirates	971	Abu Dhabi 2, Ajman 6	9	10	11	12
Uruguay	598	Canelones 332, Mercedes 532, Montevideo 2	2	3	4	5
Vatican City	39	All points	6	7	8	9
Venezuela	58	Caracas 2, Maracaibo 61, Valencia 41	1	2	3	4
West Germany	49	Berlin 30, Bonn 228, Essen 201, Frankfurt 611, Hamburg 40, Munich 89	6	7	8	9
Yugoslavia	38	Belgrade 11, Skoplje 91, Zagreb 41	6	7	8	9

For city codes not listed dial "0" (operator).

*City Codes not required.

**Military bases cannot be dialed directly.

difficult to terminate. We get many calls from viewers or listeners who spend nearly all of their time watching television or listening to the radio and, as a result, call us to offer an opinion or make a suggestion. I've answered many calls from these incessant talkers, and while I sympathize with them and often try to hear them out, I usually have a million other things that I should be doing. In most cases, if I can get a word in, I thank them for calling and offer to pass the information along to the proper person or department. One secretary whom I know has an agreement with her supervisor that if he is on a long call with someone he doesn't especially like, she should tell him there's a fire drill on their floor—not particularly diplomatic, but a crafty way of getting off the phone. One drawback is that the excuse shouldn't be used more than once with the same person!

A producer at a local New York radio station once got a call during a very busy shift and was rude to the caller and abruptly hung up. The next day the producer was called into his supervisor's office and was fired. The caller he had hung up on the previous evening was the vice president and general manager of the radio station, who, needless to say, was not too pleased that one of his employees would treat a caller so harshly. And, of course, any caller could be a friend of the chairman of the board of your company, and while a polite call probably won't stay on the caller's mind, a rude one certainly will—and the next time he sees the chairman at a cocktail party and mentions the nasty secretary in Mr. London's office, who knows what could happen?

OUTGOING CALLS

When placing a telephone call for the executive, ensure that you have the right number at hand (check the other party's company letterhead, the telephone book, or your Rolodex first). Be sure that you know the name of the person being called and that you can pronounce the name correctly. Check the time zone map(s) before placing long-distance domestic or international calls. Finally, be sure that your own superior is still in the office when you make the call: sometimes an executive will ask that a call be placed but then will step out for a minute or will become involved in an impromptu, closed-door meeting. It is extremely rude to keep the person being called hanging on the line while you try to find the vanished executive or attempt to extricate the executive from a meeting. If an unavoidable delay occurs and you cannot connect the parties right away, stay on the line with the person being called and explain the situation. Never just put the other party on hold and hang up.

Give the person being called at least ten rings, or about forty-five seconds in which to answer. Be prepared to speak as soon as the person does answer; you ought not to be talking with someone else or shuffling papers while attempting to introduce yourself. Use a pleasant tone of voice and speak clearly. Remember, when using the phone you are representing the company, and you want to project a positive image. The secretary who starts off with a staccato "Hello.Thisis Mr.London'sofficecalling.IsMs.Slocumin?" will undoubtedly have to repeat the entire message, much to the irritation of the person on the other end of the line. When the secretary to the person being called answers, you can say, "Hello. Mr. London from ZBC calling. Mr. London would like to speak with Ms. Slocum, please." As soon as Ms. Slocum comes on the line, buzz Mr. London and say,

"Ms. Slocum is on the line" or the like, and hang up your extension. If Ms. Slocum answers herself, say, "Hello, Ms. Slocum. This is Ann Beale from ZBC calling. Mr. London would like to speak with you. Shall I put him on?" If she says yes, then say, "Here he is," and buzz Mr. London. Try to avoid keeping either person waiting for more than a second or two.

If the person being called is not in, find out when he or she will be back. You can have the person return your executive's call or you can have your executive call back, depending on each person's schedule. If your superior wants to call again, find out what time would be best for both parties so as to avoid telephone tag.

Domestic Time Zone Map, United States and Canada

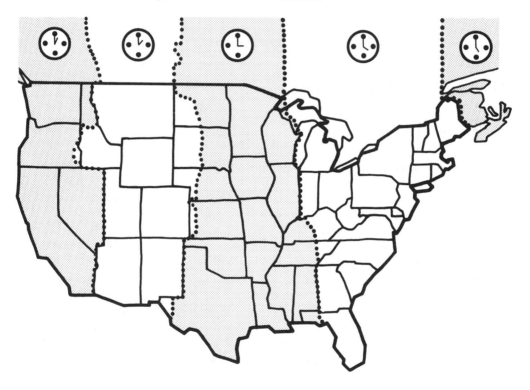

Subtract two hours from Pacific Time to obtain Alaska-Hawaii Time.

9

Conventional and Electronic Mail

Ann Elise Rubin • *Editorial Assistant to William Safire*, The New York Times *Washington Bureau ("Conventional Mail" Section of this Chapter)*
Lamont Wood • *Professional Writer; formerly Public Relations Writer, Datapoint Corporation ("Electronic Mail" Section of this Chapter)*

CONVENTIONAL MAIL

INTRODUCTION

Mail at *The New York Times* Washington Bureau

Just as the telephone and computer terminal are communication lifelines in business and industry today, so too is the mail. But written correspondence, unlike sophisticated electronic devices, is relatively inexpensive and technologically uncomplicated. In addition, conventional mail is the most private medium and the one least likely to be monitored or tampered with, without your knowledge. In today's very competitive domestic and multinational workplace, security of communications is a factor to be reckoned with as we have seen from the highly publicized activities of computer hackers and telephone eavesdroppers.

Although the expression "conventional mail" may sound somewhat less entrancing than descriptors for its more exotic electronic counterparts, its importance in keeping business moving cannot be overemphasized. And at times the mail can be anything but ho-hum. Perhaps a bit of specific corporate background will put the matter into proper perspective. *The New York Times* Washington Bureau is the largest of that company's satellite offices. Here, correspondence is often a wellspring of first-hand, hard news. Many *Times* employees receive literally pounds of letters, press releases, newsletters, journals, and other printed materials each day. Some of them have received and reported on mail from unlikely correspondents such as a would-be presidential assassin and an angry young man considering defection from the Soviet Embassy where his parents were stationed. As you can see from these two examples, the mail may be conventional in form or method of delivery, but it is often far from conventional in import or impact. Mail should never be taken lightly.

Since *The New York Times* Washington Bureau receives and posts an exceptionally high volume of mail, it was felt that some of the experience gained in this setting might be passed on to readers of this handbook. The Washington

Bureau serves merely as an example of a heavy mailer; the descriptions that follow are not intended to cover every possible working environment or situation. Of course, the volume and type of incoming and outgoing mail are directly proportional to the nature of the business and the executive's position within that business.

The Washington Bureau is staffed by about fifty news correspondents, columnists, and editors, supported by about twenty-five other individuals. My boss, William Safire, is a twice-weekly political columnist who also writes a weekly language article in the Sunday magazine section of the paper. In addition, he is the author of fiction and nonfiction books, is an occasional participant in various television and radio public affairs programs, and is often sought out for speaking engagements. In short, his is a multifaceted, high-profile position drawing more than its share of mail. For example, Mr. Safire receives about 15% of the letters and packages arriving at the Washington Bureau. This percentage translates into between 200 and 500 pieces of mail each week. Sorting, opening, reading, annotating, evaluating, logging, and routing the incoming mail alone could prove overwhelming were it not for our use of some rather uncomplicated, streamlined, commonsensical procedures—all of which are discussed in the following section together with other ideas perhaps more appropriate to your office than to ours. Similar procedures are given for treatment of outgoing mail, always with a view to fast delivery in a cost-effective manner. The procedures established for your office should be arrived at only after consultation with your employer.

INCOMING MAIL

Sorting and Opening Procedures
Some office functions still cannot be relegated completely to automation. Sorting and slicing open the mail are prime examples, not to mention reading, annotating, and evaluating the contents. The forthcoming subsections discuss these and other manual activities.

Initial sort.   Separate the letters from the periodicals and packages. With the envelopes still unopened, sort the letters into piles containing correspondence marked PERSONAL, first-class mail, bills and statements, and mass mailings (also known as *direct mail* and typically recognizable by their preprinted mailing labels). The categories in the initial sort will vary, depending on the nature of the business you're in. If you organize the mail on a daily basis, you will soon spot an emerging pattern. Define your own groupings and sort accordingly. Eventually you will become proficient enough to omit this step and sort and slice at the same time. Note that the initial sort should help you in the next stages: opening and reading. Out of respect to the writer and to my own employer, I open no mail marked PERSONAL or CONFIDENTIAL. If you open something like this inadvertently, simply say so (an initialed notation on the envelope should suffice), and take measures to prevent it from happening again. That is, look at all envelopes carefully before opening them.

Opening.   For slicing open the envelopes, the stiletto-style openers are preferable. The more functional-looking a letter opener is, the longer it will remain on one's desk. (The chances of its being liberated are reduced if it is not an attractive objet d'art.) However, if one's opener does sprout legs and march off, one can use the long blade on a Swiss Army knife. A sharp knife like this cuts through strapping tape and packaging better than scissors. An artist's knife is also handy for slicing through well wrapped parcels. Although automatic opening machines are available, you must receive a high volume of mail to justify the expense of buying one. Furthermore, in the time required to feed the letters through the device, they could have been opened manually. A simple cost-benefit analysis will determine whether an automatic opener is a necessity. Whatever method is used, care should be taken not to slice through the contents of the envelope.

During the sort, you may find accumulations of junk mail. Junk mail should be set aside and discarded later after it has been evaluated. If you have found that your employer does not wish to receive mail from certain organizations, request that his or her name be removed from their mailing lists. Before doing so, however, get permission from your employer. Because I feel uneasy about discarding unopened mail, just about everything gets opened and read in this office.

Correspondence categories. Before reading the opened letters, you should have created files corresponding to the general nature of your daily mail. This is where the emerging patterns mentioned earlier come in. Many offices can get away with file categories identical to those in the initial sort. In our office, about 70% of the usual first-class letters discuss the language column and linguistic matters; 20%, the Op-Ed political column and the national and international political scene; and the remaining 10% of the letters include social invitations, speaking engagement requests, bills, press releases, and some direct mail that has escaped my initial sort. The standard files that I have established for our mail fall under the headings "On Language" for the language column; "Daily" for the twice-weekly Essay and other topics of the day; "Other" for the newsletters, invitations, and miscellaneous letters; and "Important," into which I put the unopened letters labeled PERSONAL or CONFIDENTIAL, correspondence from prominent people in the public and private sectors, all *Times* memos and correspondence from other colleagues, social invitations, speaking engagement offers, telegrams and Mailgrams, financial statements, checks, bills, and so on. During conventions, crises, and at other times when the mail flows at flood level, I establish additional files for special press releases, newsletters, and advertisements.

Quite often I also create subsets within the major categories. For instance, on occasion Mr. Safire asks his language column readers for submissions of regionalisms, and sometimes he wants to know if anyone Out There knows the origin of an expression such as *the whole nine yards* for use in a future column. Mr. Safire's readers are precisely the types to write letters, and when he asks for help, he gets it . . . in spades . . . redoubled! Therefore, I might create a file just for correspondence relating to the expression for which he has sought input. The main purpose of the narrower categories is to save time in the future when culling the best letters and writing up a synopsis of the readers' submissions.

These categories and the date on which the mail was delivered are written on the tab at the top of the file folders, thus precluding the need for stamping each piece with the date on which it was received. (I only make a special date notation on an item when there is a large time lag between the date on which the letter was written and the date on which it was received or if it is an invitation for a function already held the night before.) However, if you prefer to stamp each piece with date and time, a variety of devices are available. They range from rubber stamps that imprint "Received" in a box large enough to accommodate the date and time of receipt written in by hand or adjustable daters that stamp the date and time, to automatic dating machines. Your own needs will dictate your choice.

As for the plethora of periodicals and packages, I obviously do not attempt to fit them into a file folder. I do thumb through the tables of contents of magazines or the media kits accompanying books and annotate them as described below. I then stack these items neatly alongside my employer's in-box. You would follow the same procedure with items such as equipment and product catalogues, technical journals, and lengthy advertising packets from outside vendors.

Reading, Annotating, and Digesting

At this point, you've got your mail sliced open and the files ready. Now comes the fun: the reading. Ideally, your employer should handle each piece of mail only once, lest he or she—and you—become unnecessarily saddled with excessive paperwork. In this single shot, the letter should be read and a decision passed on it: Does it get filed? Answered? Or is further research required? Here are some techniques that may be useful to you in helping your employer act on each piece of incoming correspondence in an expeditious manner.

Reading and highlighting. Read the letter and annotate the gist of the message. In our office each letter must be read in its entirety in order to avoid overlooking good information. (Many ideas for columns originate with our readers.) On occasion, usable information is found at the end of the letter or on page three of a four-pager. It's unfair to expect your employer to plow through the fluff to get to the pertinent material; that's your responsibility. Once you hit the mother lode in the letter, you must call attention to it. Use removable self-sticking notes. They are neat and easy to use, and they come in a variety of sizes. Mark pages and passages with them; write your remarks and references on them. When making notations directly on letters and journals (and only you can decide which ones they are), use nonrepro blue pens. They now come in felt tip, far preferable to conventional graphite. Notations made in nonrepro blue are invisible when photocopied.

Affixing envelopes and enclosures to the letters. Just as you must check the outside of the envelope for PERSONAL or CONFIDENTIAL notations, so should you examine the letter itself for the return address. If a letter arrives without the correspondent's return address, attach the envelope to it even if the address does not appear thereon. Remember, you can never give too much information; neglecting to clip an envelope to a piece of correspondence is tantamount to withholding information. And always affix enclosures to the letter. If enclosures are referred to in the letter but have not been included with it, make a notation to this effect in the margin or on a self-sticking note, and then—if necessary and appropriate—call the correspondent and request the enclosures. This can be a frustrating task, but it will make *you* more careful about your own outgoing mailings and their enclosures.

Handling hate mail. Any section dealing with incoming mail would be incomplete without a frank discussion of hate mail. Such material is not limited to media recipients, although their high profiles tend to make them rather handy targets. Hate mail, or poison-pen letters, often have the same effect on their readers as pathological or obscene telephone calls have on their recipients. Due to the often controversial, always passionate nature of William Safire's writing, we occasionally receive such mail. If you ever feel endangered by the contents of a particular letter or parcel, do not hesitate to call your company's security guard, the police, or the Postal Inspection Service. Laws proscribe such abuse of the mail system just as other statutes forbid obscene and obnoxious telephone calls. Incidentally, in our office we do not construe as hate mail the correspondence received from readers disagreeing with a perspective expressed in a given column. Yes, we do get our share of clipped columns with furious notations in the margins. These letters of disagreement are treated just as any other correspondence is: I put them in the appropriate mail file folders. My employer respects the viewpoints of others and would be alarmed if he were sheltered from them.

Maintaining a mail log.   Some offices require maintenance of a log in which the receipt of important pieces of mail is recorded. A mail log allows you to refer again to basic data about a letter without pulling it from the file. A typical log records the date and time of receipt, the date of the letter itself, the name and affiliation of the correspondent, the nature of the letter, the name of the addressee, and the nature and date of the final disposition. If filing space is limited, use of a mail log precludes the need to save originals. (Nowadays, such records can be stored in your computer system.) It also may be advisable to keep a log as a record of outgoing mail, too.

Submitting the mail.   The final step in the processing of incoming mail is submission of the sorted stack of files to your employer. Always put the most important folder(s) on top of the stack.

OUTGOING MAIL

Proofreading

The typewriting and formatting of business letters are discussed in Chapter Six. However, the final proofreading before signature and mailing is important enough to be discussed again here. You don't have to be in publishing to be a picky proofreader: the truly professional secretary scrutinizes all outgoing correspondence for correct spelling, proper syllable splits, and good syntax as well as for the presence of excessive strikeovers and corrections. Your goal is to compose or transcribe a letter calling attention to itself because of its correct format, substantive content, and original ideas—not because of a smudged correction or incorrect use of an honorific with a recipient's name. Remember that all outgoing letters represent your employer and the corporation to others. The better you make them look, the better you will look, too.

Signature

Letters, contracts, checks, or forms in need of signing may be submitted to the executive in several ways. Place all such paperwork in a file folder labeled "To Be Signed," indicate on each piece where the signature and date are to appear (use a self-sticking note), and submit the folder for signing at the executive's convenience. It is preferable to submit a stack of documents all at one time rather than seeking signatures several times throughout the day. However, a letter, contract, or form sometimes must get out posthaste, and you will not be able to wait until you've amassed numerous documents. That's when a clipboard comes in handy. A clipboard allows your employer to sign a letter in the absence of desk space, e.g., while sitting at a word processing terminal or in a reading chair. Another advantage of using a clipboard is that your employer need not be concerned with smudging the document, a primary consideration for one who handles newsprint all day. This technique works especially well for one-page letters.

A large volume of outgoing mail may justify the use of an Autopen, an automatic signature machine that reproduces original signatures. Though it is preferable to a rubber-stamp signature facsimile, it is extremely expensive. If you sign letters on your employer's behalf, it is customary to follow the employer's signature with a slash and your own initials. Sending out an unsigned letter indicates carelessness on your part. Furthermore, such a letter is technically invalid. Even though most offices recognize that slips like this do occur and treat an unsigned letter as genuine, the practice of posting such letters should be avoided.

Enclosures

If enclosures are to be included in an outgoing letter, type the standard notation *Enc.*, or one of the other conventional forms of it, flush left below the signature line. When sending two or more items, indicate the number and type it next to the enclosure notation. (See Chapter Six for specific stylings of enclosure notations.) It is also useful to itemize the enclosures and include a brief description of each one as a way of avoiding omissions. Overlooking enclosures is, at the least, annoying to the addressee and an embarrassment to you. Spare yourself some blushes: when proofreading a letter, you might want to attach a self-sticking note to the edge of the letter and jot down a list of the required enclosures if you haven't already itemized them in the enclosure notation itself.

Courtesy Copies

The abbreviated notation *cc* deserves initial comment because its changing meaning is a direct reflection of the impact of the technological revolution occurring in the workplace today. As we all know, the photocopy machine is now a permanent fixture in most offices, thus making carbon paper and pressure-sensitive copy books virtually obsolete. A question repeatedly asked of this office is: If *cc* stands for *carbon copy*, shouldn't the notation be changed to *Xc* for *Xerox copy* so as to reflect modern trends? When Mr. Safire put that question to the readers of his language column, collectively known as the Lexicographic Irregulars, we learned that *cc* now also stands for *courtesy copy*, thereby covering carbons, photocopies, and pressure-sensitive copies. The meaning of the notation is not the prime issue, though; its page placement is. The copy notation belongs below the enclosure notation (if any), flush left, and a few lines below the signature. (See Chapter Six for specific guidelines regarding the styling of copy notations, illustrated by typewritten facsimiles.) When sending copies to more than one recipient, put a check mark next to the name of each person to whom you are mailing the material.

With blind copies, the notation *bcc* appears only on the copy and not on the original. Placement of this abbreviation can vary. The typed *bcc* notation is traditionally positioned flush left with the upper or lower margin of the page. However, I write the abbreviation in nonrepro blue at the lower left margin, just below any *cc* or enclosure notations. This method is easier and is just as effective as the standard options. In addition, subsequent photocopies made from the file copy will not bear the *bcc* notation, about which you may not wish the recipient to know.

File copies.   Don't forget to retain copies for your files. Depending on the set-up of your filing system and the space available, put a copy of the letter in the alphabetical file of the correspondent's name or company, in the subject file if the letter is topical, or in the chronological file. The chronological file is a sequential file of all letters emanating from the office, and it serves as a journal or diary of business. Having letters arranged in this fashion will be convenient if your employer's memoirs are ever written. However, the immediate, short-term reason for maintaining a sequential correspondence file is retention of evidence of business transactions. Often the letters can be discarded once a transaction has been completed and a record of request is no longer needed; therefore, it is important to review regularly the contents of the chronological file. The amount of space available and the historical importance of the letters themselves dictate whether or not this approach is appropriate for your office. It also helps if your organization has archives or other ample storage facilities.

Outgoing Mail Log

My attitude toward an outgoing mail log is the same as my attitude toward an incoming mail log: if your filing system is solid, sensible, and spacious, then a mail log may not be necessary. However, if you do keep one of them, you may want to keep the other to make your records more meaningful and complete. Data to be included in an outgoing mail log are the date of issue, the name and address of the recipient, a description of the material sent, the method of dispatch (class of mail service, telegram, courier, etc.), and the description and date of any subsequent follow-up activity.

Envelope Selection and Folding

Standard letterhead.   Letters should be folded and inserted according to the kind of envelope selected. Standard letterhead and half-size, memo-style stationery are folded into traditional thirds. If you're mailing multiple sheets of the same size, attach everything together and insert them into the proper envelopes so that when the letter is open and unfolded, the text will be right side up. If you're sending several different-sized sheets, fasten everything together so that when the letter is removed from the envelope the pages, clippings, or other enclosures will not scatter. (See Chapter Six for detailed information on envelope sizes and applications.)

Envelopes and mailers made of glossy paper have been known to shed their stamps before reaching the intended recipients—a situation having several undesirable effects: the letters may be returned to you for postage, thus delaying delivery or they may be delivered to the addressee with postage due. If you have a large mailing and a problem such as this develops, notify your post office. Mail handlers will look for the problematic pieces and will help you to rectify the difficulty.

Oversized mailers. When including a letter with a larger item, you have several options. You can fold and insert the letter into its matching envelope and pack it with the enclosure in a larger mailer. Or you can put both letter and enclosure into a single large envelope. If you choose not to fold them, use a piece of corrugated cardboard to prevent damage in transit. Use padded mailers for books, small manuscripts, press kits, files, or similar materials. The mailers cushioned with plastic bubbles or Styrofoam are preferable to those lined with lint because they are neater and lighter. However, the bubble-lined bags are more costly than the ones filled with lint. It is more economical to maintain an ongoing supply of the bubble-lined bags in several sizes for use only with particularly important mailings. The cheaper shipping bags or large manila envelopes can be used for less important oversized pieces.

Specialized envelopes. Offices issuing a lot of international mail may wish to use the commercially available overseas airmail envelopes that are lighter than standard office envelopes. A rubber stamp can be used to customize them. Window envelopes, often used in mass mailings, require careful insertion of letters. If the recipient's name and address do not appear through the window, then the time you have saved by not addressing the envelope separately will have been wasted. Some letterhead stationery has a line indicating where to fold the page so that the recipient's name and address will show through the window. Generally, though, the procedure is to fan-fold the sheet in thirds with the inside address outside on the top, as opposed to folding it so that the top third folds over the bottom third with the address block on the inside. Allow about one fourth to one eighth of an inch between the edge of the window and the address to prevent blocking any part of the address. (See also the section on envelopes in Chapter Six.)

Addressing

The United States Postal Service has modernized its operations with automated scanning and sorting devices that improve dissemination of the mail. To get the most from these mail processing advancements, consider the post office's needs when addressing envelopes:

1. Use envelopes no smaller than $3\frac{1}{2}''\times 5''$ and not exceeding $6\frac{1}{8}''$ $\times 11\frac{1}{2}''$.

2. Center the address and single-space each line flush with the left edge of the line above it. This is called *blocking*. Do not indent the lines of the address.

3. Avoid the slanted address styling. Typewrite the lines parallel to the top and bottom edges of the envelope.

4. Include all information within this block in this fashion (or in one of the other ways described in Chapter Six):
   THE NEW YORK TIMES WASHINGTON BUREAU
   William Safire
   Ninth Floor
   1000 Connecticut Avenue, NW
   Washington, DC 20036

Folding and Inserting Stationery into Envelopes

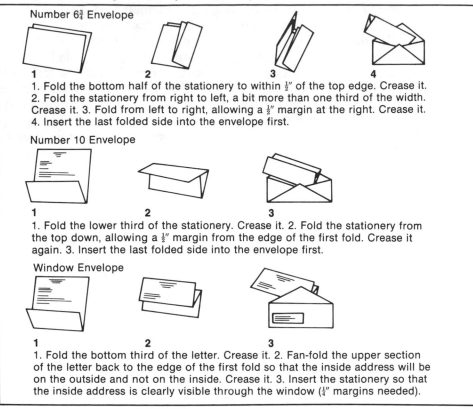

Number 6¾ Envelope

1   **2**   **3**   **4**

1. Fold the bottom half of the stationery to within ½" of the top edge. Crease it.
2. Fold the stationery from right to left, a bit more than one third of the width. Crease it. 3. Fold from left to right, allowing a ½" margin at the right. Crease it.
4. Insert the last folded side into the envelope first.

Number 10 Envelope

1   **2**   **3**

1. Fold the lower third of the stationery. Crease it. 2. Fold the stationery from the top down, allowing a ½" margin from the edge of the first fold. Crease it again. 3. Insert the last folded side into the envelope first.

Window Envelope

1   **2**   **3**

1. Fold the bottom third of the letter. Crease it. 2. Fan-fold the upper section of the letter back to the edge of the first fold so that the inside address will be on the outside and not on the inside. Crease it. 3. Insert the stationery so that the inside address is clearly visible through the window (¼" margins needed).

NOTE: Some printed letterhead intended exclusively for window applications is marked to indicate placement of the inside address. Printed fold lines are often included.

Note that attention references, suite numbers, and other nonaddress information should appear within the address block, not set apart from it. The Zip Code should appear on the same line as the city and state. (See Chapter Six for details regarding automated mail handling and addressing envelopes for automation.)

Special-handling, eyes-only, and other such notations are typed in uppercase letters below the postage line and above the top address line, one third of the way in from the right or left edge of the envelope. The name of a foreign country should appear in capitals as the last line of the address block. (Follow these fundamental guidelines also when addressing mailing labels for larger containers. Since the label can loosen from the mailer, you ought to secure it with a label cover or tape.) The return address should appear in the upper left corner or on the obverse of the envelope. Be neat and precise. Include the name of the person posting the item, his or her suite or mail stop number, department, and any other information that will ensure the parcel's safe return to sender in the event it is refused or returned by the addressee.

Make certain that the degree of color contrast between the envelope or mailing label and the typed address is sharp enough to be detected by optical character scanners. Contrast is not a problem with standard-colored stationery (white, ecru, or manila) and with single-use film typewriter ribbons. However, if the

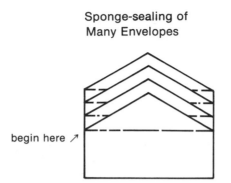

Sponge-sealing of
Many Envelopes

begin here ↗

mailer is of a color that reduces contrast or if your fabric typewriter ribbon is worn, you may inadvertently obstruct the mail's distribution.

Sealing
There are a half dozen ways to seal a mailing container. I call them the "Sibilant Six": saliva, sponge, Scotch tape, staples, strapping tape, and string. For envelopes, I use saliva. A sponge or transparent tape may be used if the quantity of the letters is excessive or if the glue is especially evil-tasting. Large numbers of outgoing envelopes can be moistened all at once by stacking them with their flaps open, glue side facing you, one behind the other, with the glue strips touching but not overlapping. Pass a wet sponge over the glue strips all at one time. Then, working from the top envelope, fold the flaps down one by one (see the figure above). For mailing bags, staples work well, as does strapping tape, especially the kind reinforced with strands of fiber. Boxes should be sealed with strapping tape and tied with string. Make sure that you have not left loose edges on the parcel that will jam up the post office's equipment.

POSTING THE MAIL

Presorting
From deposit to delivery, a letter passes through about twelve steps at the post office. By sharing the sorting workload yourself, you may obtain reduced postal rates and faster delivery. If you generate a consistently high volume of first-class letters (or a minimum of 500 pieces per mailing), presorting them yourself can save you a substantial amount of money on postage (at present, 15%).

The mail is initially sorted by Zip Code from low-numbered zones to high and each piece of mail must bear this code. When a Zip Code has been omitted or when an incorrect Zip Code appears on a parcel, mail room or postal employees must look it up or correct the error. And that's not their job; it's yours. A Zip Code directory should be part of a professional secretary's desk library. It contains the codes of course, as well as other pertinent mailing information such as the standard two-letter state abbreviations. Zip Code directories can be purchased from the post office. With the advent of the expanded nine-digit Zip Code called *Zip + 4*, directories of all the codes have become real necessities. The additional digits in Zip + 4 allow the Postal Service to process much more mail with greater speed and efficiency. The Postal Service estimates that by the year 1987, about 50% of high-volume commercial mailers will be using Zip + 4 as a matter of routine. The program is intended to eliminate all manual mail sorting. (See Chapter Six for more information regarding Zip + 4 and its use on envelopes.) Letters going to the same post office (i.e., letters bearing the same five digits in the Zip Code) should be bundled together. Mail destined for one major city (i.e., mail whose Zip Codes share the same first three digits) also ought to be bound together.

Postage for presorted mail must be paid by postage meter, permit imprint, or precanceled stamps. For mailings exceeding fifty pieces, a postage meter and/or envelopes preprinted with your permit number are preferable. If you use precanceled stamps, affix them with a roller or a wet sponge. If presorted letters have not been stamped with precanceled stamps having the printed notation "presorted first-class mail," the letters must be annotated by hand. If your office does not meet the minimum mail volume to qualify for the presort postage rate, you can still hasten the mail's delivery by separating it into broad categories (i.e., local, intrastate, interstate, and international) and by arranging the pieces from low to high Zip Codes. Separating the mail by other classes (second, third, and fourth) and by Zip Code within those classes also will speed delivery.

Stamping

You have several options for stamping outgoing mail. These include postage meters, imprints, and manual methods—all discussed in the forthcoming paragraphs. But regardless of the method chosen, you should have at hand an accurate postage scale and lists of the current postage rates applicable to the classes of mail service that your office uses if it lacks a mail room.

Postage meters.   Postage meters apply postage in any amount (you set the denominations) directly onto an envelope fed into the machine or onto a label then affixed to the parcel. Postage meters may be purchased from the manufacturer or leased and licensed from the United States Postal Service, which also sells the postage and sets the descending register to reflect the amount of postage purchased. Each time the meter is used the descending register, which keeps a current tab on the balance of postage remaining in the meter, is reduced by the denomination of postage affixed to the piece of mail. The ascending register then increases by that amount, thus reflecting the amount of postage used. If an incorrect unit of postage has been printed on the envelope or on a label or if the envelope or label has been in some way defaced after having been endowed with metered postage, a partial refund (and in some cases, a full one) can be obtained from the post office. However, you must bring the unusable pieces of mail to the post office and complete some forms within one year of the date appearing on the metered postage in order to obtain the refund.

One major benefit of a meter is that the postmarked dated item requires no further cancellation at the post office, thus bypassing another processing activity and thereby expediting delivery. Remember, though, that five or more pieces of metered mail must be bundled together; otherwise they will be processed and canceled in the usual fashion. Postage meters also allow for customized postmarks. And, of course, meters are faster than manual affixation of stamps.

Permit imprints.   Permit imprints allow an organization to print postage directly onto envelopes or post cards. Generally, the organization's return address is also printed at the same time in the upper left corner on the face of the envelope, on the obverse, or in the address block on a self-addressed stamped return envelope. Permit imprints are popular with mass mailing programs and are used in all classes of service (first through fourth). Regardless of class, permit-imprinted mail must be sorted by the sender, an extra activity that can neutralize the benefits and conveniences afforded by preprinted permit postage.

Other stamping methods.   Another stamping method includes the use of commercial postage stamp dispensers that require neither lease nor license. One such hand-held gadget called a Postafix holds a roll of stamps. A press of the hand dispenses the postage, one stamp at a time. If you have a uniform stack of envelopes or cards, you can speed matters by fanning the upper right edge with one hand and stamping them with the other. Stamps in roll form or in sheets also can be applied rapidly without a special device. Tear off a manageable number of stamps, moisten the first one while it is still attached to the rest of the section, apply it to the letter, and then tear it at the perforation.

MAIL CLASSIFICATIONS

You should be familiar with four classifications of mail: first, second, third, and fourth. To improve your service, clearly label your mail according to its appropriate classification. Mail classifications are discussed in the next few paragraphs.

First-class.   First-class mail includes letters and materials sealed against postal inspection: handwritten and typed correspondence, post cards, bills, statements, and invoices. First-class mail can be insured. Priority mail is first-class mail weighing from 12 ounces to 70 pounds. Priority is a class of mail, not a special-handling service. It receives the same treatment as first-class parcels weighing under 12 ounces. Do not use priority if you expect some sort of preferential service.

Second-class.   Unsealed second-class mail is used for posting periodicals such as newspapers, journals, and subscription forms. Because second-class mail is the cheapest, organizations must obtain a special permit to mail items at this rate.

Third-class.   Third-class mail is most frequently used by direct-mail purveyors but it is available to anyone. Essentially, mail that need not go first class, that is not considered a periodical, and that weighs under one pound is third class. Since third-class mail may be opened for postal inspection, the parcels should be wrapped and sealed with this in mind. Third-class mail can be insured.

Fourth-class.   Fourth-class mail, also called parcel post, consists of pieces weighing one pound or more that are not required to be sent first class and are not classifiable as second class. No correspondence, unless it is an invoice or a statement, may be enclosed with a fourth-class parcel; first-class postage must be paid on all such enclosures. Fourth-class mail can be insured. Specific dimensions, rate structures, and other periodically changing data can be obtained from your local post office. The United States Postal Service provides detailed mailing information available free upon request.

SPECIAL SERVICES

Registered Mail
Registered Mail is used to protect highly important, often irreplaceable domestic first-class mail. A receipt is issued by the accepting post office, a card is returned to you when delivery has been made, a record of delivery is maintained at the originating and destination post offices, and the mail is monitored through all the steps in between. If the item is lost or spoiled, the post office will award restitution to the sender. The receipt issued for the cost of registered service shows the name of the recipient and the date of delivery. You may specify "restricted delivery": the piece will be delivered only to the person you've designated. Registered mail will be forwarded if the addressee has submitted a change of address notice to the post office, and the post office will report the new address to you, should you request that information. This feature is especially nice if you're trying to track a scofflaw or deadbeat.

Certified Mail
Certified mail is used when the sender of an article with no intrinsic value wishes to have proof of mailing and delivery. No receipt is issued unless you request one, so you need not bring outgoing certified mail to the post office in person; it can be dispatched with ordinary items in a collection box. For an additional fee, restricted delivery and return receipts are available for certified mailings. The major differences between certified mail and registered mail are cost and speed. Because of the manpower spent monitoring registered mail, the cost is greater and the delivery process is slower than for certified mail. Essentially, registered mail should be used for protection of extremely valuable materials.

Special Delivery Mail
Although special delivery mail will receive special handling at the destination post office, it will probably be shipped from the originating post office with the regular post. This service is available only on classes first, third, and fourth. Special delivery mail is supposed to be delivered to the addressee the day it arrives at the destination post office, even on Sundays and holidays. However, to ensure immediate—and overnight—delivery, consider the United States Postal Service's Express Mail or the services of one of its private-sector competitors.

Express Mail
Advantages of using Express Mail include insurance against loss or damage at no additional cost and the convenience of using a postage meter or stamps. Express mail is more than just next-day delivery, although that feature is by far the best known. Express Mail service includes:

1. Same-day airport service: The parcel is posted from an airport mail facility and must be claimed by the addressee at the destination airport mail facility.

2. Airport to addressee: The parcel is shipped from an airport mail facility but is delivered directly to the addressee by the post office.

3. Office to airport: Your parcel is picked up at your office by the post office, but the recipient must claim it at the destination airport mail facility.

4. Pick-up and delivery: The post office picks up and delivers the parcel, door-to-door.

5. Next-day service: A more accurate appellation would be "next-business-day delivery." Post—or have your letter picked up—prior to 5:00 p.m. (the earlier the better), and it will arrive no later than 3:00 p.m. the following business day.

6. International Express Mail: An overseas mailing will arrive at its destination in three days. Many major cities now offer this service.

Extra charges are added for collections from your office, and pick-up arrangements generally require a service contract between your organization and the United States Postal Service. Check with your post office to determine which services are offered there and which options would be best for your needs.

Mailgrams

The Mailgram provides another form of next-business-day delivery. The difference between it and Express Mail is that the Mailgram is transmitted electronically, not physically. To send one or several, call Western Union and read your message, or use a Telex if your office is so equipped. Remember to have a confirmation copy sent to you. There is an additional fee for such a copy, but surely you will want a file copy and an opportunity to check the message for any errors in transcription or transmission, in which case Western Union will send, at no additional cost to you, revised Mailgrams. Mailgrams have many uses, from amending information in a social announcement or invitation to issuing a product recall. I've even seen one correcting the spelling in another one received the day before. (See also the section of this chapter on electronic mail where Mailgrams are further discussed.)

COD

With COD (collect on delivery) mail, the cost of purchased goods and the cost of mailing the goods are absorbed by the addressee. The maximum collectible COD payment is $300.00. The COD charges also include insurance against nonpayment, damage, or loss. For an additional fee you can be notified of nondelivery before the package is returned to you. First-, third-, and fourth-class mail can be sent by COD. Some private-sector carriers also deliver COD packages.

PRIVATE-SECTOR CARRIERS

Private shipping, delivery, and courier companies offer services that rival those of the United States Postal Service and challenge its erstwhile monopoly on mail delivery. In some instances, these operations feature services that the post office does not provide. Most private carriers will establish an account providing for regular billing and will supply you with preprinted mailing forms. The urgency of your mailings and your own budgetary concerns will affect your choice of mailing methods.

Local messengers.   Local messenger services offer same-day service within your city. They will collect a parcel from your office and deliver it across town, often within the same hour. Of course, the cost can be high compared with the cost of posting the same parcel through the United States mail. However, the impact of a hand-delivered letter often offsets the expense. Many lobbyists and politicians distribute their "media advisories" (as press releases are now known) via messenger because hand-delivered items are usually treated with higher priority in the recipients' offices. Check the messenger's references carefully.

Couriers.   Courier services, like local messengers, provide rapid surface deliveries to nearby metropolitan locations. Check your local Yellow Pages for specific information.

Bus parcel.   Bus parcel service is more economical than air package delivery. Services and companies offering these services vary throughout the continental United States. Common options include door-to-door pick-up and delivery, and terminal-to-terminal pick-up and delivery wherein the parcel is taken to the bus depot by the sender and claimed at the destination bus terminal by the addressee. This second option may be combined with the services of a local messenger, who can claim delivery at the destination depot and deliver it to the appropriate office. Before sending parcels, packages, and pouches in this fashion, it is wise to check on the security measures taken at each bus terminal.

United Parcel Service.   United Parcel Service (UPS), serving intrastate and interstate destinations, is one of the Postal Service's prime competitors. The advantages of using UPS are virtually no damage or loss, fast service, and low rates. A package shipped by UPS can be taken to a UPS office or picked up at your office by a UPS driver. If you choose to have it collected from your place of business, you can call UPS to arrange for pick-up the next day. No matter how many package collections a UPS driver makes from your office each week, a one-time weekly pick-up surcharge is added to the shipping fee. If you use UPS often, it is a good idea to arrange for a driver to come by your office the same time each day, thus precluding a telephone call and a day's wait for parcel pick-up.

Air couriers.   Air courier services function as air freight forwarders. Parcels are taken to local offices or collected from yours and are shipped by regularly scheduled commercial carriers or by the courier's own fleet of planes. Federal Express, Airborne, and Purolator are among the better known air courier companies, though in recent times major commercial airlines such as United have entered the air courier market. (See also the Electronic Mail section of this chapter for information regarding air courier use of electronic mail technology.)

SPECIAL MAILING PROBLEMS

Military Mailings
Letters, packages, and other parcels destined for Army, Air Force, or Fleet Post Offices overseas are sent to the nearest domestic gateway city where they are pouched and airmailed to their destinations. Overseas government mail is treated

in a similar manner. Parcel Airlift (PAL) mail is flown from the city of origin to the point of embarkation. Space Available Mail (SAM) is transported via regular parcel post (i.e., via surface mail) to the gateway city. Both PAL and SAM mail are assessed postage for service from the point of origin to the point of overseas embarkation (the United States gateway city). PAL costs more than SAM because you pay a fee for air service plus the regular parcel post rate. (See Chapter Six for specific instructions regarding the methods of addressing military mail.)

Overseas Customs Data

Incoming mail. Incoming international mail is first shipped to United States Customs for inspection. Pieces not requiring duty payments are turned over to the Postal Service and are then delivered to the addressee. Parcels requiring payment of import tariffs are issued mail-entry forms stating the duty due. They are returned to the post office, which then delivers them and collects the fees. You may challenge the duty assessed on any international parcel if you believe the customs fee to be incorrect. This is done in one of two ways. Pay the duty and lodge your protest by sending a copy of the mail-entry form affixed to the package along with a covering letter to the customs office listed on the form. The import duty originally charged will be reviewed and a refund issued, if deemed proper. Or you may refuse the parcel and submit a letter to the holding post office objecting to the import duty levied. The original assessment will be reexamined by customs.

Freight. International freight shipments either clear customs at the initial port of entry or travel to another customs port for clearance. You are responsible for arranging clearance of international freight coming to your office. There are at least two ways to do so. For example, a freight forwarder will, for a fee, arrange clearance and forward your parcel to you. Or you may name an unpaid agent to act on your behalf. The agent must have in hand a letter addressed to the attention of the officer in charge of customs stating that the bearer of the letter is acting for you.

Express. Express shipments arriving from foreign nations are generally cleared at customs by the express carrier and then are delivered to you.

Forwarding

The best way to redirect mail is to place over the old address a label bearing the forwarding address and conforming to standard scannable format. That's how the post office does it when they've been informed of a change in address. For misdirected letters, you may cross out the incorrect address and write the correct one directly on the envelope. However, forwarding a piece of mail in this way reduces the likelihood of its being electronically scanned, thus delaying its delivery. It would be ideal both for you and for the post office if no mail had to be forwarded in this fashion. There are several ways to inform correspondents of address changes:

1. The post office provides free change-of-address kits. They're fine if you've only a handful of people to alert.

2. You can have announcements of your imminent move printed. In addition to the new address, include the effective moving date and new telephone numbers, if they also will change.

3. Preprinted Rolodex cards are a special courtesy; you may want to send them to clients and customers in addition to change-of-address notification cards.

4. And don't forget to notify your old post office and the new one, too.

TROUBLESHOOTING AND REVIEW

Incoming Mail: Recapitulation

1. Unless you are told otherwise, do not open items marked PERSONAL or CONFIDENTIAL.

2. Suspicious-looking parcels and letters should be brought to your employer's attention and to the attention of your company's security officer. If need be, contact the police and/or the Postal Inspection Service. This kind of mail includes suspected letter or package bombs and written threats.

3. If a letter and/or its envelope bear no return address, clip both items together before submitting them to your employer.

4. Maintain accurate correspondence files or mail logs. Few things are less professional than having to request from the sender a copy of a letter to your employer because it has been misfiled, discarded, or otherwise lost.

Outgoing Mail: Recapitulation

1. Inspect all outgoing letters. Are words broken into their proper syllables at the ends of lines? Do verbs agree with their subjects? Are margins neat? Take the time to retype any correspondence in which the answer to any of the above questions is "no." Sending out a letter that you know contains errors or inaccuracies is a sign of laziness. One such slip can—and often will—lead to another. Soon you will have lowered your standards and will have compromised the integrity and efficiency of your office, an unfortunate situation that can become a way of life. If you find yourself in this situation and cannot seem to reverse it, ask yourself several questions: Is the problem from within or without? Is it endogenous, or is it beyond my control? Get assistance if you need it.

2. Be sure that all required signatures are in place; that enclosures, attachments, and other referenced items have been included; that courtesy copies have been duly noted and posted; that file copies have been made; and that the mail logs are updated. Ensure that letters are inserted into their proper envelopes. Another symptom of unprofessionalism is mixing up letters or other items and their envelopes or containers.

3. Just as business correspondence prepared by an executive is always typed, so ought the envelope or address label. Remember to style all address information in block format.

4. Sharp contrast between the mailer and the address information is a requirement for faster mail processing.

5. There is not much hope for a parcel whose mailing label has fallen off unless the return address appears directly on the mailer, in which case the parcel will be returned to you. Tape labels to containers or use mailing label holders for added security.

6. Envelopes with weak glue should be sealed with tape.

7. Clearly note the desired class of service on all outgoing mail. With distinctive air mail or green-edge first-class envelopes, further designation of class is unnecessary.

8. Use a postal scale and current rate charts to determine proper postage. When in doubt of the proper rate, call your post office or private carrier. Answers to usual and unusual questions can be obtained over the telephone, in person, or from brochures.

9. Whether you use the United States Postal Service or a private carrier, consider time, expense, and indemnity. Why send a parcel by overnight air when bus parcel achieves the same result and is less costly?

10. Investigate the reliability of the company to which you plan to entrust your mail. What recourse will you have in the event of delay, spoilage, or loss?

11. Mail early in the day to reduce delivery time by almost one full day.

ELECTRONIC MAIL SYSTEMS

INTRODUCTION TO ELECTRONIC MAIL

As mentioned in Chapter One, the trend in office automation today is toward total integration of corporate facilities via communications to and from relatively low-cost user workstations. These workstations can provide users with integrated capabilities such as word processing and printing, electronic filing and retrieval, graphics, and electronic mail. What *is* electronic mail? We define *electronic mail* as written messages transmitted and received electronically between terminals linked by telephone lines or microwave relays. Electronic mail allows users to transmit information such as memos and letters, graphics, reports, or spreadsheets from one workstation terminal to another—whether the terminals be situated within one company or sited within several different companies, whether the terminals be located within the United States or found in various other countries of the world. Electronic mail also allows the user to transmit and receive mail fast. No doubt there have been times when you and your employer have waited for the arrival of and worried about the fate of an important piece of mail: Where *is* it? Frantic telephone calls. It's in the mail. But *where?* They don't know where. Well, put a tracer on it. They still can't find it. If they *don't* find it by tomorrow, we'll be dead in the water. Does that scenario ring a bell? With the global reach of today's business, the timely delivery of accurate messages has become an absolute necessity.

A truly flexible, broad-spectrum electronic mail system permits and expedites fast, accurate communication among individuals, groups, departments, and corporations from the types of workstations described earlier. With electronic mail, you can create (i.e., "write"), edit, transmit, read, and print your own mail. Conversely, you can answer your incoming mail, forward messages to other people using the system, request that return receipts be sent to your terminal, and file the mail. If your employer has such a system, he or she can do all of this, and you too can use the system. When you key in your outgoing message it is transmitted *at once*—there is no delay involving mail pickup and delivery—and the recipient of the message can read that message right away or at a later, more convenient time (an additional advantage from the standpoint of workflow and time management).

Just to give you a concrete idea of the capabilities of electronic mail, we cite here the major features of Customizable Electronic Mail as described on page III–4 of the book *Digital's Office Solutions* (Concord, MA: Digital Equipment Corporation, 1984):

Mail Preparation	–Create, Edit, Send
Mail Reception	–Read, Answer, Forward, Print, Delete
Mail Filing	–File, Search File, Read List, Print List
Mail Distribution	–Send To, Carbon Copies, Mailing Lists
Mail Utilities	–Index of Messages

If you examine carefully these features and their resultant capabilities, you will see right away that five features fulfill sixteen tasks, ten of which (i.e., Edit, Send, Answer, Forward, Delete, File, Search File, Carbon Copies, Mailing Lists, and Index of Messages) either eradicate secretarial tasks altogether or markedly reduce them. For instance, the Edit capability disposes of drafts and redrafts. Send bypasses the fold-insert-into-envelope-affix-stamp operation. Answer enables the executive to respond to a letter or memo directly without intervention of the dictation-transcription-read-correct-edit operations. File and Search File virtually eliminate one of the tasks most disliked by secretaries. And once you yourself have been freed up from mundane chores such as filing, you will have more time to devote to other, more enjoyable and challenging responsibilities.

We have seen, then, that electronic mail combines the speed of a telephone call with the permanency and impact of a letter, and at the same time liberates the secretary from the drudgery of the past. Other advantages of electronic mail stem from the ability of most equipment to operate unattended, thus eliminating "telephone tag" (people leaving telephone messages in response to previous messages but never reaching one another) and allowing overnight operation when transmission charges are lower. (An ancillary advantage to overnight transmission and unattended reception of messages is, of course, the fact that an executive returning late from a trip need not go into the office on the way home in order to obtain accumulated messages or call you for an update on the messages. The executive can, with proper equipment, dial into the mail system from any location at any time and receive the messages.)

Types of Computer-based Mail Systems (CBMS)

Basically, this form of electronic mail involves the use of computers to store and transmit messages. Written messages are transmitted to and retrieved from in-boxes and out-boxes within a computer system. The boxes aren't physical objects, but are instead special computer files earmarked for messages. Physically, a CBMS can be based either on a central computer serving as a repository for all the messages, or on a network of computers automatically transmitting messages to each other through the telephone lines, a data network, or a local area network. The next illustration shows the difference between a central computer system and a network system. If you are using a network, your computer should take care of all the details of message transmission and reception. If you are accessing a central computer using an office computer as a terminal, your office computer may be able to handle everything automatically. Otherwise, you will have to handle the details of making the connection with the computer. But in terms of how the system functions, the user may not be able to tell the difference between a centralized system and a network. Functionally, electronic mail systems can be grouped into stand-alone, integrated, and public systems. These are discussed in the next sections.

Stand-alone and Integrated Electronic Mail Systems

A stand-alone electronic mail system is really a computer that handles electronic mail and does nothing else. At the minimum, it should be able to receive messages automatically for later retrieval either from directly connected terminals or from remote sites with auto-answer modems through which the computer can answer the telephone. The integrated electronic mail system combines the mail features with word processing and other capabilities. An example of a particularly versatile electronic mail system is the Digital Equipment Corporation DECmail system. It is an electronic mail product that functions as a stand-alone mail system or as an integrated mail system with Digital's ALL-IN-1 Office Information System to provide comprehensive integrated office applications. For instance, if you work in an office equipped with a DECmate word processing system and your office also is tied into the DECmail system, you can access the mail system through your terminal. You also can send electronic messages by DECmail from any terminal (DEC or non-DEC) connected to ALL-IN-1, from any remote terminal via telephone, from a portable terminal, and in the future from the telephone itself (via DECtalk). The following scenario tells you how the DECmail functions. DECmail will inform you of any messages in your in-box. After you have read your messages they can be placed into the Read file, they can be deleted, or they can be put into any special file that you might have set up for future reference. Using the Search command described earlier, you can scan the message files for key words or phrases or you can send a tickler message that will be put into your own mailbox at a future date to remind you of something

Electronic Mail Systems

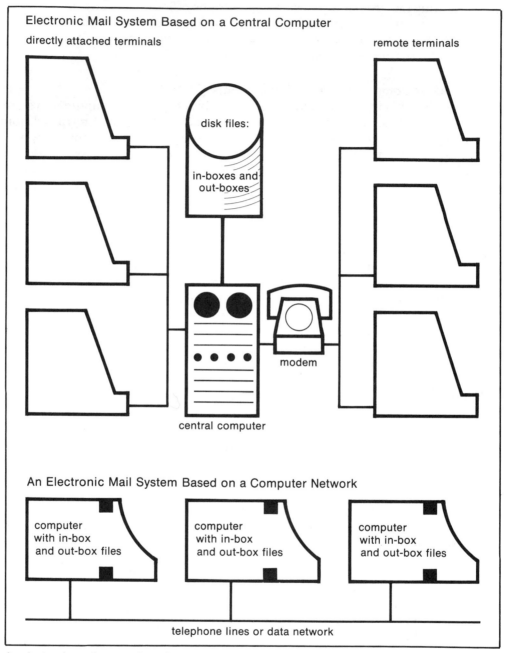

Electronic Mail System Based on a Central Computer

directly attached terminals

remote terminals

disk files:

in-boxes and out-boxes

modem

central computer

An Electronic Mail System Based on a Computer Network

computer with in-box and out-box files

computer with in-box and out-box files

computer with in-box and out-box files

telephone lines or data network

An electronic mail system based on a central computer (top) can be compared with a bulletin board on which people post and remove messages. The computer's files serve as the repository for all messages, and users can get to them through terminals attached to the system, or by calling in from remote terminals. The terminals themselves may be computers. An electronic mail system based on a computer network (bottom) can be compared with a private Telex network. The computers transmit messages to each other through the telephone lines or over a data network. The two methods overlap, since central computer systems also may exchange mail with computers in other offices.

The Datapoint Integrated Electronic Office System

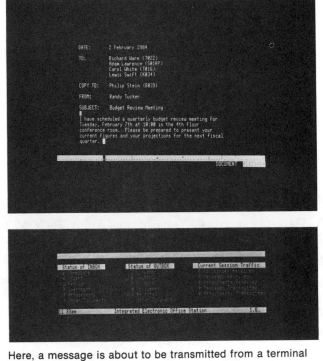

Here, a message is about to be transmitted from a terminal
running Datapoint's Integrated Electronic Office system,
which includes electronic mail.
Courtesy of Datapoint Corporation.

(another manual task deleted). Using your own terminal, you can, of course,
transmit, receive, and forward messages.

Other menu items available with DECmail include these: Attach (enabling the
user to attach a copy of one memo to another), Detach (enabling the user to break
up a memo into separate components), and Defer (enabling the user to schedule
the date and time for transmitting a memo). We have already mentioned that all
messages can be printed out as hard copy if desired. Security into the system is
regulated and maintained via user identification procedures and passwords.

Another very versatile electronic mail system is Datapoint Corporation's Integrated Electronic Office, a word processing system intended for use with
Datapoint's ARC local area network. Electronic mail is part of the main word
processing menu. You can summon electronic mail functions and send a message
to anyone in the system's directory as shown in the illustration above. You also
can attach to the message any document that you have previously prepared using
the system's word processing functions. Messages and attached documents are
stored in the user's out-box within the network's disk files. At intervals, the
computer within the network that handles distribution stops whatever it is doing, goes through the out-boxes and copies any waiting messages for delivery to
the in-boxes of the recipients. The recipients may be users of the same ARC
system, or they may be users of ARC networks or stand-alone systems at distant
locations that must be accessed through the telephone lines. Incoming messages

will be placed in your in-box after you have put your computer in standby mode and can be scanned, read, or handled like any other word processing documents by accessing the in-box with the word processing system.

Add-on features.   Having discussed two electronic products and their capabilities by brand, we sum up this section by listing those add-on features that almost any electronic mail system should make available:

1. **Append**   The system will allow you to attach pre-prepared documents to the bottom of an electronic mail message.

2. **Directory**   The system can supply a list of its users. On public systems the directory may be intentionally restrictive.

3. **Distribution**   The system can send the same message to a prestored list of recipients.

4. **Editing**   Text can be edited off-line prior to transmission.

5. **Gateway services**   You can send Telex, E-COM, or Mailgram messages through the system.

6. **Message status**   The system can list the headers of incoming messages and the status of outgoing messages, i.e., whether or not they have been transmitted.

7. **Registered mail**   The system sends you a confirmation when the recipient reads the message.

8. **Reply requested**   After you read a message, the system requires that you type a response, which immediately goes to the sender's mailbox.

9. **Security provisions**   Access can be restricted by passwords, by the encryption of messages, or by both.

10. **Store and forward**   The system can store a message for delivery at a later date.

Public Systems

A number of organizations offer public subscription electronic mail systems. These are stand-alone systems open for public use. You can exchange messages with any other subscriber, transmitting outgoing messages to the recipient's mailbox and downloading any messages you find in your own mailbox. Services like these are offered as an extra option by several packet switching networks such as Telenet and Tymnet, data service companies like The Source and CompuServe, communications carriers like MCI Communications Corporation, and specialized electronic mail companies. The gateway services offered by some Telex carriers are similar. Prices vary widely, as do service options. The mail system offered by The Source, for instance, requires that you first sign onto The Source, usually through one of the packet switching networks. To send a letter you then type MAIL SEND. The system will ask for the recipient's account name and then the subject. These items, plus the date and time, will form the header of the message. You then type or upload the text of the message, concluding with the .SEND command (pronounced dot-send). The message is immediately copied into the recipient's in-box. To check your in-box, you type the command

MAILCK. If any mail is present the system tells you, and then you can read your mail with the command MAIL READ. (MAIL SCAN will cause the system to list out just the message headers.)

Data Networks

Computer-based message systems (CBMS) often employ local area networks and packet switching networks in message transmission.

Local Area Network (LAN). A LAN is a network of computers that communicate with each other through direct wiring rather than over telephone lines. A LAN can be a system allowing the participating computers to use one another's disk files and printers automatically (as with the Xerox Ethernet or with the Datapoint ARC network), or it can be just a pathway for sending messages.

Packet switching networks. The number of nationwide data networks is growing. Although some of them use other switching techniques, *packet switching network* has become a generic term for them. Subscribers attach their computers directly to the network, and anyone can reach that computer as long as he or she has access to the network. You can usually access the network through a local telephone number. After the connection has been established, the network usually asks for a terminal identifier so that it can add special features (such as filler characters after a carriage return) to the data stream required by some terminals. Then you type in the code identifier of the computer you wish to reach. If that computer accepts your call, thereafter you will be able to act as though you were attached directly to the computer, and the packet switching network will become "invisible." The average cost for connect time is currently $6.00 an hour, regardless of distance. Most connections between a terminal and a computer are made collect.

FACSIMILE MACHINES

A facsimile (fax) machine is basically a copier that scans a full-page document and transmits a signal to a second copier, which reproduces the document on another piece of paper. Whatever is on the page will be transmitted whether it is a typed or handwritten message, a drawing, a signed legal document, or the executive's doodles. Delivery is possible within minutes between any two points served by a telephone. While fax machines previously had a reputation for low speed and low quality, this reputation now has been challenged by the computer revolution.

Types of Hardware

Fax machines from different makers were previously incompatible. But in 1976 the Consultative Committee on International Telegraph and Telephone (CCITT) established transmission standards allowing compatibility between brands. The standards divide fax machines into the four groups described here.

Group I. These machines (which have almost vanished from the market) use analog signaling techniques that require 6 minutes to transmit a page with a resolution of 96 by 96 lines per inch. They can transmit shades of gray. Also included are many older units manufactured before the CCITT standards were established, for which compatibility should not be assumed.

Exxon Office Systems Company's Digital
Facsimile Machine, Exxon 2210 Quip®

Courtesy of Exxon Office Systems Company.

Group II. These machines use analog techniques to transmit a page in 3 minutes with a resolution of 96 by 96 lines per inch. The principal difference over Group I is higher speed and the use of FM instead of AM modulation. Some cannot transmit shades of gray.

Group III. These machines use digital techniques to transmit a page with a resolution of about 200 by 200 lines per inch. They do not transmit shades of gray. Transmitting at 9,600 baud, a Group III machine can send the 200,000 bits usually required to "describe" a page in about 20 seconds. (*Baud* is a unit of data transmission speed, usually equal to one bit per second.) These machines usually come with a step-down modem that automatically switches to a lower speed if the line is too noisy due to background static caused by poor connections or other problems. The average transmission speed you can expect in the United States is 8,000 bits per second, but it is much lower over some foreign telephone systems.

Group IV. Although these machines are not currently marketed, they will use transmission speeds of 56,000 baud and will offer a resolution of 400 by 400 lines per inch. They should not be expected on the market before the late 1980s. However, laser printers with similar features are already available and should not be confused with Group IV fax machines.

Features
Most machines have the option of transmitting at higher speeds (4 minutes for Group I; 2 minutes for Group II) with less resolution. Group III and Group II

machines often have the ability to communicate with machines of a lower group. Other possible features and options are:

1. **Polling**   You can leave the machine overnight with material in it, and someone can call in and trigger the machine to start transmitting. It will answer the telephone and hang up automatically.

2. **Automatic receiving**   You can set the machine in a similar manner to receive any incoming documents automatically.

3. **Activity reports**   The machine can print out a list of the transmissions and receptions that it performed on a given day.

4. **Sender ID**   As a sort of "postmark," the machine can print the telephone number or code name of the message sender, plus possibly the date, time, and page count across the top or bottom of the page.

5. **Local copy**   The machine can be used as if it were an office photocopier.

6. **Computer printer**   Although the coding used by Group III machines is not the same as ASCII (American Standard Code for Information Interchange) or any other data communications code, some machines have the ability to receive ASCII and function as if they were computer printers. The transmission of a Group III machine can also be stored in a computer just as any other digital data can be.

Facsimile Services

A number of organizations now offer various facsimile transmission services. Usually you have to bring your documents to their offices, but high-volume customers may be given their own fax machines by the service provider.

INTELPOST.   A service of the US Postal Service and several foreign postal services, INTELPOST allows you to transmit documents from or to the INTELPOST center in Chicago, Houston, New York, San Francisco, or Washington, DC; to or from a post office in a foreign city, where it then can be forwarded by regular mail or special delivery or left for counter pickup. At this writing INTELPOST connects to points in Argentina, Canada, France, Hong Kong, the Netherlands, the United Kingdom, and West Germany. The cost is $5.00 per page. Special delivery and other services are extra. You can submit your document to the nearest INTELPOST center over the counter, by Express Mail, or through a Group III fax machine.

Data carriers.   Several data carriers offer their subscribers various value-added facsimile services. Fax transmissions can be recorded for later retransmission, converted from one CCITT standard to another, or broadcast to multiple receivers. Messages also can be received through Telex or data terminal machines and retransmitted by facsimile machines and vice versa. The vendors include ITT World Communications (Secaucus, NJ) and Graphnet Incorporated (Englewood, NJ).

Courier services.   Air Couriers International offers same-day document delivery using Group III machines, and Federal Express has announced plans for a similar service. The Air Couriers service, called Beam, offers worldwide door-to-door same-day delivery between 200 cities in 35 countries, with plans for expansion. Price for transmission within the United States is currently $5.00 per page for the first 30 pages, falling to $3.00 per page for all pages if there are more than 30. Pickup and delivery cost $15.00 each. The international charge is $4.00 per page, falling to $3.00 if there are more than 30 pages, plus the cost of the telephone call. International pickup and delivery cost $25.00 each. These costs are subject to change and are given here as a benchmark for comparison with other methods of communication.

THE TELEX NETWORK

As the descendant of the original Morse Code telegraph, the Telex network spans the globe. There are about 180,000 subscribers in North America and 1.5 million in the rest of the world. Using a standard keyboard printer often called a Teletype or teleprinter and a dial-up arrangement similar to that of the telephone system, a subscriber can print out a message on any other subscriber's machine. The illustration on the next page shows a Telex machine in use.

The Telex network is heavily relied on in Europe where language barriers limit the usefulness of long-distance telephone calls. The Telex network is also important to organizations dealing in international trade, if only because time differentials make it difficult to reach people by telephone. The drawbacks of Telex are slow and noisy operation, absence of lowercase letters, and relatively inferior print quality compared with most computer printers. In most countries the local Telex network is operated by the postal authorities. In the United States the Telex network was formerly a monopoly of Western Union, which carried all domestic traffic except in a few major cities. But Western Union was not allowed to handle overseas traffic and such messages were routed through any of several other companies called International Record Carriers (IRCs). Then in 1981 the government deregulated the industry. As a result, Western Union can now connect you directly to an overseas number and the IRCs can set up their own domestic Telex networks. Since the government requires that the networks interconnect, you can get through to anyone regardless of network affiliation.

Western Union

Western Union actually maintains two networks—Telex I and Telex II (formerly called TWX). Although the machines of the two networks are incompatible, you still can dial directly from a Telex I machine to a Telex II machine and vice versa through Western Union's central InfoMaster computer which handles speed and code conversions.

Telex I.   These machines use the five-bit Baudot code and transmit at 50 baud, or $66\frac{2}{3}$ words per minute. They can print all the uppercase letters, the ten numerals, and the characters -,:;.()'#"$&?/. The domestic charge is now 33.75¢ per minute, billed in six-second increments. Machines on the international network are essentially Telex I machines. Telex I machines generally have only three rows of keys, with numerals and punctuation marks occupying the "uppercase" portion

Electromechanical Telex Machine in Use

Courtesy of Western Union Corporation.

of the keys. Upshifting and downshifting are accomplished by the letters and figures keys that transmit upshift and downshift commands to the receiving terminal.

Telex II.   This network was originally established by AT&T under the name TWX (Teletypewriter Exchange) but was bought by Western Union. The dial-up numbers have ten digits and look like long-distance telephone numbers. Telex II machines use ASCII and transmit at 110 baud, or 100 words per minute. They use a four-row keyboard similar to an ordinary typewriter keyboard, but they do not have lowercase letters. The domestic charge is now 43¢ per minute, billed in full-minute increments.

InfoMaster.   Besides allowing connections between the two networks, the InfoMaster computer allows some "value added" services. RediList is available on special subscription, and allows you to send the same message to a prestored list of recipients. NiteCast works on the same principle, done overnight at a reduced rate. FYI supplies the latest news in various categories. Telegrams, Mailgrams, and Cablegrams also can be sent through InfoMaster.

Operating pointers.   Careful study of the instructions provided by Western Union or your international record carrier (IRC) is required before you can use the Telex network successfully. But basically, Telex machines are not very mysterious. They are just remotely connected electric typewriters with dial-up mechanisms. The only thing you might not immediately understand is the answer-back mechanism and the tape reader-puncher.

The answer-back mechanism is a metal cylinder with studs, similar to the one that you might find in a music box. When you push the HERE IS key, the cylinder revolves and causes the machine to send the characters encoded by the studs. This is your machine's answer-back message, and is listed with your number in the Telex directory. Pushing WRU (Who Are You) causes the machine at the other end to transmit its own answer-back. Usually you begin a message with an exchange of answer-backs. This ability to identify positively both parties has allowed Telex messages to serve as legal contracts in many countries. The paper tape mechanism allows you to code the message onto tape while the machine is off-line. The tape is fed into the tape reader and transmitted after the connection is made. This device allows you to save on connect charges since you cannot type as fast as the machine's transmission speed—slow as it may seem.

The International Record Carriers (IRCs)

The IRCs, no longer restricted to offering international connections, offer many of the services available through Western Union. The IRCs having their own Telex networks are: FTC Communications Incorporated, Graphnet Incorporated, ITT World Communications Incorporated, RCA Global Communications Incorporated, TRT Telecommunications Corporation, and Western Union International. Western Union International is a subsidiary of MCI Communications Corporation and is not connected with Western Union. Other IRCs include Comsat Corporation and Consortium Communications International.

The IRCs have about 40,000 total subscribers. A directory listing the combined Telex subscribers of the IRCs is available from U.S. Telecommunications Subscribers, 250 Hudson Street, 14th Floor, New York, NY 10013. The Western Union Telex directory lists Western Union subscribers only.

Gateway Services

A recent trend has been for the Telex carriers to enable subscribers to use office computers in place of Telex machines. Many IRC subscribers do this, and the Western Union gateway service is called EasyLink. All you have to do is rig your office computer for communication through a modem and dial into the Telex carrier's central computer (usually through a toll-free number). When the connection has been made, you then have full access to the resources of the Telex network. Incoming messages can be stored within the central computer for later retrieval, with the computer supplying your answer-back. Or the incoming message can be forwarded to you real-time through a telephone call to an electronic mail system in your office.

Inmarsat

The Telex network can be used to send messages via satellite to ships and off-shore oil platforms equipped with radioteletypes. This service is offered by Western Union, Comsat Corporation, ITT, RCA, and Western Union International. You should consult your Telex directory for instructions.

Teletex

In Europe where greater reliance is placed on the Telex network, the Teletex standard has been developed to combine the idea of Telex with the advantages offered by the computer revolution. Teletex is not a physical network, but rather a standard that allows properly equipped and programmed office computers to send and receive messages automatically as though they were advanced Telex machines. The standard involves a transmission speed of 2,400 baud through whatever connections are available. Teletex allows lowercase letters, with the text formatted to look like a standard business letter. It also allows interconnection to the Telex network.

Western Union currently offers Teletex service among 25 United States cities and between those cities and West Germany for a connection fee of $300.00 per month. The current domestic price is 85¢ for the first page and 35¢ for each additional page. The cost for pages sent to West Germany is $1.34 for the first page and 84¢ thereafter. A page requires about seven seconds to transmit, but if the receiver is a Telex machine the transmission takes place at Telex speed. Teletex should not be confused with Teletext, a system that involves transmitting text to home television sets.

Hybrid Services ("Time Sensitive Mail")
A number of services combine electronic mail with some other form of delivery. This field, too, has seen the emergence of competition and a proliferation of services.

Domestic telegrams.   A domestic telegram is basically a Telex message sent to someone without a Telex machine. A Western Union clerk telephones the recipient and reads the text, and then the printed copy is forwarded by mail if requested. Delivery by messenger is available in most cities for an extra charge. You can send a telegram directly from your Telex machine or through your local Western Union office. Attempted delivery is guaranteed within two hours for telephone-delivered telegrams and five hours for hand-delivered telegrams. The minimum price is $7.90 for 15 words, and 18¢ per word thereafter. The price for physical delivery is $5.95. Domestic telegrams cannot be considered cost-effective if there is any hope of getting through with a long-distance telephone call. But telegram notification is often required in legal contracts.

Cablegrams.   International telegrams (Cablegrams) are similar to domestic telegrams except that they are handled at the receiving end in whatever manner is standard in the local country. Cablegrams can be sent from a Telex terminal, or through a Western Union office or an IRC offering Cablegram service. Either way, the charge is based on the number of words in the message, with a minimum of seven words. Since the charge per word can be more than 30¢, it is important that anyone who regularly writes Cablegrams understand the word-count rules.

Information on word-count rules is available from your Cablegram carrier, but the basic rule is that any word in any language that can be found in a dictionary counts as one word, to a maximum of fifteen letters. Code words count as one word for every five letters, as do combinations of letters and numbers, and numbers by themselves. Every space counts as a new word, so that names like *De La Garza* would be counted as three words, and should be written as *DeLaGarza*. Short words can be combined (*tobe* instead of *to be*), but such combinations count as code words and the five-letter rule applies. Do not use the characters $#&%¢ in Cablegrams, since they are not used overseas. Other punctuation marks can be used but they count as one word each, with certain exceptions. Every word in the recipient's address is counted except for the destination country and any routing symbol. Therefore, it pays to use one-word cable addresses. These can be found on company letterhead, or from the annually updated *Marconi's International Register*, available in libraries. Cable addresses should not be confused with Telex answer-backs.

If the first word in the Cablegram is LT, then it becomes a letter telegram. A letter telegram costs up to 50% less and will be delivered the next business day in the receiving city (or whatever is standard). Some countries will not accept LTs, and code words cannot be used. The minimum length is twenty-two words. Other Cablegram options include prepaid responses, night delivery, delivery by mail, telephone or Telex, notification of delivery, and the inclusion of a list of alternate addresses.

Mailgrams.   A joint venture of Western Union and the Postal Service, Mailgrams are Telex messages sent to the Telex-equipped post office nearest the recipient, where the message is removed from the machine and delivered as mail. Mailgrams sent during business hours should be delivered the next day. Mailgrams sent early in the morning may be delivered the same day. They can be sent from a Telex terminal or by calling Western Union. The cost is $4.95 for the first 50 words and $2.25 for each additional 50 words. Confirmation copies are available at an extra cost.

E-COM.   A service designed for high-volume mailers, E-COM allows you to transmit letters to one of twenty-five specially equipped serving post offices (SPOs), where they will be printed out and mailed in distinctive blue-and-white envelopes. They will be delivered within two days, provided that they have been addressed to the area served by that SPO. (The current cost is 26¢ for the first page of each letter, and 5¢ for each additional page.) The letters can be unique messages to individual addresses, a common message to a list of addresses, or a mix of common and unique text for each addressee. However, you must have at least 200 letters to use the service. Your equipment and software also must be certified as workable by the Post Office, you must pay a $50.00 yearly fee, and you must set up a trust fund with the post office that will be debited as you make each mailing.

A specific example of the tie-in between electronic mail and E-COM is the Digital Electronic Mailroom. Messages are transmitted to E-COM in standard E-COM format, thus bypassing the manual operations of dictation, transcription, checking, correcting, and mail sorting/handling. The writer can write, format, edit, print, file, and mail the letter from a DEC terminal or a workstation connected to a VAX system. As soon as the letters arrive at the E-COM terminal, E-COM will print them out, fold and insert the letters into the envelopes, sort them by Zip Code, pay the first-class postage, and mail them. Electronic Mailroom capabilities are particularly attractive if your company has high-volume mailings such as these: communications to shareholders, financial and legal announcements, price-change notifications, broad-spectrum sales promotions, sales bulletins, product maintenance/recall bulletins, credit collections, subscription renewals, invoices, fund-raising campaign material, and surveys or polls.

10
Copying

Harold Bogdonoff • *Engineering Fellow, Xerox Corporation*

INTRODUCTION

Making copies may not be your favorite task as a secretary, but it's infinitely faster and easier today than it was a few decades ago. With modern photocopying equipment, you can accomplish in minutes what would have required hours of retyping and pages of carbon paper—if it could have been done at all. The trend toward more efficient copying continues, as equipment becomes increasingly sophisticated and powerful. Furthermore, the copier in the automated office has taken over many other functions besides simple copying. It can produce finished documents of the highest quality, and some copiers can also serve as output devices for electronic communications systems. High-speed copiers are even taking over the function of lower-volume offset duplicators. This chapter describes many of the special features that have been added to copiers in recent years in order to speed the copying task and enlarge the capabilities of photocopying machines. The emphasis is on xerographic copiers, since this is the kind you're most likely to find in an administrative office. Other copying technologies are described briefly.

FIFTY YEARS OF OFFICE COPYING

Office copying needs and systems have changed dramatically over the years. In the 1930s most companies used spirit or mimeo equipment located in the mail room. Carbon paper was used to make multiple copies of outgoing correspondence. Since photographic copies on sensitized paper were very expensive, only the most important items such as legal documents were copied by those methods. With the 1940s and World War II, cost became less important than speed and copy quality in reproducing engineering designs and other war-related material. This factor spurred development of small offset presses that used either direct-image masters typed by secretaries, or metal plates created photographically. As peace returned, the businesses of the 1950s became more cost-conscious—yet they were no longer satisfied with the carbon copy methods of the 1930s. Wet-process sensitized paper processes such as diazo and dry thermal processes were used in attempts to meet the growing demand for inexpensive, good quality office copies. Xerography entered the market in 1950. Offset equipment was simplified, and the offset process grew rapidly, replacing older technologies in many in-plant and commercial printing shops.

The 1960s saw radical changes in the reprographics industry. Fast, dry copies using electrostatic copying principles and zinc oxide-coated copy paper were introduced at the beginning of the decade. Xerography moved to the office setting with copiers that would produce dry copies on plain bond paper and thus revolutionized office copying. Improvements in offset master-making reduced costs for offset printing as well, and enabled the offset process to be automated and combined with on-line sorters. The office manager's problem during the sixties was deciding which of the many copying technologies to use for particular jobs. By the end of the decade, however, xerographic copying on bond paper was becoming the standard for short runs, and offset printing on bond paper dominated the market for long runs.

The 1970s saw the universal adoption of plain paper copying. High-speed copiers started to compete with offset duplicating in medium-length runs because they required no master. At the same time offset presses were becoming more automated. Xerography and offset were both heavily used in many offices and in-plant print shops. Many machines using older copying and duplicating processes are still performing satisfactorily in offices today. But the 1980s are likely to see xerography and electronic printing producing most of the copies used for administrative purposes. By the end of this decade it is likely that offset printing will be used mostly for very long runs and very high-quality printing. Furthermore, as offices become more and more automated, the distinction between copying and printing will be blurred. Sometimes the same machine will be used to produce conventional photocopies and to print out material transmitted from hundreds of miles away. Despite discussions of the paperless office, however, paper will continue to be an important medium for communication and data storage in the foreseeable future.

DIFFERENT COPIERS FOR DIFFERENT NEEDS

The variety of copiers and optional features available is enormous—and confusing. If you are involved in the process of selecting a copier for your office, here are some things to consider.

Choosing a Copier

In today's office, copying equipment is selected on the basis of two criteria: volume of copying required and special copying needs.

Copier volume ranges.   Copiers can be classified in three general volume ranges: low, medium, and high. Although these volume bands overlap considerably, low-volume copiers may make up to 5,000 copies per month; medium-volume copiers, up to 75,000 copies per month; and high-volume copiers, 100,000 or more copies per month.

Special copying needs.   A large and often confusing variety of features is available on modern copiers to meet many kinds of specialized office copying needs. Higher-volume copiers offer the greatest copy speed and range of special features, but more and more of these features are becoming available on lower-volume and lower-cost machines. A copier should be chosen on the basis of a careful analysis of the kind of copying an office requires. The investment should be balanced against the amount of time and expense it can be expected to save.

Typical Office Requirements
If you work in a small law office, your total volume of copying may not exceed 2,000 copies per month. Clearly, you need a low-volume convenience copier. But a large proportion of your 2,000 copies may represent a few very long legal documents. With an automatic document handler and collator you can continue with other work while the copies are being made. Similarly, a medium-sized organization that relies on computer printouts for communication may choose a mid-volume copier that can feed unburst computer forms automatically and reduce and collate the copies, while still serving as an all-purpose copier for general office needs.

Centralized reproduction department. In a large organization with many departments and high copy volumes, you are likely to find a centralized reproduction department (CRD) and satellite reproduction centers for high-volume work and individual copying machines elsewhere in the building for mid- or low-volume use. The centralized reproduction department may have both high-volume photocopying equipment and offset presses, plus machines for various support and finishing operations such as offset platemaking, collating, binding, drilling, padding, and folding.

The high-speed copying machines in a CRD are likely to have many special features such as computer forms feeders, automatic document handlers, automatic two-sided copying, variable reduction, and collating. The CRD will have a manager and trained staff to operate the equipment. Sometimes a word processing center is associated with the CRD for document preparation. Satellite centers are smaller than the CRD. They usually have mid- or high-volume copying equipment staffed by a trained operator. They are generally located at a distance from the CRD for the greater convenience of users, and are able to relieve the CRD of smaller and less complex jobs.

Decentralized copiers. Decentralized copying machines are individual units located in work areas for walkup use. In a large company they may be mid-volume copiers used by departmental staffs for general administrative work, or low-volume desktop units located in executive suites. In order to save secretarial time, heavily used decentralized equipment often has automatic document feeding, collating, and stapling capabilities, plus other features depending on the special needs of the department.

Special-purpose Copiers
Oversize originals. Professional organizations such as engineering and architectural firms or scientific and medical groups often require specialized copying equipment. Xerographic and diazo copiers designed for engineers and architects can copy drawings up to 34″ × 44″ or even larger. If the copier has a reduction feature, the oversize originals can be reduced for easier distribution and filing.

Some of these specialized copiers use roll paper instead of cut paper, allowing copies to be made from original documents of any reasonable length. The operator sets the desired length of the copy, and the machine cuts it. Some copiers designed for cut-paper copies can be adapted to use roll paper. A few copiers designed for general office use also use roll paper. Using roll copy paper is convenient because you don't have to change paper trays when you need copy paper in a different size. But roll paper also means you can't readily copy onto company letterhead or other special stock.

Color copiers.   There are two main kinds of color copiers: full-color copiers that can reproduce color photographs and transparencies, and highlight copiers that make one-color copies in any of several colors. Full-color copiers are specialized machines generally found in the centralized reproduction department or in commercial printing shops. The need to copy full-color originals depends upon the nature of the business. Advertising and art departments often find this capability useful in making layouts and presentations to customers. A growing number of organizations are using full-color copiers to reproduce charts and graphs created by computer-driven color plotters.

Highlight color copiers create single-color copies of an original. The color of the copy depends on the color of the toner in the cartridge. The key operator can normally change the color cartridge in a few minutes without tools. Color copies can be used for advertising posters, brochures, and similar items that benefit from an eyecatching color. If you want two colors on a copy, you can run one color, change the cartridge, and run the second color or regular black toner to complete the job.

MAKING COPIES

Making good copies depends on several factors: the original must be copyable, the machine must have the features to produce the kind of copies you need, and it must be properly maintained and supplied with toner and copy paper. Last but not least, you have to know how to operate the machine.

Originals

Good copies start with good originals. For best results on most copiers:

1. Use clean dark type on smooth white bond paper.
2. Use adequate margins of at least $\frac{1}{4}$" on all sides.
3. Avoid wrinkling or curling the originals.
4. If you use correction fluid, thin it so that it doesn't leave bumps on the page.
5. Make sure that the correction fluid is dry before copying.
6. Remove all paper clips and staples.
7. Make sure that taped or pasted sections are securely attached at all edges.

If your copier has a semiautomatic or automatic document handler, remember that the machine must move the original into position mechanically. It's especially important that the original be flat, and not curled or creased. Some machines are designed to feed lighter or heavier paper automatically. Others are limited to twenty-pound paper, and pasteups or tape on the original should be avoided. Most automatic document handlers will take originals between 8" × 10" and $8\frac{1}{2}'' \times 14''$ in size. All originals in a set should be the same size. If you're preparing originals to be copied by a centralized reproduction department, ask the CRD manager for any additional guidelines.

Planning Your Copying Job

There are three operating variables among copiers of all speeds. The first involves how the original document is received by the copier. The second concerns the kind of copy paper the machine uses and how it is stored and fed into the copier. The final variable involves how the copies are to be delivered to the user and any finishing procedures such as stapling.

Depending on the capabilities of your copier, you may have several decisions to make at each variable area about what features of the machine to use. These decisions are reviewed below in the order that you would normally make them. They are based on the assumption that the machine in question has the necessary features. Once you've made the decisions about your job, you have to tell the copier what to do. Most copiers today have pushbutton control panels for this purpose. Often the buttons bear symbols intended to help you understand their functions. A great deal of study has gone into making the symbols and instructions as clear as possible so that users worldwide will find the machines easy to operate. Some of the more common symbols are shown in the accompanying chart. Don't be embarrassed to ask questions and don't hesitate to look up information in the copier instructions. Copiers differ greatly in the way they accept originals and deliver finished copies, so if you've been accustomed to a different machine it's natural that you will need to learn new techniques. Many copying problems can be avoided if users read and follow instructions.

Input Decisions

First, check your originals:

1. Is the image blue or unusually light, such as carbon copy or pencil? Set the copier to make darker copies.

2. Is the original on darkened or colored stock? Set the copier to make lighter copies.

3. Are you copying original photographs? Use a dot screen overlay of 65 to 133 lines per inch. (Some machines can copy photos without a screen.)

4. Does the copy run right to the edge of the original? Set the reduction feature to 98%. The copy image will be slightly smaller than the original.

5. Are any originals pasted up or taped? Make a single copy manually, using the light copy setting to avoid edge marks. Then use this copy as the original in the set that you feed automatically.

6. Are you copying unburst computer forms? Use the automatic computer forms feeder and the reduction feature.

Next, decide what special features of the machine you need to use.

Standard Symbols for Duplicators and Document Copying Machines

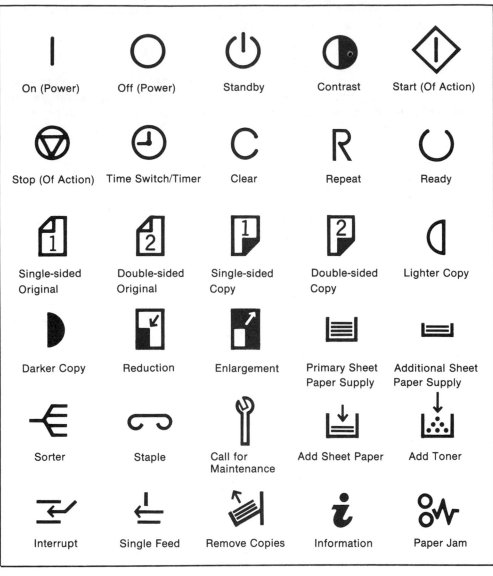

Reduction. Most machines that can reduce originals offer several fixed reduction percentages. The most common percentages are 98%, 77%, 74%, and 65%. The 98% mode avoids information losses when the image runs close to the edge of the original, or when you are copying onto predrilled paper. The 77% mode reduces legal-size originals to letter-size copies. The 74% and 65% modes are especially useful for reducing computer printouts and accounting worksheets to standard size for distribution and filing. Table 1 shows which setting to select for standard reductions.

Some copiers also have a variable reduction selector that lets you choose the exact percentage of reduction you want. Table 2 shows the percentage to select in order to reduce material to a specific dimension. You also can use the reduction

Table 1. **Standard Reduction Percentages**

Original Size	Reproduce on 8½ × 11 inch	Reproduce on 8½ × 14 inch
8½ × 11 inch	100%	100%
8½ × 14 inch	77%	100%
11 × 15 inch	74%	77%
11 × 17 inch	65%	77%
8½ × 11 inch with a narrow margin	98%	98%

feature to create newsletter formats, booklets, or other special documents. For example, you can place two standard 8½″ × 11″ documents side-by-side on the platen glass and reduce them using the 65% mode, to create a new 8½″ × 11″ original. If you want even more reduction than your machine will provide through the standard settings, you can use a reduced copy as your original for still another reduction.

Enlargement. Copiers that have reduction capability may also offer enlargement. This capability is useful for special purposes such as making overhead projection transparencies from small original diagrams or creating headlines to be pasted down on a different original. The enlargement and reduction features also

Table 2. **Determining Variable Reduction Percentages**

% Reduction Chart

Original Dimension (INCHES) vs. Copy Paper Dimension (INCHES)

Original ↓ / Copy →	5	5.5	6	6.5	7	7.5	8	8.5	9	9.5	10	10.5	11	11.5	12	12.5	13	13.5	14
17												62	65	68	71	74	76	79	82
16.5												64	67	70	73	76	79	82	85
16											62	65	69	72	75	78	81	84	87
15.5											65	68	71	74	77	81	84	87	90
15										63	67	70	73	77	80	83	87	90	93
14.5									62	65	69	72	76	79	83	86	90	93	96
14									64	68	71	75	79	82	86	89	93	96	100
13.5								63	67	70	74	78	81	85	89	93	96	100	
13							61	65	69	73	77	81	85	88	92	96	100		
12.5							64	68	72	76	80	84	88	92	96	100			
12						62	67	71	75	79	83	87	92	96	100				
11.5						65	69	74	78	83	87	91	96	100					
11					64	68	73	77	82	86	91	95	100						
10.5					67	71	76	81	85	90	95	100							
10				65	70	75	80	85	90	95	100								
9.5			63	68	74	79	84	90	95	100									
9.0			67	72	78	83	89	94	100										
8.5		65	71	76	82	88	94	100											
8	62	69	75	81	87	93	100												

Copy Paper Dimension

are used in engineering and architectural drafting departments, allowing drafters to rescale parts of existing drawings rather than redraw repetitive information.

Two-sided copying (duplexing). The most sophisticated models can make two-sided copies automatically from one-sided originals or two-sided originals. All you have to do is press the correct button. Other machines require you to turn over the originals manually and to reorient and refeed the copies at the paper tray in order to do the second side. If your machine is not fully automatic, be sure to follow the instructions carefully when you're making two-sided copies. Some machines have printed instructions, while others show a visual display describing each step. It's essential to orient both the originals and the copy paper correctly at the beginning and also when you turn them over, so that the pages will be in order and right-side up.

What Kind of Copy Paper?

Plain paper. Your copier is probably supplied with standard $8\frac{1}{2}'' \times 11''$ bond paper. Many copiers have an alternate paper tray or cassette that you can select if you want another size. Usually the alternate tray has legal-size ($8\frac{1}{2}'' \times 14''$) paper, although it could be any other size or weight used by your organization that will fit the machine.

Special stocks. At times you may want to make copies on other kinds of stock. These are just a few of the options:

1. preprinted letterhead and forms (Be sure the stock is oriented so that the copies will be right-side up.)
2. predrilled paper (Fan the paper first to remove plugs left in the holes and then use 98% reduction.)
3. colored paper
4. card stock for durable covers or dividers
5. transparent film for overlays and overhead projector slides
6. adhesive-backed labels
7. envelopes

If you're using the special stock for many copies, you'll need to remove the paper that's in the paper tray and replace it with your stock. For just one copy on some machines you can place the special stock on top of same-size paper already in the tray, or use the single-sheet feeder.

Loading the copy paper. Many low- to mid-volume copiers have feed trays or cassettes for copy paper. Usually a release lever allows you to remove the tray from the machine. On higher-volume copiers the paper is often stored in non-removable slide-out trays. Bend and fan your copy paper to make sure that the pages are not stuck together before you put the stack into the tray. Follow the manufacturer's directions for placing the paper into the tray. Return the tray or cassette to its slot if applicable, being sure to latch the release lever.

Output Decisions

All but the simplest copiers will make more than one copy of an original at a time. You may be able to choose how you want the multiple copies delivered and finished.

Loading the Paper Cartridge   Loading the Paper Tray

Courtesy of Xerox Corporation.   Courtesy of Xerox Corporation.

Stacks. All copies of each original page are stacked together at the output tray in the order that the copies were made. This is the most common method for low-volume copiers without special features. Some machines offset the stacks—that is, the tray moves slightly after the final copy of each page has been delivered, thus making it easier for you to separate the stacks for collating.

Sorted. With this option, a full set of the copied document is delivered to each bin of the sorter one page at a time.

Precollated. An entire document is copied one page at a time before the next set is copied. Full sets are delivered at the output tray. On many such machines the output tray will move slightly to offset each complete set.

Stapled. Some copiers will staple each collated set if you select this option on the control panel.

Feeding the Original
Now that you've selected the kind of copies you want and how you want them delivered, it's time to make the copies. There are many different ways to feed originals, depending on the manufacturer and on the options available for your copier.

Manual feeding. This is the simplest method. Usually you will lift a cover to expose the platen glass. Place the original face down on the glass: most copiers have guide marks along the edge of the glass to show you where to put the document. Close the platen cover slowly so as not to disturb the placement of the original. Then you're ready to make your copies.

Stream-feeding. Some low-volume machines allow you the option of feeding single originals more rapidly by stream-feeding. A special assembly containing a

The Sorter Receiving Multipage
Original Document

Courtesy of Xerox Corporation.

set of rollers carries the original document past a slot where the exposure is made while the document is in motion. The originals can be fed in rapid succession, without your having to press a button each time. Advantages of stream-feeding are its speed compared with manual copying and its delivery of the copies in collated sets if you process them in the proper order. A disadvantage is that you can copy only single sheets, not books or bound material, unless the stream-feeder assembly can be raised out of the way. If your originals are fragile or taped, it's a good idea to use a clear plastic document carrier to avoid damaging them.

Semiautomatic document feeder.   This device further automates the feeding process by placing the original on the platen glass and removing it after the copies are made. The semiautomatic document feeder uses a series of rollers to pass the original across the surface of the platen glass to the correct copying position and to move the document to the exit tray after the copies have been made. As soon as one document has moved onto the platen glass you can place the next one in position on the feeder. It will be fed automatically after the previous document has been copied. The semiautomatic document feeder is different from stream-feeding for two reasons: you can make more than one copy of each original at a time, and the original is stationary on the platen glass while the copies are being made.

Like the stream-feeder, however, the semi-automatic document feeder doesn't allow you to copy books or bound volumes. Some machines allow you to copy thick documents manually by raising the semi-automatic document feeder and placing the documents directly on the platen glass.

Automatic document feeders.   The fully automatic document feeders allow you to put an entire set of originals on the feed tray at once, instead of placing them there one at a time. The automatic document feeder will take an original,

Semi-automatic Document Feeder   Automatic Document Feeder

Courtesy of Xerox Corporation.   Courtesy of Xerox Corporation.

usually from the bottom of the stack, move it to the platen glass, copy it, and eject it while at the same time moving the next original into place on the platen glass.

There are two major types of fully automatic document feeders. One type makes all copies of each original page at one time. So if you want ten copies of your original set, each page will wait on the platen glass until ten copies have been exposed. An advantage of this method is that the originals are handled only once, thus reducing the chance of damage or jamming. But if you want collated sets, your machine must be equipped with a collator. Otherwise the copies will come out in stacks, with all copies of each page together.

The other type of fully automatic document feeder is called a *recirculating document handler* because it recirculates the set of originals, making one copy of each page at every pass until the required quantity has been exposed. This device eliminates the need for a separate collating feature, since the copies will be delivered in complete sets. Clean, flat originals are especially important with this device, however, in order to avoid jams and document damage since the originals are handled more often. Advantages of both kinds of fully automatic document handlers are their speed and their ability to process a stack of originals, so that you don't have to stand at the copier feeding originals one at a time.

Continuous-form feeder.   The tremendous growth of computer use in offices has made the continuous-form feeder a welcome feature in many organizations. The continuous-form feeder will automatically feed unburst computer forms into the copier. This avoids the time-consuming process of unfolding, positioning, and copying each printout page individually, or bursting and collating the printout before copying. It also avoids the need for multipart computer forms. Multipart forms are often used for low-volume distribution, but copy quality of the last copies is often poor, and corrections are inconvenient to make.

Continuous Forms Feeder

Courtesy of Xerox Corporation.

Copiers with continuous-form feeders often have reduction capability as well, so that continuous computer printouts on 11″ × 14″ or 11″ × 17″ paper can be copied onto standard 8½″ × 11″ paper for distribution and filing. The copies are made on separate sheets, not on continuous forms. Most continuous-form feeders use technology similar to that of semiautomatic document feeders. The operator selects the continuous-form option at the control panel along with reduction or whatever output options are desired, feeds the printout into the device, and starts the machine. The printout is pulled through automatically, a page at a time. After the desired exposures have been made, the printout is advanced to the next page. A wire basket collects the printout after it exits the feeder. With some continuous-form feeders you can start and stop copying in the middle of a continuous document if you don't need copies of the entire printout.

"I have a rush job. Will you be long?"
This question is familiar to anybody who has just started running a long, complicated job on a busy copier. Many copiers at all volume levels now offer a feature that solves the problem.

Interrupt. When you press the "interrupt" button, the copier automatically stores all the information it needs about your job: how many copies you have ordered, how many it has run, what special instructions and output options you have selected, and where it is in the copying cycle. Now you can run another job without losing your place in the first one. To resume the first job, you will normally press the interrupt button again and restart the machine. On some low-volume copiers you can run only one relatively simple job during the interruption. On more powerful copiers, however, you can run as many and as complex projects as you want before recalling the original one from the machine's memory.

DO'S AND DON'TS

Many copier problems are really people problems. Here's how to avoid some of the most common ones:

1. Read the directions.

2. If the "add paper" message comes on, do it.

3. If the copies are too light, check the toner level before you call service.

4. If you're using special stock such as mailing labels or colored stock, remove what's left from the paper tray when you've finished.

5. If you get a misfeed, clear it if you can or call the key operator. (Remember, your copies left in the machine are evidence of who caused the problem!)

6. Put the original on the platen glass correctly (see #1).

7. Spots on the copies? Clean the platen glass (or avoid the problem entirely by doing it before you start).

8. Reset the copy counter and other controls to standard settings after you've finished, if the machine doesn't do it automatically.

ELECTRONIC PRINTING

Electronic printers represent a three-way marriage of xerography and computer and laser technology. Instead of making copies of an original paper document, electronic printers print images that they receive in digital form from a computer or terminal. No conventional hard-copy original or master is needed. The largest and most powerful electronic printers are usually found in commercial printing establishments and in the CRDs of large organizations. These printers are parts of systems that computerize or bypass steps such as graphic design, layout, typesetting, platemaking, printing, and collating. Smaller and less costly electronic printers are becoming common in the automated office as well, where they serve as printers for both word processing and data processing. Some can also be used to make conventional xerographic copies. As office automation brings more and more computing power and communications capability to the workplace, the need for distributed printing is also increasing. Digital information can be transmitted to an electronic printer in the same way as it is to a computer: by telephone, satellite, local area network, or other communications technology. In today's automated office you are likely to find electronic printers performing several typical functions. These functions are discussed in the next few paragraphs.

Customized formats.   Some electronic printing systems can be programmed to generate complete pages with different typestyles and typesizes, graphics, signatures, company logos, and so on, customized to fit the particular need. Variable data such as billing information can be included automatically when a standardized form is being generated with no loss of speed and no need for preprinted forms.

Printing on demand. Since forms, letterhead, etc., can be generated immediately whenever needed, the office does not have to maintain an inventory of printed stock. Price lists, catalogs, and similar time-sensitive publications can be updated whenever a change occurs, and all subsequent distributed copies will be current.

Correspondence. The quality of some electronic printing is comparable to that of letter-quality printers and offset presses. This means that electronically printed material is appropriate for most administrative purposes including correspondence and executive communications.

Data processing. Because of its speed, electronic printing is also suitable for data processing printing. An advantage of electronic printers over conventional data processing line printers is that computer output can be formatted in a variety of typestyles and layouts for better readability and printed on $8\frac{1}{2}'' \times 11''$ cut paper instead of on oversize continuous forms.

Telecommunications. Because it prints from digital input, the electronic printer can serve as a remote output device for electronic mail or distributed data processing in addition to its other uses.

THE KEY OPERATOR

The *key operator* is a person designated by management to be responsible for day-to-day maintenance and supervision of the copier. If you're the key operator you will get special training from the manufacturer in the machine's normal operation, supplies, and troubleshooting procedures. You'll also get lots of questions and requests from users in your office who need help to run a special job or to solve a machine problem. Often you'll find yourself in a teaching role, helping your coworkers learn what the capabilities and limitations of the copier are so that they can use it more productively. These are the usual responsibilities of a key operator.

Daily
1. Keep the machine supplied with paper and toner.
2. Clean the platen glass, feed and exit trays, covers, and other areas as specified by the manufacturer.

Periodically
3. Clean other parts of the copier as specified by the manufacturer.
4. Send copy meter information to the manufacturer for billing if you are on a rental plan.
5. Report departmental usage if you have an internal metering or chargeback system.
6. Check paper and toner supplies and place orders.

As needed

7. Answer questions from users about how to run the copier.

8. Correct machine problems that you have been trained to fix, such as misfeeds, copies that are uneven or too dark or too light, and so on.

9. Call for service if you can't correct the problem yourself. If your machine displays a diagnostic message, report it when you call.

A key operator who is given the time, authority, and training to do the job and who treats the machine with normal care and respect can do a great deal to increase the productivity of the copier and cut service calls.

The role of the key operator has become more complex, yet in some ways easier with the introduction of powerful, microprocessor-based smart copiers having many special features. The key operator's role is more complex because the copiers have more functions that must be understood. Where a mid-volume copier once might have had a semiautomatic document handler and a collator, today a comparable machine may have automatic two-sided copying, reduction, and a continuous-form feeder as well. It's a good idea to get acquainted with the sales and service representatives of the copier manufacturer. They're knowledgeable about your equipment and can often save you time and effort with their suggestions.

Diagnostic messages. The key operator's job is made easier, however, by the ability of the newer machines to diagnose their own problems and identify them on diagnostic displays. Some copiers display a diagram showing where the problem is and actually walk you through the recovery process. Others give an alphanumeric message that you can look up in the key operator's guide. The result is that the key operator or even the casual user can now resolve many machine problems previously requiring service calls. Here's a tip that can save you time and frustration when you're following a self-help diagnostic procedure on a smart copier: don't take shortcuts or do the steps out of order. If the machine display instructs you to open a cover or move an assembly, do it even if you can see that there's no problem. The machine is programmed to wait until the latch has been opened and closed before continuing to the next step.

CONTROLLING COSTS

The ease of operation that makes xerographic copiers convenient for office use also makes them subject to unnecessary wasteful use and to abuse. Part of your responsibility in making copies is to do this task efficiently, which means in the most cost-effective way that will produce the desired results. There are a number of ways to control copying costs. Before you go to the copier, ask yourself these questions:

1. Do I truly need copies?

2. How many copies do I really need? Could I circulate the same copy to several people?

3. Can I save supplies and mailing costs by copying on both sides of the paper or by reducing the document to a smaller format?

4. Would it be more efficient to send the job to the CRD instead of using my time to make copies?

When management feels the need for greater security, the company's copiers can be fitted with control devices. These include keys or cards that authorized users insert into the copier to unlock it. Machines in public places such as libraries may be coin-operated. If several departments share a copier and management wants to charge back copier usage to the appropriate group, an automatic auditor can be installed. On some copiers the auditor is programmed into the machine software; on others the user inserts a hand-held device that enters the user's code and counts the copies. At the end of each accounting period, the person in charge of the monitoring system records the number of copies made by each group and resets the auditor to zero.

IT'S ILLEGAL!

It's against the law in the United States to copy certain documents. The following list is not all-inclusive but is intended to give you a general overview of the kinds of things that should not be reproduced:

1. obligations or securities of the United States Government, including paper money, bonds, notes, certificates of deposit, postage stamps, and postal money orders

2. adjusted compensation certificates for veterans of the World Wars

3. obligations or securities of any foreign government, bank, or corporation

4. copyrighted material, without permission

5. certificates of United States citizenship or naturalization

6. United States passports

7. immigration papers

8. draft registration cards

9. selective service induction papers bearing certain personal information (United States Army and Navy discharge certificates may be copied)

10. badges, identification cards, passes, or insignia carried by military personnel or members of various federal departments and bureaus such as the Treasury or Federal Bureau of Investigation

In some states it's also illegal to copy driver's licenses, automobile registrations, and automobile certificates of title. If you have questions about any document you're about to copy, ask your manager or supervisor to check with the company's law department or attorney.

The Xerographic Process

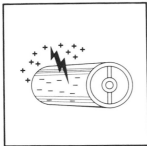

1. Charge

2. Expose

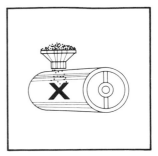

3. Develop

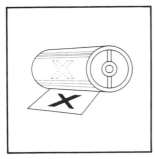

4. Transfer
Courtesy of Xerox Corporation.

5. Fuse

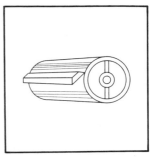

6. Clean

COPIER TECHNOLOGY

Xerography

Most likely, the copier in your office is a conventional xerographic copier that uses dry toner to make copies on plain paper. Xerography is based on two physical principles: materials of opposite electrical charges attract, and some materials behave as electrical insulators when kept in darkness but become conductive when they are exposed to light. Such materials are called *photoconductors*. The diagrams show how these principles are applied to make xerographic copies. First, the photoreceptor (a belt or drum coated with a photoconductive substance) is given a uniform electrostatic charge across its entire surface. The charge may be positive or negative, depending upon the photoconductive material (#1). The photoreceptor is then exposed to the projected image of a document. Light from the white background areas of the document dissipates the electrostatic charge on the photoreceptor surface. But a charge pattern—constituting a latent image— remains on the photoreceptor in the dark areas where no light was reflected from the original (#2). Developer or toner charged to the opposite polarity is spread over the photoreceptor surface. Particles adhere to the latent image area because of electrostatic attraction, making it a visible image (#3). A sheet of paper charged opposite to the toner polarity is brought into contact with the photo-receptor, and the image is transferred, again by electrostatic attraction (#4). The image is then fused to the paper by heat or pressure, or both (#5). Any remaining

Automatic Document Transport - Xerox 9500

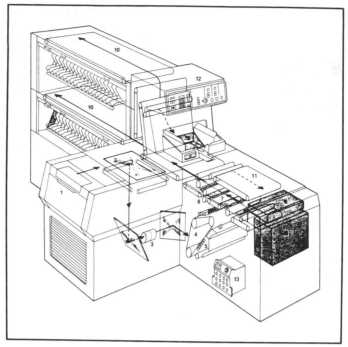

Courtesy of Xerox Corporation.

developer or toner is then cleaned from the photoreceptor (#6). The xerographic process is used by most dry copiers and by most electronic printers on the market today.

Transport systems.   In order to make a copy, the copier must transport the copy paper, and in many cases the original document as well, through the machine. On high-speed copiers with many capabilities, this becomes a high-precision task. The original document automatically moves from the document handler (1) to the platen glass (2). It is exposed by lamps and mirrors through a lens (3) focusing the image (in same or reduced sizes) onto the photoreceptor belt (4). Magnetic rollers (5) brush the belt with toner, which clings to the image area. A sheet of copy paper moves from either the main or auxiliary tray (6) to the belt, where the toner is transferred to it (7). The copy then goes between two rollers (8), where the toner image is fused to it by heat and pressure. A copy of a single-page document emerges in the receiving tray (9). Copies of multipage documents go to the sorter (10) for collating into sets. If the sheet is to be copied on both sides, it returns by conveyor (11) to the auxiliary tray to repeat the process. The copier also has a control console (12) with lighted instructions, and a maintenance module (13) where the service representative can adjust and test the machine's systems. Many xerographic copiers are much simpler than this one, of course. But they all have the basic functions of positioning the original for exposure, transporting copy paper to the photoreceptor area, transferring the image, and delivering the copy to the exit tray.

Copying colors.   You probably know that some xerographic copiers can't make black-and-white copies of certain colors of type or ink, while others can. These differences result from the varying photoconductive materials used. Four basic types of photoconductive materials are used: selenium, zinc oxide, cadmium sulfide, and manmade organic materials. Each has its advantages and disadvantages. For example, selenium is durable, but it won't "see" some tones of blue unless it has been specially treated. Zinc oxide copies all colors well but tends to be short-lived and hard to maintain. Cadmium sulfide copies tones of blue very well but has problems with some reds and yellows. Organic materials are excellent for all colors in certain applications, but have a shorter life than selenium.

Other Dry Copying Processes

Coated paper.   Some inexpensive copiers have used zinc oxide-coated copy paper. The image of the original document in such a machine is formed and developed directly on the copy paper instead of being transferred from a photoreceptor. Development is usually by toner in a liquid solution. Such copiers are rather simple mechanically, but they are limited to copying on expensive coated stock, which has a distinctive texture and appearance that is not always appropriate to the intended use and can be marred by metal objects like paper clips.

Dual spectrum.   This is a fully dry process that uses both light and heat to create copies. It requires a coated, heat-sensitive copy paper stock and a thin, intermediate light-sensitive sheet. The intermediate sheet is placed against the original, and both are exposed to light. The light creates a latent image of the original on the intermediate sheet. The intermediate sheet is then placed against the coated copy paper, and both are exposed to heat. This transfers and develops the image on the copy stock. The dual spectrum process copies colors and photographs well. Supplies have a short shelf life and are relatively expensive, however, and making copies requires two steps.

Thermal process.   In this dry process, heat-sensitive paper and the original are placed together and are exposed to infrared light. The light heats dark areas on the original, which in turn darkens the copy paper. Thermal copies tend to become brittle with age, and original images that are not printed with carbon or metallic media do not copy well.

Wet Photocopying Processes

Several methods of making photocopies require wet chemicals or vapors to develop the image on the copy. Sometimes the copy itself emerges damp.

Diazo.   The diazo process has been used since the 1940s by engineers and architects to copy large drawings. Original documents to be copied by the diazo method must be translucent: that is, they must be on film, vellum, or linen thin enough for light to shine through. The image must be as opaque (dark) as possible, and must be on one side only. The translucent original is placed against sensitized paper. Both are then exposed to ultraviolet light, which desensitizes the coating on nonimage areas of the copy paper. The development process involves the use of ammonia fumes to develop the image on the copy.

Other wet methods.   You also may encounter machines that use diffusion transfer (also called *silver* or *photo-transfer*), dye transfer, or stabilization processes.

Spirit Duplicating Process

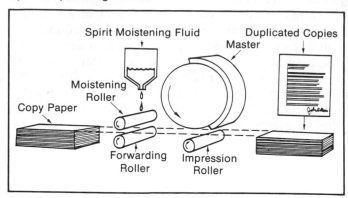

These processes require the use of masters, intermediate sheets or negatives, and liquid developers. They are rarely found in today's office environment.

DUPLICATING AND OFFSET PRINTING

The terms *copying, duplicating,* and *printing* are often used to mean almost the same thing. In general, however, *copiers* make copies directly from an original. Older forms of duplicating require the use of a special master.

Spirit Duplicating

Spirit duplicating is one of the oldest of these processes. It is an inexpensive and fast way to make a relatively small number of prints. The most common print color is purple, although red, green, blue, and black also can be printed. More than one color can be printed on each copy if desired. The spirit master set has three parts: a master sheet, a slip sheet, and a carbon sheet covered with a thin layer of aniline dye. The slip sheet keeps dye from being transferred inadvertently to the master sheet. The image can be created on the master sheet by typing or drawing with a stylus, ballpoint pen, or other hard smooth implement. Images also can be transferred automatically with an infrared copying machine and special spirit master sets.

The spirit duplicating process is quite simple. The master is clamped to the master cylinder, which is a hollow drum. The spirit fluid (alcohol) flows through a wick onto the moistening roller and the forwarding roller. The moistening roller applies an even coating of fluid to the copy paper. The impression roller presses the copy paper against the master. The fluid on the copy paper dissolves a small amount of the aniline dye image on the master. The dye is transferred to the copy paper to produce the image.

To avoid blurred copies, hard-surface twenty-pound duplicator paper should be used rather than a soft porous paper. Duplicator master sets come in several grades for different run lengths. Using long-run masters you can make up to 300 or more copies, but most people use spirit duplicators to make fewer than 100 copies. Spirit duplicating is simple and useful for short runs of certain types of

The Stencil (Mimeo) Process

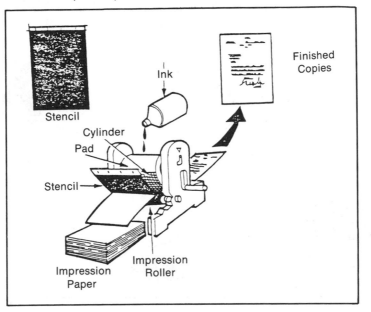

Stencil

Ink

Cylinder

Pad

Stencil

Finished
Copies

Impression
Paper

Impression
Roller

copies for internal use. The copies are not of high quality, however, and the process itself can be messy because of the spirit fluid and the dye on the master. Although spirit duplicating equipment runs copies quite rapidly, the need to create a master significantly slows the process as a whole.

Stencil Duplicating

Stencil duplicating offers better-quality copies and longer run lengths than the spirit process, but it is more costly and less convenient to use. The stencil master has three parts: the stencil itself, which is a fine mesh coated with a waxy material; a cushion sheet; and the backing sheet, which is light card stock. The stencils can be cut by typing or drawing on them with a stylus. Typing or marking on the stencil pushes the wax aside, exposing the mesh and allowing ink to flow through. You can put a film sheet over the stencil when you're typing on it, to keep the typewriter keys from getting gummed with wax from the stencil. Stencils also can be made with electronic stencil cutters and thermal stencil makers. Electronic stencils are quite fragile. Stencil duplicators are operated by hand or electric motor. The stencil is attached to the cylinder—a hollow drum with ink inside. As the drum rotates, centrifugal force presses some of the ink through holes in the cylinder drum and onto an ink pad. The pad distributes the ink over the stencil. When paper is fed between the impression roller and the cylinder drum, ink passes through the image areas of the stencil onto the paper. Since the paper used in stencil duplicating is highly absorbent, the ink dries rapidly.

Inks used in the stencil process may be fluid or paste. In either category, some are designed to dry quickly while others dry more slowly in order to produce a sharper image. Quick-drying inks are convenient for long runs of more than 200

The Offset Process

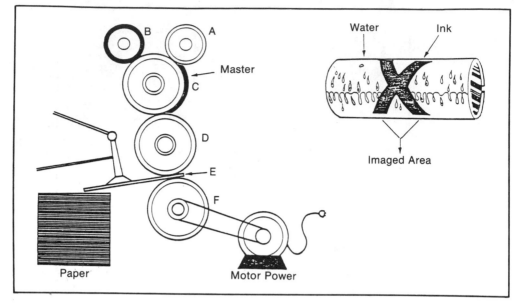

impressions. If you are using slower-drying inks, you will usually need a slip sheet—a clean sheet of paper between the printed sheets—as the copies arrive in the receiving tray. This sheet will prevent smearing of the ink on the back of the next copy in the stack. Stencils can be removed from the duplicator, cleaned, and filed for reuse. With proper care some will last for several thousand impressions. The stencil duplicating process itself is reasonably fast and simple, but it takes time and skill to prepare a good stencil. And it's easy to make an inky mess when you're setting up and operating the duplicator.

Offset Printing

Offset printing is based on the principle that water and grease do not mix. It uses a grease-based ink that sticks to the dry image area on the offset master (also called the *plate*). The nonimage areas of the master are kept wet in order to repel the ink. Offset is a high-speed process that can create thousands of impressions of consistently excellent quality. It is used by commercial printers, publishers, and centralized corporate reproduction departments for long runs in which multiple colors or photographs are being printed, and in cases where very high quality is desired.

The offset master is a specially coated sheet. The image can be created directly on a paper master with typing, pen, pencil, rubber stamp, carbon paper, or xerographic copying. Special electrostatic platemaking equipment also can be used to make masters quickly and inexpensively. These masters must be handled with care because they can be smudged or marked. Direct-image masters can be created by several automatic processes as well. Some xerographic copiers will copy a typed or etched original image onto a direct-image master. Direct-image masters are economical, easy to create, and suitable for relatively short run jobs.

More durable and precise offset masters are created photographically on sensitized metal plates. These may be photo-direct masters which create the master directly from camera-ready original copy, or they may be photo-indirect masters which require creation of an intermediate negative. Several manufacturers offer platemaking equipment. Offset presses come in a range of sizes, ranging from compact units that will produce several thousand impressions per hour to large automated presses that will produce 10,000 or more impressions per hour and require a skilled operator.

Regardless of size and complexity, offset presses all apply the same principle—that water and grease do not mix. The master is prepared, moistened, and attached to the master cylinder (C), and the press is started. A water-based solution on the water roller (A) wets the master, except for the image, which by its nature repels water. After the master is wet, the ink roller (B) applies grease-based ink. The ink sticks to the dry image but is repelled by the wet, nonimage area. The inked image is then transferred to the rubber blanket cylinder (D) by contact pressure. The paper (E) is pressed against the blanket cylinder by the impression cylinder (F) to transfer the image. Offset printing produces consistent, high-quality impressions at reasonable cost for long runs. It is less economical for short runs, however, because of the initial investment in equipment and the time and skill involved to create masters, set up the job, and clean up afterward.

11

A Guide to Business English

Jeff Blyskal • *Staff Writer*, Forbes *Magazine*
Marie Blyskal • *Co-author*, Agri Selling; *Contributor*, The New York Times
Magazine, Reader's Digest, New York, Harper's Bazaar,
and Kirkus Review

Business is only as dull as some of those who write about it manage to make it sound. The problem is, there tend to be so many numbers, statistics, and hard-to-understand phrases, that many who have to read about business tend to hunker down and just force themselves through it. Worse, those who have to write for business—secretaries, report writers, and technical people—often take on the task as though they were braving a minus-fifty-degree winter wind gusting through Chicago: bundle up, lean to, walk briskly, and hope there's a quick cup of hot coffee on the other side of the whole unpleasant experience.

But business writing need not be so terrible, certainly not if you get yourself excited about it. After all, that's why business people are themselves so interested in all this seemingly boring stuff: they are excited about the sportslike "thrill of victory and the agony of defeat" inherent in their work. As major communication links in that drama, secretaries perform several crucial tasks. Your own speed and that of the technology at your command can greatly influence events. Your ability to communicate accurately, concisely, and professionally, and to catch the errors of those who don't can enhance or hurt the entire operation. Your interest in and excitement about your role can convey an impression of a vital, can-do company, or your performance can, on the other hand, indicate an uncaring sloppy attitude adversely reflecting on the company. Central to all of this are basic abilities required in ensuring that the message you are trying to communicate is the same message that actually gets heard. Thus, what follows is a kit of tools and a guide to their use that will help you put together the building blocks of effective communication. In this way you will be able to speak the company's language loudly and clearly.

GUIDELINES TO CAPITALIZATION, PUNCTUATION, ITALICIZATION, AND USE OF NUMERALS

The importance of proper capitalization, punctuation, italicization, and numeral use cannot be overemphasized. These are the fasteners holding together business communications. Improper use of them can result in a rickety construction that detracts from the content of the letter, memo, report, speech, or press release you are responsible for. Worse, it can detract from the image of your company. Of course, not every reader will be sophisticated enough to spot each misplaced comma or incorrectly styled scientific name: in the final analysis you yourself will instinctively know whether or not you have used meticulous care in producing the documents you are responsible for. And while it is true that the readers with the highest standards will not applaud a document devoid of errors (that's the way it *should* be), neither will your documents draw attention to themselves through glaring errors in syntax and style. The trick to excellence in business writing is impeccable use of the language to achieve a product admired for its architecture, its sound construction, and its attractive packaging. Refer to the following guidelines when you have a style problem in a document.

Capitalization

Capitalization should be used in the following instances:

beginnings

1. For the first word of a sentence:

   The evening offered barbecued chicken, cornpones, iced tea, and Jesse Helms.

   Personal income rose 0.9% in December from November.

   Fabergé agreed definitively to be acquired by McGregor Corp. for $32 a share, or $179.8 million. (*The Wall Street Journal*)

2. The first word of a direct quotation (however, lowercase is used for the continuation of a split quotation or a quotation closely woven into the sentence):

   "I was there and I shook hands with the Chinese foreign minister," he said.

   "It is not a matter of what they want," commented one knowledgeable observer, "but a question of timing and tactics."

3. The first word of every line in a poem in traditional verse:

   "He said: 'My name's Rupert
             Murdoch . . .'
   He says: 'Boys, I've made a life

   Out of buyin' old newspapers,
   Changed around each format,
   Added lots of sex and crimes.
   When the news is a sensation
   It increases circulation . . .'."
   (*Forbes*, quoting Mike Royko in the Chicago *Sun-Times*)

proper names

4. The names of people, of corporations, of organizations and their members, of councils and congresses, and of historical periods and events:

   Lee Iacocca
   The Natural Resources Defense
     Council
   Nuclear Regulatory Commission
   the Civil War
   the Industrial Revolution
   Roman Catholic Church
   a Republican
   the Democratic Party
   General Dynamics Corp.
   Delta Air Lines

   The bleak situation of the American steel industry is drawing the United Steelworkers and U.S. Steel Corp. into their sharpest conflict since the 116-day steel strike of 1959. (*Business Week*)

5. The names of places and geographic divisions, districts, regions, and locales:

Wall Street	North Pole
New York	the South

Pennsylvania
George Washing-
   ton Bridge
Silicon Valley
the Sunbelt

China
Greenwich
   Village
New England
Division Street

This is the Corn Belt, heart of the most efficient agriculture in the world . . . . (*Farm Journal*)

Do not capitalize words indicating compass points unless a specific region is referred to:

Turn north onto Interstate 84.

6. The names of rivers, lakes, mountains, seas, and oceans:

Atlantic Ocean
Mississippi River
Blue Ridge Mountains
Lake Superior

[The] ill-fated drillship, the *Glomar Java Sea* . . . [sank] in the South China Sea recently with 81 crew members. (*Oil & Gas Journal*)

7. The names of ships, airplanes, and space vehicles:

U.S.S. *Enterprise*
Lindbergh's *Spirit of St. Louis*
British Airways' *Concorde*
Skylab
the spy satellite Ferret-D

The Soviet Union launched a Progress tanker spacecraft to Salyut 7 Oct. 20 to refuel the space station that suffered a serious propulsion system problem Sept. 9. (*Aviation Week & Space Technology*)

8. The names of nationalities, races, tribes, and languages:

Americans
Caucasian
Bantu
French
Gaelic
Old Church Slavonic

"Every time I see an Arab," says Sylvester Tinker, principal chief of Oklahoma's Osage tribe, "I don't care who he is or what he looks like. I want to run up and kiss him, because he has done more for the Osage people in 4

years than the federal government has done in 150." (*Forbes*)

9. Words that are derived from proper names, when used in their primary senses:

European cities   British royalty

But do not capitalize these derivations if they are used as integral elements of compound words having their own distinct meaning:

chinese red (i.e., a specific shade of red)
moroccan leather (i.e., a specific kind of leather)

titles of people

10. Words indicating familial relationships when preceding a person's name and forming a title:

Aunt Millie   Uncle Ed

but:

my aunt, Millie Martin

11. Titles—civil, corporate, military, royal and noble, religious, and honorary—when preceding a name:

Chief Justice Warren Burger
General George S. Patton
Mayor Koch
Pope John Paul II
Remington Products President Victor Kiam II
Prince Charles and Princess Diana

"There was no cash up front, no margin calls and no interest accrued on the principal," recalls Louisiana-Pacific Chairman Harry Merlo. . . . (*Forbes*)

12. All references to the President and the Vice President of the United States:

President Reagan
Vice President Bush
the President
the Vice President

titles of publications and artistic works

13. All key words in titles of literary, dramatic, artistic, and musical works:

> the book *The One Minute Manager*
> the short story "The Gift of the Magi"
> the *Fortune* article entitled "Winners (and Losers) from IBM's PC Jr."
> the poem "The Highwayman"
> the play *Cats*
> Van Gogh's *A Sidewalk Cafe at Night*
> the Beatles' album *Sgt. Pepper's Lonely Hearts Club Band*
> the movie *Gone With the Wind*

14. *The* in the title of a newspaper if considered an integral part of the publication's entire title:

> *The Wall Street Journal*
> the *Washington Post*

> Missing a deadline is bad for any newspaper, but it's worse for the *Odessa* (Tex.) *American.* (*Editor & Publisher*)

salutations and complimentary closes

15. The first word of the salutation and of the complimentary close of a letter:

> Dear Lee,
> To whom it may concern:
> All hands:
> Yours truly,
> Kind regards,

epithets

16. Epithets used as substitutes for the names of people or places:

> the Father of Capitalism
> the City by the Bay
> the Oval Office

> Yes, Virginia, there finally ·was a Peanut, and the pint-size personal computer wearing Big Blue's [International Business Machines'] daunting logo turned out pretty much as the rumor mill had described it. (*Fortune*)

personifications

17. Words used in personification:

> I met Murder in the way—/He had a mask like Castlereagh. (Percy Bysshe Shelley)

the pronoun I

18. The pronoun *I*:

> I know Sir John Gielgud does a wine commercial where he plays the butler, but I couldn't tell you whose wine it is. (*Advertising Age*)

names for the Deity and sacred works

19. Names for the Deity, for a Supreme Being, and for sacred books:

> God and His blessings
> the Almighty
> the Savior
> the Holy Spirit
> Jehova
> Allah
> the Messiah
> the Bible
> the Koran
> the Talmud

days, months, and holidays

20. Days of the week, months of the year, holidays, and holy days:

> Monday   Passover
> March   Ramadan
> July Fourth   Christmas

courts

21. The names of specific judicial courts:

> The Supreme Court of the United States

the United States Court of Appeals for the Seventh Circuit

The New York State Supreme Court heard oral argument on the publishers' motion December 22. (*Publishers Weekly*)

treaties and laws

22. The names of treaties, pacts, accords, acts, laws, and specific amendments:

the Fifth Amendment to the Constitution
the Civil Rights Act of 1964
the Strategic Arms Limitation Talks II Treaty
Warsaw Pact
the Equal Rights Amendment
Labor Management Relations Act

Truckmakers say that the recovery of sales of Class 8 rigs . . . was slowed last year by confusion over the Surface Transportation Assistance Act of 1982. (*Business Week*)

trademarks and service marks

23. Registered trademarks and service marks:

Xerox	Kleenex
Band-Aid	Ping-Pong
Teletype	Plexiglas
Scotch Post-it	TelePrompTer

In addition to Seven Up's Like cola, now available in more than half the country, other new caffeine-free sodas on the market are Pepsi Free, Pepper Free and Coca-Cola's caffeine-free Coke, Diet Coke and Tab. (*Chain Store Age Supermarkets*)

scientific terms

24. The names of geologic eras, periods, epochs, and strata and the names of prehistoric divisions:

Paleozoic Era	Age of Reptiles
Precambrian	Bronze Age
Pleistocene	

Israeli firms are watching a step-out [oil well] that awaits testing in the Zuk Tamrur area, site of the 1 Zuk Tamrur well, the country's first production from the Triassic [geologic period] formation that underlies most of Israel. (*Oil & Gas Journal*)

25. The names of constellations, planets, stars, and other celestial bodies:

the Milky Way	Pleiades
Earth	Neptune

In addition the Spacelab 1 issue has both cost and hardware implications affecting the Spacelab 2 and 3 missions, and the Astro ultraviolet telescope mission that has Halley's Comet as one target. (*Aviation Week & Space Technology*)

26. Genus—but not species—names in binomial nomenclature:

Chrysanthemum leucanthemum
Macaca mulatta
Rana pipiens

27. New Latin names of classes, families, and all groups higher than genera in botanical and zoological nomenclature:

Gastropoda   Nematoda

But do not capitalize adjectives and nouns derived from these New Latin names:

a gastropod   a nematode

abbreviations and acronyms

28. Many abbreviations and acronyms:

Dec.
Wed.
Dr. Jones
Lt. Gov. Smith
1600 Pennsylvania Ave.
IBM
FBI
OPEC

During the preceding 44 years, the Civil Aeronautics Board (CAB) had exercised tight controls over the ability of new airlines to start service. . . . (*Black Enterprise*)

Punctuation

Apostrophe   ,

1. Indicates the possessive case of singular and plural nouns, indefinite pronouns, and surnames combined with designations such as *Jr.*, *Sr.*, and *II*:

Mr. and Mrs. Postman could be anyone's lovable grandparents.

Investors also applauded XYZ Corporation's purchase of a new personal computer company.

The partnership owns 40 per cent of Dustin Hoffman's latest triumph [*Tootsie*] . . . . (*Barron's*)

And just what was it that woke Wall Street from its uneasy six months' sleep?

2. Indicates joint possession when used with the last of two or more nouns in a series:

Standard and Poor's data
Coke and Pepsi's battle
Jane and Bob's law firm

3. Indicates individual possession when used with each of two or more nouns in a series:

Smith's, Roe's, and Doe's reports

4. Can be used to indicate the plurals of figures, letters, or words:

poorly formed *a*'s and *e*'s
88's and *12*'s transposed
the 1900's

but also possible:

*a*s and *e*s
*88*s and *12*s
the 1900s

Indeed, major companies seeking to recruit MBAs at the business schools . . . . (*Madison Avenue*)

Note: The Associated Press and United Press International stylebooks for magazines and newspapers call for an *s*, not an *'s*, as do the style guides for various publishing houses.

5. Indicates omission of letters in contractions:

isn't (is not)
it's (it is)
wouldn't (would not)

Tax shelters have been around "ever since we've had tax law," said William L. Raby . . . . (*Journal of Accountancy*)

6. Indicates omission of figures in dates:

the class of '84

The mistake we made in the '70s was to assume there was only one possible course. (*Canadian Business*)

Brackets   [ ]

1. Enclose words or passages in quotations to indicate insertion of material written by someone other than the original writer:

I don't think [increasing the Court's membership to ease the workload for each Justice] would solve the problem. (Retired Supreme Court Justice Potter Stewart, quoted in *Forbes*)

2. Enclose material inserted within matter already in parentheses:

(The return on equity [ROE] is 35 per cent.)

Colon   :

1. Introduces words, phrases, or clauses that explain, amplify, or summarize what has preceded:

You know what I mean: The idea that we should all be happy all of the time . . . . (*Advertising Age*)

A big question hangs over one major vocational group: clerical workers. (*Fortune*)

The Buckingham Corporation ... and a company within the Beverage Group of Beatrice Foods have announced the appointment of D'Arcy-MacManus & Masius, Inc. as the advertising agency for Finlandia as well as for its other exclusive U.S. imports: Cutty Sark and Cutty 12 Scots Whiskies . . . . (*Beverage World*)

2. Introduces a rather long quotation:

   Says Warner: "The deficit is more destructive than any enemy we face. National defense cannot be stronger than the economy on which it rests." (*Nation's Business*)

3. Introduces a list:

   The session also gives major insights into:
   * current consumption data
   * sales projections
   * the competitive situation
   (*Chemical Week*)

4. Separates chapter and verse numbers in references to biblical quotations:

   Esther 2:17

5. Separates city from publisher in footnotes and bibliographies:

   Boston: Houghton Mifflin, 1984

6. Separates hour and minute in time designations:

   3:45 P.M.   a 7:30 meeting

   So when I left the mill at 9:30 and walked toward the big back door where the trucks unload, one of the millwrights said, "I hope you're not going to close the company today." (*Inc.*)

7. Follows the salutation in a business letter:

   Ladies and Gentlemen:
   To whom it may concern:
   Dear Mr. or Ms. Kane:

Comma ,

1. Separates the clauses of a compound sentence connected by a coordinating conjunction:

   Instead, they'll point up the good parts of the idea, and only then might they discuss a potential problem with the idea.

   "A lot of people are trying to catch us, but we're a moving target," says founder and [Lotus Development Corp.] President Mitchell D. Kapor. (*Industry Week*)

   The comma may be omitted in short compound sentences:

   We have prepared the case and we are ready to present it.

2. Can be used to separate *and* or *or* from the final item in a series of three or more:

   Want to boost employee morale? Then give your employees a New Year's present that helps them save for: retirement, a new house, college tuition, unexpected medical expenses, or other major expenses. (*ABA Banking Journal*)

   Note: In accordance with the AP and UPI stylebooks, most magazines and newspapers drop the last comma before the *and* or *or* in simple series.

3. Separates two or more adjectives modifying the same noun if *and* could be used between them:

   The short, khaki-clad guest of honor works the room like the politician he is . . . . (*The Wall Street Journal*)

   but:

   a polished mahogany desk (*and* could not be placed between *polished* and *mahogany*)

4. Sets off a nonrestrictive clause or phrase (one that if eliminated would not affect the meaning of the sentence):

Clearly, there is a fine line between editing and formatting, which is covered in the following section. (Harry Katzan, Jr.)

But the comma should not be used when the clause is restrictive (essential to the meaning of the sentence):

One railroad that already knows what will work is the Southern. . . . (*Railway Age*)

5. Sets off words or phrases in apposition to a noun or noun phrase:

Dennis R. Tourse, a partner in the Boston firm of Fitch, Miller and Tourse, [says] "your office has to look the way people picture a business lawyer's office." (*Black Enterprise*)

In this example, *partner* is in apposition to *Dennis R. Tourse.*

Note: The comma should not be used if such words or phrases precede the noun they modify:

The Navy, said ex-Chief of Naval Operations Elmo (Bud) Zumwalt, assumes "that everyone below the rank of commander is immature." (Thomas J. Peters and Robert H. Waterman, Jr.)

not

"ex-Chief of Naval Operations, Elmo (Bud) Zumwalt"

6. Sets off transitional words and short expressions that require a pause in reading or speaking:

Unless safeguards are put in place, the computer age, at least for a while, could resurrect some of the class barriers that liberals spent much of this century trying to tear down. (Heather Menzies)

7. Sets off words used to introduce a sentence:

Indeed, southern Florida does have warm winters.

At best, commodity trading is a high risk game where the only consistent winners are the brokers who charge you commissions. (*Money*)

8. Sets off a subordinate clause or a long phrase that precedes a principal clause:

If we state, then, that champions and systems of champions are the single most important key to sustained innovative success in the excellent companies, how do we reconcile repeated failure and overall success? (Thomas J. Peters and Robert H. Waterman Jr.)

Weighing in base form 1,630 lbs. (739 kg.), CRX has plastic fenders and lower body panels. (*Ward's Auto World*)

9. Sets off short quotations and sayings:

"We plan to reincarnate Elvis," says Joseph Rascoff, the New York accountant who is masterminding it all. (*Forbes*)

10. Indicates omission of a word or words:

To err is human; to forgive, divine.

11. Sets off the year from the month in full dates:

February 6, 1985

But note that when only the month and the year are used, no comma appears:

February 1985

12. Sets off city and state in geographic names:

A case in point is the Panther Valley Apartments in Allamuchy, N.J. . . . (*Professional Builder*)

13. Separates series of four or more figures into thousands, millions, and so on:

Every time bulk diesel fuel goes up a penny, it costs us $100,000.

The plant still produces 155,000 lb/week of dyed sewing thread plus about 50,000 lb/week of dyed yarn. . . . (*Textile World*)

14. Sets off words used in direct address:

    Mr. Stone, please be ready to submit your report in one hour.

    I have received your report, Ms. Smith, and I have these comments.

15. Separates a tag question from the rest of the sentence:

    Didn't take long for Jesse Jackson to get into the political mainstream of America, did it? (*Advertising Age*)

16. Sets off any sentence elements that might be misunderstood if the comma were not used:

    Dole has already held hearings, and hopes to introduce the measure in the next month or two. (*Forbes*)

17. Follows the salutation in a personal letter and the complimentary close in a business or personal letter:

    Dear Lee,   Sincerely,

18. Sets off some titles, degrees, and honorifics from surnames and from the rest of a sentence:

    Sandra Maynard, Esq.
    John Kennedy, Jr.
    Susan P. Green, MD, presented the case.

Dash ▬

1. Indicates a sudden break or change in continuity:

    Last year Presley's Graceland attracted over 500,000 people—more than Thomas Jefferson's Monticello—at $6 a head for adults. (*Forbes*)

2. Sets apart a defining or emphatic phrase:

    Only one sector—public transit—fared badly in 1983 . . . . (*Engineering News Record*)

    More important than winning the election, is governing the nation. That is the test of a political party—the acid, final test. (Adlai E. Stevenson)

3. Sets apart parenthetical material:

    . . . newspapers' 1982 income from retail ads was five times as much as from national ads—$15 billion vs. $3 billion. (*Advertising Age*)

4. Marks an unfinished sentence:

    "I demand we take a vote on—" the shareholder insisted during the annual meeting before his microphone was shut off.

5. Sets off a summarizing phrase or clause:

    Now GM, Ford, Chrysler, American Motors—it's up to you. (*Broadcasting*)

    The vital measure of a newspaper is not its size but its spirit—that is its responsibility to report the news fully, accurately, and fairly. (Arthur H. Sulzberger)

6. Can be used to set off the name of an author or source, as at the end of a quotation:

    "We have not given up on the U.S. small car. Despite all the statements by our competitors and the doomsayers, we did not give up."—Roger B. Smith, 58, chairman of General Motors (*Fortune*)

Ellipses ▪ ▪ ▪

1. Indicate, by three spaced points, omission of words or sentences within quoted matter:

    "No, I would not say things like that again, even after some of the things that have been done recently . . . I would like to convince the Soviets that no one in the world has aggressive intentions toward them." (Ronald Reagan in *Time* magazine, quoted by *Forbes*)

2. Indicate, by four spaced points, omission of words at the end of a sentence:

    "There might be an argument for doing nothing . . . . " (Kissinger Commission on Central America, quoted by *Forbes*)

3. Indicate, when extended the length of a line, omission of one or more lines of poetry:

Come away, O human child!
. . . .
For the world's more full of weeping
Than you can understand.
(William Butler Yeats)

4. Are sometimes used as a device to catch and hold the reader's interest, especially in advertising copy:

Sergeant Major Zack Carey believed in Truth, Justice, and the American Way . . . until a small-town sheriff set him up. (advertisement for the James Garner movie *Tank*, in *Variety*)

Exclamation Point !

1. Terminates an emphatic or exclamatory sentence:

"No money can buy the workers here!" (*Forbes*)

2. Terminates an emphatic interjection:

No! I won't go.
Encore!

Hyphen -

1. Indicates that part of a word or more than one syllable has been carried over from one line to the next:

. . . Chemical [Bank] and other litigants are expected to make a separate legal effort. . . .
(*Dun's Business Month*)

2. Joins the elements of some compounds:

cost-of-living index
foot-dragging
cost-effectiveness

3. Joins the elements of some compound modifiers preceding nouns:

a cattle-feeding enterprise
a heavy-duty press

. . . disease ravaged [Jim] Power's 65-sow farrow-to-finish operation. . . .
(*Farm Journal*)

4. Indicates that two or more compounds share a single base:

three- and four-ton stamping machines
eight- and ten-year-old foundries

5. Separates the prefix and root in some combinations:

- prefix + proper noun or adjective (an *anti-American* protestor; engaged in a *pro-capitalism* quest)

- some prefixes ending in a vowel + root beginning with a vowel (presidential *re-election*; *co-author*)

- stressed prefix + root word if absence of hyphen could cause misunderstanding of meaning (*re-form/reform; re-cover/recover; re-creation/recreation*)

6. Substitutes for the word *to* between figures or words:

. . . 33.1 per cent have owned [a home] only 1-2 years . . . . (*Professional Builder*)

7. Punctuates written-out compound numbers from 21 through 99 (note, however, that house styles differ on this point):

a thirty-five per cent return on equity
fifty-seven clients
ninety-nine computer companies

Parentheses ()

1. Enclose material that is not an essential part of the sentence and that if not included would not alter its meaning:

But Kansas City television (KCTV-5) anchor Wendall Anschutz said he would ask the source . . . .

Also named as defendant in the suit (filed in federal court in San Francisco) was the San Francisco Newspaper Printing Co. . . . (*Editor & Publisher*)

2. Often enclose letters or figures to indicate subdivisions of a series:

It seems our choices are (a) launch a counteroffensive marketing attack; (b) press ahead to get our new model out six months ahead of schedule; or (c) run like hell.

3. Enclose figures following and confirming written-out numbers, especially in legal and business documents:

Attempts were made to get in touch with the defendant, but he hung up on the plaintiff's telephone calls twelve (12) times in a single afternoon.

4. Enclose abbreviations of written-out words when the abbreviations are used for the first time in a text and may be unfamiliar to the reader:

According to Kevin Feeney, a practice-management official for the American Medical Association (AMA), hospitals provide another avenue for financing. (*Black Enterprise*)

Period   .

1. Terminates a complete declarative or mild imperative sentence:

A new fad in consumer stroking seems to be hotline telephone numbers.

"Boulder Beer should be made in Boulder," claims Jerry Smart, president of Boulder Beer Company. (*Beverage World*)

Would you please sign here.

2. Follows some abbreviations:

Inc.	Calif.
etc.	Jan.
a.k.a.	Ltd.
Ave.	F.Y.I.

Question Mark   ?

1. Terminates a direct question:

. . . why should anyone want to come to him for a service they can get through a toll-free number? (*ABA Banking Journal*)

but:

I wonder who said, "Speak softly and carry a big stick."

I asked if they planned to leave early.

2. Indicates uncertainty:

Ferdinand Magellan (1480?–1521)

Quotation Marks:
"   " and '   '

double quotation marks "   "

1. Enclose direct quotations:

"We discovered that we couldn't efficiently manufacture copiers at the low number of units we were producing," explains George Bradbury . . . . (*Madison Avenue*)

When advised not to become a lawyer because the profession was already overcrowded, Daniel Webster replied, "There is always room at the top."

2. Enclose words or phrases to clarify their meaning or to indicate that they are being used in a special way:

The theme "Reaching out in new directions" was revealed in an eight-page blockbuster spread . . . . (*Madison Avenue*)

ALCOA is finding that it "deep discounts" its own prices even more . . . And common alloy grades continue to be discounted "four fives," or four progressive 5% cuts, which amounts to about 18%. (*Business Week*)

3. Set off the translation of a foreign word or phrase:

déjà vu, "already seen"

4. Set off the titles of series of books, of articles or chapters in publications, of essays, of short stories and poems, of individual television and radio programs, and of songs and short musical pieces:

"The Horizon Concise History" series an article entitled "Electronic Mail in the Small Business"

Chapter Nine, "Voice Mail Technology"
Pushkin's short story "The Queen of Spades"
Tennyson's "Ode on the Death of the Duke of Wellington"
ABC's "Good Morning America"
NPR's "All Things Considered"
Schubert's "Death and the Maiden"

single quotation marks ' '

Enclose quotations within quotations:

The blurb for the piece proclaimed, "Two years ago at Geneva, South Vietnam was virtually sold down the river to the Communists. Today the spunky little . . . country is back on its own feet, thanks to 'a mandarin in a sharkskin suit who's upsetting the Red timetable.'" (Frances FitzGerald)

Note: Put commas and periods inside closing quotation marks; put semicolons and colons outside. Other punctuation, such as exclamation points and question marks, should be put inside the closing quotation marks only if it is part of the matter quoted.

Semicolon ;

1. Separates the clauses of a compound sentence having no coordinating conjunction:

   Some firms went bankrupt; others scrambled to leave the community development business altogether. (*Barron's*)

2. Separates the clauses of a compound sentence in which the clauses contain internal punctuation, even when the clauses are joined by a conjunction:

   Lewis reckons that each of these depressions lasted 10 years, except for the 1929 one; it lasted 12 years. (*Forbes*)

3. Separates elements of a series in which the items already contain commas:

The issues that top security analysts favor include SmithKline Beckman (NYSE, $58) and Bristol Myers (NYSE, $42), among drug concerns; McDonald's (NYSE, $72) and Chart House (recently traded over the counter at $20) in restaurants; and retailers Associated Dry Goods (NYSE, $67) and Dayton Hudson (NYSE, $31). (*Money*)

4. Separates clauses of a compound sentence joined by a conjunctive adverb such as *nonetheless, however,* or *hence*:

   We will produce the product; however, it will cost $15, not $12.

5. May be used instead of a comma to signal longer pauses for dramatic effect:

   But I want you to know that when I cross the river my last conscious thoughts will be of the Corps; the Corps; and the Corps. (General Douglas MacArthur)

Virgule /

1. Separates successive divisions in an extended date:

   the fiscal year 1984/85

2. Represents the word *per*:

   CRX achieves an awesome 51 mpg (4.6L/100 km) rating in EPA city tests . . . . (*Ward's Auto World*)

3. Means *or* between the words *and* and *or* (and/or) and sometimes between other words to indicate possible options or choices:

   In working with a Chevrolet stamping plant in Cleveland, Case Western Reserve's Dr. Berrettoni found that existing "go/no go" gages were inadequate . . . . (*Industry Week*)

Italics

1. Indicate titles of books, plays, and very long poems:

   the book *In Cold Type*
   the play *A Man for All Seasons*
   the epic poem *Paradise Lost*

2. Indicate the titles of magazines and newspapers:

Jeffrey Gluck, publisher of *Saturday Review* and other magazines, has signed a definitive agreement with the Newhouse family to acquire the *St. Louis Globe-Democrat*. (*Editor & Publisher*)

3. Set off the titles of motion pictures and radio and television series:

ABC's regular Wednesday schedule of *Fall Guy*, *Dynasty*, and the new *Hotel* won with ease . . . . (*Broadcasting*)

4. Indicate the titles of long musical compositions:

Messiah
Die Götterdämmerung
Bartok's *Concerto for Orchestra*

5. Set off the names of paintings and sculpture:

Mona Lisa
Pietà
American Gothic

6. Indicate words, letters, or numbers that are referred to:

I think *don't* would be more forceful than *shouldn't*.
You form your *n*'s like *u*'s.
The *60* in an earlier memo should be a *600* instead.

7. Are used to indicate foreign words and phrases not yet assimilated into English:

garçon
pâtissiers
Sturm und Drang
c'est la vie

8. Indicate the names of plaintiff and defendant in legal citations:

Franklin v. *Madison*

9. Emphasize a word or phrase:

. . . too many of those studies *weren't* being implemented. (*Inc.*)

Note: Use this device sparingly.

10. Distinguish the New Latin names of genera, species, subspecies, and varieties in botanical and zoological nomenclature:

Homo sapiens

Do not italicize phyla, classes, orders, and families in botanical and zoological nomenclature:

Gastropoda
Nematoda

11. Set off the names of ships and planes, but not space vehicles:

U.S.S. *Kitty Hawk*
Spirit of St. Louis
Apollo 11
the space shuttle Challenger
the spy satellite Ferret-D

Numerals

1. Use figures to express specific dates, measures, hours, addresses, page numbers, and coordinates:

$35 a share
10 per cent (*or* 10%) after-tax profit margin
January 22, 1984
80° north latitude
4:00 P.M.
30 Rockefeller Plaza
p. 12
Vol. 3
76 tons
0.5 microns
2.5 ml.

2. Generally, spell out numbers from zero to ninety-nine and use numerals for numbers 100 or larger (styles can and do vary):

forty-seven applicants
371 tons of iron ore

3. When a sentence begins with a number, do not use figures; spell it out:

Fifteen thousand feet of wire was lost.

but:

We lost 15,000 feet of wire.

Calendar years, however, are the exception:

1985 promises double last year's earnings.

We expect double earnings in 1985.

4. When two or more numbers appear in one sentence, spell them out consistently or use figures regardless of whether the numbers are larger or smaller than ninety-nine:

Fifteen thousand feet of wire was delivered on two trucks.
About 15,000 feet of wire was delivered on 2 trucks.

Note: House styles vary considerably on this point.

5. Spell out numbers used casually:

A thousand times No!
Thanks a million.
I traveled a half mile.

6. Spell out ordinals in texts:

the nineteenth century
the tenth meeting

Ordinals in business correspondence address blocks may be spelled out or abbreviated:

Fifth Avenue
5th Avenue

7. Sometimes a number (or numbers) forms part of a corporate name or a set phrase; style corporate names and phrases associated with them exactly as shown on letterhead or in reference works such as *Thomas Register*:

Ten Speed Press
20th Century-Fox Studios
42nd Street Photo
Pier 1 Imports
Saks Fifth Avenue
Fortune 500

8. Rounding out large numbers is often acceptable:

$116.7 million sales (instead of *$116,698,447*)

a $200 billion federal deficit (instead of the unwieldy *$200,000,000,000* federal deficit)

9. Use numerals for all decimal fractions:

100.23 mm. (not *one hundred point twenty-three mm.* or *one hundred and twenty-three one-hundredths mm.*)

THE BASICS OF GRAMMAR AND USAGE

This section contains the most basic rules of English grammar presented within the context of business writing, supplemented by a guide to English usage adapted from the usage notes in *The American Heritage Dictionary*, Second College Edition, and tailored to the needs of the business person. Since the eight parts of speech—verbs, nouns, pronouns, adjectives, adverbs, prepositions, conjunctions, and interjections—are the building blocks on which phrases, clauses, sentences, and paragraphs are constructed, our initial discussion centers on the parts of speech and common problems relating to them. The grammar section concludes with a brief discussion of phrases, clauses, sentences, and paragraphs, after which there is a section on English usage.

The Verb

A verb (*perform* or *be*, for instance) is a word that expresses action or a state of being:

Action: She *performs* well under pressure.

State of Being: He *is* the chief operating officer.

A verb can indicate tense (present, past, or future, for example), person (first, second, or third), number (singular or plural), and voice (active or passive). It can also indicate mood (indicative, subjunctive, imperative).

Regular verbs are inflected by the addition of -ed, -ing, and -s or -es to the base form (mix, mixed, mixing, mixes), while irregular verbs are inflected (do, did, done, doing, does; be, am, is, are, was, were, being, been) by way of major changes in the base form. When you are uncertain about a particular inflected form, look up the word in The American Heritage Dictionary, Second College Edition, where you will find the principal parts of all regular and irregular verbs entered.

The tense of the verb specifies the time or the nature of the action that occurs. The following chart conjugates the verb to write through the past, present, and future tenses.

Tense	I	He/She/It	We/You/They
present	write	writes	write
present progressive	am writing	is writing	are writing
past	wrote	wrote	wrote
past progressive	was writing	was writing	were writing
perfect	have written	has written	have written
past perfect	had written	had written	had written
future	will write	will write	will write
	am going to write	is going to write	are going to write
future perfect	will have written	will have written	will have written

A verb may be marked for person and number. For example:

> I have no time for this.
> You have no time for this.
> He has no time for this.
> We have no time for this.
> They have no time for this.

Voice indicates whether the verb is active or passive. For example:

> *Active:* The two companies *have merged.*

> *Passive:* The two companies *have been merged.*

The mood of a verb is used to express a statement of fact, a condition contrary to fact, or a command. The indicative mood is used for statements of fact: *The two companies have merged* (i.e., they've done it and the merger is a reality). The subjunctive mood indicates a conditional situation—one contrary to what we know is the case right now: *If the two companies were to merge, managerial heads would roll* (i.e., the two companies haven't merged yet). The imperative mood expresses a command: *See that you are not late for the meeting.*

Verbs can be transitive or intransitive. A transitive verb takes an object: *The FTC issued an important ruling last week.* In this sentence, *issued* is the transitive verb and *ruling* is its object. On the other hand, an intransitive verb (or a verb used intransitively) does not take an object: *No new information issued from the press conference.* In this example, the verb *issue* has been used intransitively. The subject is *information* and there is no object for the verb.

Linking verbs connect subjects and predicate nouns, pronouns, and adjectives and express a condition or a state of being. The most common linking verb is *to be*. Also included in the linking verb category are the "sense" verbs *feel, look, smell,* and *taste* together with *appear, become, continue, grow, prove, remain, seem, stand,* and *turn* when used in specific senses. Remember to use adjectives and not adverbs after linking verbs. For example: *He felt uncomfortable about making a presentation on such short notice. Those projected figures seem erroneous to me. They became obstinate when we asked them to change their advertising copy.* This, then, is a brief description of our verb system. Now let's look at a few of the problems that can arise.

Subject/verb agreement.   The verb must agree with its subject in number and person. *The company officers were unavailable for comment* (plural subject, plural verb). *The company president was unavailable for comment* (singular subject, singular verb). However, certain words and expressions sometimes pose problems in connection with subject/verb agreement:

1. Collective nouns
   Collective nouns such as *committee, jury,* and *group* usually take singular verbs but can take plural verbs if the constituents of the collective unit are being considered individually: *The Publishing Committee has unanimously vetoed the project.* Or, *The Publishing Committee were divided about the viability of the project.* See also the discussion about collective nouns that appears under the subsection on nouns herein. (Additional information may be found in the usage notes for **number, per cent,** and **percentage.**)

2. *One* and *one of those*
   Constructions employing *one* often raise questions about whether verbs should be singular or plural. One such construction is exemplified by this sentence: *One in every ten applicants was found deficient.* Although the plural verb *were* is sometimes used in such a sentence, a singular verb, in agreement with the subject *one,* is the acceptable usage in formal writing.
   A more controversial construction involves *one of those who* or a variant: *He is one of those managers who always complain about their expense accounts.* Most experts feel that only the plural verb (in this case, *complain*) is possible, since the antecedent of *who* is a plural noun (in this example, *managers*). In other examples, however, *one* may be construed as the subject of the verb in the relative clause: *The manager is the only one of those people who has* (not *have*) *complained.*
   The construction *more than one* is always singular despite the fact that logic would seem to require a plural verb: *More than one of the applicants has failed to complete the test.* Conversely, *fewer than two* is always plural: *fewer than two have completed the test.*

3. Singular subjects, the verb *to be,* and plural complements
   The number of the verb *to be* must agree with the subject and

not with the complement (a complement is a predicate noun or adjective coming after the verb): *The topic of my memorandum is fiscal irresponsibility and managerial incompetence.* In this example, *topic* is the singular subject, with which the singular verb *is* agrees. The compound phrase, *fiscal irresponsibility and managerial incompetence,* is the complement.

4. *There*
There frequently precedes a linking verb such as *be, seem,* or *appear* at the beginning of a sentence or a clause: *There has been a great deal of uncertainty as to the exact meaning of the law.* The number of the verb is governed by the subject, which in such constructions follows the verb: *There is a storage facility across the street. There seem to be many options.* But a singular verb is also possible before a compound subject whose parts are joined by a conjunction or conjunctions, especially when the parts are singular: *There is* (or *are*) *much work and planning involved.* When the first element of such a subject is singular, a singular verb is also possible even though the other element may be plural: *There were* (or *was*) *a box and two bags in the back of the truck.* But, *There were two bags and a box in the back of the truck.*

5. Extraneous expressions
Don't be misled by the presence of plural nouns in phrases that intervene between the true subject and its verb; the subject and verb must agree in person and number. *The executive, together with two secretaries, a chauffeur, and four bodyguards, has arrived. She, and not any of her associates, is responsible for the litigation. The parent company, as well as its affiliate, was named in the indictment.* The expressions set off by commas in the previous sentences do not constitute additions to the real subject, since the elements linking them to the subject do not have the force of conjunctions. Therefore, the singular subjects in the respective sentences require singular verbs. See also the entries **together with** and **well** in the usage section.

6. Singular subjects preceded by *each, every, many a, such a,* or *no*
A singular subject preceded by *each, every, many a, such a,* or *no* takes a singular verb even when several such subjects are linked by *and: Each manager and each division chief has urged the employees to invest in the thrift plan. No department head and no divisional manager has ever commented on that.*
See also the entry **each** in the usage section.

7. *Either/or* and *neither/nor*
If the subjects so joined are both singular, use a singular verb: *Either the general manager or the publisher decides that.* If both subjects are plural, use a plural verb: *Neither the man-*

agers nor their secretaries have responded. If one subject is singular and the other plural, the number of the verb is usually governed by the number of the subject closest to it: *Neither the supervisor nor the union members are willing to negotiate. Neither the union members nor the supervisor is willing to negotiate.*

8. Unitary compounds and singular verbs
When referring to a unit, such as an organization or corporate entity, a singular verb is correct: *Hutchins/Young & Rubicam has prepared an elaborate presentation. Little, Brown is a Boston publisher.*

Split infinitives.   The split infinitive, as in *to readily accept,* is not a grammatical error, and it has ample precedent in literature. But many writers and editors still feel that it should be avoided, especially in its more extreme form. It is least desirable when *to* and its verb are separated by a succession of modifying words that slows the reader's comprehension and produces a clumsy effect: *We are seeking a plan to gradually, systematically, and economically expand our plant.* In this example (deemed unacceptable by many), placement of the adverbs at the end of the sentence would improve the clarity and style without changing the desired sense: *We are seeking a plan to expand our plant gradually, systematically, and economically.* Most splits are not so extreme, and in such cases opinion as to acceptability is often divided: *If you want to really help patients, you must respect their feelings. To better understand the miners' plight, the coal company president lived among them for a week.* The split infinitive has greatest acceptance when it expresses concisely and clearly a sense that could not be expressed so concisely and clearly by another phrasing: *We expect our output to more than double in a year.* Many writers also feel that it is better to split an infinitive than to displace an adverb from what is felt to be its natural position in the sentence, a practice that can make the sentence appear stilted or ambiguous. If the sentence *the supervisor wanted to really help the trainee* is rewritten either as *the supervisor wanted really to help the trainee* or as *the supervisor wanted to help the trainee really,* it is unclear whether *really* modifies *wanted* or *help.* Expressions involving the verbs *be* and *have,* such as *to be really sure* and *to have just seen,* are often taken to be split infinitives. They are not, because *to* is not separated from the infinitive *be* or *have.*

Participles.   When a participle is used as a modifier, there should be no ambiguity or illogicality about the element it modifies. Special care should be taken to avoid the dangling participle—a participle that is wrongly attached to (and seemingly modifies) a noun, pronoun, or other such word and thus produces an absurdity: *Turning the corner, the view was much changed.* (Since it was not the view that turned the corner, a better phrasing would be: *Turning the corner, we discovered that the view was much changed.*) Similarly: *Lacking a better candidate, it was decided to postpone the election.* This is better rewritten: *In the absence of a better candidate, it was decided . . . .* Many participlelike constructions are well established as prepositions, however, and may be used freely. These include *speaking of, owing to, concerning, failing, considering, granting,* and *judging by.* Thus, we may write: *Speaking of politics, the election has been postponed. Considering the hour, it is surprising that the morning newspaper arrived at all.*

The verbless sentence.   Not all sentences must have main verbs to be grammatically acceptable. In memos, letters, and especially in advertising copy we often see quite effective sentence fragments. The following examples are taken from a business magazine and a newspaper, respectively:

> At long last, a word processing and mailing list program that might have been heaven-sent since it can do so much and yet costs so little. (Advertisement in *PC World* for Paperwork, Harris Micro Computers, Inc.)

In this example, the sentence fragment lacks a main verb, although verbs have been included in the subordinate clause beginning with the word *since.*

In the next example, the advertisement begins and ends with full sentences but all the matter in between is fragmentary:

> Looking for a new job is a hassle. Expensive, too. The cost of resumes, mailings, and phone calls. The cost of wasted time; sneaking around at job fairs. And the fear that it might cost you your present job. There is an easier way. (Advertisement in *The Boston Globe* for JobLine.)

Other typical examples of verbless sentences include these:

> Are you coming? *Yes.*
> *Hello.* My name is Jane.
> *Encore!*
> These, then, are the problems. *What to do?*

The Noun

A noun is traditionally described as a word that names a person, place, thing, or abstraction. Proper nouns name specific persons, places, or things (Silicon Valley; Telex); common nouns are sometimes classified as abstract nouns that name ideas, beliefs, or qualities (capitalism); and concrete nouns that name tangible things (typewriter). Nouns can show possession (the treasurer's report) and they can show number (singular or plural).

The problem of number.   Nouns usually form their plurals by addition of *-s* or *-es* to the base form (president, presidents; box, boxes). Another large group of nouns with a final *-y* follows the pattern of *query, queries.* There are irregular nouns that indicate the plural by a change in the base form (mouse, mice) or that undergo no change at all (sheep, sheep). Still other nouns have variant forms in the plural, all of which are acceptable (memorandum, memorandums, or memoranda; phenomenon, phenomena, or phenomenons). When you are uncertain about a particular plural form, consult *The American Heritage Dictionary,* Second College Edition, in which all noun plurals other than those formed by addition of *-s* or *-es* are shown. Some nouns ending in *-s* are plural in form but may function as either singular or plural or as both in number. By way of illustration, below is *The American Heritage Dictionary* entry for the word *politics,* in which the first four senses require use of a singular verb while the last two require use of a plural verb:

> **pol·i·tics** (pŏl′ĭ-tĭks) *n.* **1.** *(used with a sing. verb).* The art or science of government; political science. **2.** *(used with a sing. verb).* The activities or affairs of a government, politician, or political party. **3.** *(used with a sing. verb).* **a.** The conducting of or engaging in political affairs, often professionally. **b.** The business, activities, or profession of a person so involved. **4.** *(used with a sing. verb).* The methods or tactics involved in managing a state or government. **5.** *(used with a pl. verb).* Intrigue or maneuvering within a group: *office politics.* **6.** *(used with a pl. verb).* A person's general position or attitude on political subjects: *His politics are conservative.*

When you are unsure whether words such as *acoustics, aerobics,* or *economics* take singular or plural verbs, look them up in the dictionary. *The American Heritage Dictionary* gives the appropriate information about all such words.

Collective nouns. A collective noun denotes a collection of persons or things regarded as a unit. A collective noun takes a singular verb when it refers to the collection as a whole and a plural verb when it refers to the members of the collection as separate persons or things: *The committee was in executive session. The committee have all left for the day.* (In British usage, however, collective nouns are most often construed as plural: *The government are committed to a liberal policy.*) A collective noun should not be treated as both singular and plural in the same construction. Thus: *The company is determined to press its* (not *their*) *claim.* Among the most common collective nouns are *committee, company, clergy, enemy, group, family, flock, people,* and *team.*

Uses of nouns.   A noun can be the subject of a sentence: *The housing industry is in trouble;* the direct object of a verb: *Spiraling interest rates and inflation have softened the housing industry;* the object of a preposition: *This is one of the hottest issues in the housing industry;* or the indirect object of a verb: *Give the housing industry a chance and it may recover.*

Nouns as modifiers. Nouns often occur as modifiers of other nouns in such terms as *office systems* management, *product* quality, *cost* analysis, *work distribution* chart, and *photodiode sensor array* scanner. In the preceding examples, the italicized words are nouns functioning as modifiers. Long strings of such modifiers can sometimes be confusing, as demonstrated by the following sentence: *Network intercommunications and intersystem address specifications have been established and implemented via a computer data transport system.* Rewriting will remove any unclarity about the subject of the sentence: *Specifications for network intercommunications and intersystem addressing have been established. These specifications are implemented via a computerized data transport network.*

The Pronoun

A pronoun is a word that substitutes for a noun and refers to a person or thing that has been named or understood in a particular context. Pronouns have grammatical case (subjective or objective), number (singular or plural), person (first, second, or third), and gender (masculine, feminine, or neuter).

Personal pronouns.   Personal pronouns refer to people or objects and must agree with their antecedents (i.e., the nouns or other pronouns that they refer to) in person, number, and gender:

> Has the *supervisor* finished dictating *his* memo?
>
> The *management* and *union negotiators* refused to budge from *their* positions.
>
> The *Publishing Committee* has given us *its* unanimous approval.
>
> The *CEO* has not given us *her* comments yet.

This is the general rule with regard to pronoun/antecedent agreement. But there are a large number of words and expressions in English that are singular in form but felt to be plural in sense, so that speakers are uncertain whether to use a singular or plural pronoun in referring to them. For example, strict grammarians have long insisted that it is correct to say *everyone took his coffee break*, not *their coffee break* or *their coffee breaks*, and that we must say *no one is happy when he is fired* and not *when they are fired*. Yet speakers persist in using the plural pronouns, and the most thoughtful grammarians have recognized that there is no entirely happy solution to the problem. The constructions affected fall into three classes. First, there are words formed with the word elements *-one* and *-body*, such as *anyone, somebody, everyone, nobody*, together with the two-word form *no one*. Second, there are the words *either, each, none*, and *any* used alone (as in *each found his seat*) or together with a noun (as in *each of the participants has his notebook* and *none of the notebooks has its cover intact*). Finally, there are the words *whoever, whatever*, and *whichever*, either used as indefinite pronouns (as in *whoever reveals privileged information will have his security clearance revoked*, or together with a noun, as in *whichever nation is attacked first will find itself at a disadvantage*. The traditional rule is that only a singular pronoun can be used in referring back to these constructions, as in the preceding examples of correct usage. But the rule as stated creates grammatical complications. For one thing, a pronoun outside the sentence containing the element it refers to *cannot* be in the singular. Thus, it is simply not English to say: *Everybody left in a hurry. He took his coat with him.* Nor can one say, *No one could be seen. The individual must have been hiding behind a wall.* Constructions with *whoever* are exceptions. One says: *Whoever is elected will take office in January. I am sure he will do a good job.* Writers who do not want to risk violation of the traditional rule will have to find other ways of expressing the meaning. One may rephrase so as to get the pronoun into the same sentence as its antecedent, saying, for example, *Everybody left carrying his raincoat with him.* One may also substitute other words, such as the plural *all*, as in *All the visitors left. They took their coats with them.*

Each presents some special problems. When it precedes the noun, a following pronoun is correctly singular: *Each of the actors has learned his* (not *their*) *part.* When *each* follows the noun, however, the pronoun is generally plural: *The actors have each learned their parts* (not *his part*). It also should be noted that *none* has for centuries been used by the best writers as if it were a plural form, taking both plural verb and plural pronouns: *None of them have learned their parts* must be considered an entirely acceptable variant of *None of them has learned his part.* Only the mixture of singular verb and plural pronoun would be considered incorrect, as in *None of them has learned their parts.* The traditional rule may also be politically offensive to many speakers. When referring to a mixed-gender group, strict grammarians have insisted that the masculine singular *him* or *his* be used as a "neutral" form; one is thus required to say *Every one of the actors and actresses has learned his part.* Since the last century, however, feminists and their allies have objected to this presumption. The writer who finds the singular *he* and *his* distasteful in these cases has the choice of flying in the face of traditional grammar and using *they* and *their* or of using the somewhat clumsier variants *his and her* (or *her and his*); attempts to introduce new pronouns like *s/he* appear unlikely to win general acceptance.

Case is determined by the grammatical function of the pronoun in the sentence:

If *you* will give *me* the book, *I* can return *it* to the library.
(subject)   (indirect object)   (subject)   (direct object)

The question as to when to use the nominative pronouns *I, he, she, we,* and *they* and when to use the objective pronouns *me, him, her, us,* and *them* has always been a source of controversy among grammarians and a source of uncertainty among speakers. When the subject of a sentence is a complex phrase in which a pronoun is joined to other elements by *and* or *or,* grammarians are unanimous in considering it a part of the subject proper, so that the nominative form must be used. *Pat and I* (not *me*) *will be there to greet you. Either Dale or he* (not *him*) *will come in first.* Some grammarians have gone so far as to extend this rule to cover the use of pronouns as one-word answers to questions that ask about the identity of the subject of a verb; that is, as an answer to *Who developed this new chemical compound?* we are supposed to say *I* (as in *I did*) rather than *Me.* But such sentences are likely to occur only in informal speech or in written dialogue; in either case, the use here of a nominative, such as *I,* can only be viewed as pedantic.

When pronouns follow a form of the verb *to be,* the nominative is traditionally required, on the grounds that the pronoun denotes the same entity as the subject. Thus, the rules require *it is I, that must be she,* and so forth. The rules create problems, however, when the pronoun after *to be* denotes an entity that is also understood to be the object of some other verb or preposition. Shall we say *it is I she loves* or *it is me she loves?* There is no strict rule, but given the natural tendency to use objective forms like *me* rather than nominatives like *I* in uncertain cases, the use of *me* is entirely defensible here. It also should be noted that the use of the nominative following *to be* sounds stilted when the verb has been contracted. Nevertheless, a purist would say *it's I* rather than *it's me,* or *that's they* rather than *that's them.*

Mistakes in pronoun choice come in two varieties. There is a natural tendency to use objective forms like *me* and *him* where nominatives like *I* and *he* would be strictly required: *He has more seniority than me* instead of the correct *than I. In the end, it turned out to have been them all along* instead of the technically correct *turned out to have been they.* Strict grammarians are likely to regard such mistakes as the result of a carelessness that no one ever manages entirely to avoid. But in an effort to get the pronouns right, some people err in the opposite direction, substituting nominatives like *I* where the objective *him* would be correct. The result is constructions like *between you and I* (properly *between you and me*) or *it surprised the dealer more than the customer or I* (properly, *the customer or me*). Mistakes of this second sort are likely to be regarded as overcorrections that betray a fundamental linguistic insecurity on the part of the speaker. While there is no entirely safe course for the speaker who is in doubt as to which form to use, the difference between the risks in incorrect use of the nominative and the objective should be kept in mind. Some points to remember:

1. Do not confuse the possessive form of the pronoun with a contraction formed from a pronoun and a verb form:

Keep the calculator in *its* case.	(possession)
It's a very small calculator.	(contraction for *it is*)
Whose call did you take?	(interrogative/possession)
Who's calling?	(interrogative/contraction for *who is*)
Their TV sets are broken.	(possession)

They're fixing their TV sets.   (contraction for *they are*)

Your book is on our list.   (possession)

You're on our list.   (contraction for *you are*)

2. *I* (or *me*) should be placed at the end of a series of names or other pronouns:

Mr. Lee, Ms. Trilby, and *I* attended the convention together.

Send copies to Bill, Bob, Jean, and *me*.

Just between you and *me*, they're dead wrong.

3. Avoid vague personal pronoun constructions such as "they say" or "it indicates," as in

They say on the news that the economy is in trouble.

It indicates in the study that our TV ratings are down.

Who are *they* and *it?* Recast for greater precision and clarity:

The UBC nightly newscast says that the economy is in trouble.

Page 4 of the study indicates that our TV ratings are down.

Reflexive pronouns.   Reflexive pronouns are used only with the possessive case of the first and second person pronouns (*myself, ourselves, yourself, yourselves*) and with the objective case of the third person pronouns (*himself, herself, itself, themselves*). Therefore, nonstandard combinations such as *hisself* and *theirselves* are to be avoided. A reflexive pronoun is used for emphasis:

The systems analyst himself couldn't solve the problem, so how could we be expected to deal with it?

A reflexive pronoun is also used when the subject of a verb and the receiver of the action are identical:

He did *himself* a great disservice by being uncooperative.

Here, *himself* functions as indirect object of the verb and refers to the subject *he*. Use a reflexive pronoun only with an antecedent. In formal writing avoid sentences like *My colleagues and myself attended the meeting*, even though such constructions commonly occur in informal speech. Say instead, *My colleagues and I attended the meeting*. See also the entry **myself** in the usage section.

Indefinite pronouns.   Among the indefinite pronouns are *all, another, any, anybody, anything, both, each, each one, either, everybody, everyone, everything, few, many, much, neither, nobody, none, no one, one, other, several, some, somebody, someone,* and *something*. See the beginning of this section for a detailed discussion of the problems of number and gender in connection with the use of pronouns such as these.

Reciprocal pronouns.   Reciprocal pronouns, such as *one, another,* or *each other,* denote interaction between two or more members of a group:

They helped *one another* with the mailing lists.

The two secretaries answer *each other's* phones.

According to some traditional grammarians, *each other* is used of two; *one another*, of more than two. This distinction has been ignored by many of the best writers, however, and these examples are considered acceptable: *The four partners regarded each other with suspicion. A parent and child should trust one another.* When speaking of an ordered series of events or stages, only *one another* can be used: *The Caesars exceeded one another* (not *each other*) *in cruelty* means that each Caesar was crueler than the last. *Each other* cannot be used as the subject of a clause in formal writing. Instead of *we know what each other are thinking,* one should write *each of us knows what the other is thinking.* Instead of the *executives know that each other are coming,* write *each of the executives knows the other is coming.* Instead of *we are all each other has,* write *each of us is all the other has.* The possessive forms of *each other* and *one another* are written *each other's* and *one another's: The secretaries answer each other's* (not *each others'*) *phones. They had forgotten one another's* (not *one anothers'*) *names.*

Demonstrative pronouns.   The demonstrative pronouns are *this, that, these,* and *those.*

> *This* is my workstation. *That* is yours.

> *These* are my diskettes. *Those* are yours.

It is a mark of nonstandard usage to insert *here* or *there* after *this* or *that,* as in "This here pen is mine" or "That there pen is mine." Say instead, "*This* pen is mine" or "*That* pen is mine."

It is a common stylistic error to introduce a sentence with a demonstrative pronoun referring to something in a previous sentence:

unclear/vague

Audioconferencing consists of several people in two or more sites involved in simultaneous communication via microphones and speakers connected through a telephone network. *This* saves on travel expenses and enhances productivity.

What does *this* refer to? Audioconferencing itself? Simultaneous communication? Use of a telephone network? To avoid vagueness, such a passage should be rewritten:

clear/precise

Audioconferencing consists of several people in two or more sites involved in simultaneous communication via microphones and speakers connected through a telephone network. The use of audioconferencing results in savings in travel expenses and enhancement of productivity.

Relative pronouns.   The relative pronouns *who/whom/whose, which, what,* and *that* introduce dependent clauses functioning as nouns or adjectives. Some of them can be combined with -*ever* to yield *whoever, whomever, whichever,* and *whatever.* The next paragraphs discuss in detail two major problems of usage involving the relative pronouns.

The standard rule is that *that* should be used only to introduce a restrictive (or "defining") relative clause, which serves to identify the entity being talked about; in this use it should never be preceded by a comma. Thus, we say *the factory that we built in 1969 has been remodeled,* where the clause *that we built* tells which factory was built; or, *I am looking for a book that is easy to read*, where *that is easy to read* tells what kind of book is desired. Only *which* is to be used with nonrestrictive (or "nondefining") clauses, which give additional information about an entity that has already been identified in the context; in this use, *which* is always preceded by a comma. Thus we say, *The secretaries in the Administrative Department have been complaining about the heat, which* (not *that*) *has been deficient ever since the old boiler was replaced.* The clause *which has been deficient ever since the old boiler was replaced* does not indicate which heat is being complained about; even if it were omitted, we would know that the phrase *the heat* refers to "the heat in the Administrative Department." Similarly we say, *The product managers wanted to go to the marketing seminar entitled "The Power of Product Positioning," which* (not *that*) *I had already attended.* The title "The Power of Product Positioning" is by itself sufficient to identify the seminar that the product managers wanted to go to; the clause *which I had already attended* merely gives further information about the seminar. The use of *that* in nonrestrictive clauses like these last, while once common in writing and still frequent in speech, is now generally held to be an error that should be avoided in written prose. Some grammarians have argued that symmetry requires that *which* should be used in nonrestrictive clauses, as *that* is to be used only in restrictive clauses. Thus, they suggest that we should avoid sentences like *I need a book which will tell me all about the shipping industry*, where the clause *which will tell me all about the shipping industry* indicates which sort of book is needed. But the use of *which* in such clauses is widely supported by general usage and is in no sense incorrect. It is particularly useful where two or more relative clauses are joined by *and* or *or*, as in *It is a conclusion in which our strategic planners may find solace and which many have found reason to praise.* Which is also preferred to introduce a restrictive relative clause when the preceding phrase itself contains a *that*, as in *I can only give that which I don't need* (not *that that I don't need*) or *We want to use only that word processing system which will be the most cost-effective* (preferred to *that word processing system that will be the most cost-effective*).

According to traditional grammarians, *who* is the appropriate form to use in contexts where other subjective pronouns, such as *we* or *he* would also occur: *Who is in charge of this department? He who hesitates is lost.* As the subject of *is* and *hesitates* respectively, in the two sentences *who* is quite properly in the subjective case. In contexts requiring an objective form, such as *us* or *him*, then *whom* is appropriate to a formal style: *To whom did you speak? All the people whom we invited are planning to attend.* Although the rules are straightforward enough, problems can arise when the pronoun is at a distance from the elements of a phrase or sentence that determine the choice of case: *She interviewed the artist whom the committee had insisted that the mayor hire.* In constructing such a sentence, it is necessary to keep in mind the fact that *whom* will be the direct object of *hire*. Writing, which tends to be a more formal medium than speech, has the virtue of allowing a review of what has been produced in order to eliminate errors and inconsistencies. In speech or in the representation of speech, however, the distinction between *who* and *whom* is often not preserved: "*Who are you speaking of?*" (Thomas Hardy, *Far From The Madding Crowd*). When a preposition and its pronoun object are separated from each other, the latter is often in the technically incorrect subjective case. This usage is a common occurrence in the works of the best writers and has been defended by many grammarians and students of language on the grounds that rigid adherence to the rules, especially in informal contexts, yields sentences which sound stilted and pedantic. The same considerations as the foregoing apply to the choice between *whoever* and *whomever*. See also the next subsection.

Interrogative pronouns.   The interrogative pronouns include *who, whom, whose, which,* and *what*. Interrogative pronouns are used in direct questions.

> Who is calling?
>
> Which is your typewriter?
>
> What are your feelings about this situation?
>
> Whose is this blotter?
>
> Who (or whom) did you travel with?

but:

> With whom did you travel?

The Adjective

An adjective modifies a noun or pronoun. In modifying another word, an adjective serves to describe it, qualify it, limit it, or make it distinct and separate from something else (a *tall* building; a *reasonable* offer; a *two-story* house; a *red* fox). Most adjectives can be compared in three degrees (positive, comparative, and superlative). Adjectives can be compared by addition of the suffixes *-er* or *-est* to the unchanged base form (cold, colder, coldest); by doubling the final consonant before the addition of the suffixes (hot, hotter, hottest); by addition of *-er* or *-est* to a base form in which a terminal *-y* becomes *-i-* (fuzzy, fuzzier, fuzziest); and by the use of *more, most, less,* or *least* before the unchanged base form (more important, most important, less important, least important). And some adjectives can be compared in two ways (clear, clearer, clearest or clear, more clear, most clear). A small class of adjectives are extremely irregular (bad, worse, worst). Still other adjectives, called *absolutes*, represent ultimate conditions and therefore are not compared. Examples of absolute adjectives are *prior, maximum, minimal, unanimous,* and *chief*. If you are unsure how to compare an adjective, consult *The American Heritage Dictionary*, Second College Edition, where you will find regular and irregular comparisons entered.

Avoid making double comparisons:

wrong	right
the more commoner flu symptoms	the commoner flu symptoms
	or
	the more common flu symptoms
the most riskiest venture ever contemplated	the riskiest venture ever contemplated
	or
	the most risky venture ever contemplated

Incomplete comparisons (i.e., comparisons that are not directly expressed or that are understood) are often used in advertising and promotional writing. The famous slogan "Ford has a better idea" is a prime example. While such usage is effective in special contexts, it is often considered inappropriate in formal writing.

Some adjectives, because they are derived from proper names, are capitalized (*Machiavellian* judicial politics; *Churchillian* prose; *Russian* emigrés). To find out whether a particular adjective should be capitalized, look it up in the dictionary.

The Adverb

An adverb modifies a verb (read *fast*), an adjective (a *very* fast reader), or another adverb (read *very* fast). Most adverbs, like adjectives, can be compared in three degrees (positive, comparative, superlative). Many adverbs are compared by insertion of the words *more, most, less,* or *least* before the base form (*more soundly, most soundly, less soundly,* or *least soundly*). Others can be compared two ways (*loud, more loud, most loud* or *loud, louder, loudest*). Still others can't be compared (*extremely, very, there*).

Adverbs specify time (Please come into the office *now*); duration (I plan to stay here *indefinitely*); place (They are employed *here*); direction (Press the print key *downwards*); manner (The production line moves the cars *fast*); and degree (*Extremely* humid air can damage word processing equipment). Some adverbs can be used to link clauses (We automated the office; *nevertheless* some tasks must still be performed manually). See the section on conjunctions for full discussion of these conjunctive adverbs.

Remember that adverbs modify verbs: The salesperson talked *smoothly* (not *smooth*). Remember also that the linking and sense verbs discussed earlier take adjectives, not adverbs: Stock prices remain *erratic* (not *erratically*). And adverbs, not adjectives, modify adjectives and other adverbs: I feel *awfully* (not *awful*) tired.

The double negative.

A double negative is properly used when it makes an affirmative statement: *The doctor cannot just do nothing* (that is, the doctor must do something). An affirmative meaning is also found when *not* is used before an adjective or adverb having a negative sense: *a not infrequent visitor; a not unwisely conceived plan.* In these expressions the double negative is used deliberately to convey a weaker affirmative sense than would the adjective *frequent* or the adverb *wisely*.

A double negative is generally considered unacceptable when it is intended to convey or reinforce a negative meaning, especially in a short sentence: *The inspector didn't say nothing* (meaning the inspector said nothing). *We aren't going neither* (meaning we aren't going). Such constructions were once common in good writing as a form of intensified meaning. An example is Hamlet's advice to the players: *"Be not too tame neither, but let your discretion be your tutor."* A double negative is still occasionally acceptable when it reinforces a negative: *I will not resign, not today, not tomorrow.*

The Preposition

A preposition is used to indicate relationships between a noun or pronoun and another word or expression in a sentence. Prepositional phrases can indicate accompaniment (Joe attended the meeting *with several colleagues*); cause (The trip was canceled *because of bad weather*); support (Those who are not *for us* are *against us*); destination (We drove *to the city*); exception (I have everything *but a private office*); possession (The arrogance *of that official* defies description); constituency or makeup (I want a desk *of polished mahogany*); means or instrument (I worked out the problem *with my personal computer*); manner (Treat all visitors *with courtesy*); direction (I ran *across the hall* to find you); location (John is *in the office*); purpose or intention (They'll do anything *for a quick profit*); the goal of an action (Don't take pot shots *at me*); origin (The new manager is *from Chicago*); and time (Call me *at noon*; He arrived *on Monday*).

Between and among.   These are two prepositions that are often confused. *Between* is the only choice when just two entities are involved: *between* (never *among*) *good and evil; the rivalry between* (never *among*) *Ford and General Motors.* When more than two entities are involved, the choice of *between* or *among* depends on the intended meaning. *Among* is used to indicate that an entity has been chosen from the members of a group: *the first among* (not *between*) *equals; Among* (not *between*) *the three executives, Pat seems most likely to become the next president. Among* is also used to indicate a relation of inclusion in a group: *He is among the best engineers of our time; She took her place among the clients waiting outside the door. Between,* on the other hand, is used to indicate the area bounded by several points: *We have narrowed the search to the area between* (not *among*) *Philadelphia, New York, and Scranton.* In other cases, either *between* or *among* may be used; one may speak of *an agreement between or among several merchants,* and one may say either that *the telephone pole was lost among the trees* (in the area of the trees) or *between the trees* (in which case we infer that the trees had hidden the pole from sight).

Between and the objective case.   Note that all pronouns that follow *between* must be in the objective case: *Between you and me* (not *I*), *the problem is hopeless. This conflict is strictly between him and me* (not *he and I*).

Prepositions in phrases.   When two or more phrases used together share the same preposition, you need not repeat the preposition: *The testimony is equal and tantamount to perjury.* However, if two different prepositions are required, retain both of them: *Our interest in and concern for the welfare of our employees has led us to take steps to improve their working conditions.*

The Conjunction

A conjunction links words, phrases, or clauses. Coordinating conjunctions such as *and, or, but, nor, for,* or *so* link words, phrases, or clauses of equal rank.

> The staff includes a secretary, an assistant, and a receptionist.

> My life is busy but lonely.

> You can go or you can stay.

Remember to link equal elements with coordinating conjunctions: adjectives with adjectives, adverbs with adverbs, clauses with other clauses of equal rank, and so on:

unbalanced séntence	balanced sentence
You are an organized person and your time well spent. (faulty coordination between independent clause and phrase)	You are an organized person *and* your time is well spent. (two independent clauses linked by *and*)

Avoid excessive coordination, however, which often results in strung out, monotonous sentences in which precise relationships are obscured, and varying degrees of emphasis are needlessly clouded:

strung out	tightened
XYZ Corporation is a multinational petrochemical producer and has its corporate headquarters in Los Angeles and ten subsidiary offices in the United States, South America, and the Middle East.	XYZ Corporation, a multinational petrochemical producer with headquarters in Los Angeles, has ten subsidiary offices throughout the United States, South America, and the Middle East.

The comma fault.   The comma fault occurs when two independent clauses are separated by a comma instead of being linked by a coordinating conjunction:

> The chemical industry in the United States has contributed much to our economy, it should not be condemned on the basis of isolated instances of pollution.

The following sentences illustrate ways of eliminating the comma fault:

> The chemical industry in the United States has contributed much to our economy, and it should not be condemned on the basis of isolated instances of pollution.

> The chemical industry in the United States has contributed much to our economy. It should not be condemned on the basis of isolated instances of pollution.

> The chemical industry in the United States has contributed much to our economy; it should not be condemned on the basis of isolated instances of pollution.

> The United States chemical industry, having contributed much to our economy, should not be condemned on the basis of isolated instances of pollution.

The run-on sentence.   The failure to use proper punctuation or the appropriate coordinating conjunction between independent clauses will result in a run-on sentence:

run-on
The automobile had faulty brakes it was therefore recalled.

correct
The automobile had faulty brakes and it was therefore recalled.

The automobile had faulty brakes; therefore, it was recalled.

The automobile, having faulty brakes, was recalled.

Since the automobile had faulty brakes it was recalled.

Correlative conjunctions.   Correlative conjunctions work in pairs to link equal or parallel sentence elements. Correlative conjunctions include *either . . . or, neither . . . nor, whether . . . or, both . . . and,* and *not only . . . but also.* Correlative conjunctions should appear as close as possible to the equal elements that they link. In *either . . . or* constructions, the two conjunctions should be followed by parallel elements. The following is held to be incorrect: *You may either have the ring or the bracelet* (properly, *you may have either the ring or the bracelet*). The following is also incorrect: *He can take either the examination offered to all applicants or ask for a personal interview* (properly, *he can either take . . .*).

When all the elements in an *either . . . or* construction are singular, the verb is singular: *Either the executive or the assistant is coming.* When one element is singular and the other plural, it is sometimes suggested that the verb should agree with whichever element is closest to it: *Either the department head or the line managers are going.* But: *Either the line managers or the department head is going.* Some traditionalists, however, insist that such constructions should be avoided entirely, and that substitutes must be found for them. For example: *Either the department head is going or the line managers are.* There is no generally accepted rule in these cases.

Neither is supposed to be followed by *nor*, not *or*: *Neither prayer nor curses brought relief* (not *or curses*). When *neither . . . nor* connects two singular elements, the following verb is singular: *Neither the executive nor the assistant is coming.* When both elements are plural, the verb is plural: *Neither the line managers nor the department heads have read the report.* When one element is singular and the other is plural, many have suggested that the verb should agree with the element closest to it. Thus we would write: *Neither the line managers nor the department head has read the report.* But: *Neither the department head nor the line managers have read the report.* Other grammarians, however, have insisted that these sentences must be avoided entirely and that one must instead seek a paraphrase in which the problem does not arise. For example: *The line managers have not read the report, and neither has the department head.*

Not only . . . but also constructions should be used in such a way that each of the elements is followed by a construction of the same type. Instead of *She not only bought a new car but a new lawnmower*, write *She bought not only a new car but also a new lawnmower.* In the second version, both *not only* and *but also* are followed by noun phrases. In the *not only* construction, *also* is often omitted when the second part of the sentence merely intensifies the first: *She is not only smart but brilliant. He not only wanted the promotion but wanted it desperately.*

Similarly, when *both* is used with *and* to link parallel elements in a sentence, the words or phrases that follow them should correspond grammatically: *in both India and China* or *both in India and in China* (not *both in India and China*).

Subordinating conjunctions.   Subordinating conjunctions introduce dependent clauses. Subordinating conjunctions include terms such as *because* and *since; although, if,* and *unless; as, as though,* and *however; in order that* and *so that; after, before, once, since, till, until, when, whenever,* and *while; where* and *wherever;* and *that.* Examples:

> *Since* the Management Committee has approved the plan, we can move forward.

> *If* you don't have the facts straight, your argument is worthless.

> Keep the text in memory *so that* you can make corrections later.

> *After* he was promoted, he spent all his time in meetings.

Do you have any idea *where* they have gone?

It is hard to tell *whether* the market will really take off as predicted.

The newscaster said *that* John Green has been nominated for Governor's Council.

The use of subordinating conjunctions can help to achieve emphasis as well as variety. Put your main ideas into independent clauses and your less important ideas into subordinate clauses: *Although market predictions are bullish, stock prices continue to drop.*

Conjunctive adverbs.   A conjunctive adverb can be used to connect and relate two independent clauses separated by a semicolon: *Market predictions are bullish; nevertheless, stock prices continue to drop.* A semicolon precedes the conjunctive adverb, and a comma often follows it. *I proofread the letter carefully; therefore, the typos were detected.* Commas always separate the conjunctive adverb *however* from the rest of the sentence:

I proofread the letter; however, I did not catch all the typos.

I proofread the letter. I did not, however, catch all the typos.

Do not use commas with *however* when it means "no matter how": *However hard you try, management won't let you succeed.*

The Interjection

An interjection is an independent sentence element that can express a sound (Ouch!), and emotion (Oh, rats!). Interjections can be used alone (Bravo!) or with other words (Oh, you've got to be kidding!).

Phrases, Clauses, Sentences, and Paragraphs

The phrase.   A phrase is a group of words that does not have both a subject and verb:

Having addressed the sales force, we then took questions from the floor.

Approaching that issue was tricky.

We will be delighted *to attend.*

The clause.   A clause is a group of words with a subject and predicate. A dependent, or subordinate, clause usually functions as part of a sentence:

Those *who have signed their performance reviews* will receive their salary adjustments on schedule (modifies *those*).

When the fourth quarter ends our books will be closed (modifies *closed*).

That you have performed unsatisfactorily is reflected in your performance review (subject of sentence).

The sentence.   A sentence is usually defined as a group of words having a subject and a verb; in writing, the sentence begins with a capital letter and ends with a period, question mark, or exclamation point: *The Board of Directors has unanimously voted a dividend increase.* As we have seen in the section on verbs, a sentence may be fragmentary as long as it makes sense and is idiomatic.

A sentence may be declarative (it makes a statement), interrogative (it asks a question), imperative (it requests or commands), or exclamatory (it expresses strong feeling):

> The applicants signed the forms.
>
> Did you sign the form?
>
> Sign the form here.
>
> I wish they'd sign the forms and shut up!

Grammatically speaking, there are four kinds of sentences: simple, compound, complex, and compound-complex. Examples of each follow:

simple sentence

Some people complain.

Some people complain because of dissatisfaction on the job.

compound sentence

Some people complain, and others don't.

Some people complain, some people brood, and others don't care at all.

complex sentence

When people become dissatisfied with their jobs, they often complain.

compound-complex sentence

When people become dissatisfied with their jobs, they often complain; and then management has a problem that it must address.

Sentence style.   From the standpoint of style, there are two types of sentences—the periodic and the cumulative. The periodic sentence places the main idea at the very end, so that the previous matter serves as a buildup. A good example of a periodic sentence is this one, taken from page 374 of Leonard Shatzkin's book *In Cold Type* (Boston: Houghton Mifflin, 1982):

> Meeting the economic pinch by cutting overhead and   ← buildup
> publishing programs has brought temporary relief here
> and there, but some publishers have already passed
> through that palliation to realize that *they are now*   ← main point
> *worse off than before.*

Here is an example of a very short periodic sentence, quoted from page 200 of Thomas J. Peters and Robert H. Waterman Jr.'s book *In Search of Excellence: Lessons from America's Best-Run Companies* (New York: Harper & Row, 1982):

> The most discouraging fact of big corporate life is the   ← buildup
> loss of what got them big in the first place: innovation.   ← main point

In the last example, everything up to the last word in the sentence is really a buildup to the punch line or main point—*innovation*.

In the cumulative sentence the writer states the main point first, followed by supporting data: This example, also taken from Leonard Shatzkin's *In Cold Type* (page 3 this time), exemplifies a cumulative sentence:

> No other consumer industry produces 20,000 different,   ← main point
> relatively low-priced products each year, each with its
> own personality, requiring individual recognition on the   ← supporting ideas
> market.

The paragraph.   A paragraph is a distinct division of a written work that expresses a thought or point relevant to the whole but complete in itself; it may consist of a single sentence or several sentences. A paragraph should contain a topic sentence expressing the main thought which is developed and supported by the other sentences of the paragraph. While it is possible for the topic sentence to be placed anywhere within the paragraph, it is most often found at the beginning as a statement that is enlarged upon by the sentences that follow. A topic sentence at the end of a paragraph usually functions as a cohesive summation of the ideas and arguments in the sentences leading up to it. The topic sentence is the cement binding a paragraph together into a coherent whole.

Paragraphing can be rather easy if you follow a few simple guidelines. First, keep your paragraphs unified: every sentence therein should be related to the main topic. Avoid needless digressions from the main point; irrelevancies can muddy the prose and destroy unity. Second, avoid overly short or overly long paragraphs. A short paragraph will not give sufficient scope to cover a topic adequately, while a long paragraph is uninviting to the reader and is often difficult to assimilate. It is important to keep this point in mind especially when preparing business reports and memos. Sometimes it is possible to split long paragraphs into shorter ones and, conversely, short paragraphs can be collapsed into a single longer one. A third, and very important issue has to do with transition. Transitional words and phrases (such as conjunctions, conjunctive adverbs, and demonstratives) are an invaluable aid in guiding the reader from one sentence to another. The following example of the use of smooth, logical transition comes from Peters and Waterman's *In Search of Excellence* (pages 3–5):

> Early in 1977, a general concern with the problems of management . . .
> effectiveness *led us to* . . . .
>
> *A natural first step was to talk* extensively *to executives* around the
> world who were known for their skill, experience, and wisdom . . . .
>
> *In fact, the most helpful ideas were coming* from . . . .
>
> *But as we explored the subject* . . . .
>
> *Our next step in 1977 was* . . . .

As you can see from the italicized terms in the example, each new paragraph is tied in with the one preceding it so as to provide smooth transition from one topic to another.

Another way of achieving smooth transition is repetition of key words. The key words serve as guides to the reader. A good example of the use of this technique occurs in Harry Katzan, Jr.'s book *Office Automation: A Manager's Guide* (New York: AMACOM, a division of American Management Associations, 1982, p. 18):

> The term *word processing* refers to *text* preparation through the use of a computer or its equivalent. Historically, it referred to . . . .
>
> The concept of *word processing* originated with . . . .
>
> Modern *word processing* systems permit textual information to be . . . .
>
> The key element in the *word processing* cycle is the output functions . . . .
>
> The hardware components that make up a modern *word processing* unit are . . . .

Notice the repetition of the central term *word processing* throughout the first sentences of each paragraph. Keeping the vocabulary limited to a finite number of terms that are used over and over again reinforces the message and enables the reader to understand the material more easily.

You can develop your own paragraphs in any number of other ways that will make them lucid and effective. For example, you can start off with a definition, as Harry Katzan, Jr., does on page 6 of *Office Automation: A Manager's Guide:*

> The term "office automation" refers to the use of a computer in an office environment to facilitate normal operating procedures. The impact of office automation upon work flow can be very small or very great, depending on the extent to which organizational structures are affected.

The first sentence defines *office automation*. The second sentence in the paragraph then goes on to talk about the impact of office automation in the workplace.

Another way of paragraph development is the use of comparison, contrast, and analogy. For example, you can make two points, and discuss one and then the other from comparative and/or contrastive standpoints. Or you can use analogy to explain one thing in terms of another, similar, thing. Still another technique is the use of cause and effect: you describe a given state of affairs and then discuss its underlying causes. Alternatively, you can set out the underlying causes and then build up to the result or consequence.

Still another useful technique is inclusion of examples by way of support or illustration for an idea or point of view that you have already expressed. Finally, you can set down classes, sets, or categories relating to a topic and then sort them for the reader. For example, a writer wishing to explain the secretary's role as an information broker could categorize the various aspects of information management first. These categories might be described as generation of information, modification of information, collection of information, storage of information, retrieval of information, analysis of information, communication of information, and output/distribution of information. When each category has been defined and distinguished, the writer could then go on to discuss the secretary's managerial roles with respect to each of these broad categories and activities.

A CONCISE GUIDE TO USAGE

The following notes, adapted from those in *The American Heritage Dictionary,* Second College Edition, are intended to help you with usage problems commonly encountered in writing. They are entered in alphabetical order according to key words.

a

A is used before a word beginning with a consonant (*a building*) or a consonant sound (*a university*); *an* is used before a word beginning with a vowel (*an earphone*) or a vowel sound (*an hour*). *An* should not be used before words like *historical* and *hysterical* unless the *h* is not pronounced, a practice now uncommon in American speech.

about

The construction *not about to* is often used to express determination: *We are not about to negotiate with strikebreakers.* Many consider this usage acceptable in speech but not in formal writing.

above

The use of *above* as an adjective or noun in referring to a preceding text is most common in business and legal writing. In general writing its use as an adjective (*the above figures*) is acceptable, but its use as a noun (*read the above*) is often objected to.

acquiesce

When *acquiesce* takes a preposition, it is usually used with *in* (*acquiesced in the ruling*) but sometimes with *to* (*acquiesced to management's wishes*).

admission

Admission has a more general meaning than *admittance*, which is used only to denote the obtaining of physical access to a place. To *gain admittance to the board* is to enter its chambers; to *gain admission to the board* is to become a member. One pays *admission* to a theater (to become a member of the audience) in order to be allowed *admittance* (physical entry to the theater itself).

adopted

One refers to an *adopted* child but to *adoptive* parents.

advance

Advance, as a noun, is used for forward movement (*the advance of our salespeople into the new market*) or for progress or improvement in a figurative sense (*a sales advance of 35% this year*). *Advancement*

is used mainly in the figurative sense (*career advancement*). In the figurative sense, moreover, there is a distinction between the two terms deriving from the transitive and intransitive forms of the verb *advance*. The noun *advancement* (unlike *advance*) often implies the existence of an agent or outside force. Thus, *the advance of research and development* means simply the progress of the company's R & D efforts, whereas *the advancement of research and development* implies progress resulting from the action of an agent or force: *The addition of $1.5 million to last year's budget has resulted in the advancement of our research efforts.*

advise

Advise in the sense of "to inform" or "to notify" is generally acceptable in business contexts: *All retailers are hereby advised that our deluxe product line has been expanded.* Avoid this usage in formal general writing.

affect

Affect and *effect* have no sense in common. As a verb, *affect* is most commonly used in the sense of "to influence" (*how bad weather affects deliveries*). *Effect* means "to bring about or execute" (*layoffs designed to effect savings*).

affinity

Affinity may be followed by *of, between,* or *with*—thus, *affinity of persons, between two persons,* or *with another person.* In technical writing, *affinity* (meaning "a chemical or physical attraction") is followed by *for* (*a dye with an affinity for synthetic fabrics*). In general usage *affinity* retains some sense of the mutual relationship, and therefore its use with *for* is less widely accepted (e.g., *Even in school he had an affinity for politics*, but not *The product manager's affinity for living in California resulted in his rejecting a chance to return to the New York office*).

affirmative

The expressions *in the affirmative* and *in the negative,* as in *The client answered in the affirmative,* are generally regarded as pompous. *The client answered yes* would be more acceptable even at the most formal levels of style.

agenda

Agenda, meaning "list" or "program," is well established as a collective noun taking a singular verb.

ago

Ago may be followed by *that* or *when: it was a week ago that* (or *when*) *I saw the invoice.* It may not be followed by *since: It was a week ago since the order arrived. Since* is properly used without *ago*, as in *It has been a week since the order arrived.*

ain't

Ain't has acquired such a stigma over the years that it is beyond rehabilitation, even though it would serve a useful function as a contraction for *am not* and even though its use as an alternative form for *isn't, hasn't, aren't,* and *haven't* has a good historical justification. In questions, the variant *aren't I* is acceptable in speech, but in writing there is no generally acceptable substitute for the stilted *am I not.*

alibi

Alibi (noun) in its nonlegal sense of "an excuse" is acceptable in written usage, but as an intransitive verb (*they never alibi*), it is generally unacceptable in writing.

all

Constructions like *all us employees* are somewhat more informal than the corresponding *all of us employees.* The construction *all that* is used informally in questions and negative sentences to mean "to the degree expected" as in *The annual meeting was not all that exciting this year.* Many people find examples like this unacceptable in formal writing.

alleged

An *alleged burglar* is someone who is said to be a burglar but against whom no charges have yet been proved. An *alleged incident* is an event that is said to have taken place but which has not yet been verified. In their zeal to protect the rights of the accused, newspapers and law enforcement officials sometimes misuse *alleged.* A man arrested for murder may be only an *alleged murderer,* for example, but he is a real, not an *alleged, suspect* in that his status as a suspect is not in doubt.

Similarly, if a murder is known to have taken place, there is nothing alleged about the crime.

all right

It is still not acceptable to write *all right* as a single word, *alright,* despite the parallel to words like *already* and *altogether* and despite the fact that in casual speech the expression is often pronounced as if it were one word.

allude

Allude and *allusion* are often used where the more general terms *refer* and *reference* would be preferable. *Allude* and *allusion* apply to indirect reference that does not identify specifically. *Refer* and *reference,* unless qualified, usually imply direct, specific mention.

alternative

Alternative is widely used to denote simply "one of a set of possible courses of action," but many traditionalists continue to insist that its use be restricted to situations in which only two possible choices present themselves. In this stricter sense, *alternative* is incompatible with all numerals (*there are three alternatives*), and the use of *two,* in particular, is held to be redundant (*the two alternatives are life and death* would be unacceptable to traditionalists). Similarly, traditionalists reject as unacceptable sentences like *there is no other alternative* on the grounds that it is equivalent to the simpler *there is no alternative.*

altogether

Altogether should be distinguished from *all together. All together* is used of a group to indicate that its members performed or underwent an action collectively: *The seven unions stood all together. The new computers were stored all together in an empty office. All together* can be used only if it is possible to rephrase the sentence so that *all* and *together* may be separated by other words: *All of the unions stood together. The new computers were all stored together.*

alumni

Alumni is generally used to refer to both the *alumni* (masculine plural) and *alumnae* (feminine plural) of a coeducational institution.

and

Although frowned upon by some, the use of *and* to begin a sentence has a long and respectable history: "And it came to pass in those days . . ." (Luke 2:1).

and/or

And/or is widely used in legal and business writing. Its use in general writing to mean "one or the other or both" is also acceptable.

ante meridian

In general, *12 A.M.* denotes midnight and *12 P.M.* denotes noon, but there is sufficient confusion over them to make it advisable to use *12 noon* and *12 midnight* where absolute clarity is required.

anticipate

Some traditionalists hold that *anticipate* should not be used simply as a synonym for *expect*. They would restrict its use to senses in which it suggests some advance action, either to fulfill (*anticipate my desires*) or to forestall (*anticipate the competition's next move*). Others accept its use in the senses of "to feel or realize beforehand" and "to look forward to" (often with the implication of foretasting pleasure): *They are anticipating a sizable dividend increase.*

any

The phrase *of any* is often used in informal contexts to mean "of all," as in *That scientist is the best of any living authority on the subject.* Many find this construction unacceptable. *Any* is used to mean "at all" before a comparative adjective: *Are the field office reports any better this month?* This use is entirely proper, but the related use of *any* all by itself to mean "at all" is considered informal. In writing, one should avoid sentences like *It didn't hurt any* or *It didn't matter any to the supervisor.*

anyone

The one-word form *anyone* is used to mean "whatsoever person or persons." The two-word form *any one* is used to mean "whatever one (person or thing) of a group." *Anyone may join* means admission is open to everybody. *Any one may join* means admission is open to one person only. When followed by *of*, only *any one* (two words) can be used: *Any one of*

them could do the job. Anyone is often used in place of *everyone* in sentences like *Dale is the most thrifty person of anyone I know.* Such usage is generally unacceptable in formal writing.

apparent

Used before a noun, *apparent* means "seeming": *For all its apparent wealth, the company was leveraged to the hilt.* Used after a form of the verb *to be*, however, *apparent* can mean either "seeming" (as in *the virtues of the deal were only apparent*) or "obvious" (as in *the effects of the drought are apparent to anyone seeing the parched fields*). Writers should take care that the intended meaning is clear from the context.

as

Traditionally, a distinction has been drawn between comparisons using *as . . . as* and comparisons using *so . . . as.* Comparisons with *as . . . as* may be used in any context, as in *Their marketing is as good as ours.* The *so . . . as* construction is restricted to use in negative contexts (as in Hamlet's *'Tis not so deep as a well*), in questions (*Is it so bad as all that?*), and in clauses introduced by *if* or similar words (as in *If it is so bad as all that, why don't you leave?*). The distinction between the two types of comparison is fast disappearing in American usage, however, as the *so . . . as* construction becomes increasingly rare. The *as . . . as* comparison may be considered correct in any context. • In a comparison involving both *as . . . as* and *than*, the second *as* should be retained in written style. One writes *he is as bright as, or brighter than, his brother*, not *he is as bright or brighter than his brother*, which is unacceptable in formal style. • In many dialects, *as* is used instead of *that* in sentences like *we are not sure as we want to go* or *it's not certain as she left.* This construction is not sufficiently established to be used in writing. • In comparisons, a pronoun following *as* may be either nominative (*I, he*) or objective (*me, him*). Traditionally, the nominative is used when the pronoun would be the subject of an "understood" verb that has been omitted; we should say *Pat is as happy as I* because the sentence has an equivalent version *Pat is as happy as I am.* By the same token, we should say *It surprised her as much as me*, using the objective pronoun, on the grounds that there is an equivalent sentence *It surprised her as much as it surprised me.* In sentences like these, the use of *me* where *I* would be considered correct is regarded as careless by traditionalists. The use of *I* where *me* would be correct, however, is likely to be regarded as a pretentious overcorrection. • *As* should be preceded by a comma when it expresses a causal relation, as in *He won't be coming, as we didn't invite him.* When used to express a time relation, *as* is not preceded by a comma: *She was finishing the painting as I walked into the room.* When a clause introduced by *as* begins a sentence, care should be taken that it is clear whether *as* is used to mean "because" or "at the same time as." The sentence *As they were leaving, I walked to the door* may mean either that *I walked to the door because they left* or *at the same time that they were leaving.* The connectives *since* and *while* can be ambiguous in the same way, as in examples like *Since she has been living abroad, she has been speaking a lot of French* and *While your income is low, you should buy insurance.* When these clauses are moved to the end of the sentence, the proper placement of commas will serve to distinguish the meanings.

assure

Assure, ensure, and *insure* all mean "to make secure or certain." Only *assure* is used with references to a person in the sense of "to set the mind at rest": *They assured the leader of their loyalty.* Although *ensure* and *insure* are generally interchangeable, only *insure* is now widely used in the commercial sense of "to guarantee persons or property against risk."

averse

Averse and *adverse* are often confused. *Averse* indicates opposition or strong disinclination on the subject's part: *The graduate was averse to joining the company.* *Adverse* is used to mean something that opposes or hinders progress: *an adverse economy; adverse circumstances.*

awhile

Awhile, an adverb, is never preceded by a preposition such as *for,* but the two-word form *a while* may be preceded by a preposition. In writing, each of the following is

acceptable: *stay awhile; stay for a while; stay a while* (but not *stay for awhile*).

back

The expression *back of* is an informal variant of *in back of* and should be avoided in writing: *There was a small loading dock in back of* (not simply *back of*) *the factory.*

backward

The adverb may be spelled *backward* or *backwards,* and the forms are interchangeable; *stepped backward; a mirror facing backwards.* Only *backward* is an adjective: *a backward view.*

badly

The adverb *badly* is often used idiomatically as an adjective in sentences like *I felt badly about the ruined press run,* where grammar would seem to require *bad.* This usage is parallel to the use of the adverb *well* in sentences like *you're looking well* and is acceptable. The use of *bad* and *good* as adverbs, while common in informal speech, should be avoided in writing. Formal usage requires: *My tooth hurts badly* (not *bad*). *He drives well* (not *good*).

bait

The word *bait* is sometimes used improperly for *bate* in the phrase *bated breath.*

baleful

Baleful and *baneful* overlap in meaning, but *baleful* usually applies to that which menaces or foreshadows evil (*a baleful look*). *Baneful* is used most often of that which is actually harmful or destructive (*the baneful effects of government regulations*).

because

Because is the most direct of the conjunctions used to express cause or reason. It is used to state an immediate and explicit cause: *The company went bankrupt because the management was incompetent.* *Since, as,* and *for* are all less direct than *because;* they often express the speaker's or writer's view of the causal relation between circumstances or events. The clause introduced by *since* most frequently comes first in the sentence: *Since they stayed behind, they must have had something more important to do* (their staying behind leads the speaker to conclude that they must have had something important to do). *As,* like *since,* often indicates that what follows is the speaker's basis for coming to a certain conclusion: *As I have something more important to do, I would prefer to stay behind. For* is a coordinating conjunction, linking two independent statements. It expresses the speaker's reason for having said or concluded the previous statement: *The messenger definitely arrived at 11:30, for I was there and I saw him walk in. As* and *for* are now used primarily in formal levels of style. • *Because* is sometimes used in informal speech to mean "just because," as in *Because there's snow on the roof doesn't mean the fire is out in the furnace.* This use of *because* should be avoided in writing. Traditional grammar holds that the expression *the reason is because* is redundant and so should be avoided at all levels. This usage is well established, however, and has perfectly acceptable equivalents in expressions like *the time was when.* • When *because* follows a negative verb or verb phrase, it should be preceded by a comma when the *because* clause gives the subject's reason for not doing something: *I didn't leave, because I was busy* means roughly "I stayed because I had a lot of work to do." When no comma is used, the *because* clause is understood as part of what is being negated. *I didn't leave because I was busy* means "My reason for staying was not because of work, but because of something else." The conjunctions *since, as,* and *for,* when used to express a causal relation, must be preceded by commas: *She had a hurried breakfast, since she had to go to the office. I must have this phone repaired, as I have a lot of sales calls to make tomorrow. Everything at headquarters stopped, for the snowstorm had forced everyone home early.*

behalf

In behalf of and *on behalf of* have distinct senses and should not be used interchangeably. *In behalf of* means "in the interest of" or "for the benefit of": *We raised money in behalf of the United Way. On behalf of* means "as the agent of" or "on the part of": *The lawyer signed the papers on behalf of the client.*

besides

In modern usage the senses "in addition to" and "except for" are conveyed more often by *besides* than *beside.* Thus: *We had few options besides the course we ultimately took.*

better

Better is normally used in a comparison of two: *Which accounting firm does the better job?* However, *best* is used idiomatically with reference to two in certain expressions: *Put your best foot forward. May the best man or woman win!* The phrase *had better* is accepted, so long as the *had* or its contraction is preserved: *You had better do it* or *you'd better do it,* but not *you better do it.* The use of *better* for *more,* as in *the distance is better than a mile,* should be avoided in writing.

bias

Bias has generally been defined as "uninformed or unintentional inclination"; as such, it may operate either for or against someone or something. Recently *bias* has been used in the sense of "adverse action or discrimination": *Congress included a provision in the Civil Rights Act of 1964 banning racial bias in employment.*

bimonthly

Bimonthly and *biweekly* mean "once every two months" and "once every two weeks." For "twice a month" and "twice a week," the words *semimonthly* and *semiweekly* should be used. But there is a great deal of confusion over the distinction, and a writer is well advised to substitute expressions like "every two months" or "twice a month" whenever possible. However, the words with *bi-* are unavoidable when used as nouns to denote "a publication that appears every two months."

black

The preferred term for a person today is *black* rather than *Negro.* Another acceptable term is *Afro-American.* The noun and the adjective *black* are usually but not invariably lowercased: "Together, blacks and whites can move our country beyond racism." (Whitney Young, Jr.)

blatant

Blatant and *flagrant* are often confused. In the sense that causes the confusion, *blatant* has the meaning of "outrageous" or "egregious." *Flagrant* emphasizes wrong or evil that is glaring or notorious. Therefore, one who blunders may be guilty of a *blatant* (but not a *flagrant*) *error*; one who intentionally and ostentatiously violates a pledge commits a *flagrant act.*

born

In its literal sense the past participle *born* is used only of mammals and only in construction with *to be: The baby was born.* (It may also be used figuratively: *A great project was born.*) *Borne,* said of the act of birth, refers only to the mother's role, but it can be used actively or passively: *She has borne three children. Three children were borne by her* (but *born to her*). In all other senses of *bear* the past participle is *borne: The soil has borne abundant crops. Such a burden cannot be borne by anyone.*

borrow

In many American English dialects, the expression *borrow off* is used in place of *borrow from.* This usage is not sufficiently established to be used in writing, however; one writes *Gale borrowed $500.00 from* (not *off*) *the bank.*

both

Both is used to underscore that the activity or state denoted by a verb applies equally to two entities, where it might have been expected that it would apply only to one. *Both the employees have exasperated me,* for example, emphasizes that neither employee escapes my impatience. As such, *both* is improperly used with a verb that can apply only to two or more entities. It is illogical to say *they are both alike,* since neither could be "alike" if the other were not. Similarly, *both* is unnecessary in a sentence like *they both appeared together,* since neither one can "appear together" by himself. • The expression *the both,* as in *the office manager gave it to the both of them,* should be avoided in formal writing and speech. • In possessive constructions, *of both* is usually preferred: *the shareholders of both companies* (rather than *both their shareholders*); *the fault of both* (rather than *both their fault* or *both's fault*).

bring

In most American English dialects, *bring* is used to denote movement toward the place of speaking or the point from which the action is regarded: *Bring the letter to me now. The Wall Street Journal brought*

good news about the economy. Take denotes movement away from such a place. Thus, one normally *takes* checks to the bank and *brings* home cash, though from the banker's point of view, one has *brought* him checks in order to *take* away cash.

burgeon

The verb *burgeon* and its participle *burgeoning,* used as an adjective, are properly restricted to the actual or figurative sense of "to bud or sprout," or "to newly emerge" (*the burgeoning talent of the young attorney*). They are not mere substitutes for the more general *expand, grow,* or *thrive.*

but

But is used to mean "except" in sentences like *No one but a company officer can read it.* Some traditionalists have suggested that *but* is a conjunction in this use and so should be followed by nominative pronouns like *I* and *he* when the phrase in which it occurs is the subject of the sentence. But this use of *but* is perhaps better thought of as a preposition, since the verb always agrees with the subject preceding *but;* we say *no one but the middle managers has left* (not *have left*), and traditionalists themselves do not say *everyone but I am leaving,* which is clearly ungrammatical. Accordingly, this use of *but* should properly be accompanied by pronouns in the objective case, like *me* and *him: Everyone but me has received an answer. But* is redundant when used in combination with *however,* as in *But the division, however, went on with its own plans* (eliminate either *but* or *however*). *But* is often used in informal speech together with a negative in sentences like *It won't take but an hour.* The construction should be avoided in formal style; write *It won't take an hour. But what* is informal in sentences like *I don't know but what we'll get there before the boys do.* In writing, substitute *whether* or *that* for *but. But* is also informal when used in place of *than* in sentences like *It no sooner started but it stopped* (in writing use *than*). *But* is usually not followed by a comma. Write *Kim wanted to go, but we didn't want to,* not *Kim wanted to go, but, we didn't want to,* which is incorrect. *But* may be used to begin a sentence, even in formal style. But it should not be followed by a comma here, either.

callous

The noun is spelled *callus* (*a callus on my foot*), but the verb and adjective are spelled *callous* (*calloused skin; a callous disregard for human rights*).

can

Generations of grammarians and schoolteachers have insisted that *can* should be used only to express the capacity to do something, while *may* must be used to indicate permission. Technically, correct usage therefore requires: *The supervisor said that anyone who wants an extra day off may* (not *can*) *have one. May* (not *can*) *I have that pencil?* In speech, however, *can* is used by most speakers to express permission, and the "permission" use of *can* is even more frequent in British English. The negative contraction *can't* is frequently used in coaxing and wheedling questions like *Can't I have the car tonight?* Avoid *mayn't*, for it is awkward and unnatural.

cannot

In the phrase *cannot but*, which is sometimes criticized as a double negative, *but* is used in the sense of "except": *One cannot but admire the takeover strategy* (that is, "one cannot do otherwise than admire the strategy"). Thus, the expression is not to be classed with the double negative that occurs when *but* in the sense of "only" is coupled with a negative. Alternative phrasings are *can but admire, can only admire, cannot help admiring.*

capital

The term for a town or city that serves as a seat of government is spelled *capital.* The term for the building in which a legislative assembly meets is spelled *capitol.*

celebrant

Celebrant should be reserved for an official participant in a religious ceremony or rite (*the celebrant of a Mass*). In the general sense of "participant in a celebration" (*New Year's Eve celebrants*) it is unacceptable to many. *Celebrator* is an undisputed alternative.

center

Center as an intransitive verb may be used with *on, upon, in,* or *at.* Logically, it should not be used with *around,* since the word *center* refers to a point of focus. Thus: *The discussion centered on* (not *around*) *the meaning of the law* (with a possible alternative being *revolved around*).

ceremonial

Ceremonial (adjective) is applicable chiefly to things; *ceremonious,* to persons and things. *Ceremonial* means simply "having to do with ceremony": *ceremonial occasions; ceremonial garb. Ceremonious,* when applied to a person, means "devoted to forms and ritual" or "standing on ceremony": *a ceremonious chief of protocol.*

certain

Although *certain* appears to be an absolute term, it is frequently qualified by adverbs, as in *fairly certain.* An acceptable sentence is *Nothing is more certain than death and taxes.*

close

Strictly speaking, the expression *close proximity* says nothing that is not said by *proximity* itself.

commentate

The verb *commentate* has been in use for several hundred years in the sense of "to give a commentary." But in the sense "to provide a running commentary on," as in *Howard Cosell commentated the Super Bowl,* it is usually unacceptable.

compare

Compare usually takes *to* when it denotes the act of stating or representing that two things are similar: *They compared the odor from the smokestack to the smell of rotten eggs.* It usually takes *with* when it denotes the act of examining the ways in which two things are similar. *The painter compared the new batch of red paint with the old one. The investigators compared the forged will with the original.* When *compared* means "worthy of comparison," *with* is used: *The plastic imitation can't be compared with the natural wood cabinet.*

complement

Complement and *compliment,* though quite distinct in meaning, are sometimes confused because of the context. *Complement* means "something that completes or brings to perfection": *The thick carpet was a perfect complement to the executive suite. Compliment* means "an expression of courtesy or praise": *We paid them a supreme compliment at the testimonial banquet.*

complete

Complete is sometimes held to be an absolute term like *perfect* or *chief*, which is not subject to comparison. It can be qualified by *more* or *less*, however, when its sense is "comprehensive, thorough," as in *A more complete failure I could not imagine.* Also acceptable: *That book is the most complete treatment of the subject available today.*

comprise

The traditional rule states that the whole *comprises* the parts; the parts *compose* the whole. In strict usage: *The Union comprises fifty states. Fifty states compose* (or *constitute* or *make up*) *the Union.* While this distinction is still maintained by many writers, *comprise* is increasingly used, especially in the passive, in place of *compose: The Union is comprised of fifty states.* That use of *comprise* should be avoided, especially in formal prose.

continuance

Continuance, except in its legal sense, is sometimes interchangeable with *continuation. Continuance*, however, is used to refer to the duration of a state or condition, as in *the president's continuance in office. Continuation* applies especially to prolongation or resumption of action (*a continuation of the board meeting*) or to physical extension (*the continuation of the railroad spur beyond our plant*). *Continuity* is used to refer to consistency over time; one speaks of *the continuity of foreign policy. The continuity of a story* is its internal coherence from one episode to the next; *the continuation of a story* is that part of the story that takes up after a break in its recitation.

convince

According to a traditional rule, one *persuades* someone to act but *convinces* someone of the truth of a statement or proposition: *By convincing me that no good could come of continuing the project, the director persuaded me to shelve it altogether.* If the distinction is accepted, then *convince* should not be used with an infinitive: *They persuaded* (not *convinced*) *me to go.*

council

Council, counsel, and *consul* are never interchangeable as such, though their meanings are related. *Council* and *councilor* refer principally to a deliberative assembly (such as a city council or student council), its work, and its membership. *Counsel* and *counselor* pertain chiefly to advice and guidance and to a person who provides it (such as an attorney). *Consul* denotes an officer in the foreign service of a country.

couple

Couple, when used to refer to a man and a woman together, may take either a singular or a plural verb, but the plural is more common. Whatever the choice, usage should be consistent: *The couple are now finishing their joint research* (or *the couple is now finishing its joint research*).

criteria

Criteria is a plural form only, and should not be substituted for the singular *criterion.*

critique

Critique is widely used as a verb (*critiqued the survey*), but is still regarded by many as pretentious jargon. The use of phrases like *give a critique* or *offer a critique* will forestall objections.

data

Data is the plural of the Latin word *datum* (something given) and traditionally takes a plural verb: *These data are nonconclusive.* In casual speech the singular construction is acceptable but should be avoided in formal writing.

debut

Debut is widely used as a verb, both intransitively in the sense "to make an appearance" (*The play debuts at our new downtown theater tonight.*) and transitively in the sense "to present for the first time": *We will debut a new product line next week.* However, both of these usages are widely objected to.

depend

Depend, indicating condition or contingency, is always followed by *on* or *upon*, as in *It depends on* (or *upon*) *who is in charge.* Omission of the preposition is typical of casual speech.

deprecate

The first and fully accepted meaning of *deprecate* is "to express disapproval of." But the word has steadily encroached upon the meaning of *depreciate.* It is now used, almost to the exclusion of *depreciate,* in the sense "to belittle or mildly disparage": *The cynical employee deprecated all of the good things the company had to offer.* This newer sense is acceptable.

dilemma

Dilemma applies to a choice between evenly balanced alternatives, most often unattractive ones. It is not properly used as a synonym for *problem* or *predicament.* A sentence such as the following, therefore, is unacceptable: *Highjacking has become a big dilemma for our trucking subsidiary.*

disinterested

According to the traditional rule, a *disinterested* party is one who has no stake in a dispute and is therefore presumed to be impartial. By contrast, one is *uninterested* in something when one is indifferent to it. These two terms should not be used interchangeably despite an increasing tendency among some writers to do it.

distinct

A thing is *distinct* if it is sharply distinguished from other things (*a distinct honor*); a property or attribute is *distinctive* if it enables us to distinguish one thing from another. *This carpeting has a distinctive feel to it* means that the feel of the carpet enables us to distinguish it from other carpets. *Thick-pile carpeting is a distinct type of floor covering* means that the thick-pile carpeting falls into a clearly defined category of floor coverings.

done

Done, in the sense of "completely accomplished" or "finished," is found most often, but not exclusively, in informal usage. It is acceptable in writing in the following example: *The entire project will not be done until next year.* In some contexts this use of *done* can be unclear, as in *The work will be done next week.* Alternatives, dependent on the meaning, would be: *The work will get done next week. The work will be done by next week.*

doubt

Doubt and *doubtful* are often followed by clauses introduced by *that, whether,* or *if.* A choice among the three is guided by the intended meaning of the sentence, but considerable leeway exists. Generally, *that* is used when the intention is to express more or less complete rejection of a statement: *I doubt that they will even try* (meaning "I don't think they will even try"); or, in the negative, to express more or less complete acceptance: *I don't doubt that you are right.* On the other hand, when the intention is to express real uncertainty, the choice is usually *whether: We doubt whether they can succeed. It is doubtful whether our opponents will appear at the hearing.* In fact, *whether* is generally the only acceptable choice in such examples, though some experts would accept *if* (which is more informal in tone) or *that. Doubt* is frequently used in informal speech, both as verb and as noun, together with *but: I don't doubt but* (or *but what*) *they will come. There is no doubt but it will be difficult.* These usages should be avoided in writing; substitute *that* or *whether* as the case requires.

dove

Dove as a past tense of the verb *dive* is actually a more recent form than the historically correct *dived. Dove* is widely used in speech.

drunk

Drunk (adjective) is used predicatively; *The guard was drunk.* For attributive use before a noun, the choice is usually *drunken: a drunken guest.* The attributive use of *drunk,* as in *drunk driver,* is generally unacceptable. But in its legal sense it is supported by usage and statute to the extent that the two expressions *drunk driver* (one who has exceeded the legal limit of alcohol consumption while driving) and *drunken driver* (one who is inebriated) are not synonymous.

due

The phrase *due to* is always acceptable when *due* functions as a predicate adjective following a linking verb: *Our hesitancy was due to fear.* But objection is often made when *due to* is used as a prepositional phrase: *We hesitated due to fear.* Such a construction is unacceptable in writing, though it is widely used. Generally accepted alternatives are *because of* or *on account of*.

each

When the subject of a sentence begins with *each*, it is traditionally held to be grammatically singular, and the verb and following pronouns must be singular as well: *Each of the designers has* (not *have*) *his or her* (not *their*) *distinctive style.* When *each* follows a plural subject, however, the verb and following pronouns generally remain in the plural: *The secretaries each have their jobs to do.* The expression *each and every* is likewise followed by a singular verb and singular pronouns in formal style: *Each and every packer knows what his or her job is supposed to be.*

each other

According to some traditional grammarians, *each other* is used of two, *one another* of more than two. This distinction has been ignored by many of the best writers, however, and the following examples are considered acceptable: *The four partners regarded each other with suspicion. A husband and wife should confide in one another.* When speaking of an ordered series of events or stages, only *one another* can be used: *The Caesars exceeded one another* (not *each other*) *in cruelty* means that each Caesar was crueler than the last. *Each other* cannot be used as the subject of a clause in formal writing. Instead of *we know what each other are thinking,* one should write *each of us knows what the other is thinking.* Instead of *the individuals know that each other are coming,* write *each of the individuals knows that the other is coming.* Instead of *we are all each other has,* write *each of us is all the other has.* The possessive forms of *each other* and *one another* are written *each other's* and *one another's: The machinists wore each other's* (not *each others'*) *hard hats. The district managers had forgotten one another's* (not *one anothers'*) *names.*

either

Either is normally used to mean "one of two," although it is sometimes used of three or more: *either corner of the triangle.* When referring to more than two, *any* or *any one* is preferred. • *Either* takes a singular verb: *Either plant grows in the shade.* Sometimes it is used informally with a plural verb, especially when fol-

lowed by *of* and a plural: *I doubt whether either of them are available.* But such use is unacceptable to many in formal writing.

elder

Elder and *eldest* apply only to persons, unlike *older* and *oldest,* which also apply to things. *Elder* and *eldest* are used principally with reference to seniority: *elder statesman; Pat the Elder.* Unlike *older, elder* is also a noun (*the town elders; ought to listen to your elders*).

else

Else is often used redundantly in combination with prepositions such as *but, except,* and *besides: No one* (not *no one else*) *but that witness saw the accident.* • When a pronoun is followed by *else,* the possessive form is generally written thus: *someone else's* (not *someone's else*). Both *who else's* and *whose else* are in use, but not "whose else's": *Who else's appointment book could it have been? Whose else could it have been?*

errata

The plural *errata* is sometimes employed in the collective sense of a list of errors. Nevertheless, *errata* always takes a plural verb: *The errata are* (not *is*) *noted in an attached memo.*

everyplace

Everyplace and *every place* used adverbially for *everywhere* are appropriate principally to informal writing or speech: *Everyplace* (or *every place*) *I go, I hear raves about our product* (in formal writing, preferably *everywhere I go*). *Every place* as a combination of adjective and noun is, of course, standard English: *I searched in every place possible.*

everywhere

The only acceptable word is *everywhere* (not *everywheres*). The use of *that* with *everywhere* (*everywhere that I go*) is superfluous.

except

Except in the sense of "with the exclusion of" or "other than" is generally construed as a preposition, not a conjunction. A personal pronoun that follows *except* is therefore in the objective case: *No one except them knew it. Every member of the committee was called except me.*

excuse

The expression *excuse away* has no meaning beyond that of *excuse* (unlike *explain away*, which has a different meaning from *explain*). *Excuse away* is unacceptable: *The general manager's behavior cannot be excused* (not *excused away*).

explicit

Explicit and *express* both apply to something that is clearly stated rather than implied. *Explicit* applies more particularly to that which is carefully spelled out (*the explicit terms of ownership contained in the licensing agreement*). *Express* applies particularly to a clear expression of intention or will: *The corporation made an express prohibition against dealers' selling cars below list prices.*

farther, further

According to many traditional grammarians, the historical distinction between *farther* ("more far") and *further* ("more to the fore") should be preserved. In that case *farther* should be used only for physical distance as in *The freight train went farther down the line. Further* should be used in most other senses, especially when referring to degree, quantity, or time (*further in debt; further steps to advertise our product*). In some cases, however, either word is acceptable; one may say *further from the truth* or *farther from the truth.*

fatal

Although the senses of *fatal* and *fateful* have tended to merge in recent times, each has a different core of meaning. The contrast between *fatal*, in the sense of "leading to death or destruction," and *fateful*, in the sense of "affecting one's destiny or future," is illustrated by the following sentence: *The fateful decision to relax safety standards led directly to the fatal car crash.*

fault

Fault as a transitive verb meaning "to criticize or find fault with" is attested as far back as the 16th century but has recently come into much wider use. This usage is acceptable: *One cannot fault management's performance. To fault them is grossly unfair.*

few

Few and *fewer* are correctly used in writing only before a plural noun (*few cars; few of the books, fewer reasons, fewer gains on the stock market*). *Less* is used before a mass noun (*less music; less sugar; less material gain*). *Less than* is also used before a plural noun that denotes a measure of time, amount, or distance (*less than three weeks; less than sixty years old; less than $400.00*).

finalize

Finalize is frequently associated with the language of bureaucracy and so is objected to by many writers. The sentence *we will finalize plans to remodel twelve stores this year* is considered unacceptable. While *finalize* has no single exact synonym, a substitute can always be found among *complete, conclude, make final,* and *put in final form.*

firstly

Firstly may be used in a sequence: *firstly, secondly, thirdly,* and so on. However, it has fallen into disuse among many writers, who prefer this sequence: *first, secondly, thirdly.* Another alternative, since all these ordinal numbers can be used adverbially, is the somewhat more forceful *first, second,* or *third.*

fit

Either *fitted* or *fit* is correct as the past tense of *fit: The title fitted* (or *fit*) *my job responsibilities perfectly a year ago.* When the verb is used to mean "to cause to fit," only *fitted* is used as the past tense: *The maintenance worker fitted* (not *fit*) *the file cabinet right into the space between my desk and the wall.*

flammable

Flammable and *inflammable* are identical in meaning. *Flammable* has been adopted by safety authorities for the labeling of combustible materials because the *in-* of *inflammable* was understood by some people to mean "not." *Inflammable* is nevertheless widely used by writers, even though *flammable* is now established as a substitute.

flaunt

Flaunt and *flout* are often confused. *Flaunt* as a transitive verb means "to exhibit ostentatiously": *The manager flaunted a* corporate credit card and expense account. To *flout* is "to defy openly": *They flouted all social proprieties.*

follow

As *follows* (not *as follow*) is the established form of the phrase, no matter whether the noun that precedes it is singular or plural: *The new operating procedures are as follows* (or *procedure is as follows*).

forbid

Forbid may be used with an infinitive: *I forbid you to smoke in the elevators*; or a gerund: *I forbid your smoking*; but not with *from*: *I forbid you from smoking.*

forceful

Forceful, forcible, and *forced* have distinct, if related, meanings. *Forceful* is used to describe something that suggests strength or force (*a forceful marketing campaign*). *Forceful* measures may or may not involve the use of actual physical force. *Forcible,* by contrast, is most often used of actions accomplished by the application of physical force: *There had clearly been a forcible entry into the storeroom. The suspect had to be forcibly restrained. Forced* is used to describe a condition brought about by control or by an outside influence (*forced labor; a forced landing; a forced smile*).

former

The former is used when referring to the first of two persons or things mentioned. It is not used when referring to the first of three or more. For that purpose one may use *the first* or *the first-named* or repeat the name itself.

fortuitous

Fortuitous is often confused with *fortunate. Fortuitous* means "happening by chance." A *fortuitous* meeting may have either fortunate or unfortunate consequences. In common usage, some of the meaning of *fortunate* has rubbed off on *fortuitous* so that even when it is properly used, *fortuitous* often carries an implication of lucky chance rather than unlucky chance. But the word is not synonymous with *fortunate* and should not be used unless it refers to something that came about by chance or accident. The following example is unacceptable: *The meeting proved fortuitous; I came away with a much better idea of my responsibilities.*

forward

Forwards may be used in place of *forward* only in the adverbial sense of "toward the front" (*move forward* or *move forwards*). In specific phrases the choice of one or the other is often idiomatic (*look forward; from that day forward; backwards and forwards*).

founder

The verbs *founder* and *flounder* are often confused. *Founder* comes from a Latin word meaning "bottom" (as in *foundation*) and originally referred to a ship's sinking; it is now used as well to mean "to fail utterly, collapse." *Flounder* means "to move clumsily; thrash about" and hence "to proceed in confusion." If *the railroad's business between Chicago and Peoria is foundering,* expect that the line will be shut down. If *the run is floundering,* improved operating procedures and pricing policies may still save the service.

fulsome

Fulsome is often misused, especially in the phrase *fulsome praise,* by those who think that the term is equivalent merely to *full and abundant.* In modern usage *full* and *abundant* are obsolete as senses of *fulsome.* The modern sense of *fulsome* is "offensively flattering or insincere"; hence, *fulsome praise* really means insincere, unctuous compliments.

get

Get has a great number of uses, some of which are acceptable at all levels and others of which are generally felt to be informal (though never incorrect). Some uses to be avoided in writing are (1) the use of *get* in place of *be* or *become* in sentences such as *The executive got promoted*; (2) the use of *get* or *get to* in place of *start* or *begin,* as in *Let's get* (or *get to*) *working now*; and (3) the use of *have got to* in place of *must* in sentences like *I have got to go now.*

gift

Gift (verb) has a long history of use in the sense "to present as a gift; to endow": *We gifted the charity with a $1,000 donation.* In current general use, however, *gift* in this sense is sometimes regarded as affected and should be avoided.

good

Good is properly used as an adjective with linking verbs such as *be, seem,* or *appear: The future looks good. The soup tastes good.* It should be used as an adverb with other verbs: *The plant runs well* (not *good*). Thus: *The designer's new suits fit well and look good.*

government

In American usage *government* always takes a singular verb. In British usage *government*, in the sense of a governing group of officials, is usually construed as a plural collective and therefore takes a plural verb: *The government are determined to maintain strict reigns on industry but not on labour.*

group

Group as a collective noun can be followed by a singular or plural verb. It takes a singular verb when the persons or things that make up the group are considered collectively: *The planning group is ready to present its report. Group* takes a plural verb when the persons or things that make it up are considered individually: *The group were divided in their sympathies.*

hail

The first word of the phrase *hail fellow well met* is often misspelled *hale* in the mistaken belief that it means "sound," as in *hale and hearty.* It was originally part of a greeting, *Hail, fellow!*

half

The phrases *a half, half of,* and *half a* are all correct, though they may differ slightly in meaning. For example, *a half day* is used when *day* has the special sense "a working day," and the phrase then means "four hours." *Half of a day* and *half a day* are not restricted in this way and can mean either four or twelve hours. When the accompanying word is a pronoun, however, the phrase with *of* must be used: *half of them.* The phrase *a half a,* though frequently heard, is held by some to be unacceptable.

hanged

Hanged, as the past tense and past participle of *hang,* is used in the sense of "put to death by hanging." In the following example *hung* would be unacceptable: *Frontier courts hanged many a prisoner after a summary trial.* In all other senses of the word, *hung* is the preferred form as past tense and past participle.

hardly

Hardly has the force of a negative; therefore, it is not used with another negative: *I could hardly see* (not *couldn't hardly see*). *They listened to the presentation with hardly a smile* (not *without hardly a smile*). • A clause following *hardly* is introduced by *when* or, less often, by *before: We had hardly merged with one restaurant chain when* (or *before*) *a second chain made us an attractive offer.* Such a clause is not introduced by *than* in formal style: *Hardly had I walked inside when* (not *than*) *the downpour started.*

harebrained

The first part of the compound *harebrained* is often misspelled "hair" in the belief that the meaning of the word is "with a hair-sized brain" rather than "with no more sense than a hare." Though *hairbrained* has a long history, this spelling is not established usage.

head

The phrase *head up* is sometimes used in place of the verb *head: The committee is headed up by the city's most esteemed business leader.* The use of *head up* is unacceptable to many, and should be avoided.

headquarter

The verb *headquarter* is used informally in both transitive and intransitive senses: *Our European sales team will headquarter in Paris. The management consulting firm has headquartered its people in the New York Hyatt.* Both of these examples are unacceptable in formal writing.

headquarters

The noun *headquarters* is used with either a singular or a plural verb. The plural is more common: *Corporate headquarters are in Boston.* But the singular is sometimes preferred when reference is to authority rather than to physical location: *Headquarters has approved the purchase of desktop computers for our engineers.*

help

Help in the sense "avoid" or "refrain from" is frequently used in an expression such as *I cannot help but think.* In formal writing, use either *I cannot help thinking* or *I cannot but think.* • Another common use of *help* is exemplified by the sentence *Don't change it any more than you can help* (that is, any more than you have to). Some grammarians condemn this usage on the ground that *help* in this sense means "avoid" and logically requires a negative. But the expression is a well-established idiom.

here

In formal usage *here* is not properly placed before a noun in a phrase such as *this here house.* In constructions introduced by *here is* and *here are* the number of the verb is governed by the subject, which appears after the verb: *Here is the annual report. Here are the quarterly reports.*

historic

Historic and *historical* are differentiated in usage, although their senses overlap. *Historic* refers to what is important in history (*the historic first voyage to outer space*). It is also used of what is famous or interesting because of its association with persons or events in history (*Edison's historic lab*). *Historical* refers to whatever existed in the past, whether regarded as important or not: *a historical character.* Events are *historical* if they happened, *historic* only if they are regarded as important. *Historical* refers also to anything concerned with history or the study of the past (*a historical society; a historical novel*). The differentiation between the words is not complete, though: they are often used interchangeably, as in *historic times* or *historical times.*

hopefully

The use of *hopefully* to mean "it is to be hoped," as in *hopefully we'll exceed last year's sales volume,* is grammatically justified by analogy to the similar uses of *happily* and *mercifully.* However, you should avoid using this word because it is objected to by so many people.

how

How is often used in informal speech where strict grammar would require *that,* as in *The president told us how he was* *penniless when he started in this business.* The use of *as how* for *that* in sentences like *they said as how they would go* is informal and should be avoided in writing. Similarly, one should avoid in writing the expressions *seeing as how* and *being as how.*

however

However is redundant in combination with *but.* One or the other but not both should be used in the following examples: *We had an invitation but didn't go. We had an invitation; however, we didn't go.* The use of *however* as the first word of a sentence is now generally considered to be acceptable.

identical

Some authorities on usage specify *with* as the preferred preposition after *identical.* But either *with* or *to* is now acceptable: *a model identical with* (or *to*) *last year's.*

idle

Idle is now accepted in the transitive sense of "to make idle." The following example is accepted on all levels of speech and writing: *The dock strike had idled many crews and their ships.*

if

Either *if* or *whether* may be used to introduce a clause indicating uncertainty after a verb such as *ask, doubt, know, learn,* or *see: We shall soon learn whether* (or *if*) *it is true.* If should be avoided when it may be ambiguous, as in the following: *Let me know if the vice-chairman is invited.* Depending on the meaning, that could be better phrased: *Let me know whether the vice-chairman is invited. Let me know in the event that the vice-chairman is invited.* Often the phrase *if not* is also ambiguous: *The discovery offered persuasive, if not conclusive, evidence.* This could mean "persuasive and perhaps conclusive" or "persuasive but not conclusive." A clause introduced by *if* may contain either a past subjunctive verb (*if I were going*) or an indicative verb (*if I was going*) depending on the meaning intended. Traditionally, the subjunctive is used to describe a situation that is known to be contrary to fact, as in *if America were still a British colony* or *if Napoleon had been an Englishman.* The main clause of such a sentence must then contain the modal verb *would* or (less frequently) *should: If America were still a British colony, we would drink more tea than we do. If I were the President, I should* (or *would*) *make June 1 a national holiday.* When the situation described by the *if* clause is not known to be false, however, that clause must contain an indicative verb, and the choice of verb in the main clause will depend upon the intended meaning: *If Hamlet was really written by Marlowe, as many have claimed, then we have underestimated Marlowe's genius. If the main switchboard was out all day, as you say, then I understand why we didn't get any responses to our advertisement.* The indicative is also required when the situation described by the *if* clause is assumed to be true: *If I was short with you a moment ago, it is only because I wasn't paying attention. If Rome is the loveliest city in Italy, Milan is the most elegant.* When an *if* clause is preceded by *ask* or *wonder,* only the indicative should be used: *He asked if Napoleon was* (not *were*) *a great general. I wonder if the tax attorney was* (not *were*) *serious.* There is a growing tendency to use *would have* in place of the subjunctive in contrary-to-fact *if* clauses, but this usage is still considered incorrect. Instead of *if I would have been promoted two years earlier,* write *if I had been promoted;* instead of *if I would have been president,* write *if I were.*

impact

Impact (verb) has been used principally in the sense of "to pack together": *Traffic impacts the area during rush hour.* Recently it has come into more general use in the sense of "to have an impact on." Sometimes it is used transitively: *These taxes impact small businesses.* At other times it is used intransitively (with *on*): *Social pathologies, common to the inner city, impact most heavily on a plant operating in such a location.* The preceding example is unacceptable to many.

important

The following sentence may be written with the adjective *important: The shareholders' opinion is evident; more important, it will prevail.* It also may be written with an adverb: *The shareholders' opinion is evident; more importantly, it will prevail.* Most grammarians prescribe the adjective form, in which *important* stands

for "what is important." But the adverbial form is also acceptable.

impracticable

Impracticable applies to that which is not capable of being carried out or put into practice: *Building a highway to the moon is impracticable. Impractical* refers to that which is not sensible or prudent: *Your suggestion that we use balloons to convey messages across town is impractical.* A plan may be impractical if it involves undue cost or effort and still not be impracticable. The distinction between these words is subtle, and *impractical* is often used where *impracticable* would be more precise.

infer

Infer is sometimes confused with *imply,* but the distinction is a useful one. To *imply* is "to state indirectly." To *infer* is "to draw a conclusion." The use of these two terms interchangeably is entirely unacceptable. One should write: *The quarterly report implies* (not *infers*) *that sales are down because of the recession. Because of that implication, investors have inferred* (not *implied*) *that we have something to hide, and our stock has fallen three points.*

input

Input has gained currency in senses not related to physics or computer technology. Example: *The report questioned whether, in such a closed administration, a president thus shielded had access to a sufficiently varied input to have a realistic picture of the nation* (input here meaning "a flow of information"). Example: *The nominee declared that he had no input, so far as he knew, in the adoption of the plank on abortion* (input here meaning "an active role, a voice in policy making"). These newer uses are unacceptable to many.

inside

Inside and *inside of* have the same meaning. *Inside* is generally preferred, especially in writing, when the reference is to position or location (*inside the warehouse*). *Inside of* is used more acceptably when the reference is to time: *The 300-page report was photocopied inside of* (not *inside*) *10 minutes.*

intend

Intend may be followed by an infinitive (*intended to go*) or a gerund (*intended going*), by a *that* clause with a subjunctive verb (*intended that he be present*), or by a noun and an infinitive (*intended him to receive the prize*).

intensive

Intensive is often used interchangeably with *intense*. However, it has the special meaning of "concentrated" (the opposite of *extensive*). Thus, one speaks of *intense heat* but *intensive study*.

intrigue

Intrigue is fully established as a noun and as a verb in all meanings except that of "to arouse the interest or curiosity of." In that sense it has been resisted by writers on usage, who regard it as an unneeded French substitute for available English words such as *interest, fascinate, pique,* or *puzzle.* Nevertheless, it has gained increasing acceptance because no single English word has precisely the same meaning. The following example is therefore acceptable: *The announcement of a special press conference intrigued the financial writers in the manner of a good suspense novel.*

its

Its, the possessive form of the pronoun *it,* is never written with an apostrophe. The contraction *it's* (for *it is* or *it has*) is always written with an apostrophe.

kind

The use of the plurals *these* and *those* with *kind* as in *these kind of films,* has respectable literary antecedents and has often been defended as a sensible idiom by British grammarians. But the usage will raise the hackles of those who go strictly by the rules and probably should be avoided in writing, if only to avoid offending the sensibilities of traditionalists. It is easy enough to substitute *this* (or *that*) *kind of* or *these* (or *those*) *kinds of* and see that the following nouns and verbs agree in number with *kind: This kind of film has had a lot of success in foreign markets. Those are the kinds of books that capture the public imagination.* • When *kind of* is used to mean "more or less," it is properly preceded by the indefinite article *a* in formal writing: *a kind of genius* (not *kind of a genius*). • The use of *kind of*

to mean "somewhat," as in *we were kind of sleepy,* is generally regarded as informal.

kudos

Kudos is one of those words, like *congeries,* that look like plurals but are historically singular, and so it is correctly used with a singular verb: *Kudos is due the committee for organizing a successful company picnic.*

lack

As an intransitive verb, *lack* is used chiefly in the present participle with *in: You will not be lacking in support from the finance committee.* As a transitive verb it requires no preposition but is sometimes used with *for: You will not lack* (or *lack for*) *support from the finance committee.* In that example, *lack* is preferred over *lack for.* In some cases, however, the two phrasings can convey different meanings: *The millionaire lacks nothing* (the millionaire has everything). *The millionaire lacks for nothing* (the millionaire has everything he needs).

latter

Latter, as used in contrast to *former,* refers to the second of two: *Jones and Smith have been mentioned for transfer to our London office, but the latter may decline the post. Latter* is not appropriate when more than two are named: *Jones, Smith, and Kowalski have been nominated.* Kowalski should then be referred to as *the last, the last of these, the last named,* or simply *Kowalski.*

lay

Lay ("to put, place, or prepare") and *lie* ("to recline or be situated") are frequently confused. *Lay* is a transitive verb and takes an object. *Lay* and its principal parts (*laid, laying*) are correctly used in the following examples: *The messenger laid* (not *lay*) *the computer printouts on the desk. The executive dining room table was laid for four. Lie* is an intransitive verb and does not take an object. *Lie* and its principal parts (*lay, lain, lying*) are correctly used in the following examples: *The founder of the company often lies* (not *lays*) *down after lunch. When I lay* (not *laid*) *down, I fell asleep. The rubbish had lain* (not *laid*) *in the dumpster for a week. I was lying* (not *laying*) *in bed when I received the call. The valley lies to the east.*

There are a few exceptions to these rules. The idioms *lay low, lay for,* and the nautical sense of *lay,* as in *lay at anchor,* though intransitive, are well established.

learn

Learn in modern usage is nonstandard in the sense of "to teach": *The instructor taught* (not *learned*) *them cardiopulmonary resuscitation.*

leave

Leave alone is acceptable as a substitute for *let alone* in the sense of "to refrain from disturbing or interfering." The following examples are acceptable: *Leave the secretaries alone and they will produce. Left alone, they were quite productive.* Those who do not accept these examples generally feel that *leave alone* should be restricted to the sense of "to depart and leave one in solitude": *They were left alone in the wilderness.* • In formal writing *leave* is not an acceptable substitute for *let* in the sense "to allow or permit." Only *let* is acceptable in these examples: *Let me be. Let us not quarrel. Let matters stand.*

let's

In colloquial speech *let's* has increasingly come to be used as a mere indicator that a suggestion is being proffered, and its connection with the more formal *let us* has become correspondingly attenuated, so that one hears usages like *let's us go, don't let's get all excited,* and *let's get yourself ready for the doctor.* These usages are to be avoided in formal writing.

lighted

Lighted and *lit* are equally acceptable as past tense and past participle of *light.* When used as an adjective, *lighted* is usual (*a lighted window*), but *lit* is the regular combining form (*a moonlit sky; starlit nights*).

like

Like has been used by the best writers as a conjunction since Shakespeare's time. But the usage has been so vehemently attacked by purists in recent times that the sensible writer will avoid it lest the readers pay more attention to the words than to the content. Prudence requires *The machine responds as* (not *like*) *it should.*

Constructions like *looks like, sounds like,* and *tastes like* are less likely to offend, but *as if* is better used in formal style: *It looks as if* (not *like*) *there will be no action on the bill before Congress recesses.* There can be no objection to the use of *like* as a conjunction when the following verb is not expressed: *The new senator took to politics like a duck to water.* This usage is acceptable.

likewise

Likewise, not being a conjunction, cannot take the place of a connective such as *and* or *together with,* as in *The mayor risked his credibility, likewise his honor.* Properly, *The mayor risked his credibility and* (or *and likewise*) *his honor.*

literally

Literally means "in a manner that accords precisely with the words." It is often used to mean "figuratively" or "in a manner of speaking," which is almost the opposite of its true meaning. Thus, it is not correct to say *The boss was literally breathing fire* unless, of course, the person in question is a dragon.

loan

Loan has long been established as a verb, especially in business usage, though some hold that *lend* is the preferred form, in general as well as formal writing. *Lend* is preferred over *loan* in the following examples: *One who lends* (not *loans*) *money to a friend may lose a friend. When I refused to lend* (not *loan*) *my car, I was kicked out of the carpool.* Many phrases and figurative uses require *lend* (*lend an ear; distance lends enchantment*).

lost

The phrase *lost to* can sometimes be ambiguous, as in *As a result of poor preparation, the court battle was lost to the defense attorney* (lost by the defense attorney or lost by the plaintiff's attorney to the defense attorney?). Unless the context makes the meaning clear, the sentence should be reworded.

majority

When *majority* refers to a particular number of votes, it takes a singular verb: *Her majority was five votes.* When it refers to a group of persons or things that are in the majority, it may take either a plural or singular verb, depending on whether the group is considered as a whole or as a set of people considered individually. So we say *the majority elects* (not *elect*) *the candidate it wants* (not *they want*), since the election is accomplished by the group as a whole; but *the majority of our employees live* (not *lives*) *within five miles of the office*, since living within five miles of the office is something that each employee does individually. • *Majority* is often preceded by *great* (but not by *greater*) in expressing, emphatically, the sense of "most of": *The great majority has decided not to throw good money after bad.* The phrase *greater majority* is appropriate only when considering two majorities: *A greater majority of the workers has accepted this year's contract than accepted last year's.*

man

The use of *man* to mean "a human being, regardless of sex" has a long history, but is now much less generally accepted. For many people, its use in the primary sense of "adult male human being" has made it no longer broad enough to serve as the superordinate term: *The men who settled America's frontier were a sturdy race. Twentieth-century man has made great strides in improving health care. The man of the future will eat his meals in tablet form.* Many people feel that in such cases the sense of "male" is predominant over that of "person." Other means of expressing the idea while avoiding this possible confusion are: *men and women, humans,* and *human beings. Man* in the sense of "mankind" is also sometimes felt to be too exclusive. Its use in phrases such as *the evolution of man* can be avoided with similar substitutions: *the evolution of humans.* Many occupational titles in which *man* occurs as an element are being replaced, sometimes officially, by terms considered neutral. For example, *firefighter* is used instead of *fireman,* or *Members of Congress* instead of *Congressmen.* Caution is, however, advisable in recasting such terms with the use of *-person.* For example, *policeperson* as an alternative for *policeman* might sound awkward or strained to some people; use *police officer* instead.

masterful

Masterful has the undisputed meaning of "strong-willed, imperious, domineering."

It is widely used also as a substitute for *masterly* in the sense of "having the skill of a master." However, many feel that the distinction between the two words should be respected, as in *a masterly* (not *masterful*) *sales presentation.*

materialize

Materialize as an intransitive verb has the primary sense of "to assume material form" or, more generally, "to take effective shape": *If our plans materialize, we will be ready to corner the market.* Though it is widely used in the sense of "appear" or "happen," as in *Three more witnesses testified, but no new evidence materialized,* such a usage is still considered unacceptable.

means

In the sense of "financial resources," *means* takes a plural verb: *Our means are quite adequate for this acquisition.* In the sense of "a way to an end," it may take a singular or plural verb; the choice of a modifier such as *any* or *all* generally determines the number of the verb: *Every means was tried. There are several means at our disposal.*

meantime

Meantime serves principally as a noun: *In the meantime we made plans for an unfavorable Federal Communications Commission ruling.* In expressing the same sense as a single adverb, *meanwhile* is more common than *meantime: Meanwhile, we made plans for an unfavorable ruling.*

might

In many Southern varieties of English, *might* is used in the "double modal" construction with *could,* as in *We might could build over there.* Less frequently, one hears *may can* and *might should.* These constructions are not familiar to the majority of American speakers and are to be avoided in formal writing.

migrate

Migrate is used with reference to both the place of departure and the destination and can be followed by *from* or *to.* It is said of persons, animals, and birds and sometimes implies a lack of permanent settlement, especially as a result of seasonal or periodic movement. *Emigrate* pertains to a single move by a person, and implies permanence. It refers specifically to the place of departure and emphasizes movement from that place. If the place is mentioned, the preposition is *from*: *Since many people have emigrated from the Soviet Union, we see a new demand for Russian-language books.* *Immigrate* also pertains to a single move by persons and likewise implies permanence. But it refers to destination, emphasizes movement there, and is followed by *to*: *Many illegal aliens have immigrated to the United States in recent months.*

minimize

According to traditional grammar, *minimize* can mean only "to make as small as possible" and is therefore an absolute term, which cannot be modified by *greatly* or *somewhat*, which are appropriately used only with verbs like *reduce* and *lessen*. The newer use of *minimize* to mean "to make smaller than before," which can be so modified, is best avoided in formal writing.

most

The adverb *most* is sometimes used in the sense of "almost": *Most all the clients accepted the provisions in the contract.* However, this usage is generally considered unacceptable in formal writing. • In the sense of "very," as an intensive where no explicit comparison is involved, *most* is acceptable both in writing and in speech: *a most ingenious solution.*

mostly

Mostly is used at all levels of style to refer to the largest number of a group: *The trees are mostly evergreens. The police arrested mostly juveniles.* In speech and informal writing, it is also used to mean "in the greatest degree" or "for the most part," but this usage is to be avoided in formal writing: *Those most* (not *mostly*) *affected are the lathe operators in Building C. For the most part* (not *Mostly*), *Northern Telecom is the supplier of our communications equipment.*

movable

Something is *movable* if it can be moved at all (*movable office furniture; a movable partition*): it is *mobile* if it is designed for easy transportation (*a mobile electric generating unit*) or if it moves frequently (*a mobile drilling rig*).

mutual

Mutual is usually used to describe a relation between two or more things, and in this use it can be paraphrased with expressions involving *between* or *each other.* Thus, *their mutual relations* means "their relations with each other" or "the relations between them." *Common* describes a relationship shared by the members of a group to something else, as in *their common interest in accounting* or in the expression *common knowledge,* "the knowledge shared by all." The phrase *mutual friend,* however, has been used since Charles Dickens to refer to a friend of each of the several members of a group: *The business partners were originally introduced by a mutual friend.* *Reciprocal,* like *mutual,* applies to relations between the members of a group, with an added suggestion that an exchange of goods or favors is involved, as in *reciprocal trade.* *Joint* is usually used to describe an undertaking in which several partners are involved, as in *The joint efforts of federal and local officials will be required to eradicate acid rain.*

myself

In informal speech, reflexive pronouns like *myself* and *yourself* are often used for emphasis in compound subjects and objects: *The utility's board of directors and myself are undecided about the cost benefits of building a nuclear reactor. I would assign the new project to either Pat or yourself.* Both constructions are to be avoided in writing.

nauseous

Traditionally, *nauseous* means "causing nausea"; *nauseated* means "suffering from nausea." The use of *nauseous* in the sense of *nauseated* is unacceptable to many and should be avoided in writing.

need

When combined with another verb, *need* has two forms, one regular and one irregular. The regular form is marked for person and is followed by the infinitive with *to*: *He needs to go. Does she need to go?* The irregular form occurs only in questions, negations, and *if* clauses. Like the "modal verbs" (*must, can,* etc.), it is not marked for person and is followed by a bare verb with no *to*; moreover, its negated and questioned forms are not formed with *do.* Thus we say *he need not go,* not *he doesn't need go, he need not to go,* or *he needs not go.* Similarly, the questioned form with the irregular *need* would be *Need it be done in a hurry?* rather than *Does it need be done?* or *Need it to be done?* • The two forms of *need* are subtly different in meaning. The irregular form is roughly equivalent to "to be obliged to" and is generally reserved for situations in which there is some question as to whether its subject is under an externally imposed obligation to perform the action named by the accompanying verb. Thus, *you needn't come* means "you are under no obligation to come." Where the subject is under no external compulsion to perform the action of the accompanying verb, the regular form of *need* is used. Thus, we would say: *Since I was there at the site of the accident, I don't need to read the newspaper accounts* (not *needn't read,* since the decision not to read the newspaper is entirely the subject's own). But a product safety commission might say, *If the auto company has sent letters to all owners of the defective car, has notified the press, and has alerted state motor vehicle departments about the models in question, it needn't take any further steps to get in touch with those owners who have not yet brought their cars in for free repair of the problem* (not *doesn't need to take,* since it is the company's obligations by law and not its interests that are at issue).

neither

According to the traditional rule, *neither* should be construed as singular when it occurs as the subject of a sentence: *Neither of the reports is* (not *are*) *finished.* Accordingly, a pronoun with *neither* as an antecedent also must be singular: *Neither of the doctors in the lawsuit is likely to reveal his or her* (not *their*) *identity.*

no

When *no* introduces a compound phrase, its elements should be connected with *or* rather than with *nor.* Thus we write: *The candidate has no experience or interest in product development* (not *nor interest*). *No modification or change in operating procedures will be acceptable to them* (not *nor change*).

nominal

Nominal in one of its senses means "in name only." Hence a *nominal payment* is a token payment, bearing no relation to the real value of what is being paid for. The word is often extended in use, especially by sellers, to describe a low or bargain price: *We acquired 600,000 barrels of new oil reserves at a nominal extra cost.*

not

Care should be taken with the placement of *not* and other negatives in a sentence in order to avoid ambiguity. *All issues are not speculative* could be taken to mean either "all of the issues are not speculative" or "not all of the issues are speculative." Similarly, the sentence *We didn't sleep until noon* could mean either "We went to sleep at noon" or "We got up before noon."

nothing

Nothing takes a singular verb, even when it is followed by a phrase containing a plural noun or pronoun: *Nothing except your fears stands* (not *stand*) *in your path.*

number

As a collective noun, *number* may take either a singular or a plural verb. It takes a singular verb when it is preceded by the definite article *the: The number of skilled workers is small.* It takes a plural verb when preceded by the indefinite article *a: A number of the workers are unskilled.*

numerous

Numerous is not used as a pronoun in standard English. In writing, expressions like *numerous of the firefighters* should be avoided.

obligate

Obligate has fewer meanings than *oblige.* *Obligate* is used chiefly to mean "to bind, compel, or constrain." In that sense it is often but not always interchangeable with *oblige.* When the constraint is from the outside, either is appropriate: *I am obliged* (or *obligated*) *to fulfill the terms of the contract.* When the constraint is in one's mind, *oblige* is the choice: *I feel obliged to give two weeks' notice.* • *Obligate* used to be interchangeable with *oblige* in the sense of "to put under debt of gratitude." Although this meaning is not wholly obsolete, *oblige* is preferred in that sense: *I am obliged* (better than *obligated*) *to you for all you have done.*

odd

Odd, when used to indicate a few more than a given number, should be preceded by a hyphen in order to avoid ambiguity: *thirty-odd salespeople in the showroom. Odd* in that sense is used only with round numbers.

off

Particularly in written usage, *off* should not be followed by *of* or *from: The speaker stepped off* (not *off of* or *off from*) *the platform.* Nor should *off* be used for *from* to indicate a source in a sentence such as: *I got a loan from* (not *off*) *the credit union.*

on

To indicate motion toward a position, both *on* and *onto* can be used: *The guard dog jumped on the counter. The dog jumped onto the desk. Onto* is more specific, however, in indicating that the motion was initiated from an outside point. *The child wandered onto the field* means that the child began wandering at some point off the field. *The child wandered on the field* may mean that the wandering began somewhere on the field. • In constructions where *on* is an adverb attached to a verb, it should not be joined with *to* to form a single word *onto: The meeting moved on to* (not *onto*) *the next subject; hold on to* (not *onto*) *the railing as you climb the stairs.* • In their uses to indicate spatial relations, *on* and *upon* are often interchangeable: *The container was resting on* (or *upon*) *the flatcar. The welder took it on* (or *upon*) *himself to finish the job before nightfall. We saw a robin light on* (or *upon*) *the lawn.* To indicate a relation between two things, however, instead of between an action and an end point, *upon* cannot always be used: *Hand me the book on* (not *upon*) *the file cabinet.* Similarly, *upon* cannot always be used in place of *on* when the relation is not spatial: *We will be in Des Moines on* (not *upon*) *Tuesday. A good book on* (not *upon*) *word processing has just come out.*

onetime

Onetime (single word) means "former." *One-time* (hyphenated) means "only once." Thus *a onetime employee* is a former employee; *a one-time mayor* was mayor only once.

only

When used as an adverb, *only* should be placed with care to avoid ambiguity. Generally this means having *only* adjoin the word or words that it limits. Variation in the placement of *only* can change the meaning of the sentence, as the following examples show: *Dictators respect only force; they are not moved by words. Dictators only respect force; they do not worship it. She picked up the receiver only when he entered, not before. She only picked up the receiver when he entered; she didn't dial the number.* Though strict grammarians insist that the rule for placement of *only* should always be followed, there are occasions when placement of *only* earlier in the sentence seems much more natural. In the following example, *only* is placed according to the rule: *The committee can make its decision by Friday of next week only if it receives a copy of the latest report.* Placement of *only* earlier in the sentence, immediately after *can*, would serve the rhetorical function of warning the reader that a condition on the statement follows. *Only* is often used as a conjunction equivalent to *but* in the sense of "were it not that": *They would have come, only they were snowed in.* Many experts consider this example unacceptable in writing.

ought

Ought to is sometimes used without a following verb if the meaning is clear: *Should we begin soon? Yes, we ought to.* The omission of *to*, however (as in *no, we ought not*) is not standard. • Usages like *one hadn't ought to come* and *one shouldn't ought to say that* are common in many varieties of American English. They should be avoided in written English, however, in favor of the more standard variant *ought not to.*

pair

Pair as a noun can be followed by a singular or plural verb. The singular is always used when *pair* denotes the set taken as a single entity: *This pair of shoes is a year old.* A plural verb is used when the members are considered as individuals: *The pair are working more harmoniously now.* After a numeral other than *one*, *pair* itself can be either singular or plural, but the plural is now more common: *Six pairs* (or *pair*) *of stockings are defective.*

parent

The use of *parent* as a verb is unacceptable to many people. Since there is no acceptable one-word substitute for it, paraphrases like "perform the duties of parenthood" are recommended.

partly

Partly and *partially* are not always interchangeable. *Partly* is the better choice when reference is made to a part as opposed to the whole, especially when speaking of physical objects: *The letterhead is partly red and partly green. Partially* is used to mean "to a degree" when referring to conditions or states: *Our marketing efforts have only partially penetrated into New England.*

party

A person may be called a *party* in the sense of "participant" (*a party to the industrial espionage ring*) or in a humorous sense (*a wise old party*). But except in legal usage, *party* should not be used as a general synonym for *person*, as in this example: *The party who stole $12,000 worth of inventory was taken into custody.*

pass

The past tense and past participle of *pass* is *passed: They passed (or have passed) right by the front gate. Time had passed slowly. Past* is the corresponding adjective (*in centuries past*), adverb (*drove past*), and preposition (*past midnight; past the crisis*).

peer

Peer is sometimes misused in the sense of "a superior": *That manager is the equal, if not the peer, of any executive on the committee. Peer* refers to an equal, not a superior. Its misuse may stem from the fact that English noblemen are called *peers;* but they are so called because they are equals of each other, not because they are the superiors of English commoners. *Peer* is properly used in the expressions *peer group* and *a jury of one's peers.*

people

People and *persons* are distinguished in usage. *People* is the proper term when referring to a large group of individuals, collectively and indefinitely: *People use a wide variety of our products at work and at home. Persons* is applicable to a specific and relatively small number: *Ten persons were fired.* In modern usage, however, *people* is also acceptable with any plural number: *I counted twenty people.* • The possessive form is *people's (the people's rights)* except when *people* is used in the plural to refer to two or more groups considered to be political or cultural entities: *the Slavic peoples' history.*

per

Per is used with reference to statistics and units of measurement (*per mile; per day; per person*). Its more general use (as in *per the terms of the contract*) is acceptable in business writing.

per cent

Per cent, which also may be written as one word (*percent*), is generally used with a specific figure. The number of a noun that follows it or is understood to follow it governs the number of the verb: *Twenty per cent of the stock is owned by a conglomerate. Forty-seven percent of our sales come from consumer appliances.*

percentage

Percentage, when preceded by *the,* takes a singular verb: *The percentage of unskilled workers is small.* When preceded by *a,* it takes either a singular or plural verb, depending on the number of the noun in the prepositional phrase that follows: *A small percentage of the workers are unskilled. A large percentage of the defective press run was never shipped.*

perfect

Perfect has traditionally been considered an absolute term, like *chief* and *prime,* and not subject to comparison with *more, less, almost,* and other modifiers of degree. The comparative form nonetheless has the sanction of the United States Constitution, in the phrase *a more perfect union,* and must be regarded as entirely correct, especially when *perfect* is used to mean "ideal for the purposes," as in *A more perfect spot for our broadcasting station could not be found.*

perfectly

In writing, *perfectly* is sometimes objected to when it is used as a mere intensive denoting "quite," "altogether," or "just," as in *perfectly good* and *perfectly dreadful.*

But it is widely used by educated speakers in this sense.

permit

Permit of is sometimes used for the transitive verb *permit* (to allow, to admit) as in *permits of two interpretations.*

person

Person is increasingly used to create compounds that may refer to either a man or a woman: *chairperson; spokesperson; anchorperson; salesperson.* These forms can be used when reference is to the position itself, regardless of who might hold it: *The committee should elect a new chairperson at its meeting.* They are also appropriate when speaking of the specific individual holding the position: *She was the best anchorperson the local station had ever had. The group asked him to act as its spokesperson.* In such cases, the alternatives *anchorwoman* and *spokesman* also would be appropriate, and sometimes are preferred by the holder of the position.

personality

Personality, meaning "celebrity" or "notable," is widely used in speech and journalism. In more formal writing, however, it is considered unacceptable by many.

personnel

Personnel is a collective noun and never refers to an individual; therefore, it is unacceptable when used with a numeral. It is acceptable, however, to use another qualifying word: *A number of armed forces personnel* (not *six armed forces personnel*) *testified.*

plead

In strict legal usage, one is said to *plead guilty* or *plead not guilty,* but not to *plead innocent.* In nonlegal contexts, however, *plead innocent* is well established.

plus

Traditionally, *plus* as a preposition does not have the conjunctive force of *and.* Therefore, when *plus* is used after a singular subject, the verb remains singular: *Two* (the numeral considered as a single noun) *plus two equals four. Our production efficiency plus their excellent distribution system results in a new industry leader. Plus* is sometimes used loosely as a conjunction to connect two independent clauses: *We had terrible weather this year, plus the recession affected us adversely.* Such use in writing is considered unacceptable by many, and should be avoided.

poor

Poor is an adjective, not an adverb. In formal usage it should not be used to qualify a verb, as in *did poor* or *never worked poorer. Poorly* and *more poorly* are required in such examples.

practicable

Practicable describes that which can be put into effect. *Practical* describes that which is also sensible and worthwhile. It might be *practicable* to build a bullet train between New York and Omaha, but it would not be *practical.*

practically

Practically is used unexceptionally in its primary sense of "in a way that is practical." In other senses it has become almost interchangeable with *virtually.* Such use is acceptable when the meaning is "for all practical purposes." Thus, a man whose liabilities exceed his assets may be said to be *practically bankrupt,* even though he has not been legally declared insolvent. By a slight extension of this meaning, however, *practically* is often used to mean "nearly" or "all but": *They had practically closed the deal by the time I arrived.* Such use should be avoided in writing, because it is disapproved of by many experts.

precipitate

Precipitate (adjective) and *precipitately* apply primarily to rash, overhasty human actions. *Precipitant* (adjective) and *precipitantly* are also used in the foregoing sense, with stress on rushing forward or falling headlong (literally or figuratively). *Precipitous* and *precipitously* are used primarily of physical steepness, as in *a precipitous slope* or in the figurative extensions of such literal uses, as in *a precipitous drop in interest rates.*

première

Première as a verb is unacceptable to a great number of people, despite its wide usage in the world of entertainment.

presently

Presently is now used primarily in the sense of "soon." Confusingly, it is also used in the sense of "at the present time."

Writers who use the word should take care that the meaning is clear from the context.

principal

Principal and *principle* are often confused but have no meanings in common. *Principle* is only a noun, and all its senses are abstract. *Principal* is both a noun and an adjective. As a noun (aside from its specialized meaning in law and finance), it generally denotes a person who holds a high position or plays an important role (*a meeting between all the principals in the transaction*). As an adjective it has the same sense of "chief" or "leading."

protagonist

Protagonist denotes the leading figure in a theatrical drama or, by extension, in any work or undertaking. Sometimes in modern usage the sense of singularity is lost: *There are three protagonists in the takeover fight.* This watered-down meaning, though well established, is unacceptable to a great many people. *Protagonist* is informally used to indicate a champion or advocate.

prove

The regular form *proved* is the preferred past participle: *You have proved your point. The theory has been proved by our physicists.* The alternative *proven* in such examples is unacceptable to many experts. *Proven* is a Scots variant made familiar through its legal use: *The charges were not proven.* But *proven* is more widely used as an adjective directly before a noun (*a proven talent; a proven point*).

quick

Both *quick* and *quickly* can be used as adverbs. *Quick* is more frequent in speech: *Come quick!* In writing, the slightly more formal *quickly* is preferred: *When the signal was relayed to our parts center, we responded quickly.* In the latter example, *quick* would be unacceptable to many experts.

quote

Quote (transitive verb) is appropriate when words are being given exactly as they were originally written or spoken. When the reference is less exact, *cite* is preferable. • *Quote* (noun) as a substitute for *quotation* is considered unacceptable by many traditionalists.

raise

Raise is properly used as a transitive verb: *Raise the loading bay doors.* For intransitive uses, *rise* is standard: *The platform rises.* However, *raise* is sometimes used as an intransitive verb: *The window raises easily.* • *Raise* (noun), rather than *rise*, is now standard in the United States for an increase in salary, though one still speaks of a *rise in prices.*

rare

Rare and *scarce* are sometimes interchangeable, but *scarce* carries an additional implication that the quantities involved are insufficient or inadequate. Thus we speak of *rare books* or of *the rare qualities* of someone we admire, but of *increasingly scarce oil reserves.*

rarely

The use of *ever* after *rarely* or *seldom* is considered redundant. Thus, the example *he rarely* (or *seldom*) *ever makes a mistake* is unacceptable in speech and writing to a majority of experts. The following constructions, using either *rarely* or *seldom*, are standard, however: *rarely if ever; rarely or never* (but not *rarely or ever*).

rather

Rather is usually preceded by *should* or *would* in expressing preference: *They would rather not diversify the company.* But *had* is equally acceptable: *I had rather be dead than be unemployed.* In a contraction such as *he'd*, either *would* or *had* can be understood.

regard

Regard is traditionally used as a singular in the phrase *in* (or *with*) *regard to* (not *in regards to*). *Regarding* and *as regards* are used in the same sense of "with reference to" but are not acceptable to a great number of people. In the same sense *with respect to* is acceptable, but *respecting* is not. • *Respects* is sometimes preferable to *regards* in the sense of "particulars": *In some respects* (not *regards*) *we are similar to our competition.*

relatively

Relatively is appropriate when a comparison is stated or implied: *The first question was relatively easy* (that is, in comparison to the others). In formal style *relatively* should not be used to mean simply "fairly," as *I am relatively sure of it.*

repel

The verbs *repel* and *repulse* both have the physical sense of driving back or off. *Repulse* also may apply to rebuffing or rejecting discourteously, but only *repel* is used in the sense of causing distaste or aversion: *Your arrogance repelled us. He repulsed with rudeness all of our attempts to help him.*

replete

Replete means "abundantly supplied": *a takeover battle replete with scandal, mudslinging, and threats.* It should not be used to mean simply "complete" or "equipped": *a club replete with pool, tennis courts, and golf courses* (better, *complete with*).

responsible

Some usage experts say that *responsible* should be used only with reference to persons, not things, since only persons can be held accountable. The word is commonly used, however, with reference to things: *Defective welds were responsible for the buckled axle.*

restive

Restive and *restless* are now commonly used as equivalent terms. *Restive,* however, implies more than simply "nervous" or "fidgety": it implies resistance to some sort of restraint. Thus, a patient who is sleeping poorly may be *restless;* but the same patient is *restive* only if kept in bed against his or her will.

sacrilegious

Sacrilegious, the adjective of *sacrilege,* is often misspelled through confusion with *religious.*

said

The adjective *said* is seldom appropriate to any but legal writing, where it is equivalent to *aforesaid: the said tenant* (named in a lease); *said property.* In similar contexts in general usage, *said* is usually unnecessary and *the tenant* or *the property* will suffice.

same

Only in legal writing is *the same* or just *same* used as a substitute for *it* or *them.* In general writing, one should avoid sentences like *The charge is $5.00; please remit same.*

scarcely

Scarcely has the force of a negative; therefore, it is not properly used with another negative: *I could scarcely believe it* (not *I couldn't scarcely believe it*). A clause following *scarcely* is introduced by *when* or, less often, by *before* but not by *than: The meeting had scarcely begun when* (or *before* but not *than*) *it was interrupted.*

seasonal

Seasonal and *seasonable,* though closely related, are differentiated in usage. *Seasonal* applies to what depends on or is controlled by the season of the year: *a seasonal rise in unemployment. Seasonable* applies to what is appropriate to the season (*seasonable clothing*) or timely (*a seasonable intervention in the dispute*). Rains are *seasonal* if they occur at a certain time of the year. They are *seasonable* at any time if they save the crops.

see

The phrase *see where* sometimes occurs in speech as an informal equivalent of *see that,* as in this sentence: *I see that everything is running smoothly at the grain elevator.* The same applies to *read where.* These informal usages, permissible in speech, should be avoided in formal writing.

set

Originally *set* meant "to cause (something) to sit," so that it is now in most cases a transitive verb: *The worker sets his shovel down. One sets the table. Sit* is generally an intransitive verb: *They sit at the microphone.* There are some exceptions: *The sun sets* (not *sits*). *A hen sets* (or *sits*) *on her eggs.*

shall

In formal writing, *shall* is employed in the first person to indicate futurity: *I shall leave tomorrow.* In the second and third persons, the same sense of futurity is expressed by *will: He* (or *she*) *will come this afternoon.* Use of the auxiliaries *shall* and *will* is reversed when the writer wants to indicate conditions such as determination, promise, obligation, command, compulsion, permission, or inevitability; *will* is then employed in the first person and *shall* in the second and third. Thus, *I will leave tomorrow* (meaning, I am determined, or obligated, or compelled, or fated to leave). *He* (or *she*) *shall come this afternoon* likewise can express any of the conditions enumerated, such as promise, permission, command, or compulsion. Such, at least, are the rules of traditional grammar. However, these distinctions are only rarely observed in American English, even in formal writing. In general usage, *will* is widely employed in all three persons to indicate futurity: *We will be in New York next week* (acceptable in writing on all levels). *Shall* is largely neglected, except in some interrogatives, such as *Shall we go?* *Where shall we have our sales conference this year?* and in a few set phrases: *We shall overcome. Will*, in all three persons, is employed more often than *shall* in expressing any of the forms of emphatic futurity. In speech, the degree of stress of the auxiliary verb is usually more indicative of the intended meaning than the choice of *shall* or *will*. In writing, a condition other than mere futurity is often expressed more clearly by an alternative to *shall* or *will*, such as *must* or *have to* (indicating determination, compulsion, or obligation) or by use of an intensifying word, such as *certainly* or *surely*, with *shall* or *will*. Informally, contractions such as *I'll, we'll*, and *you'll* are generally employed without distinction between the functions of *shall* and *will* as formally defined.

should

In traditional grammar the rules governing the use of *should* and *would* were based on the rules governing the use of *shall* and *will*. In modern times and especially in American usage, these rules have been greatly eroded, even more in the case of *should* and *would* than in the case of *shall* and *will*. Either *should* or *would* is now used in the first person to express conditional futurity: *If I had known that, I should* (or *would*) *have made a different reply.* In that example either *should* or *would* is acceptable. But in the second and third persons only *would* is acceptable: *If he had known that, he would have made a different reply. Would* cannot always be substituted for *should*, however. *Should* is used in all three persons in a conditional clause: *if I* (or *you* or *he* or *she*) *should decide to go. Should* is also used in all three persons to express duty or obligation (the equivalent of *ought to*): *I* (or *you* or *he* or *she*) *should go.* On the other hand, *would* is used to express volition or prom-

ise: *I agreed that I would do it.* Either *would* or *should* is possible as an auxiliary with *like, be inclined, be glad, prefer*, and related verbs: *I would* (or *should*) *like to call your attention to an oversight in the accountant's report.* Here *would* is acceptable on all levels and is more common in American usage than *should. Should have* is sometimes incorrectly written *should of* by writers who have mistaken the source of the spoken contraction *should've.*

slow

Slow sometimes may be used as a variant form of the adverb *slowly*, when it comes after the verb: *We drove the car slow.* In formal writing *slowly* is generally preferred. *Slow* is often used in speech and informal writing, especially when brevity and forcefulness are sought: *Drive slow! Slow* is also the established idiomatic form with certain senses of common verbs: *The watch runs slow. Take it slow.*

so

In formal writing the conjunction *so* is preferably followed by *that* when it introduces a clause stating the purpose of or reason for an action: *The supervisor stayed late so that he could catch up on his paperwork.* If *that* were omitted in the preceding example, the sentence would be unacceptable. • *So* generally stands alone, however, when it is used to introduce a clause that states the result or consequence of something: *The canning process kills much of the flavor of the food, so salt is added.*

sometime

Sometime as an adjective is properly employed to mean "former." It is also used colloquially with the meaning "occasional" (*the team's sometime pitcher*). This latter use, however, is unacceptable to a great many experts and should be avoided.

sooner

No sooner, as a comparative adverb, should be followed by *than*, not *when*, as in these typical examples: *No sooner had I arrived than I had to leave for an emergency meeting. I had no sooner made an offer than they said the property had been sold to another person.*

special

Special and *specially* have wider application than *especial* and *especially*. In the senses that it shares with *especial*, the adjective *special* is now much more commonly used. *Especial* is increasingly rare and is used chiefly to stress pre-eminence or an outstanding quality: *a work of especial ingenuity.* The adverb *especially*, on the other hand, has not been similarly displaced by *specially*. *Specially* is used with reference to a particular purpose (*specially trained; specially arranged*). *Especially* is used in the sense of "particularly" or "pre-eminently": *Their writers are especially talented. The first defendant especially is implicated in the fraud. Prudence is the best policy, especially now.*

stratum

The standard singular form is *stratum*: the standard plural is *strata* (or sometimes *stratums*) but not *stratas*.

tend

Tend is an informal variant of *attend* in the phrase *tend to*, meaning "to apply one's attention to": *A special session of the legislature has been called to tend to the question of a windfall profits tax.* This example is unacceptable in writing that is not expressly informal.

than

In comparisons, a pronoun following *than* or *as* may be taken as either the subject or the object of a "missing" verb whose sense is understood. Thus, in a sentence such as *John is older than I*, the nominative *I* is traditionally required on the grounds that the sentence is equivalent to *John is older than I am.* In *It does not surprise me as much as him*, the use of the objective *him* is justified by analogy to the sentence *It does not surprise me as much as it surprises him.* • On the other hand, pronouns introduced by *but* or *except* should properly be regarded as objective, demonstrated by the following sentence whose subject is a complex phrase of which a pronoun is a part: *Everybody but us* (not *we*) *has* (and not, of course, *have*) *left.* Since the verb in such a sentence always agrees in person and number with the element preceding *but*, logic similarly favors *No one except them* (not *they*) *has* (not *have*) *seen the report.* Some grammarians nonetheless illogically insist on the nominative in sentences like these and require *no one but they, everyone but he*, and so forth. When the phrase with *but* or *except* is moved to the end of the sentence, however, the objective form of the pronoun is universally acceptable: *Everyone left but me. No one left except us.*

there

There (adverb) meaning "in that place" comes after the noun in constructions introduced by the demonstrative *that: That truck there should be moved away from the front gate.* Use of *there* before the noun, as in *that there truck*, is inappropriate in formal English.

this

This and *that* are both used as demonstrative pronouns to refer to a thought expressed earlier: *The door was unopened; that* (or *this*) *in itself casts doubt on the guard's theory. That* is sometimes prescribed as the better choice in referring to what has gone before (as in the preceding example). When the referent is yet to be mentioned, only *this* is used: *This* (not *that*) *is what bothers me. We have no time to consider late applications.* • *This* is often used in speech as an emphatic variant of the indefinite article *a: This friend of mine inquired about working here. I have this terrible headache.* This usage should be avoided in writing.

thusly

Thusly was formerly used and is now occasionally employed humorously for mock-stylish effects. Otherwise, as a variant of *thus* (itself an adverb), *thusly* is termed unacceptable by most experts.

tight

Tight as an adjective appears after the verb when it is used to qualify the process denoted by the verb (*hold on tight; close it tight*). In a few cases *tight* is the only form that may be used (*sit tight; sleep tight*). In most cases the adverb *tightly* also may be used in this position (*close it tightly*). Before a verb only the adverb is used: *The money supply will be tightly* (not *tight*) *controlled.*

together

Together with, like *in addition to*, is often employed following the subject of a sentence or clause to introduce an addition.

The addition, however, does not alter the number of the verb, which is governed by the subject: *The chairman (singular), together with two aides, is expected in an hour.* The same is true of *along with, as well as, besides, in addition to,* and *like: Common sense as well as training is a requisite for a good job.*

too

Too preceded by *not* or another form of negative is frequently employed as a form of understatement to convey humor or sarcasm: *The workers were not too pleased with the amount of their raises. This applicant is not too bright.* When used for effect, it is employed on all levels. *Not too,* when used to mean approximately "not very," is generally considered informal: *Passage of the bill is not now considered too likely* (unacceptable in written usage to many). *Too* can often be eliminated from such sentences without loss, but if deletion gives undue stress to the negative sense, the writer may find *not very* or *none too* preferable choices. *Too* is often used in writing in place of *moreover* or *in addition* to introduce a sentence, as in *There has been a cutback in oil production. Too, rates have been increasing.* This usage is not so well established as to be entirely acceptable.

torn

Torn, never *tore,* is the standard past participle of the verb *tear. I have torn the book* (not *tore*).

tortuous

Although *tortuous* and *torturous* have a common root, their primary meanings are distinct. *Tortuous* means "twisting" (*a tortuous road*) or by extension "extremely strained or devious" (*tortuous reasoning*). *Torturous* refers primarily to the pain of torture. However, *torturous* also can be used in the sense of "twisted" or "strained," and *tortured* is an even stronger synonym (*tortured reasoning*).

transpire

Transpire has long been used in the sense of "to become known": *It soon transpired that they intended to gain a controlling interest in the corporation.* The meaning "to happen" or "to take place" has come into use more recently: *The board wondered what would transpire next.* This use, though widespread, is unacceptable to a majority of traditionalists and should be avoided so as not to incur criticism.

try

Try and is common in speech for *try to,* especially in established combinations such as *try and stop me* and *try and get some rest.* In most contexts, however, it is not interchangeable with *try to* unless the level is clearly informal. For instance in formal writing, the following would be unacceptable to many critics: *It is a mistake to try and force compliance with a regulation that is so unpopular* (preferably *try to force*).

type

Type is followed by *of* in constructions like that *type of leather.* The variant form omitting *of,* as in *that type leather,* is considered unacceptable, though it is common in many varieties of American English. *Type* is most appropriate when reference is being made to a well-defined or sharply distinct category, as in *that type of chassis, this type of aspirin.* When the categorization is vaguer or less well accepted, *kind* or *sort* is preferable: *That is not the sort of analysis one can trust. This is the kind of annual report that puts you to sleep after the first page.*

unexceptional

Unexceptional is often confused with *unexceptionable.* When the desired meaning is "not open to objection" or "above reproach," the term is *unexceptionable: unexceptionable arguments.*

various

Various, sometimes appearing as a collective noun followed by *of,* as in *He spoke to various of the members,* is an unacceptable usage.

verbal

In the sense "by word of mouth," *verbal* is synonymous with oral. In other senses *verbal* has to do with words, whether written or spoken: *verbal communication* (as opposed, say, to gestures). *Verbal,* when applied to terms such as *agreement, promise, commitment,* or *understanding,* is well established in the sense of *oral.* But anyone who fears misunderstanding may use *oral* instead.

wait

Wait on is correctly used in the sense of "to serve." Though some dialects use *wait on* as an equivalent of *wait for*, in general usage this variation has not yet become established: *We will wait for* (not *on*) *the purchaser's decision.*

want

When *want* is followed immediately by an infinitive construction, it does not take *for: I want you to go* (not *want for you*). When *want* and the infinitive are separated in the sentence, however, *for* is used: *What I want is for you to finish that one first. I want very much for you to take the other company's offer.*

–ward *or* –wards

Since the suffix *–ward* indicates direction, there is no need to use *to the* with it: *The containerized cargo ship is sailing westward* (or *to the west* but not *to the westward*).

way

Way, not *ways,* is the generally accepted form in writing when the term refers to distance: *a long way to go.* The phrase *under way* (meaning "in motion" or "in progress") is written thus in all contexts, including the nautical (not as *under weigh*). Confusion sometimes arises because an anchor is *weighed* and, when off the bottom, is *aweigh.*

well

As well as in the sense of "in addition to" does not have the conjunctive force of *and.* Consequently, in the following examples the singular subjects remain singular and govern singular verbs: *The parent company, as well as its affiliate, was named in the indictment. Harris, as well as Lewis, has bought a personal computer. As well as* is held to be redundant in combination with *both.* Therefore, the following example should be avoided: *Both in theory as well as in practice, the idea is unsound.* Acceptable alternatives are *both in theory and in practice; in theory, as well as in practice.*

what

When *what* is the subject of a clause, it may be construed either as singular or as plural, depending on the sense. It is singular when it is taken as equivalent to *that which* or *the thing which: What seems to be a mechanical problem in the stamping equipment is creating defective panels.* It may be plural when it is equivalent to *those which* or *the things which: What were at first minor incidents have now become major problems in the chemical disposal system.* But when a *what* clause is the subject of a sentence, it will not in general take a plural main verb unless it is the subject of a plural verb in its own clause. Thus we say *what most surprise me are the remarks at the end of the study,* where the main verb *are* is plural because the verb *surprise* is plural in the subordinate clause. But we say *what the person was holding in his lap was* (not *were*) *four letters,* because *what* is not the subject of a plural verb in its own clause. In the same way, we say *what were called predicates by traditional grammarians are called verb phrases by modern linguists,* but *what I am most interested in is* (not *are*) *the latest stock quotations.*

whatever

Whatever (pronoun) and *what ever* are used in questions and statements: *Whatever* (or *what ever*) *made them say that?* Both forms are used, although some meticulous writers prefer the two-word form. The same is true of *whoever, whenever, wherever,* and *however* when used in corresponding senses. For the adjective, only the one-word form is used: *Take whatever office supplies you need.* • When a clause beginning with *whatever* is the subject of its sentence, no comma should be used: *Whatever you do is right.* Otherwise, a comma may be used: *Whatever you do, don't forget to record your expenses.* • When the phrase preceding a restrictive clause is introduced by *whichever* or *whatever, that* should not be used in formal writing. It is held to be incorrect to write *whatever book that you want to look at;* one should write instead *whatever book you want to look at will be sent to your office* or *whichever book costs less* (not *that costs less*) *is fine with us.*

when

In informal style *when* is often used to mean "a situation or event in which," as in *A dilemma is when you don't know which way to turn.* This usage should be avoided in formal writing.

where

When *where* refers to "the place from which," it requires the preposition *from*: *Where did you come from?* When it refers to "the place to which," it requires no preposition: *Where did they go* (better than *where did they go to?*). When *where* refers to "the place at which," it also requires no preposition: *Where are they* (not *where are they at?*).

which

Which sometimes refers to an entire preceding statement rather than to a single word: *The drilling failed to turn up any new reserves, which disturbed the geologist.* In this acceptable example, the reference is clear. But when *which* follows a noun, the antecedent may be in doubt and ambiguity may result: *The inspector filed the complaint, which was a surprise.* If *which* is intended to refer to the entire first clause rather than to *complaint*, the desired sense would be expressed more clearly by this construction: *We learned that the inspector had filed the complaint, and that discovery came as a surprise to us.*

whose

Whose, as the possessive form of a relative pronoun, can refer to both persons and things. Thus, it functions as the possessive of both *who* and *which*. The following example, in which *whose* refers to an inanimate object, is acceptable on all levels: *The car, whose design is ultramodern, is typical of the new styles.* The alternative possessive form *of which* is also used in referring to things but is sometimes cumbersome in application.

why

Why is sometimes held to be redundant in *the reason why*. Although the expression is frequently used, it is found unacceptable by many in this example: *The reason why they opposed the new policy is not clear.* Alternative phrasings include: *Why they opposed the new policy is not clear.*

Their reasons for opposing the new policy are not clear.

win

Win used as a noun in the sense of "victory" or "success" is frequently used in sports reporting and other informal contexts. Some object to its use in more formal writing, as in *An impressive win in the primary would strengthen his position greatly.*

–wise

The suffix *–wise* has a long history of use in the sense "in the manner or direction of" (*clockwise, likewise, otherwise,* and *slantwise*). In recent times, *–wise* has been in vogue as a suffix meaning "with relation to" and attachable to any noun: *saleswise, inflationwise.* But indiscriminate use of these coinages can lead to confusion, as the exact nature of the relation the writer intends is not always clear from the context. Most new or temporary coinages of this sort are thus unacceptable in writing and are considered by many to be inappropriate in speech. The following typical examples are unacceptable in general speech: *The report is not encouraging saleswise. Taxwise, it is an unattractive arrangement.*

with

With does not have the conjunctive force of *and*. Consequently, in the following example the verb is governed by the singular subject and remains singular: *The governor, with his aides, is expected at the trade show on Monday.*

wreak

Wreak is sometimes confused with *wreck*, perhaps because the wreaking of damage may leave a wreck: *The storm wreaked* (not *wrecked*) *havoc along the coast.* The past tense and past participle of *wreak* is *wreaked*, not *wrought*, which is an alternative past tense and past participle of *work*. Thus, the Bible says *God wreaked punishment on sinners*, but Samuel F. B. Morse properly asked, *"What hath God wrought?"*

CLICHÉS

Make no bones about it, the word *cliché* means "a trite or overused expression or idea." The English language is, of course, literally awash and maybe even up to its ears in clichés, many of which originated as metaphors, proverbs, or brief quotations. But it's an open and shut case which is as plain as the nose on your face that historical changes in the language through the ages have taken the stuffing (as well as much of the starch) out of many of these expressions, and, without a doubt, have rendered them virtually meaningless. They are simply often not worth the paper they're printed on. A case in point: What does *fell* in *one fell swoop* mean? As if that's not enough to add insult to injury, *do one's thing* and *keep a low profile* illustrate that such expressions have become old before their time through relentless use and are now as stale as yesterday's bread. They are like a broken record, and a little of that, as everyone knows full well, goes a long way—as the crow flies, that is.

But if we may be so bold as to play devil's advocate, we must warn you that one man's meat is another man's poison and, strictly speaking, to pooh-pooh clichés altogether will only throw more fuel on the fire and stir up a hornet's nest of controversy. Since most clichés express rather clear meanings, every writer is in the same boat and will have to determine whether a cliché, all things being equal, doesn't actually offer a shade of meaning that is hard to convey by fresher alternative wording. After all, one doesn't want to compare apples to oranges—or write that way—does one? It all boils down to the fact that the choice is really six of one, half a dozen of the other. If the process of substitution is too hard a row for the writer to hoe then rest assured that use of some of the phrases that follow may be advisable and well worth one's while; sooner or later, lest we forget, writing around the formulaic expressions may produce a fate worse than hackneyed language: strained, wordy, or ambiguous discourse that will put you out of the frying pan and into the fire. Foregoing the use of clichés may be pennywise and pound foolish, and in so doing one might cut off one's nose to spite one's face—hardly a viable option under any circumstances.

But, all things considered, you can bet your bottom dollar that few on the following list are truly indispensable. We can certainly live without them, and— a word to the wise—writers of fresh, original prose who have the courage of their convictions, practice what they preach, stick to their guns, and dot all their *i*'s and cross all their *t*'s will avoid most clichés like the plague!

a little of that goes a long way	as the crow flies	bend (*or* lean) over backward
absence makes the heart grow fonder	at a loss for words (*or* never at a loss . . . .)	best foot forward
add insult to injury	at first blush	best-laid plans
age before beauty	at one fell swoop	best of all possible worlds
agonizing reappraisal	(an) axe to grind	best of both worlds
agree to disagree	babe in the woods	better late than never
albatross around one's neck	backhanded compliment	between a rock and a hard place
all in a day's work	bag and baggage	between the devil and the deep blue sea
all in all	bark up the wrong tree	beyond the call of duty
all in the same boat	bated breath	beyond the pale
all over but the shouting	bathed in tears	bigger than all outdoors
all things being equal	battle of the giants	bigger than both of us
all things considered	battle royal	bigger (*or* larger) than life
all things to all men (*or* people)	beard the lion in his den	bite off more than one can chew
all work and no play	beat a dead horse	bite the bullet
apple of one's eye	beat a hasty retreat	bite the hand that feeds one
apple-pie order	beat around the bush	bitter pill to swallow
armed to the teeth	before hell freezes over	black-and-white issue
arms of Morpheus	beg to disagree	bloody but unbowed
as luck would have it	beggar description	bloom is off the rose

bloom of youth
blue-sky thinking (or idea)
blush of shame
blushing bride
boggle the mind
bolt from the blue
bone of contention
boom to bust
born with a silver spoon in one's
  mouth
bosom of the family
brave the elements
breathe a sigh of relief
bright and early
bright as a button
bright-eyed and bushy-tailed
bright future
bring home the bacon
brown as a berry
budding genius
bull in a china shop
burn the midnight oil
busy as a bee
butter wouldn't melt in one's
  mouth
by leaps and bounds
by the same token
calm before the storm
can't see the forest for the trees
carry (or have) a chip on one's
  shoulder
carry its share of the burden
(a) case in point
cash cow
caught on the horns of a dilemma
caught red-handed
chip off the old block
clear as a bell
clear as mud
coals to Newcastle
coin a phrase
cold as ice
(a) cold day in July (or Hell)
come (with) hat in hand
compare apples to oranges
conspicuous by one's absence
cool as a cucumber
cross the Rubicon
crying need
crying shame
cut a long story short
cut off one's nose to spite one's
  face
cynosure of all eyes
daily repast
David and Goliath
dead as a doornail
dead giveaway
dead in the water
deaf as a post
death warmed over
defend to the death one's right
  to . . . .
depths of despair
diamond in the rough

die in harness
die is cast
distaff side
do it up brown
do one's thing
dog in the manger
dog of a company
dollars to doughnuts
doom is sealed
doomed to disappointment
down in the dumps
down in the mouth
down one's alley
down-side risk
draw the line
drown one's sorrows
drunk as a lord (or skunk)
dull thud
dyed in the wool
ear to the ground
early bird gets the worm
early to bed, early to rise . . . .
easier said than done
eat one's hat (or words)
epoch-making
eternal reward
eyes of the world
face the music
fair sex
fall between the cracks
fall on deaf ears
far be it from me
(a) far cry
fast and loose
fate worse than death
fat's in the fire
feather in one's cap
feather one's nest
feel one's oats
festive board
few and far between
few well-chosen words
fiddle while Rome burns
fight like a tiger
fill the bill
filthy lucre
fine and dandy
first and foremost
fit as a fiddle
flash in the pan
flat as a flounder (or pancake)
flesh and blood
fly off the handle
fond farewell
food for thought
fool's gold
fool's paradise
fools rush in
foot in one's mouth
foot in the door
foot the bill
foregone conclusion
forewarned is forearmed
frame of reference
free as a bird (or the air)

fresh as a daisy
generous to a fault
gentle as a lamb
get a jump on the competition
get down to brass tacks
get one's back (or dander) up
get one's ducks in a row
get one's feet wet
gift of gab
gild the lily
go belly up
(a) good time was had by all
goose that laid the golden egg
grain of salt
grand and glorious
graphic account
green-eyed monster
grin like a Cheshire cat
grind to a halt
hail fellow well met
hale and hearty
hand that rocks the cradle
handsome is as handsome does
handwriting on the wall
hapless victim
happy as a lark
happy pair
hard row to hoe
haughty stare
haul (or rake) over the coals
have a foot in the door
have a leg up
head over heels
heart of gold
heave a sigh of relief
heir apparent
hew to the line
high and dry
high as a kite
high on the hog
hit the nail on the head
hit the spot
hitch one's star to
hook, line, and sinker
hook or crook
horse and pony show
hot as a firecracker (or pistol or
  six-shooter)
hue and cry
hungry as a bear (or lion)
if (the) truth be told
in full swing
in no uncertain terms
in on the ground floor
in seventh heaven
inspiring sight
in the final (or last) analysis
in the limelight
in the long run
in the nick of time
in this day and age
iron out a difficulty
irons in the fire
irony of fate
irreparable damage (or loss)

it goes without saying
it is interesting to note
it never rains but it pours
it's a small world
it's an ill wind
it's six of one and a half a dozen of
the other
it stands to reason
it takes all kinds to make a world
it takes two to tango
(the) jig is up
just deserts
keep a low profile
keep a stiff upper lip
keep one's chin up
keep (or lose) one's cool
keep one's ear to the ground
knock into a cocked hat
knock on wood
labor of love
land of milk and honey
land of opportunity
land office business
land war in Asia
last but not least
last straw
law unto one's self
lead to the altar
lean and hungry look
lean over backward
leave holding the bag
leave in the lurch
leave no stone unturned
left-handed compliment
leg up on the competition
lend a helping hand
lest we forget
let one's hair down
let the cat out of the bag
let well enough alone
lick into shape
lick one's wounds
lid of secrecy
light at the end of the tunnel
like a house afire (or on fire)
like a newborn babe
limp as a dish rag
lock, stock, and barrel
long arm of the law
look a gift horse in the mouth
look for a needle in a haystack
(as) luck would have it
mad as a hatter (or March hare)
mad as a hornet (or wet hen)
mad dash
make a clean breast of
make a long story short
make a virtue of necessity
make bricks without straw
make ends meet
make hay while the sun shines
make no bones about
mantle of snow
matter of life and death
meaningful dialogue

meek as Moses
meet one's Waterloo
method in one's madness
milk of human kindness
mince words
mind one's p's and q's
miss the boat
moment of truth
monarch of all one surveys
month of Sundays
moot question (or point)
more easily said than done
more sinned against than sinning
more than meets the eye
(the) more the merrier
motley crew
naked truth
name is legion
necessary evil
needs no introduction
neither fish nor fowl
neither here nor there
neither hide nor hair
never a dull moment
never say die
nip in the bud
none the worse for wear
no holds barred
no sooner said than done
not to be sneezed (or sniffed) at
not wisely but too well
not worth its salt
not worth the paper it's printed
on
nothing new under the sun
of a high order
old before one's time
on cloud nine
on one's uppers
on the ball (or stick)
on the best (or unimpeachable)
authority
on the bum (or the fritz)
on the lam
on the other hand
on the QT
on the wagon
once in a blue moon
one man's meat is another man's
poison
one's own worst enemy
open and shut case
open secret
opportunity knocks
other side of the coin
other things being equal
out of the frying pan and into the
fire
over a barrel
overcome with emotion
paint the town red
pandemonium reigned
part and parcel
pay the piper
paying its own freight

penny for one's thoughts
pennywise, pound foolish
perfect gentleman
pet peeve
pillar of society
pillar to post
pinch pennies
plain and simple
plain as day
plain as the nose on one's face
play fast and loose
play hardball
play it by ear
play second fiddle
play the devil's advocate
(a) plum of a job (or position)
plumb the depths
(at this) point in time
point with pride
poor but honest
(the) powers that be
pretty as a picture
pretty kettle of fish
pretty penny
psychological moment
pull no punches
pull the wool over one's eyes
pure as the driven snow
put on the dog
put on the Ritz
quick and dirty
quick as lightning (or a flash)
quiet as a mouse
rack one's brains
rain cats and dogs
raise Cain
raise the roof
read the riot act
(the) real McCoy
red as a beet
red-letter day
reign supreme
render a decision
rest assured
ring true
ripe old age
rising star
roll up one's sleeves
rollercoaster earnings
rub one the wrong way
run it up the flagpole and see if
anyone salutes it
sadder but wiser
sad to relate
save for a rainy day
seal one's fate (or doom)
second to none
seething mass
sell like hot cakes
separate the men from the boys
separate the sheep from the goats
shoot from the hip
short end of the stick
(a) shot in the arm
shout from the rooftops

show one's hand
show one's true colors
show the white feather
sick and tired
sight to behold
silver lining
sing like a bird
skeleton in one's closet
small world
smell a rat
sow one's wild oats
spinning (or turning over) in one's
  grave
spinning straw into gold
stagger the imagination
stair-step earnings
start (or get) the ball rolling
steal one's thunder
stem to stern
stick in one's craw
stick out like a sore thumb
stick to one's guns
stick to one's knitting
stir up a hornet's nest
straight and narrow
straight from the shoulder
straw in the wind
straw that broke the camel's back
strictly speaking
strong as an ox
stubborn as a mule
sweat of one's brow
sweet sixteen

sweet smell of success
sweeten the pot (or kitty)
take a dim view of
take a raincheck
take it easy
take off one's hat to
take the bull by the horns
take up the cudgels
talk through one's hat
tell someone who cares
that is to say
that's for sure
throw caution to the wind
throw in the towel (or sponge)
throw one's hat in the ring
throw the book at
time hangs heavy
time immemorial
time of one's life
tip the scales
tired as a dog
tit for tat
to tell the truth
to the manner born
too funny for words
too little, too late
tried and true
trip the light fantastic
true blue
turn over a new leaf
ugly duckling
uncharted seas

up and comer
up the creek without a paddle
up to one's ears
up-side potential
usually reliable source(s)
vale of tears
viable option
view with alarm
walk on eggshells
wash one's hands of
wax poetic (or eloquent)
wear two hats
wee (small) hours
well worth one's while (or trouble)
wet behind the ears
wet to the skin
what makes the world go 'round
when all is said and done
when you come right down to it
whistle Dixie
whistle in the dark
wide-open spaces
wise as an owl
without a doubt
without further ado
wolf in sheep's clothing
work one's fingers to the bone
worst-case scenario
you can bank on that
you can bet your bottom dollar
you can take that to the bank

REDUNDANT EXPRESSIONS

Redundancy—needless repetition of ideas—is one of the principal obstacles to writing clear, precise prose. The list below gives some common redundant expressions. The elements repeated in the phrases and in the brief definitions are italicized. To eliminate redundancy, delete the italic elements in the phrases.

anthracite *coal*
(a hard *coal* having a high carbon content)

old **antique**
(an object having special value because of its *age*, especially a work of art or handicraft more than 100 years *old*)

ascend *upward*
(to go or move *upward*)

assemble *together*
(to bring or gather *together*)

pointed **barb**
(a sharp *point* projecting in reverse direction to the main point of a weapon or tool)

first **beginning**
(the *first* part)

big *in size*
(of considerable *size*)

bisect *in two*
(to cut *into two* equal parts)

blend *together*
(to combine, mix, or go well *together*)

capitol *building*
(a *building* in which a legislative body meets)

coalesce *together*
(to grow or come *together* so as to form a whole)

collaborate *together* or *jointly*
(to work *together*, especially in a *joint* effort)

fellow **colleague**
(a *fellow* member of a profession, staff, or academic faculty)

congregate *together*
(to bring or come *together* in a crowd)

connect *together*
(to join or fasten *together*)

consensus *of opinion*
(collective *opinion*)

courthouse *building*
(a *building* in which judicial courts or county government offices are housed)

habitual **custom**
(a *habitual* practice)

descend *downward*
(to move, slope, extend, or incline *downward*)

doctorate *degree*
(the *degree* or status of a doctor)

endorse a check *on the back*
(to write one's signature *on the back of*, e.g., a check)

erupt *violently*
(to emerge *violently* or to become *violently* active

explode *violently*
(to burst *violently* from internal pressure)

real **fact**
(something with *real*, demonstrable existence)

passing **fad**
(a *transitory* fashion)

few *in number*
(amounting to or made up of a *small number*)

founder *and sink*
(to *sink* beneath the water)

basic **fundamental**
(a *basic* or essential part)

fuse *together*
(to mix *together* by or as if by melting)

opening **gambit**
(a remark intended to *open* a conversation)

gather *together*
(to come *together* or cause to come *together*)

free **gift**
(something bestowed voluntarily and *without compensation*)

past **history**
(a narrative of *past* events; something that took place *in the past*)

hoist *up*
(to raise or haul *up* with or as if with a mechanical device)

current or *present* **incumbent**
(one *currently* holding an office)

new **innovation**
(something *new* or unusual)

join *together*
(to bring or put *together* so as to make continuous or form a unit)

knots *per hour*
(a unit of speed, one nautical mile *per hour*, approximately 1.15 statute miles *per hour*)

large *in size*
(greater than average *in size*)

merge *together*
(to blend or cause to blend *together* gradually)

necessary **need**
(something *necessary* or wanted)

universal **panacea**
(a remedy for *all* diseases, evils, or difficulties)

continue to **persist**
(to *continue* in existence)

individual **person**
(an *individual* human being)

advance **planning**
(detailed methodology, programs, or schemes worked out *beforehand* for the accomplishment of an objective)

chief or *leading* or *main* **protagonist**
(the *leading* character in a Greek drama or other literary form; a *leading* or *principal* figure)

original **prototype**
(an *original* type, form, or instance that is a model on which later stages are based or judged)

protrude *out*
(to push or thrust *outward*)

recall *back*
(to summon *back* to awareness; to bring *back*)

recoil *back*
(to kick or spring *back*; to shrink *back* in fear or loathing; to fall *back*)

new **recruit**
(a *new* member of a body or organization, especially of a military force)

recur *again* or *repeatedly*
(to occur *again* or *repeatedly*)

temporary **reprieve**
(a *temporary* relief, as from danger or pain)

revert *back*
(to *return* to a *former* state)

short *in length* or *height*
(having very little *length* or *height*)

shuttle *back and forth*
(to move, go, or travel *back and forth*)

skirt *around*
(to move or pass *around* rather than across
or through)

small *in size*
(characterized by relatively little *size* or
slight dimensions)

tall *in height*
(having greater than average *height*)

two **twins**
(one of *two* offspring born at the same
birth; one of *two* identical or similar persons, animals, or things)

completely **unanimous**
(being in *complete* harmony, accord, or
agreement)

visible *to the eye*
(perceptible *to the eye*)

from **whence**
(*from* where; *from* what place; *from* what
origin or source)

THE BUSINESS LETTER

Most of us have been late or forgetful in paying a bill at one time or another and
perhaps have received one of these letters:

> Dear Mr. and Mrs. McKenzie:
>
> Perhaps it has slipped your mind, but your account with
> our store is now sixty days past due. Unless you get in
> touch with us, or mail your payment within five days of
> the date of this notice [and the letter is always dated three
> weeks ago], we will have no choice but to close your ac-
> count to further purchases.
>
> If your payment and this letter have crossed in the
> mail, however, please consider this as our thank-you to
> an especially valued customer.
>
> Sincerely,
>
>
> Credit Department

And have you wondered what kind of letter a loan shark might send out under
the same set of circumstances?

> Dear McKenzie:
>
> Perchance it has slipped your mind, but you have not yet
> made good on the $5,000 PLUS 18% monthly interest. If
> you do not pay up tomorrow, we will be forced to rub you
> out with a steamroller. Get the point?
>
> If your payment and this letter have crossed in the
> mail, however, please consider this as our thank-you to
> an especially valued client.
>
> Warm regards,
>
>
> Loans R Us

What does all this have to do with business letter writing in general? Plenty. The two letters shown here fail to fulfill their objectives because they try to do too much. On the one hand, each letter is intended as a threat to a deadbeat. But on the other hand, the writers, clearly mindful of the fact that the billings might not have gone out on time, have tried to be courteous to the recipients—just in case. The incongruous combination of threat-cum-thank-you results in unclear signals to the reader—signals that cause confusion on the part of the reader. Confusion and opaqueness are just two of many characteristics that you do not want to have in your own letters, regardless of the content of the message.

We have said before in this book that the business letter speaks for you, your employer, and your entire company. If the letter is muddled, the writer is seen to be muddled; if the letter is long, boring, and diffuse, the writer is viewed in the same light. If the letter makes one point and then contradicts itself in the next paragraph, the writer looks incompetent. However, if the letter is crisp, clean, neat, and complete, and if it gets right to the point and speaks loud and clear, it— and everyone associated with its writing—will convey the desired impression. *That* is the kind of letter you want to be responsible for.

Writing Effective Business Letters

The main stylistic features of business letters have been explained and illustrated in detail in Chapter Six. This section discusses the actual techniques used in composing good letters for your employer. At times you will have to write letters for the employer or in the name of the company. When doing so, keep in mind that the reader will most likely be as busy as, or busier than you; hence, keep the message short and right to the point. W. Somerset Maugham is said to have described the process of good writing thus: "Cut, cut, cut. And when you've finished cutting, cut some more." This rule is especially appropriate to today's business correspondence: remember, somebody's meter is always running and the costs of writing time, keyboarding time, and reading time do mount up. Here are some specific points to keep in mind when composing letters:

1. Get right to the point; the reader may have a pile of mail to get through.

2. Keep your sentences short and crisp; break down overly long ones into separate sentences if you can do so without making the prose choppy.

3. Use the active voice (as *We are excited about your proposal*) instead of the passive voice (*Your proposal has been met with excitement on our part*); while the active voice conveys the idea straightforwardly and precisely, the passive voice often blunts the intended effect and requires more words.

4. Precede the bad news with the good news whenever possible; this makes the recipient feel better:

```
Thank you, Bob, for your proposal with regard to the
product marketing survey. I really think it's great
that you want to use the FRT Research Corporation's
sampling techniques: this shows that your research
plan is state-of-the-art. However, we simply don't
have that kind of money in the budget at this point.
```

> I will bring the matter up with Mr. Lee as soon as he returns; perhaps some fiscal adjustment can be made during the next Operating Committee meeting.

5. Avoid the use of bureaucratic jargon (*Operational lifecycle statistics re the configuration of this weapons system belie the system's estimated utility vis-à-vis strategic plans* et cetera) but at the same time try not to be folksy or cutesy (*Gosh, we'd love to talk to you guys about your proposal*). A straightforward businesslike approach is always acceptable.

6. Try to order your thoughts and the paragraphs containing them in a logical, coherent manner. (See the material on paragraphing at the end of the section on business grammar earlier in this chapter.)

7. Use—but don't overuse—the recipient's name in the body of the letter (see the example in #4 above). Overuse of the recipient's name in direct address will make your message sound like a canned sweepstakes announcement.

Types of Business Letters

The letters that follow are intended to help you in the composition of some of the communications often written in offices. You can use them as guides in formulating messages in your own words:

1. A sales letter, page 402
2. A collection letter, page 403
3. An order letter, page 403
4. An inquiry letter, page 404
5. A cancellation letter, page 404
6. A letter of appreciation, page 405
7. An application letter, page 405
8. A reservation letter, page 406
9. An adjustment letter, page 406
10. A transmittal letter, page 407
11. An invitation response, page 407
12. A letter of introduction, page 408

A Sales Letter

Ms. Laura Fennimore
President
Monroe Publishing Co.
458 LaSalle Street
City, US 98765

Dear Ms. Fennimore:

What would you say if someone offered you a way to cut
your workload by 50%? Word processing equipment can do
just that, according to several studies on office productivity.

I understand from our computer representative, who
deals regularly with your company, that Monroe Publishing does not use word processing equipment. You may not
be aware of it, Ms. Fennimore, but American Data Processors is more than the third largest mainframe computer
maker. We are also the leading word processing company
whose equipment is used by more Fortune 500 companies
than any other.

I'm sure you have heard about the benefits of word processing equipment to an operation such as yours. To provide you with still more information, I am enclosing a
brochure of the latest studies on word processing and
office productivity. I am also enclosing a brochure of
our line of word processors.

Should you need more information about word processing
and our products in particular, I would be glad to meet
with you. Better yet, I would like to invite you to our
ADP demonstration center where you can see our models in
action. I will call you in several days to see if you
would like me to make the arrangements for a visit.

Yours truly,

William Warner
District Sales Director

A Collection Letter

Mr. Howard Lewitt
Western New York Hardware
737 State Street
Anywhere, US 12345

Dear Mr. Lewitt:

While we understand that the recession has been hard on
many retailers during the past year, it is important
that all members of our buyers' cooperative live up to
the terms of our credit agreement.

Your account is now 90 days past due, and we must request that you bring it up to date. If special circumstances surround this delinquency, circumstances preventing you from meeting your obligations, please call
me at (216) 589-3300, and explain the matter to me.

Sincerely,

Mike Hotchkiss
Credit Manager

An Order Letter

Mr. Anthony DiDominici
Manager
Legg & Greene Inc.
5475 Geary Boulevard
City, US 12345

Dear Mr. DiDominici:

Please accept the following order for shipment to Medical Associates, 12 State Street, City, US 98765:

Quantity	Item	Unit price	Total
1	balance beam scale (to 400 pounds) Cat. No. 133-6466-01	$250	$250

We would like to receive this in less than the normal
two-week delivery time mentioned in your catalog. Could
you please ship this via UPS Second Day Delivery?

Sincerely,

Melanie Nelson, MD

An Inquiry Letter

Ms. Jane Prince
Executive Director
Department of Transportation
One Statehouse Plaza
City, US 12345

Dear Ms. Prince:

I understand from the newspapers that the state Department of Transportation has recently published a study
entitled ''The Impact of Trucking Deregulation on Missouri Common Carriers.'' Would you please send two
copies of that study to me at the above address? Thank
you for your help.

Cordially,

Lewis Shepard
President
Shepard Shippers

A Cancellation Letter

Mr. Howard Lewitt
Western New York Hardware
737 State Street
Anywhere, US 12345

Dear Mr. Lewitt:

We regret to inform you that as of today, your credit
line has been closed to further purchases. Mr. Lewitt,
we have approached you many times by mail and by telephone to remind you of the importance of keeping your
account current. Unfortunately, you have failed to do so
and your account is now 120 days in arrears. This leaves
us no other choice but to take drastic action.

We will not be able to reopen your account until it is
brought back up to date. Please call me to discuss how
you intend to repay this debt.

Regretfully,

Mike Hotchkiss
Credit Manager

A Letter of Appreciation

Melanie Nelson, MD
Medical Associates
12 State Street
City, US 98765

Dear Dr. Nelson:

Thank you for your recent order, which we have shipped
out via our express service according to your request.
It is always a pleasure to welcome a new customer to
Legg & Greene.

We know the extent to which joint medical practices such
as yours are expanding in your city and we stand ready
to serve whatever equipment needs you may have in the
months and years ahead. I'm enclosing a copy of our
spring/summer catalogue, just off the press.

Sincerely,

Anthony DiDominici
Manager

An Application Letter

Stanley Broughton, Esq.
Society of City Trial Attorneys
4790 Memorial Drive
City, US 56789

Dear Mr. Broughton:

It was a pleasure meeting with you and Leslie Maguire
during lunch Tuesday. It's always nice to find other
Brooklyn Law School graduates in our city.

I was particularly impressed with what you had to say
about the Society of City Trial Attorneys, and I am taking you up on your offer to become a member. Please consider this my application so that you may recommend me
to the membership committee.

Enclosed is a copy of my résumé, as well as several letters of recommendation. Thank you for your interest; I
hope to be hearing from you soon.

Yours truly,

James Newton, Esq.

A Reservation Letter

Mr. William Sewell
Reservations Manager
Queen Mary Hyatt Hotel
P.O. Box 20396
Anywhere, US 12345

Dear Mr. Sewell:

This is to confirm our telephone conversation of April 24, 1984. Mary Wasser, President of Wasser Communications, and her husband, John Wasser, will require an executive stateroom beginning the afternoon of May 15, 1984. They will be departing on May 20.

As discussed, Wasser Communications will also require four one-bedroom suites for John Sullivan, Vice President; Sarah Washington, Treasurer; William Searsima, Accountant; and Jack Schrager, Administrative Assistant. All billing will be to Wasser Communications' American Express account, number _____. Please call me at (123)456-7890, if there are any complications.

Sincerely,

Jack Schrager

An Adjustment Letter

Ms. Julius Schorsch
Office Manager
First Federal Savings & Loan Association
887 First Avenue
Metropolis, US 33440

Dear Ms. Schorsch:

We were very sorry to learn about the terrible condition of the electronic typewriters we sent you on September 1; the damage was apparently caused by the shipper, but I have personally seen to it that replacement models will be shipped out immediately at no cost to you.

I understand the inconvenience you have undergone and so am sending the new typewriters via Express Freight. I also have enclosed in the shipment a small token of our appreciation for your patience.

I hope that this takes care of a very unfortunate situation. Should you need additional office equipment and supplies from our extensive line, I hope you will continue to think of Meenan Office Supply.

Sincerely,

Richard Meenan, Jr.

A Transmittal Letter

Mr. Frank Hart
Staff Writer
The City *Times-Republic*
5811 River Street
City, US 98765

Dear Mr. Hart:

Thank you for your interest in interviewing our chairman, Mr. Clements. While Mr. Clements would be delighted
to meet with you to discuss Midwest Barge and Shipping,
all press interviews are scheduled through our Public
Relations department. I am therefore forwarding your
request to Jane LaRosa, Director of Corporate Communications. You should be hearing from her via telephone
shortly.

Thank you again for your interest, and I look forward to
meeting you when an appointment has been arranged.

Sincerely,

Deloris Martin
Secretary to Mr. Clements

An Invitation Response

The Honorable Harriet Hay
Governor of State
Governor's Mansion
City, US 12345

Dear Governor Hay:

Congratulations on your recent election victory. We all
look forward to six more years of your sensible steward-
ship.

Of course, I will be honored to attend dinner at 8:00
p.m. on December 1. As you already know, I always find
our periodic meetings extremely enjoyable, and I will be
most interested in discussing the particulars of the
legislature's bill on a corporate tax increase.

Cordially yours,

James A. Kirby

A Letter of Introduction

```
Stanley Broughton, Esq.
Society of City Trial Attorneys
4790 Memorial Drive
City, US 56789

Dear Mr. Broughton:

This is a letter of introduction for James Newton, Esq.,
who has worked for this firm for the past two years. I
understand he is interested in joining the Society of
City Trial Attorneys, and I wholeheartedly endorse his
application.

Mr. Newton is a bright, hard-working attorney who has
taken on several difficult cases for us and has per-
formed superbly. He is clearly one who will make a name
for himself in your area.

As you may know, Mr. Newton's credentials and law school
record are impeccable, and he is well-versed in your
state law, since he served as a judicial assistant to
criminal court Judge John M. Mahoney before being em-
ployed in our locale.

If you need any further information about Mr. Newton,
please feel free to call me at (123)673-5000.

Sincerely,


Clifford Taylor Ingraham, III
```

FOOTNOTES AND BIBLIOGRAPHIES

Footnotes

Footnotes may be a major part of a study—especially an academic one. Although the members of our Advisory Board inform us that they do not have to typewrite footnotes and bibliographies, we have nevertheless included this section for the benefit of those of you who are employed in academic or research settings where such material is often used. Footnotes may be included at the bottom of the text page on which the quoted matter appears, or they may be grouped at the very end of the paper. Footnotes are numbered in the order of their appearance in the text. The first line of a footnote is indented by five spaces and runover lines are typed flush with the left margin. (For detailed typewriting guidelines see Chapter Six under the section on corporate report formats.)

The author's given name appears first, followed by the surname, a *comma*, and the title of the work cited. The publishing data (location of publisher, name of publisher, date of publication, etc.) appear next in the note, followed by the pages cited. Here are some sample footnotes ordered according to the kind of publication and nature of the authorship. Follow these examples when styling your employer's footnotes.

books:

one author

[1]Samuel Barash, *How to Reduce Your Real Estate Taxes* (New York: Arco, 1979), p. 78.

two or three authors

[2]James Sinclair and Harry Schhultz, *How You Can Profit From Gold* (Westport, CT: Crown/Arlington House, 1980), p. 50.

more than three authors

[3]Kiril Sokoloff, et al., *Investing in the Future: 10 New Industries and over 75 Key Growth Companies That Are Changing the Face of Corporate America* (Garden City, NY: Doubleday, 1982), p. 121.

translation

[4]Aleksandr I. Solzhenitsyn, *The Gulag Archipelago*, trans. Thomas P. Whitney (New York: Harper & Row, 1973), p. 25.

later edition

[5]Lloyd G. Reynolds, *Labor Economics and Labor Relations*, 7th ed. (Englewood Cliffs, NJ: Prentice-Hall, 1978), p. 364.

corporate author

[6]*Report of the Commission on the Humanities* (New York: American Council of Learned Societies, 1964), p. 3.

anonymous

[7]*The American Heritage Dictionary*, 2nd college ed. (Boston: Houghton Mifflin, 1982), p. 1101.

articles:

from a journal paged consecutively throughout its annual volume

[8]Gordon Young, ''The Miracle Metal Platinum,'' *National Geographic*, Vol. 164, No. 5 (Nov. 1984), 686–706.

from a journal paged separately for each of its issues

[9]Roscoe L. Egger, Jr., ''Maintaining the Viability of the U.S. Tax System,'' *Journal of Accountancy*, 156, No. 6 (Dec. 1983), 84–90.

from a monthly magazine

[10]Henry Eason, ''Environmentalists Take the Offensive,'' *Nation's Business*, Apr. 1983, p. 26.

from a weekly magazine

[11]Paul G. Engel, ''Leasing Wins New 'Respectability,' '' *Industry Week,* 12 Dec. 1983, pp. 53–56.

from a daily newspaper

[12]L. Erik Calonius, ''Why Are Japanese Cultivating Coffee in Jamaican Hills?'' *The Wall Street Journal,* 2 Feb. 1984, p. 1, col. 4.

letter to the editor

[13]Martin Frost, Letter, *Forbes* (30 Jan. 1984), p. 14.

Bibliography

A bibliography is an alphabetically ordered list of publications appearing at the end of a study or other long paper. The bibliography may contain works cited by the author, but it also may contain works of general interest to the reader. While a bibliography contains essentially the same data as those found in footnotes, the two styles differ markedly. For one thing, bibliographic entries are unnumbered. For another, the authors' names are ordered alphabetically by surname: the surname appears first followed by a comma, the given name, and a *period*. Pagination in books need not always be shown. And bibliographies, unlike footnotes, are hanging-indented: the first line is typed flush left, and all runover lines are block indented by five character spaces. In the following examples you can see the proper format and style of a bibliography. The titles used in the section on footnotes have been used here, too, so that you can better see the differences in styling. We have not entered the titles in alphabetical order by authors' surnames, however, because we feel that you, the reader, will be more interested in the types of entries and their stylings:

books:

one author

Bladen, Ashby. *How to Cope with the Developing Financial Crisis.* New York: McGraw–Hill, 1979.

two or three authors

Sinclair, James, and Harry Schhultz. *How You Can Profit From Gold.* Westport, CT: Crown/Arlington House, 1980.

more than three authors

Sokoloff, Kiril, et al. *Investing in the Future: 10 New Industries and over 75 Key Growth Companies That Are Changing the Face of Corporate America.* Garden City, NY: Doubleday, 1982.

translation

Solzhenitsyn, Aleksandr I. *The Gulag Archipelago.* Trans. Thomas P. Whitney. New York: Harper & Row, 1973.

later edition

Reynolds, Lloyd G. *Labor Economics and Labor Relations.*
7th ed. Englewood Cliffs, NJ: Prentice-Hall, 1978.

corporate author

Report of the Commission on the Humanities. New York:
American Council of Learned Societies, 1964.

anonymous

The American Heritage Dictionary, 2nd college ed. Boston: Houghton Mifflin, 1982.

articles:

from a journal paged consecutively throughout its annual volume

Young, Gordon. ''The Miracle Metal Platinum.'' *National
Geographic* Vol. 164, No. 5 (Nov. 1984), 686–706.

from a journal paged separately for each of its issues

Egger, Roscoe L., Jr. ''Maintaining the Viability of the
U.S. Tax System.'' *Journal of Accountancy,* 156, No.
6 (Dec. 1983), 84–90.

from a monthly magazine

Eason, Henry. ''Environmentalists Take the Offensive.''
Nation's Business, Apr. 1983, p. 26.

from a weekly magazine

Engel, Paul G. ''Leasing Wins New 'Respectability.' ''
Industry Week, 12 Dec. 1983, pp. 53–56.

from a daily newspaper

Calonius, L. Erik. ''Why Are Japanese Cultivating Coffee in Jamaican Hills?'' *The Wall Street Journal,* 2
Feb. 1984, p. 1, col. 4.

letter to the editor

Frost, Martin. Letter, *Forbes* (30 Jan. 1984), p. 14.

12

Preparing Technical and Scientific Material

Palmer T. Van Dyke • *Writer/Editor, Lawrence Livermore
National Laboratory*

INTRODUCTION

The role of the professional secretary in preparing technical and scientific material is not well established and may vary over a broad range of responsibilities, depending on the employer's needs and the nature of the organization. In this respect the secretary's role is more fluid than it is in traditional business settings. Because such a role presents both challenges and opportunities, it is important that the secretary try to establish the employer's expectations as early as possible.

Many institutions that deal routinely with technical and scientific material, such as government or private organizations and large aerospace companies, employ a staff of technical writers or editors who are responsible for turning draft manuscripts into finished products. Such organizations often have, in addition, a technical typing pool especially trained to deal with technical and scientific material. In such cases, the secretary's role may be limited to typing from handwritten material rough-draft manuscripts that are then sent to the editorial staff for further processing. In other institutional settings, such as colleges or universities, the secretary's role may be significantly expanded, with the employer relying more heavily on the secretary to produce a final manuscript.

Whatever the institutional setting, however, the secretary who is expected to deal with technical and scientific material in any capacity faces special challenges. These challenges can be frustrating or surprisingly rewarding, depending on how you approach them. First, it is misleading to think of "science" as a single cohesive body of knowledge. There are many sciences, each with its own subject matter, tradition, specialized vocabulary, guiding principles, and techniques. Being exposed to a science for the first time is a little like being confronted with a new language and the underlying ideas it expresses. The sooner you learn the language of whatever field you are working in, the more interesting your job will become and the more effectively you will carry out your assignments. A number of books have been written for the scientific layperson in almost every field. Don't hesitate to ask the scientists you work with to recommend one that deals with their subject. In addition, several good general periodicals are devoted to explaining advances in the sciences. *Scientific American*, available on most newsstands, is one of the oldest and most comprehensive of these.

Most sciences have two aspects, basic science and applied science. Basic science attempts to understand how the things in the natural world come to be as they are and why things happen as they do: the origin of mountain chains, the causes of the weather, the shape of a galaxy, the pattern of a snowflake, the source of the sun's light, the reasons that objects have different colors, the origin of the universe, and countless other problems. Applied science uses this understanding to devise new or improved ways of doing things. Many of our modern technologies—computers, stereo systems, space flight, lasers, new fabrics and materials, new energy sources, to mention only a few—were made possible by new insights into why things happen.

Another challenge to the secretary employed in a technical setting arises from the fact that many of the sciences rely heavily on the language of mathematics, which embodies a special notation that at first may seem strange and forbidding. As we shall see, however, it is possible to understand much of this notation without formal training in mathematics and without a detailed understanding of the more complex mathematical procedures that scientists use. This chapter explains the role of some of the notation used in the sciences, provides some rules of style, and describes procedures for preparing various kinds of scientific and technical material. It is by no means comprehensive, and you will find that, as in any field, much of what you will need to know will be acquired on the job by asking questions in the same spirit of adventure that scientists bring to their work.

FORMATTING MATHEMATICAL MATERIAL

This section introduces you to some of the basic ideas and notations used in mathematics and to some of the rules of style for formatting mathematical material. You will find it very helpful if you learn to recognize some of the different kinds of mathematical expressions and understand the roles played by the various signs and symbols they contain. Although it is not feasible in a brief survey to discuss all of the special symbols and notations you are likely to encounter, this section is designed to convey some of the flavor of what mathematics is about. The ability to see the *form* of a mathematical expression will help you to type it more accurately.

Some Basic Mathematical Ideas

The commonest form of mathematical "statement" in the sciences is the equation. An equation may be thought of as a kind of symbol machine that transforms one number (or set of numbers) into another. We can write an algebraic equation in the general form

$$y = f(x) \, ,$$

where $f(x)$ means "a function of x." When used to designate a function, it does *not* mean "x multiplied by f" (and thus should not be broken at the end of a line). A function of x stands for any mathematical expression in which x is the only variable. (A *variable* is a letter that takes on the value of any number we substitute for it.) Because the numerical value of x can be any number, it is known as the *independent* variable. The letter y is called the *dependent* variable because its numerical value is equivalent to, and depends on, the value of $f(x)$. As we have not yet specified the particular mathematical expression that $f(x)$ stands for, our imaginary function machine for $f(x)$ looks like this:

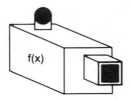

If we now replace $f(x)$ with a specific function of x, say $2x$ (x multiplied by 2), the function machine looks like this:

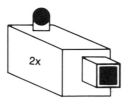

Substituting a numerical value for x is like dropping it into our imaginary function machine. Suppose this number is 4. If we drop 4 into the hopper of the machine and turn the crank, the machine grinds away and multiplies 2 and 4 to produce the resulting value of y:

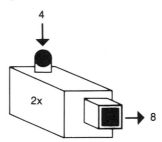

and the result is different for each number that we drop into the hopper. We can make the function $f(x)$ as complicated as we please; we can even add terms containing other variables w and z so that our original equation becomes

$$y = f(x, w, z) .$$

The principle is the same: every time we drop a number or set of numbers into a particular function machine and turn the crank, we get another value of y.

The use of equations in the sciences depends on this number-generating property of functions. For example, when a scientist studying a physical system (such as an atom) can write down an equation describing the time behavior of the system in the form of a specific mathematical function, he or she can predict how the system will change over time by substituting numbers for the independent variables. Because the quantities they contain can be precisely manipulated, equations also enable us to find the values of quantities that we cannot directly measure by using the values of quantities that we can directly measure.

How to Read a Mathematical Expression

Although a mathematical expression may appear complicated, with a little practice it can be mentally broken down into smaller units. This way of looking at an equation enables us to see its general *form* and can be very helpful when an equation is being typed. Mathematics, like music, uses a special notation to convey information. The mathematical expressions used in the sciences are made up of several kinds of signs and symbols: English (or Roman) and Greek letters, signs of operation, fences, and special symbols.

Letter symbols.   The letters in a mathematical expression may stand for variables (whose values range over a set of numbers), constants (whose numerical values are fixed and must be specified in a particular context), abbreviations of English words such as *sin* or *exp*, or other kinds of symbols such as index numbers. The meaning of each letter, abbreviation, or symbol should be clearly defined the first time it is used, with an indication of whether it is a variable, a constant, or another kind of symbol.

In addition to Roman letters, letters of the Greek alphabet are often used in mathematical expressions. (Greek letters are used for certain kinds of quantities for historical reasons.) Table 1 lists the letters of the Greek alphabet, their names and pronunciations, and their English equivalents. Because they are used extensively, you should learn to recognize them. However, even the Roman and Greek alphabets together may not contain enough letters for an author's needs. Further, an author may wish to use similar symbols for closely related but different quantities. The solution to both of these problems is the use of superscripts, subscripts, or primes. Thus, an author may mean completely different things by a and a_o or p_{ij} and p_{ik} or f' and f''. This means that the secretary must be *very* careful to type every character as the author wants it. Typographical errors in mathematics are much more serious than in ordinary text. An error like "typwriter" is easy to spot in a draft, and the meaning is still clear; but dropping an e from a mathematical quantity may go unnoticed and can make an equation wrong.

It is also important to note that letter symbols maintain their identities throughout a discussion. In algebra, we are taught that the unknown is always x (or some other letter), no matter what the variable stands for. This does not mean that a symbol can stand for anything at different places. Most characters used in a paper or article mean the same thing, whatever it is, throughout. For example, if the author writes "the Boltzmann constant, k," at one point in a paper, you can be reasonably sure that when k appears again it still stands for the Boltzmann constant. (This does not necessarily apply to superscripts and subscripts used as indexes, such as i, j, or k, which may stand for different numbers in different places.)

In handwritten equations, authors often do not distinguish between the letter "oh" (uppercase or lowercase) and the numeral zero. Ordinarily, the secretary can guess the meaning from the context. When "oh" or zero is used in a superscript or subscript, however, the context may not help. If you cannot decide, ask. Thereafter, you can assume that the character is the same in identical contexts.

A word about the displayed expressions in this chapter.   Displayed mathematical expressions, when typeset, conventionally appear with the symbols representing entities such as variables styled in *italics*. But in this book we have purposely set the symbols in our *displayed* expressions in Roman, for that is the

Table 1.   **Greek Alphabet**

Uppercase	Lowercase	Name	Pronunciation*
A	α	alpha	(ăl'fə)
B	β	beta	(bā'tə)
Γ	γ	gamma	(găm'ə)
Δ	δ	delta	(děl'tə)
E	ε	epsilon	(ĕp'sə-lŏn')
Z	ζ	zeta	(zā'tə)
H	η	eta	(ā'tə, ē'tə)
Θ	θ	theta	(thā'tə)
I	ι	iota	(ī-ō'tə)
K	κ	kappa	(kăp'ə)
Λ	λ	lambda	(lăm'də)
M	μ	mu	(myo͞o, mo͞o)
N	ν	nu	(no͞o, nyo͞o)
Ξ	ξ	xi	(zī, sī)
O	ο	omicron	(ŏm'ĭ-krŏn')
Π	π	pi	(pī)
P	ρ	rho	(rō)
Σ	σ, ς	sigma	(sĭg'mə)
T	τ	tau	(tou, tô)
Y	υ	upsilon	(ŭp'sə-lŏn', yo͞op'sə-lŏn')
Φ	φ	phi	fi (fī)
X	χ	chi	ki (kī)
Ψ	ψ	psi	(sī, psī)
Ω	ω	omega	(ō-měg'ə)

*The pronunciations shown here are taken from *The American Heritage Dictionary*, Second College Edition.

way you may encounter them in handwritten or typewritten draft formats. When you keyboard a document for typesetting, use an italic font for the symbols or underscore them. (Mathematical expressions that have been run into the text itself have been italicized in order to set them off from the rest of the text.)

Signs of operation.   Signs of operation (sometimes called *operators* or *operational signs*) indicate specific mathematical operations, such as addition ($+$), subtraction ($-$), multiplication ($\times$), or division ($\div$), that are to be carried out on the letter symbols. In multiplication and division, the signs $\times$ and $\div$ are usually implicit rather than written out. For example, instead of writing $a \times b \times c$, we write *abc*, where the multiplication signs between the letters are understood. Another way of indicating multiplication is used when a symbol is multiplied by itself; rather than writing *aaa*, we write a^3 ("*a* cubed" or "*a* to the third power"). Similarly, in division, instead of writing $x \div y$ we use the fractional form x/y (read as "*x* divided by *y*" or "*x* over *y*").

Expressions that appear complicated often consist of the familiar operations of arithmetic carried out on various letter symbols. For example,

$$ax + by + 4x^2 - 2y + y/x$$

means "*ax* (or *a* times *x*) plus *by* (or *b* times *y*) plus $4x^2$ (4 times *x* squared) minus $2y$ (2 times *y*) plus the quantity *y* divided by *x* (or *y* over *x*)." The constants *a*, *b*, 4, and 2 are known as the *coefficients* of the variables they multiply.

Operations are also indicated by the superscript (exponent) of a quantity. For example, a^n ("a raised to the nth power" or "a to the nth") means n of the quantities a multiplied together. The symbol for the root of a quantity ($\sqrt{}$) is called the *radical* symbol, as in $\sqrt{x}$, read as "the square root of x." The same quantity also can be written as $x^{1/2}$, read as "x raised to the one-half power." Similarly, $\sqrt[4]{x}$ ("the fourth root of x") can be written as $x^{1/4}$ ("x raised to the one-fourth power"). Using this same notation, we can write the expression $\sqrt[3]{x^2}$ ("the third root of the quantity x squared") as $x^{2/3}$, or "x to the two-thirds power."

Mathematical expressions also can have more complicated exponents; for example, x^{2n+1}, read as "x raised to the power $2n$ plus 1" or "x to the quantity $2n$ plus 1." One special function often used in mathematics is called the exponential function, e^x, where e is a fixed quantity called the base of natural logarithms and the exponent x can be any expression. If the exponent of e is a complicated expression that includes a fraction, as in

$$e^{t^2/4k^2} ,$$

writing it in this form can be awkward, especially if the expression occurs in text. Scientists therefore sometimes use *exponential* notation, in which "exp" replaces e and the exponent is written on the same line. In this notation, the expression above is written $\exp(t^2/4k^2)$.

Other signs of operation stand for more complicated mathematical processes such as *differentiation* and *integration*. These are operations that change the *form* of a function. They may be thought of as changing the machinery in the function machine. Roughly speaking, differentiation is a procedure that enables us to study the rate at which the value of a function changes with respect to a change in its independent variable. If our equation, in functional form, is

$$y = f(x) ,$$

differentiation is often indicated by the symbols

$$\frac{dy}{dx} = f'(x)$$

(read as "the derivative of y with respect to x equals f prime of x" or "dy over dx equals. . .”), where $f'(x)$ is the new function arrived at by differentiation. If y represents distance traveled as a function of time t, for example, differentiating $f(t)$ will tell us how distance changes with time, or in other words, the *velocity* of whatever it is that we are describing.

Similarly, if we differentiate the function in our example a second time, indicated by

$$\frac{d^2y}{dx^2} = f''(x) ,$$

we obtain the rate at which the velocity *changes*, or the *acceleration.*

Differentiation can also be symbolized by what is called the "dot" notation. For example,

$$\dot{y} = f'(x)$$

means the same as

$$\frac{dy}{dx} = f'(x)$$

and

$$\ddot{y} = f''(x)$$

means the same as

$$\frac{d^2y}{dx^2} = f''(x).$$

Finally, functions with more than one independent variable can be differentiated by a process called *partial differentiation*, in which one variable at a time is differentiated while the others are held constant. Partial differentiation of a function $y = f(x, z)$ is indicated by the symbolism

$$\frac{\partial y}{\partial x} = f_x(x, z)$$

$$\frac{\partial y}{\partial z} = f_y(x, z) \, ,$$

where the symbol $\partial y / \partial x$ is read as "the partial derivative of y with respect to x" or "partial y over partial x."

Because the operation of *integration* is the reverse of differentiation, it is sometimes known as *antidifferentiation*. Integration may be thought of as a procedure that sums up an infinite number of elements whose size becomes gradually smaller; it is indicated by the symbol $\int$. For example, in the function

$$y = \int x^2 \, dx$$

(read as "integral of x squared dx"), the function to be integrated (called the *integrand*) is x^2. (The dx specifies the variable x on which the operation is to be performed; it does *not* mean "d multiplied by x").

The last expression is called an *indefinite integral* because it does not specify the range of values of x over which integration is carried out. When such a range of values is specified, the resulting expression is called a *definite integral*. An example is the function

$$y = \int_0^\infty 2x^3 \, dx \, .$$

The symbols for zero and infinity (∞) at the bottom and top of the integral sign are said to indicate the *limits* of the integration (that is, the two ends of the range). Each integral may have its own limits. You also may see an integral sign with a circle at its center: $\oint$. This is known as a *contour integral* and represents integration over a closed path. As in differentiation, we can also integrate a function of more than one variable; for example,

$$y = \iint (x^2 + 2y) \, dxdy$$

or

$$y = \iiint (x^2 + 2y - z) \, dxdydz$$

Other signs of operation are the product sign Π (capital Greek *pi*) and the summation symbol Σ (capital Greek *sigma*). These are used when a series of mathematical terms is multiplied or added, respectively. For example,

$$\prod_{i=1}^{n} x_i \, ,$$

read as "the product from *i* equals one to *n* of *x* sub *i*," means that we start with x_1 and multiply each term by the next (x_2, x_3, etc.) and end with x_n, whatever number *n* may be: $x_1 \times x_2 \times x_3 \times x_4 \times \ldots \times x_n$. The expression operated on by the product sign is called the *multiplicand*. In summation, we simply add the terms

$$\sum_{i=1}^{n} x_i$$

(read as "summation from *i* equals 1 to *n* of *x* sub *i*") instead of multiplying them. The expression operated on by the summation sign is called the *summand*.

The summation and product signs are *large* Greek capital letters, larger than those you may have on a typing element. You should therefore hand-letter these symbols or use rub-ons. Since the integral sign is unique, you can use the sign on a scientific typing element, especially for in-text expressions. However, any of these signs must always be as high as the expressions they apply to.

Trigonometric functions also specify operations that are performed on letter symbols that represent angles. Some of the simpler trigonometric functions are $x = \sin \theta$, $y = \cos \theta$, and $z = \tan \theta$, where "sin" is the abbreviation for "sine," "cos" for cosine," "tan" for "tangent," and θ is an angle (other characters may be used for the angle). In the right-angle triangle, the lengths of the three sides are *a*, *b*, and *c*. The sine of the angle θ is defined as b/c, the cosine of θ is defined as a/c, and the tangent of θ is defined as b/a.

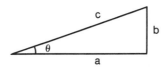

Another sign of operation you may often encounter (especially in the mathematics of probability) is the *factorial* symbol !, as in *n*! (read as "*n* factorial"). In mathematical notation, ! is not an exclamation point but indicates the product of all the integers (whole numbers) from *n* to 1. For example, if $n = 6$, $n! = 6 \times 5 \times 4 \times 3 \times 2 \times 1 = 720$. We have described in this section only a few of the most common mathematical operations; there are many others. Table 2 includes some additional operators and their meanings.

Signs of relation.   In contrast to signs of operation, signs of relation indicate the relationships among the various terms in a mathematical expression. We have already seen how one common sign of relation, the equality sign, is used. Other often used signs of relation play similar roles. For example, < and > mean "less than" and "greater than," respectively; the expression $a < b$ is read as "*a* is less

Table 2. **Common Mathematical Operators**

$+$	plus
$-$	minus
$\pm$	plus or minus
$\mp$	minus or plus
$\times$	multiplication sign
Σ	summation
Π	product symbol
∂	backcurling delta (partial derivative sign)
∇	del (vector operator)
$\boldsymbol{\nabla}$	bold del
$\forall$	inverted sans serif aye (for all)
$\exists$	inverted sans serif ee (there exists)
$\wedge$	wedge, roof (outer product sign; conjunction sign)
$\vee$	inverted wedge or roof (disjunction sign)
$\cap$	intersection sign
$\cup$	union sign
$\sqrt{}$	radical
$\int$	integral
$\oint$	contour integral

Adapted with permission from the American Institute of Physics *Style Manual* (3rd ed.).

than b," and $a > b$ is read as "a is greater than b." Table 3 includes some additional signs of relation.

Fences.   Fences, sometimes called *symbols of inclusion*, are the punctuation marks of mathematics. Their role is to prevent ambiguity by setting off from one another the different terms in a mathematical expression. Fences include left and right parentheses ( ), brackets [ ], braces { }, and other specialized symbols. The accepted convention for the order in which fences are used is { [( )] }. If more fences are needed, this order may be repeated with larger fences. An example illustrates the way fences are used. In the expression

$$n + 2n + 1^2 - 2n + a - 1^3 u - n$$

it is not clear, in the absence of fences, on which terms the operations are to be performed. Proper use of fences makes the meaning clear:

$$\{[(n + 2)(n + 1)^2 - 2n + (a - 1)^3]u\} - n^2 .$$

There is one important rule about fences: except in very special cases, every left fence of a given kind must have a corresponding right fence. In complicated expressions, we can be sure that every kind of fence has a mate by counting the fences. If we find that an expression has, say, five parentheses, we can be reasonably sure that somewhere a parenthesis has been omitted. The same rule applies to special symbols that define what they enclose, such as the symbol for absolute value $|a|$ (read as "the absolute value of a"), where the vertical bars mean that the quantity a is to be used without regard for its sign (positive or negative). Another set of such symbols is the angle brackets $\langle a \rangle$ (not to be confused with the "less than" or "greater than" symbols), which indicate that the quantity they enclose is an average. Another notation for showing an average is the overbar $\bar{a}$. The overbar should extend over the entire expression to which it applies. Fences

Table 3.   Common Mathematical Signs of Relation

$=$	equals; double bond
$\neq$	not equal to
$\triangleq$	corresponds to
$\equiv$	identically equal to; equivalent to; triple bond
$\not\equiv$	not identically equal to; not equivalent to; not always equal to
$\sim$	asymptotically equal to; of the order of magnitude of
$\approx$	approximately equal to
$\simeq$	approximately equal to
$\cong$	congruent to; approximately equal to
$\propto$	proportional to
$<$	less than
$>$	greater than
$\nless$	not less than
$\ngtr$	not greater than
$\ll$	much less than
$\gg$	much greater than
$\leq$	less than or equal to
$\geq$	greater than or equal to
$\lesssim$	less than or approximately equal to
$\gtrsim$	greater than or approximately equal to
$\subset$	included in, a subset of
$\supset$	contains as a subset
$\not\subset$	not included in, not a subset of
$\subseteq$	contained within
$\supseteq$	contains
$\in$	an element of
$\ni$	contains as an element
$\notin$	not an element of
$\rightarrow$	approaches, tends to; yields; is replaced by
$\leftrightarrow$	mutually implies
$\perp$	perpendicular (to)
$\parallel$	parallel (to)

Adapted with permission from the American Institute of Physics *Style Manual* (3rd ed.).

should be as high as the expressions they enclose. Rub-on or hand-drawn fences should be used if an expression is taller than a single letter symbol with a superscript and subscript, such as a_i^2.

Rules of Style for Mathematical Material

In typing mathematical material, you not only will be dealing with signs and symbols that may be unfamiliar, but you also may be working with handwritten drafts that are barely legible. Perhaps the most effective way of coping with this situation, and the one you may find the most rewarding, is to familiarize yourself with the subject matter you will be dealing with.

If you simply cannot make out a symbol in a handwritten draft, you can guess, leave a space with a question mark, or ask the author. In the last case it is preferable, if there are several questionable symbols, to mark them for clarification in a single conference with the author. If you are fortunate enough to work on a word processing system (see Chapter Four), especially one linked to a dual-head printer or—better yet—a computerized phototypesetter, the range of mathematical symbols that you can conveniently key will be much greater than if you are using an electric typewriter with an interchangeable element.

In typing mathematical material, decisions about the use of typed, hand-lettered, or rub-on symbols will depend on the variety of typing elements available, the kind of manuscript you are preparing (rough draft, camera-ready copy, journal article, conference paper, etc.), and the stage of a particular draft (preliminary, intermediate, or final). In some cases you may find it more convenient, unless otherwise instructed, to hand-letter all symbols in each successive draft except for the final, where you may need to use rub-on symbols or carefully annotated hand-lettered symbols (see the section on preparing journal articles).

When hand-lettering the symbols or using rub-ons, you will find that it is distressingly easy to drop some of them inadvertently in successive drafts, especially if you are working with a computer-linked printer not equipped with a special symbol element. One way to avoid this problem is to write or draw in the symbols neatly in each draft with a highly visible ink (such as red).

Although mathematics has been called the universal language of the sciences, it is fair to say that there is no generally observed standard for formatting mathematical expressions. Stylistic conventions may differ from one science to another and even from journal to journal within a particular science. Whatever set of rules is used, however, the result must be clear, consistent, and unambiguous. Many technical journals provide a style sheet for authors; if you know you will be preparing materials mostly for a particular journal or set of journals, you should obtain such a guide, either from your employer or from the journal (see the section on preparing journal articles). The American Institute of Physics, for example, publishes a useful *Style Manual*. Companies that produce their own technical reports often provide a style guide for authors, editors, and secretaries. You should ask whether such a guide is available. The rules of style given here thus should be regarded as default rules; they can be used if no other formal guidance is available.

Use of typing elements.   Mathematical elements are available for most interchangeable-element typewriters. Though it is unlikely that such an element will contain all the characters in the appropriate sizes that you will need, it should be used whenever feasible. Letter symbols in mathematical expressions are normally printed in italic type. Unless you are working with a computer-driven phototypesetter, you probably need not be concerned with the use of italics.

Because they can appear frequently in mathematical expressions, and thus require changing a typing element, Greek letters can be troublesome for the secretary. A workable approach is to mark Greek letters in an expression before you type it, and then to make two passes through the expression (without removing the paper), once with a Roman element and once with a Greek element, again leaving spaces for any hand-lettered characters. This may be done on the final draft only, but in that case it is a good idea to make sure that you understand each Greek letter indicated. Again, you should be clear about what is expected in your own work situation.

Mathematical expressions sometimes contain variables that represent quantities called *scalars, vectors,* and *tensors.* By convention, vectors, tensors, and certain other symbols appear in boldface (heavy) type. If a boldface element is unavailable, an alternative method (especially in journal submissions) is to underscore with a wavy line each symbol to be set in boldface; for example, $\underset{\sim}{v}$. Sometimes a vector quantity is also indicated by a right arrow above it, as in $\vec{v}$. Again, you should inquire as to the convention you are expected to use and follow it consistently.

Spacing of symbols.   Proper spacing of mathematical symbols is important both to avoid ambiguity and to give a clean, uniform appearance to a manuscript. Although the rules given here may seem tedious at first, with a little practice you should be able to apply them almost automatically in most cases. There is one important caveat in deciding how to space symbols: unless you know that an author is meticulous about writing mathematics (and, surprisingly, most are not), *you cannot rely on what you see,* either in a handwritten draft or in one that has been typed by the author. This is one of those cases in which you probably will be more familiar with the rules than the author is and thus can provide a valuable service.

1. Do not space:
   - between quantities multiplied together when no multiplication sign is used, as in xy, $2ab$, or $2x_r e^x$.
   - between a symbol and its subscript and superscript, as in x^n, x^{2y+c}, or Q_{max} .
   - before and after fences, as in $(2x + b)(6y + c)$ or $[(x_i^2 - 2y^2)(x + 2)]u_i$.
   - in names of functions or between names of multiplied functions, as in $f(x)$ or $f(x)f(y)$.
   - between a sign and its quantity in signed quantities: ± 6, -7, $+10$.
   - when a sign of relation is used with a single quantity: "a value >6," "a length of ~ 3 metres."

2. Use one space:
   - before and after a binary sign of operation (an operation involving two quantities), as in $a + b$ or $a - b$ (note that this is different from a signed quantity). An exception is when a binary operator or sign of addition appears in a superscript, subscript, or limit, in which case no spaces are used: u^{n-1}, $\sum_{i=1}^{\infty}$.
   - before and after a sign of relation: $a = 2b$, $x < y$, $g \subset r$.
   - before and after abbreviations that are set in Roman type: $2 \sin \theta$, $\log b$, $2x \exp 4y$. An exception to this is when the abbreviation is preceded or followed by an expression in fences or a superscript or subscript. In such cases, use no space: $(6n - m)\log a$, $\exp[(2x - y)/4]$, $\sin^2\theta$.

- before and after a unary sign of operation (an operation on one expression), as in

$$\omega \int_0^\infty (6x^2 - 4y)\, dx, \quad iq\, \frac{\partial \psi}{\partial t}, \quad \sum_{n=1}^{\infty} x_n, \text{ or } \frac{dy}{dx}\, f(x).$$

Note: if an expression includes limits, count one space before and after the beginning and end of the limit, as in

$$\lim_{y \to \infty} f(y).$$

If limits are written as superscripts or subscripts, count one space after the last character to the right, as in

$$g(t) = \frac{1}{2\pi i} \int_{a-i\infty}^{a+i\infty} e^{xt} f(x)\, dx.$$

- after commas in sets of symbols, as in (r, θ, ϕ) and $f(x, y)$.

3. Use three spaces:
   - between two or more equations that are in sequence on the line: $z = a^2 + b^2 + c^2, \quad x = 2a + 3b + c.$
   - between an equation and a condition on that equation:
     $$d = u_a k \quad (a = 1, 2, 3, \ldots, n).$$
   - between an equation and any parenthetical unit of measure:
     $$a = v/t \quad (\text{m·s}^{-2}).$$
   - between an equation and a following phrase in a displayed expression: $f(x) \to 0 \quad \text{as } x \to \infty.$

In-text and displayed equations.   To avoid awkwardness or to conserve space, equations or expressions set in text are often formatted differently from equations set on a separate line (displayed). For example, in

$$\frac{h^2}{4\pi^2 k e^2 m} = \frac{a_0}{Z}$$

the fractions are "built up." In text, such an equation should be typed with the solidus (slash) instead of the fraction bar: $h^2/4\pi^2 k e^2 m = a_0/Z$. When reformatting, however, it is sometimes necessary to add fences to avoid ambiguity. For example,

$$z = \frac{a + y}{b}$$

does not mean the same as $z = a + y/b$. In such a case it is necessary to place the numerator in parentheses to preserve the meaning: $z = (a + y)/b$. Similarly, the expression

$$\frac{2\pi i}{e^{\sqrt{(x^2 + y^2)}}}$$

can be typed in text as $\exp[2\pi i/\sqrt{(x^2 + y^2)}]$, but the brackets are necessary. If an in-text expression is sufficiently complex, however, it is preferable to display it. You should seek the author's advice when reformatting an equation. Even in displayed equations, it is best to avoid expressions that are doubly built up. For example,

$$y = \frac{x}{b} + \frac{x^2}{4/a}$$

is preferable to

$$y = \frac{x}{b} + \frac{x^2}{\frac{4}{a}} .$$

Displayed equations are often numbered. The rule of thumb is that if a displayed equation is subsequently cited, it should be numbered. All numbered equations should be displayed, but not all displayed equations need be numbered.

The rules for indenting displayed equations vary from style to style; equations are sometimes centered, sometimes indented slightly to the right, and sometimes typed flush left. In the absence of specific guidance, you will probably find it convenient to indent them or type them flush left, a practice that avoids counting the spaces to the center and tabbing. Whatever spacing you use, be consistent. In numbered equations, the equation number is enclosed in parentheses and set flush with the right margin:

$$f' = \sum_{n=0}^{\infty} na_n u^{n-1} . \tag{1}$$

Punctuation after in-text mathematical expressions is the same as in ordinary English. In a displayed equation, however, leave one space between the last character and any following punctuation (period, comma, or semicolon).

Breaking an equation.   If they will not fit on a single line, lengthy displayed equations may be broken (carried over to the next line). An equation should be broken, if at all possible, only preceding a sign of relation (equal, less than, etc.) or preceding a sign of operation (plus, minus, integral symbol, etc.):

$$u'(t) = b^0 a_0^{-1} \sum_{r=1}^{\infty} \exp(srt)p_r t \; (line\ break\ can\ come\ here)$$

$$- b_1 a_0^{-1} \sum_{r=1}^{\infty} \exp[s_r(t - \omega)]p_r (t - \omega) . \tag{2}$$

The second line may be typed as a standard indentation from the left margin (to allow space for an equation number) or, as in Eq. (2), aligned one space to the right of a sign of relation. Whatever style you use, however, consistency is the watchword.

If a displayed equation is broken between multiplied numbers, the multiplication sign (which is usually implicit) should be inserted at the beginning of the new line. Thus,

$$\Delta m = m_2 - 2m_1 = 2m_1\left[\left(1 - \frac{u^2}{c^2}\right)^{-1/2} - 1\right]$$

becomes

$$\Delta m = m_2 - 2m_1 = 2m_1$$

$$\times \left[\left(1 - \frac{u^2}{c^2}\right)^{-1/2} - 1\right].$$

Fractions, expressions within fences, and expressions within a radical sign $(\sqrt{})$ should not be broken unless absolutely necessary. Do not break an expression containing an integral sign until $d(\text{variable})$ occurs, as in

$$\overline{K}(s, t) = -K(s, t) + \int_a^b K(s, r)K(r, t)\, dr$$

$$- \int_a^b\int_a^b K(s, r)K(r, w)K(w, t)\, dr\, dw .$$

"Where" lists.   Displayed equations are often followed by lists that define the symbols they contain, called "where" lists since they are preceded by the word *where*. If a where list contains few or only simple definitions, it may be run into the text, as in

$$"L = n\,\frac{h}{4\pi} = n\hbar ,$$

where $\hbar$ is Planck's constant and n is an integer."

When a list is lengthy (say, four or more lines) or itself contains built-up expressions, it should be displayed separately and the definitions aligned with the "equals" sign. For example, an author might say:

"We may write

$$F^{3/4} = \left(\frac{bW_v - c}{2yL}\right)^m ,$$

where
$$\begin{aligned}
b &= \text{proportionality constant,} \\
W_v &= \text{vapor mass rate,} \\
c &= \text{intercept as } W_v = 0, \\
2yL &= \text{cross-sectional area normal to flow,} \\
L &= \text{tube length per crosspass,} \\
m &= \text{positive exponent."}
\end{aligned}$$

The symbol definitions are listed in the same order in which they appear in the equation. Note that each line is punctuated by a comma except for the last, which ends with a period because it is the end of the sentence. Some miscellaneous rules:

- Fraction bars should extend over or under the longest expression in a fraction, with the shorter expression centered on the bar. For example, in

$$\frac{2E_0(P_1 - P_2)}{2}$$

the bar extends under the entire numerator, and the denominator is centered.

- In a signed fractional expression, the sign should be aligned on the fraction bar, as in

$$X = -\frac{mA}{R}$$

- Complicated expressions involving a radical sign, as in

$$\sqrt{[3J/(J + 1)]T_N m^2} \, ,$$

are more conveniently typed as

$$\sqrt{\{[3J/(J + 1)]T_N m^2\}} \, .$$

However, note the added braces, which are essential to indicate the extent of the radical. Alternatively, an expression such as

$$\sqrt{\frac{[3J/(J + 1)]T_N m^2}{E_n - B_n^2 b^2 T_N}}$$

may be written as

$$\left\{\frac{[3J/(J + 1)]T_N m^2}{E_n - B_n^2 b^2 T_N}\right\}^{1/2} \, .$$

However, if the radical sign is used, it must extend over the entire expression it applies to.

- To avoid awkward spacing, limits for in-text signs of operation (integration, summation, etc.) may be written as superscripts or subscripts rather than above or below the operator without causing confusion. For example,

$$\prod_{n=0}^{\infty} a_n$$

can be typed as $\prod_{n=0}^{\infty} a_n$. This is *always* done with the limits of an integral sign.

- In a symbol having both a superscript and a subscript, they should be aligned, as in x_n^2 (not $x^2{}_n$), unless the author specifies otherwise.

FORMATTING CHEMICAL MATERIAL

What Is an Atom?

The basic unit of matter is the *atom*. There are many different kinds of atoms. Each kind of atom is called an *element*. The chemical properties of an element are governed by its atomic structure. Every atom has a central part, the *nucleus*, in which most of its mass (or weight) is concentrated. The nucleus consists of two kinds of particles: the *proton*, which has one positive unit of electrical charge, and the *neutron*, which is electrically neutral. The number of protons in the nucleus is called its *atomic number*. The total number of neutrons and protons in a nucleus is called its *atomic mass number*. The nucleus is surrounded by a swarm of much lighter, fast-moving particles called *electrons*, each of which carries one negative unit of electrical charge. The electrons are bound to the nucleus by the attractive force between their negative charges and the positive charge on the nucleus.

However, an electron is not free to move anywhere in the space around the nucleus. Each electron is constrained by a set of rules to move only in a certain volume of space around the nucleus called a *shell*. The rules partition the space around the nucleus so that only a certain number of electrons can occupy a particular shell. Some shells are relatively close to the nucleus and some are farther away. After the innermost shell (which has no more than two electrons), each shell can accommodate various numbers of electrons (with the number varying from shell to shell). The outermost shell is known as the *valence shell*, and its electrons are called the *valence electrons*. The electrons in the outermost shell are those that give an atom its chemical properties.

When the number of protons (positively charged) in the nucleus equals the number of electrons (negatively charged) around the nucleus, the charges cancel one another and the atom is electrically neutral. In general an atom is more stable if its valence shell contains eight electrons. Hence, an atom of chlorine, which has seven electrons in its valence shell, is more stable if it accepts an electron from another atom (filling its valence shell for a total of eight electrons). Because the resulting chloride atom has one more electron than proton, it carries one unit of negative charge. Similarly, an atom of sodium, which has one electron in its valence shell, is more stable if it gives up an electron (so that the next shell in contains eight electrons). The resulting sodium atom carries one unit of positive charge.

An atom that has one or more units of charge, positive or negative, is called an *ion*. The transfer of an electron from one atom to another forms an *ionic bond*. Ordinary table salt (sodium chloride) consists of sodium and chlorine atoms bonded to one another. Other atoms *share* their valence electrons to fill up their valence shell, forming *covalent bonds*. A nitrogen atom, for example, has five valence electrons. If two nitrogen atoms share three electrons apiece, they form three covalent bonds and effectively fill their valence shells. The process by which atoms form chemical bonds is called a *chemical reaction*. Atoms can undergo a chemical reaction with other atoms, or groups of atoms, combining to form a *molecule*. Likewise, molecules can combine chemically with other molecules or atoms.

The chemical properties of the various elements depend, as we have noted, on the number of electrons in their valence shells and also the readiness with which

Periodic Table of the Elements

KEY

Atomic Number — **1**
H — Symbol
Hydrogen
1.00797
Atomic Weight
(or Mass Number
of most stable
isotope if in
parentheses)

1a	2a	3b	4b	5b	6b	7b		8		1b	2b	3a	4a	5a	6a	7a	0
1 **H** Hydrogen 1.00797																	2 **He** Helium 4.0026
3 **Li** Lithium 6.939	4 **Be** Beryllium 9.0122											5 **B** Boron 10.81\	6 **C** Carbon 12.01115	7 **N** Nitrogen 14.0067	8 **O** Oxygen 15.9994	9 **F** Fluorine 18.9984	10 **Ne** Neon 20.183
11 **Na** Sodium 22.9898	12 **Mg** Magnesium 24.312											13 **Al** Aluminum 26.9815	14 **Si** Silicon 28.086	15 **P** Phosphorus 30.9738	16 **S** Sulfur 32.064	17 **Cl** Chlorine 35.453	18 **Ar** Argon 39.948
19 **K** Potassium 39.102	20 **Ca** Calcium 40.08	21 **Sc** Scandium 44.956	22 **Ti** Titanium 47.90	23 **V** Vanadium 50.942	24 **Cr** Chromium 51.996	25 **Mn** Mangenese 54.9380	26 **Fe** Iron 55.847	27 **Co** Cobalt 58.9332	28 **Ni** Nickel 58.71	29 **Cu** Copper 63.546	30 **Zn** Zinc 65.37	31 **Ga** Gallium 69.72	32 **Ge** Germanium 72.59	33 **As** Arsenic 74.9216	34 **Se** Selenium 78.96	35 **Br** Bromine 79.904	36 **Kr** Krypton 83.80
37 **Rb** Rubidium 85.47	38 **Sr** Strontium 87.62	39 **Y** Yttrium 88.905	40 **Zr** Zirconium 91.22	41 **Nb** Niobium 92.906	42 **Mo** Molybdenum 95.94	43 **Tc** Technetium (97)	44 **Ru** Ruthenium 101.07	45 **Rh** Rhodium 102.905	46 **Pd** Palladium 106.4	47 **Ag** Silver 107.868	48 **Cd** Cadmium 112.40	49 **In** Indium 114.82	50 **Sn** Tin 118.69	51 **Sb** Antimony 121.75	52 **Te** Tellurium 127.60	53 **I** Iodine 126.9044	54 **Xe** Xenon 131.30
55 **Cs** Cesium 132.905	56 **Ba** Barium 137.34	51–71* Lanthanides	72 **Hf** Hafnium 178.49	73 **Ta** Tantalum 180.948	74 **W** Tungsten 183.85	75 **Re** Rhenium 186.2	76 **Os** Osmium 190.2	77 **Ir** Iridium 192.2	78 **Pt** Platinum 195.09	79 **Au** Gold 196.967	80 **Hg** Mercury 200.59	81 **Tl** Thallium 204.37	82 **Pb** Lead 207.19	83 **Bi** Bismuth 208.980	84 **Po** Polonium (210)	85 **At** Astatine (210)	86 **Rn** Radon (222)
87 **Fr** Francium (223)	88 **Ra** Radium (226)	89–103** **Actinides															

*Lanthanides

57 **La** Lanthanum 138.91	58 **Ce** Cerium 140.12	59 **Pr** Praseodymium 140.907	60 **Nd** Neodymium 144.24	61 **Pm** Promethium (145)	62 **Sm** Samarium 150.35	63 **Eu** Europium 151.96	64 **Gd** Gadolinium 157.25	65 **Tb** Terbium 158.924	66 **Dy** Dysprosium 162.50	67 **Ho** Holmium 164.930	68 **Er** Erbium 167.26	69 **Tm** Thulium 168.934	70 **Yb** Ytterbium 173.04	71 **Lu** Lutetium 174.97

**Actinides

89 **Ac** Actinium (227)	90 **Th** Thorium 232.038	91 **Pa** Protactinium (231)	92 **U** Uranium 238.03	93 **Np** Neptunium (237)	94 **Pu** Plutonium (244)	95 **Am** Americium (243)	96 **Cm** Curium (247)	97 **Bk** Berkelium (247)	98 **Cf** Californium (251)	99 **Es** Einsteinium (254)	100 **Fm** Fermium (257)	101 **Md** Mendelevium (256)	102 **No** Nobelium (254)	103 **Lw** Lawrencium (257)

their atoms accept, give up, or share electrons. As we increase the number of protons and electrons in an atom, the number of electrons in the valence shell repeats in a regular pattern. Atoms having the same number of valence electrons tend to have similar chemical properties. This periodic pattern enables us to group elements with similar chemical properties; the result is known as the *periodic table of the elements*, shown above.

The table also lists the names of the elements, their chemical symbols, their atomic numbers, and their atomic mass numbers. (Since a chemical symbol is *not* an abbreviation, it is *not* followed by a period.) The atomic mass number is not always a whole number because the nuclei of atoms of the same element can contain different numbers of neutrons (such atoms are called *isotopes*). The atomic mass numbers in the table thus represent an *average* for a particular element as it is found in nature.

Chemical Notation

Chemists generally divide all chemical compounds into two major kinds, *inorganic* compounds and *organic* compounds. Inorganic compounds are those that are composed of elements other than the element carbon (atomic number 12). Organic compounds are those that contain carbon atoms. The reason for this division is twofold. Historically, the first carbon compounds studied were products of the human body; hence, they were called organic compounds. Secondly, because of its chemical properties, the element carbon forms a countless variety of different compounds, and the molecules of carbon compounds can be very large. Such compounds have given rise to a separate field of study. In observing this division, we first discuss the notation for inorganic compounds and then the notation for organic compounds (which has some special features), although the notation overlaps in many respects.

Inorganic chemistry.   The *name* of a chemical element appearing in text should be spelled out the first time it is used. The name of an element is not capitalized (unless, of course, it is the first word in a sentence):

Oxygen and hydrogen react to form water.

The first letter of each chemical *symbol* is always capitalized; the second letter, if there is one, is never capitalized:

The material was found to consist of C, H, Cl, and Br.

There is a conventional notation for indicating the atomic number, atomic mass number, ionic charge, and number of atoms of an element in a compound. This is done by the use of appropriate index numbers (superscripts and subscripts) attached to the chemical symbol. As in mathematical notation, there is no space between a chemical symbol and its index number.

1. The atomic number is indicated by a lower-left index number: $_1H$, $_8O$, $_{12}Mg$, $_{50}Sn$. (The atomic number is usually omitted in a chemical formula, as it is unique to an element.)

2. The atomic mass number is indicated by an upper-left index number: ^1H, ^{16}O, ^{24}Mg, ^{118}Sn. Another way of indicating the atomic mass number of an element, usually when it stands alone or is mentioned in text, is to place it after the hyphenated name or chemical symbol of the element: uranium-238, curium-247, carbon-14. Note that we may infer the number of neutrons in a nucleus by subtracting the atomic number from the atomic mass number. Hence, the isotope ^{235}U has 143 neutrons (235 minus 92) and ^{238}U has 146 neutrons (238 minus 92).

3. Ionic charge is indicated by an upper-right index number: H^+, F^-, O^{2-}, Fe^{3+}, Co^{3+}, U^{5+}, Mn^{4+}.   If an ion has only one plus or minus charge, the numeral 1 is omitted. When an atom gives up valence electrons, it is said to be *oxidized* or in an *oxidation state*. Some atoms can give up different numbers of valence electrons. The *oxidation number*, which specifies how many electrons have been given up, is indicated by a Roman numeral in parentheses following the chemical symbol: Fe(II), Fe(III), Co(III), U(V), Mn(IV). There is no space between the chemical symbol and the parenthetical numeral.

4. The number of atoms of an element in a molecule is indicated by a lower-right index number: H_2, O_2, $C_{16}H_{34}$, K_2CO_3.

The same notation, with some additional features, is used for chemical compounds or molecules. Such an expression is known as a *chemical formula*. For example, the formula for the water molecule, which consists of two atoms of hydrogen and one atom of oxygen, is expressed in chemical notation by H_2O. (Note that we use only the index numbers that are relevant in a particular context. Atomic number and atomic mass number are usually included in a formula only when we deal with reactions of the nucleus. To write the formula for the carbon dioxide molecule when we wish to draw attention to the atomic mass number of the carbon atom because it is radioactive, we would write $^{14}CO_2$.)

Some molecules are also ions; that is, they have a net electrical charge, indicated by using fences (parentheses and brackets) in much the same way as they are used in mathematical notation. For example, $Fe[(CN)_6]^{4-}$ indicates an ion composed of one iron atom (Fe^{2+}) and six cyano groups (CN^-), and the ion has a net charge of -4. The unshared electron of a free radical is indicated by a raised period to the right of the chemical symbol: $H_3C\cdot$, $C_6H_5\cdot$, $HO\cdot$. The same notation is used to indicate water of hydration: $Na_2SO_4\cdot H_2O$.

The physical state—solid (s or c), liquid (ℓ or l), or gas (g)—of an element or compound is specified by including the abbreviation in parentheses after the chemical symbol: $H_2(g)$, $Br_2(l)$, $S(s)$. Note that there is no space between the abbreviation and the chemical symbol. A chemical reaction (that is, the chemical combination of atoms or molecules) is indicated by linking the reacting species with a "plus" symbol, followed by an arrow indicating the direction of the reaction, and finally by the formula(s) of the reaction product(s). The number of each species participating in the reaction is given by a coefficient preceding the chemical symbol:

$$Ca_3(PO_4)_4 + 3H_2SO_4 \rightarrow 2H_3PO_4 + 3CaSO_4$$

$$2AgCl + 2Hg \rightarrow Hg_2Cl_2 + 2Ag.$$

The first of these expressions tells us that one molecule of $Ca_3(PO_4)_4$ combines with three molecules of H_2SO_4 (sulfuric acid) to form two molecules of H_3PO_4 and three molecules of $CaSO_4$. The second expression tells us that two molecules of $AgCl$ combine with two atoms of Hg (mercury) to form one molecule of Hg_2Cl_2 and two atoms of Ag (silver). As in mathematical notation, we leave one space on both sides of the "plus" symbol and on both sides of the arrow (chemical sign of relation). If a reaction proceeds in both directions, two single-headed arrows are used to indicate a balance in which the forward and reverse reactions are proceeding at equal rates:

$$Zr + H_2 \rightleftharpoons ZrH_2.$$

An expression for a chemical reaction may also contain additional information describing the conditions of the reaction, the physical state of the reactants, or other reaction products:

$$WF_6(g) + 3H_2(g) \xrightarrow[\text{Excess } H_2]{\text{Heat}} W(s) + 6HF(g)\ .$$

Organic chemistry.   As mentioned previously, organic chemistry is the study of the compounds of the element carbon. Because a carbon atom can form covalent bonds with as many as four other atoms, it is known as a *tetravalent* element. The spatial orientation of other atoms when they bond to carbon, and the number of bonds they form with carbon, strongly affect the properties of the resulting molecule. For example, two molecules containing carbon may have the same chemical formula (with regard to the total number of atoms in the molecule) but may have quite different physical or chemical properties because of the way the other atoms are attached to the carbon atoms. For this reason, formulas describing carbon compounds are often given in *structural* form. A *structural formula* displays the spatial relationships among the atoms in a unique and unambiguous way. A structural formula thus contains more *information* about a compound than does its chemical formula. This becomes especially important when we deal with the very large molecules that carbon is capable of forming. (The long and complex molecules that comprise the genetic material in a biological cell, for example, can contain many thousands of carbon atoms.) In general, a carbon atom can bond to its neighbors in four different ways; each kind of bond is represented by a special notation:

1. a single bond, in which two electrons are shared, is represented by a single line drawn from the carbon atom to another atom, as in

2. a double bond, in which four electrons are shared, as in

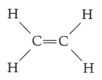

3. a triple bond, in which six electrons are shared, as in

$$H—C\equiv C—H$$

4. a hydrogen bond, represented by a dotted line, in which a hydrogen atom bonded to atom A in one molecule makes an additional bond to atom B in either the same or another molecule, as in

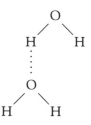

Hydrogen bonds are generally not shown unless they are specifically discussed.

Especially in biological molecules, carbon tends to bond with oxygen, nitrogen, and hydrogen. As we have already seen, a hydrogen atom has one electron to share, and thus forms a single bond with carbon. Oxygen shares one or two electrons and can form a single or double bond with carbon:

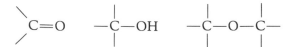

Nitrogen can share one, two, or three electrons to form a single, double, or triple bond:

We are now able to see the importance of structural formulas, for the same formula, for example, C_3H_6O, can represent more than one geometrical structure, as in

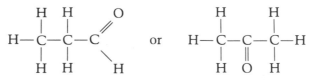

Some of the bonds in a structural formula can be omitted if it can be done without ambiguity. The resulting formula is a hybrid between a chemical formula and a structural formula. For example, $CH_3(CH_2)_6CH_3$ is a shortened form of

$$CH_3—CH_2—CH_2—CH_2—CH_2—CH_2—CH_2—CH_3.$$

However, when bonds are shown explicitly, they are always drawn *between* atoms and not to the center of a *group* of atoms:

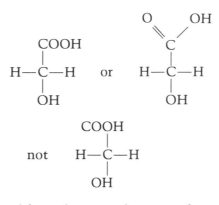

We know that the second formula cannot be correct because it shows an oxygen atom, which has two bonding electrons, sharing electrons with three other atoms (top) and hydrogen, which has one bonding electron, sharing electrons with two other atoms (bottom).

This simplification can be carried even further when no ambiguity results. For example, besides the straight-chain carbon molecules we have so far discussed, carbon can form other kinds of chemical structures. A *ring structure* is one common form, as in the benzene ring, which can be drawn as

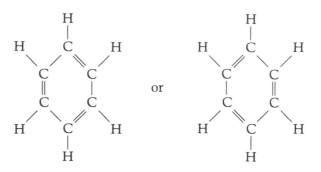

Note that the alternating double bonds that link the carbon atoms appear in a different position in each molecule, although the structures are chemically

equivalent. This representation can be further simplified to

without loss of information. Finally, the same structure can be shown as

We have so far discussed organic compounds as if they all lay in the plane of the page. Actually, carbon's four bonds are arranged in a three-dimensional tetrahedral structure, and to distinguish among different possible configurations in space, we sometimes wish to show this structure. In one widely accepted convention, three different kinds of lines are used: solid lines for atoms (or groups) in the plane of the page, dashed lines for atoms behind the plane of the page, and wedge-shaped lines for atoms that lie above the plane of the page. For example,

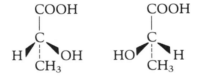

Ring structures may also be represented in three dimensions with the same conventions:

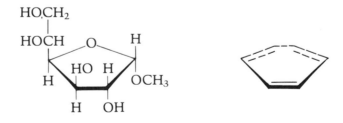

SCIENTIFIC NOTATION

Because scientists often deal with very large or very small numbers, they have developed a special *scientific notation* that enables them to name such numbers without using an excessive number of zeros. This notation is based on powers of 10 (10^n, where the exponent n is any number). For example, the number 1000 (one followed by three zeros) is written more compactly as 10^3 ("ten to the third power") because $10 \times 10 \times 10 = 1000$. We can see the usefulness of this notation when we consider a larger number such as one billion (1 000 000 000 or one followed by nine zeros). In scientific notation, this is written as 10^9. Using this notation, we can quickly write numbers as large as we please without bothering to count zeros, even numbers that are so large they have no name, such as 10^{28} ("ten to the 28th power"), or one followed by 28 zeros. We can use this notation to write numbers less than one. The general form for numbers less than 1 is 10^{-n} (read as "ten to the minus n"), where the minus sign means 1 divided by 10^n, or $1/10^n$. For example, one billionth is written 10^{-9} $(1/10^9)$. We also can combine this notation with decimal numbers to express numbers that lie between powers of ten. This is done by multiplying the base number by another number, or in general, $m \times 10^n$. For example, 240 000 may be written 240×10^3. Using this notation, we can easily rewrite numbers in whatever form is most convenient by moving the decimal point in m any number of spaces to the left or right and increasing or decreasing the exponent by the same number. For example, 240×10^3 can be rewritten as 24×10^4 (moving the imaginary decimal point after 24 one place to the left and increasing the exponent by 1). Similarly, 3.5×10^8 can be written as 35×10^7 (moving the decimal point one space to the right and reducing the exponent by 1). The same rules hold for negative exponents.

Scientific notation also makes it easy to multiply or divide large or small numbers quickly. The general form for multiplication is

$$10^a \times 10^b = 10^{a+b},$$

where a and b are added algebraically. For example, $10^{16} \times 10^4 = 10^{(16+4)}$ or 10^{20}. Similarly, $10^{-16} \times 10^8 = 10^{-16+(8)}$ or 10^{-8}. (Remember that we add *algebraically*.) For division, the general form is $10^a/10^b = 10^{a-b}$, where again the subtraction is algebraic. For example, $10^{16}/10^{-4} = 10^{16-(-4)}$ or 10^{20}. Here we have subtracted -4 algebraically, changing its sign and adding. With a little practice, numbers written in scientific notation can be easily manipulated. As we shall see, this system of notation is very useful when we use the metric system of measurement, which is based on units of ten.

THE METRIC SYSTEM

The metric system, also called the International System of Units (or SI for short), is a standardized system of expressing units of measurement. SI units have been officially adopted in nearly every country in the world because of their simplicity and ease of manipulation. Although the use of metric weights and measures was legalized in the United States as long ago as 1866, Americans have in general preferred the traditional English system of measurement (such as *foot*, *pound*, and *degree Fahrenheit*), and conversion to SI has gone more slowly here than elsewhere. (However, even English measures are now officially defined in SI units.) In 1975, the United States Congress passed legislation to coordinate a voluntary policy of increasing the use of SI in this country as well. This means that eventually all measurements in the United States will be expressed in SI units. (Liquid and weight measures are now often listed on labels in both English and SI units.)

Base Units

Table 4 gives the SI base and supplemental units and their abbreviations. You may find that the SI units for mass (the kilogram), length (the metre), and time (the second) are the most familiar of these. However, the other base units (and their derived units) are used extensively in the scientific literature. Each SI base

Table 4.   **SI Base and Supplemental Units**

Quantity	Unit	Symbol
length	metre	m
mass	kilogram	kg
time	second	s
electric current	ampere	A
thermodynamic temperature	kelvin	K
amount of substance	mole	mol
luminous intensity	candela	cd
plane angle	radian	rad
solid angle	steradian	sr

unit has been defined with great precision in terms of measurable physical quantities. As measuring techniques become more precise, the base units occasionally have been redefined by decision of international scientific meetings. For example, the metre, previously defined as 1 650 763.73 wavelengths of the light emitted by krypton-86 gas, now has been redefined as the distance light travels in 1/299 792 458 of a second. To deal with very large and very small measurements, SI provides prefixes for the base units. Table 5 gives the SI prefixes, their equivalents in scientific notation, and their official symbols.

Derived Units and Conversion
The derived units of SI are obtained by combining the base and supplementary units. Table 6 gives the approved derived units that have special names. For those accustomed to the traditional English units, it may help to understand SI units by comparing them to their equivalents in the English system. Table 7, called a *conversion table*, lists some common SI units and their English equivalents. To convert from English to SI, we multiply the number of English units by their equivalent in SI units. For example, to convert 6 miles to kilometres, we multiply 6 by 1852 to obtain 11 112 metres, or 11.112 kilometres.

Table 5.   **SI Prefixes**

Symbol	Prefix	Multiplication Factor
E	exa	10^{18}
P	peta	10^{15}
T	tera	10^{12}
G	giga	10^{9}
M	mega	10^{6}
k	kilo	10^{3}
h	hecto	10^{2}
da	deca	10^{1}
d	deci	10^{-1}
c	centi	10^{-2}
m	milli	10^{-3}
μ	micro	10^{-6}
n	nano	10^{-9}
p	pico	10^{-12}
f	femto	10^{-15}
a	atto	10^{-18}

Table 6. Some Common SI-derived Units*

Quantity	Unit	Symbol
acceleration	metre per second squared	m/s^2
angular acceleration	radian per second squared	rad/s^2
angular velocity	radian per second	rad/s
area	square metre	m^2
concentration (of amount of substance)	mole per cubic metre	mol/m^3
current density	ampere per square metre	A/m^2
density, mass	kilogram per cubic metre	kg/m^3
electric charge density	coulomb per cubic metre	C/m^3
electric field strength	volt per metre	V/m
electric flux density	coulomb per square metre	C/m^2
energy density	joule per cubic metre	J/m^3
entropy	joule per kelvin	J/K
heat capacity	joule per kelvin	J/K
heat flux density irradiance	watt per square metre	W/m^2
luminance	candela per square metre	cd/m^2
magnetic field strength	ampere per metre	A/m
molar energy	joule per mole	J/mol
molar entropy	joule per mole kelvin	$J/(mol \cdot K)$
molar heat capacity	joule per mole kelvin	$J/(mol \cdot K)$
moment of force	newton metre	$N \cdot m$
permeability	henry per metre	H/m
permittivity	farad per metre	F/m
radiance	watt per square metre steradian	$W/(m^2 \cdot sr)$
radiant intensity	watt per steradian	W/sr
specific heat capacity	joule per kilogram kelvin	$J(kg \cdot K)$
specific energy	joule per kilogram	J/kg
specific entropy	joule per kilogram kelvin	$J/(kg \cdot K)$
specific volume	cubic metre per kilogram	m^3/kg
surface tension	newton per metre	N/m
thermal conductivity	watt per metre kelvin	$W/(m \cdot K)$
velocity	metre per second	m/s
viscosity, dynamic	pascal second	$Pa \cdot s$
viscosity, kinematic	square metre per second	m^2/s
volume	cubic metre	m^3
wavenumber	1 per metre	$1/m$

*Adapted with permission from *Standard for Metric Practice*, a publication of the American Society for Testing and Materials.

Some conversion tables give the conversion factor as a decimal number followed by the letter E plus or minus a two-digit number: 4.184 E + 03. This notation means that the conversion factor 4.184 is multiplied by 10^3. As a rough rule of thumb, we suggest the following reminders:

A litre is a quart and a little more.
A kilogram is two pounds and a little more.
A kilometre is $\frac{1}{2}$ mile and a little more.

SI Style
Because a small change in the way SI units are written or typed can change their meaning completely, it is important to type them correctly. Adherence to a few simple rules can avoid confusion.

Table 7. Measurement

Length

U.S. Customary Unit	U.S. Equivalents	Metric Equivalents
inch	0.083 foot	2.540 centimeters
foot	⅓ yard, 12 inches	0.305 meter
yard	3 feet, 36 inches	0.914 meter
rod	5½ yards, 16½ feet	5.029 meters
mile (statute, land)	1,760 yards, 5,280 feet	1.609 kilometers
mile (nautical, international)	1.151 statute miles	1.852 kilometers

Area

U.S. Customary Unit	U.S. Equivalents	Metric Equivalents
square inch	0.007 square foot	6.452 square centimeters
square foot	144 square inches	929.030 square centimeters
square yard	1,296 square inches, 9 square feet	0.836 square meters
acre	43,560 square feet, 4,840 square yards	4,047 square meters
square mile	640 acres	2.590 square kilometers

Weight

U.S. Customary Unit (Avoirdupois)	U.S. Equivalents	Metric Equivalents
grain	0.036 dram, 0.002285 ounce	64.798 milligrams
dram	27.344 grains, 0.0625 ounce	1.772 grams
ounce	16 drams, 437.5 grains	28.350 grams
pound	16 ounces, 7.000 grains	453.592 grams
ton (short)	2,000 pounds	0.907 metric ton (1,000 kilograms)
ton (long)	1.12 short tons, 2,240 pounds	1.016 metric tons

Apothecary Weight Unit	U.S. Customary Equivalents	Metric Equivalents
scruple	20 grains	1.296 grams
dram	60 grains	3.888 grams
ounce	480 grains, 1.097 avoirdupois ounces	31.103 grams
pound	5,760 grains, 0.823 avoirdupois pound	373.242 grams

Volume or Capacity

U.S. Customary Unit	U.S. Equivalents	Metric Equivalents
cubic inch	0.00058 cubic foot	16.387 cubic centimeters
cubic foot	1,728 cubic inches	0.028 cubic meter
cubic yard	27 cubic feet	0.765 cubic meter

U.S. Customary Liquid Measure	U.S. Equivalents	Metric Equivalents
fluid ounce	8 fluid drams, 1,804 cubic inches	29.573 milliliters
pint	16 fluid ounces, 28.875 cubic inches	0.473 liter
quart	2 pints, 57.75 cubic inches	0.946 liter
gallon	4 quarts, 231 cubic inches	3.785 liters
barrel	varies from 31 to 42 gallons, established by law or usage	

U.S. Customary Dry Measure	U.S. Equivalents	Metric Equivalents
pint	½ quart, 33.6 cubic inches	0.551 liter
quart	2 pints, 67.2 cubic inches	1.101 liters
peck	8 quarts, 537.605 cubic inches	8.810 liters
bushel	4 pecks, 2,150.420 cubic inches	35.239 liters

British Imperial Liquid and Dry Measure	U.S. Customary Equivalents	Metric Equivalents
fluid ounce	0.961 U.S. fluid ounce, 1.734 cubic inches	28.413 milliliters
pint	1.032 U.S. dry pints, 1.201 U.S. liquid pints, 34.678 cubic inches	568.245 milliliters
quart	1.032 U.S. dry quarts, 1.201 U.S. liquid quarts, 69.354 cubic inches	1.136 liters
gallon	1.201 U.S. gallons, 277.420 cubic inches	4.546 liters
peck	554.84 cubic inches	0.009 cubic meter
bushel	1.032 U.S. bushels, 2,219.36 cubic inches	0.036 cubic meter

The Metric System

Length

Unit	Number of Meters	Approximate U.S. Equivalent	Unit	Number of Meters	Approximate U.S. Equivalent
myriameter	10,000	6.214 miles	meter	1	39.370 inches
kilometer	1,000	0.621 mile	decimeter	0.1	3.937 inches
hectometer	100	109.361 yards	centimeter	0.01	0.394 inch
decameter	10	32.808 feet	millimeter	0.001	0.039 inch

Area

Unit	Number of Square Meters	Approximate U.S. Equivalent	Unit	Number of Square Meters	Approximate U.S. Equivalent
square kilometer	1,000,000	0.386 square mile	deciare	10	11.960 square yards
hectare	10,000	2.477 acres	centare	1	10.764 square feet
are	100	119.599 square yards	square centimeter	0.0001	0.115 square inch

Table 7. *(continued)*

Volume

Unit	Number of Cubic Meters	Approximate U.S. Equivalent	Unit	Number of Cubic Meters	Approximate U.S. Equivalent
decastere	10	13.079 cubic yards	decistere	0.10	3.532 cubic feet
stere	1	1.308 cubic yards	cubic centimeter	0.000001	0.061 cubic inch

Capacity

Unit	Number of Liters	Cubic	Approximate U.S. Equivalents Dry	Liquid
kiloliter	1,000	1.308 cubic yards		
hectoliter	100	3.532 cubic feet	2.838 bushels	
decaliter	10	0.353 cubic foot	1.135 pecks	2.642 gallons
liter	1	61.024 cubic inches	0.908 quart	1.057 quarts
deciliter	0.10	6.102 cubic inches	0.182 pint	0.211 pint
centiliter	0.01	0.610 cubic inch		0.338 fluid ounce
milliliter	0.001	0.061 cubic inch		0.271 fluid dram

Mass and Weight

Unit	Number of Grams	Approximate U.S. Equivalent	Unit	Number of Grams	Approximate U.S. Equivalent
metric ton	1,000,000	1.102 tons	gram	1	0.035 ounce
quintal	100,000	220.462 pounds	decigram	0.10	1.543 grains
kilogram	1,000	2.205 pounds	centigram	0.01	0.154 grain
hectogram	100	3.527 ounces	milligram	0.001	0.015 grain
decagram	10	0.353 ounce			

Metric Conversion Chart—Approximations

When You Know	Multiply By	To Find	When You Know	Multiply By	To Find
Length			**Volume**		
millimeters	0.04	inches	liters	1.06	quarts
centimeters	0.39	inches	liters	0.26	gallons
meters	3.28	feet	cubic meters	35.32	cubic feet
meters	1.09	yards	cubic meters	1.35	cubic yards
kilometers	0.62	miles	teaspoons	4.93	milliliters
inches	25.40	millimeters	tablespoons	14.78	milliliters
inches	2.54	centimeters	fluid ounces	29.57	milliliters
feet	30.48	centimeters	cups	0.24	liters
yards	0.91	meters	pints	0.47	liters
miles	1.61	kilometers	quarts	0.95	liters
			gallons	3.79	liters
Area					
square centimeters	0.16	square inches	**Volume**		
square meters	1.20	square yards	cubic feet	0.03	cubic meters
square kilometers	0.39	square miles	cubic yards	0.76	cubic meters
hectares (10,000m^2)	2.47	acres			
square inches	6.45	square centimeters	**Speed**		
square feet	0.09	square meters	miles per hour	1.61	kilometers per hour
square yards	0.84	square meters	kilometers per hour	0.62	miles per hour
square miles	2.60	square kilometers			
acres	0.40	hectares	**Temperature (exact)**		
			Celsius temp.	9/5, +32	Fahrenheit temp.
Mass and Weight			Fahrenheit temp.	− 32, 5/9 × remainder	Celsius temp.
grams	0.035	ounce			
kilograms	2.21	pounds			
tons (100kg)	1.10	short tons			
ounces	28.35	grams			
pounds	0.45	kilograms			
short tons (2000 lb)	0.91	tons			

Temperatures in degrees Celsius, as in the familiar Fahrenheit system, can only be learned through experience. The following temperatures are ones that are frequently encountered:

When You Know	Multiply By	To Find
Volume		
milliliters	0.20	teaspoons
milliliters	0.06	tablespoons
milliliters	0.03	fluid ounces
liters	4.23	cups
liters	2.12	pints

0°C	Freezing point of water (32°F)
10°C	A warm winter day (50°F)
20°C	A mild spring day (68°F)
30°C	A hot summer day (86°F)
37°C	Normal body temperature (98.6°F)
40°C	Heat wave conditions (104°F)
100°C	Boiling point of water (212°F)

1. The full names of SI units are always written in lowercase letters (unless being the first word in a sentence). Some SI units (newton, kelvin, watt, pascal) are named after famous scientists; if so, the *symbol* begins with an uppercase letter (N, K, W, Pa). An exception is the (non-SI but commonly used) unit for temperature, the degree Celsius, which is always capitalized.

2. SI units are not italicized because they are not mathematical symbols.

3. Do not put a period after SI symbols, except at the end of a sentence; they are *not* abbreviations.

4. Do not mix unit names and their symbols. For example, do not write km/second. Write either km/s or kilometre/second.

5. Do not pluralize symbols. For example, write 800 km, not 800 kms. Full unit names are pluralized normally, by adding an *s* (metres, kilograms). NOTE: We spell *metre, centimetre,* etc., in the European fashion, which is the approved SI style. You will, however, often see these units with their American spellings. Unless you are preparing material for a journal requiring or permitting the American spelling, the European spelling is preferred. (The metric ton is always spelled *tonne*).

6. Always space between a symbol and its numerical value; 500 s, not 500s (which appears to be the plural of 500). The exception is the degree Celsius (°C), where the degree and Celsius symbols are written flush with the numerical value (40°C).

7. When a prefix symbol (M, G, etc.) is combined with a unit symbol, do not leave a space between them: GHz, not G Hz.

8. Derived units involving multiplication, such as Newton metre, should be separated from one another with a raised dot (N·M) or, if your typing element lacks this symbol, with a period (N.M).

9. Derived units involving division can be written using either the solidus (/) or the negative exponent combined with the dot multiplier. For example, kilograms per cubic metre may be written kg/m^3 or $kg \cdot m^{-3}$. When preparing a manuscript for a journal, you should consult its style specifications on this point. Whatever style is used, it is best to be consistent.

10. When numerical values are written in SI, use a space rather than a comma to separate groups of three digits to the left and to the right of the decimal point, as in the standard American style. Thus, ten thousand is typed 10 000 rather than 10,000 and one millionth as 0.000 000 1 rather than 0.000,000,1. This convention was adopted because Europeans traditionally use a comma where we use a decimal point and periods to space groups of three numbers. However, numbers

with only four digits to the right or left of the decimal point are written without either a space or a comma (9856 and 0.0011). In decimal numbers less than one, the decimal point is *always* preceded by a zero: 0.068, not .068.

PARTS OF A SCIENTIFIC MANUSCRIPT

Like any other narrative account, a scientific or technical report must have a beginning, a middle, and an end. This seems elementary, but it is surprising how many professional scientists ignore this precept in practice. Although you cannot be expected to rewrite a paper (that is the author's or the editor's job), you can be alert to obvious omissions, especially when preparing material for a professional journal. There are, of course, many different forms of scientific and technical writing, from an article written for popular consumption to a journal paper, a meeting paper, an internal document, a published report, a grant application, etc. Each has its own special format and requirements. Here, we focus on the parts of a typical scientific report.

A report can serve a variety of purposes: it can present the results of experiment, it can be a purely theoretical study, it can compare the results of experiment with theory, or it can survey and review the current status of a particular topic. In addition to its substantive portions—the beginning, middle, and end—a report contains certain parts that may be regarded as "housekeeping"; that is, it contains parts that provide the standard information normally included in scholarly writing. These usually brief parts may be some or all of the following:

1. **Title**   Titles may be subject to restrictions (especially by journals). For example, some journals limit the number of words in a title or specify that a title cannot be a question.

2. **By-line and supplementary information**   This includes the name of the author or authors, address or institutional affiliation, etc.

3. **Abstract**   An abstract summarizes in a few sentences the research problem addressed and the author's principal conclusions. Abstracts serve a twofold purpose: printed with the paper, they provide a brief overview of its content; abstracts are also printed in journals dedicated solely to abstracts of work in a particular field.

4. **Acknowledgments**   In the acknowledgments, an author may give credit to others who contributed significantly to the work reported; these may be individuals, institutions, or funding agencies.

5. **References**   Many authors are careless about the accuracy, completeness, and style of their references. The secretary may be asked to verify references or to complete fragmentary references by consulting the source. (Nearly all journals specify a style for references; your institution may have a preferred style for its reports.) Make sure that every reference cited appears in the list of references and that every reference listed is cited.

6. **Index codes or key words** These list the principal topics addressed in a report in a form appropriate for computerized search. In most sciences there is a standard index from which index codes or key words may be drawn.

PREPARING MATERIALS FOR SCIENTIFIC JOURNALS

The number of specialized scientific and technical journals and their publication costs have grown enormously over the past few decades. As a result, the editorial resources of many journals have been stretched so thin that most submitted manuscripts cannot be edited, and careless preparation may be cause for rejection. Although authors are aware of their responsibility for a paper's content and technical accuracy, many are careless about details of style. The secretary is often the one person who must ensure proper formatting and perform routine copyediting—tasks that require thorough familiarity with the style requirements of specific journals.

All journals provide, in some form, specifications that detail format and style requirements. These usually include instructions governing length, title, abstract, types of headings used, numbering of sections, abbreviations, mathematical conventions, use of metric units, preparation of artwork and photographs, and so on. Such a guide may appear in each issue of a journal or at intervals throughout the publication cycle. Some journals (or institutions publishing several journals) provide a more comprehensive style guide which may be ordered, and still others refer their authors to a general style guide such as the University of Chicago's *Manual of Style* (13th ed.).

The secretary preparing a manuscript for a journal should obtain a copy of its current style specifications. These should be followed as closely as possible. However, no journal is likely to provide complete guidance on every aspect of style. Accordingly, it is important for you to obtain copies of one or more recent issues of the journal and to follow these when in doubt. If the articles vary in details of style that are not covered in the journal's style guide, choose any standard guide and follow it consistently. Another good general guide to the preparation of technical papers is John H. Mitchell's *Writing for Technical and Professional Journals*, published by John Wiley & Sons, New York.

What the Secretary Can Contribute to a Journal Article

The most important contributions that you can make to a manuscript being prepared for journal submission are adherence to style specifications, notational consistency, neatness, and legibility. Keep in mind that you are not designing an article for the compositor: the journal editor will mark up the manuscript for typesetting and in doing so will indicate size and styles of type for text, subheads, figure captions, and so forth. Your job is to ensure that the manuscript is as complete and as accurate as possible. Signs and symbols should be typed whenever feasible. When they are not available on a typing element, or when typing them would require continual changing of elements, they may be entered neatly and legibly in the text with a black pen. The first time a sign or symbol (other than an English letter) is used, its name enclosed in a circle should be noted opposite it in the margin. This enables the compositor, who will be typesetting the manuscript, to interpret the symbols in the text. Some signs and symbols,

Table 8.* Some Easily Confused Symbols†

Symbol	Identification	As typeset	Symbol	Identification	As typeset
a	cap aye	A	ψ	lc psi	ψ
a	lc aye	a	Ψ	cap psi	Ψ
α	lc alpha	α	ϕ	lc phi	φ
$\propto$	proportional to	∝	Φ	cap phi	Φ
∞	infinity	∞		cap sigma	Σ
c	lc cee	c	Σ	summation	Σ
C	cap cee	C	s	lc ess	s
|	vertical bar	|	S	cap ess	S
/	solidus	/	V	cap vee	V
′	prime	′	v	lc vee	v
I	one	1	ν	lc nu	ν
l	lc ell	l	γ	lc gamma	γ
e	lc ee	e	υ	lc upsilon	υ
∈	an element of	∈	u	lc you	u
ε	lc epsilon	ε	μ	lc mu	μ
ε	eh	ε	W	cap double-you	W
K	cap kay	K	w	lc double-you	w
k	lc kay	k	ω	lc omega	ω
κ	lc kappa	κ	x	lc ex	x
n	lc en	n	X	cap ex	X
η	lc eta	η	×	multiplication sign	×
°	degrees	°	χ	lc chi	χ
o	lc oh	o	z	lc zee	z
O	cap oh	O	Z	cap zee	Z
0	zero	0	2	two	2
ρ	lc rho	ρ	⟨⟩	angle brackets	⟨⟩
p	lc pee	p	<,>	less than, greater than	<, >
P	cap pee	P	†	dagger	†
π	lc pi	π	+	plus	+
Π	cap pi	Π			
Π	product symbol	Π			

*Adapted with permission from the American Institute of Physics *Style Manual* (3rd ed.).
†The second column gives acceptable ways of spelling out a symbol in the margin when marking copy for typesetting.

especially if they are hand-lettered, are easily confused. Table 8 shows some of these symbols. If you are uncertain what the author intends, ask. Remember that the compositor will typeset what he or she thinks is there, not what you (or the author) know is there. In addition to annotating a symbol in the margin, you may be asked to prepare a list of all symbols used in the manuscript, together with their names. (Most journals require such a list.) Provision of a list of symbols affords additional insurance that they will be typeset correctly. Underscoring of Roman letters used in a mathematical context may be required if they are to be italicized in print. Follow the specifications of the individual journal, for house styles vary.

Neatness, legibility, and correctness are especially important when the paper being submitted is camera-ready copy (that is, it will be photographically copied for publication rather than typeset). This method is often used with symposium proceedings, for example. In other words, what you see is what you get. In such a case, marginal annotation and symbol lists are dispensed with, but it is wise to use rub-on symbols in the interest of appearance when symbols are unavailable on a typing element. It is also important in such a case to follow specifications for manuscripts *exactly*.

Illustrations

All journals provide specifications for illustrations submitted with manuscripts. These can include charts and graphs, line drawings, and photographs. Normally, graphs and other drawn illustrations will be produced by a professional technical illustrator prior to manuscript submission. You should provide a copy of a journal's specifications along with the hand-drawn illustrations when submitting them to an illustrator. Most journals will reject a paper if the illustrations have not been drawn to their specifications. For example, many journals must photographically reduce artwork to fit space limitations and format requirements. If the correct typesize has not been used on labels and callouts, these will appear either too small or too large when reduced and therefore will be unacceptable. It is the technical illustrator's job to ensure that such requirements are met. Photographs, if used, also should satisfy the journal's specifications regarding size, callouts, and so on. Since very few professional journals print color photographs, it is best to submit black-and-white glossy prints to ensure that the salient features will be visible in black-and-white reproduction. Previously screened photographs (i.e., images that have been treated to produce a dot pattern) are usually unacceptable. Placement of figures in a manuscript is indicated by simply making a note in the margin, such as "Fig. 2," or "Fig. 3 should appear about here," at an appropriate point (normally the first time a figure is mentioned). Circle these notations.

Submitting a Manuscript

After a final check of the manuscript against the journal's specifications, the original and any extra copies requested by the journal can be packaged for submission. *Always* keep at least one file copy of the manuscript, in case the original is lost or damaged. A manuscript is usually accompanied by a covering letter.

Proofs

Before a journal prints a paper, it will send typeset galley or page proofs to the author. (Galley proofs are uncut text; page proofs are fully laid-out pages.) This is the author's last chance to correct any errors; therefore, the proofs must be read with great care, especially if the paper contains mathematical material. Compositors and editors can make errors or misinterpret instructions. After reading the proofs, the author may ask you to proofread the typeset copy as a double check. Any errors that you find should be called to the author's attention and corrected neatly and legibly in the margin, using standard proofreaders' marks. In the days when the volume of scientific publications was smaller and costs were lower, journals normally provided galley proofs to an author. Any errors were reset by the typesetter before the text was set in page size for publication. Today the practice of most journals is to provide page proofs only. This means that any author-generated changes (adding a sentence, for example) other than corrections of typographical errors could require the resetting of an entire page or more.

Table 9. Examples of Selected Proofreaders' Marks

Mark	Instruction
Copper is highly toxic␣*to*␣many aquatic organisms.	Insert indicated letter, word, phrase, or sentence.
Copper is highly toxic␣#␣to many aquatic organisms.	Insert space.
Copper is highly toxic to many aquatic organisms⊙	Insert period.
Copper is highly toxic to many aquatic organisms␣and . . .	Insert punctuation (or subscript).
We have measured the mussels sensitivity to copper.	Insert apostrophe (or superscript).
Copper is highly toxic to many aquatic organisms.5	Raise to superscript.
Copper (29Cu) is highly toxic to many aquatic organisms.	Lower to subscript.
Copper is highly toxic to to many aquatic organisms.	Delete.
Copper is highly toxic to *many* all aquatic organisms.	Delete and insert.
Copper is highly toxic to many aqua tic organisms.	Close space.
Copper is highly toxic to many aquaatic organisms.	Delete and close.
Copper is highly toxic to many (STET) aquatic organisms.	Let it stand.
copper is highly toxic to many (U.C.) aquatic organisms.	Capitalized letter.
Copper is highly toxic to many aquatic Organisms. (lc.)	Lowercase letter.
Copper is highly toxic to many AQUATIC organisms.	Lowercase word.
Copper is highly toxic to many aquatic organisms.	Transpose letters.
Copper is highly (to toxic) many aquatic organisms.	Transpose words.
¶ Copper is highly toxic to many aquatic organisms.	Begin new paragraph.
No ¶ Copper is highly toxic to many aquatic organisms.	No new paragraph.
Copper is highly toxic to many ⌐aquatic organisms.	Move left as indicated.
Copper is highly toxic to many aquatic organisms. ⌐	Move right as indicated.

Table 9.   *(continued)*

Mark	Instruction
Copper is highly toxic to many aquatic organisms.	Raise as indicated.
Copper is highly toxic to many aquatic organisms.	Lower as indicated.
⌐APPENDIX A⌐	Center.
Copper is highly toxic to many aquatic organisms.	Run in.
APPENDIX A	Italics or underscore.
APPENDIX A	Boldface.

Since resets are costly, the author (or institution) may be billed for any such changes or additions. Nearly all journals today levy page charges for papers accepted. Page charges are normally billed to the institution rather than to the author, but a bill may be included along with the page proofs. You should find out how your organization handles these charges. At the time the corrected proofs are returned to the journal, the author may request reprints of the paper for distribution to colleagues. The publisher ordinarily includes with the proofs a form for ordering reprints. However, widespread use of photocopying has reduced the demand for reprints.

13

Time Management: Appointments, Meetings, and Conferences

Linda Noble Gutierrez • *Confidential Secretary, Human Resources Department*, The Times Mirror Company

Remember that time is money.
—Benjamin Franklin
Advice to a Young Tradesman
(1748)

The March Hare took the watch and looked at it gloomily; then he dipped it into his cup of tea and looked at it again.
—Lewis Carroll
Alice's Adventures in Wonderland
(1865)

Some meetings should be long and leisurely. Some should be mercifully brief. A good way to handle the latter is to hold the meeting with everybody standing up. The meetees won't believe you at first. Then they get very uncomfortable and can hardly wait to get the meeting over with.
—Robert Townsend
Further Up the Organization
(1984)

EXECUTIVE CALENDAR MANAGEMENT

Helping an executive manage time is an integral part of a secretary's duties. Many of the things that a secretary does for the executive, in one way or another, lend to enhanced management of time. Effective time management can be achieved through many means, some of which can be very detailed and others very simple, depending on the needs and requirements of the individual executive and the practices followed within the company. As a believer in "simplify, simplify," I tend to eliminate as many steps as possible to accomplish a given task. (But at the same time, the desired result of the activity must not be changed because of my own wish for simplification.) Since ours is a very busy and generally hectic office, I use as many timesaving methods and procedures as possible, within limitations. Undoubtedly, you too have realized that some practices and procedures have come to be "set in concrete," thus precluding introduction of more streamlined approaches. In this chapter I discuss some of the methods I have found to be useful in assisting the executive with appointments, schedules, and meetings.

Daily, Weekly, and Monthly Scheduling

One of your primary considerations as a time manager should be ensuring that the executive is in the proper location at the proper time, regardless of whether the location is within your own facility or at an outside site. Appropriate scheduling of meetings and appointments and confirmation or cancellation of them is critical in maintaining efficient use of the executive's time. Having a large, desk-type monthly calendar is a good start. Tentative schedules, indicated in pencil, can be logged in as far in advance as possible. If a business trip or meeting is scheduled during a particular month, for instance, it can be marked on the calendar along with all available information such as the destination or location, the time, travel arrangements, and so on. As the details are confirmed, appropriate notations can then be added to the calendar. Another method also may be helpful to you in this respect. I keep a monthly calendar book, and the executive to whom I report keeps a duplicate calendar book. We sit down from time to time and go over the calendar, scheduling as far into the future as possible in *both* books. Our own schedules require us to do this only occasionally; however, you may have to do it on a daily, weekly, or monthly basis, depending on the nature of the executive's schedule and the practices or needs of your company. Again, as confirmations are received or other details are arranged, we note them in the appropriate places in both books. If the executive's schedule often changes erratically and without notice, you should note all activities in the books in pencil to facilitate quick, neat changes.

Confirmations and cancellations.   A prompt telephone call to confirm or cancel an appointment or meeting is a simple way to eliminate no-shows on both sides. The call should take only a moment or two of your time. This, of course, avoids wasting the executive's time later on and precludes any possibility of the executive or a caller appearing at a particular place and time without a confirmed appointment. If a meeting or appointment remains unconfirmed or has been cancelled, that block of time then becomes open to all of the parties involved for still other appointments or other activities.

You may be confronted with a situation in which the executive leaves for a meeting that overruns its allotted time, in which case appointments throughout the rest of the day could become hopelessly backed up. Think ahead: if you know that meetings with certain people tend to run long, call the conference room or office in which the meeting is taking place and confer with the executive. You can then call the scheduled visitors and reschedule their appointments. If you know that some of the visitors have rather flexible schedules, you can call them on your own without conferring with the executive, and say, "Ms. Lee is in a meeting that may last well into the afternoon. I doubt very much that she will be able to see you at one o'clock today, but her schedule tomorrow morning looks very good. Could you come in about 9:30?" If the executive is in a high-level meeting with, say, the chairman or the president, call the secretary to this officer, explain the situation, and ask that a message be conveyed to your superior regarding the upcoming appointments. Your superior can then call you back at a convenient time.

Some executives are very well organized and are always aware of their upcoming activities. They have an excellent sense of time. Managing the time of such a person is relatively easy. Others, however, especially those who are involved in numerous high-priority projects, seem unable to schedule themselves realistically and really entrust their days to their secretaries. If you are in this situation, you'll have to become very familiar with all of the executive's associates and outside visitors so that you can make spot decisions regarding rescheduling and cancellation of appointments. You may be faced with five visitors pacing in the outside office, impatiently waiting for an Executive Who Isn't There and you have no idea where to find him or her. You can put a tracer on the executive by calling all of the offices frequently visited, or you can save yourself a lot of time by suggesting that the executive purchase a beeper. You can beep the executive on or off the company site with reminders that certain activities are scheduled during the rest of the day. Or, you can use the beeper to alert the executive that visitors are waiting in the office.

Tickler files.   Use of a tickler or "suspense" file has been very helpful to me in my daily, weekly, and monthly scheduling. When I know that a particular item (e.g., correspondence, a note, or a reminder) is due on a certain date, I put a notation to this effect into a tickler file in my desk and I mark my daily calendar "suspense." This notation reminds me that an item in the suspense file will need attention on a certain date. Some of you may wish to use an expansion file tabbed by day, month, or full date, as appropriate. Another extremely useful item is a control sheet that tells me when reports or other materials are to be issued. I simply use a sheet marked with grid lines. The date is written across the top, either by day or month, and the reports or other projects are listed down the left-hand side. Progress on each can be noted within the grid. The control sheet lets me know at first glance where I stand with upcoming activities from start to finish. It therefore serves as a comprehensive reminder and a progress report.

Our legal department is responsible for our company's corporate calendar. At the beginning of each year the legal department solicits input from various executives and departments as to what activities, such as meeting dates or deadlines for particular documents or reports, should be noted on that calendar. Recurring events and projects with predetermined dates and deadlines, such as shareholders' meetings and the issuance of annual reports, are, of course, already indicated on the corporate calendar. This calendar, when made final, is then issued to all of the executives and secretaries concerned, followed by updated monthly versions reflecting revisions or other changes as appropriate. In this way, high-level corporate communication regarding such activities is ensured. The same system could be used on a smaller scale for the secretary's own needs or as an aid to the executive in outlining daily, weekly, monthly, or annual planning and reporting. Such a calendar would provide a broad outline of the matters to be taken care of by day, week, month, or at any given time during the year. The daily, weekly, or monthly update (as required by the circumstances) will allow progress, changes, or adjustments to be recorded and acted on.

Communication between executive and secretary.   Communication between executive and secretary concerning calendar planning and scheduling is imperative to ensure accurate and effective time management. Imagine the embarrassment that could ensue if the executive schedules an appointment with one guest or client, while in the meantime the secretary unwittingly schedules another appointment for the same hour with another guest or a competitive client. This kind of communication breakdown should not happen. One way of avoiding double bookings is to have an understanding with the executive whereby you schedule *tentative* appointments. With this system you notify the visitor that the meeting or appointment is tentative and that confirmation will follow. After having checked with the executive as to the schedule for that date and time, you then can confirm the appointment. The confirmed appointment should be noted in both calendar books. This procedure, while preventing overbooking of appointments, also precludes the possibility of your scheduling unwanted or unscreened appointments. It is far wiser to spend a few minutes on a daily or weekly basis in going over the tentative or confirmed appointment schedule or meeting to avoid situations embarrassing for all concerned. Try to set a specific time for this activity.

"Do not disturb" or quiet time blocks.   Every executive should try to set aside quiet or "do not disturb" time periods, either during each day or at some point once or twice each week. However, in reality, it can be more difficult to accomplish than one might think. For example, members of our staff were fortunate enough to participate in a time management seminar a number of years ago. Stressed during the seminar was the importance of the "do not disturb" time periods, preferably in the morning hours. Although quiet hours would have been very beneficial to all of us, we were unable to put it into effect in our department.

If you and the executive are able to set aside such blocks of time, the executive can use it for planning, paperwork, formulating thoughts and ideas, and problem-solving. Staff members should be informed that "Ms. Doe is, from now on, reserving the time from 9:15 a.m. to 10:15 a.m. [or whatever] for concentrated, undisturbed work and will see no visitors and will take only the most urgent calls during that period." The executive should shut the door—a closed door usually will cause even the more aggressive visitors to pause. You will have to be firm with visitors and callers at first until they realize the executive is truly serious about the need for quiet time.

An ancillary advantage to this arrangement is that it may give you an opportunity to catch up on miscellaneous correspondence, paperwork, filing, and other matters. If you have an assistant, the assistant could answer the telephone for you during this period.

Time Wasters

When we attended the time management seminar mentioned earlier, we also learned that an enormous amount of time is wasted, particularly but not exclusively, by the executives themselves. A recent study of management by Henry Mintzberg of McGill University shows that executives' biggest time wasters are telephone interruptions, drop-in visitors, ineffective delegation of tasks, and meetings with two or more people in attendance, in that order. And the members of the Secretarial Advisory Board of this book have indicated in their answers to questionnaires that meetings consume most of the chief executive officers' time. The situation may seem utterly hopeless; however, you and the executive can work together to alleviate it as much as possible. For example, you should display initiative in handling as many administrative details as possible and in coordinating effective procedures for an easy flow of paper. This, of course, turns on the willingness of the executive to delegate these responsibilities to you and to rely on your good judgment in fulfilling them. As we have learned in Chapter Nine, you can and should sort, read, and annotate incoming mail and other documents. Attaching the appropriate files or back-up information to incoming documents will facilitate later action by the executive. If an incoming letter is a response to a letter from the executive, attach a copy of the executive's original letter to the incoming reply. Include with them any other relevant material, such as a memo. In this way you can save the executive expensive time otherwise wasted while wading through masses of mail, some items of which probably could have been handled by another person or department.

Interruptions. Of course, no office is free of interruptions. But the number of interruptions tends to increase proportionally to the extent that the executive's ongoing responsibilities and projects escalate. Your job is to shield the executive from all unnecessary and extraneous interruptions by screening and redirecting telephone calls as appropriate and by screening visitors. If you are cognizant of the executive's priority projects and the importance of various callers as they relate to the executive's position and projects, you should be able to control and modulate the flow of incoming calls and visitors.

Compile a list of frequent callers and the level of priority of their calls. The executive will always talk to certain people whenever they call, but there will be others to whom the executive may or may not wish to talk. This list should be kept next to the phone, in full view so that you or anyone else covering for you can see it at a glance. Confer with the executive from time to time to ensure that the list is kept revised and current.

Our office receives numerous telephone calls that really should be redirected to other departments. Many of the callers ask for "my old pal so and so" but then mispronounce the executive's name. Obviously, those callers are not really old friends or business associates of the executive at all but wish to appear to be so that the executive will take the call. With calls like this, try to assist the caller and whenever possible, forward the call to the proper person or department. If the caller is insistent, take a message and let the executive decide later whether or not to return the call.

A log of incoming telephone calls can be prepared by the secretary, as shown in Chapter Eight. When giving the list to the executive, the secretary can include precise information about the nature of the call together with any relevant attachments and back-up material. Difficult and unfamiliar names should be accompanied by phonetic spellings to aid the executive in pronouncing them correctly—a useful public relations gesture.

Our time management seminar recommended that a predetermined period during the day be set aside for making or returning telephone calls. If the executive could block out such a time, either before or after lunch or even late in the day, frequent callers would become accustomed to expecting a return call at a certain time and others could be advised accordingly.

Organizing your own tasks. Set your own task priorities by keeping a list of specific things to be done on a given day and then do them. Divide your tasks into small time blocks and handle each one in order of importance. Try to schedule short, simple tasks between other activities. Arrange schedules around high-priority projects and do first things first. Extra time always should be allowed for concentration on high-priority matters, and the time of day during which you are at your best should be reserved for such activities. If working on figures, for example, early in the morning might be the best time for you.

If you report to more than one executive, you may have a time management problem that could evolve into a people problem unless you do the following:

1. Find out which executive is higher in rank; the work that you do for the higher-ranking executive will take priority. For example, if you work for the chairman and the president, the

chairman's assignments should be carried out first. And at the outset, everyone concerned should reach an understanding about priorities-by-rank.

2. If possible, obtain colored in- and out-boxes and assign them to each executive. Label them clearly with the executives' names. Try to get the executives to use these boxes rather than dropping materials onto the middle of your desk.

3. If the executives hand you top-priority tasks all at the same time, ask for the assistance of a temporary worker. You can offload the less complicated tasks onto this person.

4. Set up a back-up system with another secretary who can fill in for you during breaks and on occasions when you are in meetings or are away from the office.

5. Establish set time blocks for performing time-consuming tasks such as mail sorting and annotating. Whenever possible, keep up with filing chores on a daily basis so that you are not swamped with unfiled papers at week's end.

Meetings

Although meetings are vital to the conduct of business, many are unnecessary. Some meetings are now being eliminated through the use of telephone conference calls, videoconferencing, and electronic mail. All of these alternatives are, in the long run, less costly and more efficient than meetings. When a meeting or conference is being discussed, many factors should be considered to determine whether the meeting is truly necessary in the first place. The secretary is normally not in a position to make such determinations; however, input from the secretary can, at times, be of great assistance to the executive. Is there a real objective for the meeting or conference? If the meeting is for gathering or dispersing of information, what will be accomplished as a result? If no concrete actions will be taken, or if the participants will not leave the meeting better informed, why have the meeting in the first place?

Let's consider at the outset what Stephanie Winston, author of *The Organized Executive: New Ways to Manage Time, Paper, and People* (New York: W.W. Norton & Company, 1983), tells us on pages 148 and 149 of her book:

> According to a recent study by the management consulting firm Booz, Allen & Hamilton, 299 managers with an average salary of $40,000 spent half their time in meetings. And a sizable chunk of that time was absorbed by rambling discussions, political maneuvering, excessive socializing, and special-interest conflicts. Nor is time the only casualty. Five $50,000-a-year people spending ten useless hours a week in meetings can cost your firm well over $1,000 a week.

If asked, you can encourage your executive to use more time- and cost-efficient methods of discussion and decision-making. These include a quick one-on-one phone call, a conference or videoconferencing call, a short memo, or a scaled-down and tightly controlled meeting devoted only to the pertinent topics. In a scaled-down meeting, the agenda itself can contain specific time limitations for discussion of topics. Example: Marketing Plan — Software (10:30–11:00 a.m.).

But once a meeting has definitely been decided upon, a few simple ploys can be used to make it efficient, controlled, and effective. First of all, the attendee list should be scaled down: only those who are essential to the objective of the meeting should attend. Ten or twelve people at the most should attend a discussion-style meeting. However, if the intent is to give or hear a speech, with or without a question-and-answer period, the number of participants need be restricted only by seating and space availability. After having determined the number of participants, an agenda should be prepared. For meetings that we have been involved with, a preliminary (or "working") agenda is circulated to the prospective participants. In some cases, the host may wish to solicit input from those participants as to what items might be included or excluded. We have had cases in which an individual received and reviewed a preliminary agenda and then decided that he or she was really not the appropriate person to attend. That person might wish to send another representative, or might not want to be represented at the meeting at all. Use of a preliminary agenda enables the host to cut out as much extraneous subject matter as possible. The final agenda is, of course, developed from the preliminary model and is distributed to the participants in advance.

Responses from the Advisory Board Regarding Time Management Problems

In a questionnaire sent to the members of our Secretarial Advisory Board, we asked the respondents to "list, according to degree of irritation, the prime wasters of [their] executives' time," with number 1 being the worst culprit and number 5, the least offensive. We have already mentioned earlier in this chapter that meetings took the number 1 slot with no contest. Look now at the *percentage* of executive time actually spent in meetings:

1. meetings/business lunches (an average of 70.9% of the executive's day spent in this activity)
2. paperwork (reading/writing/digesting memos, letters, and reports)
3. backed-up mail
4. too many trips
5. too many overlong phone calls

Only one respondent had no problems with these activities: she stated that "he doesn't waste time on any of the above. That's what I'm there for."

When asked to list, in order of time consumption, the five tasks that occupy most of their own work days, the majority of the executive secretaries/assistants on the Board listed the following items in this order:

1. scheduling appointments and greeting guests
2. answering the telephone
3. incoming mail management
4. making meeting/conference/travel arrangements
5. running the office in the executive's absence

Keep in mind that the Board members are the secretaries/assistants to presidents and chief executive officers of large corporations. Three fourths of them have at least one clerical assistant who is typically assigned some, or all of these tasks:

1. keyboarding documents
2. filing
3. photocopying
4. ordering/maintaining supplies
5. opening/sorting/distributing mail
6. keeping an outgoing mail log
7. handling routine, "informational" phone calls and serving as a "telephone back-up" person
8. research

Undoubtedly these lists pose no surprises to experienced secretaries. However, they present all of us with food for thought if we consider that, of five tasks in the list of most time-consuming secretarial activities, only one task can really be eradicated by office automation. That activity is, of course, incoming *paper* mail management. (In the future the executive will be able to deal much more directly and much faster with the mail by way of electronics.) The other four activities— appointment management, telephone management, meeting/conference/travel arrangements, and running the office in the absence of the executive—require highly developed organizational and decision-making skills. Conversely, two major items in the list of activities assigned to the secretaries' clerical assistants have been markedly impacted by the advent of office automation: document keyboarding and photocopying. And filing won't be far behind, when many more companies adopt electronic filing systems tied in with their electronic mail systems. In total, five out of the eight clerical tasks have been or will be further streamlined and reduced in scope by OA. There are several messages here: hone down your organizational competency and strive for a top-level position by being a superb time manager. (Incidentally, "excellent organizational skills" was listed by a majority of our Board as the most significant attribute of an exceptional secretary. Close behind came "initiative and willingness to assume responsibility," "cooperation," "a true interest in the corporation and the executive's goals," "confidentiality and trustworthiness," and "excellent attendance.") If you are currently experiencing an overloaded work schedule, try to hire an assistant on whom you can offload some of the more routine tasks. If your company cannot or will not hire a full-time assistant to help you, try for a student intern or a part-time temporary worker.

ARRANGEMENTS FOR FORMAL MEETINGS AND CONFERENCES

Using the Services of Hotel Meeting Coordinators

Setting up a formal meeting or conference may be simple or complicated, depending on the nature of the event and the kind of advance planning you do. The easiest and most direct way to plan off-site meetings is to get in touch with the hotel or facility where the event will be held. Major domestic and foreign hotels and conference centers usually have individuals or staff responsible for setting up and coordinating meeting arrangements. Why spend time and energy making arrangements that can be handled by others who are trained and paid exclusively to do just that? They may be able to suggest innovative arrangements that you have not even considered. As an example, we held a recent meeting in Palm Springs, California. About a dozen executives from around the nation attended. When determining the hotel or conference site, we simply called many hotels in the Palm Springs area, selected the most appropriate one, and let the meeting coordinator handle the arrangements that we requested. Most of the hotels in that particular area do not charge for meeting rooms, but may or may not levy additional charges for extras, such as audiovisual equipment. After we had outlined the requirements for this meeting, the hotel representative provided us with printed preregistration cards, which we sent to the participants. They, in turn, made their own reservations directly with the hotel—a process that saved an enormous amount of our time. When the event drew near, we checked with the hotel to find out who had made reservations and verified their count with our list of respondents. Discrepancies were straightened out with the participants by telephone. Had we chosen to do so, we could have had the participants get in touch with us concerning their hotel reservations, and then we could have taken further steps to coordinate them with the hotel representative.

Other meetings or conferences may require that all arrangements be made in a more personal fashion. Regardless of whether this is the case or whether the hotel or conference site representative does the coordinating, it is extremely important that all possible requirements be known well in advance of the event.

Making Arrangements for Off-site Meetings and Conferences Yourself

You can't always rely on the availability of hotel meeting planners at every single meeting site. Furthermore, you will have to have planned the activities in advance to a certain degree so that you can tell the hotel people—whoever they may be—the following essential things:

> the date(s) of the meeting
>
> the number of participants
>
> the size of the conference room(s) and dining room(s) needed and the desired seating plans
>
> the meals (i.e., the number, locations, times, and menus)
>
> the special equipment (if any) required
>
> the nonbusiness events planned

Obviously, you must know well in advance the inclusive dates of the event. The number of participants must be worked out and confirmed well in advance, too, for this figure affects all other planning—the budget for the entire event, the number of hotel reservations required, the selection of conference and dining rooms, the type of seating, the group rates for meals, and so forth. Determine with the hotel the final cutoff date for receipt of acceptances and changes in the list of participants and stick to it. Otherwise, chaos will reign—rooms will not be available, the hotel staff will be upset, and participants arriving without reserved

Meeting Activity Sheet

```
TO:     International Hotel              SUBJECT:        Affiliates' Meeting

FROM:   Janice Sale                     INCLUSIVE DATES:  May 1, 19— through
        Executive Assistant to Mart Miller               May 4, 19—
        UBC TV Network
        45 Green Mountain Tower
        Anywhere, US 98765
        (123) 456-7890

DATE:   February 1, 19—
```

DAY-BY-DAY ACTIVITY CHART

date	time	room	activity	setup	attendees	equipment	food
5/4	9:00 a.m. to noon	Colonial	Ratings Review	Panel Plan seats for 200	200	1 dias mike 25 aisle mikes 4 video machines	
	10:30 a.m. to 10:45 a.m.	Colonial	Break	4 buffet tables	200		fruit bowl pastries coffee/ tea/milk/ juice
	1:00 p.m. to 2:00 p.m.	Lee	Luncheon	20 round tables each seating 10 persons	200		vichy- soisse veal roast green salad rolls apple pie coffee/ tea/milk
	2:15 p.m. to 5:00 p.m.	Colonial	New Programs	same as 9-12	200	same as 9-12	
	3:45 p.m. to 4:00 p.m.	Colonial	Break	same as 10:30- 10:45 a.m.	200		cheese crackers coffee/ tea/milk/ juice
	6:00 p.m. to 7:30 p.m.	Jeffer- son	Cocktail Party	4 buffet tables 4 open bars	200		see attached bar and hors d'oeuvres lists

rooms will be angry. Take bids from at least three hotels based on the data in the list above. You and the executive can then decide together which hotel is the most competitive. At this point you should give the hotel detailed information on a day-by-day chart showing exactly what is expected of them. Base your chart on the agenda that the executive has written for the meeting. See the illustration for a sample of one day's activities.

A detailed conference package ought to be mailed to all participants well in advance. If the conference involves several days of long meetings, type up a separate agenda for each day, allowing ample space between agenda items as explained and illustrated in Chapter Five. Also in the package should be:

a map indicating the location of the meeting site

ground transportation data

registration materials including name tag

information regarding hotel check-in and check-out times, room reservations and payments, meal plans, and payment procedures

description of planned entertainment and a précis of available activities and points of interest to be seen during free time

sports facilities described

list of doctors in the area

Seating plans.   Various seating plans should be studied with a view toward the nature of the meeting (Is it a panel discussion? A formal sales presentation? An informal brainstorming session? A meeting at which a VIP will give a speech?) and the number of participants. The next illustration shows you some of the more typical seating plans used at meetings.

When developing the seating plans, set up separate smoking and nonsmoking areas. An attractive way to indicate them is by affixing the international "smoking permitted" and "smoking forbidden" press-on signs to pieces of folded poster board and placing them on the appropriate tables. Consider round tables for meals—such tables allow for more relaxed conversation. The long rectangular tables of the T and U Formations are more appropriate for formal gatherings, especially those during which video or slide shows are to be presented.

Companies usually plan morning and afternoon breaks during meetings. For the morning break, usually lasting fifteen minutes, you will have to arrange for coffee, tea, juice, and milk as well as snacks. Ensure that decaffeinated coffee is available. Try to get away from serving only sweet rolls at the morning break— sweet rolls at such gatherings have become a gastronomic cliché. A large crystal bowl of melon balls mixed with various other fresh fruits would be a welcome alternative or at least an interesting supplement to the rolls. Perhaps some hot turnovers would also be appealing. Consult with the hotel or an outside caterer for innovative ideas.

Ensure that all tables are covered and that they are set with water pitchers, glasses, ashtrays, pens, and writing tablets. If placecards are to be used, check them against your seating charts just before the meeting begins. If audiovisual equipment, screens, flipcharts and markers, slide projectors, lecterns, microphones, recorders, or video machines are needed, give the hotel a list of these items and then ensure later on that they are on hand in the right rooms at the right times. With overhead projectors, you should find out the dimensions of the screens so that the people preparing the transparencies will tailor them to fit the equipment. If the hotel cannot supply all the equipment that you need, check the Yellow Pages for equipment rentals. *Reconfirm* delivery of all rental equipment.

Your role at the meeting.   If you are slated to attend the meeting, you will fulfill many responsibilities which could be grouped under the general heading of *expediter* or *troubleshooter*. You should have several checklists with you on which you have noted the particulars of the meeting plans for each day. Go to the meeting rooms and check the seating, the ventilation, the placecards, the positioning of the equipment, and the arrangements for morning and afternoon break refreshments. Stay in contact with the hotel staff members assigned to your company's event and work closely with them to resolve any last-minute problems. If registration is to take place the night before and early on the first official

Seating Plans for Meetings

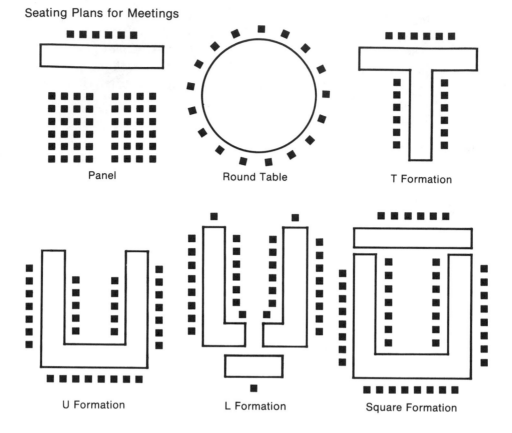

Panel

Round Table

T Formation

U Formation

L Formation

Square Formation

day of the meeting, be at the desk along with the other participants so that you can assist in getting the attendees settled. It is a good idea to hand out a card with your name and room number on it, so that if anyone does have a problem with a room or a bill, that person can call you for assistance.

You may be asked to assist a speaker with a slide projector or an audiovisual projector during a presentation. Take enough time in advance to familiarize yourself with the equipment so that the presentation will run smoothly and professionally. If possible, rehearse the presentation at least once before it is given, especially if you are using a slide projector keyed to a running tape recorder. Be sure that all electrical cords are out of the way; speakers have been known to become entangled in such wiring and then fall while walking back and forth during presentations—most embarrassing and hazardous incidents.

If the company has booked a hospitality suite for informal gatherings between events, see to it that Housekeeping cleans and airs the room at least one time, and preferably two times during the day. Stale cigarette smoke and stale leftover drinks combine to create a rather unpleasant atmosphere for people who might want to use the suite for phone calls, small informal meetings, or just for relaxation.

You may have to arrange for special secretarial or translation services. Discuss these problems with the hotel; if no help is forthcoming, check the Yellow Pages for temporary secretarial persons and for foreign-language translators or schools. Universities are also good sources for translators, as is the United States State

Department, which maintains a list of qualified people to accompany foreign visitors on government-sponsored itineraries.

Perhaps the meeting will feature a VIP from the private, political, government, or entertainment sector as a keynote speaker or performer. If this is the case, talk to that person's staff and the hotel staff about any special security arrangements required. (See also Chapter Fourteen on executive security arrangements, most of which apply equally well here.)

On-site Meetings

On-site meetings can include the following:

1. sales and other meetings held at corporate headquarters (these involve hotel, restaurant, travel, and entertainment arrangements as indicated in the previous sections)

2. shareholders' and directors' meetings

3. regularly scheduled management and executive committee meetings

4. special staff, management, and executive meetings

5. employee meetings (such as those called by management to make important announcements)

For regularly scheduled and special meetings you should:

1. obtain the date, time of day, and location

2. reserve an on-site meeting room

3. obtain the list of attendees

4. prepare and distribute a meeting announcement and an agenda (the distribution list of the agenda may or may not be controlled)

5. alert the attendees and/or presenters of any special materials that they may have to bring with them

6. notify the chair of any prospective absentees

7. just before the meeting is to start (i.e., about thirty minutes ahead of time) check the room for proper ventilation, pens and writing tablets, and the presence of any special equipment that has been requested by the participants)

Sometimes only the members of high-level corporate committees receive copies of the agenda and of the minutes of previous meetings. In such cases, you would send only a brief memo to the presenters and guests, informing them of the date, time, and location of the meeting and the time at which they are expected to make their presentation(s):

```
There will be a meeting of the Publishing Committee at
9:00 a.m., Tuesday, May 23, 19—, in the Board Room on the
30th floor. Mr. Smith asks that you be prepared to give
your presentation from 9:15 a.m. to 9:45 a.m.
```

Shareholders' meetings.   Invitations to shareholders' meetings are very formal and are usually preprinted. They are issued on behalf of the company officers about four weeks prior to the event or at a set time stipulated in the company's by-laws. A proxy form usually accompanies the invitations, for use by the shareholders who cannot attend in person. The corporate secretary or general counsel usually handles invitations to these kinds of meetings.

Directors' meetings.   If you work in the office of the company chairman or president, you may be called on to issue notices of forthcoming meetings to the board of directors. These gatherings usually occur at a set time during the fiscal year and the procedures in preparation for them are predetermined. Keep a current list of the directors' full names, corporate and home addresses, corporate titles, and telephone numbers. Notify them of the meeting, preferably in writing, at least two or three weeks in advance or in accordance with the provisions of the company's by-laws. Keep a separate list of the directors, in order of seniority on the board, with notations as to the date on which they were notified of the meeting, and a check mark indicating whether or not each person will or will not be able to attend. Total the number of attendees and indicate whether or not a quorum is assured.

You also may have to make arrangements for outside sites for shareholders' meetings. Follow the guidelines given in previous sections of this chapter when doing so. With directors' meetings, you will probably have to make hotel reservations for those living at a distance, and you will be expected to arrange dinners and luncheons for them—this, if your position is in the office of the president or the chairman and chief executive officer.

14

International and Domestic Travel

M. Sue Strachan • *Executive Assistant to the Chairman of the Board, Pan American World Airways, Inc. ("Travel Arrangements" Section of this Chapter)*

Kaethe Ellis • *Editor, Houghton Mifflin Company, Reference Division (Global Travel and Holidays Chart)*

David R. Pritchard, *Associate Editor, Houghton Mifflin Company, Reference Division (Global Travel and Holidays Chart)*

TRAVEL ARRANGEMENTS

INTRODUCTION

A great percentage of executive time is spent in travel, both domestic and foreign. Of course, the amount of time spent on the road or in the air varies according to the type of business and the responsibilities of the individual manager. These factors, in turn, dictate the amount of pretravel planning time allotted to executive and secretary. Since the vast majority of trips involve air travel, we concentrate on that mode of transport in this chapter. It is hoped that the years of experience accrued as an executive assistant to a chief executive officer and the accompanying insights gained as an employee of Pan American World Airways will provide you with a double-prismed view, as it were, of executive travel. The chapter concludes with a Global Travel and Holidays Chart that should be invaluable to you and the executive in working out optimal travel times, planning for climate and weather, and learning a bit about currency and language in foreign countries.

THE FORTHCOMING TRIP

"I need to go to Dubrovnik for the Tex-Lab meeting."

You smile and say, "Certainly" . . . and now all you have to do is figure out what "Dubrovnik" is and where it is located. And that is only a small part of the information you will require in order to give the executive the problem-free trip that is expected of you. Some, but not all, of the questions that must be answered right away are:

1. Where is the destination?

2. How does one get there from here?

3. Where do I look for the necessary travel information or whom do I call?

4. What is the departure date?

5. What is the estimated date of arrival at the destination?

6. What is the date of return?

7. Where is the best place to stay?

8. What travel documents are required (if an international trip)?

9. How much luggage is allowed?

10. What currency is used and what is the basic exchange rate?

To begin, you will need to know *where* the executive is going. (Dubrovnik, by the way, is in Yugoslavia). In order to locate cities and countries with which you might be initially unfamiliar, we suggest at the outset that you devote one shelf of your bookcase to travel guides, at least two atlases—one international, and the other domestic (i.e., a U.S. road atlas), and current editions of the airline guides discussed later in this section. In many instances you may not have time to go to a library for this sort of information, for the executive who travels frequently may have to plan a trip on the spur of the moment with very little time to spare.

Travel Guides

We recommend several titles, some of which are published by Pan American World Airways by arrangement with the DR Group, Inc. and McGraw-Hill Book Company: *Pan Am's World Guide: The Encyclopedia of Travel*, 26th ed. (New York: McGraw-Hill, 1982) and *Pan Am's USA Guide: Everything You Need to Know About 50 Great States—and U.S. Territories*, 4th ed. (New York: McGraw-Hill, 1982). These two volumes, which are updated regularly, can be purchased directly from Pan Am. The local Pan Am office in your city maintains a supply, or they may be requested from Pan Am, Pan Am Building, 200 Park Avenue, New York, NY 10166 (Attention: Public Relations Department). They are also available at your local bookstore. We also recommend the *American Tourist Manual: People's Republic of China*, by John E. Felber, published by International Intertrade Index, Box 636, Newark, NJ 07101. With increasing trade between the United States and the People's Republic of China, such a book may come in very handy if your executive has to travel to that nation. The international travel books contain vital information: geographic capsules as to locations, capitals, and climates; types of government; religions, holidays, and currency; customs regulations and entry requirements; airport and hotel information; locations of money exchange bureaus and branches of American banks within countries abroad, plus banking hours; mail and telephone information; availability of English-language newspapers; tipping customs; electricity; local public and rental transportation facilities available; food and restaurants; shopping, entertainment, sports, and points of interest; and dress and drinking restrictions where applicable.

Houghton Mifflin Company publishes a very comprehensive, annually updated set of travel books entitled *The Get 'em and Go Series*, edited by Stephen Birnbaum. These books include, in separate volumes, coverage of Europe; Great Britain and Ireland; South America; Mexico; the Caribbean, Bermuda, and the

Bahamas; the United States; Hawaii; and Canada. Also included in the series is *USA for Business Travelers*. Particularly useful sections in these guides are the cost calculations; entry requirements and documents; insurance; hints for handicapped travelers, travelers accompanied by children, single travelers, and elderly travelers; foreign exchange; time zones and business hours; and local customs regarding drinking and drugs. Judicious use of the travel guides and a good world atlas will enable you to answer question one and part of question two: Where is the destination city or country and how does the executive get there?

Airline Guides

The next essential book is a current copy of the *Official Airline Guide (OAG)*. This publication comes in two editions—the North American Edition and the Worldwide Edition. The *OAG* is also supplemented by several pocket editions limited to certain geographic areas. The *OAG* is easy to interpret once you have taken a few minutes to familiarize yourself with its format and symbols. The North American Edition applies to travel within the United States and to and from the United States and Mexico, Central America, Canada, and the Caribbean. The larger Worldwide Edition is for travel to and from and within virtually every city in the world served by air *excluding* those in the United States. Pocket editions of the *OAG* contain only nonstop, or direct, flight service information relating to areas of North America, Europe and the Middle East, and the Pacific. Connection schedules are *not* included in the pocket editions. While the *OAG*, obtained via subscription, is expensive, its cost can be more than offset if your personnel travel regularly and if you do not rely totally on a travel agent. European travelers rely upon the *ABC Worldwide Airline Guide*.

Hotel Indexes

An absolutely essential book for the secretary whose executive travels a lot is a complete up-to-date hotel and motel index. A particularly useful volume is the *Hotel and Motel Red Book* issued annually in May by the American Hotel and Motel Association. This—the official directory of the American Hotel and Motel Association—lists hotels, motels, and resorts in the United States; Central and South America; Canada; the Bahamas, Bermuda, and the Caribbean; Europe; Asia; the Near and Middle East; Africa; and Australia and the South and Central Pacific. The book also includes a special section on meeting and conference centers. It can be purchased by writing to the American Hotel Association Directory Corporation, 888 Seventh Avenue, New York, NY 10019. Most hotel indexes also list various hotel representatives together with their telephone numbers. Representatives make reservations for accommodations at the properties they represent. Their services are free to the customer, since the hotel properties they represent pay them a fee or commission for their services. The hotel index also includes a list of hotel chains, together with toll-free or local telephone numbers through which one can make reservations. The reservation centers can confirm room reservations and room rates and can answer most basic questions concerning the hotels, such as location, proximity to major airports or convention/conference centers, and proximity to major downtown locations or places of interest. The hotel index itself also provides information such as room rates (usually figured in terms of the minimum to maximum rate), address, distance from airport or town centers, telephone numbers of the hotel property itself, and the name of the general manager.

Date of Travel

The next thing to do is to determine the degree of flexibility, if any, in the executive's travel plans, for fares can fluctuate, depending not only on the day of the week of travel, but also on the date (or month). The fare differences applicable to day of week or time of day apply mostly to domestic travel (i.e., travel completely within the United States and some resort destinations, such as those in the Caribbean, Acapulco, or Cancún). Because the executive's time is often limited and is always precious, he or she must often travel during the peak times, but it is certainly worth your while to find out if an off-peak time would still fit the proposed travel schedule.

Making reservations.   If you have already used the *OAG* and/or a hotel index, your time on the phone will be reduced to a minimum during the pretravel stage. Since your own time is also valuable, the less spent asking basic questions will allow you more time to attend to other travel details. If you don't have access to the *OAG* or a hotel index, you can still keep your telephone waiting time to a minimum if you know these things in advance: the date of travel, the preferred departure time (such as morning, afternoon, or evening), and the length of stay (approximate, if actual dates are not known; this information may be used to determine fare savings/costs).

When making the actual reservations, you have several options. You can make the reservations direct with the airline, through a travel agency, or through your company's own corporate travel department. If your company's employees travel extensively, the company may have its own Travel Department—an arrangement similar to having a travel agency on the property. Most corporate travel departments are managed either by a former travel agent or airline reservations person, or they are run by a company employee who has been trained by a travel agent or airline. In some instances travel agencies have branch offices in large corporations that assist company personnel in the myriad of details required in dealing with high-volume travel.

If you find that your company (or even one department within the company) is becoming increasingly involved with travel, I suggest that you investigate several travel agencies in your area and have one of the agencies set up an account to handle all travel arrangements for you. Most travel agencies, depending upon their size and proximity to your office, will set up such an account for billing purposes, will make all travel and travel-related arrangements for you, will deliver the tickets to your office (and in emergency situations will arrange for airport ticket pickup), and will assist you with international documentation such as visas and tourist cards. They also will provide itinerary sheets with day-by-day reservations and accommodations information. Travel agents are staffed and equipped to make airline, rail, ship, hotel, rental car, tour, and transfer arrangements.

It should be mentioned here that a travel agency does not charge for the majority of its services, for the airlines and hotels pay the agency on a commission basis. As an example, the fares charged for an airline ticket purchased from a travel agency will be the same as if the ticket had been purchased directly from the airline. But if the travel agency incurs unusual expenses such as long-distance or international telephone calls for last-minute arrangements or changes, then those additional expenses are normally charged back to your company's account.

Of course, you can always make the reservations directly with the airline. In the case of international travel, it is best to get in touch with the airline responsible for the international segment of the itinerary because you know that they have facilities in the destination country through which you can book additional reservations for connecting or continuing travel and hotel accommodations. The airline also can reserve rental cars, request tours, and arrange transfers. As an added convenience, the tickets may be charged to your executive's airline credit card or a major credit card and then mailed to your office or held for pickup at one of the airline's ticket office locations.

How much will it cost?   Before making reservations, it is wise to become familiar with pricing. Fares can vary greatly depending upon the day of the week, the time of day, the month of the year, the length of stay, and the nature of the flight (i.e., one way or round trip). As mentioned earlier, business travelers are usually limited in flexibility as to travel time, so your options regarding reservations may be reduced greatly even before you start.

Classes of airline travel.   First class is by far the ultimate way to travel. The accommodations, especially for international or transcontinental travel, are superior. The seating configuration is more spacious than that provided for other classes. Some airlines have first-class seating with adjustable foot rests that extend full length to afford a roomy, comfortable seat approximating a bed (in fact, some international airlines do have beds)—a feature greatly appreciated by travelers on long flights, such as transatlantic or transpacific ones. The meal service offered in first class is gourmet fare and is attractively served in several courses. The courses include appetizers and hors d'oeuvres (such as caviar), fresh salads, prime cuts of meat, seafood, desserts that will tempt even the most serious dieter, fruits and cheeses from around the world, coffee, tea, champagne and wine, and after-dinner liqueur. Of course, on most flights longer than three hours, in-flight entertainment of first-run movies is offered and the stereo headsets in first class are complimentary. Other amenities in first class include "slipper socks" (for use while sleeping to avoid swollen feet the next day); an overnight kit with toothbrush, toothpaste, shaving paraphernalia, hand lotion, spot remover, and comb. Since first-class service is very competitive among the airlines, the executive can be assured of a deluxe flight, after which he or she should arrive relaxed and ready to start doing business.

Business class is less expensive than first class but slightly more expensive than economy class. However, the difference in price over economy can be well worth the extra dollars because of the desirable accommodations. The roomy seating is usually identical to the first-class seats of those airlines not offering sleeper seats. The meal service is more diversified than that of economy, usually with a choice of entrees and complimentary wines and champagne. The service is also more personalized than that of economy. In-flight entertainment headsets are usually complimentary in business class as well. Business class also affords the executive the larger, quieter aircraft cabin for attending to last-minute business details while en route. The executive should arrive at the final destination relaxed and refreshed.

Economy class is the least expensive and its seating is slightly smaller than that found in the business class section. Also, because of the popularity of special fares and tours, the economy-class cabin (or main cabin) is usually more crowded than either first class or business class. The meal service normally does not offer choices, the servings are smaller, and beverages such as wine and beer are offered at a nominal charge. First-run movies are shown on virtually all international flights and the headsets for viewing in-flight entertainment must be rented in economy class. However, depending on the executive's schedule on the arrival day, economy class can be a smart choice. Of course, some companies restrict the classes of travel to various management levels. You'll have to act within these guidelines if they exist.

Fare categories.   Several fare categories should be considered. Normal, or all-year, fares are usually unrestricted, in that they allow you complete flexibility in making travel arrangements. The fares are valid for one full year from the date of purchase (or the date of travel), and can be changed at any time en route without penalty. No additional fare is charged if the routing remains basically the same. All-year fares apply to all three classes of service—first, business, and economy.

Fare seasons, the next category, are classed as peak, low, and "shoulder." Peak season rates are in force between May 15 and September 14. The fares are highest during this, the most popular travel season. Low season rates apply between October 1 and April 30 (or September 15 and May 14). These are the least popular travel months; however, much business travel takes place during this time. Fortunately for businesses, the air fares are cheapest during the low season. "Shoulder" season rates are in effect between May 1 and May 14 and between September 15 and September 30. Fares during this time are less than peak but higher than the low season. Fares within all seasons can and do vary. At the same time, though, the all-year fares remain the same and therefore are the least restrictive.

Special fares are available, usually in all three classes of service, but have some restrictions. There are "apex" fares (advance purchase excursion fares), excursion fares, special interest fares (such as those for large groups traveling together), tour fares, group inclusive fares (a combination air fare/hotel accommodations/tour fare for one set price), and so on. However, the excursion fare can offer the most flexible alternate arrangements for business travelers, provided that some basic requirements are met. These requirements usually stipulate a minimum number of days that the traveler must be away from the origin city and the maximum number of days that travel is allowed. Some excursion fares allow one or two, and sometimes several, stopovers en route, while others permit no stopovers. Still other excursion fares must be purchased a minimum number of days prior to travel, and most of them assess a penalty if the reservations are changed either after the tickets have been purchased or after the travel has begun. If the executive qualifies for a special or excursion fare, be sure that you understand the restrictions (if any) so as to avoid misunderstandings. Taking advantage of these fares can result in significant cost savings for your company.

Sometimes work-schedule flexibility is virtually impossible and the all-year fares will apply. Obviously, the all-year fares will afford the executive the greatest amount of travel flexibility and may, even in the long run, prove to be the best travel bargain. The executive's meeting might last longer than the maximum number of days allowed on an excursion ticket, in which case when the reservations are changed, the tickets reissued, and the penalty assessed, the amount paid may end up being as much as a normal ticket would have cost in the first place. Had the executive traveled on an all-year fare, he or she would not have had to stand in line while the fares and routings were being refigured and the tickets reissued. If you have the slightest doubt as to the executive's business agenda on the trip, your wisest choice will be the all-year fare.

Accommodations

The next travel consideration is the type of hotel accommodations. When traveling internationally, the executive should take into account several hotel rate plans:

1. *Full American Plan* With this plan, breakfast, lunch, and dinner are included in the price of the room. However, the meals usually must be taken on the hotel property itself and most of the time a particular restaurant within the hotel is stipulated. There may be occasions when several hotels have arranged trades among themselves, offering the traveler diversified meals at different sites. The hotel, of course, can tell you what other hotels, if any, participate in such "trade" plans.

2. *Modified American Plan*   With the Modified American plan, two meals—breakfast and either lunch or dinner—are included in the price of the room. Again, the hotel normally requires that the meals be taken on the hotel property itself, but as with the Full American Plan, reciprocal agreements with other properties in the same city may exist.

3. *Continental Plan* With this plan, a light breakfast (or continental breakfast) consisting of coffee, juice, and pastries is included in the price of the room.

4. *European Plan* With the European Plan, no meals are included in the price of the room.

Depending on the individual travel and business schedule, cost savings can be achieved through judicious use of these plans. Adding the cost of the meals to the room rate increases the cost of the room; however, it could be less expensive in the long run than if the meals were purchased separately. At some locations such as resorts during the peak season, one has no choice of the plans. The various meals are included in the bill whether they are taken or not, and it should be understood that in such a case there is no refund for unused meal plans. This point is particularly important when planning a meeting at a resort during the peak season.

In suggesting hotel accommodations, you will need to keep in mind the nature and scope of the planned activities. Will meetings or appointments be held downtown, or in the "town center," as most European business districts are called? Will the meetings be held at a conference center? Will the scheduled appointments be at several different places throughout a large area? You should have some idea of the type of mobility required before firming up hotel reservations. If the executive has one appointment and then is scheduled to depart on another flight, suggest accommodations close to the airport or near the train station if the connections out of the city are via rail. If the executive is to be attending a conference, determine the location of the conference hall so that convenient accommodations in the immediate vicinity can be requested. If meetings are to be held in several locations within a large area, suggest accommodations close or readily accessible to one or more of the meeting places. Good restaurants and shopping areas also ought to be near at hand. Be sure to find out whether or not ground transportation will be required. Most airlines and travel agencies can tell you if taxi service is obtainable. Of course, most large metropolitan areas around the world have excellent taxi services. However, taxis can become quite scarce late in the evening, during inclement weather, and during rush hours. If the executive has several appointments scheduled close together, suggest hiring a private car and driver. The airline or travel agent can arrange that service and provide cost estimates. A private car and driver will be particularly desirable for an executive operating under a tight schedule.

Hotels normally have noon or early afternoon check-out/check-in times. And most flights to and from the United States and European cities depart the United States gateway city in the evening, arriving at their destinations the following morning. Therefore, during peak travel time or when large conventions are under way, the hotels might be booked up and rooms might not be available until some of the guests have checked out. As a result, the executive may have to wait for several hours before the rooms have been cleaned and have been made available for check-in . . . not the best way to spend the first few hours at a destination after a long flight. If an appointment has been scheduled for the same day as the executive's arrival, and if you know that the hotel is heavily booked, I suggest that you reserve a room for the evening *before* the day of the first appointment and that you ensure that the booking is guaranteed and available for immediate check-in upon the executive's arrival. This procedure will allow the executive time to freshen up, relax, and get settled prior to the first appointment. Otherwise, after a long flight and another long wait in a hotel lobby, the proper business mood may have evaporated. The extra cost is sometimes half the normal room tariff, but even at the full room rate it is well worth the money. Of course, if the hotel is not filled to capacity, rooms should be readily available for immediate check-in upon arrival. Your job, then, is to find out what the situation is ahead of time.

Travel Documents

When traveling to a foreign country, a valid United States passport is a must. While some countries require only proof of citizenship, a passport is essential in others, and is, therefore, recommended across the board—especially if several trips are to be made in the course of a few months. The requirements for obtaining a United States Passport follow.

A passport may be obtained by completing the Passport Application Form DSP-11, which must be *personally* presented to and executed by: A Passport Agent, a clerk of any federal court or state court of record, a judge or clerk of any probate court accepting applications, or a postal employee designated by the postmaster at a post office selected to accept passport applications. If your executive wishes to apply for the passport by mail, the form DSP-82 must be completed. However, the executive must have had another United States passport in his or her name within the past eight years and that passport must be available for submission with the by-mail application. The documents required in order to

Table 1. Addresses of Passport Agencies for Use in Passport Renewal Applications

BOSTON PASSPORT AGENCY
Room E 123, John F. Kennedy Bldg.,
Government Center
Boston, MA 02203

CHICAGO PASSPORT AGENCY
Suite 380, Kluczynski Federal Bldg.,
230 South Dearborn Street
Chicago, IL 60604

HONOLULU PASSPORT AGENCY
Room C-106, New Federal Bldg.,
300 Ala Moana Boulevard
P.O. Box 50185
Honolulu, HI 96850

HOUSTON PASSPORT AGENCY
One Allen Center
500 Dallas Street
Houston, TX 77002

LOS ANGELES PASSPORT AGENCY
Room 13100, 11000 Wilshire Blvd.,
Los Angeles, CA 90024

MIAMI PASSPORT AGENCY
16th Floor, Federal Office Bldg.
51 S.W. First Avenue
Miami, FL 33130

NEW ORLEANS PASSPORT AGENCY
Room 400, International Trade Mart
2 Canal Street
New Orleans, LA 70130

NEW YORK PASSPORT AGENCY
Room 270, Rockefeller Center
630 Fifth Avenue
New York, NY 10111

PHILADELPHIA PASSPORT AGENCY
Room 4426, Federal Bldg.,
600 Arch Street
Philadelphia, PA 19106

SAN FRANCISCO PASSPORT AGENCY
Room 1405, Federal Bldg.,
450 Golden Gate Avenue
San Francisco, CA 94102

SEATTLE PASSPORT AGENCY
Room 906, Federal Bldg.,
915 Second Avenue
Seattle, WA 98174

STAMFORD PASSPORT AGENCY
One Landmark Square
Broad and Atlantic Streets
Stamford, CT 06901

WASHINGTON PASSPORT AGENCY
1425 K Street, NW.
Washington, D.C. 20524

obtain a passport are proof of citizenship, proof of identity, two photographs, and payment of required fees. When completing the form by mail, send it together with the most recent passport, two photographs, and the fee to one of the Passport Agencies listed in Table 1.

Traveler's Advisory: **Travelers should always carry their passports on the person, never packed in their luggage.**

Many countries require a visa or tourist card for entry. The visas are issued by the embassies and consulates of the various countries for a small fee, or in some cases they are free of charge. Be certain to check with the appropriate consulate or embassy or with your airline or travel agent to learn which visas or tourist cards are required for a particular trip; these regulations can change without notice. Since consulates are not located in all United States cities, be sure to allow sufficient time for securing the proper visa application forms, completing them, and applying by mail, especially if several visas are required. It is helpful to maintain a current District of Columbia telephone book if your executive travels abroad a lot; you can find the addresses and telephone numbers of all the embassies in Washington therein. Under World Health Organization regulations, many countries require that visitors be vaccinated against smallpox, cholera, and yellow fever. While some vaccinations are not required by the World Health Organization, they may be recommended for the traveler's protection. Be sure to consult with your local Public Health Service, your travel agent, or the airline. All vaccinations must be contained in a World Health Organization certificate, obtainable from the Public Health Service in your city. Should the executive be concerned with the possibility of becoming ill during a foreign trip, it is suggested that you contact Intermedic or IAMAT (International Association for Medical Assistance to Travelers) prior to departure from the United States. Both organizations publish international directories of English-speaking physicians. Intermedic's United States headquarters is at 777 Third Avenue, New York, NY 10017. The IAMAT directory is available by writing to IAMAT, 350 Fifth Avenue, New York, NY 10001.

If the executive is taking special medication, he or she should carry enough of the medication for the duration of the trip, as well as a doctor's certificate verifying the need for the medication. The family physician can provide information relating to prescription refills in case of an emergency. It is a good idea to take along extra medication just in case a business trip lasts longer than expected or in case inclement weather or other untoward circumstances delay the return schedule. As with a passport, the executive should *never* pack medication in luggage that is to be checked, in the event that the luggage does not arrive on the same flight.

Packing and Luggage

Traveling light can add considerably to the comfort and ease of a trip. The travel agent or airline reservations office can assist with updated weather information and can offer suggestions as to the general type and weight of clothing needed. Some countries such as those in the Middle East and parts of Africa have very strict clothing requirements, especially for women, and you should be sure to familiarize the executive with the various social customs and restrictions pertaining to attire. Detailed information can be obtained from the embassies or consulates of these countries. In dressing for the trip itself, the executive should consider what the weather conditions will be upon arrival at the first destination. If the origination city is warm but the destination is cold, suggest that the executive wear heavier clothing to the airport and carry a coat on board the flight so that it will be at hand as soon as the flight arrives. The reverse will be true for trips from cold areas to warmer ones. See the Global Travel and Holidays Chart at the end of this chapter for general guidance regarding weather conditions in all of the countries of the world.

Choice of luggage is a matter of personal preference, but it is suggested that if possible the luggage be of a size and weight to be carried on board the flight. If the business trip is fairly short, usually all that is needed will be a strong soft garment bag that can be hung in one of the coat closets on board the aircraft or that will fit, folded, into one of the overhead storage bins. A small light bag that will fit beneath the airplane seat can be used for smaller articles. Check with the airline or travel agent for regulations concerning size, weight, or amount of carry-on luggage. If luggage must be checked, be sure that the executive allows sufficient time for airport check-in. The airline or travel agent will provide information concerning minimum check-in times. If the luggage is to be locked, be sure that the executive carries an extra set of keys. The airline or travel agent can tell you the maximum weight allowable and pieces that can be checked. This point applies especially to long trips or to trips in which the executive may have to carry special product samples in oversize bags. Obviously, carry-on luggage is best: upon arrival there is no need to wait at the baggage claim area for all the luggage to be unloaded and transported into the claim area. Another useful tip: if your executive travels extensively and sometimes with little prior notice, suggest that he or she maintain a prepacked flight bag and overnight kit, or, if this is not feasible, a series of packing lists—one for overnighters, another for two- or three-day trips, and still another for trips of four days or more. This method has been used for years by military personnel and it saves much time and last-minute rushing. A prepacked travel briefcase is another way of expediting takeoff; include in it an appointment book, address book, writing materials, dictation equipment with cassettes, stamps, envelopes, and calculator.

Electric current abroad.   Throughout Europe, the Mediterranean, and the Far East, the standard electric current is generally 220 volts/50 cycles and the plugs to appliances as well as the electrical outlets differ markedly from ours. Therefore, if an electric appliance such as a shaver or hair dryer is carried along, the traveler also should take a lightweight, all-purpose transformer and plug adaptor, available at most department or hardware stores.

Currency

Before leaving home, it is always good to have some currency of the host country. Most banks maintain international departments and will exchange dollars for foreign currency. We suggest that a minimum of $500.00 be exchanged (for very short trips). Thus, upon arrival the executive does not have to wait at the airport for a bank to open or queue up to exchange currency. Taxis, buses, and trains are ready to depart for town and hotel, or for connections to other cities away from the airport, and with local currency in hand, one has no delay in getting out of the airport area. Also, with local currency in hand upon arrival, one has money for tipping porters and bellhops, taking transportation, and using pay phones.

The bank, when exchanging dollars into foreign currency, will usually provide a guide on the foreign currency purchased, such as denominations and conversion rates. Conversion rates are based on the current buying rate and therefore fluctuate. One day's rate may be slightly more or less on another day. Conversion from dollars to local currency also can be accomplished after arrival at most major cities abroad. Banks and currency exchange booths are located in major airports throughout the world. However, it should be kept in mind that banking hours vary in different countries. The executive should be prepared by having at least a small amount of foreign currency on hand before departing on the trip. Most hotels abroad can exchange dollars if necessary. However, the conversion rate there may not be as attractive as it is in the United States since the hotels must pay a percentage to have dollars converted back into the local currency.

AIRLINE LOUNGES AND CLUBS

Another item in the list of passenger conveniences is the special private lounge that most airlines maintain at major airports, especially at locations where the airline operates a significantly large number of scheduled flights. The traveler can purchase an annual or lifetime membership. The clubs offer a quiet, relaxed setting with easy chairs, sofas, tables, desks, beverage service (in most cases complimentary), snacks, and so on, away from the noise and hustle-bustle of the main passenger terminal. After having checked the luggage at the main ticket counter, the traveler can go to the club and check in for the flight. During check-in, the passenger can secure a seat assignment and a boarding pass and then can enjoy a cup of coffee, juice, cocktail, or other beverage in a pleasant atmosphere while waiting for the flight to be announced. Telephones are readily accessible. Several types of clubs and lounges are available. Some first-class lounges are free of charge for first-class passengers. Most of the clubs, however, assess a membership fee, especially in the case of United States airlines, whether domestic or international. Several years ago, the Civil Aeronautics Board found that the practice of allowing free access to first-class lounges for first-class passengers only was discriminatory. The United States airlines decided to charge for membership, thereby allowing access to anyone who had paid the membership fees. But regardless of the class of travel, the atmosphere in a club prior to a trip is well worth the fee. Membership is valid for the airline's club facilities anywhere in the world that such facilities are maintained.

EXECUTIVE SECURITY PRECAUTIONS

Top corporate executives face continuous problems with inflation, the high cost of money, supply backlogs, energy crises, labor unrest, business and labor negotiations, new and amended government regulations, and perhaps domestic issues involving spouses and children. As a result, many executives are more concerned about their organizations and families than they are about themselves. This means that executive assistants and secretaries, in addition to their own responsibilities, must also be concerned about the executive's personal security. Personal security has been the topic of much editorial and news comment as a result of civil disorder and a marked increase in criminal and terrorist activities around the world. We should emphasize at the outset that personal security concerns apply at every phase of a high executive's activity, from his or her residence to the telephone and the office. However, since the executive is particularly vulnerable while moving from one place to another, our emphasis is on travel-related precautions that you, the executive assistant, should be aware of and the role that you can play in ensuring the security and safety of the executive.

Of paramount importance is the relationship and open communication that exist among the executive assistant, the corporate security staff, and, if applicable, chauffeurs and the household staff. All travel, regardless of distance involved or mode of transportation, should be coordinated among this group, especially if your superior is a company chief executive or operating officer. Since each executive's lifestyle, habits, priorities, and travel plans vary, we address the issue of your role, as executive or administrative assistant, as it relates to this matter in general terms. The following precautions are by no means inclusive, nor are they uniformly applicable to all travel conditions. It is hoped, however, that these guidelines will stimulate thoughtful planning for forthcoming trips that the executive may make.

Established patterns or routines are the greatest threats to personal security and safety. Hence, a regular route and time of travel should not be adhered to. Frequent changes of direction, travel time, and mode of transportation, coordinated within an overall protection plan, will make it more difficult for a potential abductor or attacker to plan an ambush or interception. One of the most important things to remember is *not* to announce travel plans: keep all such arrangements confidential. For instance, travel information concerning the executive or the executive's family should not be released to the media. Information for the local newspapers (top executives and their families are newsworthy) can be carried after the *return* from a trip. Press releases with photographs and travel details could create unnecessary exposure and should be evaluated very carefully. Telephone calls, mail, or personal inquiries from unknown sources and/or persons seeking travel information or personal data about the executive and the family should be refused.

Whenever possible, especially in the case of high-level executives of multinational organizations, bookings for hotels, rental cars, limousines, or chauffeur services should be made in the name of the manager of the local office in the host country, in the company name only, or in a name other than the executive's (perhaps in the name of an associate traveling with the executive). This procedure will preclude unnecessary interest on the part of unknown people in the travel plans and whereabouts of the executive. Arrangements and agreements between the executive and assistant should be made with a view toward ensuring that the assistant is continually aware of *all* itineraries and *all* changes in itineraries (regardless of when any changes are made), *all* arrival times, destinations, departure times, excursions, and so forth.

Airline regulations require that personal identification be carried on the outside of all checked luggage in the event that the luggage is misdirected at some point during the journey. Top executives should *not* put luggage tags bearing the residence address or even the office address on their luggage. No one besides the family and close associates needs to know that the executive is going on a trip. For travel identification, executives should use one of the many commercial identification tags that bear only a name and an identification number. Some of the private clubs maintained by the airlines issue special luggage tags with a name (initials only rather than first names) and the traveler's identification number. If the luggage is misdirected en route and is subsequently found, the airline locating the luggage will contact the other airline's office whose luggage identification tags are on the suitcases to determine how to reroute or return them. Special tags are also issued by various credit card companies. These companies follow the same basic procedures with regard to the data on the tags. The offices issuing the cards maintain the utmost security concerning their clients. If the executive has to have an address on the identification tag, it is recommended that the corporate address be used, but not the company name or executive title.

Evaluate the political atmosphere of a foreign government and/or the mood of its populace as they relate to Americans or American enterprise. If political or economic unrest is evident, confer with the government's foreign affairs office or with our State Department prior to departure. Have the executive check in with foreign governmental representatives upon arrival. When possible, give our embassy or consulate a copy of the executive's itinerary, at least on a per-city basis. Take the advice of the embassy or consulate personnel as to maintenance of any special security procedures. For each country on the executive's itinerary prepare a list of phrases in the local language such as, "I need the police (or doctor, telephone, ambulance, hospital, U.S. embassy, etc.)." Include *numerals* in the host country's language on the same list. For instance, while 1, 2, 3, 4, etc., are fine in most countries, Egypt, China, Japan, and most Middle Eastern countries have totally different numeral systems. Prepare instructions on the use of local pay telephones, for telephone services in many countries abroad are not what we might be familiar with. The local consulate of the country being visited or the United States embassy or consulate there will be of valuable assistance in this regard. Be sure that the executive has a supply of local currency in coins for use with the pay telephones.

Most corporate executives travel worry-free around the globe with never a hint of trouble. But by keeping your eyes and ears open to political situations, many tense moments can be avoided both for you and for the executive. Chances are that you might never have the occasion to be concerned, but if these few guidelines are followed to some extent, you will have gone the extra mile to ensure a successful trip for the executive.

LANGUAGE

Most first-time travelers to a foreign country are a little skeptical about language barriers. Every bookstore has foreign-language phrase books for the traveler who is unfamiliar with the language of the country to be visited. While most Europeans speak several languages, English included, many Americans speak only English. Therefore, it is a courtesy to one's hosts to take a few minutes to learn just a few words and phrases in their native language.

The executive who has mastered a few common words and phrases not only will please the hosts but also will be almost certain to get the meeting off to a good start. I find that most Americans are somewhat timid about attempting to speak foreign languages. Perhaps it is our inherent desire always to be correct that sometimes prohibits us from attempting to make ourselves understood in another language. But fluency is not expected; it is the diplomacy and the thought that counts. And no one should be afraid to try. If the executive travels a lot, your office should buy a set of pocket-size foreign phrase books that can be taken along on trips. Of course, professional interpreters can be contracted in advance to translate during meetings and appointments when accuracy is particularly important. The embassy or consulate of the host country can assist in arranging for interpreters' services.

If the company plans major commitments to a given country or area of the world, then a language course is recommended. It is estimated that approximately 100,000 companies are currently engaged in business or business deals abroad. Hence, many executives in multinational companies are taking language courses providing them a degree of fluency in a foreign language (or languages). Adult education language classes are offered by most universities, colleges, and high schools in the evenings and on weekends. Private and semiprivate classes are available through most language schools such as Berlitz or Inlingua. Self-teaching cassettes and records are available, as is private instruction from tutors. Again, the amount of international corporate involvement will determine the amount of fluency required, but learning a foreign language is never a wasted talent and will serve the executive well through life. If time does not permit a crash course in another language, it is highly recommended and almost essential that a few words and phrases in that language become a part of the executive's vocabulary: *Hello, goodbye, please, thank you, where is the* (hotel/hospital/police station?) . . . and one of the most important, *Do you speak English?* In most European countries, and especially in the major cities, almost all of the people speak some English. However, good manners dictate that we attempt the language of the host country. One should always remember that the American is the foreigner when away from the United States.

SPECIAL SERVICES

If, during a trip, the executive calls you and asks for an important document or other item, there are ways of sending a package abroad quickly and efficiently. Most international airlines have a small package service. A package can be shipped on the next flight for a nominal fee. Special customs clearances are included, but the package should be available for pickup at the destination within a few minutes of its arrival. Check with the airline's small package service for complete details. If you do not find a separate listing in the telephone directory for such a service, the airline reservations office or your travel agent will be able to assist you with the arrangements via telephone. Some of the overnight delivery services such as Federal Express, Purolator, and Emery offer similar overseas courier services. Special arrangements can be made through them for electronic transmittal of documents to domestic as well as to international destinations (see the section on electronic mail in Chapter Nine).

UNITED STATES CUSTOMS INFORMATION

If the executive's permanent residence is in the United States, he or she is allowed an exemption of US$400.00 (retail value) on items for personal use only, providing that he or she has been outside the United States for at least 48 hours and has not claimed an exemption within 30 days. Articles accompanying the traveler in excess of the exemption, but under US$1,400.00 in value will be assessed at a flat duty rate of 10%. There is no limit if one is arriving from Mexico or the Virgin Islands. Everything acquired abroad is subject to duty, including items that are used or worn. The goods must accompany the traveler to qualify for exemption. Anything shipped is subject to duty (except gifts under US$50.00). Included in the exemption are 100 cigars (Cuban cigars may be brought in, provided they were acquired by the traveler in Cuba) and 200 cigarettes (one carton). If the traveler is over twenty-one years of age, one quart (.95 liter) of alcoholic beverages may be included in the exemption. However, some states have restrictions on the number of cigarettes and the amount of liquor that residents may bring back. If the purchases have been made in Guam, American Samoa, or the Virgin Islands, the exemption jumps to US$800.00. Families from one household traveling together may pool their exemptions. If the traveler is not a United States resident, an exemption of US$100.00 is allowed for gifts accompanying the traveler, providing the stay in the United States is in excess of 72 hours and an exemption has not been claimed within six months. Adults are allowed 50 cigars and 200 cigarettes (one carton) for personal use.

Antiques and original works of art produced 100 years before the date of entry may be brought into the United States duty free, provided the proper documentation has been obtained to prove authenticity. Galleries and antique dealers where the purchases are made can provide the proper documents with the purchases. Gifts valued under US$50.00 retail may be sent to the United States free of duty if not more than one parcel per day is addressed to the same person. Mark the package: "Gift—Value under $50.00." These gifts (no alcohol, tobacco, or alcoholic perfume, however) need not be declared upon arrival. Fruits, vegetables, plants, seeds, meats, and pets must meet Department of Agriculture or Public Health Service requirements. No one may bring in articles valued over

US$100.00 or for other than their personal use from Cuba, North Korea, Vietnam, or Cambodia without having a license from the Treasury Department. Wildlife products, such as furs of the cat species and skins of alligators and crocodiles, require special documents to enter the United States. Call the nearest consulate for further details.

There is no limitation in terms of total amount of monetary instruments which may be brought into or taken out of the United States, nor is it illegal to do so. However, if one transports or causes to be transported (including by mail or other means), more than US$5,000.00 in monetary instruments on any occasion into or out of the United States, or if one receives more than that amount, one must file a report (Customs Form 4790) with Customs. Monetary instruments include United States or foreign currency, coin, travelers checks, money orders, and negotiable instruments of investment securities in bearer form. Reporting is required under the Currency and Foreign Transactions Reporting Act of 1970 (Public Law 91–508. 31U.S.C.1101, et seq.). Failure to comply can result in civil and criminal penalties.

Traveler's Advisory: **On trips abroad, be sure to register dutiable items, such as cameras and watches, before departure. This simple step will save you from paying duty on "prior possessions" upon reentry. Registration can be done at the airport or local customs houses in major cities, and is valid for life. We suggest keeping all purchases together and having the receipts handy for customs inspection.**

BUSINESS ASSISTANCE

Throughout the world, the traveler will rarely be too far from communication with an embassy or consulate where expert assistance in arranging local business contacts can be obtained. United States Chamber of Commerce offices that also can be helpful are located in many international cities. Major sources of information in the United States are

World Trade Information Center
Department 1AB
One World Trade Center
New York, NY 10048
(202) 466–3063

Bureau of International Commerce
U.S. Department of Commerce
Washington, DC 20230
(202) 377–5341
(or one of the 43 district offices)

Market Research Clearinghouse
500 Fifth Avenue
New York, NY 10036
(212) 354–2424

Common Market Information
Director of European Community
2100 M Street, NW
Washington, DC 20037
(202) 872–8350

Additionally, information or guidance on business matters may be obtained from the Economic or Commercial Attaché of any United States embassy or consulate, special overseas trade office, or Chamber of Commerce office abroad.

International Marketing Centers are located in many cities. The marketing centers can provide free information, and, for a nominal fee (e.g., $25.00–$50.00 per day) office space, a desk, telephone, secretarial services, and an interpreter for a maximum of five days. (The secretarial and interpretative services, however, involve an additional fee.) This service also includes the use of audiovisual equipment and a display rack for samples or brochures. Free local telephone service and access to telecommunications are usually provided too.

A telephone call or visit to the Commerce Department District Office in your state will enable you to make arrangements in advance. A similar service is also available at Export Development Offices, Trade & Commercial Offices, East-West Trade Support Offices, and Chamber of Commerce Offices in many countries. Other useful information can be gained by contacting the commercial officer at the embassy or consulate of the host country.

ITINERARIES AND APPOINTMENT CALENDARS

One of the best aids to the traveling executive is a well-prepared itinerary and schedule of appointments. It is always good to note on the appointment schedule the time differences, if any, so that the executive will know what time it is at home. During a business meeting, if something should arise that warrants a telephone call, the executive can decide when to call the home office. The appointment list also should include the name, address, and telephone number of the limousine service (if any); the name of the driver (if known); the name, address, and telephone number of the hotel; and the name, address, and telephone number of each appointment.

In developing business relationships with strangers, it is always advisable to learn in advance as much about the people being visited as possible. Some information can be obtained from the person who has originally set up or suggested the meeting. Another source of information is the international edition of *Who's Who.* If the host is a government official, the local consulate or embassy can usually provide appropriate personal background information. This information should be listed in the order that the appointments are to occur and can be put on small index cards for the executive to review while en route to the appointments, en route to the office, or while at the hotel. Having some knowledge of a foreign colleague's interests and family can be of great assistance in getting a meeting off to a pleasant, diplomatic start.

TRANSPORTATION ABROAD

Public transportation is far more widely used abroad than it is in the United States. Urban and interurban bus travel, especially within Europe, is excellent, and if time permits between appointments, it is an excellent alternate means of travel. Europe and the Far East have some of the most modern, efficient, comfortable, and well-run train networks in the world. Another mode of transportation to consider is a rental car. Reservations for rental cars can be made through your local travel agent, the airline, or the car rental office in your city, for most of the major rental car agencies have offices throughout the world. All countries of Western and Central Europe and the Far East accept a valid driver's license from any state in the United States. An International Driving Permit, required by some countries, can be obtained for a small fee through the American Automobile Association. Driving is not as difficult as might be expected. One drives on the right-hand side of the road in most countries except ones such as the United Kingdom and Ireland. All countries have adopted the International Road Signs.

TRIP FOLLOW-UP

Expense Reports

Sit down with the executive and go over the itinerary sheet as soon as possible after the trip is over. Having kept a copy of the itinerary and having made pertinent notes as the executive has called in during the trip, your own follow-up tasks now should be easier. No doubt the executive will have made notes on the itinerary regarding expenses. If additional currency exchanges have taken place abroad, the rates will usually differ, either from day to day or from city to city. This factor will obviously affect the bottom line of the expense reports. In converting foreign currency to dollars, be sure to use the currency conversion rate that was charged. Remember to take into consideration tips for porters at airports and hotels, and doormen at hotels and clubs. Any cash paid out as tips should be noted. If you remind the executive about the tips, other cash expenses that might not be supported by receipts will come to mind at the same time. If payment for hotels, meals, or limousines was made with a major credit card, it is advisable to complete as much of the expense report as possible and hold it, pending receipt of the credit-card charges. (The credit-card accounting office converts the foreign currency to dollars for billing.) If your company prefers that all expenses be submitted immediately upon return, always mention in the Purpose of Trip section of the expense report that a supplemental expense record will follow as soon as all credit-card billings have been received.

Follow-up Correspondence

While going over the itinerary with the executive after the trip, request all business cards that the executive has received during the course of the trip. Put the names, addresses, corporate titles, and phone numbers of the card bearers into the executive's Rolodex. During the review, make a note of any letters of appreciation that should be written. Were any special arrangements made by the host, such as limousine transportation, flowers or fruit baskets in the hotel room, dinners at the host's home or at a club or restaurant, special tours, etc.? Just a short note of thanks will suffice:

> Dear Mr. Giraud:
>
> My sincere thanks for the courtesies you extended on my behalf during my recent visit to Paris. The welcome that I received from your fine staff on check—in certainly made me feel right at home. It was especially thoughtful of you to provide the excellent bottle of wine, which made the long journey much less tiring.
>
> The kindness of your personnel was greatly appreciated, and I am looking forward to returning to Paris soon.
>
> Sincerely yours,
>
>
> Martin I. Benson
> President

If the executive has called in during the trip, review any notes made during the course of the conversations. Will some time elapse before plans or agreements made abroad can be put into final form? If so, a note to this effect is called for, thereby reassuring the foreign business colleague that while some work still may be pending, the arrangements discussed are nevertheless proceeding on track:

> Dear Mr. Johnson:
>
> Thank you again for the time afforded me on Thursday, January 19, to discuss our proposal. I have passed the information and changes along to our legal staff for incorporation into the final analysis. As soon as these changes have been approved by the Board, we will be in contact with you.
>
> In the meantime, the many courtesies and kindnesses extended on my behalf during the course of our discussions are greatly appreciated.
>
> Sincerely yours,
>
>
> Martin I. Benson
> President

Written Reports

In reviewing the itinerary, take the opportunity to typewrite all notes or comments made by the executive. Type up these notes immediately for the executive's review, together with a list of all business cards received. In this way the executive will have raw travel data in a readable, well organized format for reference in writing any post-trip reports. As soon as the executive has given you the full information for the post-trip report, type a draft for editing, additions, and other changes. By following the suggestions outlined, you will be in a position to provide the executive with a problem-free, efficiently scheduled, and productive business trip. Many happy flights.

GLOBAL TRAVEL AND HOLIDAYS CHART

Variable holidays are indicated with an asterisk (*), and wherever possible the formula for determining the actual date of observance is included in parentheses after the holiday name. Variable holidays are of three types:

- Fixed holidays that are observed on a nearby variable date.
- Movable holidays that fall in a particular month or months.
- Islamic holidays, which cannot be fixed to any month on the standard calendar. Islamic holidays are listed separately in the order in which they occur on the Islamic lunar calendar.

Abbreviations used in this chart include: EC (Eastern Caribbean currency association), CFA (Communauté Financière Africaine currency association), IDC (International Dialing Code), and DDC (Direct Dialing Code).

Afghanistan

Official Name:	Democratic Republic of Afghanistan
Capital:	Kabul
Nationality:	Afghan
Language:	Pashto, Dari (both official)

Religion:	Moslem (chiefly Sunni)
Currency:	afghani = 100 puls
Location:	S central Asia
Climate:	dry temperate, with seasonal extremes

Mar.	21	Now Rooz (Afghan New Year)
Apr.	27	Sawr Revolution Day
May	1	International Labor Day
Aug.	21	Independence Day
Sep.	1 *	Pashtunistan Day

Islamic Holidays
*	Prophet's Birthday

*	First of Ramadan
*	Eid Ramadan (End of Ramadan, 3 days)
*	Eid Adha (Feast of Pilgrimage, 4 days)
*	Ashura

Albania

Official Name:	People's Socialist Republic of Albania
Capital:	Tiranë
Nationality:	Albanian
Language:	Tosk, Gheg, Greek

Religion:	officially atheist; Moslem, Greek Orthodox, Roman Catholic
Currency:	lek = 100 quintar
Location:	SE Europe
Climate:	mild temperate

Jan.	1	New Year's Day
Jan.	11	Republic Proclamation Day
May	1	May Day

Nov.	28	Independence Day
Nov.	29	Liberation Day

Algeria

Official Name:	Democratic & Popular Republic of Algeria
Capital:	Algiers
Nationality:	Algerian
Language:	Arabic (official); French

Religion:	Sunni Moslem
Currency:	dinar = 100 centimes
Location:	NW Africa
Climate:	Mediterranean in coastal areas to desert inland

Jan.	1	New Year's Day
May	1	Labor Day
June	19	National Day
July	5	Independence Day
Nov.	1	Revolution Day

Islamic Holidays
*	First of Muharram (Islamic New Year)

*	Ashura
*	Prophet's Birthday
*	Id al-Fitr (End of Ramadan)
*	Id al-Adha (Feast of Pilgrimage)

Andorra

Official Name:	Principality of Andorra
Capital:	Andorra la Vella
Nationality:	Andorran
Language:	Catalan (official); French, Spanish

Religion:	Roman Catholic
Currency:	French franc = 100 centimes; Spanish peseta = 100 centimos
Dialing Code:	IDC 33
Location:	SW Europe
Climate:	mild temperate with snowy winters

Jan.	1	New Year's Day
Jan.	6	Epiphany
*		Carnival
Mar.	19	St. Joseph's Day
*		Holy Thursday (half day)
*		Good Friday
*		Easter Monday
*		Ascension Day
*		Whitmonday
*		Corpus Christi

June	24	St. John's Day
Aug.	15	Assumption Day
Sep.	8	Our Lady of Meritxell Day
Nov.	1	All Saints' Day
Nov.	4	St. Charles' Day
Dec.	8	Immaculate Conception
Dec.	24	Christmas Eve (half day)
Dec.	25	Christmas Day
Dec.	26	St. Stephen's Day
Dec.	31	New Year's Eve (half day)

Angola

Official Name:	People's Republic of Angola	Religion:	Christian, animist
Capital:	Luanda	Currency:	kwanza = 100 lwei
Nationality:	Angolan	Location:	SW Africa
Language:	Portuguese (official); Bantu	Climate:	subtropical

Jan.	1	New Year's Day	Sep.	17	National Hero Day
Feb.	4	Commencement of the	Nov.	11	Independence Day
		Armed Struggle	Dec.	10	MPLA Foundation Day
May	1	Labor Day	Dec.	25	Family Day

Antigua and Barbuda

Official Name:	Antigua and Barbuda	Religion:	Protestant (chiefly Anglican)
Capital:	St. John's	Currency:	EC dollar = 100 cents
Nationality:	Antiguan, Barbudan	Dialing Code:	DDC 809
Language:	English	Location:	E Caribbean Sea
		Climate:	tropical marine

Jan.	1	New Year's Day	*		Whitmonday
Feb.	14	Valentine's Day	Aug.	*	Carnival (1st Mon. &
*		Good Friday			Tues.)
*		Easter Monday	Nov.	1	State Day
May	*	Labor Day (1st Mon.)	Dec.	25	Christmas Day
June	*	Queen's Birthday	Dec.	26	Boxing Day

Argentina

Official Name:	Argentine Republic	Religion:	Roman Catholic
Capital:	Buenos Aires	Currency:	New Argentine peso = 200
Nationality:	Argentine, Argentinean		centavos
Language:	Spanish	Dialing Code:	IDC 54
		Location:	SE South America
		Climate:	temperate, with wide
			regional variations

Jan.	1	New Year's Day	July	9	Independence Day
Apr.	2	Malvinas Islands Memorial	Aug.	17	San Martin Day
*		Holy Thursday	Oct.	12	Day of the Race
*		Good Friday	Dec.	8	Immaculate Conception
May	1	Labor Day	Dec.	25	Christmas Day
May	25	May Revolution Day	Dec.	31	Bank Holiday
June	20	Flag Day			

Australia

Official Name:	Commonwealth of Australia	Religion:	Protestant (chiefly Anglican),
Capital:	Canberra		Roman Catholic
Nationality:	Australian	Currency:	dollar = 100 cents
Language:	English	Dialing Code:	IDC 61
		Location:	continent between Pacific &
			Indian Oceans
		Climate:	widely varied, subtropical to
			mild temperate

Jan.	1	New Year's Day	Apr.	25	Anzac Day
Jan.	26 *	Australia Day (1st Mon. on	June	*	Queen's Birthday
		or after the 26th)	Aug.	*	Bank Holiday (1st Mon.)
*		Good Friday	Dec.	25	Christmas Day
*		Easter Saturday	Dec.	26	Boxing Day
*		Easter Monday			

Austria

Official Name:	Republic of Austria	
Capital:	Vienna	
Nationality:	Austrian	
Language:	German	

Religion:	Roman Catholic, Protestant
Currency:	schilling = 100 groschen
Dialing Code:	IDC 43
Location:	central Europe
Climate:	mild summers, cold snowy winters

Jan.	1	New Year's Day	Aug.	15	Assumption Day
Jan.	6	Epiphany	Oct.	26	National Holiday
*		Easter Monday	Nov.	1	All Saints' Day
May	1	Labor Day	Dec.	8	Immaculate Conception
*		Ascension Day	Dec.	24	Christmas Eve
*		Whitmonday	Dec.	25	Christmas Day
*		Corpus Christi	Dec.	26	St. Stephen's Day

Bahamas

Official Name:	Commonwealth of the Bahamas	
Capital:	Nassau	
Nationality:	Bahamian	
Language:	English	

Religion:	Protestant, Roman Catholic
Currency:	dollar = 100 cents
Dialing Code:	DDC 809
Location:	Atlantic Ocean, off SE Florida
Climate:	subtropical

Jan.	1	New Year's Day	July	10	Independence Day
*		Good Friday	Aug.	*	Emancipation Day
*		Easter Monday	Oct.	12	Discovery Day
*		Whitmonday	Dec.	25	Christmas Day
June	*	Labor Day (1st Fri.)	Dec.	26	Boxing Day

Bahrain

Official Name:	State of Bahrain	
Capital:	Al Manamah	
Nationality:	Bahraini	
Language:	Arabic (official); English	

Religion:	Moslem
Currency:	dinar = 1,000 fils
Dialing Code:	IDC 973
Location:	Persian Gulf, off E Arabian Peninsula
Climate:	hot and humid

Jan.	1	New Year's Day	*		Ashura (2 days)
Dec.	16	National Day	*		Prophet's Birthday
Dec.	31	Year-end Closing	*		Id al-Fitr (End of Ramadan, 3 days)
Islamic Holidays			*		Id al-Adha (Feast of Pilgrimage, 3 days)
*		First of Muharram (Islamic New Year)			

Bangladesh

Official Name:	People's Republic of Bangladesh	
Capital:	Dacca	
Nationality:	Bangladeshi	
Language:	Bengali (official); English	

Religion:	Moslem, Hindu
Currency:	taka = 100 paisas
Location:	S Asia
Climate:	tropical monsoon

Feb.	21	National Mourning Day (Shaheed)	Dec.	25	Christmas Day
			Dec.	31	Bank Holiday
Mar.	26	Independence Day	*Islamic Holidays*		
Apr.	*	Bengali New Year	*		Ashura
*		Good Friday	*		Prophet's Birthday
May	1	May Day	*		Eid-ul-Fitr (End of Ramadan, 3 days)
July	1	Bank Holiday			
Nov.	7	Revolution Day	*		Eid-ul-Azha (Feast of Pilgrimage, 3 days)
Dec.	16	Victory Day			

Barbados

Official Name:	Barbados	Religion:	Protestant (chiefly Anglican),
Capital:	Bridgetown		Roman Catholic
Nationality:	Barbadian	Currency:	dollar = 100 cents
Language:	English	Dialing Code:	DDC 809
		Location:	E Caribbean Sea
		Climate:	tropical marine

Jan.	1	New Year's Day	Aug.	6	Caricom Day
*		Good Friday	Oct.	1	United Nations Day
*		Easter Monday	Nov.	30	Independence Day
May	1	May Day	Dec.	25	Christmas Day
*		Whitmonday	Dec.	26	Boxing Day
Aug.	3	Kadooment Day			

Belgium

Official Name:	Kingdom of Belgium	Religion:	Roman Catholic, Protestant
Capital:	Brussels	Currency:	franc = 100 centimes
Nationality:	Belgian	Dialing Code:	IDC 32
Language:	French, Flemish, German (all	Location:	NW Europe
	official)	Climate:	temperate, often cool and
			rainy

Jan.	1	New Year's Day	Aug.	15	Assumption
*		Easter Monday	Nov.	1	All Saints' Day
May	1	Labor Day	Nov.	11	Armistice Day
*		Ascension Day	Nov.	15	Dynasty Day
*		Whitmonday	Dec.	25	Christmas Day
July	21	Independence Day	Dec.	26	Bank Holiday

Belize

Official Name:	Belize	Religion:	Roman Catholic, Protestant
Capital:	Belmopan	Currency:	dollar = 100 cents
Nationality:	Belizean	Dialing Code:	IDC 501
Language:	English (official); Spanish,	Location:	Central America
	Mayan	Climate:	humid tropical

Jan.	1	New Year's Day	Sep.	10	National Day
Mar.	9	Baron Bliss Day	Sep.	21	Independence Day
*		Good Friday	Oct.	12	Columbus Day
*		Holy Saturday	Oct.	14	Pan-American Day
*		Easter Monday	Nov.	19	Garifuna Day
May	1	Labor Day	Dec.	25	Christmas Day
May	24	Commonwealth Day	Dec.	26	Boxing Day

Benin

Official Name:	People's Republic of Benin	Religion:	animist, Christian, Moslem
Capital:	Porto-Novo	Currency:	CFA franc = 100 centimes
Nationality:	Beninese	Location:	W Africa
Language:	French (official); tribal	Climate:	tropical, with rainy/dry
	languages		seasons

Jan.	1	New Year's Day	*		Whitsunday
Jan.	16	Martyrs' Day	Oct.	26	Armed Forces Day
Apr.	1	Youth Day	Nov.	30	National Day
*		Easter	Dec.	25	Christmas Day
May	1	Labor Day	Dec.	31	Feed Yourself Day
*		Ascension Day			

Bhutan

Official Name:	Kingdom of Bhutan	
Capital:	Thimbu	
Nationality:	Bhutanese	
Language:	Dzongka (official); Nepalese	

Religion:	Buddhist, Hindu
Currency:	ngultrum = 100 chetrums (Indian rupee also used)
Location:	S Asia
Climate:	temperate to subtropical

May	5	Jigme Dorji Wangchuck's Birthday	Nov.	11	Jigme Singye Wangchuck's Birthday (3 days)
June	6	Jigme Singye Wangchuck's Coronation Day	Dec.	17	National Day
July	21	Jigme Dorji Wangchuck's Death Anniversary			

Bolivia

Official Name:	Republic of Bolivia
Capital:	La Paz (administrative); Sucre (legal and judicial)
Nationality:	Bolivian
Language:	Spanish (official); Quechua, Aymara

Religion:	Roman Catholic
Currency:	peso = 100 centavos
Dialing Code:	IDC 591
Location:	central South America
Climate:	varies with altitude from tropical to dry and cool

Jan.	1	New Year's Day	July	16	Civic Holiday (La Paz)
*		Carnival (2 days)	Aug.	6	Independence Day
*		Holy Thursday	Oct.	12	Day of the Race
*		Good Friday	Nov.	2	All Souls' Day
May	1	Labor Day	Dec.	25	Christmas Day
*		Corpus Christi			

Botswana

Official Name:	Republic of Botswana
Capital:	Gaborone
Nationality:	Botswana
Language:	English (official); Setswana

Religion:	Christian, animist
Currency:	pula = 100 thebe
Location:	S central Africa
Climate:	subtropical

Jan.	1–3	New Year's Holiday	July	16	President's Day (2 days)
*		Good Friday	Sep.	30	Botswana Day (2 days)
*		Holy Saturday	Dec.	25	Christmas Day
*		Easter Monday	Dec.	26	Boxing Day
*		Ascension Day			

Brazil

Official Name:	Federative Republic of Brazil
Capital:	Brasília
Nationality:	Brazilian
Language:	Portuguese

Religion:	Roman Catholic
Currency:	cruzeiro = 100 centavos
Dialing Code:	IDC 55
Location:	E South America
Climate:	widely varied from tropical to mild temperate

Jan.	1	New Year's Day	*		Corpus Christi
Jan.	20	Foundation Day (Rio de Janeiro)	Sep.	7	Independence Day
			Oct.	12	Religious Holiday
Jan.	25	Foundation Day (São Paulo)	Nov.	2	Memorial (All Souls') Day
*		Carnival (2 days)	Nov.	15	Proclamation of the Republic
*		Ash Wednesday (half day)			
*		Holy Thursday	Dec.	24	Christmas Eve (half day)
*		Good Friday	Dec.	25	Christmas Day
Apr.	21	Tiradentes Day	Dec.	31	New Year's Eve (half day)
May	1	Labor Day			

Bulgaria

Official Name:	People's Republic of Bulgaria		Religion:		Officially atheist; Eastern Orthodox, Moslem
Capital:	Sofia				
Nationality:	Bulgarian		Currency:		lev = 100 stotinki
Language:	Bulgarian		Location:		SE Europe
			Climate:		temperate, with dry summers and damp winters

Jan.	1	New Year's Day	May	24	Bulgarian Culture Day
Mar.	8	Women's Day	Sep.	9	Liberation Day (2 days)
May	1	Labor Day (2 days)	Nov.	7	Soviet Revolution Day

Burma

Official Name:	Socialist Republic of the Union of Burma		Religion:		Buddhist, Hindu, Christian
			Currency:		kyat = 100 pyas
Capital:	Rangoon		Location:		SE Asia
Nationality:	Burmese		Climate:		tropical monsoon
Language:	Burmese (official); English				

Jan.	4	Independence Day	Apr./May	*	Full Moon of Kason (Birth of Buddha)
Feb.	12	Union Day			
Feb.	21	National Mourning Day	July	*	Full Moon of Waso (Buddhist Lent)
Mar.	2	Peasants Day			
Feb./Mar.	*	Full Moon of Tabaung	July	19	Martyrs' Day
Mar.	27	Resistance Day	Oct.	*	Full Moon of Thadingyut (End of Buddhist Lent)
Apr.	*	Maha Thingan (Burmese New Year, 3 days)			
			Nov.	*	Tazaungdaing Festival
May	1	May Day	Dec.	25	Christmas Day

Burundi

Official Name:	Republic of Burundi		Religion:		Christian (chiefly Roman Catholic), animist
Capital:	Bujumbura				
Nationality:	Burundian		Currency:		franc = 100 centimes
Language:	Kirundi, French (both official); Swahili		Location:		E central Africa
			Climate:		mild equatorial, cooler in highlands

Jan.	1	New Year's Day	Aug.	15	Assumption Day
May	1	Labor Day	Sep.	18	UPRONA Victory Day
*		Ascension Day	Nov.	1	All Saints' Day
July	1	Independence Day	Dec.	25	Christmas Day

Cameroon

Official Name:	United Republic of Cameroon		Religion:		Christian, animist, Moslem
			Currency:		CFA franc = 100 centimes
Capital:	Yaoundé		Location:		W central Africa
Nationality:	Cameroonian		Climate:		tropical in coastal areas to hot & dry inland
Language:	French, English (both official); tribal languages				

Jan.	1	New Year's Day	Dec.	25	Christmas Day
Feb.	11	Youth Day	*Islamic Holidays*		
*		Good Friday	*		Djoulde Sonmae (End of Ramadan)
May	1	Labor Day			
May	20	Constitution Day	*		Id-el-Kibir (Feast of Pilgrimage)
*		Ascension Day			
Aug.	15	Assumption Day			

Canada

Official Name:	Canada		Religion:	Roman Catholic, Protestant	
Capital:	Ottawa		Currency:	dollar = 100 cents	
Nationality:	Canadian		Location:	N North America	
Language:	English, French (both official)		Climate:	temperate to arctic	

Jan.	1	New Year's Day	July	1	Dominion Day
Jan.	3	Civic Holiday (Quebec)	Aug.	*	Civic Holiday (1st Mon.)
*		Good Friday	Sep.	*	Labor Day (1st Mon.)
*		Easter Monday	Oct.	*	Thanksgiving Day
May	24 *	Victoria Day	Nov.	11	Remembrance Day
June	24	St. John the Baptist's Day	Dec.	25	Christmas Day
		(Quebec)	Dec.	26	Boxing Day

Cape Verde

Official Name:	Republic of Cape Verde		Religion:	Roman Catholic, animist	
Capital:	Praia		Currency:	escudo = 100 centavos	
Nationality:	Cape Verdian		Location:	Atlantic Ocean, off NW	
Language:	Portuguese (official); Crioulo			Africa	
			Climate:	dry temperate	

Jan.	1	New Year's Day	June	1	Children's Day
Jan.	20	National Heroes Day	July	5	Independence Day
Mar.	8	Women's Day	Sep.	12	Nationality Day
*		Good Friday	Dec.	24	Christmas Eve
May	1	Labor Day	Dec.	25	Christmas Day

Central African Republic

Official Name:	Central African Republic		Religion:	Protestant, Roman Catholic,	
Capital:	Bangui			animist, Moslem	
Nationality:	Central African		Currency:	CFA franc = 100 centimes	
Language:	French (official); Sango		Location:	central Africa	
			Climate:	mild temperate, with	
				rainy/dry seasons	

Jan.	1	New Year's Day	*		Whitmonday
Mar.	29	Anniversary of President	Aug.	13	Independence Day
		Boganda's Death	Aug.	15	Assumption Day
*		Easter Monday	Nov.	1	All Saints' Day
May	1	Labor Day	Dec.	1	National Day
*		Ascension Day	Dec.	25	Christmas Day

Chad

Official Name:	Republic of Chad		Religion:	Moslem, animist, Christian	
Capital:	Ndjamena		Currency:	CFA franc = 100 centimes	
Nationality:	Chadian		Location:	N central Africa	
Language:	French (official); Arabic,		Climate:	tropical (rainy/dry) to desert	
	tribal languages			in north	

Jan.	1	New Year's Day	Dec.	25	Christmas Day
*		Easter Monday	*Islamic Holidays*		
May	1	Labor Day	*		Prophet's Birthday
May	25	Africa Freedom Day	*		Aid-el-Sakkhair (End of
June	7	Chad Liberation Day			Ramadan)
Aug.	11	Independence Day	*		Aid-el-Adha (Feast of
Nov.	1	All Saints' Day			Pilgrimage)
Nov.	28	Proclamation of the			
		Republic			

Chile

Official Name:	Republic of Chile	Religion:	Roman Catholic
Capital:	Santiago	Currency:	peso = 100 centavos
Nationality:	Chilean	Dialing Code:	IDC 56
Language:	Spanish	Location:	SW South America
		Climate:	temperate (central) to dry (north) to cool & wet (south)

Jan.	1	New Year's Day	Sep.	19	Armed Forces Day
★		Good Friday	Oct.	12	Day of the Race
May	1	Labor Day	Nov.	1	All Saints' Day
May	21	Battle of Iquique Day	Dec.	8	Immaculate Conception
Aug.	15	Assumption Day	Dec.	25	Christmas Day
Sep.	11	National Liberation Day	Dec.	31	Bank Holiday
Sep.	18	Independence Day			

China

Official Name:	People's Republic of China	Religion:	Confucian, Buddhist, Taoist
Capital:	Beijing (Peking)	Currency:	renminbi = 100 chiao
Nationality:	Chinese	Location:	E Asia
Language:	Mandarin Chinese (official); regional dialects	Climate:	widely varied from temperate to subtropical

Jan.	1	New Year's Day	May	1	Labor Day
Jan./Feb.	★	Chinese New Year (4 days)	Oct.	1–2	National Day

China, Republic of. *See* TAIWAN.

Colombia

Official Name:	Republic of Colombia	Religion:	Roman Catholic
Capital:	Bogotá	Currency:	peso = 100 centavos
Nationality:	Colombian	Dialing Code:	IDC 57
Language:	Spanish	Location:	NW South America
		Climate:	tropical in coastal areas to cool & dry in mountains

Jan.	1	New Year's Day	June	30 ★	Mid-Year Balance (half day)
Jan.	6	Epiphany	July	20	Independence Day
Mar.	19	St. Joseph's Day	Aug.	7	Battle of Boyacá
★		Holy Thursday	Aug.	15	Assumption Day
★		Good Friday	Oct.	12	Day of the Race
May	1	Labor Day	Nov.	1	All Saints' Day
★		Ascension Day	Nov.	11	Independence of Cartagena
★		Corpus Christi	Dec.	8	Immaculate Conception
★		Sacred Heart of Jesus	Dec.	25	Christmas Day
June	29	Sts. Peter & Paul Day	Dec.	31 ★	Year-End Bank Closing

Congo

Official Name:	People's Republic of the Congo	Religion:	Christian (chiefly Roman Catholic), animist
Capital:	Brazzaville	Currency:	CFA franc = 100 centimes
Nationality:	Congolese	Location:	W central Africa
Language:	French (official); Lingala, Kongo	Climate:	tropical

Jan.	1	New Year's Day	Aug.	13–15	The Three Glorious Days
Mar.	18	Supreme Sacrifice Day	Nov.	1	Day of the Dead
May	1	Labor Day	Dec.	25	Children's Day
July	31	Revolution Day	Dec.	31	Proclamation of the Republic

Costa Rica

Official Name:	Republic of Costa Rica	
Capital:	San José	
Nationality:	Costa Rican	
Language:	Spanish	

Religion:	Roman Catholic	
Currency:	colon = 100 centimos	
Dialing Code:	IDC 506	
Location:	Central America	
Climate:	tropical, with rainy/dry seasons	

Jan.	1	New Year's Day	July	25	Annexation of Guanacaste Day
Mar.	19	St. Joseph's Day			
Apr.	11	Battle of Rivas Day	Aug.	2 *	Our Lady of the Angels Day
*		Holy Thursday			
*		Good Friday	Aug.	15	Assumption (Mother's) Day
*		Holy Saturday			
May	1	Labor Day	Sep.	15	Independence Day
*		Corpus Christi	Oct.	12	Day of the Race
June	29	Sts. Peter & Paul Day	Dec.	8	Immaculate Conception
			Dec.	25	Christmas Day

Cuba

Official Name:	Republic of Cuba	
Capital:	Havana	
Nationality:	Cuban	
Language:	Spanish	

Religion:	Roman Catholic
Currency:	peso = 100 centavos
Location:	N Caribbean Sea
Climate:	tropical marine

Jan.	1–2	Liberation Day	July	26	Revolution Day (3 days)
May	1	Labor Day	Oct.	10	Beginning of Wars of Independence

Cyprus

Official Name:	Republic of Cyprus	
Capital:	Nicosia	
Nationality:	Cypriot, Cyprian	
Language:	Greek, Turkish (both official)	

Religion:	Greek Orthodox, Moslem, Christian
Currency:	pound = 1,000 mils
Dialing Code:	IDC 357
Location:	E Mediterranean Sea
Climate:	mild, with hot summers

Jan.	1	New Year's Day	Dec.	26	Boxing Day
Jan.	6	Epiphany	*Islamic Holidays*		
Mar.	1	Green Monday	*		Prophet's Birthday
Mar.	25	Greek Independence Day	*		Ramazan Bairam (End of Ramadan)
*		Good Friday			
*		Holy Saturday	*		Kurban Bairam (Feast of Pilgrimage)
*		Easter Monday			
May	1	Labor Day			
Oct.	28	Greek National Day			
Oct.	29	Turkish National Day	*Note:* Easter Week holidays determined		
Dec.	25	Christmas Day	according to Julian calendar.		

Czechoslovakia

Official Name:	Czechoslovak Socialist Republic	
Capital:	Prague	
Nationality:	Czechoslovakian	
Language:	Czech, Slovak (both official)	

Religion:	Roman Catholic, Protestant, Eastern Orthodox
Currency:	crown (koruna) = 100 halers
Location:	central Europe
Climate:	cool temperate

Jan.	1	New Year's Day	Dec.	24	Day of Rest
*		Easter Monday	Dec.	25	Christmas Day
Apr.	30	Day of Rest	Dec.	26	Christmas Holiday
May	1	Labor Day	Dec.	31	Day of Rest
May	9	National Day			

Denmark

Official Name:	Kingdom of Denmark		Religion:		Lutheran
Capital:	Copenhagen		Currency:		krone = 100 öre
Nationality:	Danish		Dialing Code:		IDC 45
Language:	Danish		Location:		NW Europe
			Climate:		cool temperate, with mild winters

Jan.	1	New Year's Day	June	5	Constitution Day
★		Holy Thursday	★		Whitmonday
★		Good Friday	Dec.	24	Christmas Eve
★		Easter Monday	Dec.	25	Christmas Day
May	18	General Prayer Day	Dec.	26	Boxing Day
★		Ascension Day			

Djibouti

Official Name:	Republic of Djibouti		Religion:	Moslem
Capital:	Djibouti		Currency:	franc = 100 centimes
Nationality:	Djibouti		Location:	NE Africa
Language:	French (official); Somali, Afar, Arabic		Climate:	hot & dry

Jan.	1	New Year's Day	★	Prophet's Birthday
May	1	Labor Day	★	Al-Isra-Wal-Mira'age (Prophet's Ascension)
June	27–28	Independence Feast Days	★	Aid-El-Fitre (End of Ramadan, 2 days)
Dec.	25	Christmas Day		
Islamic Holidays			★	Aid-El-Adha (Feast of Pilgrimage, 2 days)
★		First of Muharram (Islamic New Year)		

Dominica

Official Name:	Commonwealth of Dominica		Religion:	Roman Catholic, Protestant
Capital:	Roseau		Currency:	EC dollar = 100 cents
Nationality:	Dominican		Dialing Code:	DDC 809
Language:	English (official); French patois		Location:	E Caribbean Sea
			Climate:	tropical marine

Jan.	1	New Year's Day	June	★	Queen's Birthday
★		Carnival (2 days)	Aug.	★	Bank Holiday (1st Mon.)
★		Good Friday	Nov.	3–4	Independence Day
★		Easter Monday	Dec.	25	Christmas Day
May	1	Labor Day	Dec.	26	Boxing Day
★		Whitmonday			

Dominican Republic

Official Name:	Dominican Republic		Religion:	Roman Catholic
Capital:	Santo Domingo		Currency:	peso = 100 centavos
Nationality:	Dominican		Dialing Code:	DDC 809
Language:	Spanish		Location:	N Caribbean Sea (E portion of Hispaniola)
			Climate:	tropical, cooler in mountains

Jan.	1	New Year's Day	★		Corpus Christi
Jan.	6	Epiphany	Aug.	16	Restoration Day
Jan.	21	Our Lady of Altagracia	Sep.	24	Feast of Our Lady of Mercy
Jan.	26	Duarte's Day	Oct.	12	Day of the Race
Feb.	27	Independence Day	Nov.	6	Constitution Day
★		Good Friday	Dec.	25	Christmas Day
May	1	Labor Day			

East Germany

Official Name:	German Democratic Republic		Religion:	Protestant, Roman Catholic		
Capital:	East Berlin		Currency:	mark = 100 pfennigs		
Nationality:	East German		Dialing Code:	IDC 37		
Language:	German		Location:	N central Europe		
			Climate:	cool temperate		

Jan.	1	New Year's Day	Oct.	7	Constitution Day
★		Good Friday	Dec.	25	Christmas Day
May	1	Labor Day	Dec.	26	Boxing Day
★		Whitmonday			

Ecuador

Official Name:	Republic of Ecuador		Religion:	Roman Catholic		
Capital:	Quito		Currency:	sucre = 100 centavos		
Nationality:	Ecuadorian		Dialing Code:	IDC 593		
Language:	Spanish		Location:	W South America		
			Climate:	tropical in coastal areas to cool & dry in mountains		

Jan.	1	New Year's Day	Aug.	10	Independence Day
Jan.	6	Epiphany	Oct.	9	Independence of
★		Carnival (2 days)			Guayaquil
★		Holy Thursday	Oct.	12	Day of the Race
★		Good Friday	Nov.	1	All Saints' Day
May	1	Labor Day	Nov.	2	All Souls' Day
May	24	Battle of Pichincha Day	Nov.	3	Independence of Cuenca
June	30 ★	Bank Holiday	Dec.	6	Civil Holiday (Quito)
July	24	Bolívar's Day	Dec.	25	Christmas Day
July	25	Civic Holiday (Guayaquil)	Dec.	31	Bank Holiday

Egypt

Official Name:	Arab Republic of Egypt		Religion:	Sunni Moslem, Coptic		
Capital:	Cairo		Currency:	pound = 100 piasters		
Nationality:	Egyptian		Location:	NE Africa		
Language:	Arabic		Climate:	hot & dry, with mild winters		

Jan.	7	Eastern Orthodox Christmas	*Islamic Holidays*		
★		Palm Sunday	★		First of Muharram (Islamic New Year)
★		Easter Sunday	★		Prophet's Birthday
Apr.	23	Sham El Nessim	★		Ramadan Bairam (End of Ramadan, 2 days)
Apr.	25	Sinai Liberation Day			
May	1	Labor Day	★		Wakfet Arafet
June	18	Evacuation Day	★		Kurban Bairam (Feast of Pilgrimage, 2 days)
July	1	Bank Holiday			
July	23	National Day			
Oct.	6	Armed Forces Day	*Note:* Easter Week holidays determined according to Julian calendar.		
Oct.	24	Suez National Day			

El Salvador

Official Name:	Republic of El Salvador		Religion:	Roman Catholic		
Capital:	San Salvador		Currency:	colon = 100 centavos		
Nationality:	Salvadoran		Dialing Code:	IDC 503		
Language:	Spanish		Location:	Central America		
			Climate:	tropical, with rainy/dry seasons		

Jan.	1	New Year's Day	June	22	Teachers' Day
Apr.	14	Pan-American Day	June	30 ★	Bank Holiday (2 days)
★		Holy Thursday	Aug.	3–6	Feast of San Salvador
★		Good Friday	Sep.	15	Independence Day
May	1	Labor Day	Oct.	12	Day of the Race

El Salvador (Continued)

Nov.	2	All Souls' Day	Dec.	24	Christmas Eve (half day)
Nov.	5	Anniversary of First Call	Dec.	25	Christmas Day
		for Independence	Dec.	31 ★	Bank Holiday (2 days)

England. *See* GREAT BRITAIN.

Equatorial Guinea

Official Name:	Republic of Equatorial Guinea	Religion:	Christian (mainly Roman Catholic), animist
Capital:	Malabo	Currency:	ekpwele = 100 cents
Nationality:	Equatorial Guinean	Location:	W Africa
Language:	Spanish (official); Fang, Bubi	Climate:	humid tropical

Jan.	1	New Year's Day	Aug.	3	Armed Forces Day
★		Good Friday	Oct.	12	National Day
May	1	Labor Day	Nov.	1	All Saints' Day
May	25	Organization of African Unity Day	Dec.	10	Human Rights Day
			Dec.	25	Christmas Day
June	25	President's Birthday			
★		Corpus Christi			

Ethiopia

Official Name:	Ethiopia	Religion:	Christian (chiefly Coptic), Moslem, animist
Capital:	Addis Ababa		
Nationality:	Ethiopian	Currency:	birr = 100 cents
Language:	Amharic (official); Arabic	Location:	E Africa
		Climate:	tropical in coastal areas to mild inland

Jan.	7	Ethiopian Christmas	Sep.	28 ★	Feast of the True Cross
Jan.	19	Ethiopian Epiphany	*Islamic Holidays*		
Mar.	2	Aduwa Victory Day	★		Prophet's Birthday
Apr.	6	Patriots Victory Day	★		Id al-Fitr (End of Ramadan)
★		Good Friday	★		Id al-Adha (Feast of Pilgrimage)
★		Easter Sunday			
May	1	Labor Day			
Sep.	11 ★	Ethiopian New Year	*Note:* Easter Week holidays determined according to Julian calendar.		
Sep.	13	Popular Revolution Day			

Fiji

Official Name:	Fiji	Religion:	Christian (chiefly Methodist), Hindu
Capital:	Suva		
Nationality:	Fijian	Currency:	dollar = 100 cents
Language:	English (official); Fijian, Hindi	Dialing Code:	IDC 679
		Location:	SW Pacific Ocean
		Climate:	tropical marine

Jan.	1	New Year's Day	Oct./Nov.	★	Diwali (Festival of Lights)
★		Good Friday	Nov.	14	Prince of Wales' Birthday
★		Holy Saturday	Dec.	25	Christmas Day
★		Easter Monday	Dec.	26	Boxing Day
June	★	Queen's Birthday			
Aug.	★	Bank Holiday (1st Mon.)	*Note:* The Islamic holiday of the Prophet's Birthday is also celebrated.		
Oct.	★	Fiji Day (1st Mon.)			

Finland

Official Name:	Republic of Finland	Religion:	Lutheran
Capital:	Helsinki	Currency:	markka = 100 penni
Nationality:	Finnish	Dialing Code:	IDC 358
Language:	Finnish, Swedish (both official)	Location:	N Europe
		Climate:	cool temperate

Finland (Continued)

Jan.	1	New Year's Day	Nov.	1 ★	All Saints' Day (nearest
★		Holy Thursday (half day)			Sat.)
★		Good Friday	Dec.	6	Independence Day
★		Easter Monday	Dec.	24	Christmas Eve
May	1	Labor Day	Dec.	25	Christmas Day
June	24 ★	Midsummer Holiday	Dec.	26	Boxing Day
		(nearest Fri. & Sat.)	Dec.	31	New Year's Eve (half day)

France

Official Name:	French Republic	Religion:	Roman Catholic
Capital:	Paris	Currency:	franc = 100 centimes
Nationality:	French	Dialing Code:	IDC 33
Language:	French	Location:	W Europe
		Climate:	temperate (north) to Mediterranean (south)

Jan.	1	New Year's Day	July	14	Bastille Day
★		Good Friday	Aug.	14	Assumption Day Eve (half day)
★		Holy Saturday			
★		Easter Monday	Aug.	15	Assumption Day
May	1	Labor Day	Oct.	31	All Saints' Day Eve (half day)
May	8	Armistice Day			
★		Ascension Day Eve (half day)	Nov.	1	All Saints' Day
			Nov.	11	Armistice Day
★		Ascension Day	Dec.	24	Christmas Eve
★		Whit Holiday Eve (half day)	Dec.	25	Christmas Day
★		Whitmonday	Dec.	31	New Year's Eve
July	13	Bastille Day Eve (half day)			

French Guiana

Status:	French Overseas Department	Religion:	Roman Catholic
Capital:	Cayenne	Currency:	franc = 100 centimes
Nationality:	French Guianese	Location:	NE South America
Language:	French	Climate:	humid tropical

Jan.	1	New Year's Day	★		Whitmonday
★		Carnival (Mon. & Tue. before Lent)	July	14	Bastille Day
			Aug.	15	Assumption Day
★		Ash Wednesday	Nov.	1	All Saints' Day
★		Good Friday	Nov.	2	All Souls' Day
★		Easter Monday	Nov.	11	Armistice Day
May	1	Labor Day	Dec.	24	Christmas Eve
★		Ascension Day Eve (half day)	Dec.	25	Christmas Day
			Dec.	31	New Year's Eve
★		Ascension Day			

Gabon

Official Name:	Gabonese Republic	Religion:	Christian, animist, Moslem
Capital:	Libreville	Currency:	CFA franc = 100 centimes
Nationality:	Gabonese	Location:	W central Africa
Language:	French (official); Fang, other Bantu languages	Climate:	humid tropical, with rainy/dry seasons

Jan.	1	New Year's Day	Nov.	1	All Saints' Day
Mar.	12	Renovation Day	Dec.	25	Christmas Day
★		Easter Monday	*Islamic Holidays*		
May	1	Labor Day	★		Id al-Fitr (End of Ramadan)
★		Whitmonday	★		Aid El Kebir (Feast of Pilgrimage)
Aug.	17	Independence Day			

Gambia

Official Name:	Republic of The Gambia	Religion:	Moslem, Christian
Capital:	Banjul	Currency:	dalasi = 100 bututs

Gambia (Continued)

Nationality:	Gambian		Location:		W Africa
Language:	English (official); Malinke, Wolof		Climate:		dry tropical

Jan.	1	New Year's Day	Aug.	15	St. Mary's (Assumption) Day
Feb.	18	Independence Day			
⋆		Good Friday	Dec.	25	Christmas Day
May	1	Labor Day			

Germany. *See* EAST GERMANY; WEST GERMANY.

Ghana

Official Name:	Republic of Ghana	Religion:		Christian, Moslem, animist
Capital:	Accra	Currency:		cedi = 100 pesewa
Nationality:	Ghanaian	Location:		W Africa
Language:	English (official); tribal languages	Climate:		humid tropical

Jan.	1	New Year's Day	June	4 ⋆	Revolution Day
Mar.	6	Independence Day	July	1	First Republic Day
⋆		Good Friday	Dec.	25	Christmas Day
⋆		Holy Saturday	Dec.	26	Boxing Day
⋆		Easter Monday	Dec.	31 ⋆	Revolution Day
May	1	May Day			

Great Britain

Official Name:	United Kingdom of Great Britain & Northern Ireland	Religion:		Protestant (chiefly Church of England), Roman Catholic
Capital:	London	Currency:		pound = 100 pence
Nationality:	British	Dialing Code:		IDC 44
Language:	English	Location:		British Isles
		Climate:		maritime temperate

Jan.	1	New Year's Day	July	12	Orangeman's Day (Northern Ireland)
Mar.	17	St. Patrick's Day (Northern Ireland)	Aug.	⋆	Summer Bank Holiday (Scotland: 1st Mon.)
⋆		Good Friday	Aug.	⋆	Summer Bank Holiday (except Scotland: last Mon.)
⋆		Easter Monday			
May	⋆	Early May Bank Holiday (1st Mon.)			
May	⋆	Late May Bank Holiday (last Mon.)	Dec.	25	Christmas Day
			Dec.	26	Boxing Day

Greece

Official Name:	Hellenic Republic	Religion:		Greek Orthodox
Capital:	Athens	Currency:		drachma = 100 lepta
Nationality:	Greek	Dialing Code:		IDC 30
Language:	Greek	Location:		SE Europe
		Climate:		mild temperate

Jan.	1	New Year's Day	⋆		Whitmonday
Jan.	6	Epiphany	Aug.	15	Assumption Day
⋆		Shrove Monday	Oct.	28	National Day
Mar.	25	Independence Day	Dec.	25	Christmas Day
⋆		Good Friday	Dec.	26	Boxing Day
⋆		Easter Monday			
May	1	Labor Day			

Note: Movable holidays determined according to Julian calendar.

Grenada

Official Name:	Grenada	Religion:		Roman Catholic, Protestant
Capital:	St. George's	Currency:		EC dollar = 100 cents
Nationality:	Grenadian	Dialing Code:		DDC 809

Grenada (Continued)

Language:		English (official); French patois	Location:		E Caribbean Sea
			Climate:		tropical marine

Jan.	1–2	New Year's Holiday	*		Queen's Birthday
Feb.	7	Independence Day	*		Corpus Christi
Mar.	13	National Day	Aug.	*	Emancipation Day (1st
*		Good Friday			Mon. & Tue.)
*		Easter Monday	Aug.	*	Carnival (3rd Mon.)
May	1	Labor Day	Dec.	25	Christmas Day
*		Whitmonday	Dec.	26	Boxing Day

Guadeloupe

Status:		French Overseas Department	Religion:		Roman Catholic
Capital:		Basse-Terre	Currency:		franc = 100 centimes
Language:		French (official); Creole	Dialing Code:		IDC 596
			Location:		E Caribbean Sea
			Climate:		tropical marine

Jan.	1	New Year's Day	July	13	Bastille Day Eve (half day)
*		Carnival (Mon. & Tue. before Lent)	July	14	Bastille Day
			Aug.	14	Assumption Day Eve (half
*		Ash Wednesday			day)
*		Holy Thursday (half day)	Aug.	15	Assumption Day
*		Good Friday	Oct.	31	All Saints' Day Eve (half
*		Easter Monday			day)
May	1	Labor Day	Nov.	1	All Saints' Day
May	8	Armistice Day	Nov.	2	All Souls' Day
*		Ascension Day Eve (half day)	Nov.	11	Armistice Day
			Dec.	24	Christmas Eve
*		Ascension Day	Dec.	25	Christmas Day
*		Whitmonday	Dec.	31	New Year's Eve

Guatemala

Official Name:		Republic of Guatemala	Religion:		Roman Catholic
Capital:		Guatemala City	Currency:		quetzal = 100 centavos
Nationality:		Guatemalan	Dialing Code:		IDC 502
Language:		Spanish (official); Maya-Quiché dialects	Location:		Central America
			Climate:		humid tropical, cooler in highlands

Jan.	1	New Year's Day	Aug.	15	Assumption Day
Mar.	23	National Day	Sep.	15	Independence Day
*		Holy Wednesday (half day)	Oct.	12	Day of the Race (bank
*		Holy Thursday			holiday)
*		Good Friday	Oct.	20	Revolution Day
May	1	Labor Day	Nov.	1	All Saints' Day
June	30	Army Day	Dec.	24	Christmas Eve (half day)
July	1	Bank Employees' Day (bank holiday)	Dec.	25	Christmas Day
			Dec.	31	New Year's Eve (half day)

Guinea

Official Name:		People's Revolutionary Republic of Guinea	Religion:		Moslem, animist
			Currency:		syli = 100 cory
Capital:		Conakry	Location:		NW Africa
Nationality:		Guinean	Climate:		humid tropical, with
Language:		French (official); Fulani, Mandé			rainy/dry seasons

Jan.	1	New Year's Day	Dec.	25	Christmas Day
May	1	Labor Day	*Islamic Holidays*		
May	14	Anniversary of Guinean Democratic Party	*		Prophet's Birthday
			*		Id-ul-Fitr (End of
Sep.	28	Referendum Day			Ramadan)
Oct.	2	Republic Day	*		Tabaski (Feast of
Nov.	22	National Day			Pilgrimage)

Guinea-Bissau

Official Name:	Republic of Guinea-Bissau			Religion:	animist, Moslem, Christian	
Capital:	Bissau			Currency:	peso = 100 centavos	
Nationality:	Guinean			Location:	W Africa	
Language:	Portuguese (official); Criolo			Climate:	tropical, with rainy/dry seasons	

Jan.	1	New Year's Day	Aug.	3	Martyrs of Colonialism Day
Jan.	20	National Heroes Day			
Feb.	28	Bank Holiday	Sep.	12	National Day
Mar.	8	Women's Day	Sep.	24	Republic Day
May	1	Labor Day	Nov.	14	Readjustment Day
			Dec.	25	Christmas Day

Guyana

Official Name:	Cooperative Republic of Guyana		Religion:	Christian, Hindu, Moslem
			Currency:	dollar = 100 cents
Capital:	Georgetown		Dialing Code:	IDC 592
Nationality:	Guyanese		Location:	NE South America
Language:	English (official); Hindi		Climate:	tropical, with rainy/dry seasons

Jan.	1	New Year's Day	Oct./Nov.	★	Deepavali (Festival of Lights)
Feb.	23	Republic Day			
Mar.	★	Phagwah Day	Dec.	25	Christmas Day
★		Good Friday	Dec.	26	Boxing Day
★		Easter Monday	*Islamic Holidays*		
May	1	Labor Day	★		Prophet's Birthday
July	★	Caribbean Community Day (1st Mon.)	★		Eid-ul-Azah (Feast of Pilgrimage)
Aug.	★	Freedom Day (1st Mon.)			

Haiti

Official Name:	Republic of Haiti		Religion:	Roman Catholic, Protestant
Capital:	Port-au-Prince		Currency:	gourde = 100 centimes
Nationality:	Haitian		Dialing Code:	IDC 509
Language:	French (official); Creole		Location:	N Caribbean Sea (W portion of Hispaniola)
			Climate:	tropical, semiarid

Jan.	1	New Year's & Independence Day	★		Ascension Day
			★		Corpus Christi
Jan.	2	Ancestors' Day	June	22	President's Day
★		Mardi Gras (3 days before beginning of Lent)	Aug.	15	Assumption Day
			Oct.	17	Dessalines' Day
★		Good Friday	Oct.	24	United Nations Day
Apr.	14	Pan-American Day	Nov.	18	Armed Forces (Vertières) Day
May	1	Labor Day			
May	18	Flag Day	Dec.	5	Discovery Day
May	22	National Sovereignty Day	Dec.	25	Christmas Day

Honduras

Official Name:	Republic of Honduras		Religion:	Roman Catholic
Capital:	Tegucigalpa		Currency:	lempira = 100 centavos
Nationality:	Honduran		Dialing Code:	IDC 504
Language:	Spanish		Location:	Central America
			Climate:	tropical, with rainy/dry seasons

Jan.	1	New Year's Day	May	1	Labor Day
Feb.	3	Virgin of Suya's Day	Sep.	15	Independence Day
★		Holy Thursday	Oct.	3	Francisco Morazán's Birthday
★		Good Friday			
Apr.	14	Pan-American Day	Oct.	12	Discovery Day

Honduras (Continued)

Oct.	21	Armed Forces Day	Dec.	31	Bank Holiday
Dec.	25	Christmas Day			

Hong Kong

Status:	British Crown Colony	Religion:	Buddhist, Taoist, Confucian, Christian
Capital:	Victoria (unofficial)		
Language:	Chinese, English (both official)	Currency:	dollar = 100 cents
		Dialing Code:	IDC 852
		Location:	SE China coast
		Climate:	subtropical

Jan.	1	New Year's Day	June	★	Dragon Boat Festival
Jan.	2 ★	First Weekday in January	July	1	Half-year Holiday
Jan./Feb.	★	Chinese New Year (3 days)	Aug.	★	Saturday before Liberation Day
Apr.	5	Ching Ming (Tomb-Sweeping Day)	Aug.	★	Liberation Day (last Mon.)
★		Good Friday	Sep.	★	Mid-Autumn Festival
★		Holy Saturday	Oct.	★	Chung Yeung Festival
★		Easter Monday	Dec.	25	Christmas Day
Apr.	21	Queen's Birthday	Dec.	26	Christmas Holiday

Hungary

Official Name:	Hungarian People's Republic	Religion:	Roman Catholic, Protestant
Capital:	Budapest	Currency:	forint = 100 fillér
Nationality:	Hungarian	Location:	E central Europe
Language:	Hungarian (Magyar)	Climate:	temperate

Jan.	1	New Year's Day	Aug.	20	Constitution Day
Apr.	4	Liberation Day	Nov.	7	October Revolution Day
★		Easter Monday	Dec.	25	Christmas Day
May	1	Labor Day	Dec.	26	Christmas Holiday

Iceland

Official Name:	Republic of Iceland	Religion:	Lutheran
Capital:	Reykjavik	Currency:	krona = 100 aurar
Nationality:	Icelandic	Location:	N Atlantic Ocean
Language:	Icelandic	Climate:	temperate, with cool damp summers

Jan.	1	New Year's Day	★		Whitmonday
★		Holy Thursday	June	17	Independence Day
★		Good Friday	Aug.	★	Bank Holiday (1st Mon.)
★		Easter Monday	Dec.	24	Christmas Eve (half day)
Apr.	22 ★	First Day of Summer	Dec.	25	Christmas Day
May	1	Labor Day	Dec.	26	Boxing Day
★		Ascension Day	Dec.	31	New Year's Eve (half day)

India

Official Name:	Republic of India	Religion:	Hindu, Moslem, Christian
Capital:	New Delhi	Currency:	rupee = 100 paise
Nationality:	Indian	Location:	S Asia
Language:	Hindi (official); English, many regional languages	Climate:	subtropical monsoon, with wide regional variations

Jan.	1	New Year's Day (regional)	Oct.	2	Mahatma Gandhi's Birthday
Jan.	26	Republic Day			
★		Good Friday (regional)	Dec.	25	Christmas Day
May	1	May Day (regional)	Dec.	31	Bank Holiday
June	30	Bank Holiday			
Aug.	15	Independence Day			

Note: Many local and religious holidays are also observed in different states.

Indonesia

Official Name:	Republic of Indonesia	Religion:	Moslem, Christian
Capital:	Djakarta	Currency:	rupiah = 100 sen
Nationality:	Indonesian	Dialing Code:	IDC 62
Language:	Bahasa Indonesian (official); English	Location:	SE Asia (Malay Archipelago)
		Climate:	tropical monsoon

Jan.	1	New Year's Day	*Islamic Holidays*	
Feb./Mar.	*	Hari Raya Haji	*	First of Muharram (Islamic
*		Good Friday		New Year)
Apr./May		Wesak (Birth of Buddha)	*	Prophet's Birthday
*		Ascension Day	*	Ascension of the Prophet
Aug.	17	Independence Day	*	Idul Fitri (End of Rama-
Oct.	5	Army Day		dan)
Dec.	25	Christmas Day	*	Idul Adha (Feast of Pil-
				grimage)

Iran

Official Name:	Islamic Republic of Iran	Religion:	Shiah Moslem
Capital:	Teheran	Currency:	rial = 100 dinars
Nationality:	Iranian	Dialing Code:	IDC 98
Language:	Persian (Farsi)	Location:	SW Asia
		Climate:	dry temperate, with seasonal extremes

Feb.	11	Revolution Day	*	Prophet's Birthday
Mar.	21/22	Now Rooz (Iranian New	*	Birth of Imam Ali
		Year, 5 days)	*	Mission of the Prophet
Apr.	1	Islamic Republic Day	*	Birth of the 12th Imam
Apr.	2	13th of Farvardin	*	Martyrdom of Imam Ali
June	5	15th Khordad Uprising	*	Id-al-Fetre (End of Ram-
Islamic Holidays				adan)
*		Ashura	*	Death of Imam Jaffar
*		Arbain		Sadeq
*		Death of the Prophet &	*	Birth of Imam Reza
		Martyrdom of Imam	*	Id-E-Ghorban
		Hassan	*	Id-E-Ghadir

Iraq

Official Name:	Republic of Iraq	Religion:	Sunni & Shiah Moslem
Capital:	Baghdad	Currency:	dinar = 1,000 fils
Nationality:	Iraqi	Dialing Code:	IDC 964
Language:	Arabic	Location:	Middle East
		Climate:	hot & dry, with mild winters

Jan.	1	New Year's Day	*Islamic Holidays*	
Jan.	6	Army Day	*	First of Muharram (Islamic
Feb.	8	Ramadan Revolution Day		New Year)
Mar.	21	Spring Day	*	Ashura
May	1	Labor Day	*	Prophet's Birthday
July	14	1958 Revolution Day	*	Id El-Fitr (End of
July	17	1968 Revolution Day		Ramadan, 3 days)
			*	Id El-Adha (Feast of
				Pilgrimage, 4 days)

Ireland

Official Name:	Republic of Ireland	Religion:	Roman Catholic
Capital:	Dublin	Currency:	pound = 100 pence
Nationality:	Irish	Dialing Code:	IDC 353
Language:	English, Irish (Gaelic), both official	Location:	W British Isles
		Climate:	temperate, with mild wet winters

Ireland (Continued)

Jan.	1	New Year's Day	Aug.	*	Bank Holiday (1st Mon.)
Mar.	17	St. Patrick's Day	Oct.	31	Allhallows Eve
*		Good Friday	Dec.	25	Christmas Day
*		Easter Monday	Dec.	26	St. Stephen's Day
June	*	Irish Bank Day (1st Mon.)	Dec.	27	Christmas Holiday

Israel

Official Name:	State of Israel	Religion:	Jewish, Moslem, Christian,
Capital:	Jerusalem		Druse
Nationality:	Israeli	Currency:	shekel = 100 agorot
Language:	Hebrew (official); English,	Dialing Code:	IDC 972
	Arabic	Location:	Middle East
		Climate:	Mediterranean

Jan.	1	Bank Holiday	Sep./Oct.	*	Rosh Hashanah
Feb./Mar.	*	Purim	Sep./Oct.	*	Yom Kippur
Mar./Apr.	*	Passover (7 days)	Sep./Oct.	*	Succoth
May	*	Independence Day	Nov./Dec.	*	Chanukah
May/June	*	Shavuot			

Italy

Official Name:	Italian Republic	Religion:	Roman Catholic
Capital:	Rome	Currency:	lira = 100 centesimi
Nationality:	Italian	Dialing Code:	IDC 39
Language:	Italian	Location:	S Europe
		Climate:	Mediterranean to temperate in north

Jan.	1	New Year's Day	Nov.	1	All Saints' Day
*		Easter Monday	Dec.	8	Immaculate Conception
Apr.	25	Liberation Day	Dec.	24	Christmas Eve (half day)
May	1	Labor Day	Dec.	25	Christmas Day
June	2	Republic Day	Dec.	26	St. Stephen's Day
Aug.	15	Assumption Day	Dec.	31	New Year's Eve (half day)

Ivory Coast

Official Name:	Republic of Ivory Coast	Religion:	animist, Moslem, Christian
Capital:	Abidjan	Currency:	CFA franc = 100 centimes
Nationality:	Ivorian	Dialing Code:	IDC 225
Language:	French (official); tribal	Location:	W Africa
	languages	Climate:	humid tropical

Jan.	1	New Year's Day	Dec.	7	Independence Day
*		Easter Monday	Dec.	25	Christmas Day
May	1	Labor Day	*Islamic Holidays*		
*		Ascension Day	*		End of Ramadan
*		Whitmonday	*		Tabaski (Feast of Pilgrimage)
Aug.	15	Assumption Day			
Nov.	1	All Saints' Day			

Jamaica

Official Name:	Jamaica	Religion:	Protestant (chiefly Anglican),
Capital:	Kingston		Roman Catholic
Nationality:	Jamaican	Currency:	dollar = 100 cents
Language:	English (official); Creole	Dialing Code:	DDC 809
		Location:	N Caribbean Sea
		Climate:	tropical marine

Jan.	1	New Year's Day	Aug.	*	Independence Day (1st Mon.)
*		Ash Wednesday			
*		Good Friday	Oct.	*	National Heroes' Day (3rd Mon.)
*		Easter Monday			
May	23 *	Labor Day	Dec.	25	Christmas Day
			Dec.	26	Boxing Day

Japan

Official Name:	Japan	Religion:	Buddhist, Shintoist
Capital:	Tokyo	Currency:	yen = 100 sen
Nationality:	Japanese	Dialing Code:	IDC 81
Language:	Japanese	Location:	NW Pacific Ocean
		Climate:	temperate monsoon

Jan.	1	New Year's Day	May	5	Children's Day
Jan.	2	Bank Holiday	Sep.	15	Respect for the Aged Day
Jan.	15	Adults' Day	Sep.	23 ★	Autumnal Equinox Day
Feb.	11	Foundation Day	Oct.	10	Physical Education Day
Mar.	20 ★	Vernal Equinox Day	Nov.	3	Culture Day
Apr.	29	Emperor's Birthday	Nov.	23	Labor Thanksgiving Day
May	3	Constitution Memorial			

Jordan

Official Name:	Hashemite Kingdom of Jordan	Religion:	Sunni Moslem
Capital:	Amman	Currency:	dinar = 1,000 fils
Nationality:	Jordanian	Location:	Middle East
Language:	Arabic	Climate:	warm & dry, with mild winters

Jan.	1	New Year's Day	*Islamic Holidays*	
Jan.	15	Arbor Day	★	First of Muharram (Islamic New Year)
Mar.	22	Arab League Day	★	Prophet's Birthday
May	1	Labor Day	★	Lailat al-Miraj (Prophet's Ascension)
May	25	Independence Day	★	Id al-Fitr (End of Ramadan)
Aug.	11	King Hussein's Accession Day	★	Id al-Adha (Feast of Pilgrimage)
Nov.	14	King Hussein's Birthday		
Dec.	25	Christmas Day		

Kenya

Official Name:	Republic of Kenya	Religion:	Christian, animist, Moslem
Capital:	Nairobi	Currency:	shilling = 100 cents
Nationality:	Kenyan	Dialing Code:	IDC 254
Language:	Swahili (official); English	Location:	E Africa
		Climate:	moderate inland to hot & humid on coast

Jan.	1	New Year's Day	Dec.	12	Jamhuri (Independence) Day
★		Good Friday			
★		Easter Monday	Dec.	25	Christmas Day
May	1	Labor Day	Dec.	26	Boxing Day
June	1	Madaraka Day			
Oct.	20	Kenyatta Day			

Note: The Islamic holiday Id-ul-Fitr is also observed.

Korea. *See* SOUTH KOREA.

Kuwait

Official Name:	State of Kuwait	Religion:	Sunni Moslem
Capital:	Kuwait	Currency:	dinar = 1,000 fils
Nationality:	Kuwaiti	Dialing Code:	IDC 965
Language:	Arabic (official); English	Location:	NE Arabian Peninsula
		Climate:	hot & dry

Jan.	1	New Year's Day	★	Lailat al-Miraj (Prophet's Ascension)
Feb.	25	National Day	★	Eid al-Fitr (End of Ramadan, 4 days)
Islamic Holidays				
★		First of Muharram (Islamic New Year)	★	Standing on Mt. Arafat
★		Prophet's Birthday	★	Eid al-Adha (Feast of Pilgrimage, 4 days)

Lebanon

Official Name:	Republic of Lebanon	
Capital:	Beirut	
Nationality:	Lebanese	
Language:	Arabic (official); French, English	

Religion:	Moslem, Christian, Druse	
Currency:	pound = 100 piasters	
Location:	Middle East	
Climate:	Mediterranean	

Jan.	1	New Year's Day	
Feb.	9	St. Maron's Day	
*		Good Friday	
May	1	Labor Day	
Aug.	15	Assumption Day	
Nov.	22	Independence Day	
Dec.	25	Christmas Day	

Islamic Holidays

*	First of Muharram (Islamic New Year)
*	Ashura
*	Prophet's Birthday
*	Id al-Fitr (End of Ramadan)
*	Id al-Adha (Feast of Pilgrimage, 2 days)

Lesotho

Official Name:	Kingdom of Lesotho
Capital:	Maseru
Nationality:	Basotho (pl.), Mosotho (sing.)
Language:	Sesotho, English (both official)

Religion:	Christian, animist
Currency:	loti = 100 lisente
Location:	enclave within E South Africa
Climate:	mild

Jan.	1	New Year's Day	*		Ascension Day
Mar.	12	Moshoeshoe's Day	July	2 *	Family Day
Mar.	23	National Tree Planting Day	Oct.	4	Independence Day
*		Good Friday	Oct.	5	National Sports Day
*		Easter Monday	Dec.	25	Christmas Day
May	2	King's Birthday	Dec.	26	Boxing Day

Liberia

Official Name:	Republic of Liberia
Capital:	Monrovia
Nationality:	Liberian
Language:	English (official); tribal languages

Religion:	animist, Moslem, Christian
Currency:	U.S. dollar = 100 cents
Dialing Code:	IDC 231
Location:	W Africa
Climate:	humid tropical

Jan.	1	New Year's Day	July	26	Independence Day
Feb.	11	Armed Forces Day	Aug.	24	Flag Day
Mar.	2	Decoration Day	Nov.	*	Thanksgiving Day (1st Thurs.)
Mar.	15	J. J. Roberts' Birthday			
Apr.	12	Redemption Day	Nov.	29	President Tubman's Birthday
Apr.	13	National Fast & Prayer Day			
May	14	National Unification Day	Dec.	25	Christmas Day

Libya

Official Name:	Socialist People's Libyan Arab Jamahiriya
Capital:	Tripoli
Nationality:	Libyan
Language:	Arabic

Religion:	Sunni Moslem
Currency:	dinar = 100 dirhams
Dialing Code:	IDC 218
Location:	N Africa
Climate:	Mediterranean in coastal areas to desert inland

Mar.	8	Syrian Revolution Day
Mar.	28	Evacuation of British Army
May	25	Sudanese Revolution Day
June	11	Evacuation of U.S. Army
July	23	Arab Revolution Day
Sep.	1	Libyan Revolution Day
Oct.	7	Evacuation of Italian Fascists

Islamic Holidays

*	First of Muharram (Islamic New Year)
*	Prophet's Birthday
*	Eid el-Fitr (End of Ramadan, 3 days)
*	Eid el-Adha (Feast of Pilgrimage, 4 days)

Liechtenstein

Official Name:	Principality of Liechtenstein	Religion:	Roman Catholic
Capital:	Vaduz	Currency:	Swiss franc = 100 centimes
Nationality:	Liechtensteiner	Dialing Code:	IDC 41
Language:	German (official); Alemannic	Location:	W central Europe
		Climate:	temperate, with snowy winters

Jan.	1	New Year's Day	*		Ascension Day
Jan.	6	Epiphany	*		Whitmonday
Feb.	2	Candlemas Day	*		Corpus Christi
Mar.	19	St. Joseph's Day	Aug.	15	Assumption Day
Mar.	25	Annunciation Day	Nov.	1	All Saints' Day
*		Good Friday	Dec.	8	Immaculate Conception
*		Easter Monday	Dec.	25	Christmas Day
May	1	Labor Day	Dec.	26	St. Stephen's Day

Luxembourg

Official Name:	Grand Duchy of Luxembourg	Religion:	Roman Catholic
Capital:	Luxembourg	Currency:	franc = 100 centimes
Nationality:	Luxembourger, Luxembourgian	Dialing Code:	IDC 352
		Location:	W Europe
Language:	French (official); German, Letzeburgesch	Climate:	mild temperate, rainy

Jan.	1	New Year's Day	Sep.	3	Bank Holiday (Luxembourg City)
*		Shrove Monday			
*		Easter Monday	Nov.	1	All Saints' Day
May	1	Labor Day	Nov.	2	All Souls' Day (bank holiday)
*		Ascension Day			
*		Whitmonday	Dec.	24	Christmas Eve (half day)
June	23	Grand Duke's Birthday	Dec.	25	Christmas Day
Aug.	15	Assumption Day	Dec.	26	St. Stephen's Day

Macao

Status:	Portuguese Administered Territory	Religion:	Buddhist
		Currency:	pataca = 100 avos
Capital:	Macao	Location:	SE China coast
Language:	Chinese, Portuguese	Climate:	humid subtropical

Jan.	1	New Year's Day	June	24	Civic Holiday
Jan.	2	First Weekday in January	Aug.	15	Assumption Day
Jan./Feb.	*	Chinese New Year	Aug.	25	Holiday
Apr.	4	Ching Ming	Sep.	*	Chinese Mid-Autumn Festival
*		Good Friday			
*		Holy Saturday	Oct.	1	Chinese Republic Day
*		Easter Sunday	Oct.	*	Festival of Ancestors
*		Easter Monday	Oct.	5	Portuguese Republic Day
Apr.	25	Anniversary of Portuguese Revolution	Nov.	1	All Saints' Day
			Nov.	2	All Souls' Day
May	1	Labor Day	Dec.	1	Restoration of Independence
June	*	Dragon Boat Festival			
June	10	Portuguese Community Day	Dec.	8	Immaculate Conception
			Dec.	22 *	Winter Solstice
*		Corpus Christi	Dec.	24–26	Christmas Holiday

Madagascar

Official Name:	Democratic Republic of Madagascar	Religion:	animist, Christian, Moslem
		Currency:	franc = 100 centimes
Capital:	Antananarivo	Location:	SW Indian Ocean
Nationality:	Malagasy, Madagascan	Climate:	tropical in coastal areas, moderate inland
Language:	Malagasy, French (both official)		

Madagascar (Continued)

Jan.	1	New Year's Day	June	26	Independence Day
Mar.	29	Memorial Day	Aug.	14	Assumption Day Eve
*		Good Friday	Aug.	15	Assumption Day
*		Easter Monday	Oct.	31	Allhallows Eve (half day)
Apr.	30	Labor Day Eve (half day)	Nov.	1	All Saints' Day
May	1	Labor Day	Dec.	24	Christmas Eve (half day)
*		Ascension Day Eve (half day)	Dec.	25	Christmas Day
*		Ascension Day	Dec.	30	Anniversary Day
*		Whitmonday	Dec.	31	New Year's Eve (half day)
June	25	Independence Day Eve (half day)			

Malawi

Official Name:	Republic of Malawi	Religion:	animist, Christian, Moslem
Capital:	Lilongwe	Currency:	kwacha = 100 tambala
Nationality:	Malawian	Location:	SE Africa
Language:	English (official); Chichewa	Climate:	mild

Jan.	1	New Year's Day	July	6	Republic Day
Mar.	3	Martyrs' Day	Aug.	*	Bank Holiday (1st Mon.)
*		Good Friday	Oct.	17	Mother's Day
*		Holy Saturday	Dec.	25	Christmas Day
*		Easter Monday	Dec.	26	Boxing Day
May	14	Kamuzu Day			

Malaysia

Official Name:	Federated States of Malaysia	Religion:	Moslem, Hindu
Capital:	Kuala Lumpur	Currency:	ringgit = 100 sen
Nationality:	Malaysian	Dialing Code:	IDC 60
Language:	Malay (official); English, Tamil, Chinese	Location:	SE Asia
		Climate:	tropical monsoon, rainy year round

Jan.	1	New Year's Day	Aug.	31	National Day
Feb.	3 *	Federal Territory Holiday (Kuala Lumpur)	Oct./Nov.	*	Deepavali
Jan./Feb.	*	Chinese New Year (2 days)	Dec.	25	Christmas Day
May	1	Labor Day			
Apr./May	*	Wesak			
June	2	Yang di-Pertuan Agong's Birthday			

Note: The sultan's birthday is observed on varying dates by different states. Many other local and Islamic holidays are also celebrated.

Maldives

Official Name:	Republic of Maldives	Religion:	Sunni Moslem
Capital:	Male	Currency:	rupee = 100 larees
Nationality:	Maldivian	Location:	E Indian Ocean
Language:	Divehi (official); Arabic, English	Climate:	tropical monsoon

Jan.	1	New Year's Day	*		Prophet's Birthday
Jul.	26–28	Independence Holiday	*		First of Ramadan (2 days)
Nov.	11–12	Republic Day Holiday	*		Id al-Fitr (End of Ramadan, 3 days)
Nov.	24–25	National Day Holiday			
Islamic Holidays			*		Hajj (Pilgrimage) Day
*		First of Muharram (Islamic New Year)	*		Id al-Adha (Feast of Pilgrimage, 4 days)

Mali

Official Name:	Republic of Mali	Religion:	Moslem, animist
Capital:	Bamako	Currency:	franc = 100 centimes
Nationality:	Malian	Location:	W Africa
Language:	French (official); tribal languages	Climate:	dry tropical

Mali (Continued)

Jan.	1	New Year's Day	Nov.	19	Liberation Day
Jan.	20	Army Day	Dec.	25	Christmas Day
*		Easter Monday	*Islamic Holidays*		
May	1	Labor Day	*		Prophet's Birthday
May	25	African Liberation Day	*		End of Ramadan
Sep.	22	Independence Day	*		Tabaski (Feast of Pilgrimage)

Malta

Official Name:	Republic of Malta	Religion:	Roman Catholic
Capital:	Valletta	Currency:	pound = 100 cents
Nationality:	Maltese	Location:	Mediterranean Sea, S of Sicily
Language:	Maltese, English (both official); Italian	Climate:	Mediterranean

Jan.	1	New Year's Day	Aug.	15	Assumption
Mar.	31	National Day	Dec.	13	Republic Day
*		Good Friday	Dec.	25	Christmas Day
May	1	May Day			

Martinique

Status:	French Overseas Department	Religion:	Roman Catholic
Capital:	Fort-de-France	Currency:	franc = 100 centimes
Language:	French (official); Creole	Dialing Code:	IDC 596
		Location:	E Caribbean Sea
		Climate:	tropical marine

Jan.	1	New Year's Day	July	13	Bastille Day Eve (half day)
*		Carnival (Mon. & Tue. before Lent)	July	14	Bastille Day
*		Ash Wednesday	Aug.	14	Assumption Day Eve (half day)
*		Holy Thursday (half day)	Aug.	15	Assumption Day
*		Good Friday	Oct.	31	All Saints' Day Eve (half day)
*		Easter Monday			
May	1	Labor Day	Nov.	1	All Saints' Day
May	8	Armistice Day	Nov.	2	All Souls' Day
*		Ascension Day Eve (half day)	Nov.	11	Armistice Day
			Dec.	24	Christmas Eve
*		Ascension Day	Dec.	25	Christmas Day
*		Whitmonday	Dec.	31	New Year's Eve

Mauritania

Official Name:	Islamic Republic of Mauritania	Religion:	Moslem
		Currency:	ouguiya = 5 khoums
Capital:	Nouakchott	Location:	NW Africa
Nationality:	Mauritanian	Climate:	hot & dry
Language:	French (official); Arabic		

Jan.	1	New Year's Day	*Islamic Holidays*	
May	1	Labor Day	*	First of Muharram (Islamic New Year)
May	25	African Liberation Day		
July	10	Armed Forces Day	*	Prophet's Birthday
Nov.	28	Independence Day	*	Idul Fitr (End of Ramadan)
Dec.	25	Celebration for the Organization of African States	*	Idul Adha (Feast of Pilgrimage)

Mauritius

Official Name:	Mauritius	Religion:	Hindu, Christian, Moslem
Capital:	Port Louis	Currency:	rupee = 100 cents
Nationality:	Mauritian	Location:	SW Indian Ocean
Language:	English (official); French, Creole	Climate:	tropical rainy

Mauritius (Continued)

Jan.	1	New Year's Day	Dec.	25	Christmas Day
Jan./Feb.	*	Chinese Spring Festival	Dec.	26	Boxing Day
Mar.	12	Independence Day	*Islamic Holidays*		
*		Easter Monday	*		Prophet's Birthday
May	1	Labor Day	*		Id al-Fitr (End of Ramadan)
Aug.	15	Assumption Day	*		Id al-Adha (Feast of
Oct./Nov.	*	Divali			Pilgrimage)
Oct.	24	United Nations Day			
Nov.	1	All Saints' Day	*Note:* Many Hindu holidays also observed.		

Mexico

Official Name:	United Mexican States
Capital:	Mexico City
Nationality:	Mexican
Language:	Spanish

Religion:	Roman Catholic
Currency:	peso = 100 centavos
Dialing Code:	DDC 905 (Mexico City)
	DDC 903 (NW Mexico)
Location:	S North America
Climate:	widely varying, from tropical to highland desert

Jan.	1	New Year's Day	Oct.	12	Day of the Race (bank holiday)
Feb.	5	Constitution Day			
Mar.	21	Benito Juarez' Birthday	Nov.	2	All Souls' Day (bank holiday)
*		Holy Wednesday (half day)			
*		Holy Thursday	Nov.	20	Anniversary of the Revolution
*		Good Friday			
May	1	Labor Day	Dec.	12	Our Lady of Guadalupe
May	5	Battle of Puebla Day	Dec.	24	Christmas Eve (half day)
Sep.	1	Presidential Message Day	Dec.	25	Christmas Day
Sep.	16	Independence Day	Dec.	31	Bank Holiday

Monaco

Official Name:	Principality of Monaco
Capital:	Monaco
Nationality:	Monacan, Monégasque
Language:	French (official); Monégasque, English, Italian

Religion:	Roman Catholic
Currency:	French franc = 100 centimes
Dialing Code:	IDC 33
Location:	N Mediterranean coast
Climate:	Mediterranean

Jan.	1	New Year's Day	Jul.	13	National Holiday Eve (half day)
Jan.	27	St. Dévote Day			
*		Shrove Tuesday (half day)	Jul.	14	National Holiday
*		Mid Lent (half day)	Aug.	15	Assumption Day
*		Good Friday	Sep.	3	Liberation of Monaco
*		Easter Monday	Nov.	11	Armistice
May	1	Labor Day	Nov.	19	National Day
*		Ascension Eve (half day)	Dec.	8	Immaculate Conception
*		Ascension Day	Dec.	24	Christmas Eve
*		Whitmonday	Dec.	25	Christmas Day
*		Corpus Christi	Dec.	31	New Year's Eve

Mongolia

Official Name:	Mongolian People's Republic
Capital:	Ulan Bator
Nationality:	Mongolian
Language:	Mongolian

Religion:	Lamaistic Buddhist
Currency:	tugrik = 100 mongo
Location:	N central Asia
Climate:	dry continental, with seasonal extremes

Jan.	1	New Year's Day	July	11–12	National Holiday
Mar.	8	International Women's Day	Nov.	7	October Revolution Day
May	1–2	International Socialist Workers' Day			

Morocco

Official Name:	Kingdom of Morocco
Capital:	Rabat

Religion:	Sunni Moslem
Currency:	dirham = 100 centimes

Morocco (Continued)

Nationality:	Moroccan		Location:		NW Africa
Language:	Arabic (official); French, Berber		Climate:		mild to hot in coastal areas, desert inland

Jan.	1	New Year's Day	*Islamic Holidays*		
Mar.	3	Feast of the Throne	*		First of Muharram (Islamic New Year)
May	1	Labor Day			
May	23	Fête Nationale	*		Prophet's Birthday
Aug.	14	Oued Eddahab	*		Idul-Fitr (End of Ramadan, 2 days)
Nov.	6	Anniversary of the Green March			
Nov.	18	Independence Day	*		Idul-Adha (Feast of Pilgrimage, 2 days)

Mozambique

Official Name:	People's Republic of Mozambique		Religion:	animist, Christian, Moslem
			Currency:	metical = 100 centavos
Capital:	Maputo		Location:	SE Africa
Nationality:	Mozambican		Climate:	hot & humid in coastal areas, mild inland
Language:	Portuguese (official); Bantu languages			

Jan.	1	New Year's Day	June	25	Independence Day
Feb.	3	Heroes' Day	Sep.	25	Mozambican Popular Forces Liberation Day
Apr.	7	Mozambican Women's Day			
May	1	Workers' Day	Dec.	25	Family Day

Nauru

Official Name:	Republic of Nauru		Religion:	Christian
Capital:	Yaren		Currency:	Australian dollar = 100 cents
Nationality:	Nauruan			
Language:	Nauruan (official); English		Location:	central Pacific Ocean
			Climate:	tropical marine

Jan.	1	New Year's Day	May	17	Constitution Day
Jan.	31	Independence Day	July	1	Takeover Day
*		Good Friday	Oct.	26	Angam Day
*		Easter Monday	Dec.	25	Christmas Day
*		Easter Tuesday	Dec.	26	Boxing Day

Nepal

Official Name:	Kingdom of Nepal		Religion:	Hindu, Mahayana Buddhist
Capital:	Katmandu		Currency:	rupee = 100 paisas
Nationality:	Nepalese		Location:	central Asia
Language:	Nepalese (official); English, local languages		Climate:	varies with altitude, subtropical to temperate

Jan.	*	Prithbi Jayanti	Sep.	*	Indrajatra (Rain God Festival)
Jan.	26	Indian Republic Day			
Jan./Feb.	*	Maha Shivaratra	Oct.	*	Durga Puja (Divine Mother Festival)
Feb.	18	Democracy Day			
Apr.	*	Ram Nawamee	Nov.	*	Diwali (Festival of Lights)
Apr.	*	New Year's Day	Nov.	8	Queen's Birthday
Apr./May	*	Buddha Jayanti (Birth of Buddha)	Dec.	16	Constitution Day
			Dec.	28	King Birendra's Birthday
Aug.	*	Teej Women's Festival			
Aug.	*	Gaijatra (Cow Festival)			

The Netherlands

Official Name:	Kingdom of the Netherlands		Religion:	Roman Catholic, Protestant
Capital:	Amsterdam (constitutional); The Hague (de facto)		Currency:	guilder = 100 cents
			Dialing Code:	IDC 31
Nationality:	Dutch		Location:	NW Europe
Language:	Dutch (official); Frisian		Climate:	northern maritime

The Netherlands (Continued)

Jan.	1	New Year's Day	*		Ascension Day
*		Good Friday	*		Whitmonday
*		Easter Monday	Dec.	25	Christmas Day
Apr.	30	Queen's Birthday	Dec.	26	Boxing Day
May	5	Liberation Day			

Netherlands Antilles (Aruba, Bonaire, Curaçao, Saba, St. Eustatius, St. Maarten)

Status:	Autonomous Part of the Kingdom of the Netherlands	Religion:	Roman Catholic, Protestant, Jewish
		Currency:	guilder = 100 cents
Capital:	Willemstad (Curaçao)	Dialing Code:	IDC 599
Nationality:	Netherlands Antillean	Location:	E & S Caribbean Sea
Language:	Dutch (official); Pipiamento, English, Spanish	Climate:	tropical marine (Saba, St. Eustatius, St. Maarten); semiarid tropical (Aruba, Bonaire, Curaçao)

Jan.	1	New Year's Day	*		Ascension
*		Carnival Monday	Sep./Oct.	*	Yom Kippur
*		Good Friday	Dec.	15	Statute Day
*		Easter Monday	Dec.	25	Christmas Day
Apr.	30	Queen's Birthday	Dec.	26	Boxing Day
May	1	Labor Day	Dec.	31	Bank Holiday

New Zealand

Official Name:	New Zealand	Religion:	Protestant, Roman Catholic
Capital:	Wellington	Currency:	dollar = 100 cents
Nationality:	New Zealander	Dialing Code:	IDC 64
Language:	English	Location:	S Pacific Ocean
		Climate:	temperate

Jan.	1	New Year's Day	*		Easter Monday
Jan.	21	Provincial Anniversary (Wellington)	Apr.	25	Anzac Day
Jan.	29	Provincial Anniversary (Auckland, Northland, Nelson)	June	*	Queen's Birthday (1st Mon.)
			Oct.	*	Labor Day (4th Mon.)
Feb.	6	New Zealand Day	Dec.	25	Christmas Day
*		Good Friday	Dec.	26	Boxing Day

Nicaragua

Official Name:	Republic of Nicaragua	Religion:	Roman Catholic
Capital:	Managua	Currency:	cordoba = 100 centavos
Nationality:	Nicaraguan	Dialing Code:	IDC 505
Language:	Spanish	Location:	Central America
		Climate:	tropical, with rainy/dry seasons

Jan.	1	New Year's Day	Sep.	14	Battle of San Jacinto
*		Holy Thursday	Sep.	15	Independence Day
*		Good Friday	Dec.	8	Immaculate Conception
May	1	Labor Day	Dec.	25	Christmas Day
July	19	Sandinist Revolution Day			

Niger

Official Name:	Republic of Niger	Religion:	Moslem
Capital:	Niamey	Currency:	CFA franc = 100 centimes
Nationality:	Nigerois	Location:	W Africa
Language:	French (official); tribal languages	Climate:	hot & dry

Jan.	1	New Year's Day	Aug.	3	Independence Day
Apr.	15	National Day	Dec.	18	Proclamation of the Republic
*		Easter Monday			
May	1	Labor Day	Dec.	25	Christmas Day

Niger (Continued)

Islamic Holidays

⋆	Prophet's Birthday	⋆	Tabaski (Feast of Pilgrimage)
⋆	Korité (End of Ramadan)		

Nigeria

Official Name:	Federal Republic of Nigeria	Religion:	Moslem, Christian, animist
Capital:	Lagos	Currency:	naira = 100 kobos
Nationality:	Nigerian	Dialing Code:	IDC 234
Language:	English (official); Hausa, Yoruba, Ibo, Edo	Location:	W Africa
		Climate:	tropical, with rainy/dry seasons

Jan.	1	New Year's Day	Dec.	26	Boxing Day
⋆		Good Friday	*Islamic Holidays*		
⋆		Easter Monday	⋆		Prophet's Birthday
May	1	Labor Day	⋆		Id-el-Fitr (End of Ramadan)
Oct.	1	Independence Day	⋆		Id-el-Kabir (Feast of Pilgrimage)
Dec.	25	Christmas Day			

Norway

Official Name:	Kingdom of Norway	Religion:	Lutheran
Capital:	Oslo	Currency:	krone = 100 öre
Nationality:	Norwegian	Dialing Code:	IDC 47
Language:	Norwegian	Location:	N Europe
		Climate:	cool temperate

Jan.	1	New Year's Day	⋆		Ascension Day
⋆		Holy Wednesday (half day)	⋆		Whitmonday
⋆		Holy Thursday	Dec.	24	Christmas Eve
⋆		Good Friday	Dec.	25	Christmas Day
⋆		Easter Monday	Dec.	26	Boxing Day
May	1	Labor Day	Dec.	31	New Year's Eve (half day)
May	17	Constitution Day			

Oman

Official Name:	Sultanate of Oman	Religion:	Moslem
Capital:	Muscat	Currency:	rial-omani = 1,000 baiza
Nationality:	Omani	Location:	SE Arabian Peninsula
Language:	Arabic	Climate:	hot & dry

July	23	Accession of the Sultan	⋆	Lailat al Miraj (Prophet's Ascension)
Nov.	18–19	National Days		
Dec.	31	Bank Holiday	⋆	Eid al-Fitr (End of Ramadan, 4 days)
Islamic Holidays			⋆	Eid al-Adha (Feast of Pilgrimage, 5 days)
⋆		First of Muharram (Islamic New Year)		
⋆		Prophet's Birthday		

Pakistan

Official Name:	Islamic Republic of Pakistan	Religion:	Moslem
Capital:	Islamabad	Currency:	rupee = 100 paisas
Nationality:	Pakistani	Location:	S Asia
Language:	Urdu (official); English, Punjabi, Sindhi	Climate:	dry temperate

Mar.	23	Pakistan Day	Dec.	25	Christmas & Birthday of Quaid-e-Azam
May	1	May Day			
July	1	Bank Holiday	Dec.	31	Bank Holiday
Aug.	14	Independence Day	*Islamic Holidays*		
Sep.	6	Defense of Pakistan Day	⋆		Ashura (2 days)
Sep.	11	Death of Quaid-e-Azam	⋆		Prophet's Birthday
Nov.	9	Iqbal Day	⋆		First of Ramadan

Pakistan (Continued)

*	Eid-ul-Fitr (End of Ramadan, 3 days)	*	Eid-ul-Azha (Feast of Pilgrimage, 3 days)	

Panama

Official Name:	Republic of Panama
Capital:	Panama City
Nationality:	Panamanian
Language:	Spanish

Religion:	Roman Catholic
Currency:	balboa (U.S. dollar) = 100 centesimos)
Dialing Code:	IDC 507
Location:	Central America
Climate:	tropical, with rainy/dry seasons

Jan.	1	New Year's Day	Oct.	11	Revolution (Columbus) Day
Jan.	9	Martyrs' Day			
*		Carnival (Mon. & Tue. before Lent)	Oct.	12	Hispanic Day
			Nov.	3	Independence from Colombia
*		Ash Wednesday			
*		Holy Thursday (half day)	Nov.	4	Flag Day (bank holiday)
*		Good Friday	Nov.	28	Independence from Spain
May	1	Labor Day	Dec.	8	Mother's Day
Aug.	15	Founding of the City (Panama City)	Dec.	25	Christmas Day

Papua New Guinea

Official Name:	Papua New Guinea
Capital:	Port Moresby
Nationality:	Papuan New Guinean
Language:	English (official); Melanesian Pidgin

Religion:	animist, Protestant, Roman Catholic
Currency:	kina = 100 toea
Dialing Code:	IDC 675
Location:	SW Pacific Ocean
Climate:	humid tropical to cool in highlands

Jan.	1	New Year's Day	June	*	Queen's Birthday
*		Good Friday	Sep.	16	Independence Day
*		Easter Saturday	Dec.	25	Christmas Day
*		Easter Monday	Dec.	26	Boxing Day

Paraguay

Official Name:	Republic of Paraguay
Capital:	Asunción
Nationality:	Paraguayan
Language:	Spanish (official); Guarani

Religion:	Roman Catholic
Currency:	guarani = 100 centimos
Dialing Code:	IDC 595
Location:	S central South America
Climate:	temperate, with hot summers

Jan.	1	New Year's Day	*		Corpus Christi
Feb.	3	Feast of St. Blas	Aug.	15	Foundation of Asunción (Assumption Day)
Mar.	1	Heroes' Day			
*		Holy Thursday	Aug.	25	Constitution Day
*		Good Friday	Sep.	29	Battle of Boquerón Day
May	1	Labor Day	Oct.	12	Day of the Race
May	14–15	National Independence Days	Nov.	1	All Saints' Day
			Dec.	8	Immaculate Conception
June	12	Chaco Peace Day	Dec.	25	Christmas Day

Peru

Official Name:	Republic of Peru
Capital:	Lima
Nationality:	Peruvian
Language:	Spanish, Quechua (both official)

Religion:	Roman Catholic
Currency:	sol = 100 centavos
Dialing Code:	IDC 51
Location:	W South America
Climate:	arid & mild in coastal areas to temperate in highlands

Peru (Continued)

Jan.	1	New Year's Day	Aug.	30	St. Rose of Lima Day
★		Holy Thursday (half day)	Oct.	9	National Day of Dignity
★		Good Friday	Nov.	1	All Saints' Day
May	1	Labor Day	Dec.	8	Immaculate Conception
June	24	Indian Day	Dec.	25	Christmas Day
June	29	Sts. Peter & Paul Day	Dec.	31	Bank Holiday
June	30	Bank Holiday			
July	28–29	Independence Days			

Philippines

Official Name:	Republic of the Philippines	Religion:	Roman Catholic	
Capital:	Manila	Currency:	peso = 100 centavos	
Nationality:	Filipino	Dialing Code:	IDC 63	
Language:	Pilipino, Spanish, English (all official)	Location:	SW Pacific Ocean	
		Climate:	tropical monsoon, with rainy/dry seasons	

Jan.	1	New Year's Day	July	4	Philippine-American Friendship Day
★		Holy Thursday			
★		Good Friday	Nov.	1	All Saints' Day
May	6	Araw Ng Kagitingan Memorial Day	Nov.	30	National Heroes' Day
			Dec.	25	Christmas Day
June	12	Independence Day	Dec.	30	Rizal Day
			Dec.	31	Bank Holiday

Poland

Official Name:	Polish People's Republic	Religion:	Roman Catholic	
Capital:	Warsaw	Currency:	zloty = 100 groszy	
Nationality:	Polish	Location:	E central Europe	
Language:	Polish	Climate:	temperate, with cold winters	

Jan.	1	New Year's Day	July	22	National Liberation Day
★		Easter Monday	Nov.	1	All Saints' Day
★		Labor Day	Dec.	25	Christmas Day
May	9	Victory Day	Dec.	26	Christmas Holiday
★		Corpus Christi			

Portugal (includes Azores & Madeira)

Official Name:	Portuguese Republic	Religion:	Roman Catholic	
Capital:	Lisbon	Currency:	escudo = 100 centavos	
Nationality:	Portuguese	Dialing Code:	IDC 351	
Language:	Portuguese	Location:	SW Europe	
		Climate:	mild temperate	

Jan.	1	New Year's Day	July	1	Regional Holiday (Madeira)
★		Shrove Tuesday			
★		Holy Thursday (half day)	Aug.	15	Assumption Day
★		Good Friday	Oct.	5	Republic Day
Apr.	25	Liberty Day	Nov.	1	All Saints' Day
May	1	Labor Day	Dec.	1	Independence Restoration Day
June	10	National Day			
June	13	Feast of St. Anthony of Padua (Lisbon)	Dec.	8	Immaculate Conception
			Dec.	24	Christmas Eve
★		Corpus Christi	Dec.	25	Christmas Day
June	24	St. John the Baptist Day (Oporto)	Dec.	26	Boxing Day (Madeira)

Puerto Rico

Official Name:	Commonwealth of Puerto Rico	Religion:	Roman Catholic	
		Currency:	U.S. dollar = 100 cents	
Capital:	San Juan	Dialing Code:	DDC 809	
Nationality:	Puerto Rican	Location:	N Caribbean Sea	
Language:	Spanish, English (both official)	Climate:	tropical marine	

Puerto Rico (Continued)

Jan.	1	New Year's Day	July	17	Muñoz-Rivera's Birthday
Jan.	6	Epiphany	July	25	Constitution Day
Jan.	11	Hostos' Birthday	July	27	Barbosa's Birthday
Feb.	*	Washington's Birthday (3rd Mon.)	Sep.	*	Labor Day (1st Mon.)
			Oct.	12	Day of the Race
Mar.	22	Emancipation Day	Nov.	11	Veterans Day
Apr.	16	De Diego's Birthday	Nov.	19	Discovery of Puerto Rico
*		Good Friday	Nov.	*	Thanksgiving (4th Thurs.)
May	*	Memorial Day (last Mon.)	Dec.	25	Christmas Day
July	4	U.S. Independence Day			

Qatar

Official Name:	State of Qatar	Religion:	Sunni Moslem
Capital:	Doha	Currency:	riyal = 100 dirhams
Nationality:	Qatari	Dialing Code:	IDC 974
Language:	Arabic	Location:	E Arabian Peninsula
		Climate:	hot & dry

Sep.	3	Independence Day	*		Id al-Fitr (End of Ramadan, 4 days)
Dec.	31	Yearly Closing			
Islamic Holidays			*		Id al-Adha (Feast of Pilgrimage, 4 days)
*		First of Muharram (Islamic New Year)			

Rumania

Official Name:	Socialist Republic of Rumania	Religion:	Rumanian Orthodox
		Currency:	leu = 100 bani
Capital:	Bucharest	Dialing Code:	IDC 40
Nationality:	Rumanian	Location:	SE Europe
Language:	Rumanian	Climate:	temperate, with cold winters

Jan.	1–2	New Year's Day	Aug.	23–24	Liberation Day
May	1–2	Labor Day			

Russia. *See* SOVIET UNION.

Rwanda

Official Name:	Republic of Rwanda	Religion:	Roman Catholic, animist, Moslem
Capital:	Kigali		
Nationality:	Rwandan	Currency:	franc = 100 centimes
Language:	Kinyarwanda, French (both official); Kiswahili	Location:	E central Africa
		Climate:	mild temperate

Jan.	1	New Year's Day	July	5	Peace & Unity Day
Jan.	28	Democracy Day	Aug.	1	Harvest Day
*		Easter Monday	Aug.	15	Assumption
May	1	Labor Day	Sep.	25	Referendum Day
*		Ascension Day	Oct.	26	Armed Forces Day
*		Whitmonday	Nov.	1	All Saints' Day
July	1	Independence Day	Dec.	25	Christmas Day

Saint Kitts-Nevis

Official Name:	Saint Christopher and Nevis	Religion:	Christian, chiefly Anglican
Capital:	Basseterre	Currency:	EC dollar = 100 cents
Language:	English	Dialing Code:	DDC 809
		Location:	E Caribbean Sea
		Climate:	tropical marine

Jan.	1	New Year's Day	June	*	Queen's Birthday (2nd Sat.)
*		Good Friday	*		Whitmonday
*		Easter Monday	Aug.	*	August Monday (1st Mon.)
May	*	Labor Day (1st Mon.)			

Saint Kitts-Nevis (Continued)

Sep.	19	Independence Day	Dec.	26	Boxing Day
Dec.	25	Christmas Day	Dec.	31	Carnival Day

Saint Lucia

Official Name:	Saint Lucia	Religion:	Roman Catholic	
Capital:	Castries	Currency:	EC dollar = 100 cents	
Nationality:	Saint Lucian	Dialing Code:	DDC 809	
Language:	English	Location:	E Caribbean Sea	
		Climate:	tropical marine	

Jan.	1–2	New Year's Day	Aug.	*	Emancipation Day (1st
Feb.	22	Independence Day			Mon.)
*		Carnival Monday	Oct.	*	Thanksgiving Day (1st
*		Good Friday			Mon.)
*		Easter Monday	Dec.	13	Feast of St. Lucia
May	1	Labor Day	Dec.	25	Christmas Day
*		Whitmonday	Dec.	26	Boxing Day
*		Corpus Christi			

Saint Vincent and the Grenadines

Official Name:	Saint Vincent and the	Religion:	Protestant, Roman Catholic	
	Grenadines	Currency:	EC dollar = 100 cents	
Capital:	Kingstown	Dialing Code:	DDC 809	
Nationality:	Saint Vincentian	Location:	E Caribbean Sea	
Language:	English	Climate:	tropical marine	

Jan.	1	New Year's Day	July	*	Carnival (1st Mon. &
Jan.	22	Discovery Day			Tue.)
*		Good Friday	Aug.	*	Emancipation Day (1st
*		Easter Monday			Mon.)
May	1	Labor Day	Oct.	27	Independence Day
*		Whitmonday	Dec.	25	Christmas Day
			Dec.	26	Boxing Day

San Marino

Official Name:	Most Serene Republic of San	Religion:	Roman Catholic	
	Marino	Currency:	Italian lira = 100 centesimi	
Capital:	San Marino	Dialing Code:	IDC 39	
Nationality:	San Marinese	Location:	enclave in N central Italy	
Language:	Italian	Climate:	moderate	

Jan.	1	New Year's Day	Aug.	15–16	Summer Holiday
Jan.	6	Epiphany	Sep.	3	San Marino Day
Feb.	5	Feast of St. Agatha	Oct.	1	Captain Regents Day
Mar.	19	St. Joseph's Day	Nov.	1	All Saints' Day
Mar.	25	Arengo Anniversary Day	Nov.	2	Memorial Day
Apr.	1	Captain Regents Day	Dec.	8	Immaculate Conception
May	1	Labor Day	Dec.	24	Christmas Eve
June	29	Sts. Peter & Paul Day	Dec.	25	Christmas Day
July	28	Fall of Fascism Day	Dec.	26	St. Stephen's Day

São Tomé and Principe

Official Name:	Democratic Republic of São	Religion:	Roman Catholic	
	Tomé and Principe	Currency:	dobra = 100 centimos	
Capital:	São Tomé	Location:	Gulf of Guinea, off W Africa	
Nationality:	São Toméan		coast	
Language:	Portuguese	Climate:	tropical, with rainy/dry	
			seasons	

Jan.	1	New Year's Day	Sep.	*	Armed Forces Day (1st
Feb.	4	Martyrs' Day			week on varying days)
May	1	Labor Day	Sep.	30	Nationalization Day
July	12	Independence Day	Dec.	21	Power of the People's Day
			Dec.	25	Family Day

Saudi Arabia

Official Name:	Kingdom of Saudi Arabia	Religion:	Sunni Moslem
Capital:	Riyadh	Currency:	riyal = 20 qurush
Nationality:	Saudi Arabian	Dialing Code:	IDC 966
Language:	Arabic	Location:	Arabian Peninsula
		Climate:	hot & dry, with mild winters on coast

Sep.	23	National Unification Day	*	Id al-Adha (Feast of Pilgrimage, 8 days)
Islamic Holidays				
*		Id al-Fitr (End of Ramadan, 6 days)		

Senegal

Official Name:	Republic of Senegal	Religion:	Moslem, animist, Christian
Capital:	Dakar	Currency:	CFA franc = 100 centimes
Nationality:	Senegalese	Dialing Code:	IDC 221
Language:	French (official); Wolof, Fulani	Location:	W Africa
		Climate:	tropical, with rainy/dry seasons

Jan.	1	New Year's Day	Dec.	25	Christmas Day
Apr.	4	Independence Day	*Islamic Holidays*		
*		Easter Monday	*		Prophet's Birthday
May	1	Labor Day	*		Korité (End of Ramadan)
*		Ascension Day	*		Tabaski (Feast of Pilgrimage)
*		Whitmonday			
Aug.	15	Assumption Day	*		Tamkharit
Nov.	1	All Saints' Day			

Seychelles

Official Name:	Republic of the Seychelles	Religion:	Roman Catholic
Capital:	Victoria	Currency:	rupee = 100 cents
Nationality:	Seychellois	Location:	W Indian Ocean
Language:	English, French (both official); Creole	Climate:	tropical marine

Jan.	1–2	New Year's Day	June	29	Independence Day
*		Good Friday	Aug.	15	Assumption Day
*		Easter Saturday	Nov.	1	All Saints' Day
May	1	Labor Day	Dec.	8	Immaculate Conception
*		Corpus Christi	Dec.	25	Christmas Day
June	5	Liberation Day			

Sierra Leone

Official Name:	Republic of Sierra Leone	Religion:	animist, Moslem, Christian
Capital:	Freetown	Currency:	leone = 100 cents
Nationality:	Sierra Leonean	Location:	W Africa
Language:	English (official); Krio Pidgin	Climate:	tropical, with rainy/dry seasons

Jan.	1	New Year's Day	*Islamic Holiday*	
Apr.	19	Republic Day	*	Prophet's Birthday
*		Good Friday	*	Eid-ul-Fitr (End of Ramadan)
*		Easter Monday		
Dec.	25	Christmas Day	*	Eid-ul-Adha (Feast of Pilgrimage)
Dec.	26	Boxing Day		

Singapore

Official Name:	Republic of Singapore	Religion:	Buddhist, Moslem, Hindu, Christian
Capital:	Singapore		
Nationality:	Singaporean	Currency:	dollar = 100 cents

Singapore (Continued)

Language:	Malay, English, Chinese, Tamil (all official)	Dialing Code:	IDC 65
		Location:	SE Asia
		Climate:	tropical monsoon, rainy year round

Jan.	1	New Year's Day	Dec.	25	Christmas Day
Feb./Mar.	*	Chinese New Year (2 days)	*Islamic Holidays*		
*		Good Friday	*		Prophet's Birthday
May	1	Labor Day	*		Hari Raya Puasa (End of
Apr./May	*	Wesak			Ramadan)
Aug.	9	National Day	*		Hari Raya Hiji (Feast of
Oct./Nov.	*	Deepavali			Pilgrimage)

Solomon Islands

Official Name:	Solomon Islands	Religion:	Protestant, Roman Catholic
Capital:	Honiara	Currency:	dollar = 100 cents
Nationality:	Solomon Islander	Location:	SW Pacific Ocean
Language:	English (official); Melanesian Pidgin	Climate:	tropical monsoon

Jan.	1	New Year's Day	June	*	Queen's Birthday
*		Good Friday	July	7	Independence Day
*		Holy Saturday	Dec.	25	Christmas Day
*		Easter Monday	Dec.	26	Boxing Day
*		Whitmonday			

Somalia

Official Name:	Somali Democratic Republic	Religion:	Sunni Moslem
Capital:	Mogadishu	Currency:	shilling = 100 cents
Nationality:	Somalian	Location:	E Africa
Language:	Somali (official); Arabic, English, Italian	Climate:	hot & dry

Jan.	1	Bank Holiday	*Islamic Holidays*	
May	1	Labor Day	*	Id al-Fitr (End of Ramadan)
June	26	Independence Day	*	Id al-Adha (Feast of Pil-
July	1	Union Day		grimage, 3 days)
Oct.	21–22	Anniversary of the Revolution	*	Prophet's Birthday

South Africa

Official Name:	Republic of South Africa	Religion:	Protestant
Capital:	Pretoria (administrative); Cape Town (legislative); Bloemfontein (judicial)	Currency:	rand = 100 cents
		Dialing Code:	IDC 27
		Location:	S Africa
Nationality:	South African	Climate:	mild temperate
Language:	Afrikaans, English (both official)		

Jan.	1	New Year's Day	May	31	Republic Day
Apr.	6	Founder's Day	Sep.	*	Settlers' Day (1st Mon.)
*		Good Friday	Oct.	10	Kruger Day
*		Easter Monday (Family Day)	Dec.	16	Day of the Covenant
			Dec.	25	Christmas Day
*		Ascension Day	Dec.	26	Boxing Day

Southern Yemen

Official Name:	People's Democratic Republic of Yemen	Religion:	Sunni Moslem
		Currency:	dinar = 1,000 fils
Capital:	Aden	Location:	SW Arabian Peninsula
Nationality:	Southern Yemenite or Yemeni	Climate:	hot & dry
Language:	Arabic		

Southern Yemen (Continued)

Jan.	1	New Year's Day	*Islamic Holidays*
Mar.	8	Women's Day	
May	1	Labor Day	* First of Muharram (Islamic New Year)
Sep.	26–28	Revolution Days	
Oct.	14	National Day	* Prophet's Birthday
Nov.	30	Independence Day	* Id al-Fitr (End of Ramadan, 2 days)
			* Id al-Adha (Feast of Pilgrimage, 3 days)

South Korea

Official Name:	Republic of Korea
Capital:	Seoul
Nationality:	South Korean
Language:	Korean
Religion:	Buddhist, Confucian, Christian, shamanist
Currency:	won = 100 chon
Dialing Code:	IDC 82
Location:	NE Asia
Climate:	temperate

Jan.	1–3	New Year Holiday	July	17	Constitution Day
Mar.	1	Independence Movement Day	Aug.	15	Liberation Day
			Sep.	*	Moon Festival (Choosuk)
Mar.	10	Labor Day	Oct.	1	Armed Forces Day
Apr.	5	Arbor Day	Oct.	3	Foundation Day
May	5	Children's Day	Oct.	9	Alphabet Day (Hangul)
Apr./May	*	Lord Buddha's Birthday	Dec.	25	Christmas Day
June	6	Memorial Day			

Soviet Union

Official Name:	Union of Soviet Socialist Republics
Capital:	Moscow
Nationality:	Soviet
Language:	Russian, many regional languages
Religion:	officially atheist; Russian Orthodox
Currency:	rouble = 100 kopecks
Dialing Code:	IDC 7
Location:	N Eurasia
Climate:	widely varied temperate conditions

Jan.	1	New Year's Day	Oct.	7	Constitution Day
Mar.	8	International Women's Day	Nov.	7–8	October Revolution Holiday
May	1–2	International Labor Day			
May	9	Victory Day			

Spain

Official Name:	Spanish State
Capital:	Madrid
Nationality:	Spanish
Language:	Spanish
Religion:	Roman Catholic
Currency:	peseta = 100 centimos
Dialing Code:	IDC 34
Location:	SW Europe
Climate:	Mediterranean to temperate

Jan.	1	New Year's Day	Aug.	15	Assumption Day
Jan.	6	Epiphany	Sep.	24	Our Lady of Mercy (Barcelona)
Mar.	19	St. Joseph's Day			
*		Good Friday	Oct.	12	Hispanic Day
*		Easter Monday	Nov.	1	All Saints' Day
May	1	Labor Day	Nov.	9	Our Lady of Almudena (Madrid)
May	15	St. Isidro's Day (Madrid)			
*		Whitmonday (Barcelona)	Dec.	8	Immaculate Conception
*		Corpus Christi	Dec.	25	Christmas Day
June	24	St. John the Baptist's Day (Barcelona)	Dec.	26	St. Stephen's Day (Barcelona)
July	25	St. James' Day			

Sri Lanka

Official Name:	Democratic Socialist Republic of Sri Lanka
Capital:	Colombo
Religion:	Buddhist, Hindu, Moslem, Christian
Currency:	rupee = 100 cents

Sri Lanka (Continued)

Nationality:	Sri Lankan		Dialing Code:	IDC 94	
Language:	Sinhala (official); Tamil, English		Location:	Indian Ocean	
			Climate:	tropical monsoon	

Jan.	14	Tamil Thai Pongal Day	Dec.	25	Christmas Day
Feb.	4	Independence Day	Dec.	31	Bank Holiday
Feb./Mar.	*	Maha Sivarathri Day			
Apr.	13 *	Sinhala & Tamil New Year's Day (2 days)	*Islamic Holidays*		
			*		Prophet's Birthday
*		Good Friday	*		Id al-Fitr (End of Ramadan)
May	1	May Day	*		Id al-Adha (Feast of Pilgrimage)
Apr./May	*	Wesak (2 days)			
May	22	National Hero's Day			
June	30	Bank Holiday			
Oct./Nov.	*	Deepavali			

Note: There are 12 Full Moon Poya Days on which many stores & businesses are closed.

Sudan

Official Name:	Democratic Republic of the Sudan		Religion:	Moslem, animist, Christian	
Capital:	Khartoum		Currency:	pound = 100 piasters	
Nationality:	Sudanese		Location:	NE Africa	
Language:	Arabic (official); English, tribal languages		Climate:	hot & dry north to tropical south	

Jan.	1	Independence Day	*		Ashura
Mar.	3	Unity Day	*		Prophet's Birthday
Apr.	23	Sham Al-Naseem	*		Rajab
May	25	Revolution Day	*		15th Sha'ban
Dec.	25	Christmas Day	*		27th Ramadan
			*		Ramadan Bairam (End of Ramadan, 4 days)
Islamic Holidays			*		Kurban Bairam (Feast of Pilgrimage, 5 days)
*		First of Muharram (Islamic New Year)			

Surinam

Official Name:	Republic of Suriname		Religion:	Christian, Hindu, Moslem	
Capital:	Paramaribo		Currency:	guilder = 100 cents	
Nationality:	Surinamese		Dialing Code:	IDC 597	
Language:	Dutch (official); English, Creole		Location:	NE South America	
			Climate:	tropical rainy	

Jan.	1	New Year's Day	July	1	Freedom Day
Feb.	25	Revolution Day	Nov.	25	Independence Day
Feb./Mar.	*	Holi Day (Phagwa)	Dec.	25	Christmas Day
*		Good Friday	Dec.	26	Christmas Holiday
*		Holy Saturday			
*		Easter Monday	*Note:* Hindu & Islamic holidays are also observed.		
May	1	Labor Day			

Swaziland

Official Name:	Kingdom of Swaziland		Religion:	Christian, animist	
Capital:	Mbabane		Currency:	lilangeni = 100 cents	
Nationality:	Swazi		Location:	SE Africa	
Language:	English, si-Swati (both official)		Climate:	subtropical	

Jan.	1	New Year's Day	July	22	King's Birthday
Mar.	*	Commonwealth Day (2nd Mon.)	Sep.	6	Independence Day
			Oct.	24	United Nations Day
*		Good Friday	Dec.	25	Christmas Day
*		Easter Monday	Dec.	26	Boxing Day
Apr.	25	Flag Day			
*		Ascension Day			
July	*	Reed Dance Festival (2nd Mon.)			

Sweden

Official Name:	Kingdom of Sweden		Religion:	Lutheran	
Capital:	Stockholm		Currency:	krona = 100 öre	
Nationality:	Swedish		Dialing Code:	IDC 46	
Language:	Swedish		Location:	N Europe	
			Climate:	cool temperate	

Jan.	1	New Year's Day	Nov.	1 ⋆	All Saints' Day (nearest Sat.)
Jan.	6	Epiphany			
⋆		Good Friday	Dec.	24	Christmas Eve
⋆		Easter Monday	Dec.	25	Christmas Day
May	1	Labor Day	Dec.	26	Boxing Day
⋆		Ascension Day	Dec.	31	Bank Holiday
⋆		Whitmonday			
June	22 ⋆	Midsummer Holiday (nearest Fri. & Sat.)			

Note: Days preceding public holidays are half-day bank holidays.

Switzerland

Official Name:	Swiss Confederation		Religion:	Protestant, Roman Catholic	
Capital:	Bern		Currency:	franc = 100 centimes	
Nationality:	Swiss		Dialing Code:	IDC 41	
Language:	German, French, Italian, Romansch (all official)		Location:	central Europe	
			Climate:	temperate, varying with altitude	

Jan.	1	New Year's Day	Aug.	15	Assumption Day
Jan.	2	Berchtoldstag	Sep.	6	Jeune Genevois (Geneva)
Feb./Mar.	⋆	Carnival (regional)	Nov.	1	All Saints' Day (regional)
Apr.	⋆	Sechseläuten (Zurich)	Dec.	8	Immaculate Conception (regional)
⋆		Good Friday			
⋆		Easter Monday	Dec.	24	Christmas Eve (half day)
May	1	Labor Day (regional)	Dec.	25	Christmas Day
⋆		Ascension Day	Dec.	26	St. Stephen's Day
⋆		Whitmonday	Dec.	31	St. Sylvester's Day (half day)
⋆		Corpus Christi (regional)			
Aug.	1	Confederation Day			

Syria

Official Name:	Syrian Arab Republic		Religion:	Sunni Moslem	
Capital:	Damascus		Currency:	pound = 100 piasters	
Nationality:	Syrian		Location:	Middle East	
Language:	Arabic		Climate:	Mediterranean, with seasonal extremes inland	

Jan.	1	New Year's Day	*Islamic Holidays*	
Mar.	8	Revolution Day	⋆	First of Muharram (Islamic New Year)
Apr.	17	Independence Day		
⋆		Easter Sunday	⋆	Prophet's Birthday
May	1	Labor Day	⋆	Id al-Fitr (End of Ramadan, 4 days)
May	6	Martyrs' Day		
July	23	Egyptian Revolution Day	⋆	Id al-Adha (Feast of Pilgrimage, 5 days)
Sep.	1	Libyan Unity Day		
Dec.	25	Christmas Day		

Tahiti (French Polynesia)

Status:	French Overseas Territory		Religion:	Protestant, Roman Catholic, Buddhist, Confucian	
Capital:	Papeete (Tahiti)				
Language:	Tahitian, French		Currency:	franc = 100 centimes	
			Dialing Code:	IDC 689	
			Location:	S Pacific Ocean	
			Climate:	tropical marine	

Jan.	1–3	New Year Holiday	⋆		Good Friday
Mar.	5	Arrival of the Holy Scriptures	⋆		Easter Monday
			May	1	Labor Day

Tahiti (Continued)

May	8	Armistice Day	Aug.	15	Assumption Day
*		Ascension Eve (half day)	Oct.	31	All Saints' Eve (half day)
*		Ascension Day	Nov.	1	All Saints' Day
*		Whitmonday	Nov.	11	Armistice Day
Jul.	13	Bastille Day Eve (half day)	Dec.	24	Christmas Eve
Jul.	14	Bastille Day	Dec.	25	Christmas Day
Aug.	14	Assumption Eve (half day)	Dec.	31	New Year's Eve

Taiwan (Nationalist China)

Official Name:	Republic of China	Religion:	Buddhist, Confucian, Taoist
Capital:	Taipei	Currency:	yuan = 100 cents
Nationality:	Chinese	Dialing Code:	IDC 886
Language:	Mandarin Chinese (official); Amoy dialect	Location:	Pacific Ocean, off S China coast
		Climate:	subtropical

Jan.	1–2	New Year's Day & Founding of the Republic of China	Sep.	*	Mid-Autumn Festival
			Sep.	28	Confucius' Birthday
			Oct.	10	Double Tenth National Day
Feb./Mar.	*	Chinese New Year (3 days)			
Mar.	8	Women's Day	Oct.	25	Taiwan Restoration Day
Mar.	29	Youth Day	Oct.	31	Chiang Kai-Shek's Birthday
Apr.	5	Ching Ming (Tomb-Sweeping Day)	Nov.	12	Sun Yat-Sen's Birthday
June	*	Dragon Boat Festival	Dec.	25	Constitution Day
July	1 *	Bank Holiday (1st Mon.)			

Tanzania

Official Name:	United Republic of Tanzania	Religion:	Moslem, Christian, animist
Capital:	Dar es Salaam	Currency:	shilling = 100 cents
Nationality:	Tanzanian	Location:	E Africa
Language:	English, Swahili (both official); Bantu languages	Climate:	tropical in coastal areas to temperate & semiarid inland

Jan.	12	Zanzibar Revolution Day	Dec.	25	Christmas Day
Feb.	5	Chama Cha Mapinduzi Anniversary	*Islamic Holidays*		
*		Good Friday	*		Idd El Fitr (End of Ramadan, 2 days)
*		Easter Monday	*		Idd El Hajj (Feast of Pilgrimage)
Apr.	26	Union Day			
May	1	Labor Day			
July	7	Saba Saba (Farmers') Day			
Dec.	9	Independence & Republic Day			

Thailand

Official Name:	Kingdom of Thailand	Religion:	Hinayana Buddhist
Capital:	Bangkok	Currency:	baht = 100 satang
Nationality:	Thai	Dialing Code:	IDC 66
Language:	Thai	Location:	SE Asia
		Climate:	tropical monsoon

Jan.	1	New Year's Day	July	*	Asalhabuja
Feb.	*	Makhabuja	July	*	Buddhist Lent
Apr.	6	Chakri Day	Aug.	12	Queen's Birthday
Apr.	13	Songkran (Thai New Year)	Oct.	23	King Chulalongkorn Day
May	1	Labor Day	Dec.	5	King's Birthday
May	5	Coronation Day	Dec.	10	Constitution Day
May	*	Royal Ploughing Ceremony	Dec.	31	New Year's Eve
May/June	*	Visakhabuja			

Togo

Official Name:	Republic of Togo	Religion:	animist, Christian, Moslem
Capital:	Lomé	Currency:	CFA franc = 100 centimes
Nationality:	Togolese	Location:	W Africa
Language:	French (official); tribal languages	Climate:	tropical

Jan.	1	New Year's Day	Nov.	1	All Saints' Day
Jan.	13	Liberation Day	Dec.	25	Christmas Day
Jan.	24	Economic Liberation Day	*Islamic Holidays*		
Apr.	24	Victory Day	*		Id al-Fitr (End of Ramadan)
Apr.	27	Independence Day	*		Id al-Adha (Feast of Pilgrimage)
May	1	Labor Day			
*		Ascension Day			
June	21	Pya Martyrs' Day			
Aug.	15	Assumption Day			

Note: Banks close at noon on days preceding holidays.

Tonga

Official Name:	Kingdom of Tonga	Religion:	Christian, chiefly Methodist & Mormon
Capital:	Nukualofa		
Nationality:	Tongan	Currency:	pa'anga = 100 seniti
Language:	Tongan, English	Location:	South Pacific Ocean
		Climate:	tropical marine

Jan.	1	New Year's Day	July	4	King's Birthday & Coronation Day
*		Good Friday			
*		Easter Monday	Nov.	4	Constitution Day
Apr.	25	Anzac Day	Dec.	4	King Tupou I Day
May	4	Crown Prince's Birthday	Dec.	25	Christmas Day
June	4	Emancipation Day	Dec.	26	Boxing Day
			Dec.	31	Bank Holiday

Trinidad and Tobago

Official Name:	Republic of Trinidad and Tobago	Religion:	Christian, Hindu, Moslem
Capital:	Port of Spain	Currency:	dollar = 100 cents
Nationality:	Trinidadian, Tobagonian	Location:	SE Caribbean Sea
Language:	English	Climate:	tropical, with rainy/dry seasons

Jan.	1	New Year's Day	Aug.	*	Discovery Day (1st Mon.)
Feb./Mar.	*	Carnival (Mon. & Tue. before Lent)	Aug.	31	Independence Day
			Sep.	24	Republic Day
*		Good Friday	Oct./Nov.		Divali (Festival of Lights)
*		Easter Monday	Dec.	25	Christmas Day
*		Whitmonday	Dec.	26	Boxing Day
June	19	Labor Day			
*		Corpus Christi			

Note: The Islamic holiday of Id al-Fitr is also observed.

Tunisia

Official Name:	Republic of Tunisia	Religion:	Moslem
Capital:	Tunis	Currency:	dinar = 1,000 milliemes
Nationality:	Tunisian	Dialing Code:	IDC 216
Language:	Arabic (official); French	Location:	N Africa
		Climate:	Mediterranean in coastal areas to desert inland

Jan.	1	New Year's Day	June	2	Youth Day
Jan.	18	Revolution Day	July	25	Republic Day
Mar.	20	Independence Day	Aug.	3	President's Birthday
Apr.	9	Martyrs' Day	Aug.	13	Women's Day
May	1	Labor Day	Sep.	3	Commemoration Day
June	1	National Holiday	Oct.	15	Evacuation of Bizerte Day

Tunisia (Continued)

Islamic Holidays

★	First of Muharram (Islamic New Year)
★	Prophet's Birthday

★	Aid El Seghir (End of Ramadan, 2 days)
★	Aid El Kebir (Feast of Pilgrimage, 2 days)

Turkey

Official Name:	Republic of Turkey	Religion:	Sunni Moslem
Capital:	Ankara	Currency:	pound = 100 kurus
Nationality:	Turkish	Dialing Code:	IDC 90
Language:	Turkish	Location:	SW Asia & SE Europe
		Climate:	mild in coastal areas, with seasonal extremes inland

Jan.	1	New Year's Day	
Apr.	23	Children's Day	
May	1	Spring Day	
May	19	Youth & Sports Day	
May	27	Constitution Day	
Aug.	30	Victory Day	

Oct.	28–29	Republic Days

Islamic Holidays

★	Sheker Bairam (End of Ramadan, 4 days)
★	Kurban Bairam (Feast of Pilgrimage, 5 days)

Uganda

Official Name:	Republic of Uganda	Religion:	Christian, animist, Moslem
Capital:	Kampala	Currency:	shilling = 100 cents
Nationality:	Ugandan	Location:	E central Africa
Language:	English (official); Swahili, tribal languages	Climate:	mild, with rainy/dry cycles

Jan.	1	New Year's Day	Oct.	9	Independence Day
★		Good Friday	Dec.	25	Christmas Day
★		Holy Saturday	Dec.	26	Boxing Day
★		Easter Monday			
May	1	Labor Day			

Note: The Islamic holiday Id al-Fitr is also observed.

United Arab Emirates

Official Name:	United Arab Emirates	Religion:	Sunni Moslem
Capital:	Abu Dhabi	Currency:	dirham = 100 fils
Nationality:	Emirian	Dialing Code:	IDC 971
Language:	Arabic (official); English	Location:	E Arabian Peninsula
		Climate:	hot & dry

Jan.	1	New Year's Day
Aug.	6	Accession of Ruler of Abu Dhabi
Dec.	2	National Day (2 days)

Islamic Holidays

★	First of Muharram (Islamic New Year)

★	Prophet's Birthday
★	Lailat al-Miraj (Prophet's Ascension)
★	Id al-Fitr (End of Ramadan, 3 days)
★	Id al-Adha (Feast of Pilgrimage, 4 days)

United Kingdom. *See* GREAT BRITAIN.

Upper Volta

Official Name:	Republic of Upper Volta	Religion:	animist, Moslem, Christian
Capital:	Ouagadougou	Currency:	CFA franc = 100 centimes
Nationality:	Upper Voltan	Location:	W Africa
Language:	French (official); Niger-Congo languages	Climate:	hot & semiarid

Jan.	1	New Year's Day	Aug.	15	Assumption Day
★		Easter Monday	Nov.	1	All Saints' Day
May	1	Labor Day	Nov.	30	Youth Day
★		Ascension Day	Dec.	11	National Holiday
★		Whitmonday	Dec.	25	Christmas Day

Upper Volta (Continued)

Islamic Holidays

*	Ashura	*	End of Ramadan
*	Prophet's Birthday	*	Tabaski (Feast of Pilgrimage)

Uruguay

Official Name:	Oriental Republic of Uruguay
Capital:	Montevideo
Nationality:	Uruguayan
Language:	Spanish

Religion:	Roman Catholic
Currency:	peso = 100 centesimos
Dialing Code:	IDC 598
Location:	SE South America
Climate:	moderate

Jan.	1	New Year's Day	
Jan.	6	Epiphany	
Feb./Mar.	*	Carnival (Mon. & Tue. before Lent)	
*		Holy Week (Mon.–Sat. before Easter Sunday)	
Apr.	19	Landing of the 33 Patriots	
May	1	Labor Day	
May	18	Battle of Las Piedras	

June	19	Artigas Day
July	18	Constitution Day
Aug.	25	Independence Day
Oct.	12	Discovery of America Day
Nov.	2	All Souls' Day
Dec.	24	Christmas Eve (half day)
Dec.	25	Christmas Day
Dec.	31	New Year's Eve (half day)

U.S.S.R. *See* SOVIET UNION.

Vanuatu

Official Name:	Republic of Vanuatu
Capital:	Vila
Nationality:	Vanuatuan
Language:	English, French, Bislama Pidgin (all official)

Religion:	Christian
Currency:	franc = 100 centimes
Location:	S Pacific Ocean
Climate:	tropical marine

Jan.	1	New Year's Day
*		Good Friday
*		Easter Monday
May	1	Labor Day
*		Ascension Day
July	30	Independence Day

Aug.	15	Assumption Day
Oct.	5	Constitution Day
Nov.	29	Unity Day
Dec.	25	Christmas Day
Dec.	26	Family Day

Vatican City

Official Name:	State of the Vatican City
Language:	Italian, Latin

Religion:	Roman Catholic
Currency:	Italian lira = 100 centesimi
Dialing Code:	IDC 39
Location:	Rome, Italy
Climate:	mild

Jan.	1	New Year's Day
Jan.	6	Epiphany
Feb.	11	Anniversary of Lateranensi Pacts
Mar.	19	St. Joseph's Day
*		Holy Week (Holy Thursday to Easter Tuesday)
May	1	St. Joseph the Worker's Day
*		Ascension Day
*		Corpus Christi
June	29	Sts. Peter & Paul Day

Aug.	14–16	Mid-August Holiday
Sep.	28	Anniversary of John Paul I's Death
Oct.	22	Anniversary of John Paul II's Pontificate
Nov.	1	All Saints' Day
Nov.	2	All Souls' Day
Nov.	4	John Paul II's Name Day
Dec.	8	Immaculate Conception
Dec.	24–27	Christmas Holiday
Dec.	31	Year-end Holiday

Venezuela

Official Name:	Republic of Venezuela
Capital:	Caracas
Nationality:	Venezuelan
Language:	Spanish

Religion:	Roman Catholic
Currency:	bolivar = 100 centimos
Dialing Code:	IDC 58
Location:	N South America
Climate:	varies with altitude, tropical to mild temperate

Venezuela (Continued)

Jan.	1	New Year's Day	*			Corpus Christi
Jan.	6	Epiphany	June	24	Battle of Carabobo
*		Carnival (Mon. & Tue. before Lent)	June	29	Sts. Peter & Paul Day
			July	5	Independence Day
Mar.	19	St. Joseph's Day	July	24	Bolívar's Birthday
*		Holy Thursday	Aug.	15	Assumption Day
*		Good Friday	Sep.	24	Public Functionary Day
Apr.	19	Declaration of Independence	Oct.	12	Discovery of America Day
			Nov.	1	All Saints' Day
May	1	Labor Day	Dec.	8	Immaculate Conception
*		Ascension Day	Dec.	25	Christmas Day

Virgin Islands (St. Croix, St. John, St. Thomas)

Status:	U.S. Unincorporated Territory	Religion:	Roman Catholic, Protestant
		Currency:	U.S. dollar = 100 cents
Capital:	Charlotte Amalie (St. Thomas)	Dialing Code:	DDC 809
		Location:	N Caribbean Sea
Nationality:	Virgin Islander	Climate:	subtropical marine
Language:	English		

Jan.	1	New Year's Day	July	3	Emancipation Day
Jan.	6	Epiphany	July	4	Independence Day
Jan.	15	Martin Luther King's Birthday	Sep.	*	Labor Day (1st Mon.)
Feb.	12 *	Lincoln's Birthday	Oct.	12	Puerto Rico Friendship Day
Feb.	22 *	Washington's Birthday (3rd Mon.)	Oct.	*	Hurricane Thanksgiving Day (3rd Mon.)
Mar.	*	Transfer Day (last Mon.)	Nov.	1	Liberty Day
*		Good Friday	Nov.	11	Veterans Day
*		Easter Monday	Nov.	*	Thanksgiving (4th Thurs.)
May	*	Carnival/Children's Parade	Dec.	25	Christmas Day
May	*	Memorial Day (last Mon.)	Dec.	26	Christmas Holiday
June	*	Organic Act Day (3rd Mon.)			

Western Samoa

Official Name:	Independent State of Western Samoa	Religion:	Protestant (chiefly Congregationalist), Roman Catholic
Capital:	Apia		
Nationality:	Western Samoan	Currency:	tala = 100 sene
Language:	Samoan, English (both official)	Location:	S Pacific Ocean
		Climate:	tropical marine

Jan.	1–2	New Year's Day	June	1–3	Independence Holidays
*		Good Friday	Oct.	11 *	National Day
*		Holy Saturday	Nov.	4	Arbor Day
*		Easter Monday	Dec.	25	Christmas Day
Apr.	25	Anzac Day	Dec.	26	Boxing Day

West Germany

Official Name:	Federal Republic of Germany	Religion:	Protestant, Roman Catholic
Capital:	Bonn	Currency:	deutsche mark = 100 pfennigs
Nationality:	West German		
Language:	German	Dialing Code:	IDC 49
		Location:	Central Europe
		Climate:	temperate

Jan.	1	New Year's Day	*		Ascension Day
Jan.	6	Epiphany (Baden-Württemburg, Bavaria)	*		Whitmonday
			*		Corpus Christi (most states)
*		Carnival (regional; Mon. & Tue. before Lent)	June	17	Day of Unity
*		Good Friday	Aug.	15	Assumption Day (regional)
*		Easter Monday	Nov.	1	All Saints' Day (most states)
May	1	Labor Day			

West Germany (Continued)

Nov.	*	Repentance Day (Wed. before 3rd Sun.)		Dec.	25	Christmas Day
				Dec.	26	Boxing Day
Dec.	24	Christmas Eve (bank holiday)		Dec.	31	New Year's Eve (half day)

Yemen

Official Name:	Yemen Arab Republic		Religion:	Moslem
Capital:	Sana		Currency:	riyal = 100 fils
Nationality:	Yemeni, Yemenite		Location:	SW Arabian Peninsula
Language:	Arabic		Climate:	hot & dry coastal, moderate inland

May	1	Labor Day		*	Prophet's Birthday
Sep.	26	Revolution Day		*	Id al-Fitr (End of Ramadan, 4 days)
Oct.	14	Southern Yemen Day			
Islamic Holidays				*	Id al-Adha (Feast of Pilgrimage, 5 days)
*		First of Muharram (Islamic New Year)			

Yemen, People's Democratic Republic of. *See* SOUTHERN YEMEN.

Yugoslavia

Official Name:	Socialist Federal Republic of Yugoslavia		Religion:	Orthodox, Roman Catholic, Moslem
Capital:	Belgrade		Currency:	dinar = 100 para
Nationality:	Yugoslavian; officially, Serbian, Croatian, Slovene, Macedonian, Montenegrin		Dialing Code:	IDC 38
			Location:	SE Europe
Language:	All national languages are official		Climate:	Mediterranean coastal to temperate inland

Jan.	1–2	New Year Holiday		Nov.	29–30 Republic Days
May	1–2	International Labor Day			
July	4	Partisans Day			

Note: People's Uprising Day is celebrated on separate dates in each federal republic.

Zaire

Official Name:	Republic of Zaire		Religion:	Christian (chiefly Roman Catholic), animist
Capital:	Kinshasa			
Nationality:	Zairian		Currency:	zaire = 100 makuta
Language:	French (official); regional & tribal languages		Location:	W central Africa
			Climate:	tropical, with rainy/dry cycles

Jan.	1	New Year's Day		Oct.	14	Youth Day & President's Birthday
Jan.	4	Martyrs of Independence Day		Oct.	27	Anniversary of Zaire's Name Change
May	1	Labor Day			
May	20	M.P.R. Day		Nov.	17	Armed Forces Day
June	24	Proclamation of the Constitution		Nov.	24	Anniversary of the New Regime
June	30	Independence Day		Dec.	25	Christmas Day
Aug.	1	Parents' Day			

Zambia

Official Name:	Republic of Zambia		Religion:	animist, Christian
Capital:	Lusaka		Currency:	kwacha = 100 ngwee
Nationality:	Zambian		Location:	E central Africa
Language:	English (official); Bantu languages		Climate:	mild temperate

Zambia (Continued)

Jan.	1	New Year's Day	July	★		Heroes' Day (1st Mon.)
Mar.	14	Youth Day	July	★		Unity Day (1st Tue.)
★		Good Friday	Aug.	3	★	Farmers' Day
★		Holy Saturday	Oct.	24		Independence Day
May	1	Labor Day	Dec.	25		Christmas Day
May	25	Africa Freedom Day				

Zimbabwe

Official Name:	Republic of Zimbabwe	Religion:		Christian (chiefly Anglican), animist
Capital:	Harare (formerly Salisbury)			
Nationality:	Zimbabwean	Currency:		dollar = 100 cents
Language:	English (official); Bantu languages	Location:		S central Africa
		Climate:		moderate

Jan.	1	New Year's Day	May	1	Workers' Day
Apr.	18	Independence Day	May	25	Africa Freedom Day
★		Good Friday	Aug.	11–12	Heroes' Day
★		Easter Saturday	Dec.	25	Christmas Day
★		Easter Monday	Dec.	26	Boxing Day

15

Accounting and Data Processing

Susan W. Hass, MBA, CPA • *Assistant Professor, Simmons College Graduate School of Management*

The evolution, over several hundred years, of the practice of accounting as a means of enabling businesses to keep track of past events and provide them with useful information for making future decisions has been key to business expansion in the 1980s. Every business must handle certain financial and tax matters, and subsequently keep records of these transactions as well as report them to various persons and groups outside the organization, including government agencies. A secretary is often required to perform many of the daily functions related to these types of financial transactions. This chapter is intended to help you become familiar with certain accounting principles and definitions, as well as with specific procedures related to recording the transactions in the company's books.

BASIC ACCOUNTING PRINCIPLES

Accounting is called the language of business. The first step in mastering any language is to learn its rules and the meanings of its terms. Present-day accounting practice has produced a number of generally accepted principles which standardize both terminology and methods of recording the activities of the business. This standardization allows a company's accounting reports to be meaningful to managers, bankers, stockholders, creditors, government agencies, and others interested in its financial reports. These generally accepted principles provide the "language of business" which is understood by a diverse group of individuals.

Dual Aspect Concept

If you had to determine the financial status of a business or individual, you might ask, "What does it (or the individual) own of value?" The items of value that a company owns are called *assets*. A company's assets are entered in the records at their original cost to the company, indicating that the value of the assets is equal to their cost. Over time, certain items owned by a company increase or decrease in value. However, once an asset is recorded at its original cost, it is almost never adjusted to a current market value. Such adjustment could require continual revaluation to reflect the almost daily changes in the real or current market values of a company's numerous assets. Moreover, who could determine the real worth to a company of its desks, carpets, or calculators? This would be a difficult and time-consuming task. Therefore, accounting records are rarely adjusted to reflect the actual or current market value of an asset as opposed to its book (cost) value. Assets owned by a company may include the following:

Cash (in the bank as well as petty cash)

Accounts Receivable

Marketable Securities (stocks, bonds, certificates of deposit)

Prepaid Items (insurance, rent deposits)

Property, Plant, and Equipment (land, buildings, equipment, furniture, fixtures)

Inventory (raw materials, work in process, finished goods)

The money or funds used to acquire assets is provided either by the owners of the company or by creditors of the company. Creditors are individuals or companies that lend money or extend credit to a business for a period of time. When this occurs, they acquire a claim of that amount against the business. Because a business will use its assets to pay off these claims, the claims are *claims against assets.* If a business refuses to pay a claim, the person to whom it is due can sue the business in a court of equity. Thus, *all* claims against assets are called *equities.* A court of equity will usually hold the business liable for the amount of the claim. This helps explain the accounting term for the equity of a creditor, *liability.* Any asset not claimed by a creditor will be claimed by the owners of the business. These claims are called *owners' equity.* However, the total of all claims cannot exceed what there is to be claimed. This leads to the dual aspect concept: *Assets = Equities* or *Assets = Liabilities + Owners' Equity,* also known as the basic accounting equation:

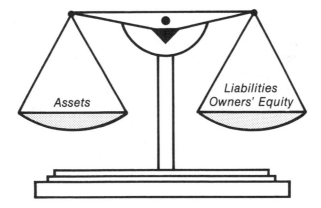

Monetary Concept

An accounting system records only those events that can be expressed in terms of dollars; e.g., the purchase of land or equipment, or the sale of inventory for cash or on account. On the other hand, the morale and health of company personnel cannot be expressed in dollar terms and the accounting system does not consider such factors. Thus, a company's accounting records do not reveal all the facts, or even all the important facts, about a business. The records show only events that have taken place and that can be expressed in monetary terms. The belief that accounting reports tell everything that one needs to know about a business is, therefore, incorrect.

The Business Entity

Accounting records are maintained for the business entity, as opposed to the persons who own, operate, or are otherwise associated with the business. Records reflect only what is happening to the company and not the personal transactions entered into by the people related to the company. For example, if the owner of a business buys a home, this purchase has no bearing on what is happening to the business, since the owner is an entity distinct from the business entity. A business may be operated under any one of several legal forms, such as a corporation, a partnership (two or more owners), or a proprietorship (one owner). Regardless of legal status, the business entity concept applies.

The Accrual Principle

The accrual principle is based on the fact that net income of a business is not related to the flow of cash but rather to changes in the owners' equity resulting from operations of a business. Revenue of a business adds to the owners' equity and expenses decrease the owners' equity. The difference between revenue and expenses is the company's net income. (See later sections of the chapter for additional explanations.)

Other Concepts

Two other generally accepted principles relate to the accrual concept. The first one states that *revenue* is recognized when goods are delivered or when services are performed. This is called the *realization concept.* It does not specifically relate to when cash is received for the sale of goods or services. The second concept, called the *matching concept,* states that *expenses* of a period are costs associated with the revenues or activities of that period. The expenses do not relate to the actual cash disbursements for those expenses.

Most entities account for revenues and expenses as well as cash receipts and cash payments. Many individuals and some small businesses keep track only of cash receipts and cash payments. This type of accounting is called *cash accounting.* If you record your deposits, the checks you write, and your balance in a bank account, you are doing cash accounting. However, in order to measure the income of a period, we must measure revenues and expenses, and this requires the use of accrual accounting. Accrual accounting is more complex than cash accounting, but it is the only one that measures true changes in owners' equity.

ACCOUNTING REPORTS

Accounting information is given to third parties external to the company on three main financial statements. The first, called the balance sheet, shows a company's assets and liabilities and owners' equity at a given point in time. It is like a snapshot, capturing the company's financial position at a specific moment, while recognizing that events may soon occur that will change certain aspects of the items of value that a company owns, as well as claims against those assets by

Andrew Manufacturing Company
Balance Sheet
December 31, 1984

Assets

Current Assets		
Cash		$ 10,000
Marketable Securities		13,000
Accounts Receivable, net		72,000
Inventories		101,000
Prepaid Insurance		3,000
Total Current Assets		199,000
Fixed Assets		
Land	$120,000	
Buildings	500,000	
Furniture and Fixtures	73,000	
Equipment	104,000	
	797,000	
Less: Accumulated Depreciation	407,000	
Total Fixed Assets		390,000
Other Assets		
Long-term Investments	93,000	
Long-term Receivables	10,000	
Goodwill, net	72,000	
Other Assets	17,000	
Total Other Assets		192,000
TOTAL ASSETS		$781,000

Liabilities & Owners' Equity

Current Liabilities		
Accounts Payable		$ 53,000
Bank Loan Payable		100,000
Accrued Wages and Salaries Payable		7,000
Current Portion of Mortgage Payable		5,000
Taxes Payable		10,000
Total Current Liabilities		175,000
Long-term Liabilities		
Mortgage Payable	$200,000	
Bonds Payable	150,000	
Total Long-term Liabilities		350,000
Total Liabilities		525,000
Owners' Equity		
Common Stock	100,000	
Retained Earnings	156,000	
Total Owners' Equity		256,000
TOTAL EQUITIES		$781,000

creditors and owners. The presentation shown in the first illustration is fairly typical, although it is also common to find the assets listed on the left-hand side and the liabilities on the right-hand side of a page. In any event, the dual aspect principle is followed, and the total dollar amount of assets will equal the total amount of liabilities and owners' equity. The totals, however, are not indicative of the company's financial condition. It is only after analysis of the various accounts listed on the balance sheet that we can come to any conclusions about the financial health of a company.

The second statement, the income statement, presents the results of a company's operations for a given period of time—a month, three months, or a year. The last day of that period will be the date of the balance sheet information accompanying the income statement. The income statement is also known as the profit and loss report, P & L, or operating statement. In any case, the statement shows sales, the cost of the specific goods or services sold, the other costs associated with selling the goods or services, and the resulting profit or loss (net income, bottom line, or net profit). Thus, this statement shows all sources of revenue generated by the company's operations as well as all related expenses incurred to generate that revenue, following the accrual, matching, and realization concepts. The format and specific revenue and expense classifications will vary but the income statement in the illustration on page 529 is fairly typical.

The third financial statement (see page 530) is the statement of changes in financial position. Although this financial statement is required by certified public accountants, it is not commonly used by persons within a company. The statement presents the results of financing and investing activities of a company for the same period of time covered by the income statement. This information helps inform its readers about events that have occurred within the company but that are not reflected in the other two financial statements (i.e., are not related to the items a company owns at a specific point in time and are not related to the results of operations for a period of time). This financial statement is also known as the source and application of funds statement, or the "where got-where gone" statement. Because it is not commonly used within a business, we will not go into any more detail about its construction or use. Refer to an accounting text for additional information about the statement of changes in financial position.

Before we go into more depth about the types of accounts included in the balance sheet and income statement, we should elaborate on the accounting period being covered by the income statement. For most businesses, the official accounting period is one year. However, income statements, called interim statements, usually are prepared for shorter periods as well. Most companies have income statements prepared on a monthly basis to report the operation of the business during the past month. Thus, the accounting period covered in a monthly income statement is one month. The report is prepared from information accumulated in the accounts of the business. Information often must be reported to various government agencies and banks on a monthly or quarterly basis, so income statements are often generated for these reasons as well.

As we mentioned earlier, the official accounting period is usually one year and for most companies, it is the calendar year; that is, the year which ends on the last day of the calendar, December 31. Some companies, however, end their year at the end of their busy season. This is called a fiscal year end. For example, colleges and universities usually have a June 30 year end. Retailers often end their year at the end of January. Sports-related businesses end their year at the end of

Andrew Manufacturing Company
Income Statement
for the year ended December 31, 1984

Gross Sales		$3,600,000
Less Sales Returns, Allowances, and Discounts		250,000
Net Sales		3,350,000
Less Cost of Goods Sold		1,650,000
Gross Profit		1,700,000
Less Operating Expenses		
Selling, General, and Administrative Expenses		
Insurance	$ 12,000	
Office Salaries	311,000	
Selling Expense	175,000	
Heat, Light, and Power	23,000	
Advertising	165,000	
Telephone	57,000	
Office Supplies	17,000	
Automobile Expense	30,000	
Bad Debt Expense	97,500	
Travel Expense	133,000	
Depreciation Expense	20,000	
Miscellaneous Expense	53,500	
Total Selling, General and Administrative Expenses		1,094,000
Research and Development Costs		250,000
Other Operating Expenses		16,000
Total Operating Expenses		1,360,000
Operating Profit		340,000
Other Income and Expenses		
Interest Expense	100,000	
Interest Income	(73,000)	
Miscellaneous Income	(10,000)	
Total Other Income and Expenses		17,000
Profit Before Taxes		323,000
Provision for Corporate Income Taxes		147,000
Net Income		$ 176,000

the month that their season ends. The accounting period for these businesses is the natural business year, not a calendar year. Of course, companies do not fire their employees and cease operations at the end of an accounting period; they continue from one accounting period to the next. The fact that accounting chops the stream of events into a set period makes the problem of measuring revenue and expenses into that period one of the most difficult problems in accounting,

Andrew Manufacturing Company
Statement of Changes in Financial Position
for the year ended December 31, 1984

Resources Were Provided by:		
Operations	$176,000	
Add: Items Not Affecting Working		
Capital		
Depreciation	20,000	
Total Resources Provided by Operations		$196,000
Increase in Mortgages Payable		75,000
Sale of Common Stock		50,000
Total Resources Provided		321,000
Resources Were Used To:		
Purchase Fixed Assets	153,000	
Acquire Long–term Investments	43,000	
Pay Mortgages Payable	25,000	
Total Resources Used		221,000
Net Change in Working Capital		$100,000

Changes in Working Capital	Increase (Decrease) in Working Capital
Current Assets	
Cash	$ 30,000
Marketable Securities	(10,000)
Accounts Receivable	30,000
Inventories	(19,000)
Prepaid Insurance	3,000
Current Liabilities	
Accounts Payable	(30,000)
Bank Loan Payable	100,000
Accrued Wages and Salaries Payable	(2,000)
Current Portion of Mortgage Payable	— — —
Taxes Payable	(2,000)
Change in Working Capital	$100,000

but it does not affect the daily operations of the company. In rare instances, an accounting period may extend beyond one year if the business activities of the company extend beyond twelve months from the time the transaction is initiated until it is completed. This situation occurs in companies dealing with long-term contracts or in those companies whose production processes are lengthy. If your company falls into this category, the accounting period and the income statement covered by it may extend beyond twelve months.

Balance Sheet Accounts

A balance sheet showing a number of items becomes more useful when the items are classified into significant groups of assets and liabilities. It would, of course, be possible to list each individual account receivable, each inventory item owned, each piece of equipment, and each account payable, but this usually provides much more detail than is needed for a balance sheet analysis. For the practical purpose of making the balance sheet more informative, items are grouped into classifications. There is no limit to the number of classifications, but the ones shown in the facsimile are the common ones.

Current assets.   The first balance sheet classification is current assets. The current assets classification includes cash and other assets which can reasonably be expected to be realized in cash or sold or consumed during the normal operating period of the business, usually one year. Current assets can be subclassified as indicated in the following list:

1. *Cash*   This includes all cash owned by a company, including cash in the bank (in a checking or savings account), petty cash, and so on. The amount of cash a company has will change through the receipt of cash for sales and the payment of bills with cash (or checks). An adequate amount of cash is vital to a company's survival and sufficient amounts should be available to meet the immediate needs of the company's operations.

2. *Marketable Securities*   If a company has more cash on hand than is needed for the immediate future, it may use the excess cash to purchase short-term investments such as certificates of deposit or stock or indebtedness of other companies. The investing company earns short-term returns such as interest or dividends just as an individual's savings account in a bank earns interest. These investments can be readily sold in the marketplace and converted back into cash on very short notice.

3. *Accounts Receivable*   This account often comprises a large portion of a company's current assets and represents amounts of money owed to the company by its regular customers. It is collectible within the next twelve months. This account is reported at its net value, which means that the actual value of the receivables has been reduced by an amount equivalent to the company's expectations of receivables that will not be paid. A company maintains detailed records of accounts receivable by customer in a subsidiary accounts receivable ledger. This subsidiary record has a page devoted to each customer and lists all sales "on account" as well as cash collections related to these sales. The total of every page balance in the subsidiary ledger is shown as the amount owed to the company as total accounts receivable.

4. *Inventories*   Inventories often represent the largest portion of current assets for a company. For manufacturing firms, inventories include raw materials to be converted into a finished

product, work-in-process inventories that include partially completed products, and finished products ready for sale. Inventories generally cannot be converted into cash as quickly as receivables, since it takes time for the goods to be sold (usually resulting in an account receivable) and for the cash to be collected.

5. *Prepaid Items* This represents prepayments for resources such as rent, interest, insurance, deposits, and so on, that will be used up during the next twelve months. Since they have not yet been used up or consumed, they still are assets (items of value) to the company. They are rarely converted into cash (although conversion is possible) and are therefore listed last under current assets.

Fixed assets.   The next major asset classification is fixed assets which may also be called plant assets; property, plant, and equipment; or tangible fixed assets. Fixed assets are relatively long-lived assets that are held for use by the business in the production of goods or sale of goods or services. They are not acquired for resale in the ordinary course of business but must have a useful life of at least one year. The reported value of fixed assets is based on the amount it cost the company to acquire them, called the historical or acquisition cost. Items in this category include:

1. *Land* (on which the company may have already constructed buildings)

2. *Buildings* (office or plant locations used in routine business operations)

3. *Equipment* (office or production machines used by the company)

4. *Furniture and Fixtures* (desks, chairs, and similar furnishings used by company personnel)

Fixed assets other than land are assumed to have limited lives because time, obsolescence, and normal use eventually reduce their benefit to the business. Those assets are therefore called depreciable assets. The process of allocating the cost of these assets ratably to the accounting periods in which they are consumed and benefit the company is called depreciation. Depreciation expense is taken each accounting period as an expense on the income statement and results from an attempt to systematically allocate the asset's acquisition cost over its anticipated useful life. The depreciation accumulated from all previous periods appears on the balance sheet as a reduction of the related fixed asset account cost. This yields the presumed fixed asset value to the company at the balance sheet date.

The estimated useful life of an asset is an estimate and is subject to many uncontrollable external factors such as obsolescence, technological advancements, and unexpected wear and tear. Therefore, the balance sheet value of fixed assets does not necessarily represent the value a company would receive if the asset were to be sold at the balance sheet date.

The Internal Revenue Service does not use depreciation but has a similar, although not identical, system called the "Accelerated Cost Recovery System," or ACRS. This system allows companies to recover their asset cost by taking deductions on their tax returns at a more rapid pace than allowed for book or internal financial statements.

Other assets. This is the last major asset classification and, if used at all, contains miscellaneous assets difficult to classify as either fixed or current assets. Investments, long-term receivables, and goodwill are examples of assets that the company intends to hold for more than one year. Investments may include securities of other companies that the business has invested in or that the employer owns and/or controls. Long-term receivables may indicate the sale of expensive items for which payments are spread out over more than one year. Goodwill is associated with the price paid by one company to purchase another; the selling price paid by one company to purchase another company is often higher than the value of the net physical assets acquired. The excess amount paid is called goodwill and reflects the purchaser's belief in the company's potential to earn high profits.

Current liabilities. Recall that liabilities are claims of creditors against the assets of the business. Current debts or obligations that must be paid or otherwise settled within one year or the normal operating cycle of a business are called current liabilities. These are the company's most immediate obligations, and cash or other current assets are necessary to liquidate them. These claims are usually not against a specific asset of the company. Within the classification of current liabilities there are several subclasses:

1. *Accounts Payable*   This represents amounts owed to ordinary business creditors for unpaid bills for inventory and supplies. If the claim is evidenced by a note or other written document, it is usually segregated as a note payable.

2. *Bank Loan Payable*   This represents money owed by the company to its bank. Because it is shown as a current liability, it implies that it is payable within one year.

3. *Accrued Salaries and Wages Payable*   This refers to amounts owed to employees of the business at the time the balance sheet was drawn up. An example of this is when employees are paid on a weekly basis, and the balance sheet has been drawn up at a point during one of the pay periods. As a result, wages and salaries owed to employees but not yet paid to them are recorded as a liability.

4. *Current Portion of the Mortgage Loan Payable*   This amount represents the portion of the mortgage principal (not interest) payable within twelve months of the balance sheet date.

5. *Taxes Payable*   This amount is owed to the federal, state, or local government for taxes due on income, payroll, inventory, etc., but not yet paid.

6. *Unearned Revenues*   These are obligations to provide goods or services to customers who have made advance payments. For example, subscription receipts that have been received by a magazine publisher in advance of sending the magazine issues are unearned revenues. Rent that is received in advance by a landlord is still another example of these types of liabilities.

Long-term liabilities.   These claims against assets are due to be paid after the next twelve months. This category includes: property mortgages payable, long-term loans payable, notes payable, and bonds or debentures payable. Unlike accounts payable, these liabilities tend to be evidenced by formal documents indicating a definite obligation to pay at some future time. Often long-term liabilities are a guaranteed claim against some specific assets, known as a *lien.* Any portion of long-term payables becoming due within one year from the balance sheet date should be included in the current liabilities category. Any amount recorded here represents the principal amount due only. These types of obligations usually have an interest payment associated with them; however, the interest due is not recorded on the balance sheet because interest relates to the use of money or funds over time. Interest is not initially recorded until your company has had the use of someone else's funds for a period of time. Then the expense is recorded in the income statement and the payable recorded separately as a current liability.

Owners' equity.   This section of the balance sheet represents claims made against the assets by the owners of the business and is simply the portion of the company not claimed by anyone else. It is also known as book value or net worth. The manner of reporting owners' equity on the balance sheet depends on the type of business for which the balance sheet is prepared. As previously mentioned, a business may be organized as a single proprietorship, a partnership, or a corporation.

The owners' equity section of Andrew Manufacturing Company indicates that it is organized as a corporation. Corporations are created under and regulated by state and federal laws. These laws require that a distinction be made between the amount invested in the corporation by its owners (the original shareholders) and the increase or decrease in owners' equity due to daily operations. The former, called common stock or capital stock, is entered on the balance sheet at its stated value, which might be the price paid for the stock, its par value, or some other figure agreed upon at the time the stock was issued or sold. Subsequently, there is no relationship between the recorded value and the market value of the stock. The latter, called retained earnings, reflects the earnings of the company from daily operations in prior years that have been left in the business and have not been paid out to the owners in the form of dividends. The word *surplus* was used in place of retained earnings in the past but is not in current use today. Retained earnings or accumulated amounts of net income belong to and are a claim of the company's owners and are always shown after common stock in the owners' equity section of the balance sheet.

When a business is owned by one person, it is called a sole or single proprietorship and the single owner's equity may be reported on the balance sheet in either of the following ways:

a. Ryan Andrew, capital $256,000

b. Ryan Andrew, capital, January 1, 1984 $200,000

Net Income for the year ended		
December 31, 1984	$323,000	
Withdrawals	267,000	
Excess of earnings over withdrawals		56,000
Ryan Andrew, capital, December 31, 1984		$256,000

When two or more persons own a business as partners, changes in their equities resulting from earnings and withdrawals are normally shown in a supplementary financial statement entitled the Statement of Partners' Equity. Only the amount of each partner's equity and the total equities are shown on the balance sheet itself:

Partners' Equity

Ryan Andrew, capital	$128,000
Daniel Andrew, capital	128,000
	$256,000

Thus, in the owners' equity section of the balance sheet, capital (cash or assets) contributed by the owners of the company as well as earnings accumulated since the business began are accumulated as claims against assets.

Income Statement Accounts

Sales. The first entry on the income statement is the sales for the period. It is customary to show gross sales revenue earned by the accrual method and then to deduct any returns, allowances, and discounts given during the period to arrive at net sales. By showing sales returns and allowances separately, attention is called to any unusual amounts (increase) shown in this category.

Sales revenues are inflows of cash and other assets received from others for goods exchanged or services performed. The result is an increase in total assets, a decrease in total liabilities, or a combination thereof. Terms such as *income, revenue, earned,* and *received* preceded by a noun such as *rent, interest,* or *commissions* identify a revenue source. Revenues derived from sales to customers are often described as sales revenue, fees earned, or commissions earned in the income statement. Other revenues unrelated to customer sales include commissions earned, dividends received, interest income, rental revenue, and so forth.

Expenses. In accounting, expenses are considered as the outflow of cash or other resources of the business during a specific period of time. The accrual principle is followed. Expenses relate to the consumption of assets or the incurrence of debt for goods or services consumed by the company in order to produce revenue. The common classifications of expenses are:

1. *Cost of Goods Sold* This represents the cost of goods purchased for resale as well as the cost incurred in manufacturing products for sale to customers. This category should include, to the extent possible, only the costs associated with goods sold during the current accounting period. In a manufacturing company, they include raw materials, direct labor, and manufacturing overhead. Manufacturing overhead includes all allocated product-related costs other than raw material and direct labor including indirect labor, fringe benefits, supervision costs, plant rent, insurance, freight, light and power, plant depreciation, quality assurance, shipping, and so on. The cost of any goods remaining on hand at the end of the period is shown as inventory in the current assets section of the balance sheet.

2. *Gross Profit* This represents the amount of sales revenue recognized in excess of the cost of goods sold. This amount must exceed the amount of all remaining expenses of operating the business if the business is to be profitable. Gross profit is also known as gross margin.

3. *Operating Expenses* Operating expenses are incurred in the normal operations of the business. Operating expenses are not incurred to produce a product; rather, they are considered costs of the period. They are often subclassified by function, such as selling and distribution, research and development, and general and administration expenses. Selling expenses include all expense incurred during the period to perform the sales activities of the firm. Such expenses include salaries paid to sales people, commissions, rental of sales facilities, depreciation on sales equipment, and advertising costs. General and administrative expenses are those incurred during the year in administering overall company activities. They often include office supplies used, officers' salaries, depreciation of the office building and equipment, rental of office space, property taxes, legal fees, accounting fees, office employee salaries, and related fringe benefits. Research and development (R&D) expenses are incurred by the company in pursuit of further improvement of existing products or development of new products. These expenses include salaries of R&D personnel, facilities and equipment expense, and other like expenses incurred for research and development efforts.

4. *Operating Profit* This represents profit earned from the normal business operations of the firm. It represents sales revenues minus the cost of goods sold and operating expenses. Operating profit also may be called income from operations or net operating revenue.

5. *Other Income and Expense*   These are nonoperating sources of revenues and/or expenses, not resulting from the daily operations of the business. They include items such as interest income from investments, interest expense on loans or other outstanding debts, profit or loss on the sale of fixed assets, and revenue from nonrelated business operations. They are listed separately to highlight their difference from other revenue and expenses related to the business' primary operations.

6. *Profit Before Taxes*   This is the net difference between all revenues and expenses of the business and also may be called income before taxes.

7. *Provision for Corporate Income Taxes*   Included in this line classification are all federal corporate income taxes. Local and state taxes are sometimes included here as well. If not, they are included with general and administrative expenses. If the company is a sole proprietorship or partnership, the business pays no taxes. Rather, the owners include their pro rata share of the business profit (or loss) on their personal tax returns and pay taxes on this profit individually.

8. *Net Income*   Also known as net profit or "the bottom line," net income represents the amount of profit the company has earned for the period covered by the income statement.

PROCEDURES

Now that you are familiar with accounting as the language of business, you are better able to perform the many duties and functions that you may be called on to do. Included in them are activities related to handling cash such as recording cash receipts and disbursements, controlling petty cash, or performing a bank reconciliation; recording investments in securities; and recording the acquisition of fixed assets. We will go into some depth about performing each function, but first let's explore the various data-gathering accounting information systems.

Accounting Systems

An accounting system consists of all the business papers, records, reports, and procedures used in recording and reporting transactions. Actually an accounting system is a data processing system and it may be manual, mechanical, electronic, or, as is the usual case, a combination of all three. The three approaches may be described briefly as follows.

Manual data processing.   With this approach, the accounting work is performed by hand (i.e., manually). This type of system is used extensively in small businesses and for certain parts of the information process in medium- and large-sized businesses. In larger companies, it is useful for discussing and illustrating the application of accounting concepts and principles as well as for explaining the accounting process. The writing-copying-posting procedure when performed manually accomplishes its objectives but is often time-consuming and error-prone. Therefore, procedures that reduce the number of times information is copied and recopied improve the system.

One such system is the one-write, or pegboard, system. It is designed to process all or a large portion of the data of the transaction with one writing. This can be done with payroll, sales, purchases, cash receipts, and cash disbursements. For payroll, the paycheck, employee earnings record, and payroll register are all recorded simultaneously via a system of alignment of documents and carbon copies. Similarly for credit sales, the entry on the customer's month-end statement, the posting to his or her account, and the entry in the sales journal are all made at once.

Mechanical data processing.   When repetitive transactions occur in large numbers, mechanical processing of accounting data is often used. Cash registers, adding machines, calculators, and posting machines or punched card equipment are typical of this type of processing. One electric accounting (posting) machine can be used for sales accounting, cash receipts, cash disbursements, accounts payable, payroll, and other accounting applications. When used in sales accounting, for example, the machine will produce the invoice for each charge sale, post to the customer's individual account, update the statement to be sent to the customer at month-end, and enter the sale in the sales journal, all in one operation. Although this type of processing is still used today, it is quickly being superseded by inexpensive desktop electronic data processing via micro- and minicomputers.

Electronic data processing (EDP).   This method uses computers of varying sizes and sophistication (large mainframes to micro- and minicomputers) to process information in a rapid, usually inexpensive fashion. This equipment has a large capacity to store data and the capability to manipulate and recall data with great speed. Electronic data processing involves the use of hardware (the central processing unit and related peripherals) and software (the computer programs that give instructions to the computer as well as other related items for system operations such as training material). The EDP equipment in use today performs many functions that accounting needs, such as arithmetic procedures (add, subtract, multiply, and divide), memory storage (file maintenance), memory recall, comparison of information, repetition of the same set of instructions, and making yes/no decisions.

Computers process data with speed and accuracy. However, before a computer can do this, a human being must think through the procedures that the computer will use in processing the data, anticipate every processing exception, and then instruct the computer in great detail how to do the job. Although computers are a big help in the processing of accounting information, they are only as good as the people programming them and the correctness of the data being processed. Remember, computers—and those who input data into them—are not infallible.

The Accounting Process
The basic accounting process is the same for all businesses, large and small. The purpose of an information processing system is to facilitate the accumulation of data needed to make decisions and to prepare financial statements. The basic components of that information processing system, whether manual or elec-

tronic, are the same and are shown in the next illustration. The components of the system include:

Component	Purpose
General journals and special journals	For formally recording the data obtained from the analysis of individual transactions.
General ledger	For accumulating and summarizing the data recorded in the journals in terms of the dual aspect concept for the balance sheet and income statement accounts. There is a separate account page for each general ledger account.
Subsidiary ledgers	To provide a detailed analysis of the balance in a specific general ledger account (accounts receivable, notes receivable, marketable securities, inventories, fixed assets, and notes payable).

When a company must record hundreds or thousands of similar transactions such as credit sales or purchase of materials, it is critical that the information processing system handle the transaction as efficiently as possible. This makes the use of special journals which record and summarize like transactions advantageous.

Transaction	Special Journal
1. Purchase of merchandise or raw materials on credit	Purchases journal
2. Cash payments	Cash disbursements journal
3. Credit (and sometimes cash) sales	Sales journal
4. Cash collections	Cash receipts journal

The formats of special journals vary depending upon the needs of management. The two special journals we discuss in detail are typical examples, but may be modified to meet management's goals for cost and time savings.

The cash receipts journal.   Used to record all cash receipts of the company, this journal is designed to handle not only payments of credit and cash sales but also other revenue sources. The procedures to follow in recording cash receipts are performed daily (refer to the illustration on page 542):

1. Enter cash received in the cash receipts journal, listing the amount, date, and source (columns 1–3).

2. If the receipt is in payment of a prior credit sale, record the amount in column 5 and record the customer account number

The Basic Accounting Record-keeping System

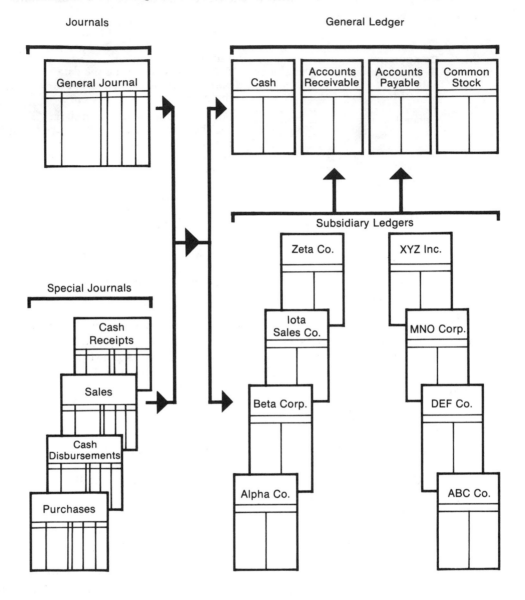

from the accounts receivable subsidiary ledger in column 4. Someone also should record the receipt on the individual customer's account card in the subsidiary ledger.

3. If the customer in #2 above paid less than the full invoice price because he or she took an allowable discount for paying within a certain period of time, note the amount of discount taken in column 6.

4. If the receipt is for a cash sale, record the amount of the sale in column 7.

5. Each miscellaneous cash receipt is recorded in columns 8–11. Record the general ledger account and account number in columns 8 and 9 (e.g., receipt of proceeds from *bank loan*, sale of old *equipment*, or sale of *marketable securities*). Record the amount in column 10 or 11. (Someone should record the receipt in the specific general ledger account as well.)

6. The columns in the cash receipts journal are totaled on a monthly basis and the totals are recorded in the general ledger accounts. (The total of the miscellaneous account column is not recorded in the general ledger since it represents the sum of amounts already recorded in several different accounts.) Each month, start a new page in the cash receipts journal. Number each page sequentially.

The cash disbursements journal. Used to list all checks written during the period, a sample format is shown in the illustration on page 543. The procedures that should be followed in recording cash disbursements are:

1. Enter each check in the journal in sequential order in columns 1–4.

2. Most checks will normally be issued in payment of a previously recorded account payable. If this is the case, record the amount in column 6 and record the vendor account number from the accounts payable subsidiary ledger in column 5. Someone also should record the payment on the individual vendor account card in the subsidiary ledger.

3. If the payment in #2 above is less than the full invoice price because the company took an allowable discount for paying within a certain period of time, note the amount of the discount taken in column 7.

4. Any other payments should be entered as a miscellaneous payment in columns 8–10. Record the general ledger account and account number in columns 8 and 9 (e.g., payment of *rent*, *repairs*, *utilities*, *notes payable*, *interest* expense). Record the amount in column 10. (Someone should also record the payment in the specific general ledger account.)

5. The columns in the cash disbursements journal are totaled on a monthly basis and the totals are recorded in the general ledger accounts. (The total of the miscellaneous amount column is not recorded in the general ledger since it represents the sum of amounts already recorded to several different accounts.) Each month, start a new page in the cash disbursements journal. Number each page sequentially.

These procedures do not change the basic accounting concepts or process discussed previously. They simply are used to make the recording and summarizing of financial/accounting information more efficient. They are shown as they would apply to a manual system, but the same journals and ledgers can be generated in an EDP system. Although such records may be simplified for a small

Andrew Manufacturing Company
Cash Receipts Journal

Cash Receipts Journal

Date	Source/ Explanation	Cash Received (Debit)	Accounts Receivable (Credit) Subsidiary Ledger Reference No.	Amount	Sales Discount Taken (Debit)	Cash Sales (Credit)	Other Miscellaneous Receipts Account Title	Acct. No.	Amount Debit	Credit
12/4/84	Alpha Co.-Invoice 412	723	1011	730	7					
12/7/84	Cash Sale	471				471				
12/12/84	Sales of Market- able Securities	2000					Marketable Securities	105		2000
12/20/84	Zeton W.-Invoice 422	973	9008	1000	27					
12/21/84	Bank Loan	4500					Bk. Loan Payable	575		4500
12/30/84	Delta Co. Invoice 425	524	2013	550	26					
		9191		2280	60	471				6500
		Col. 3	Col. 4	Col. 5	Col. 6	Col. 7	Col. 8	Col. 9	Col. 10	Col. 11

Col. 1   Col. 2

Note: Column 3 = Column 5 + Column 7 + Column 11 - Column 6
9191 = 2280 + 471 + 6500 - 60

Andrew Manufacturing Company
Cash Disbursements Journal

Cash Disbursements Journal

Date	Check Number	Explanation/ Payee/Invoice No.	Amount of Cash Paid (Credit)	Accounts Payable (Debit) Subsidiary Ledger Reference No.	Amount	Purchase Discount Taken (Credit)	Other Miscellaneous Payments Account Title	Acct. No.	Amount (Debit)
12/12/84	7031	ABC Co.–No. C3704	1313	A 1002	1313	—			
12/17/84	7032	R. W. Walp–rent	1100				Rent Expense	733	1100
12/20/84	7033	QRS Co.–No. 11078	728	Q 1772	750	22			
12/21/84	7034	Bank Loan Interest	300				Interest Expense	602	300
12/27/84	7035	Acton Water Dept.	152				Water Expense	939	152
12/30/84	7036	XYZ Co.–No. KBQ3	111	X 0001	125	14			
			3704		2188	36			1552
Col. 1	Col. 2	Col. 3	Col. 4	Col. 5	Col. 6	Col. 7	Col. 8	Col. 9	Col. 10

Note: Column 4 = Column 6 + Column 10 – Column 7
3704 = 2188 + 1552 – 36

company or greatly expanded for a larger, more sophisticated accounting system, it is critical that the system be designed to meet the needs of the company's managers and owners. Now let's continue with specific procedures that you may be asked to perform in the areas of bank reconciliations, petty cash, fixed asset control, and investment record-keeping.

Bank Reconciliation

The bank reconciliation is a comparison of the information contained in the bank's monthly statement with the company's own cash accounting records. A separate reconciliation should be prepared for each bank account. It should be prepared promptly upon receipt of the bank statement and canceled checks included with the statement. The canceled checks should be compared to the company's cash disbursements records to ensure that the checks have been made payable to the proper person or company (payee) and have been written for the proper amounts. The bank's list of deposits should be compared to the company's cash receipts records and the company's copies of the bank deposit slips to verify that all cash receipts have been properly deposited.

Due to timing differences between the company's recording of cash receipts and disbursements and those reported in the bank's statement, the ending cash balance in the company's records and the cash balance reported in the bank statement will usually differ. The sources of these differences are called *reconciling items*. The purpose of the bank reconciliation is to identify the reconciling items, and, by making the proper adjustments, to determine the correct cash balance.

The illustration on page 546 is a bank reconciliation for Andrew Manufacturing Company at December 31, 1984. Although the format for the bank reconciliation may vary from company to company, the end result is the same. Some common reconciling items are listed below.

Item	Description	Reconciliation Effect
1. Outstanding checks	Checks written by the company and sent to the payee but not recorded on the bank statement. This means that the check has not yet cleared the bank.	Deduct from the bank statement balance.
2. Deposits in transit	Deposits made by the company at the end of the month but not recorded by the bank until the following month.	Add to the bank statement balance.
3. NSF check	Nonsufficient funds (NSF) check of a customer that was deposited by the company but was not honored by the customer's bank.	Deduct from book balance; add to listing of accounts receivable.

Item	Description	Reconciliation Effect
4. Collections by the bank for the depositor	Funds collected by the bank (usually on a note receivable) for the benefit of the depositor. A reconciling item if not previously recorded by the company.	Add to book balance; reduce notes receivable.
5. Bank service charge	Charges made by the bank for services performed by them.	Deduct from book balance; add to expense.
6. Errors	Errors of the following types may be made either by the company or by the bank: Company errors:	
a. Improper amount of check or deposit recorded		Add to or deduct from the book balance depending upon the direction of the error. Correct the company's financial records.
b. Failure to record a check or deposit		Same as 6a above.
	Bank errors (notify the bank of all errors made by them immediately):	
c. Improper amount of deposit or check added or deducted		Add to or deduct from the bank balance depending upon the direction of the error.
d. Check drawn by another depositor deducted from the company's account.		Add to bank balance.
e. Company check deducted from another depositor's account.		Not detected by bank reconciliation process; the bank will ultimately find the error.
f. Company's deposit added to another depositor's account.		Add to bank balance.
g. Another depositor's deposit added to the company's account.		Deduct from bank balance.

Andrew Manufacturing Company
Bank Reconciliation
at December 31, 1984

Books		Bank	
Balance per the books	$ 9,007.00	Balance per the bank statement	$ 8,056.90
Additions:		Additions:	
Proceeds of note collected by the bank	1,100.00	Deposits in transit: December 30, 1984 December 31, 1984	1,143.07 2,000.05
			11,200.02
Error in recording check number 4033 (recorded as $151.00, should be $115.00)	36.00		
	10,143.00		
Deductions:		Deductions:	
NSF check returned	$128.00	Outstanding checks (see detailed list not shown here)	1,200.02
Bank service charge	15.00		
	143.00		
Corrected Book Balance	$10,000.00	Corrected Bank Balance	$10,000.00

Bank Reconciliation Procedures

1. Gather the current month's bank statement and canceled checks; the prior month's reconciliation; the checkbook or check register listing checks written during the period and the cash balance at month end; and the record of deposits or the company's copy of the month's deposit slips.

2. Trace all canceled checks and bank memorandums to the bank statement to ensure that there are no differences.

3. Put the canceled checks returned by the bank in numerical order.

4. Compare the canceled checks to the prior month's outstanding check list and the current month's listing of checks written by the company. Make a list of outstanding checks at the end of the current month.

5. List information from the bank memorandums for inclusion in the bank reconciliation.

6. Compare deposits per the bank statement with the company's copy of the deposit slips or other listing of cash receipts. Note differences for inclusion as deposits in transit.

7. Complete the bank reconciliation in a format similar to the one illustrated in this section.

8. Correct or adjust the company's records as needed. Notify the bank of any errors they have made.

Petty Cash Voucher

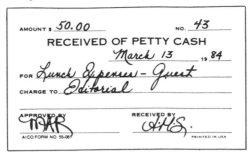

Petty Cash Fund

Many companies maintain small amounts of cash on their premises to cover small disbursements when it is impractical to write a check or when cash is needed immediately. These petty cash funds may cover the purchase of office supplies, postage, coffee, and so on. Also known as an *imprest fund*, the petty cash fund is normally established at an amount sufficient to cover two to four weeks of needs and is usually between $100.00 and $500.00. When the amount is determined, a check payable to Petty Cash is made out and cashed, and the cash is then placed in a locked box or drawer under the control of a custodian having sole responsibility for the fund. All expenditures from the petty cash fund should be made by the custodian, and adequate documentation should be maintained to support the payments. Often a petty cash voucher (purchased from any stationery store) is used for such documentation. The voucher shows the date, purpose of the expenditure, the department or account to be charged, the signature of the person receiving the cash, the signature of the person disbursing the funds, the amount disbursed, and a sequential voucher number. (This information may be maintained on a separate disbursement sheet rather than on petty cash vouchers, but that practice is less common.)

At any time, the amount of cash on hand plus the amount of disbursements noted on the petty cash vouchers should equal the established amount of the petty cash fund. When the cash in the fund is low, it should be replenished by writing a check to Petty Cash for the amount needed to restore the fund to its authorized amount. The check is cashed and the proceeds are placed in the petty cash box. The fund is now back at its original amount and is ready for use once again.

INVESTMENT TRANSACTIONS

Many organizations invest in stocks, bonds, and other vehicles to earn a return on excess funds. It is important for you to record properly all information related to these transactions not only for the company's financial records, but also to comply with governmental agency requirements. When handling security transactions, you should maintain the following documents or files:

1. A separate record should be kept for each security owned, and the records should be kept in alphabetical order. All investment activity should be posted as it occurs. (See the next illustration, "Record of Security Transactions.")

Andrew Manufacturing Company
Record of Security Transactions

Security _____

Exchange Listed on _____

Broker _____

No. of Shares	Date	Purchase/ Sale	Price/ Share	Broker's Commis.	Total Purchase Price Paid/Sales Price Rec'd	Cap. Gain or (Loss) on Sale		Bal. Shares Owned	Total Cost
						Short-term	Long-term		

2. A list of all investments in securities owned should be compiled and updated on a weekly, biweekly, or monthly basis, depending on the volume of investment activity. This list, too, should be kept in alphabetical order. (See the illustration, "List of Securities Owned.")

3. A file of all brokers' trade advices should be kept. It is the basis for recording information in the individual security records. (A *trade advice* lists the purchase or sale of a specific investment including the trade date, settlement date, purchase/sales price, broker's commission, and security being purchased/sold.)

4. A file should be kept of monthly brokers' statements that are verified by tracing to the individual security records maintained by the company and noting agreement of month-end information.

5. A record of interest or dividend income received based on actual cash receipts and deposits into the cash account should be kept. (See the illustration, "Record of Interest and Dividend Income," on page 550.)

6. Security certificates should be kept in a locked vault with access limited to a very few people. Access to the securities should never be permitted to fewer than two authorized persons accompanying each other.

Andrew Manufacturing Company
List of Securities Owned
December 31, 1984

Number of Shares or Face Value	Security Name and Description	Total Cost	Current Market Value
Stocks:			
Bonds:			
Investment Funds:			
Other:			
Totals:		$	$

Andrew Manufacturing Company

Record of Interest and Dividend Income
Period Covered _____

Interest Income (grouped by security)

Security	Date Received	Amount	Annual Total

Dividend Income (grouped by security)

Security	Date Received	Amount Received	Annual Total
	qtr 1		
	qtr 2		
	qtr 3		
	qtr 4		
	qtr 1		
	qtr 2		
	qtr 3		
	qtr 4		

FIXED ASSETS RECORDS

Records of plant assets having a productive or service life beyond one year must be maintained to ensure the proper safeguarding of company-owned assets and to allocate properly the cost of the asset to the appropriate period the asset is benefiting (depreciation). A fixed asset record should be fully completed. (See the illustration on page 551.)

The estimated life of a fixed asset is the period of time the asset is used in producing or selling other assets or services. This period of time varies by type of asset (i.e., buildings, equipment, furniture, or fixtures) but is usually standardized by company policy. Salvage value is that portion of the asset cost that is expected to be recovered at the end of the asset's productive life.

Allocating the cost of the asset over its service life (depreciation) can be done by many methods. Four of the more common methods are straight line, units of production, declining balance, and sum-of-years-digits:

1. When the straight line method is used, the cost of the asset minus the estimated salvage value is divided by the asset's productive life in years or months. This method allocates an equal share of the asset's cost to each accounting period.

2. The units of production method divides the cost of an asset after deducting estimated salvage value by the estimated units of product that the asset will produce over its service life. This process gives depreciation per unit of product. Depreciation for the period is determined by multiplying the units produced in a period by the unit depreciation.

3. Under the declining balance method, depreciation of up to twice the straight line rate, without considering salvage value, may be applied each year to the declining book value of a new plant asset having an estimated life of at least three years. If this method is followed and twice the straight line rate is used, the amount charged each year as depreciation expense is determined by (1) calculating a straight line depreciation rate (100% divided by the useful life in years) for the asset; (2) doubling this rate; and then (3) at the end of each year in the asset's life, applying the doubled rate to the asset's remaining book value.

4. Under the sum-of-years-digits method (SYD), the years in an asset's service life are added and their sum is used as the denominator of a series of fractions used in allocating total depreciation to the periods in the asset's service life. The numerator of the fractions are the years in the asset's life in their reverse order. For example, if the SYD method is used to depreciate an asset having a five-year life and a cost of $6,000.00, the following is used to calculate depreciation:

Number of years for the denominator = $1+2+3+4+5=15$

Year	Annual Depreciation Calculation	Annual Depreciation Expense
1	$5/15 \times \$6,000$	$2,000
2	$4/15 \times \$6,000$	1,600
3	$3/15 \times \$6,000$	1,200
4	$2/15 \times \$6,000$	800
5	$1/15 \times \$6,000$	400
		$6,000

Andrew Manufacturing Company
Fixed Assets Record

Asset Description _____
Purchase Date & Vendor _____
Purchase Price (including freight and installation costs)

_____

Asset Location _____
Asset Identification Number _____
Estimated Life _____
Depreciation Method _____
Annual/Monthly Depreciation (if applicable)

_____

Estimated Salvage Value _____
Disposition Date _____
Sales Price When Sold _____

Year	Original Cost	Depreciation Expense	Net Book Value	Sales Price	Gain or (Loss) Upon Disposition

16

Business Law

Gail Pennington, Esq. • *Partner, Homans, Hamilton, Dahmen & Marshall*
James C. Hamilton, Esq. • *Partner, Homans, Hamilton, Dahmen & Marshall*

LAW IN THE OFFICE ENVIRONMENT

A professional secretary in a law office will be exposed to the intricacies of the legal system and will be called on to understand the many peculiarities of legal form and style as well as some of the substantive framework of that system. While the secretary in a general business office will not have as great a need for an in-depth knowledge of law and the legal system, general knowledge of certain legal concepts will enable the secretary to deal more effectively with the legal issues that do arise in the business context. You may be called on to prepare documents intended to have legal effect, and the form chosen or the formalities followed in executing the documents may be critical. Familiarity with general principles of contract law, agency, and corporate law may assist you in dealing with various documents or issues that frequently arise in the business office. You also should be aware of a number of statutes and regulations generally applicable to the conduct of a business. In this chapter we do not attempt to address all of the issues of legal form and style or provide an exhaustive treatise on business law. Rather, we explain a number of those areas of the law that frequently arise in a business office environment in order to give you an awareness of the legal implications of your work and to assist you in understanding the meaning and purpose of common legal documents, words, and regulations.

CONTRACTS

The law of contracts is basic to business law, as the negotiation, preparation, execution, and enforcement of contracts are the foundation for much of the conduct of business. In the office, an understanding of the elements of a valid contract and its legal formalities will aid you when you are called on to prepare a document or assist in its execution, and may be helpful in connection with aspects of office management in matters ranging from ordering supplies and purchasing equipment to dealing with personnel functions.

General Principles

Stated simply, a *contract* is an agreement that is legally enforceable. It can be created by an oral promise or a written document, or it can be implied where the circumstances indicate. It is not always necessary that there be a formal, written agreement for a contract to exist. The factors necessary to create an enforceable agreement include *parties* who are competent to contract; an expression of the *terms* of the agreement; and *consideration* for the agreement. In addition, the object of the contract must not violate any public policy or statute.

There are two issues relevant in determining whether a party is competent to contract: whether the party has any legal disability and whether the party has the proper authority to enter into the particular contract in question. As a general rule, a minor or a person under guardianship or conservatorship is considered incompetent to contract as a matter of law, and any agreement with or on behalf of a person who cannot contract on his or her own behalf should be entered into in the name of the guardian, custodian, or conservator of the person. The issue of authority to enter into the particular contract depends on the circumstances of the situation. An agreement made by an individual who is legally competent will be binding on the individual. Agreements made by corporations or other business entities will be binding if they are executed by officers, agents, or employees who have been authorized to bind the company, either under rules of agency or by specific corporate action. You may want to refer to the section on Agency that appears later in this chapter for a fuller discussion of this issue.

There are no specific rules on the expression of the terms of the agreement, although this criterion is often expressed as a requirement that there must have been a "meeting of the minds" to create a binding contract. That is, there must be sufficient evidence that the parties had reached an agreement even though all of the terms and conditions are not clearly defined. Although the parties' failure to express adequately the terms of their agreement can result in a finding that no contract exists, more often a court will attempt to reconstruct what the parties intended at the time they entered into the contract. In certain instances, some of the terms of an agreement will be provided by statute if the parties have not expressed them. This is particularly true with regard to sales of goods under the Uniform Commercial Code, discussed in a later section of this chapter. It is generally more satisfactory, however, if the terms of the agreement are clearly expressed by the parties. Such a statement need not be extensive. An offer by a merchant of a certain product for a specified price and an acceptance of that offer by a customer by tendering payment or submitting a purchase order will be a sufficient expression of the terms of an agreement. More extensive provisions will be necessary in more complicated relationships.

Consideration for a contract most commonly consists of payment in exchange for services or goods or of a promise in exchange for another promise. Except in limited circumstances, if there is no consideration or if the consideration is considered inadequate, the contract will not be enforceable. The law considers that a promise not supported by consideration is a gift rather than a binding obligation and the courts will not compel a party effectively to make a gift. In spite of this rule, a contract "under seal" is considered enforceable without regard to consideration. Further, the courts will rarely look behind a statement in a contract that the parties consider the consideration to be adequate.

Formalities

A well-written agreement should follow certain rules of form, some of which relate to the elements described previously and some of which are simply good business practice. Many of the following suggestions relative to form can be varied to meet a particular situation or to suit an individual's style and are intended to serve as a general guide.

Introductory clauses.   The agreement should begin with an introductory clause that describes the agreement and identifies the parties. Some circumstances require inclusion of the full address of each of the parties and, even where such information is not required, it is good practice to include the information. The introductory clause also provides an opportunity to assign a short descriptive term to each of the parties, such as "Buyer" and "Seller," as a means of easy reference throughout the agreement. The date of the agreement also should be stated, either in this introductory clause or in the testimonium clause described later. A common form of introductory clause is as follows:

> This Agreement is made this third day of February 1984 by and between Hemingway Incorporated, a Delaware corporation with a usual place of business in Boston, Massachusetts (hereinafter called the ''Company''), and Peter F. Trombley, of 123 Park Street, Newton, Massachusetts (hereinafter called the ''Consultant'').

The manner of identifying a party will vary depending on the legal status of the party. An individual should be identified by his or her name and, usually, residence address. If, however, the individual is in business as a sole proprietor and the agreement relates to the business, the business address should be used.

A corporation should be identified by its registered name, state of incorporation, and principal place of business. The name of the corporate officer who will be signing on behalf of the corporation should not appear in the introductory clause. The description of the corporation can be in the form indicated in the preceding example, or a more formal approach may be used:

> . . . Hemingway Incorporated, a corporation duly organized and validly existing under the General Corporation Law of the State of Delaware, and maintaining a usual place of business at 73 Tremont Street, Boston, Massachusetts. . . .

For any number of reasons, a corporation may be organized under one name and actually conduct its business under an assumed name. If the information is available, it should be included as follows:

> . . . Hemingway Incorporated, a Delaware corporation doing business in California as Hemingway Business Forms, Inc., and maintaining a usual place of business at 1999 Wilshire Boulevard, Los Angeles, California. . . .

Professional corporations should be identified by their corporate names in the same manner as business corporations.

General partnerships in most jurisdictions are not considered legal entities apart from the individual partners, and for purposes of bringing suit each of the general partners must be named. A general partnership usually conducts its business under a trade name, however, and may be referred to by such trade name for purposes of most agreements, especially where there are a large number of general partners. For example:

> . . . Thayer & Crispin, Attorneys-at-Law, a general partnership engaged in the practice of law. . . .

It is also appropriate to identify each of the general partners:

> . . . Jean G. Thayer and Sandra Crispin, general partners engaged in the practice of law under the name of Thayer & Crispin. . . .

Limited partnerships are in many respects more similar to corporations than they are to general partnerships. A limited partnership consists of one or more general partners who manage the business and can bind the partnership, and one or more limited partners who have no managerial authority. The partnership must adopt a name that must be registered, usually with the secretary of state. The limited partnership should be identified by its registered name, and the state of registration should be stated.

There are a number of different types of trusts, including general trusts, business trusts, and realty trusts. Generally, a trust does not have a separate legal identity and an agreement involving a trust should be made in the name of the trustee:

> . . . James P. Overmeyer, as trustee of the Adam Thomas Family Trust and not individually . . . .

Similarly, where a contract is made by any other fiduciary, such as the guardian of a minor, the conservator of an incompetent, or the executor of a will, the fiduciary should be named as a party and clearly identified as acting in a fiduciary capacity.

Recitals.   It is common practice to recite the background of an agreement, the relationship of the parties, or other facts that tend to clarify the basis for each party entering into the agreement. In addition, a recitation of the consideration for the agreement is often made, either as part of the preliminary recitals or in the body of the agreement (or both). Recitals generally take one of the following forms, the first of which is the more traditional:

> WITNESSETH:
>
> WHEREAS, Seller has developed and markets a software program relating to legal time and billing which has been adapted for use on the XYZ personal computer; and
>
> WHEREAS, Buyer is a law firm which has need for a legal time and billing program for use on its XYZ personal computer and desires to acquire a license to use Seller's program;
>
> NOW, THEREFORE, in consideration of the payment of the licensee fee by the Buyer to the Seller and of the mutual covenants and promises set forth herein, the parties agree as follows: . . . .

or:

> ### Recitals.
>
> 1. The Seller is in the business of manufacturing headsets for use with tape recording equipment and has the capacity to produce in excess of 5,000 headsets per week;
>
> 2. The Buyer is in the business of marketing tape recording equipment to the general public and has need for headsets which can be used with its equipment;

> 3. The Buyer desires to reserve the Seller's capacity to produce 5,000 headsets per week on the terms and conditions of this Agreement.
>
> The Parties therefore agree as follows: . . . .

Body.   The body of the contract will contain all of the provisions relating to the actual terms of the agreement. There are no general rules as to form or style other than general rules applicable to all business documents, discussed elsewhere in this book.

Testimonium.   The testimonium is the clause that appears at the end of the body of the contract and prior to the signatures of the parties. Such a clause, in its various forms, serves to affirm that the parties are aware that they are entering into an agreement and that they intend to be bound by the terms of the written document they are signing. Common forms of testimonium clauses follow:

> IN WITNESS WHEREOF, the parties have hereunto set their hands and seals to this Agreement the date and year first set out above.
>
> IN WITNESS WHEREOF, the parties have executed this Agreement in duplicate the 4th day of June 1983.

For business entities:

> IN WITNESS WHEREOF, the parties have caused this Agreement to be executed by their duly authorized officers on the 1st day of February 1984.
>
> The said Joseph P. Smith, as trustee of the Smithfield Realty Trust, and the said George A. Grey, as President of George A. Grey Associates, Inc., have signed this Agreement this 3rd day of April 1984.

Frequently, the testimonium clause will state that the parties have "set their hands and seals" or that the document is to have the effect of a "sealed" document. The concept of a sealed document derives from early common law, which provided that the presence of a seal eliminated the need to prove that there was consideration to support the contract. The effect of a seal and its necessity under current law depend on the circumstances and the applicable law of the jurisdiction. Most commonly, you will see an actual seal where a corporation is a party and the seal is used to prove corporate authority. Most jurisdictions provide by statute that a statement to the effect that a document is sealed is sufficient to give it the force of a sealed document, even if no seal is actually affixed. There is usually no negative effect from the presence of a seal or where there is a recitation of a seal that gives the document the effect of a sealed document.

Signatures.   The agreement should be signed by a natural person who is a party or who is authorized to bind a party. The signatory's name should be typed below the signature line and, except where an individual is signing on his own behalf, the authority of the person who is signing should be indicated. An example of the proper form for execution of a document by a corporation is as follows:

> Hemingway Incorporated
>
> By_____
> James P. Jacobs, President

As a general rule, an agreement on behalf of the following entities should be signed by a person who fills one of the indicated positions:

Entity	Permissible Signatory
Corporation (including professional corporations)	Corporate Officer
General Partnerships	General Partner
Limited Partnerships	General Partner
Trusts	All Trustees, unless there is evidence of authority to act alone
Estates	Executor or Administrator

Frequently, one person is a party to a contract in more than one capacity and where this is the case the best practice is to have the person sign the document on separate lines for each capacity. At a minimum, the description under a single signature line should make it clear that the person is signing in more than one capacity.

Attestations.   Although not always required, signatures are often attested by witnesses to the signing. This can be helpful if later there is some doubt as to who actually signed or the circumstances under which the document was signed. An attestation can simply be the signature of the witness under the word "witness" or an attestation clause can recite any information that is relevant, such as the following:

```
      Signed, sealed and delivered by the above-named
      Peter Gregory, in my presence, at Boston, Massachu-
      setts, this 3rd day of June 1983.
```

Signatures of corporate officers are often attested by the corporate clerk or secretary to verify that the corporation has authorized the document to be signed. The attestation takes the following form and the corporate seal is embossed over the attestation:

```
      Attest:   [Corporate Seal]
      _____
      Clerk/Secretary
```

Acknowledgments.   Some documents, most notably affidavits or documents dealing with real property, must be acknowledged before a public official such as a notary public or judicial officer qualified to administer oaths. An acknowledgment executed by a public official has the effect of verifying the facts stated in the acknowledgment, without the necessity to prove them by testimony. Frequently used forms of acknowledgment follow:

```
      State of _____        December __, 19__
      County of _____

      Then personally appeared the above-named James P.
      Jacobs and acknowledged the foregoing to be his free
      act and deed, before me,

      _____
      Notary Public
```

State of _____   December __, 19__
County of _____

Then personally appeared the above named James P.
Jacobs, Vice President and General Manager of Hemingway Incorporated, and acknowledged the foregoing instrument to be the free act and deed of the corporation,
before me,

_____
Notary Public

State of _____
County of _____

On the ____ day of _____, 19__, before me personally came James P. Jacobs, to me known, who, being by me
duly sworn, did depose and say that he resides at
_____; that he is the Vice President and General
Manager of Hemingway Incorporated, the corporation
described in and which executed the above instrument;
that he knows the seal of said corporation; that the
seal affixed to said instrument is such corporate seal;
that it was so affixed by authorization of the board of
directors, and that he signed his name thereto by like
authorization.

_____
Public Official

The form of acknowledgment for an affidavit or other statement of facts should
appear substantially as follows:

State of _____
County of _____

The undersigned, Lynn F. Green, known to me and
known to be the person who executed the foregoing
document, personally appeared before me this ____ day
of _____, 19__, and stated that the facts stated
therein are true to the best of her knowledge and
belief.

_____
Notary Public

If the affidavit includes a statement by the affiant that the statements contained
therein are true to the best of his or her knowledge and belief, it is sufficient to
add just the notary jurat at the end of the document after the signature of the
party offering the statement. This should include a statement of the venue (state
and county) and the language, "Subscribed and sworn to before me," as well as
the notary's signature and seal.

AGENCY

The law of agency is concerned with a number of issues raised when an individual acts on behalf of another party. These issues should be of some concern to the
secretary from at least two perspectives. On the one hand, contract law and

business relationships raise a number of questions—such as who is able to bind a corporation contractually—which involve issues of agency. On the other hand, an employee is considered for many purposes to be an agent of the employer and, especially where he or she has administrative or managerial responsibilities, the secretary should be aware of the potential consequences of his or her actions as an agent of the employer.

Legal Principles

An *agent* is an individual authorized to act on behalf of another party. The party on whose behalf the agent acts is called the *principal.* Where a valid agency exists, the agent can bind the principal and the principal will be responsible for the acts of his agent which are within the scope of the agency or which occur in the course of the agent's fulfilling his duties as agent. In some forms of agency, the principal's liability to third parties for the acts of his agent may extend to acts not directly related to the agency, such as when an employee is involved in an automobile accident during the course of making a delivery for the employer, and to acts not expressly authorized by the principal, such as when a managerial employee refuses to hire an applicant because of the applicant's race.

The scope of authority of an agent depends on the terms of the agency. In some cases, the agent's authority is a legal consequence of the relationship of the parties. Hence, corporate officers are agents of the corporation, and general partners are agents of their fellow general partners and of the limited partners in a limited partnership. In each of these cases, the agent's authority to act for and bind the principal exists only to the extent that the agent is acting within his role as corporate officer or general partner, as the case may be. Unfortunately, it is not always clear whether the agent was acting within his role and that issue often leads to serious disputes. In other principal-agent relationships, the scope of the agent's authority is created by an express agreement and is, consequently, more clearly defined. For example, a homeowner may retain a real estate broker to find a buyer for his or her house at a certain price. The broker is the agent of the homeowner only for that limited purpose and clearly is not authorized to otherwise act for the homeowner.

Generally the agent is able to bind his principal contractually only to the extent he acts within the scope of the agency. To some extent, third parties who deal with the agent do so at the risk that the agent is acting outside the scope of his agency. Where it is not clear from principles of agency that the agent is authorized to act as a consequence of his relationship to the principal, or where there is otherwise any question of authority, a third party will often require evidence of authority, such as a certificate signed and sealed by a corporate clerk certifying the adoption of a resolution by the board of directors which authorizes a specific corporate action or certifying that the officer signing an agreement is either generally or specifically authorized to do so.

There are some circumstances under which an agent can bind his principal even without express authority. The authority to do related acts may be implied from the express authority given to the agent, such as where an office manager's authority to hire a receptionist may imply the authority to fire the employee. In addition, an apparent agency may exist where the circumstances lead a third party reasonably to believe that the apparent agent has the authority to act for another person who could but who does not do anything to deny the agency. In some situations, a person will ratify the acts of another who purported to be his agent and thereby create an agency by ratification. In each of these cases, the determination of whether an agency exists depends on the particular facts.

The extent of the principal's liability for the acts of his agent which are not within the scope of the agency depends in large part on the degree of control the principal exercises over the agent. The strictest agency relationship is commonly referred to as a *master-servant relationship*, and exists where the principal exercises significant control over the conduct of the agent, such as by setting hours of work, providing tools or equipment, and supervising the work performed. It generally applies to employer-employee relationships. As a result of the high degree of control and close supervision, the employer is liable not only for authorized contractual commitments made by its employees on its behalf but also for accidents and personal injuries caused negligently or intentionally by them in the course of their employment. The employee need not be actually performing work for the employer at the time he or she causes personal injuries or similar damage; so long as there is a reasonable link between the activity and the employment, the employer may be liable. In other types of agency relationships where the principal exercises a lesser degree of control over the actual performance by the agent, such as those involving independent contractors, the scope of the principal's liability is correspondingly smaller. Even where the principal is liable to third parties for injuries caused by its agent, however, the agent is primarily liable to the injured party or, where the injured party recovers from the principal, the agent may be required to reimburse the principal.

Powers of Attorney

Many agencies are created by the use of powers of attorney. A power of attorney is a written document by which another person is specifically authorized to act for the person signing the document. Where a person is authorized to act for a definite and specified purpose, he or she is often referred to as an *attorney in fact* for such purpose. There is no particular form that must be used to create a power of attorney, although certain governmental entities—most notably the Internal Revenue Service—have issued printed forms which they require to be used in connection with matters brought before them. Any document intending to serve as a power of attorney should contain a clear statement of the powers and duties of the attorney in fact. In executing the power of attorney, the formalities required to effectively complete the act should be observed. For instance, if the attorney in fact is given the power to execute a deed, an act requiring an acknowledgment by an official, the power of attorney must be likewise acknowledged. It is always good practice to provide an attestation by witness even though it may not be legally required, as it may avoid questions later concerning the signature of the principal granting the power of attorney.

Execution of Documents

Whenever an agent is acting for a principal in the execution of a document, whether under a power of attorney or other agency, it is important that the fact of the agency be expressed. If it is unclear whether the agent is acting for himself or for a principal, the agent may be personally liable on the contract. It is also possible that the principal will not be liable at all, which may be to the detriment of both the agent and the third party. A discussion of various forms of execution of contracts by agents on behalf of principals is contained earlier in this chapter and is applicable where the agent is acting under a power of attorney or any other agency relationship.

UNIFORM COMMERCIAL CODE

The Uniform Commercial Code (UCC), a collection of laws relating to commercial transactions, has been adopted in varying forms in most states. It is intended to provide for relatively consistent regulation of commercial transactions among the various jurisdictions. Our discussion focuses on two of the areas covered by the UCC, transactions involving sales of goods and secured transactions, as these are likely to be most relevant in the business environment.

Sales

Article 2 of the UCC applies to transactions involving sales of goods and has two basic functions. Most broadly, it establishes standards of fair dealing among buyers and sellers primarily by imposing an overriding obligation of good faith and commercial reasonableness in sales transactions. Article 2 also provides definitions of commonly used commercial terms that serve to clarify the expectations of the parties and standardize the usage of terms in the commercial world.

In addition to this general role, Article 2 has a more practical application. Although the law gives the parties wide freedom to set the terms of their agreement, it also recognizes that parties occasionally fail to provide for all contingencies. There are numerous situations where the UCC will come into play unless the parties otherwise agree. For instance, Article 2 contains rules for determining, in the absence of an express agreement, whether an offer has been made and accepted, where the goods are to be delivered, what warranties are given or implied, the buyer's right to inspect and reject goods, the seller's right to withhold shipment, and remedies for breach by either party. Frequently, the parties will intentionally omit a provision in a contract knowing that the UCC will govern or will specifically refer to the relevant section of Article 2 and incorporate its provisions into the agreement.

Security Interests

When your business finances the purchase of office equipment or similar items, or if the company takes out a loan for other purposes, the lender will usually require a security interest in the items financed or in the assets of the corporation. Article 9 of the UCC governs the creation of security interests and provides for a filing procedure by which such interests are perfected.

A security interest is created by the agreement of the parties. The agreement should be in writing and signed by the debtor. The parties are generally free to set the terms of the security agreement, although certain provisions of Article 9, primarily with respect to the rights of third parties, will override contradictory provisions in a written agreement. Generally, a security interest gives the secured party the right to repossess the collateral if payments are not made or if the debtor is otherwise in default and to receive the proceeds if the collateral is sold. If the security interest is perfected, as explained below, the secured party can repossess the collateral even if it has been sold or transferred to a third party.

A security interest is enforceable against third parties only when it has been perfected. Except in very limited circumstances, a security interest is perfected by filing a financing statement with the appropriate governmental agency. The

Uniform Commercial Code Financing Statement—UCC-1

Uniform Commercial Code — FINANCING STATEMENT — Form UCC-1

IMPORTANT — Read instructions on back before filling out form

This FINANCING STATEMENT is presented to a filing officer for filing pursuant to the Uniform Commercial Code.

4. ☐ Filed for record in the real estate records.	5. ☐ Debtor is a Transmitting Utility.	6. No. of Additional Sheets Presented:
1. Debtor(s) (Last Name First) and address(es)	2. Secured Party(ies) and address(es)	3. For Filing Officer (Date, Time, Number, and Filing Office)
Gorham Enterprises One Park Place Arlington, MA 01000	Smith Leasing Co. 155 Wagner Road Arlington, MA 01000	

7. This financing statement covers the following types (or items) of property:

Xerox Copier, Model 1045, Serial No. XPF6666666

☐ Products of Collateral are also covered.

Whichever is Applicable (See Instruction Number 9)	*Peter Gorham, President* .... Signature(s) of Debtor (Or Assignor)	*John Smith* .... Signature(s) of Secured Party (Or Assignee)

Filing Officer Copy — Alphabetical
STANDARD FORM — UNIFORM COMMERCIAL CODE — FORM UCC-1   Rev. Jan. 1980   *Forms may be purchased from Hobbs & Warren, Inc., Boston, Mass. 02101*

---

proper place of filing varies from state to state and may also depend on the type of collateral covered by the security agreement, so the statute in effect in the place where the collateral is located must be checked to assure proper filing.

Most states have adopted some version of a relatively standard financing statement which is called a Form UCC–1. There are some variations for different states and the requirements of your particular state should be checked. A completed UCC–1 relating to the purchase of office equipment appears above. The financing statement must be signed by the debtor, unless the security agreement signed by the debtor is filed with the financing statement. It is often necessary to file the financing statement with more than one office and a Form UCC–2 is designed for this purpose. It is a duplicate of the UCC–1, but has an extra sheet of carbon attached so that it can be placed over a UCC–1 and the form need only be typed once. There is also a form UCC–3 which may be used to continue, terminate, release, assign, or amend a previously filed UCC–1 financing statement.

REGULATION OF BUSINESS

Business enterprises are subject to a variety of statutes and regulations that may affect the conduct of the business generally or only specific aspects of its operation. There are statutes governing the creation of business corporations and providing rules for the basic structure and functioning of the corporation. The offering and issuance of securities is governed by another set of laws and regulations, and still other statutes regulate certain relationships between businesses. Some enterprises are subject to regulation because of the nature of their business. The most prominent examples of this specialized regulation are telephone and utility companies, insurance companies and, previously, the airline industry. Businesses dealing with consumers are generally subject to consumer protection statutes and companies involved in hazardous operations may be required by law to follow extraordinary safety precautions.

Every business with employees is also required to comply with a variety of laws and regulations relating to certain aspects of the employer-employee relationship, such as payment of wages, hours worked, discrimination, worker safety, and benefits for injured workers. It would be beyond the scope of this chapter to attempt to identify all of the regulatory statutes that may be of concern in the operation of many businesses. We felt it would be more useful to identify two areas that are likely to be relevant in the daily operation of a general business office—corporate law and the employment relationship—and to discuss some of the general policies and specific statutes in these areas.

Corporate Law

Corporations exist only if created in accordance with state law. Every state has enacted a statute that sets forth the requirements for establishing the corporation and maintaining its corporate existence. General rules relating to corporate functions such as issuance of stock and the holding of annual stockholder meetings are also found in the statute. Often, much of the paperwork relating to the creation and continued existence of the corporation is done by the corporation's counsel. There are, however, certain forms and procedures that you may see in the course of your work, and we hope that the forthcoming general explanation will be of assistance to you in understanding these matters.

The charter document for a corporation is often called a *Certificate of Incorporation, Articles of Organization,* or something similar, and usually contains the following information: the name of the corporation and its purposes; the type and number of shares of corporate stock authorized; any stock restrictions or special rules for the governing of the corporation; and the names of the initial officers and directors of the company. The charter document must be filed with the proper state office, usually the secretary of state, and becomes effective upon approval. Amendments can be made by vote of the stockholders of the corporation and also must be filed and approved to become effective.

The corporate Bylaws are the rules by which the corporation conducts its internal affairs. The Bylaws, which must be consistent with state law, generally describe the relative functions and powers of the corporate officers, board of directors, and stockholders. Bylaws do not need to be filed and are effective upon adoption by the stockholders. They also can be amended by the stockholders, or in some instances by the board of directors.

A corporation is organized in three tiers. The stockholders own the stock, elect the board of directors, and must approve certain corporate actions such as authorization of additional stock, mergers, or sale of the corporate assets. The board of directors is responsible for overseeing the operation of the corporation at all levels and elects the corporate officers to handle the day-to-day affairs of the corporation. The officers, who generally include a president, one or more vice presidents, a treasurer, and a secretary or clerk have such duties as are given them by the Bylaws or the board of directors. In a small company, the stockholders, directors, and officers are often comprised of a few individuals. Large corporations may have a very complex organization of officers and directors and usually a large number of stockholders not otherwise involved in the business.

Although the corporate structure is established pursuant to state law, one important aspect of the corporate operation—the sale of securities—is regulated under two federal securities statutes as well as securities statutes known as *Blue Sky laws* which are in effect in every state. As a general rule, the securities statutes require that stock either be registered with a regulating authority or specifically be exempt from registration under the statute. Under the federal laws, stock that is not exempt must be registered with the Securities Exchange Commission (SEC) and each state has identified a state agency which enforces its Blue Sky law. Registration requires the preparation and filing of a statement and a prospectus which fully disclose pertinent facts about the history of the corporation, its financial and business affairs, and similar information. Once stock has been registered, the company must continually update the information that was provided in the statement filed upon initial registration. Properly registered stock may be publicly traded, which means that it may be offered for sale to the general public. All stock traded on the major stock exchanges or sold over the counter is registered stock.

The federal securities law and most of the state Blue Sky laws exempt private offerings or limited offerings from the registration requirement. Strict statutory requirements must be met to qualify for this exemption, but most small corporations whose stock is owned by a few individuals and which do not offer their stock for sale to outside investors qualify for this exemption. References to "public corporations" mean those corporations which have registered their stock for sale to the general public. Private corporations with only a few stockholders actively involved in the corporate enterprise are often referred to as *closely held corporations*.

The Employment Relationship

The rights and obligations of employers and employees to one another are governed in part by the express agreement of the parties; in part by statutory regulation by federal, state, and local governments; and in part by the common law. Although the agreement of the employer and employee generally establishes the terms and conditions of the employment relationship, that agreement may intentionally or inadvertently fail to address many of the issues that arise during the course of employment. It may also include provisions that are unenforceable because they violate public policy or a specific statute.

Employment agreements. The agreement between the employer and the employee, like any contract, may be oral or written, simple or complex. It is important, from the perspective of both parties, that the agreement be as specific as possible with respect to the basic issues: What work is to be performed by the employee? Is there a formal performance review and evaluation? Is there a probationary period? What is the salary and when is it paid? Are there benefits such as medical and dental insurance, profit sharing or pension plans, and life insurance?

Within the limits of certain regulatory statutes, these are all issues that are open for negotiation, and it is a good idea to raise them early. The oral and written agreement of the parties with respect to these and similar terms and conditions of employment constitute the employment contract. If the employer has written employee policies, these too will be considered as part of the employment contract. You should be aware that if you are interviewing and/or hiring new employees, you are considered an agent of your employer and what you say will be binding on the company.

In most instances, the relationship between the employer and employee is considered a contract "at-will." This means that it can be terminated by either party for almost any reason or for no reason. The agreement may require one or two weeks' notice, but generally no reason need be given to justify or explain the termination. Problems can arise upon termination by the employer, even in an at-will contract, when the reason for terminating is prohibited by law or public policy, such as when the employer terminates an employee in order to avoid paying a large commission that is about to become due.

Wages and hours.   An employee cannot waive the protections established by the federal wage and hour laws. The National Fair Labor Standards Act, applicable to most employers having fifteen or more employees and engaged in interstate commerce, establishes minimum wages for regular and overtime work. The statute is enforced by the Wage and Hour Division of the Department of Labor. As a general rule, an employer must pay its employees not less than the minimum wage for the first forty hours of work per week. The employee must be compensated at one and one-half times his or her regular hourly rate for all hours worked in excess of forty hours for the week. In addition to the federal statute, there may be state and local laws that regulate the maximum number of hours a person can be required to work, whether work can be required on holidays and/or Sundays, under what conditions minors may work, and related issues.

Employment discrimination.   A number of federal and state laws prohibit discrimination in employment. The federal laws include Title VII of the Civil Rights Act of 1964 (Title VII), which applies to most employers having at least fifteen employees and which makes it unlawful to base employment decisions on or to discriminate with respect to terms and conditions of employment because of an individual's race, color, religion, sex, or national origin; the Age Discrimination in Employment Act (ADEA), which prohibits most employers with twenty or more employees from discriminating against employees between the ages of forty and seventy; and the Equal Pay Act, which is part of the wage and hour law and which makes it illegal to pay unequal wages to men and women who do substantially equal work. In addition to these federal laws, many states have similar statutes prohibiting employment discrimination.

The federal Equal Employment Opportunity Commission (EEOC) monitors compliance with Title VII, ADEA, and the Equal Pay Act. Many states have local agencies or commissions responsible for enforcing the state discrimination statutes. The procedure established under most discrimination statutes requires the employee to file a claim with the proper agency within a relatively short time of the incident claimed to constitute discrimination. Generally, the agency then has the option to investigate, to attempt to conciliate, to bring a legal action on behalf of the claimant, or to authorize the individual to bring legal action. The filing of the claim within the period established by the applicable discrimination statute is almost always a prerequisite of later court action.

Some forms of employment discrimination are more obvious than others. It is important to note that a pattern or practice that tends to effect any of the identified classifications can constitute prohibited discrimination, even if there was no overt discrimination against an individual. Sexual harassment is a form of sex discrimination and exists where there are sexual advances, requests for sexual favors, and other verbal or physical conduct of a sexual nature. Sexual harassment is illegal if it affects the terms and conditions of an individual's employment or if it creates a hostile or negative working environment. Where a supervisory employee is responsible for a discriminatory decision, the employer will be liable. The employer also will be liable for discriminatory acts by employees who are not in supervisory positions if the employer is or should be aware of the conduct and does nothing to correct the situation. An employer guilty of employment discrimination may be required to hire or reinstate the affected individual, to pay back wages, and, in limited circumstances, to pay compensatory damages.

Workers' compensation.   Workers' compensation laws have been enacted in every state. Although the statutes vary from state to state with respect to what kinds of employees are covered, how claims are administered, and what benefits are payable, they generally require that every employer maintain workers' compensation insurance to cover *compensable losses* of employees. Compensable losses can be very broadly defined as injuries from accidents or diseases resulting from an individual's employment.

Businesses are required to cover most employees by workers' compensation insurance, whether employed by a private business or by a public agency. A few statutes exempt businesses with fewer than three employees and some permit corporate officers, working partners, and owners of the business to be excluded from coverage. An employer can face significant penalties for failing to provide workers' compensation insurance, including fines, imprisonment, inability to raise defenses to a claim, personal liability of owners or corporate officers, and increased levels of compensation.

If an employee is injured on the job or suffers injury or disease resulting from his or her employment, the employee is entitled to receive compensation for lost wages, medical expenses, and rehabilitation costs. With few and limited exceptions, a worker's exclusive remedy against the employer for work-related injury is the recovery of workers' compensation benefits. This means that the employee cannot bring a personal injury suit against the employer, even if the employer was negligent or otherwise at fault for the injury. On the other hand, workers' compensation benefits are payable regardless of whether the employer was at fault. The theory underlying this system is that the employee is assured of a reasonable measure of compensation to be paid without delay, and the employer is relieved of the burden of defending personal injury suits in exchange for providing the insurance which pays the compensation benefits.

The amount of the benefits payable under workers' compensation is established by statute and depends primarily on the wage level of the injured employee, but also may involve other factors including the type of injury, whether the employee is totally or partially disabled, and whether the disability is temporary or permanent. There is usually a ceiling on the amount recoverable for a single injury. Workers' compensation insurance is available from private insurance companies and, in a few states, from a public fund. In addition, many states permit self-insurance by large coporations or groups of smaller businesses.

State workers' compensation statutes are governed in most states by a board or commission, and by the courts in a few states. The usual procedure is for an employee to file a claim with the employer and the employer to notify the insurance carrier. The administrative agency responsible for implementing the statute receives reports concerning claims and resolves disputes concerning the extent or duration of the injury and the amount of benefits payable.

Index